Canadian
Business
&
the Law

DOROTHY DUPLESSIS
Professor, University of New Brunswick

STEVEN ENMAN
Associate Professor, Acadia University

SALLY GUNZ
Associate Professor, University of Waterloo

SHANNON O'BYRNE
Associate Professor, University of Alberta

NELSON
™
THOMSON LEARNING

Australia • Canada • Mexico • Singapore • Spain • United Kingdom • United States

NELSON

THOMSON LEARNING ™

Canadian Business and the Law

by Dorothy DuPlessis, Steven Enman,
Sally Gunz, and Shannon O'Byrne

Editorial Director and Publisher:
Evelyn Veitch

Marketing Manager:
Anthony Rezek

Developmental Editor:
Geraldine Kikuta

Production Editors:
Tracy Bordian and Susan Calvert

Production Coordinator:
Hedy Sellers

Copy Editors:
Marcia Miron and Sarah Weber

Proofreader:
Matthew Kudelka

Art Director:
Angela Cluer

Interior Design:
Liz Harasymczuk

Cover Design:
Peggy Rhodes

Cover Image:
PhotoDisc

Compositor:
Janet Zanette

Indexer:
Edwin Durbin

Printer:
R.R. Donnelley

**Canadian Cataloguing in
Publication Data**

Main entry under title:

Canadian business and the law

Includes bibliographical references
and index.

ISBN 0-17-607372-8

1. Commercial law – Canada. I.
DuPlessis, Dorothy, 1955-   .

KE919.C36 2001   346.71'07
C00-933309-6

KF889.C36 2001

This book provides legal information of interest to those studying business law. It neither offers
nor contains legal advice of any kind. If you have a personal legal question that requires legal
advice, please consult a lawyer.

About the Authors

Dorothy Roberta Ruth DuPlessis, B. Com. (Dalhousie University), LL.B (Dalhousie University), M.B.A. (Dalhousie University), LL.M. (University of London), is a professor in the Faculty of Business Administration, University of New Brunswick (Fredericton). She is also a member of the Nova Scotia Barristers' Society. Professor DuPlessis has taught courses in business law, administrative law, and international law at both the undergraduate and graduate levels. She has also lectured at the Czech Management School and at the Institute of Professional Management. Professor DuPlessis has published articles on auditor's and director's liability, copyright, and university administration.

Steven Enman, B.B.A. (Acadia University), B.L. (Dalhousie University), Master of Commercial Laws (Bristol University), is an associate professor at the School of Business Administration, Acadia University. He is a member of the Academy of Legal Studies in Business. Admitted to the bar of Nova Scotia in 1978, Professor Enman is a member of the Nova Scotia Barristers' Society and the Canadian Bar Association, as well as acting as counsel for the firm of Waterbury Newton in Kentville, Nova Scotia. He is the editor of two editions of *Canadian Business Law Cases*.

Sally Gunz studied and then practised law in Australia. She moved to the United Kingdom to study business at the Manchester Business School, University of Manchester. In 1981 she joined the School of Accountancy, University of Waterloo, where she is now an associate professor. She is the author of *The New Corporate Counsel* (Carswell: Toronto, 1991) and a researcher and writer in the areas of legal and ethical responsibilities of public accountants and management and ethical issues concerning corporate counsel practice. Professor Gunz is a former president of the Academy of Legal Studies in Business and is the director of the Centre for Accounting Ethics, University of Waterloo.

Shannon Kathleen O'Byrne, B.A. (University of Regina), M.A., LL.B., LL.M. (University of Alberta), is an associate professor at the Faculty of Law, University of Alberta. She was admitted to the Law Society of Alberta in 1987 and is a past member of the Board of Directors of the Edmonton Bar Association. Her teaching and research areas include contract law, corporations law, and human rights law. Professor O'Byrne's articles have been cited with approval by courts across the country, including the Supreme Court of Canada. She has delivered papers at academic conferences in Japan, Ireland, and the United States. As well, Professor O'Byrne has lectured for professional organizations, including the Canadian Bar Association, the Continuing Legal Education Society of British Columbia, the Legal Education Society of Alberta, and the Saskatchewan Legal Education Association.

Contents

Part 1 The Legal Environment of Business

Chapter 1 An Introduction to the Study of Law

Chapter 2 The Canadian Legal System

Chapter 3 Managing Legal Risks

Chapter 4 Dispute Resolution

Part 5 Property

Chapter 17   Personal Property

Chapter 18   Intellectual Property

Chapter 19   Real Property

Chapter 20   Insurance

Part 7 The Market

Chapter 24 Marketing Practices:
Product and Promotion

Chapter 25 Marketing Practices:
Price and Distribution

Part 8 Financing the Business

Chapter 26 Business and Banking

Chapter 27 The Legal Aspects of Credit

Chapter 28 Bankruptcy and Insolvency

Preface

In *Canadian Business and the Law*, legal knowledge is regarded as a business asset that builds competitive advantage for the individual and the organization alike. This text demonstrates how the law can protect persons and their property as well as resolve disputes. Just as importantly, the text shows that law facilitates personal and commercial interactions. In short, the law provides both opportunities to be capitalized on and risks to be managed.

Canadian Business and the Law is written from the perspective that the law plays an integral role in all business decisions. This approach encourages students to anticipate, identify, and manage legal considerations. Topical coverage is organized as follows:

- Part 1 establishes the rationale for why students should study business law. It accounts for what the law is, where it comes from, and how the law regulates business.

- Parts 2 and 3 recognize that the most prevalent legal issues a business person will face are contained in the areas of contract law and tort law. Part 2, Contracts, and Part 3, Business Torts, provide a practical and contextualized analysis of these very important areas. Not only do students acquire an essential legal grounding in contract and tort principles, but they also attain the basic background for the specialized topics discussed in the latter part of the book.

  The fundamentals of contract law are provided in depth. Chapters 21 and 22, which deal with employment, allow further discussion of this important area. The focus on employment gives the class an opportunity to discuss the principles of contract law in relation to a particular context. By applying the law to the employment relationship, students gain insight to a form of contract that will figure prominently in their professional lives.

- In our experience, students best understand the law when it is related to core subject areas in the business curriculum, including finance, human resources, sales, and marketing. For this reason, the remaining parts of the book look at the functional areas of business and consider legal issues in relation to those activities:
  - Part 4 concerns the selection of the business vehicle.
  - Part 5 examines the creation and acquisition of property.
  - Part 6 analyzes the acquisition of human resources.
  - Part 7 focuses on the marketing and selling of goods and services.
  - Part 8 addresses financing the business activity.

Our work in *Canadian Business and the Law* focuses on meeting a number of objectives:

- Our most important aim is to explain the basic legal principles and concepts in a business context that is engaging and relevant for all readers.

- A second objective is to convey legal information in contexts geared to the practical application of knowledge. A **Business Law in Practice** scenario opens each chapter with a business situation containing both legal and managerial implications. Questions posed by the opening scenario give students direction and purpose and encourage critical thinking as they read the chapter. As a means of testing the student's comprehension and analytical skills, the scenario is revisited later in the chapter with suggested responses to the opening questions.

   The practical application of legal knowledge is reinforced through boxes provided throughout the text entitled **Business Application of the Law** and **A Business Perspective.** The former provides examples of the impact of the law on business enterprises, and the latter presents the experiences of individuals in industry. By illustrating how legal issues arise in the business environment and how these issues are managed, these features help students develop a concrete understanding of why the law matters in a business context.

- A third goal of the text is to recognize that the important legal considerations inherent in the emergence of new technologies, internationalization and globalization of the economy, and environmental concerns cut across traditional legal subjects. These topics are integrated throughout the body of the text and through features entitled **Technology and the Law**, **International Perspective**, and **Environmental Perspective**.

- A fourth objective is to reinforce that all aspects of the legal environment necessitate active management. We offer a model for identifying, evaluating, and managing legal risk in Chapter 3. Examples of the model's application to business enterprises and a risk management orientation are reflected in the treatment of legal subjects throughout the text.

- A fifth goal is to provide a pedagogically effective framework for the presentation of judicial decisions. Our special **Case** format begins with a description of the business context surrounding the legal dispute in question, followed by a concise statement of the relevant facts that led to the legal conflict. Next, a statement of the legal issues is provided as a summary of how the court resolved the conflict. The feature concludes with several questions that students are asked to consider to deepen their understanding of the case under study.

   The **Landmark in the Law** feature provides an account of pivotal case law and historical legislative initiatives, which can be essential to grasping contemporary law.

   Finally, an **Ethical Considerations** feature assists the student in assessing the sometimes uncomfortable compromises that the law forges between competing interests.

Canadian Business and the Law is offered as a modern resource for learning the fundamentals of business law from a business perspective. Rather than simply providing a summary of the law, it presents traditional business law topics in a manner that resonates with commercial reality. If you have any suggestions for improvements, additions, or clarifications, please let us know:

Dorothy DuPlessis   ddupless@unb.ca
Steve Enman   steve.enman@acadiau.ca
Sally Gunz   sgunz@uwaterloo.ca
Shannon O'Byrne   sobyrne@law.ualberta.ca

The Teaching and Learning Package

Instructor's Guide

The Instructor's Guide is designed to assist the instructor in preparing lectures and to offer lecture-tested ideas and strategies. The guide also provides suggested answers and explanations for all of the questions and problems presented in the text. Further, it gives ideas for projects, research activities, and class preparation plans.

Test Bank

The Test Bank offers instructors a rich resource of test items that have been developed specifically for the text. Questions represent a range of difficulty from recall through analysis. Multiple choice, short answer, and essay questions are provided.

Computerized Test Bank

The Computerized Test Bank provides instructors with the enhanced functionality of an electronic format, including the ability to add, modify, or delete questions; scramble multiple choice answers; and set parameters for the range and type of questions desired in the test generated.

PowerPoint Slides

A set of PowerPoint slides supports lecture preparation and presentation.

Video

The video component is composed of "lecture-launchers" that highlight key aspects of the course. The video is supported by a video guide that provides a topical overview, suggested introductions to each segment, and suggested questions to encourage in-class discussion.

Web Site

A Web site (www.businesslaw.nelson.com) accompanies *Canadian Business and the Law*. Instructors and students alike will find this site a useful resource. Instructors will be able to download instructor resources, access case summaries, and obtain key case updates. Students will be able to check their understanding of material covered in the course with interactive chapter quizzes, link to Internet resources referenced in the book, and view relevant federal and provincial legislation.

Student Study Guide

The Study Guide is designed to support mastery of the course content through reinforcement of the learning objectives and core concepts. It provides a variety of self-test opportunities with explanations for the suggested answers.

Acknowledgments

Canadian Business and the Law was a team effort, and credit for the text must be widely shared. We would like to thank our student assistants Shane Goguen, Nimanthika Kaneira, Tyler Langdon, and Kim Wylde, all of the University of New Brunswick; Dion Legge and Catherine Bradley of the University of Alberta; and Avril Lavallee of the University of Western Ontario and of Giesbrecht Griffin and Funk. Our thanks to Merle Metke for valued assistance in manuscript preparation and to Heather Harvie and Joyce O'Byrne for their help on the early drafts of many chapters.

In addition to the valued educators noted below, we extend our appreciation to our colleagues who made an important contribution by reviewing draft chapters. They include Peter Lown of the Alberta Law Reform Institute; Barbara Trenholm, Hugh Whalen, and Gunapala Nanayakkara of the University of New Brunswick; James McGinnis of Parlee McLaws; Ronald Hopp, David Percy, Gerald Gall, Lewis Klar, Moe Litman, Linda Reif, Barbara Billingsley, Rod Wood, Carol Lawrence, and Roy Suddaby of the University of Alberta; Kathryn Dykstra of Miller Thomson; Eric Spink of the Alberta Securities Commission; and Darren Charters and Warren Griffin of the University of Waterloo.

We also wish to thank Nora Batchelor, David Harrison, and Lesley Woodward of CGA-Canada, and John McReynolds of the Canadian Institute of Chartered Accountants, for their wise counsel on how to present material in a manner that best addresses the needs of Canadian accounting students. We thank Bill Goss, Tom Kaufman, Glen McCurdie, Don McCurdy, Michael H. Rayner, and Marcella Szel for their assistance in providing practical materials. To our U.S. colleagues in the Academy of Legal Studies in Business, thank you for your quick and thoughtful responses from time to time on current legal issues in the United States.

We would like to acknowledge the Faculty of Administration at the University of New Brunswick for financial assistance in having draft chapters tested in the classroom. Additionally, we would like to acknowledge research and administrative support from: the School of Accountancy and the Faculty of Arts at the University of Waterloo; the Faculty of Law at the University of Alberta; the Faculty of Administration at the University of New Brunswick; and the Fred C. Manning School of Business Administration at Acadia University.

We are grateful to Nelson's editorial, sales, and marketing team, including Tim Sellers, Marcia Miron, Susan Calvert, Anthony Rezek, Joseph Gladstone, and Evelyn Veitch for their insights and support throughout the development of this project. Special thanks to our developmental editor, Geraldine Kikuta, for her commitment, expertise, and patience.

Finally, our deep appreciation goes to those who were instrumental in the preparation of this text by providing direction through their insightful reviews of manuscript and/or participation in focus groups. They include:

Robert Beninger (Trent University)
George Cummins (Memorial University)
Maureen Donnelly (Brock University)
Elaine Geddes (University of Alberta)
Reginald Haney (Wilfrid Laurier University)
Peter Holden (Capilano College)
Ivan Ivankovich (University of Alberta)
Gilles Levasseur (Ottawa University)
Matt Lewans (University of Saskatchewan)

Geraldine Lindley (Seneca College)
Glen McCann (Brock University)
Richard Powers (University of Toronto)
Ian Restall (University of Manitoba)
David Ryan (Wilfrid Laurier University)
Mark Schwartz (York University)
Kelli Simmonds (University of New Brunswick)
Judith Stoffman (Guelph University)
Kenneth Thornicroft (University of Victoria)

By dedication of this book we thank our families for their sacrifice and support.

Dorothy's dedication is to Neil, Andrea, and Charles
Steve's dedication is to Jennie, Michael, and Edward
Sally's dedication is to John, Bill, Tommy, Mary, and Annie
Shannon's dedication is to Jamie, Kerry, and Sean

Table of Cases

The cases shown in boldface are developed in the text on the page indicated at the end of the citation.

Table of Statutes

Integrated Pedagogical System

Basic legal principles and concepts are explained and reinforced through the use of extensive pedagogy designed to help you process and learn the material.

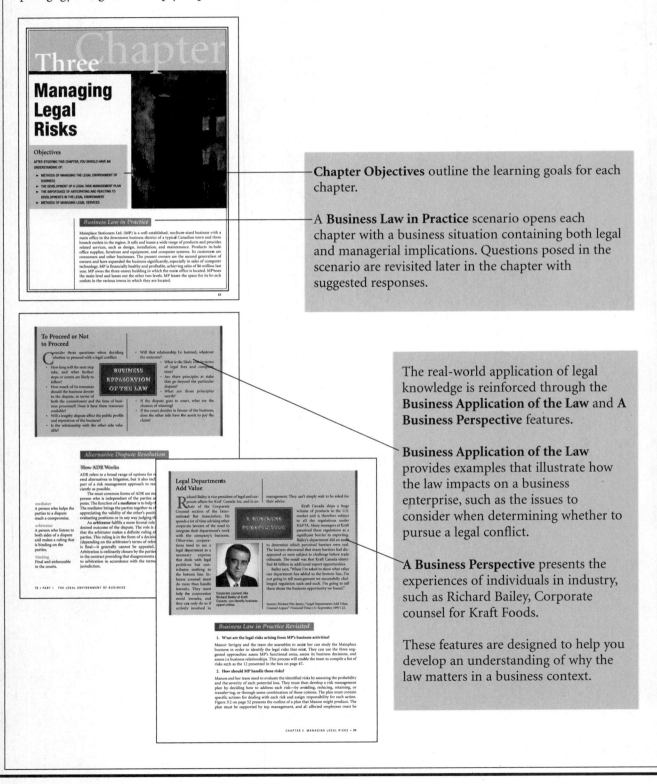

Chapter Objectives outline the learning goals for each chapter.

A **Business Law in Practice** scenario opens each chapter with a business situation containing both legal and managerial implications. Questions posed in the scenario are revisited later in the chapter with suggested responses.

The real-world application of legal knowledge is reinforced through the **Business Application of the Law** and **A Business Perspective** features.

Business Application of the Law provides examples that illustrate how the law impacts on a business enterprise, such as the issues to consider when determining whether to pursue a legal conflict.

A Business Perspective presents the experiences of individuals in industry, such as Richard Bailey, Corporate counsel for Kraft Foods.

These features are designed to help you develop an understanding of why the law matters in a business context.

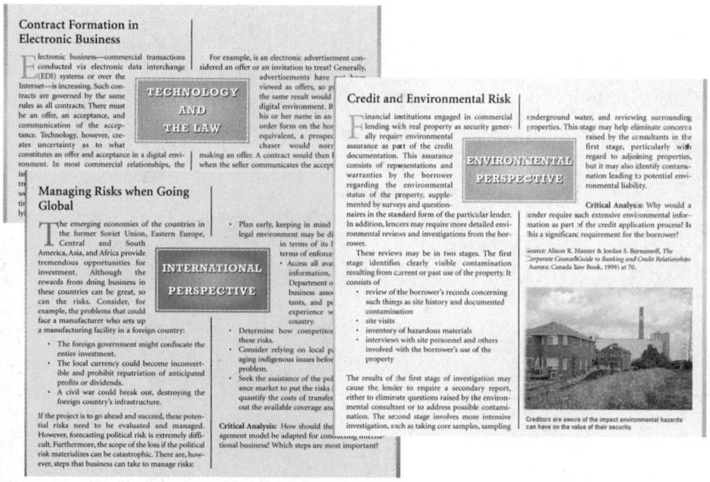

Contract Formation in Electronic Business

Electronic business—commercial transactions conducted via electronic data interchange (EDI) systems or over the Internet—is increasing. Such contracts are governed by the same rules as all contracts. There must be an offer, an acceptance, and communication of the acceptance. Technology, however, creates uncertainty as to what constitutes an offer and acceptance in a digital environment. In most commercial relationships, the

For example, is an electronic advertisement considered an offer or an invitation to treat? Generally,

TECHNOLOGY AND THE LAW

the same result when viewed as offers, so p his or her name in an order form on the hos equivalent, a proper chaser would norm making an offer. A contract would then when the seller communicates the accept

Managing Risks when Going Global

The emerging economies of the countries in the former Soviet Union, Eastern Europe, Central and South America, Asia, and Africa provide tremendous opportunities for investment. Although the rewards from doing business in these countries can be great, so can the risks. Consider, for example, the problems that could face a manufacturer who sets up a manufacturing facility in a foreign country:

INTERNATIONAL PERSPECTIVE

- The foreign government might confiscate the entire investment.
- The local currency could become inconvertible and prohibit repatriation of anticipated profits or dividends.
- A civil war could break out, destroying the foreign country's infrastructure.

If the project is to go ahead and succeed, these potential risks need to be evaluated and managed. However, forecasting political risk is extremely difficult. Furthermore, the scope of the loss if the political risk materializes can be catastrophic. There are, however, steps that business can take to manage risks:

- Plan early, keeping in mind legal environment may be d in terms of its l terms of enforce
- Access all av information, Department o business ass tants, and p experience w country.
- Determine how competi
- Consider relying on local p aging indigenous issues befor problem.
- Seek the assistance of the pol ance market to put the risks quantity the costs of transfer out the available coverage and

Critical Analysis: How should the agreement model be adapted for conducting international business? Which steps are most important?

Credit and Environmental Risk

Financial institutions engaged in commercial lending with real property as security generally require environmental assurance as part of the credit documentation. This assurance consists of representations and warranties by the borrower regarding the environmental status of the property, supplemented by surveys and questionnaires in the standard form of the particular lender. In addition, lenders may require more detailed environmental reviews and investigations from the borrower.

ENVIRONMENTAL PERSPECTIVE

These reviews may be in two stages. The first stage identifies clearly visible contamination resulting from current or past use of the property. It consists of

- review of the borrower's records concerning such things as site history and documented contamination
- site visits
- inventory of hazardous materials
- interviews with site personnel and others involved with the borrower's use of the property

The results of the first stage of investigation may cause the lender to require a secondary stage, either to eliminate questions raised by the environmental consultant or to address possible contamination. The second stage involves more intensive investigation, such as taking core samples, sampling

underground water, and reviewing surrounding properties. This stage may help eliminate concerns raised by the consultants in the first stage, particularly with regard to adjoining properties, but it may also identify contamination leading to potential environmental liability.

Critical Analysis: Why would a lender require such extensive environmental information as part of the credit application process? Is this a significant requirement for the borrower?

Source: Alison R. Manzer & Jordan S. Bernamoff, The Corporate Counsel Guide to Banking and Credit Relationships (Aurora: Canada Law Book, 1999) at 70.

Creditors are aware of the impact environmental hazards can have on the value of their security.

New technologies, globalization, and the environment all have implications for many aspects of business law. Learn how in the **Technology and the Law**, **International Perspective**, and **Environmental Perspective** features.

The **Special Case format** follows a standard analysis format for every featured case and landmark case that begins with an explanation of the BUSINESS CONTEXT that is at issue. Readers are then given the FACTUAL BACKGROUND of the case and presented with the LEGAL QUESTION before they actually read the court's RESOLUTION. Each case ends with questions for CRITICAL ANALYSIS. Each of these sections is clearly labelled for easy reference.

The **LANDMARK in the LAW** feature provides an account of pivotal case law and historical legislative initiatives.

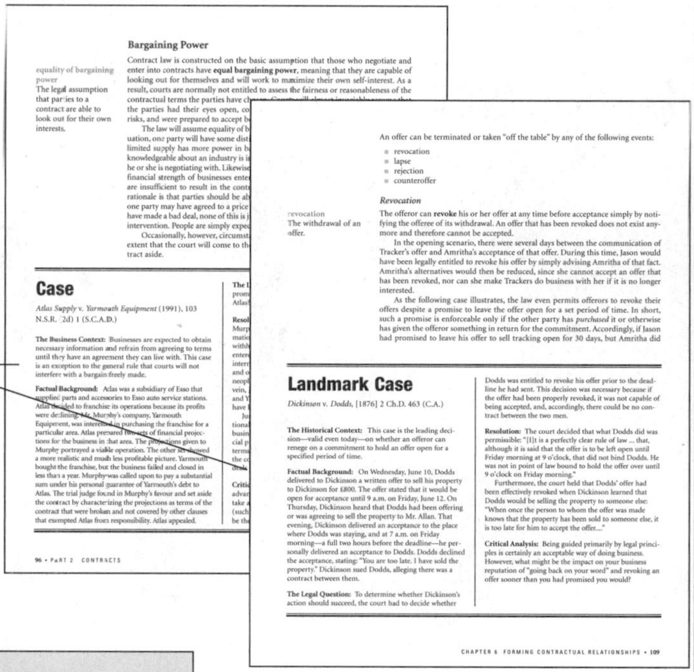

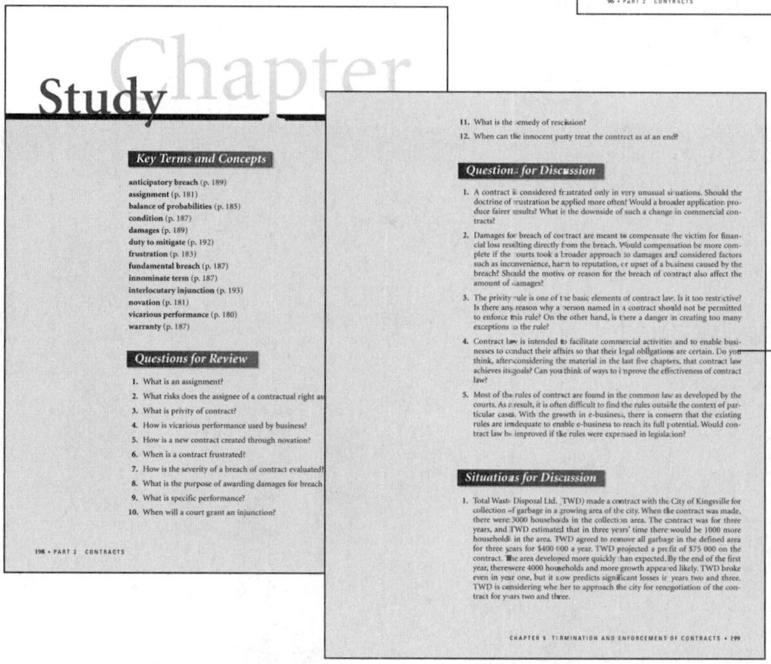

Bargaining Power

equality of bargaining power
The legal assumption that parties to a contract are able to look out for their own interests.

Contract law is constructed on the basic assumption that those who negotiate and enter into contracts have **equal bargaining power**, meaning that they are capable of looking out for themselves and will work to maximize their own self-interest. As a result, courts are normally not entitled to assess the fairness or reasonableness of the contractual terms the parties have chosen. Given that the parties had their eyes open, co risks, and were prepared to accept be

The law will assume equality of b uation, one party will have some dist knowledgeable about an industry is he or she is negotiating with. Likewise financial strength of businesses enter are insufficient to result in the court rationale is that parties should be ab one party may have agreed to a pric have made a bad deal, none of this is intervention. People are simply expec

Occasionally, however, circumst extent that the court will come to its tract aside.

Case

Atlas Supply v. Yarmouth Equipment (1991), 103 N.S.R. 2d) 1 (S.C.A.D.)

The Business Context: Businesses are expected to obtain necessary information and refrain from agreeing to terms until they have an agreement they can live with. There is an exception to the general rule that courts will not interfere with a bargain freely made.

Factual Background: Atlas was a subsidiary of Esso that supplied parts and accessories to Esso auto service stations. Atlas decided to franchise its operations because its profits were declining. Mr. Murphy's company, Yarmouth Equipment, was interested in purchasing the franchise for a particular area. Atlas pretrayed the profit of financial projections for the business in that area. The projections given to Murphy portrayed a viable operation. The other side showed a more realistic and much less profitable picture. Yarmouth bought the franchise, but the business failed and closed in less than a year. Murphy was called upon to pay a substantial sum under his personal guarantee of Yarmouth's debt to Atlas. The trial judge found in Murphy's favour and set aside the contract by characterizing the projections on terms of the contract that were broken and not covered by other clauses that exempted Atlas from responsibility. Atlas appealed.

The Legal Question: To determine whether Dickinson's action should succeed, the court had to decide whether

An offer can be terminated or taken "off the table" by any of the following events:

- revocation
- lapse
- rejection
- counteroffer

revocation
The withdrawal of an offer.

Revocation

The offeror can **revoke** his or her offer at any time before acceptance simply by notifying the offeree of its withdrawal. An offer that has been revoked does not exist anymore and therefore cannot be accepted.

In the opening scenario, there were several days between the communication of Tracker's offer and Amritha's acceptance of that offer. During this time, Jason would have been legally entitled to revoke his offer by simply advising Amritha of that fact. Amritha's alternatives would then be reduced, since she cannot accept an offer that has been revoked, nor can she make Trackers do business with her if it is no longer interested.

As the following case illustrates, the law even permits offerors to revoke their offers despite a promise to leave the offer open for a set period of time. In short, such a promise is enforceable only if the other party has *purchased* it or otherwise has given the offeror something in return for the commitment. Accordingly, if Jason had promised to leave his offer to sell tracking open for 30 days, but Amritha did

---

Landmark Case

Dickinson v. Dodds, [1876] 2 Ch.D. 463 (C.A.)

The Historical Context: This case is the leading decision—valid even today—on whether an offeror can renege on a commitment to hold an offer open for a specified period of time.

Factual Background: On Wednesday, June 10, Dodds delivered to Dickinson a written offer to sell his property to Dickinson for £800. The offer stated that it would be open for acceptance until 9 a.m. on Friday, June 12. On Thursday, Dickinson heard that Dodds had been offering or was agreeing to sell the property to Mr. Allan. That evening, Dickinson delivered an acceptance to the place where Dodds was staying, and at 7 a.m. on Friday morning—a full two hours before the deadline—he personally delivered an acceptance to Dodds. Dodds declined the acceptance, stating: "You are too late. I have sold the property." Dickinson sued Dodds, alleging there was a contract between them.

The Legal Question: To determine whether Dickinson's action should succeed, the court had to decide whether

Dodds was entitled to revoke his offer prior to the deadline he had set. Dickinson argued that because the offer had been properly revoked, it was not capable of being accepted, and, accordingly, there could be no contract between the two men.

Resolution: The court decided that what Dodds did was permissible: "[I]t is a perfectly clear rule of law ... that, although it is said that the offer is to be left open until Friday morning at 9 o'clock, that did not bind Dodds. He was not at point of law bound to hold the offer over until 9 o'clock on Friday morning."

Furthermore, the court held that Dodds' offer had "been effectively revoked when Dickinson learned that Dodds would be selling the property to someone else: "When once the person to whom the offer was made knows that the property has been sold to someone else, it is too late for him to accept the offer..."

Critical Analysis: Being guided primarily by legal principles is certainly an acceptable way of doing business. However, what might be the impact on your business reputation of "going back on your word" and revoking an offer sooner than you had promised you would?

Study Chapter

Key Terms and Concepts

anticipatory breach (p. 189)
assignment (p. 181)
balance of probabilities (p. 185)
condition (p. 187)
damages (p. 189)
duty to mitigate (p. 192)
frustration (p. 183)
fundamental breach (p. 187)
innominate term (p. 187)
interlocutory injunction (p. 193)
novation (p. 187)
vicarious performance (p. 180)
warranty (p. 187)

Questions for Review

1. What is an assignment?
2. What risks does the assignee of a contractual right as
3. What is privity of contract?
4. How is vicarious performance used by business?
5. How is a new contract created through novation?
6. When is a contract frustrated?
7. How is the severity of a breach of contract evaluated?
8. What is the purpose of awarding damages for breach
9. What is specific performance?
10. When will a court grant an injunction?

11. What is the remedy of rescission?
12. When can the innocent party treat the contract as at an end?

Questions for Discussion

1. A contract is considered frustrated only in very unusual situations. Should the doctrine of frustration be applied more often? Would a broader application produce fairer results? What is the downside of such a change in commercial contracts?

2. Damages for breach of contract are meant to compensate the victim for financial loss resulting directly from the breach. Would compensation be more complete if the courts took a broader approach to damages and considered factors such as inconvenience, harm to reputation, or upset of a business caused by the breach? Should the motive or reason for the breach of contract also affect the amount of damages?

3. The privity rule is one of the basic features of contract law. Is it too restrictive? Is there any reason why a person named in a contract should not be permitted to enforce this rule? On the other hand, is there a danger in creating too many exceptions to the rule?

4. Contract law is intended to facilitate commercial activities and to enable businesses to conduct their affairs so that their legal obligations are certain. Do you think, after considering the material in the last five chapters, that contract law achieves its goals? Can you think of ways to improve the effectiveness of contract law?

5. Most of the rules of contract are found in the common law as developed by the courts. As a result, it is often difficult to find the rules outside the context of particular cases. With the growth in e-business, there is concern that the existing rules are inadequate to enable e-business to reach its full potential. Would contract law be improved if the rules were expressed in legislation?

Situations for Discussion

1. Total Waste Disposal Ltd. (TWD) had a contract with the City of Kingsville for collection of garbage in a growing area of the city. When the contract was made, there were 3000 households in the collection area. The contract was for three years, and TWD estimated that in three years' time there would be 1000 more household in the area. TWD agreed to remove all garbage in the defined area for three years for $400 000 a year. TWD projected a profit of $75 000 on the contract. The area developed more quickly than expected. By the end of the first year, there were 4000 households and more growth appeared likely. TWD broke even in year one, but it now predicts significant losses in years two and three. TWD is considering whether to approach the city for renegotiation of the contract for years two and three.

End-of-chapter materials include **Key Terms and Concepts** with page references, **Questions for Review**, **Questions for Discussion**, and **Situations for Discussion**. **Questions for Review** will help you to check your understanding of chapter topics; **Questions for Discussion** and **Situations for Discussion** will let you apply the concepts you have learned about to other business situations.

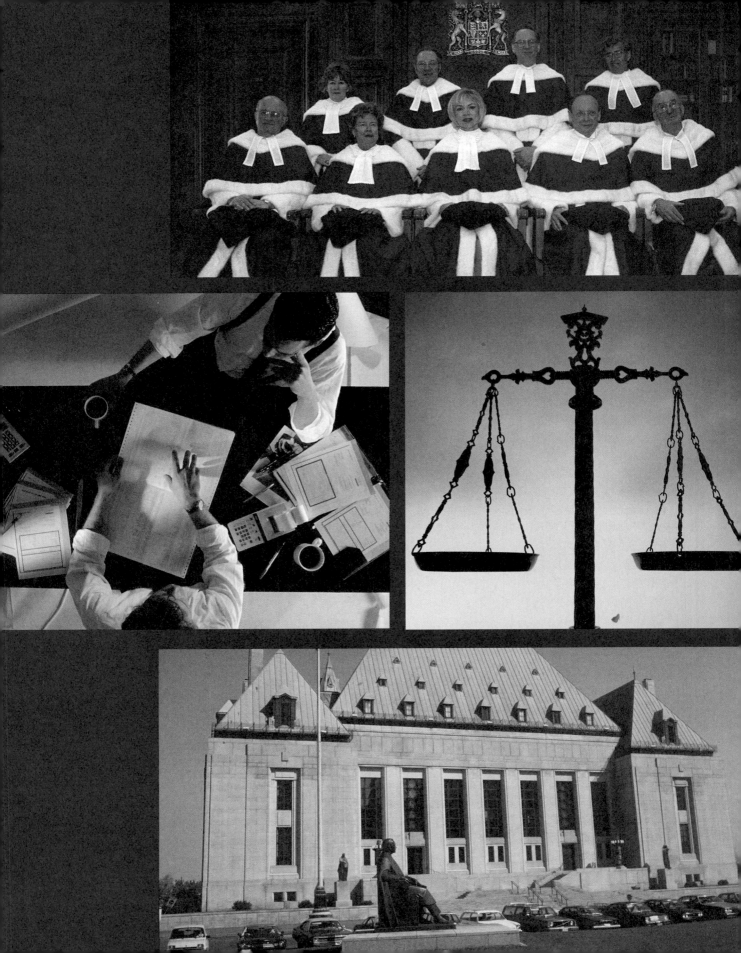

Part One

The Legal Environment of Business

THIS TEXT DEALS WITH THE IMPORTANCE OF THE LAW to business and, in Parts 2 to 8, presents fundamental legal principles in their relevant business contexts. The text contends that those engaged in business need to manage the legal environment as much as any other aspect of their business. Part 1 provides the basis for that management by introducing the foundations of business law and the concept of legal risk management. It emphasizes the importance of knowing the law, complying with the law, avoiding unexpected legal problems, and regarding law not as an obstacle, but as a way to facilitate commercial activity.

Chapter 1   An Introduction to the Study of Law

▶ Chapter 1 sets the stage for the study of law by presenting the purposes of law, describing how and why the law works, and noting how knowledge of the law can be a valuable business asset.

Chapter 2 The Canadian Legal System

▶ Chapter 2 outlines the role of the Canadian legal system in the business environment, describing the branches of government, the various sources and classifications of the law, and the way in which business is regulated by administrative law.

Chapter 3 Managing Legal Risks

▶ Chapter 3 deals with the management of legal risks by identifying and assessing risks that arise in particular businesses and describing the development of a risk management plan in response.

Chapter 4 Dispute Resolution

▶ Chapter 4 describes how legal disputes arise in business and surveys the various methods of resolving disputes, from informal negotiation to formal litigation in the courts.

One Chapter

An Introduction to the Study of Law

Objectives

AFTER STUDYING THIS CHAPTER, YOU SHOULD HAVE AN
UNDERSTANDING OF:

▶ THE ROLE OF LAW IN THE BUSINESS ENVIRONMENT
▶ THE PLANNING FUNCTION OF LAW
▶ THE VALUES ASSOCIATED WITH THE CANADIAN LEGAL SYSTEM
▶ THE IMPORTANCE OF LEGAL KNOWLEDGE AS A BUSINESS
   ASSET

Business Law in Practice

Joe has an entrepreneurial spirit and wants to fulfill his lifelong dream of owning and operating a business. Since Joe has some experience in the food service industry and has recently completed a culinary program at a community college, he has decided to open a gourmet restaurant.

One year later, Joe fulfills his dream by opening a seafood restaurant and an adjoining bar. He decides to name the restaurant Finny Friends, after a restaurant he had visited in Toronto. Outside of his restaurant, Joe has a beautiful awning with the name Finny Friends stretched across it in large, elegant letters.

Joe relies on a reputable supplier to provide him with fresh fish, but, unfortunately, Joe's refrigeration system temporarily breaks down. He decides to use the fish for his customers' meals anyway, reasoning that the fish had been recently delivered and the mechanical breakdown had lasted for less than a day.

In accordance with the law, Joe has a liquor licence from the provincial liquor commission, which limits the seating capacity in the bar to 30. As Joe's bar becomes increasingly popular, he begins to regularly allow more than 60 patrons in at one time. Eventually, he is caught, and because he had already received two warnings, his liquor licence is suspended for 30 days. Joe is flabbergasted at the severity of the penalty.

Soon thereafter, Joe is contacted by a lawyer for Finny Friends restaurant in Toronto. The lawyer says that Joe has 48 hours to take down his restaurant awning and destroy anything else with the name Finny Friends on it (including menus, invoices, placemats, napkins, and even matchbook covers); otherwise, she will bring an application for a court order to that effect. The lawyer advises that her clients are going to sue Joe for damages because Joe is misleading people into thinking that his restaurant and the Toronto restaurant are affiliated.

To make matters worse, a health inspector arrives on Joe's doorstep and says that there have been several recent reports of food poisoning originating from Joe's restaurant.

1. How does the law affect Joe's business?
2. What are the purposes of the laws that affect Joe's business?
3. What has gone wrong in Joe's business, and why?

Law in the Business Environment

The law permeates virtually every aspect of society, including the business environment. The law affects most business decisions—from development of the basic business idea through to its implementation, and all the attendant matters in between, including financing, hiring of personnel, production, marketing, and sales. As Joe starts his business, for example, he will be involved in a number of transactions and events with significant legal implications.

For instance, to get his business off the ground, Joe has to decide whether to form a corporation, operate as a sole proprietor, or find some partners. He has financing decisions to make: Should he borrow money, use his own funds, or perhaps sell shares in his venture? Joe also needs to find a location for his restaurant, whether by constructing a new building, purchasing an existing structure, or leasing premises from someone else. He requires equipment, furnishings, signage, and supplies, including food, liquor, condiments, and table napkins. He has cooks to hire, as well as helpers, servers, and cleaning staff. Joe also has to market his business in order to build and maintain a customer base. All of these decisions have legal aspects to them, whether Joe recognizes that or not.

By understanding the role of law in the multitude of business decisions that people like Joe must make, an entrepreneur can maximize the protection that the law extends while avoiding its pitfalls. Put another way, knowledge of the law is a business asset that can assist owners and managers in reaching their goals and objectives because **business law**

- defines general rules of commerce
- protects business ideas and more tangible forms of property

business law
A set of established rules governing commercial relationships, including the enforcement of rights.

- provides mechanisms that permit business people to select their desired degree of participation and exposure to risk in business ventures
- seeks to ensure that losses are borne by those who are responsible for them
- facilitates planning by ensuring compliance with commitments

Of course, a business person can function with little or no understanding of the law. This lack of knowledge, however, may result in failure to maximize opportunities or in losing out on them altogether. For example, a business that neglects to protect its intellectual property may have its ideas taken by a competitor with impunity; a business that ignores employment and human rights laws may be forced to reverse human resource decisions or pay compensation to wronged employees; a business that fails to explore different modes of carrying out business may suffer unnecessary losses. Perhaps even more seriously, this lack of legal knowledge may result in the business being subjected to regulatory and judicial sanctions, including being fined, forced to pay penalties, or closed down altogether.

Rules and Principles

law
The set of rules and principles guiding conduct in society.

Broadly defined, the **law** is a set of rules and principles intended to guide conduct in society, primarily by protecting persons and their property; facilitating personal and commercial interactions; and providing mechanisms for dispute resolution.

Protecting Persons and Their Property

Probably the most familiar purpose of the law is to provide protection. Those who violate the *Criminal Code of Canada*—such as by breaking into another person's house, assaulting someone, or driving while impaired—are subject to criminal sanctions, such as fines or imprisonment. From this vantage point, the law protects members of society in two ways: first, it sets rules with penalties in order to encourage compliance, and second, it seeks to make those who break the law accountable for their misconduct. The law also protects businesses by setting penalties and ensuring accountability. For example, if one business misappropriates another business's legally protected commercial idea, the law can step in and penalize that conduct. As well, the law ensures that losses are paid for by the parties responsible for creating them. For example, if a law firm gives negligent advice to a client, that client can sue the firm for losses associated with the advice.

Joe's business intersects with the law in both of these ways. First, the law guards his business interests. Assuming that Joe is entitled to use the name Finny Friends for his restaurant, he can protect it. Should a competitor "steal" the name of Joe's business and try to benefit from the goodwill Joe has built up, Joe can bring an action against that competitor for damages suffered and apply for a court order prohibiting the competitor from continuing to use the name. Second, if a supplier fails to deliver a product to Joe in **breach of its contract** to do so, Joe can sue for any damages he suffers as a result. However, the law also protects those who deal with Joe's business. Joe must not discriminate in hiring practices. He must not disregard health and safety regulations governing the workplace. He must pay his creditors. He must not accept bribes. In managing his operation, Joe is obliged to abide by the law on a variety of fronts, since failure to comply can have severe consequences, including financial penalties and criminal prosecution.

breach of contract
Failure to comply with a contractual promise.

Wal-Mart

In early 2000, a former vice president of apparel merchandising for Wal-Mart's Canadian subsidiary was charged with violating the *Criminal Code* by accepting secret commissions, or "kickbacks." One Toronto supplier is alleged to have paid this former executive kickbacks totalling US$60 000. *The Globe and Mail* reports Constable Doug Robinson of the Peel, Ontario, fraud squad as stating, "We don't see very many secret-commission investigations come our way ... but after learning something about the industry—not just the apparel industry but all of the purchasing industries—it's probably more common than I thought." *The Globe and Mail* also reports a statement from a Wal-Mart spokesperson that the company "is committed to the highest standards when it comes to ethical conduct, and that's well known throughout the retail industry."

Critical Analysis: Should the law prohibit under-the-table payments? How does this example illustrate the protective function of the law? What could happen to the marketplace if corrupt practices were not criminalized?

Source: Canadian Press Wire Service quoting *The Globe and Mail*, undated (31 January 2000), online: QL (CP2K).

Facilitating Interactions

The law facilitates personal interactions by providing rules concerning marriage, adoption, and the disposal of property upon the owner's death, to name a few examples. The law also facilitates commercial activity by providing rules governing the marketplace. The law of contract, for example, provides a way for parties to enter into binding agreements, thereby creating a measure of security and certainty in their business operations. **Contract law** allows business enterprises to plan for the future and to enforce their expectations.[1]

contract law
Rules that make agreements binding and therefore facilitate planning and the enforcement of expectations.

While the law addresses failed relations—as when one party fails to meet its contractual obligations or gives negligent legal advice—it is not primarily about conflict. Rather, the law functions to prevent disputes and to facilitate relationships. It provides certainty for Joe's commercial agreements and enables him to engage in transactions that might otherwise be unstructured and unpredictable.

Nor is the law primarily about rules that constrain commerce. Though the law does forbid certain activities—such as false advertising and operating without a business licence—its more significant role is facilitative. Legal rules provide definition and context to doing business. For example, assume that Joe wants to enter into a long-term relationship with a particularly reliable local wholesaler. Contract law allows him to accomplish this end by providing a mechanism through which Joe and the supplier can describe—and enforce—their commitments to each other. Therefore, Joe can agree in advance with his supplier on what kind of product is to be provided, how much product, at what price, over what period of time, and when.

---

1. For a discussion of contract law, see Part 2 of this text.

The creation of certainty in business relationships is one of the most important facilitative contributions that law can make to the commercial arena. While the necessity of creating certainty means that some anticipated contracts founder when it comes to formalizing their content, the law has not necessarily "failed." It more likely means that the business people involved were not as close to being in agreement as they had initially assumed. Further discussions, perhaps through lawyers, have simply identified problems that, although hidden under the surface, were always there.

No contract can recite and provide for all contingencies. There will be some issues left unstated, but often the parties themselves find ways of overcoming these omissions. How do the two contractors reach consensus? Generally, they will be guided by the need to achieve the original intent behind the contractual relationship, with the objective of dealing fairly with the unexpected or unaddressed event that has just occurred. In this way, the business relationship comes to the fore and "fills in the blanks" in the contractual arrangement. If one or both of the parties involve the legal system, a judge will apply established rules governing contracts that lack the necessary specificity.

The influence of the law on the business environment does not have to be exacting and literal. In fact, parties to a business contract do not always observe their agreement to the letter, preferring to maintain their relationship rather than sue for breach of contract. For example, assume that Joe has a long-term contract with a supplier of restaurant condiments. Owing to poor planning, the supplier will be unable to make its monthly delivery on time and has advised Joe of the delay. Although he may be annoyed at the default, Joe stands to lose more than he would gain from suing, particularly if the supplier is otherwise reliable and the two have

Kathryn Dykstra, Partner, Miller Thomson

Kathryn Dykstra has been advising corporate-commercial clients for over 15 years. She states:

When business clients come to see me, I know there are many issues that they haven't thought about in the push to "get the deal done." The job of a lawyer is not to send them away with ten more problems than they started with, although it is clearly our job to raise those legal issues that have to be addressed in order to complete the transaction properly. Lawyers should not be seen as "deal-breakers," that is, people who point out so many potential problems that the transaction never goes through. Rather, the lawyer is retained to act in her client's best interest, and this includes providing a range of solutions to meet that end.

A BUSINESS PERSPECTIVE

In the final analysis, it is the client who negotiates a deal that meets his objectives, with the assurance that his lawyer has given enough guidance to allow informed choices throughout the negotiation process.

Kathryn Dykstra, a partner at Miller Thomson.

litigation
The process involved when one person sues another.

established a solid working relationship. There is no good reason to risk this relationship and devote resources to **litigation**, that is, the process involved in suing someone else. In this way, the contract between Joe and the supplier provides the legal backdrop to their relationship—by defining rights and obligations—but it is the *business* relationship that determines whether strict legal rights will be insisted upon. This is an important reality that affects how the law actually operates in the business environment.

Providing Mechanisms for Dispute Resolution

Whether a conflict can or even should be resolved outside of the formal legal system depends on the circumstances. If Joe hires an on-site manager who proves to be incompetent, it is in the interests of his enterprise to terminate the person's employment. While Joe may have a case to fire the employee outright, he might also consider offering a small severance package to reduce the possibility of being sued for wrongful dismissal.[2] This is a judgment call, but the time and money saved in avoiding a court battle may more than offset the cost of the severance package. Conversely, it may be that the employee has had his hand in the till and stolen some of the restaurant's daily receipts. Joe is in a different situation now. He must not only ensure that the employee leaves the company immediately, but he also will want to involve the police and try to recover what the employee has misappropriated. In these kinds of circumstances, there are few olive branches to offer, and a full-blown legal conflict is much more likely and appropriate.

When a business encounters a legal conflict—as when a customer refuses to accept delivery of a product at the contractually agreed-upon price—solutions at various levels of formality are available. The first logical step is for the parties to try to come to a resolution between themselves and produce, if necessary, a formalized settlement agreement. If this solution proves untenable, the legal system offers **mediation** and **arbitration** as ways of circumventing litigation.[3] Thus, the law provides a number of mechanisms for settling disputes short of a courtroom battle.

mediation
A process through which the parties to a dispute endeavour to reach a resolution with the assistance of a neutral person.

arbitration
A process through which a neutral party makes a decision (usually binding) that resolves a dispute.

Some business disputes do end up in court, however, for a variety of reasons: perhaps there had been no previous agreement between the parties to refer disputes to arbitration and they have no desire to do so now; perhaps one of the parties refuses to accept mediation; perhaps one of the parties is tremendously unfair and cannot be reasoned with; or perhaps the dispute has reached the point at which a court ruling is the only way to end the matter once and for all. It is essential to a workable business environment that the last-resort solution provided by the litigation process also be available to the disputants.

How and Why the Law Works

There are any number of ways to resolve a dispute, including trial by ordeal (as in the notorious Salem witch trials of 17th-century America); pistol duel (prevalent in France and England until the 19th century); and even modern-day drive-by shootings. What these methods lack, however, is accordance with modern ideas of what is just, fair, and reasonable.

Important values associated with the Canada's legal system today stand in opposition to inequitable, arbitrary, and violent alternatives. While today's legal system is

---

2. For further discussion of the law of unjust dismissal, see Chapter 22.
3. See Chapter 4 for further information on dispute resolution.

Litigation as a Last Resort

When one party fails to keep a contractual commitment, suing that person may seem the best and only response. This is particularly true when someone feels badly treated and believes that an essential principle is at stake in the conflict. However, the desire to stand up for this principle at all costs tends to betray a short-term perspective and should be resisted. Maintaining a good business relationship with the party in breach—or at least minimizing the financial costs of the dispute—is often much more important than proving yourself to be "right" in a court of law. Questions to ask yourself before choosing litigation include:

BUSINESS APPLICATION OF THE LAW

- Are legal proceedings absolutely necessary, at least right now?
- Is there a way to resolve the problem from a larger, relationship-preserving perspective, rather than from a strictly legal viewpoint?

There are times when litigation is appropriate, and a good lawyer will be able to tell you when that is. If the other side is unwilling to compromise and is posing a threat to your economic interests, for example, then formal legal proceedings may be unavoidable.

Canadian Business and International Law

Canadian business is not confined to Canada. Although there is no doubt that the national market is of primary importance to most commercial enterprises, Canadian businesses are increasingly extending their reach beyond their national borders. Today, there are more global markets than ever before. Although the United States remains Canada's chief trading partner, Canadian businesses have contacts in many corners of the world. These countries differ in many ways—in their cultures, political systems, economic systems, level of economic development, and legal systems. Therefore, just as a Canadian business cannot assume that another country shares the same culture, it also cannot assume that it shares the same legal system. Indeed, there are major differences from one system to the next, and in some instances a business will be subjected to a legal system quite unlike the one that it is most familiar with.

INTERNATIONAL PERSPECTIVE

Canadian businesses may be subject to international law in addition to the law of a foreign jurisdiction. Because there is no world government, as such, that enacts laws, international law is somewhat different from domestic law. International law becomes law when nations agree to abide by it. The chief sources of international law affecting businesses doing business abroad are conventions and treaties, such as the Convention on the International Sale of Goods and the North American Free Trade Agreement (NAFTA), and long-standing customs and practices. These factors need to be considered in any decision to expand internationally.

Critical Analysis: What is the purpose of international law? Does it serve the same purpose as domestic law?

liability
Legal responsibility for the event or loss that has occurred.

suing
The process of instituting formal legal proceedings against someone to enforce a right. *- Civil matter*

far from perfect, it possesses essential improvements over its predecessors because it determines **liability** in accordance with certain principles and processes that are regarded as "just."

For example, assume that Joe is **suing** a supplier for breach of contract, and the matter has now come before a judge. The Canadian legal system demands that both the process for determining liability and the rules or laws that are applied in that process are fair and free from bias.

Joe, as the party who has initiated the complaint of breach of contract, is obligated to prove his case. The judge, in turn, is obligated to be as objective as possible in determining whether Joe has proven his case. Part of the judge's job is to determine what the agreement between the parties actually was, as well as the law governing the matter. The judge must then apply this law as impartially as possible to the situation. In order that the outcome of Joe's dispute with the supplier be seen as just, the law that the judge ultimately relies on must itself possess certain characteristics. In this way, both the process or procedure of the legal system (that is, *how* the law is applied) and the substantive law (that is, *what* is applied) must achieve a standard of fairness and reasonableness.

For instance, it is a rule or law that a party who suffers a breach of contract is entitled to be put in the position that he would have been in had the contract been fulfilled. If Joe can prove that as a result of the supplier's breach he lost a lucrative catering job, for example, a court may well award him damages for loss of profit. The rationale behind the rule is simple: the supplier has broken his contractual promise. The supplier must therefore assume responsibility for any direct and foreseeable financial consequences Joe experiences as a result.

The quality of the Canadian legal system is measured by the common values, attributes, and standards shown in Figure 1.1.

Figure 1.1

THE VALUES OF THE CANADIAN LEGAL SYSTEM

Broad application	The same law is to apply to everyone.
Fair and impartial judges	The law is to be applied by someone who is free from bias.
Consistency	The law must deal with similar cases in similar ways.
Accessibility	The law must be accessible and understandable.
Constancy	Any change in the law must be gradual so that the rules remain reasonably certain and predictable.
Flexibility	The law must keep up with developments in business and society and be able to change with the times.
Reasonableness	The law must set standards of behaviour that are defensible.
Enforcement	The law must be capable of enforcement. In other words, people who believe they have been wronged must have a forum at which their complaints can be heard and redressed.

Justice is the goal of the Canadian legal system. This goal is achieved when the legal question is assessed by an objective, impartial, and neutral judge who applies laws that are fair and transparent. Needless to say, the ideal of total justice is elusive, and there are serious and possibly chronic problems with how legal disputes are resolved in Canada.

The Reputation of Canada's Legal System

A 1997 Angus Reid Group survey entitled "Canada and the World" assessed how Canadians and those from other countries rate the Canadian legal system: 42 percent of the Canadians surveyed strongly or moderately agreed with the statement, "The justice system here in Canada treats all citizens fairly"; 57 percent strongly or moderately disagreed. At the same time, 71 percent of the Canadians regarded their system as being much or somewhat better than what was offered in other countries. Ukraine, France, and Mexico also rated Canada as having one of the better legal systems in the world.

Critical Analysis: What features of the Canadian legal system help to make it fair?

Source: Rob Richardson, "Most Canadians Feel Legal System Is Unfair" *Lawyers Weekly* (29 August 1997).

The goal of achieving justice is ambitious and often difficult to achieve. There are also obvious limitations to what the law can actually accomplish, even when it is most successful. Employment equity law will not end discrimination. Reform of bankruptcy law will not prevent business failures. More restrictive copyright laws will not alter the ease of unauthorized copying in everyday life. As noted earlier, the law can, however, offer itself as a mechanism for achieving the goals of protection, facilitation, and dispute resolution. For example, bankruptcy law is the vehicle for ensuring that all those affected by a failed business are treated fairly, reasonably, and according to a set of agreed-upon rules. The law is prepared to confront bigotry by providing remedies to those who are the targets. It provides rules for contract formation. And it provides a vast machinery for resolving conflict.

Knowledge of the Law as a Business Asset

Entrepreneurs like Joe can use the law to protect and advance their business interests. Conversely, they can cause themselves much anxiety, grief, and financial loss by ignoring the law.

The law forbids Joe from using the business name of the Toronto restaurant in part because there is goodwill associated with the name that belongs to the Toronto

Comme Chez Soi, a restaurant in Granby, Quebec, was shut down for 30 days in February 2000 for serving leftover food to customers.

restaurant alone. In the interests of public protection, the law makes Joe's operation subject to public health laws concerning the storage of food, as well as to safety and public order regulations limiting the number of patrons permitted in his establishment at one time. Breaching these rules and regulations has serious consequences, including fines, closure, and adverse publicity, from which his business may never recover. Furthermore, any of Joe's patrons who could prove that eating fish in his restaurant gave them food poisoning can successfully sue him for financial compensation.

While Joe's negative experience with the law is exaggerated, it illustrates the point that knowing the law is a business asset. Had Joe taken the time to inform himself about the laws governing his operations—as well as about the consequences for failing to abide by them—his business experience presumably would have been much more positive and profitable.

Business Law in Practice Revisited

1. How does the law affect Joe's business?

As Joe starts his business, he will be involved in a number of transactions and events with significant legal implications, including the following:

- *Business form.* Does Joe want to operate his business alone as a sole proprietor, or would he prefer to work with partners, or is he interested in incorporating? Each business vehicle has its own set of rules, which Joe must find out about. For instance, the incorporation process is strictly dictated by federal and provincial law.
- *Business name.* Joe must be sure to choose a name that is not confusingly similar to the name of another business. Even if he chooses such a name inadvertently, he will be subject to legal consequences, including being sued for damages by the person who has built up goodwill in the name in question.
- *Financing considerations.* If Joe decides to borrow his operating capital from the bank, he will have to enter into a specialized form of contract known as a promissory note. In this contract, he promises to repay the loan, with interest, according to a schedule. If Joe decides that he wants to raise money by selling shares, he will definitely have to incorporate a company. As well, should Joe's company end up selling shares to the public, it will have disclosure obligations under securities legislation.
- *Property.* Joe has to determine whether to buy, build, or lease premises for his business operation. Each option involves a unique set of laws. Furthermore, many aspects of the property used in Joe's business are regulated through health legislation, liquor licensing requirements, and fire regulations, to name several examples.

- *Services.* Joe must hire staff to run his business. He must become aware of the law concerning unjust dismissal and employment equity, as well as human rights legislation that prohibits discrimination.
- *Marketing.* In promoting his restaurant to the public, Joe must be sure to abide by laws prohibiting false and misleading advertising, as well as trademark and copyright law, to name two examples.
- *Selling.* Joe must be sure to provide a reasonable level of service to his customers. If customers suffer food poisoning or perhaps injure themselves by falling in his restaurant, Joe may be held liable and be required to pay damages.

Just as Joe must devote resources to monitoring his staff, attending to proper book-keeping, and keeping his loans in good standing, he also must spend time managing the legal elements of his business environment. Since the law affects Joe's business from a variety of perspectives, he is much better off accepting this responsibility from the outset, rather than fighting a rearguard action. Once he understands the law, Joe can take simple, proactive steps to ensure that he complies with it; just as importantly, he can plan for the future.

2. What are the purposes of the laws that affect Joe's business?

One of the most important functions of law in the business environment is to facilitate planning, particularly—though not exclusively—through contract law. It also has a protective function in that it seeks to ensure that those who cause a loss are held financially responsible and otherwise accountable for their actions, including through the criminal justice system. Finally, the law provides a series of mechanisms and rules for dispute resolution, thereby making an essential contribution to certainty in the marketplace.

3. What has gone wrong in Joe's business, and why?

The Business Law in Practice scenario provides a lengthy illustration of the kinds of penalties and liabilities Joe faces if he neglects to pay attention to the legal rules that govern his enterprise. Joe's blissful ignorance of his legal obligations and potential liabilities is staggering and will lead to the demise of his business.

Chapter Summary

Law is involved in all aspects of business, whether the entrepreneur is aware of it or not. The law protects persons and their property; facilitates commercial interactions, particularly through contract law; and provides mechanisms for dispute resolution. Though far from perfect, the Canadian legal system has much to recommend it. The system strives for the ideal of justice by seeking fairness both in how the law is applied (the legal process) and in how the laws are defined. Judges are expected to render impartial and fair decisions, and the laws they apply must display certain values and attributes. They must have broad application and be consistently applied. Furthermore, laws must be accessible, constant, flexible, reasonable, and enforceable. No justice system, of course, can achieve all these goals.

Indeed, there are serious limitations to what the law can realistically achieve when a legal problem arises; thus, it is imperative that a business adopt a proactive approach in managing the legal aspects of its environment. This chapter has emphasized the idea that knowledge of the law is an essential business asset. Informed owners and managers can protect their businesses by ensuring compliance with legal requirements. They can capitalize on the planning function of law to ensure the future of their business by entering into contracts. They also can seek enforcement of legal rules against those who do business or have other interactions with the enterprise. In this way, the property, contractual expectations, and profitability of the business are made more secure.

Study Chapter

Questions for Review

1. What is the function of law?

2. In what ways does law facilitate certainty in the marketplace?

3. Does the nature of the business relationship affect the enforcement of legal rights?

4. How does the law resolve disputes? Does dispute resolution always involve going to court?

5. Which values are traditionally associated with a fair legal system, and how are they achieved?

6. In what way is knowledge of the law a business asset?

Questions for Discussion

1. Do you think the Canadian justice system treats all Canadians fairly? Give examples to support your opinion.

2. What are the most important societal values today that the law should reflect?

3. What are the major weaknesses in our legal system today?

Situations for Discussion

1. Discuss the kinds of legal questions that you think might arise in the following business proposals:
   - Corporation A is planning to launch a new marketing program featuring an advertising campaign that extols the virtues of its product and denigrates the product of Corporation B.
   - Corporation C is planning to construct an oil rig at the mouth of a particular river to exploit a recent mineral find.
   - Corporation D is planning to expand its manufacturing facilities into a foreign country. In order to finance its operations, it is planning to sell shares to the public.

2. Assume that you have a major dispute with a business on the property next to yours over acceptable use of their land. You find that although zoning allows a small tool shop to operate on the property, the noise is too much for you. Your lawyer tells you that there may be a legal case for you to pursue, but it will be costly and the results are not guaranteed. What alternative approaches might address your problems more effectively?

3. Alexis owns a convenience store and has invested a lot of money in video gambling machines for the store. Recently, the government passed a law banning the machines from stores immediately, although pubs are allowed to continue operating these machines. Is this law fair? Does it violate any of the common values associated with the law? Would it make a difference if the law applied only to new businesses? Would it make a difference if government provided compensation to the convenience stores affected or phased in the law to allow for a period of adjustment?

4. How can a business person acquire legal knowledge, short of becoming a lawyer? What resources are available, and how are they accessed?

Common boundaries
- law must apply to everyone

The Canadian Legal System

Objectives

AFTER STUDYING THIS CHAPTER, YOU SHOULD HAVE AN UNDER-
STANDING OF:

► THE OPERATION OF THE CANADIAN LEGAL SYSTEM AND
ITS RELATIONSHIP TO BUSINESS

► THE THREE BRANCHES AND LEVELS OF GOVERNMENT

► THE GOVERNMENT'S LAW-MAKING POWERS

► THE JUDICIARY'S ROLE IN ASSESSING THE CONSTITUTION-
ALITY OF LEGISLATION

► THE SOURCES AND CATEGORIES OF LAW

► THE WAY THAT ADMINISTRATIVE LAW AFFECTS BUSINESS

Business Law in Practice

Terry Addison is the newly appointed director of a corporation that produces a well-
known brand of cigarettes. She is reviewing, with considerable concern, a piece of
legislation called the *Tobacco Products Control Act.* A central goal of this legislation is
to restrict how the tobacco industry can advertise its products. Terry is particularly
disturbed by a provision requiring that every package of cigarettes carry a warning

about the dangerous health effects of smoking, such as a statement that secondhand smoke causes illness. She believes that the connection between serious illness and secondhand smoke inhalation has not been established, and she wants no such warning placed on the packages. She believes that it is unfair of the government to force her company to state to the public that there is such a connection. Even more seriously, from her perspective, the Act bans virtually all advertising of tobacco products, which strikes Terry as being an unreasonable restraint on her ability to do business.

1. Is the government's law to regulate tobacco advertising a legal one?
2. What is legislation, and where does it come from?
3. Who assesses whether the legislation is permissible?
4. Are there any moral or ethical questions that arise from this scenario?
5. What can Terry do about the legislation at this point?

Introduction

liberalism
A political philosophy that elevates individual freedom and autonomy as its key organizing value.

constitutional law
The body of law governing the individual–state relationship, including the permissible scope of legislative power.

government policy
The central ideas or principles that guide government in its work, including the kinds of laws it passes.

The Canadian legal system is pledged to uphold the principles associated with a political philosophy known as **liberalism**. Briefly put, liberalism elevates individual freedom and autonomy as its key organizing value. A corollary is that any interference with freedom—including the freedom to advertise—is inherently suspect and must be justified according to the principles of **constitutional law**.

Constitutional law supplies the basic legal structure for Canadian society, providing for such matters as

- the branches of government
- the creation of legislation
- the rules constraining what kinds of laws governments can put in place
- the sources of law

While the legal system may seem to be an overly technical subject, it is critical that business people have an understanding of constitutional law, particularly the basics of governmental operations and the vocabulary used to describe those operations. This basic knowledge of the law is essential because business, in all its forms, is directly affected by **government policy** and legislation. If proactive and knowledgeable, businesses can assume a significant role in influencing how government formulates and executes its agenda. General Motors of Canada Ltd., for example, has a corporate and environmental affairs department that is charged with monitoring government policy, as well as tracking and contributing to debates over public policy that could affect G.M. operations.[1] Smaller businesses may work to influence government on a more modest scale by monitoring issues in-house, hiring lobbyists, and working through industry associations.[2]

Businesses need to be aware of government operations because governments enact a great number of rules and regulations that affect them. Failure to comply with these rules and regulations can result in fines and other penalties, including closure of the business. It also may mean that the business loses out on opportunities to influence government policy and to take advantage of favourable laws.

---

1. Interview with Ms. Miriam Christie, Manager of Government Relations, Corporate and Environmental Affairs Department, General Motors of Canada Ltd. (10 March 2000).

2. Another simple way to keep apprised of a government's agenda and its potential impact on one's business is to get a copy of the speech from the throne. This speech is prepared by the prime minister's or premier's office and sets out the government's legislative agenda for each legislative session.

The Legislative Branch of Government

Statute Law and Jurisdiction

legislative branch
The branch of government that creates statute law.

statute law
Formal, written laws created or enacted by the legislative branch of government.

jurisdiction
The power that a given level of government has to enact laws.

The *Tobacco Products Control Act*—objected to by Terry in the Business Law in Practice scenario—is created by the legislative branch of the federal government. The other two branches of government, discussed later in this chapter, are the executive branch and the judicial branch.

The **legislative branch** of government creates a form of law known as **statute law**. A familiar example of statute law is the *Criminal Code of Canada*, which prohibits a variety of offences, such as assault, theft, fraud, and impaired driving.

Three levels of government make statute law in Canada: the federal, provincial, and municipal levels. The Constitution—through a statute known as the *Constitution Act, 1867*—dictates whether each level of government can make a given law or not. Expressed in legal language, each level of government has the **jurisdiction** to pass laws within its proper authority or sphere. Jurisdiction is divided in this way because Canada is a federal state, which means that governmental power is split between the central, national authority (the federal government) and regional authorities (the provincial governments). The provincial governments, in turn, empower municipal governments to legislate in defined areas.

Constitution Act, 1867

The federal government has the right, or the jurisdiction, to make laws in those areas set out in section 91 of the *Constitution Act, 1867* (formerly known as the *British North America Act* or the *BNA Act*). Areas in which the federal government may enact laws include the following:

LANDMARK IN THE LAW

- interprovincial/international trade and commerce
- trade as a whole
- postal service
- navigation and shipping
- currency
- national defence
- criminal law
- all legislative areas not given to the provinces (Note: This is a residual category in the sense that the federal government has all the law-making power not expressly given to the provinces. For example, it is the residual power that justifies federal legislation that creates federally incorporated companies.)

The provincial governments have jurisdiction to make laws in those areas set out in section 92 of the *Constitution Act, 1867*, including the following:

- hospitals
- property and civil rights within the province (e.g., the regulation of contracts)
- administration of justice (e.g., the court system)
- local matters (e.g., highway regulation)
- incorporation of provincial companies

The municipal governments have jurisdiction to make laws as permitted by the relevant provincial government, for example, in these areas:

- zoning
- subdivision
- taxation for the benefit of the municipality
- licensing

As outlined in the Constitution, the federal government has jurisdiction over criminal law, which includes the power to define new crimes, to provide penalties for breaches of the criminal law, and to pass laws with the purpose of protecting the public. Because criminal law falls under federal jurisdiction, there is a *Criminal Code of Canada* but no provincial criminal codes. In fact, if the legislature of British Columbia were to attempt to enact a law known as the Criminal Code of B.C., for example, this law would be unconstitutional because a provincial government does not have the power to pass such a law. No court would enforce the code because it would be contrary to the Constitution to do so.

The federal government undoubtedly has the jurisdiction to pass the *Tobacco Products Control Act* under its criminal law power, given that the idea or policy behind the law is to protect the public by regulating a dangerous product.[3] This area falls squarely within federal jurisdiction.

paramountcy
A doctrine that provides that federal laws prevail when there are conflicting or inconsistent federal and provincial laws.

Legislative Bodies in Canada

Federal

The federal legislative branch is known as Parliament and has two bodies: the House of Commons and the Senate. The House of Commons is made up of representatives elected from across Canada. Part of the job of the House of Commons is to consider

Who Has Jurisdiction?

Regulation of the environment is not assigned exclusively to either the federal or provincial government. Both levels of government have jurisdiction, depending on the legislative purpose. For example, jurisdiction over criminal law permits the federal government to forbid activity that endangers the public health, as well as to put regulations in place to control pollution and other forms of environmental degradation where it is a matter of national concern. The federal government also has jurisdiction over interprovincial rivers and can therefore regulate the release of marine pollution that would be carried from one province into another. The provincial jurisdiction over property and civil rights, however, permits provincial governments to regulate business activity, such as by imposing strict emission controls. The provincial power over municipalities permits provinces to regulate zoning, water quality, and the disposal of garbage.

ENVIRONMENTAL PERSPECTIVE

Where conflicting or inconsistent federal and provincial laws cannot be reconciled, the doctrine of **paramountcy** dictates that the federal law prevails, and while the federal law remains in force, the provincial law cannot operate.[4] The doctrine of paramountcy is infrequently applied, since actual conflict between federal and provincial law is rare.

Critical Analysis: What would happen without the doctrine of paramountcy if two levels of government passed competing laws? Do you think it would be better to simply give jurisdiction over an area such as the environment to one level of government or the other? What problems might arise if that were to happen?

---

3. *RJR-MacDonald Inc.* v. *Canada (A.G.)*, [1995] 3 S.C.R. 199.

4. For a discussion of jurisdiction over the environment, see Peter Hogg, *Constitutional Law of Canada*, student edition (Scarborough: Carswell, 1998) at ss. 17.3 (b)-(d), 18.4. For a discussion of paramountcy, see ss. 16.1-16.6.

and pass legislation, which the Senate must then approve before it can become law. The Senate, in turn, is composed of appointed members. Because it assesses the work of the House of Commons, the Senate has been called "the chamber of sober second thought."

Provincial

Each province has its own law-making body. For example, British Columbia has the Legislative Assembly, and Nova Scotia has the House of Assembly. There is no Senate, or upper house, at the provincial level.

Municipal

Each municipality also has a legislative body—generally known as a city council—which exercises powers delegated to it by the relevant province.

Business is affected by all levels of government, but it is most affected at the provincial level and, through delegation, at the municipal level. The regulation of business is generally a provincial matter because the provinces have jurisdiction over property and civil rights.[5] Civil rights does not, in this context, refer to civil liberties such as freedom of expression. Rather, it refers to the rights that someone might have as a result of entering into a contract or owning a piece of property.

The Passage of a Bill

This account of how the *Tobacco Products Control Act* became law illustrates the workings of the legislative branch of the federal government.

Passage of a Federal Bill

Legislation comes into being as a result of government policy. This policy has a variety of sources, including input from lobbyists, constituents, advisory boards, consultants, committees, bureaucrats, industry associations and other interest groups, and government ministers. Once the government is in general agreement that legislation in a given area is necessary, it asks the relevant minister to draft the proposed law. The matter is now ready to proceed through the legislative phase.

Step One: The proposed legislation, known as a bill, is brought before the House of Commons for what is called first reading. Ordinarily, passage through first reading is a foregone conclusion. There is never debate at this stage. A vote is taken, and if approved by a majority of members present, the bill passes first reading. The bill is then formally placed on Parliament's agenda.

Step Two: The bill is brought before the House again for second reading. It is at this point that debate takes place, with government members seeking clarification from the minister responsible and opposition members perhaps attacking the bill. Again, a vote is taken, and the bill passes second reading through a simple majority.

Upon second reading, the bill has been approved in principle and is referred to a committee for further consideration and redrafting as necessary. Depending on the nature of the committee to which the bill is referred, public input may be accepted, including input from industry associations and other lobby groups. After the committee has completed its work, the bill moves to the next step.

---

5. *Ibid.* at section 21.6. There are, of course, exceptions to this general statement, such as the *Competition Act*, R.S.C. 1985, c. C-34. This is a federal piece of legislation governing the marketplace which prohibits a variety of anticompetitive behaviours, such as misleading advertising.

Step Three: The bill is now ready to be read for a third time. It is at this point that any proposed amendments are debated and the bill is either defeated or passed in some form.

Step Four: The whole process described in steps one to three is repeated in the Senate. If the bill is approved, it proceeds to the governor general for formal confirmation, known as royal assent. At this point, the bill has been enacted into law.

Once the *Tobacco Products Control Act* has become law, it is a difficult and time-consuming procedure to get it changed, since its amendment or repeal would also have to follow the four-step process described above. For this reason, any industry affected by proposed legislation should consider making representations to government well before the matter proceeds as a bill. Industries may lobby individually, through relevant industry associations, or through the involvement of professional lobbyists.

Passage of a Provincial Bill

The legislative phase for passing a provincial bill is the same as the process described above, with two exceptions. First, there is no requirement for senatorial approval, since provinces do not have senates, and second, formal approval is granted by the lieutenant governor rather than the governor general. Canada's three territories—Nunavut, Yukon, and the Northwest Territories—have limited self-government and are subject to ultimate control by the federal government.[6]

The jurisdiction to pass laws affecting the tobacco industry, for example, is not confined to the federal parliament. In fact, many matters—such as health—can involve jurisdictional overlap between the federal and provincial spheres.[7]

Legislation by Municipal Governments

All municipalities in Canada are created by provincial legislation—they do not spring up spontaneously. When a municipality is created by an Act, a governing body (generally known as a council) is created and given the power to enact laws within

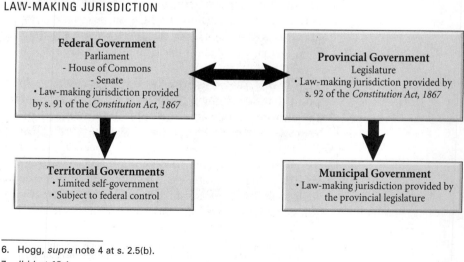

Figure 2.1

LAW-MAKING JURISDICTION

Federal Government
Parliament
- House of Commons
- Senate
• Law-making jurisdiction provided by s. 91 of the *Constitution Act, 1867*

Provincial Government
Legislature
• Law-making jurisdiction provided by s. 92 of the *Constitution Act, 1867*

Territorial Governments
• Limited self-government
• Subject to federal control

Municipal Government
• Law-making jurisdiction provided by the provincial legislature

---

6. Hogg, *supra* note 4 at s. 2.5(b).
7. *Ibid.* at 18.4.

bylaws
A law made by the municipal level of government.

the parameters defined in the Act. Municipalities have jurisdiction to legislate in a broad variety of matters, from levying appropriate taxes and regulating local zoning, parking, and subdivision, to requiring the licensing of businesses and dogs. Municipal legislation takes the form of **bylaws**.

The Executive Branch of Government

The executive branch of government has a formal, ceremonial function, as well as a political one. From a formal or ceremonial perspective, the executive branch supplies the head of the Canadian state. The **formal executive** also has a significant role in the legislative process, since the executive branch of government, represented by the governor general or lieutenant governor, issues approval as the final step in enacting a bill into law.

formal executive
The branch of government responsible for the ceremonial features of government.

The formal function of the executive branch developed as a result of the British monarch's historical role in governance when Canada was a British colony. It is for this reason that the queen—not the prime minister—is the formal head of the Canadian state, as well as the formal head of executive government. Since the queen obviously cannot be in Canada to perform her constitutional duties, representatives are appointed in her place. The queen's federal representative is the governor general, and her representative in each province is the lieutenant governor. While the governor general and lieutenant governors play an essential part in passing legislation by giving it royal assent, they have little practical power or real authority. Although the queen's representative could technically refuse to give royal assent to a bill, this would be a virtual impossibility. In short, **convention** dictates that the queen's representatives do what they are advised to do by the government of the day.

convention
Important rules that are not enforceable by a court of law but that practically determine or constrain how a given legal power is exercised.

The **political executive** is of great concern to businesses because it performs the day-to-day operations of government by formulating and executing government policy and administering all departments of government.

political executive
The branch of government responsible for day-to-day operations, including formulating and executing government policy, as well as administering all departments of government.

The chief executive of the federal government is the prime minister, while the chief executive of the provincial government is the premier. Other members of the executive—both provincial and federal—include cabinet ministers, civil servants, and the agencies, commissions, and tribunals that perform governmental functions.[8]

The **Cabinet**—made up of all the ministers of the various government departments, as well as the prime minister or premier—also has a very significant law-making function. It is often Cabinet that passes **regulations** providing detail to what the statute in question has enacted. For example, under the *Tobacco Products Control Act*, some of the regulations enacted were as follows:

Cabinet
A body composed of all ministers heading government departments, as well as the prime minister or premier.

> Every package that contains cigarettes or cigarette tobacco and that is sold or offered for sale by a manufacturer or importer of the cigarettes or cigarette tobacco shall, effective on September 12, 1994, display
>
> (a) in accordance with subsection 15(1), one of the following health messages...
>
> (i) "Cigarettes are addictive"....
>
> (ii) "Tobacco smoke can harm your children"....
>
> (iii) "Cigarettes cause fatal lung disease"....

regulations
Rules created by the political executive that have the force of law.

---

8. For example, the National Energy Board's power to approve pipeline construction in Canada is delegated by the federal government.

(iv) "Cigarettes cause cancer"....

(v) "Cigarettes cause strokes and heart disease"....

(vi) "Smoking during pregnancy can harm your baby"....

(vii) "Smoking can kill you"...., or

(viii) "Tobacco smoke causes fatal lung disease in non-smokers"....[9]

When Cabinet enacts regulations, it is known by its formal name: the Lieutenant Governor in Council (provincially) and the Governor in Council (federally). Cabinet's authority to pass the regulations referred to above, for example, is derived from Parliament through the *Tobacco Products Control Act.*

responsible government
Government that abides by conventions prescribing how governmental power is to be exercised.

Responsible government is a keystone of the Canadian system of governance. Responsible government includes the idea that the formal head of state—the queen—must always act on the advice and direction of ministers who belong to the legislative branch and who have the confidence of a majority of the elected members.[10] It also means that the prime minister—or premier, as the case may be—and other ministers must be elected members of the legislative branch.[11] Responsible government also means that the legislative branch is entitled to show, by a simple vote, that it has lost confidence in the executive. If the vote of nonconfidence is approved by a majority, the executive must resign, and an election is normally called.[12]

The rules associated with responsible government are not written down in the Constitution. Like the rule that the prime minister is the political head of the executive, they operate on the basis of tradition and convention. In this way, the Canadian Constitution is contained in a variety of sources: in the rules recited in formal constitutional documents, such as the *Constitution Act, 1867,* as well as in the rules provided by constitutional convention.

The exact wording of warnings on cigarette packages is set by regulation.

The Judicial Branch of Government

judiciary
A collective reference to judges.

It may seem surprising that the **judiciary** is a branch of government, given that the judiciary is supposed to be independent of government. Expressed more completely, however, the concept is this: the judiciary is to be independent from the legislative and executive branches of government.

---

9. *Tobacco Act; Tobacco Products Control Regulations,* S.O.R./89-21, s. 11(1). In September 2000, a Quebec court ruled that the tobacco industry must comply with federal regulations requiring bigger health warnings on cigarette packages and refused a request for a delay. A legal challenge to the warning law is expected in 2001. Imperial Tobacco, JTI-MacDonald Corp., and Rothmans, Benson and Hedges Inc. claim that the law violates their right to display their trademark logos and colour. Source: *Canadian Press Wire Service* (12 September 2000), online: QL (CP2K) and "Big Tobacco to Comply with Labelling Order" *The Toronto Star* (12 September 2000) A6.

10. Hogg, *supra* note 4 at 9.2.

11. *Ibid.* at 9.3(a). Hogg also notes that on rare occasions, someone who is not elected is appointed a minister, but that person must quickly seek election and win.

12. *Ibid.* As Hogg notes at 9.5(a), if the House of Commons passes a nonconfidence motion, this is the clearest example of when the government must resign, but defeat on any important vote is generally seen as a loss of confidence.

judges
Those appointed by
federal and provincial
governments to
adjudicate on a variety
of disputes, as well as
to preside over
criminal proceedings.

**Canadian Charter of
Rights and Freedoms**
A guarantee of specific
rights and freedoms
enshrined in the
Constitution and
enforceable by the
judiciary.

The judiciary is composed of **judges,** who are appointed by both federal and provincial governments. These judges are required to adjudicate on a variety of matters, including divorce and the custody of children, civil disputes such as those arising from a will, breach of contract, car accidents, and other wrongful acts causing damage or injury. Judges also preside over criminal proceedings.

The *Canadian Charter of Rights and Freedoms*

A key responsibility for judges is determining whether a given law meets the requirements of the Canadian Constitution, including the **Canadian Charter of Rights and Freedoms,** often referred to as simply the *Charter* (see Appendix A for the complete text). The *Charter* was created in 1982 and is intended as a judicially enforceable guarantee that the government will act consistently with the values associated with a liberal democratic state. The right to freedom of expression and of religion, the right to a fair and speedy trial, equality rights, and the right to vote are all examples of *Charter* protections that reflect a set of constitutional values founded on individual freedom and political laissez faire. Two protections that are particularly germane to business are contained in sections 2 and 15.

Fundamental Freedoms

2. Everyone has the following fundamental freedoms:

    (a) freedom of conscience and religion;

    (b) freedom of thought, belief, opinion and expression, including freedom of the press and other media of communication;

    (c) freedom of peaceful assembly; and

    (d) freedom of association.

    ...

Equality Rights

15. (1) Every individual is equal before and under the law and has the right to the equal protection and equal benefit of the law without discrimination and, in particular, without discrimination based on race, national or ethnic origin, colour, religion, sex, age or mental or physical disability.

The *Charter* is a powerful constitutional document because it provides protection from improper or oppressive *government* conduct—conduct that most often takes the form of legislation or policy. In short, section 32 of the *Charter* prohibits government and government alone from violating any of the rights or freedoms recited. By way of contrast, violation of rights in the private sector, such as through employment discrimination, is a matter for provincial and federal human rights codes and thus is addressed according to a separate set of rules.

Assume that Terry, the director of the tobacco company referred to at the beginning of this chapter, wants to mount a constitutional attack on the *Tobacco Products Control Act.* The *Charter* certainly applies, because legislation is one of the clearest forms of government action. With that hurdle passed, one of the matters that Terry must establish to a court's satisfaction is that the legislation violates a right or freedom protected by the *Charter*. In this case, it would appear that section 2

Appointment of Judges in Canada and the United States

INTERNATIONAL PERSPECTIVE

In Canada, the federal government appoints judges to the superior (higher level) courts, while the provincial governments make appointments at the provincial court level. Appointments are made after considerable consultation with a broad range of people who know the candidate well, both personally and professionally. These consultations are, however, conducted in private.

In the United States, the federal government appoints judges operating within the federal jurisdiction. The appointments are recommended by the executive arm of government and have to be approved by the Senate. The U.S. Senate is an elected body with much more authority than the Canadian Senate.

As with Canadian appointments, a good deal of private consultation takes place prior to any judicial appointment. To assist in the process, the American Bar Association ranks existing judges who are being considered for appointments at superior levels. These rankings take into account such factors as the number of times a judge's decisions have been overturned on appeal. High judicial appointments, and in particular U.S. Supreme Court appointments, are generally preceded by Senate reviews. At times, these reviews will be particularly contentious, and some candidates, as a result, have removed themselves from consideration, had presidential support removed, or failed to gain senatorial approval.

At the state level, most judicial positions are filled by way of popular election. The form of these votes varies; in some cases, it is a similar process to any political ballot, while in others it takes the form of a yes/no vote for one candidate only. These elections are the basis for the advertisements heard from time to time on U.S. television and radio. There is no equivalent to this electoral process in Canada.

Critical Analysis: Should the public have more input into the appointment of judges in Canada? If so, how might this input be accomplished?

(freedom of expression) is being violated, since the legislation does restrict how cigarettes are to be packaged by requiring health warnings and prohibits advertising altogether. Demonstrating a violation of section 2 does not mean that Terry has automatically won her case, however, because the rights and freedoms guaranteed by the *Charter* are not absolute. On the contrary, the *Charter* acknowledges that the government is entitled to restrict freedom of expression—as well as any other right recited in the *Charter*—but only if it has balanced all relevant interests carefully, as required by the very first section of the *Charter*.

1. The *Canadian Charter of Rights and Freedoms* guarantees the rights and freedoms set out in it subject only to such reasonable limits prescribed by law as can be demonstrably justified in a free and democratic society.

Section 1 requires the government to justify *why* it is infringing a right, as well as to demonstrate that in doing so, it is restricting the right in question as minimally and in as measured, controlled, and appropriate a way as possible. A court assessing the constitutionality of the *Tobacco Products Control Act*, for example, would seek to determine what the government was trying to accomplish through the legislation (i.e., protection of the public from a dangerous product) and then assess how that intent was accomplished. If there were a way that the government could achieve the same legislative goal without interfering as much with the right in question (i.e., freedom of expression), then the law would be vulnerable to legal attack since a more constitutionally palatable alternative is available.

If the tobacco company in the opening scenario can demonstrate that the *Tobacco Products Control Act* violates a *Charter* provision *and* the government cannot prove that its legislation meets the standard set by section 1, a court can order that the legislation be struck down—that is, it can declare the law to be of no force or effect. In essence, the Act is thrown out because it is unconstitutional. The court's authority to order such a powerful remedy is set out in sections 24 and 52 of the *Charter*.

That even a tobacco company could enforce constitutional rights associated with human beings is part of the essence of modern constitutional protections. In a free and democratic society, expression should be as unfettered as is reasonably possible, no matter who the speaker is and no matter what the words are. The Supreme Court of Canada has emphasized the need to protect such expression because

> [o]ver and above its intrinsic value as expression, commercial expression which, as has been pointed out, protects listeners as well as speakers plays a significant role in enabling individuals to make informed economic choices, an important aspect of individual self-fulfilment and personal autonomy. The Court accordingly rejects the view that commercial expression serves no individual or societal value in a free and democratic society and for this reason is undeserving of any constitutional protection.[13]

Not all Canadians agree with the idea that the judiciary should have the power to strike down legislation as being unconstitutional. Many believe that it is undemocratic for the courts to have the right to eliminate or amend a law duly enacted by elected representatives. However, those who support the *Charter* argue that even a majority (the elected representatives who enacted the legislation) should not have the power to infringe on the rights of others. Put another way, a liberal democratic system of government is not just about majority rule, as suggested in the following statement from Madam Justice Wilson of the Supreme Court of Canada:

> The *Charter* is predicated on a particular conception of the place of the individual in society. An individual is not a totally independent entity disconnected from the society in which he or she lives. Neither, however, is the individual a mere cog in an impersonal machine in which his or her values, goals and aspirations are subordinated to those of the collectivity. The individual is a bit of both. The *Charter* reflects this reality by leaving a wide range of activities and decisions open to legitimate government control while at the same time placing limits on the proper scope of that control. Thus, the rights guaranteed in the *Charter* erect around each individual, metaphorically speaking, an invisible fence over which the state will not be allowed to trespass. The role of the courts is to map out, piece by piece, the parameters of the fence.[14]

In "real life," the *Tobacco Products Control Act*, which concerned Terry, was successfully challenged before the Supreme Court of Canada for interfering with freedom of expression. One of the judges who heard the case, Madam Justice McLachlin, observed:

---

13. *Ford* v. *Quebec (A.G.)*, [1988] 2 S.C.R. 712 at 767.
14. *R.* v. *Morgentaler* (1988), 44 D.L.R. (4th) 385 at 485 (S.C.C.).

Commercial speech, while arguably less important than some forms of speech, nevertheless should not be lightly dismissed.... Tobacco consumption has not been banned in Canada. Yet the advertising ban deprives those who lawfully chose to smoke of information relating to price, quality and even health risks associated with different brands.[15]

On this basis, the government had unquestionably interfered with a section 2 right. Could that interference be justified under section 1? The court's answer was no, for a variety of reasons. Of central concern was that the warnings on the cigarette packages were required to be unattributed. That is, the cigarette company could not, on its package, attribute the health warning to the government—a particular irony, given that it was the government that was requiring the warning to be there in the first place. From this perspective, the government had interfered with freedom of expression more than was necessary to achieve its goal of protecting the public. Put another way, there was no evidence that an unattributed warning would protect the public any better than an attributed warning would. For reasons like this, the Supreme Court of Canada found that the legislation was unconstitutional and struck it down. Since then, the federal government has passed new legislation, which contains a revision, along with other changes, that permits the health warnings to be attributed.[16]

Though the court has the power to assess the constitutionality of legislation—and to strike down the law, if need be—it is the legislative branch of government that can have the last word in many cases. This power is enshrined in section 33.

In this way, the *Charter* permits the government to override or disregard a judicial decision that a given piece of legislation is unconstitutional or to pre-empt judicial involvement at the start. Section 33 of the *Charter* allows the government to enact legislation "notwithstanding" its unconstitutionality. While the government does not have this option with respect to all rights and freedoms guaranteed by the *Charter*, it does have this option for a great many of them, including the right to freedom of expression.[17]

There are, of course, political consequences to using section 33, as when the government of Alberta introduced legislation limiting the right of recovery to $150 000 for those wrongfully sterilized under that province's now-repealed eugenics legislation. As a result of public outcry that the government would deny sterilization victims their right to establish in court that they had suffered damages exceeding $150 000, the government quickly withdrew the bill.[18]

---

15. *Supra* note 3 at 347.

16. Section 15 of the *Tobacco Act*, S.C. 1997, c. 13, states:

  15. (1) No manufacturer or retailer shall sell a tobacco product unless the package containing it displays, in the prescribed form and manner, the information required by the regulations about the product and its emissions, and about the health hazards and health effects arising from the use of the product or from its emissions.

  (2) If required by the regulations, every manufacturer or retailer shall provide, in the prescribed form and manner, a leaflet that displays the information required by the regulations about a tobacco product and its emissions and about the health hazards and health effects arising from the use of the product and from its emissions.

  (3) The information referred to in subsections (1) and (2) may be attributed to a prescribed person or body if the attribution is made in the prescribed manner.

17. Section 33 of the *Charter* permits government to violate a large number of rights and freedoms, including freedom of conscience and religion; freedom of thought, belief, opinion, expression, and peaceful assembly; freedom of association; the right to life, liberty and security of the person; the right to be free from unreasonable search and seizure; the right to be free from arbitrary detention and imprisonment; the right not to be subject to cruel or unusual punishment; the right against self-incrimination; and the right to equality.

18. Eoin Kenny, "Klein Government Drops Bill to Compensate Victims" (11 March 1998), online: QL (CP98). Eugenics is a discredited belief that through selective breeding, the "quality" of the human race can be improved.

Sources of Law

royal prerogative
Historical rights and privileges of the Crown, including the right to conduct foreign affairs and to declare war.

common law
Rules that are formulated in judgments.

There are four sources of law in Canada: constitutional convention (discussed earlier), statute law (outlined in the preceding section), the **royal prerogative**, and the **common law**.

The royal prerogative has diminishing influence in the modern Canadian legal system. Briefly put, the royal prerogative refers to the historical rights and privileges of the Crown, including the right to conduct foreign affairs and to declare war.[19]

Figure 2.2

THE SOURCES OF LAW

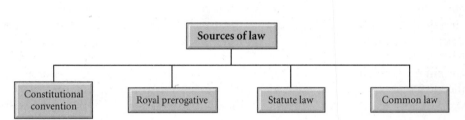

Common law, unlike statute law, is judge-made law. Common law is the end product of disputes that come before the judiciary. That is, when a judge gives a decision in determining the outcome of a given legal conflict, this is known as a judgment; judgments referred to cumulatively are called the common law.

For example, the *RJR-MacDonald* case, which involved a constitutional challenge to the *Tobacco Products Control Act,* went through the entire court system—right up to the Supreme Court of Canada—and produced a series of judicial decisions, all of which automatically became part of the common law.

Step One: The dispute, in this case, came to trial before a justice of the Superior Court of Quebec. At this stage, lawyers for both the government and the tobacco companies make representations to the trial judge. The trial judge considers the evidence and the arguments presented in favour of striking down the legislation, as well as all arguments supporting its constitutionality. In this case, Mr. Justice Chabot ruled that the legislation was unconstitutional, in part because the government could not establish that a *total* ban on advertising was necessary to achieve its goal of protecting the public, nor could it show that an unattributed health message would reduce tobacco consumption more effectively than would a message attributed to the federal Department of National Health.[20]

Ordinarily, a judge does not just give a bald resolution to the dispute in question. Rather, the judge seeks to explain, justify, and account for whatever decision she or he has reached. In doing so, the court relies on decisions made by other judges in other cases that are relevant to the matter at hand. These cases are known as **precedent**.

precedent
An earlier case used to resolve a current case because of its similarity.

The key principle of precedent can be summarized as "like cases should be treated alike." This means that judges should rule in a given case in a manner consistent with the way judges have adjudicated on or dealt with similar matters in the past. In short, the judge looks to the common law in order to resolve the matter at hand.

19. Hogg, *supra* note 4 at 1.9.
20. *RJR-MacDonald Inc.* v. *Canada (A.G.)* (1991), 82 D.L.R. (4th) 449 at 515 and following (Que. Sup. Ct.).

There are a number of rules governing the application of precedent, including the following:

- A lower court must follow a relevant precedent created by a higher court.[21]
- Not all precedents are of equal value—the higher the court that created the precedent, the more valued the decision is.
- The Supreme Court of Canada—the highest court in Canada—is entitled to decide a case in any way it sees fit.

equity
Rules that focus on what would be fair given the specific circumstances of the case, as opposed to what the strict rules of common law might dictate.

Judges are free not just to consider common law rules. There is a whole other set of rules, known as rules of **equity**, that judges also regularly apply. Equity, like common law, originated in England. The role of equity is to provide redress for the deserving person who otherwise would not receive an adequate remedy under the rules of common law. It focuses on what would be fair given the specific circumstances of the case, as opposed to what the strict rules of common law might dictate. In this way, it seeks to mitigate the harsh or unfair result that the common law might otherwise generate. This is not to suggest that "anything goes, as long as it's fair." Equity itself is constrained by rules limiting when it can render assistance. Equity also provides its own set of remedies—rectification, *quantum meruit,* rescission, specific performance, and the injunction—which will be described in more detail in later parts of this text.

While the process of applying precedent is reasonably easy to describe, it is inevitably riddled with ambiguity, uncertainty, and subjectivity. Although judges endeavour to be impartial, unbiased, and objective, such a standard is probably impossible to achieve. Furthermore, even reasonable people may differ in interpreting whether a given case from the common law applies to the dispute in question. This is not to imply that the study of law is futile or that the judicial application of precedent is without rhyme or reason. It is merely to suggest that the outcome in any case cannot be fully predicted.

Step Two: The Superior Court's judgment can be appealed; in this case, it was sent to the Quebec Court of Appeal. At this stage, the key question is whether the trial judge understood and applied precedent correctly. If not, the Court of Appeal overrules the decision of the lower court. In the *RJR-MacDonald* case, for example, the Quebec Court of Appeal ruled that the trial judge erred in his determination that the tobacco law was unconstitutional. According to the Appeal Court, though the legislation did interfere with freedom of expression, it did so in as minimal a way as was reasonably possible. The Appeal Court also ruled that the lower court had expected the government to have to prove too much with respect to the effectiveness of the measures it was taking through the legislation. According to a majority of the Court of Appeal:

> The legislator has adopted a measured solution with regard to a major public heath issue, while at the same time respecting certain social and economic realities. We are faced with an example of the difficulties of governmental action in contemporary Canadian society. The deference of the courts with regard to legislative choices made in this context is justified in this case.[22]

---

21. Chapter 4 discusses in detail the judicial hierarchy upon which the operation of precedent depends. For now, it is enough to know that not all courts are created equal—the higher the court, the more authority that court has. Lower courts must follow the decisions of the appeal courts. The appeal courts, in turn, must follow the decisions of the Supreme Court of Canada.

22. *R.J.R-MacDonald Inc.* v. *Canada (A.G.)* (1993), 102 D.L.R. (4th) 289 at 327 (Que. C.A.).

On this basis, the Court of Appeal upheld the constitutionality of the *Tobacco Products Control Act*.

Step Three: The Court of Appeal's judgment is appealable to the Supreme Court of Canada if the Supreme Court decides that the legal issue in question is of sufficient importance to the country as a whole. In this case, the Supreme Court agreed to hear the appeal and, as indicated, went on to restore the decision of the trial judge. The key problem with the legislation for a majority of the Supreme Court of Canada was that the Act went further than necessary in realizing its goal of protecting the public from a dangerous, but legal, product. As the earlier excerpt from the decision of Madam Justice McLachlin illustrates, the court held that there was a good reason for health warnings to be included on the package of a tobacco product, but there was no demonstrated reason for the health warnings to be unattributed. That is, legislation drafted with a sounder balance of interests would have permitted the packages to note that the health warning came from the Government of Canada, Department of National Health. As for the ban on advertising, a majority of the court ruled that the government had failed to establish a sufficient link between advertising bans and a decrease in tobacco consumption. Accordingly, the limitation on the industry's freedom of expression had been unjustified. For these kinds of reasons, the legislation was struck down for being unconstitutional.

This ruling left the tobacco industry free to resume all forms of advertising, pending the next move by government. As already noted, this move came in 1997 in the form of new legislation, which had not been successfully challenged as of October 2000.

Divisions/Classifications in Law

The law can be organized according to various categories. These categories help us conceptualize the diverse scope and purposes of the law.

Domestic versus International Law

domestic law
The internal law of a given country, which includes both statute and case law.

Domestic law is the internal law of a given country and includes both statute and common law. Domestic law deals primarily with individuals and corporations, and to a lesser extent, the state. In the *RJR-MacDonald* case, for example, the courts at all levels applied domestic law to determine whether the federal government had violated a right protected by the *Charter*.

international law
Law that governs relations between states and other entities with international legal status.

Conversely, **international law** governs relations between states and other entities with international legal status, such as the United Nations and the World Trade Organization. An important source of international law is **treaty** law. International law focuses mainly on states and international organizations.

treaty
An agreement between two or more states that is governed by international law.

Substantive versus Procedural Law

substantive law
Law that defines rights, duties, and liabilities.

Substantive law refers to law that defines rights, duties, and liabilities. In the *RJR-MacDonald* case, for example, at issue was the duty of the government to legislate in accordance with the *Charter*, as well as the right of the plaintiff to challenge the government for failing to meet that standard.

procedural law
The law governing the procedure to enforce rights, duties, and liabilities.

Procedural law refers to the law governing the procedure to enforce rights, duties, and liabilities. For example, the fact that a trial judge's decision can be appealed to a higher court is a procedural matter.

Public versus Private Law

public law
Areas of the law that relate to or regulate the relationship between persons and government at all levels.

Public law describes all those areas of the law that relate to or regulate the relationship between persons and government at all levels. An important aspect of public law is its ability to constrain governmental power according to rules of fairness. Examples of public law are criminal law, tax law, constitutional law, and administrative law.

Figure 2.3

EXAMPLES OF PUBLIC LAW

Criminal law	Identifies behaviour that is seriously unacceptable. In the interests of maintaining order and security in relations between citizens, the government prosecutes those who transgress basic standards of conduct, and the courts provide sanctions for that conduct, including fines and imprisonment.
Tax law	Sets the rules for the collection of revenue for governmental operation.
Constitutional law	Sets the parameters on the exercise of power by government.
Administrative law	Governs all regulatory activity of the state.

private law
Areas of law that concern dealings between persons.

Private law concerns dealings between persons. Many of the major topics in this text fall within private law, including contract law, tort law, property law, and company law.

Figure 2.4

EXAMPLES OF PRIVATE LAW

Contract law	Provides rules that make agreements between parties binding.
Tort law	Includes rules that address legal wrongs committed by one person against another, apart from a breach of contract. The wrongs may be intentional (as in an assault) or unintentional (as in a case of negligent driving).
Property law	Sets rules that define and protect property in all forms.
Company law	Provides rules concerning the rights, liabilities, and obligations of companies and other business vehicles.

The distinction between public and private law is not absolute. Most of the law of property is private, even if the government is buying, selling, or leasing. However, should the government choose to exercise its executive right to expropriate land, for example, issues of public law would be involved.

Furthermore, a single set of circumstances can have two sets of consequences, one involving private law and the other involving public law. For example, where a personal injury arises from an assault, the Crown may decide to prosecute the perpetrator of the assault under the *Criminal Code*. The victim, however, also has civil rights that can be enforced through tort law. Specifically, the victim of the assault can ask a court to order financial compensation from the perpetrator.

Figure 2.5

DIVISIONS/CLASSIFICATION OF THE LAW

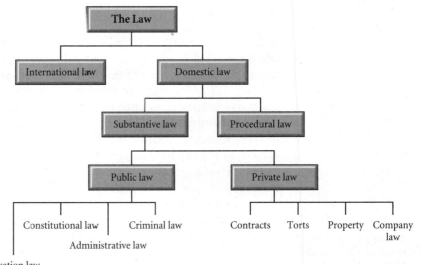

Source: Adapted from Gerald L. Gall, *The Canadian Legal System*, 4th ed. (Scarborough: Carswell, 1995).

Common versus Civil Law

Common law refers to judge-made law. It also is used in a totally different sense to describe the system of private law in place in all provinces except Quebec. A common law system is one that bases its private law on judicial decisions, which—if relevant and binding—*must* be applied to the case at issue. The private law in nine Canadian provinces, as well as the territories, is governed by common law in this sense of the word.

Quebec Civil Code
The rules of private law that govern Quebec.

The province of Quebec is, of course, bound by federal law such as the *Criminal Code,* but it has its own system of private law, which is governed by the **Quebec Civil Code**. Although there are many similarities between common law principles and what would be found in the *Civil Code,* conceptually there are significant differences between the two systems. One key difference is that judges in Quebec look to the *Civil Code* for general principles to be applied to the case at hand. They are not bound by how other judges have interpreted the *Code,* though practically speaking, these interpretations would be helpful and relevant.[23] Nor is a judge in a civil code system bound to apply a relevant provision of the code if to do so would produce an unjust outcome.[24]

Administrative Law and Business

administrative law
Rules created and applied by those having governmental powers.

Administrative law is one of the primary legal areas in which government and business interact. This area of law refers to rules created and applied by the various boards, agencies, commissions, tribunals, and individuals who exercise a governmental function as a result of legislation giving them that power. It also refers to rules of fairness that constrain how administrative bodies exercise their authority.

23. Gerald Gall, *The Canadian Legal System*, 4th ed. (Scarborough: Carswell, 1995) at 30.
24. *Ibid.*

Administrative bodies have often been established on a needs basis to deal with particular problems or difficulties as they have arisen, rather than pursuant to some overall regulatory plan. This piecemeal nature can make the area somewhat perplexing at times.

The functions of administrative bodies and officials often vary, as well. In some instances, the body or individual carries out purely administrative functions, as when the Employment Insurance Commission processes a claim for benefits; sometimes the body also has judicial functions, such as when the Labour Relations Board settles a dispute between an employer and employee; sometimes the body exercises legislative functions, as when the CRTC passes regulations concerning the amount of Canadian content on radio and TV; and sometimes the body has some combination of these functions. As a result, it is often difficult to summarize how businesses are subject to administrative regulation.

Nonetheless, this area of law has a significant impact on business because so much commercial activity is regulated by these bodies—from licensing requests to zoning and subdivision applications and human rights complaints. (See Figure 2.6 for a summary of the administrative bodies and officials that affect business.)

Figure 2.6

ADMINISTRATIVE BODIES AND OFFICIALS AFFECTING BUSINESS

Legend: F = federal; P = provincial; M = municipal

If you plan to ...	you may interact with ...	in regards to ...
establish a business	Regional and/or Municipal Licencing Tribunal, Minister, Agency, or Officer (M)	a business permit
construct new facilities or make exceptions to existing zoning regulations	Development Officer/Zoning Board (M) Building Officer (M) Development Appeal Board (M)	a development permit a building permit a denial of permit application
alter the interior or exterior of an existing building	Building Officer (M)	a building permit
hire employees	Workers Compensation Board (P) Labour Relations Board (P) Provincial Human Rights Tribunal (P)	an accident or injury unions, collective agreements discriminatory practices in the workplace
manufacture, sell, or store food or drink	Board of Health (P, M) Food and Drug Agency (F)	a food establishment permit packaging and labelling requirements
sell alcohol	Liquor Control Board or Commission (P)	a liquor licence
manufacture, sell, or advertise products	Consumer Protection Agency (F) trade practices legislation (P)	a product/item construction standards fair advertising practices
import products	Federal Import Review Agency (F)	approval
practise in architecture, pharmacy, law, dentistry, medicine, or accountancy	Professional Society (e.g., Law Society of British Columbia, Public Accountants Council for the Province of Ontario) (P)	a licence to practise the profession
sell real estate	Superintendent or Council of Real Estate (P)	a licence to sell
carry on a radio, television, or telecommunications business	Canadian Radio and Telecommunications Commission (F)	structure, scope, and content approval
sell financial products	Securities Commission, Financial Services Commission (P)	licensing and procedural requirements
engage in interprovincial trucking	National Transportation Agency (F)	a business licence
sell a particular agricultural product	Canadian Egg Marketing Agency (F) Canadian Wheat Board (F)	a production and sales licence

Source: Researched and written by Catherine Bradley.

To illustrate the workings of administrative law, consider the process involved in bringing an application for a bylaw or ordinance variance. A bylaw—sometimes known as an ordinance—is a form of legislation created by a municipality for purposes of local management, such as the regulation of parking, sanitation in restaurants, and the fitness of buildings for human habitation.

Making a Variance Application

Ms. Gourmet wants to set up a restaurant in a building that has limited on-site parking. The relevant municipal bylaw requires a minimum number of parking spots, which Ms. Gourmet cannot provide. Therefore, she must approach the municipal authority and apply for a variance of the land-use bylaw. If she succeeds, she will be able to operate her restaurant with fewer on-site parking spots than otherwise would be required.

Though details and terminology will vary from jurisdiction to jurisdiction, the basic steps in a variance application would be as follows:

Step One: Either alone or with the assistance of a lawyer, Ms. Gourmet files a formal variance application with a municipal officer—sometimes known as a development officer—to allow her proposed development to proceed, even though she cannot provide the minimum number of parking spots required by the bylaw. In her application, Ms. Gourmet provides some general background, as well as reasons why she should be granted the variance.

Step Two: The officer notifies owners of surrounding properties and invites their views on the variance matter by a fixed date.

Step Three: The officer considers the background provided by Ms. Gourmet, the input of the owners of surrounding properties, and the municipal rules and policies that govern his decision in the matter.

Step Four: The officer renders his decision, notifying Ms. Gourmet that he has refused her application because parking would spill over into the neighbourhood, to its detriment.

Step Five: Ms. Gourmet appeals the decision to a development appeal board, or another appropriate body. Whatever its name, the appeal body is usually

BUSINESS APPLICATION OF THE LAW

empowered to assess the application anew and come to its own determination. Ms. Gourmet advises the board that there would not be a huge increase in traffic with the opening of her restaurant, since many of her customers would be locals who would simply walk to her restaurant. For this reason, fewer parking spots would be required. The appeal board may also hear representations on behalf of the municipality, most often by a city solicitor.

Step Six: The board comes to its decision and, in this case, informs Ms. Gourmet that her appeal is unsuccessful because it has been persuaded by the reasoning of the development officer who first refused her application.

An important role for administrative law is regulating *how* the municipal officer and the appeal board, in our example, exercise their powers. First and foremost, administrative law principles seek to enforce a standard of fairness. For example, what if a member of the appeal board who refused the appeal were also a competitor of Ms. Gourmet? It is a conflict of interest for such a member to have heard the appeal, since, on the one hand, the board member is charged with the duty of assessing the matter on its own merits, yet, on the other hand, he or she would secure a strong personal advantage if the appeal were refused. In this circumstance, Ms. Gourmet would have what is legally referred to as a "reasonable apprehension of bias"—most people would conclude that the appeal member in question would be unable to do his job fairly.[25] When there is a reasonable apprehension of bias, the person adversely affected can go to a judge for assistance. In this example, Ms. Gourmet would likely receive a judicial order that the matter be heard again by a properly constituted appeal panel.

---

25. *Committee for Justice and Liberty* v. *Canada (National Energy Board)*, [1978] 1 S.C.R. 369 at 394.

Business Law in Practice Revisited

1. Is the government's law to regulate tobacco advertising a legal one?

The *Constitution Act*, 1867 sets out jurisdictional constraints that dictate to each level of government the areas in which it can legislate. The federal government must justify the *Tobacco Products Control Act* under the headings of section 91, most likely under the power of criminal law. It must also defend the legislation for violating freedom of expression. It must convince a court that this infringement is as minimal and as reasonable as possible, given the policy of the legislation to discourage smoking and protect the public from a dangerous product.

2. What is legislation, and where does it come from?

Legislation comes from the legislative branch of government. Federally, it must be approved by both the House of Commons and the Senate. Provincially, only the legislature is involved. Before a matter becomes law, it comes before the legislative branch of government in the form of a bill. It is read a first time, debated upon its second reading, referred to a committee for further study, and then brought back to the legislative branch for third reading. Upon approval by the queen's representative—provincially, it is the lieutenant governor, and federally, it is the governor general—the bill becomes law.

Legislation comes into existence because the government forms the opinion that a given area of society requires new or additional regulation.

3. Who assesses whether the legislation is permissible?

The judiciary makes this assessment. Under the Constitution, judges are mandated to hear challenges to the legal foundation of laws passed by all levels of government. In this example, a judge would consider whether the federal government has the jurisdiction under the *Constitution Act, 1867*, to pass the law in question, as well as whether the legislation could be justified under the *Charter*.

4. Are there any moral or ethical questions that arise from this scenario?

Given the persuasiveness of studies demonstrating that cigarettes cause death and serious illness, there are serious moral and ethical issues that arise for anyone in the tobacco industry. However, cigarettes are a legal product, and thus tobacco companies are entitled to be in business. If Terry believes that she is unable to actively advance the interests of her company, she should resign.

5. What can Terry do about the legislation at this point?

Like RJR-MacDonald and other tobacco companies, Terry can challenge the legislation for being unconstitutional. She should also consider less formal means of dealing with the matter, such as meeting with the federal Minister of Health and other governmental officials involved. Terry should consider a strategy that accepts the inevitability of some regulation while suggesting less drastic means to address the policy objectives of the legislation. She can also hire a public relations firm to ensure that she handles this sensitive matter in as palatable a way as possible.

Chapter Summary

Canadian society is bound by a set of constitutional values, many of which insist on the importance of the individual and the right to freedom from unreasonable government interference. These values restrain how government operates at all levels—federally, provincially, and municipally. Constitutional law plays an important role in *how* government does its job by defining what kinds of laws are permissible, as well as the process involved in creating those laws.

Each branch of government has its own work to do. The legislative branch creates statutes according to rules that govern the passage of a bill. The executive branch is responsible for the ceremonial features of government and for day-to-day operations, including formulating and executing government policy, as well as administering all departments of government. The judiciary has a significant role in scrutinizing the legislative and executive branches of government and can be an important resource for those who believe they have been unreasonably limited, such as in how they are permitted to carry out business, or unfairly treated by a governmental officer, board, or tribunal.

In sum, the Canadian Constitution places mandatory limits on the power of the legislature to pass any law it sees fit. The court, as required by the Constitution, insists that the power of government be exercised in a manner that is

- within that body's "jurisdiction," as defined by the *Constitution Act, 1867,* and
- consistent with the values and principles contained within the *Charter.*

The judiciary itself is bound by the rules of precedent to help ensure that any given legal dispute is resolved in a manner that is consistent with how similar disputes in the past have been resolved. Judges also have a discretion, accorded to them by the rules of equity, to ensure that each matter before them is justly resolved.

Administrative law also provides protection by ensuring that a fair process accompanies any regulatory decisions that affect a business or any other activity.

StudyChapter

Key Terms and Concepts

administrative law (p. 35)

bylaws (p. 25)

Cabinet (p. 25)

Canadian Charter of Rights and Freedoms (p. 27)

common law (p. 31)

constitutional law (p. 20)

convention (p. 25)

domestic law (p. 33)

equity (p. 32)

formal executive (p. 25)

government policy (p. 20)

international law (p. 33)

judges (p. 27)

judiciary (p. 26)

jurisdiction (p. 21)

legislative branch (p. 21)

liberalism (p. 20)

paramountcy (p. 22)

political executive (p. 25)

precedent (p. 31)

private law (p. 34)

procedural law (p. 34)

public law (p. 34)

Quebec Civil Code (p. 35)

regulations (p. 25)

responsible government (p. 26)

royal prerogative (p. 31)

statute law (p. 21)

substantive law (p. 33)

treaty (p. 33)

Questions for Review

1. What is the key idea upon which the Canadian Constitution is based?

2. What does "jurisdiction" mean?

3. Which document determines whether a government has the jurisdiction to pass a law or not?

4. What is a bill, and how does it become a law? What are the differences between the federal and provincial systems of enacting legislation?

5. How does the authority of a municipal government come into existence?

6. What is the difference between a regulation and a bylaw (or ordinance)?

7. What is the executive branch of government? How is it different from the legislative branch?

8. What is the *Canadian Charter of Rights and Freedoms*?

9. What is the common law? Who creates it?

10. What can a judge do if he or she determines that a piece of legislation is unconstitutional?

11. What is the difference between public law and private law?

12. Which Canadian province operates under a civil law system?

13. What is the role of equity?

14. What is one important function of administrative law?

Questions for Discussion

1. Canada has often been described as an overgoverned state. What features of Canada's system of government contribute to this opinion? Do you agree with this opinion?

2. What are the advantages and disadvantages of a judiciary that is appointed versus one that is elected?

3. Under a common law system, judges follow precedent when making decisions or resolving disputes. What are the advantages of following precedent? Can you think of any situations where it would be inappropriate to follow precedent?

4. Dozens of administrative tribunals, such as the Atomic Energy Commission of Canada, the Labour Relations Board, the Canadian Radio-television and Telecommunications Commission, the Occupational Health and Safety Commission, and Human Rights Tribunals, have been established by both the federal and provincial governments. Why do you think administrative tribunals are such a predominant feature in Canada? In other words, why have they been established?

1. As a result of the government's trend to privatize and outsource ser-
    vices, MNX Inc. received a government contract to provide a wide range
    of medical services to residents of nursing homes. The services provided
    include nutrition advice, massage and physiotherapy, screening for dis-
    eases prevalent in the aged, and general emotional counselling. The pro-
    gram has been very well received by the patients, with the exception of
    several patients who have complained that they can't access the services
    either because they are hearing impaired or because they do not speak
    the language in which the services are provided (several of the patients
    speak only Tamil and Hindi). MNX is concerned about the plight of
    these patients, but the cost of providing services in a manner that would
    allow hearing impaired and non-English-speaking patients to access
    them was not factored into the contract with the government. MNX has
    approached the government for additional funding, but the govern-
    ment has said that there is no more money. Could the affected residents
    of the nursing home bring a *Charter* action against MNX? On what
    basis? What would MNX's potential defence be? What kind of remedy
    would the residents seek?[26]

2. R&D, a Crown corporation, has recently completed a human resource
    audit and inventory. One of the distressing results of the exercise was
    the revelation that its workforce is aging and that young recruits are
    leaving for better opportunities elsewhere. One of the recommenda-
    tions of the consultants carrying out the review is to institute a manda-
    tory retirement age of 55. Such a course of action would open up
    opportunities in the higher ranks of the corporation and would help
    retain younger workers by providing opportunities for promotion.
    Would such a policy violate the *Canadian Charter of Rights and
    Freedoms*? What additional information would be useful?

3. In 1999, General Motors and Toyota announced that, working together,
    they would create the car engine of the future. Ford and
    DamilerChrysler have formed a partnership to improve fuel-cell engine
    technology. This initiative is in response to a California law requiring
    that by 2003, zero emission vehicles (ZEVs) must make up 10 percent of
    an auto company's total sales. What is the role of government in regu-
    lating industry and protecting the environment, particularly when
    doing so drives up the cost of the product?

---

26. Based, in part, on *Eldridge* v. *British Columbia (A.G.)*, [1997] 3 S.C.R. 624.

Three Chapter

Managing Legal Risks

Objectives

AFTER STUDYING THIS CHAPTER, YOU SHOULD HAVE AN
UNDERSTANDING OF:

- ► METHODS OF MANAGING THE LEGAL ENVIRONMENT OF
  BUSINESS
- ► THE DEVELOPMENT OF A LEGAL RISK MANAGEMENT PLAN
- ► THE IMPORTANCE OF ANTICIPATING AND REACTING TO
  DEVELOPMENTS IN THE LEGAL ENVIRONMENT
- ► METHODS OF MANAGING LEGAL SERVICES

Business Law in Practice

Mainplace Stationers Ltd. (MP) is a well-established, medium-sized business with a
main office in the downtown business district of a typical Canadian town and three
branch outlets in the region. It sells and leases a wide range of products and provides
related services, such as design, installation, and maintenance. Products include
office supplies, furniture and equipment, and computer systems. Its customers are
consumers and other businesses. The present owners are the second generation of
owners and have expanded the business significantly, especially in sales of computer
technology. MP is financially healthy and profitable, achieving sales of $6 million last
year. MP owns the three-storey building in which the main office is located. MP uses
the main level and leases out the other two levels. MP leases the space for its branch
outlets in the various towns in which they are located.

Two of the owners have recently attended a trade show where one of the seminars dealt with the concept of risk management in the office services industry. When the owners returned, they asked Manon Sevigny, a member of the management team, to explore the possible legal risks in their business.

1. What are the legal risks arising from MP's business activities?
2. How should MP handle these risks?

Assessing the Legal Environment

Many factors determine the success of a business organization. It must be able to analyze and evaluate its activities, forecast changes in the business environment, and react effectively to unexpected developments. Of central importance is the ability to strike the right balance between managing the present and planning for the future. To meet its goal of producing a product or delivering a service at a profit, the business enterprise must have a set of functions and systems in place, including finance, marketing, and human resources. To ensure the smoothest possible operation of these systems, the business also needs to deal intelligently with the legal environment. By doing so, the business is less likely to make mistakes that are

- costly in terms of the expense of legal services and damage claims
- distracting in terms of time and effort
- harmful in terms of relationships and reputation in the industry

This chapter explores how a business can manage its interaction with the law and legal issues. It considers two basic approaches—preventative and reactive. The preventative approach requires a thorough evaluation of the risks associated with the business's activities in order to minimize their impact. The emphasis is on compliance with legal requirements and anticipation of changes in the legal environment. The reactive approach recognizes that legal problems may still materialize, so the firm needs a strategy in place to deal with such developments. These two approaches are combined in a management plan that reduces the impact of **legal risks** on the organization.

legal risk
A business risk with legal implications.

Legal Risk Management Plan

Managing the intersection of law with an organization's activities requires completing a comprehensive assessment of legal risk exposure and developing a **legal risk management plan**. Large businesses may have a whole department headed by a risk manager to achieve this goal. In smaller organizations, the risk management function may be performed by the chief executive or delegate (such as Manon Sevigny for MP) or by someone outside the organization, such as an insurance agent or a risk management consultant.

legal risk management plan
A comprehensive action plan for dealing with the legal risks involved in operating a business.

Another possibility is assigning responsibility for the assessment to internal or external lawyers. However, this approach is effective only when the lawyer has the training or experience to perform such a function. If the lawyer lacks such qualifications, she or he should be involved only as a resource for the manager who is conducting the actual assessment. Regardless of where primary responsibility lies, it is not a task for one person. Risk management involves the cooperation of managers and others at every level of the organization. The challenge for Manon is to identify those inside and outside MP who can help her through the steps for developing a useful plan.

Creating a risk management plan is a four-step process:

Step One: Identify the legal risks.
Step Two: Evaluate the potential loss associated with those risks.
Step Three: Devise a legal risk management plan to address those risks.
Step Four: Implement the plan.

Applying the Four-Step Process

Identify the Legal Risks

There are several methods that a business can use to identify its potential exposure to legal risks. This section explores three possible approaches, which, although reasonably distinct, do sometimes overlap. These approaches would have Manon assessing MP's functional areas, its business decisions, and its business relationships.

Step One: Identify the legal risks.

 Assess the organization's functional areas.

 Review the organization's business decisions.

Determine the parties with whom the organization has a business relationship.

Assess Functional Areas

functional areas
Traditional departments for organizing a business.

The **functional areas** of business are those that are traditionally recognized in business organization charts and business school curricula—accounting, finance, marketing, production, human resources, and information systems. Although business and education are moving away from strictly defined functional responsibilities to a more integrated approach, functional areas still provide a useful starting point for risk analysis.

What follows are some possible risks arising in functional areas relevant to our example of Mainplace Stationers.

- Marketing programs are subject to industry codes and government regulation. For example, if MP decides to mount a large sale on excess inventory, managers should be aware of the consumer protection rules against misleading statements in advertising "regular" and "sale" prices. Without this grounding, the managers may cause the organization to break the law.
- Production decisions may entail tradeoffs between efficiency and safety. For example, cost pressures could tempt MP to cut corners in assembling and installing furniture and equipment, which could lead to claims against MP for property damage and injury.
- Human resources face a number of serious risks, including harassment, downsizing, and wrongful dismissal. If such matters are not handled according to well-developed policy, the organization runs a greater risk of being sued or having a human rights complaint made against it by a disgruntled employee.
- Information technology poses risks if records are inadequately maintained and protected. For example, timely delivery of product and services is bound to be

important to MP customers. If a proper system of monitoring customer orders is not maintained, MP may lose future orders and be subject to claims from customers for the consequences of late delivery.

Employees can provide a useful starting point for identifying risks, given their familiarity with operations. As well, Manon needs to involve managers from each functional area in her risk review process.

Assess Business Decisions

A review of decisions having possible legal implications also can be used to identify risks.

standard form contract
A form of agreement that imposes the same set of terms on every customer.

- MP must assess the risk in its decisions concerning financial arrangements. How is credit granted to customers? How does MP obtain credit from suppliers? Who assumes responsibility for defining the terms of credit?
- MP must assess the risk in its decisions on how its contracts are worded. Sales to customers may involve **standard form contracts**. These contracts set out terms and conditions that are the same in every sale or transaction. Buying goods and services from suppliers involves dealing with their terms and conditions, also often in standard form. Do the organization's employees understand the content of these documents? Is the organization unwittingly assuming unnecessary risk of loss and liability as a result of these contracts?
- MP must assess the risk in its decisions on the ownership and use of land. MP is the owner and occupier of part of its building and the landlord of the remainder, as well as the occupier of the space it leases for its branch operations. As occupier, MP is subject to claims by customers who injure themselves on its premises. As landlord, MP has leases with its tenants, which may lead to legal problems if the terms are not met (if, for example, tenants fall behind in their rent payments). As tenant in its branches, MP depends on its landlords to meet their obligations.
- MP must assess the risk in its decisions affecting personnel. MP faces legal ramifications in hiring, employing, and dismissing employees. These decisions require extensive planning, particularly in setting standards for performance, monitoring performance, and providing feedback to employees.

An inventory of such decisions will provide valuable input into the overall legal risk assessment. A team of senior managers is likely in the best position to help Manon with this part of her assessment.

Assess Business Relationships

This approach focuses on the relationships a business has both internally and externally. It has the potential of providing a broad perspective because it identifies

- those who have relationships with the business, both long and short term
- the risks involved in those relationships, in both the long and short term

Mainplace Stationers has a number of relationships, all with attendant legal risks, such as the following:

- Employees may be injured at work or experience discrimination.
- Suppliers or lenders may claim that they have not been paid.

■ Regulators may charge that the organization is failing to obey regulations related to business signs or waste disposal.

As noted earlier, there are important interrelationships among these approaches, and all three of them can be used in performing Step One of the risk management plan, as illustrated in the Business Application of the Law box, below.

This first step in developing a legal risk management program may seem to be unduly negative because it seeks to identify everything that could possibly go wrong in a business operation. The purpose of Step One, however, is to provide a realistic assessment of the potential downside of doing business, with a view toward minimizing loss.

Legal Risks in the Business of Mainplace Stationers

1. MP might have a fire in its building, causing damage to inventory, the building itself, and the property of tenants.

2. Suppliers to MP may deliver orders late, deliver defective goods, or fail to deliver the goods that were ordered.

3. Customers may fail to pay for orders delivered. They may complain about the quality of the goods or the service provided by MP.

4. A customer might slip and fall on a slippery floor and be injured.

5. MP employees may fail to do their jobs properly or make commitments to suppliers or customers that are unacceptable to MP management.

There is legal risk involved in delivering customer orders.

6. Local regulations dealing with such matters as business signs or waste disposal may change, requiring MP to make significant adjustments and incur expenses.

7. If MP buys equipment from other countries, trade regulations may change, making continued importation impossible or much more expensive.

8. MP may get into financial difficulty, which would have serious implications for the owners of MP and put their personal assets at risk.

9. Accountants (whether employed by MP or retained as professional advisors) may make a significant error that misleads creditors, owners, or investors.

10. A delivery truck may be involved in a motor vehicle accident, resulting in personal injury and property damage.

11. A customer may complain that a sale price is higher than a competitor's regular price. MP may be in violation of advertising regulations.

12. A business operated by one of the MP tenants may fail, leaving MP with several months of unpaid rent.

Evaluate and Measure the Risks

The techniques used in Step Two vary from a simple, subjective evaluation to a complex statistical approach, involving actuaries and other professionals. These techniques involve assessing both the probability and the severity of loss.

Step Two: Evaluate or measure the risks.

 Assess the probability of loss.

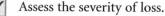 Assess the severity of loss.

Most organizations have a wealth of information available to assist in performing such assessments, including the organization's loss history, industry statistics on losses, and expert opinion, from both within and outside of the organization.

A high probability that a particular event will occur can be offset by a relatively low level of loss, should the event actually occur. Events that are unlikely to occur also may deserve close attention if the potential loss is high. In the Mainplace Stationers situation, customers may occasionally slip and fall on MP property, despite the best efforts of staff to prevent such events. However, these falls are unlikely to result in serious injuries that would be catastrophic for MP. Yet if MP seriously mishandles a major order from its most important customer, this one event may imperil the future of MP.

The point in evaluating risks is to recognize that not all risks are alike, nor should they be treated alike. Some risks crystalize into liability fairly often, but their financial and legal impact is relatively small. Other risks materialize infrequently, but when they do their impact is severe.

Devise a Risk Management Plan

There are a number of methods a business can follow to limit its exposure to risk, including risk avoidance, risk reduction, risk retention, and risk transfer. Choosing one or more approaches involves evaluating the risk matched with the resources, financial or otherwise, of the organization—in other words, doing a cost-benefit analysis.

Step Three: Devise a risk management plan.

 Avoid or eliminate the risk.

 Reduce the risk.

Retain the Risk.

Transfer the risk.

Risk Avoidance

risk avoidance
The decision to cease a business activity because the legal risk is too great.

Eliminating risk, or **risk avoidance**, is appropriate when the risk is simply too great or when the undesirable result of the activity, product, or service is greater than the advantages. In the Mainplace Stationers context, the risk that import regulations and conditions may change in ways harmful to MP may cause the company to avoid committing to an offshore firm as a major supplier. Domestic sources may be less attractive in the short term, but less risky in the long term. Depending on the circumstances, dealing with a major supplier offshore may be judged so risky that the potential downside outweighs the benefits.

Another example of risk avoidance relates to financing the business. If MP owners need capital for expansion, they may be called upon to pledge personal assets as security for a loan to the business. Despite their confidence about the future of their business, the owners may be unprepared to jeopardize their personal assets. They may, instead, seek other sources of financing—by selling shares in the company, for example—thereby reducing personal risk to themselves.

Risk Reduction

risk reduction
Implementation of practices in a business to lower the probability of loss and its severity.

A business can undertake **risk reduction** in relation to a host of operational activities. For example, MP cannot do business without extending credit to customers. The provision of credit inevitably involves the risk that some customers will not pay their accounts. To minimize that risk, MP should have procedures in place (such as regular credit checks) for evaluating and periodically reassessing the creditworthiness of customers.

As another example, MP can reduce the risk of the municipal government's changing regulations in a way that adversely affects the enterprise. MP's management should keep apprised of municipal politics, through contact with municipal representatives, bureaucrats, legal advisors, industry associations, chambers of commerce, and other businesses in the community. By doing so, MP will see regulatory changes coming and be able to make representations before they become law. At a minimum, MP will be able to plan for changes and accommodate them in the least disruptive fashion.

To minimize the chance that customers will injure themselves by slipping and falling, MP can pay extra attention to keeping walkways and other areas frequented by customers clear of possible hazards. Employees delegated to do the maintenance work can be informed about the importance of their work and the nature of the risks to MP if the work is inadequately performed. MP also might consider posting warnings for customers in hazardous areas.

MP also can reduce the risk of accounting errors by carefully hiring and training staff and by choosing professionals based on their reputation and proven performance. MP can seek professional advice on financial controls and take an active role in the work that their accounting professionals do for them. For example, before financial results are sent to the bank, MP management and the accountants should review them for cogency.

Risk Retention

risk retention
The decision to absorb the loss if a legal risk materializes.

Keeping or absorbing all or part of the risk within the organization is known as **risk retention**. In effect, the organization pays losses out of its own resources. The organization can do this in several ways:

- *Self-insurance.* The organization can establish a funded reserve.
- *Insurance policy deductibles.* The organization can retain risks to a certain dollar amount.
- *Noninsurance.* The organization can charge losses as an expense item.

There has been a marked increase recently in the use of risk retention, owing in part to significant increases in insurance premiums in many industry sectors. There are also some risks that cannot be avoided or reduced to zero. These risks must be absorbed by the business. For example, MP cannot avoid local regulations. If waste disposal rules change, MP may face significant expense, despite its best efforts to anticipate and adapt to the changes.

Another example concerns dissatisfied customers. Even if employees are thoroughly trained to deal with customers (with a view to meeting the best interests of both MP and customers), some customers will make complaints with significant financial consequences. Perhaps a customer has bought a computer system on the advice of MP, and the system has turned out to be completely inappropriate for the customer's real needs. This is a situation that MP must resolve, and it represents a risk that cannot be completely avoided.

Risk Transference

This approach involves transferring the financial risk to another by contract. Insurance, which is an integral part of most risk management plans, is discussed in detail in Chapter 20. Insurance is likely the best response to many of the risks faced by MP. Motor vehicles owned by MP will be covered by vehicle insurance. Slips and falls by customers will be covered by a general liability policy. The risk of fire will be covered by fire insurance. However, it should be noted that insurance can be costly, that some risks are difficult to insure against (such as potential environmental liability), and that insurance provides coverage only to the extent and in the amount actually purchased. As well, insurance does not prevent loss or the adverse publicity resulting from a high-profile case, even if the insurance company defends or pays the claim.

Exploding Gas Tanks

General Motors discovered that the gas tank of their 1979 Malibu was placed too close to the rear bumper. GM's own cost-benefit analysis of the gas tanks showed that it would cost $2.20 per auto to settle claims involving fatalities caused by exploding tanks, versus $8.59 per car to fix the problem beforehand.

What nonfinancial factors should GM consider in its decision as to whether to retain or avoid the risk of exploding gas tanks? Which factors are most important?

GM decided not to fix the problem, and to retain the risk and cost of injuries caused by the defect. Passengers in one of the Malibus were severely burned when the fuel tank exploded after a rear-end collision. Those injured sued GM, and in the course of the trial, the GM cost-benefit analysis was revealed.

What is the attitude of a jury likely to be? Why was it inappropriate for GM to retain this kind of risk? What kinds of damages do you think GM will be responsible for? Will GM's reputation suffer?

Source: Michael White, "Jury Orders GM to Pay Crash Victims $4.9-Billion (U.S.)" *The Globe and Mail* (10 July 1999) B3.

risk transference
The decision to shift the risk to someone else through a contract.

Although **risk transference** is usually thought of in terms of insurance, it can also involve indemnity, exemptions, waivers of liability, and other such protection that can be provided by contract (see Part 2).

The most common transaction in the business of Mainplace Stationers is the delivery of goods to customers. Many things can go wrong that may cause loss to the customer, resulting in a claim against the business. The product may be delivered late. It may fail to meet the customer's expectations. It may be defective. One common approach to such risks is to create a contract for all customers that limits the liability of the business for such claims. For example, MP might include a clause in its customer contracts providing that in event of a system failure of an MP product, MP is only liable to pay the customer a maximum of $40.00 in damages. This is called a **limitation of liability clause**.

limitation of liability clause
A term in a contract that sets a monetary limit on the financial responsibility for failure to perform as agreed.

The challenge in such a contract is to create terms and conditions that achieve the business objective of risk transference, that are acceptable to customers, and that are legally enforceable if a dispute arises. Lawyers can create these standard form contracts only if they fully understand the risks involved and are able to work closely with the business to ensure that the terms achieve their purpose in a reasonable manner.

The focus on transferring the risk to the customer in the MP example would address the following questions:

- Is the limitation of liability clause legally permissible?
- Does such a clause make business sense from the perspective of good customer relations?
- Is the contract clearly drafted?
- Has it been established which employees, if any, have authority to change the terms, and if so, to what extent?
- Have the employees been instructed on how to present and explain the standard form contract to the customer and answer questions about its contents?
- Is there a system in place for addressing consumer complaints promptly and effectively?

Any plan or program devised with Step Three in mind must be reasonable in terms of its cost and complexity. It cannot eliminate all risk. The goal is to be aware of risks and to make conscious decisions about dealing with them. To assist in this process, managers may turn to legal professionals for balanced advice, either on a lawyer–client basis or through in-house counsel. However, the lawyer must know the business and the industry in which it functions in order to provide useful input.

Implement the Plan

Once a business has devised a risk management plan, it must put the plan into action and assess its effectiveness on an ongoing basis.

Step Four: Implement the plan.

 Carry out the plan.

 Monitor and revise the plan.

Responsibility for implementing the risk management plan must be clearly assigned. Much of this allocation may be obvious. For example, if the analysis has suggested a quality-control problem, the plan must identify those responsible for both monitoring quality and delivering the service or producing the product. It will not be enough, however, to simply advise the appropriate personnel of the problem. The employees must be educated as to why the problem requires correction and what techniques should be adopted to ensure that the problem is corrected. In addition, guidelines for carrying out the procedures should be collected in a manual to allow immediate reference. The document should include, as appropriate, a schedule of inspections of facilities, a formal system of ensuring that those inspections take place as scheduled, an accident-reporting system, and information on any insurance coverage in place. Such a manual can be a two-edged sword, however. If MP is sued for injury or loss and it is shown that MP neglected its own policy on the matter, the claimant may have grounds for establishing liability.

The plan must be continually reviewed, reassessed, and revised. Management should try to determine whether the plan is working, and if not, why it is not. Risks may frequently change and practices will need to be adapted, but a routine review process can help to ensure that the requisite adjustments are made.

Figure 3.1

SUMMARY OF THE LEGAL RISK MANAGEMENT MODEL

Step One: **Identify the legal risks.**
- ✓ Assess the organization's functional areas.
- ✓ Review the organization's business decisions.
- ✓ Examine the organization's business relationships.

Step Two: **Evaluate or measure the risks.**
- ✓ Assess the probability of loss.
- ✓ Assess the severity of loss.

Step Three: **Devise a risk management plan.**
- ✓ Avoid or eliminate the risk.
- ✓ Reduce the risk.
- ✓ Retain the risk.
- ✓ Transfer the risk.

Step Four: **Implement the plan.**
- ✓ Carry out the plan.
- ✓ Monitor and revise the plan.

A risk management plan need not be a lengthy or complicated document. The key is for managers like Manon to identify and evaluate legal risks and then rely on a cost-benefit analysis to devise an action plan in response. For example, the cost of checking in detail the background of prospective tenants may outweigh the possible cost of a tenant's defaulting on the rent. The cost of prevention is a certainty, while risks and the resulting losses may never materialize. Figure 3.2 presents a possible plan for MP that Manon might develop with the management team by applying the risk management model. It addresses the risks identified earlier in the chapter.

Figure 3.2

LEGAL RISK MANAGEMENT PLAN FOR MAINPLACE STATIONERS

Risk 1: MP might have a fire in its building, causing damage to inventory, the building itself, and the property of tenants.

Action: MP should identify potential fire hazards (such as paper stored near a heat source) and implement a fire prevention plan. For example, someone should be assigned the duty of conducting and documenting regular inspections and reporting any hazards. MP should also have insurance coverage that includes the fire risks and covers losses to property, personal injury, and loss of business. MP should review its coverage with the insurance agent at least once a year.

Risk 2: Suppliers to MP may deliver orders late, deliver defective goods, or fail to deliver the goods that were ordered.

Action: MP should choose suppliers carefully, based on reputation in the trade (for example, by contacting industry associations and other firms in the industry), and carefully monitor their quality of performance. MP also should attempt to negotiate agreements with suppliers that set clear standards of performance (specific delivery dates) and specify compensation for performance failures (for example, the right to obtain the goods elsewhere and claim extra costs).

Risk 3: Customers may fail to pay for orders delivered. They might complain about the quality of the goods or the service provided by MP.

Action: MP should choose customers carefully before extending credit (by doing checks through credit-reporting agencies) and monitor payment records. In terms of quality of goods and services, MP should have detailed customer service practices in place (such as on-time delivery and time limits for response to customer complaints) and regularly gather feedback from customers (through telephone follow-up). MP should also use standard form contracts to clearly indicate who is responsible for what in their transactions.

Risk 4: A customer might slip and fall on a slippery floor and be injured.

Action: MP should identify hazards (such as a slippery floor or inventory obstructing an aisle in the showroom) and ensure that procedures are in place for regular patrol and maintenance of those areas. MP should post warning signs for visitors and should have insurance coverage in place for any injuries that do occur.

Risk 5: MP employees may fail to do their jobs properly or make commitments to suppliers or customers that are unacceptable to MP management.

Action: MP needs clear performance standards for employees (such as sales quotas or number of customer complaints). Employees should be carefully recruited and trained, as well as regularly evaluated.

Risk 6: Local regulations dealing with such matters as business signs or waste disposal might change, requiring MP to make significant adjustments and incur expenses.

Action: MP should keep attuned to local politics so that changes do not come as a surprise, be prepared to contribute to public debate over proposed changes, and be able to formulate coordinated efforts to deal with adaptation to regulatory changes. For example, if sign regulations change, the marketing manager could be assigned the task of consulting all those affected by the signs and deciding exactly what needs to be done to comply with the changes.

Risk 7: If MP buys equipment from other countries, trade regulations might change, making continued importation impossible or much more expensive.

Action: MP should obtain expert advice (legal or otherwise) on the situation in the relevant countries and be in a position to anticipate changes there, just as they would with local regulations. If the situation is deemed too unstable, MP should seek other sources of supply.

Risk 8: MP might get into financial difficulty, which would have serious implications for the owners of MP and put their personal assets at risk.

Action: MP owners need to structure their business and personal affairs to achieve a level of comfort with their degree of personal risk. This risk relates to the legal structure of the business (for example, partnership versus corporation) and the extent to which the owners accept responsibility for business losses through such vehicles as guarantees. MP management needs to keep on top of the financial position of the firm and anticipate financial problems, rather than be caught by a crisis.

Risk 9: Accountants (whether employed by MP or retained as professional advisors) may make a significant error that misleads creditors, owners, or investors.

Action: MP should choose all professional advisors carefully (based on record and reputation) by consulting professional associations and others involved in the industry and community. MP can then be confident that the professionals they retain are members in good standing of their professional societies and insured against professional errors. MP should also work closely with those advisors and not simply rely on their advice.

MP should also carefully choose accounting employees based on ability and trustworthiness and obtain professional advice about a system of financial controls to prevent mistakes.

Risk 10: A delivery truck may be involved in a motor vehicle accident, resulting in personal injury and property damage.

Action: MP should carefully recruit drivers of firm vehicles and provide appropriate specialized training programs for them. MP should also make sure that complete vehicle insurance coverage is in place and review coverage at least annually with an insurance agent.

Risk 11: A customer may complain that a sale price is higher than a competitor's regular price. MP may be in violation of advertising regulations.

Action: MP marketing personnel should be familiar with relevant advertising regulations and seek prior approval from regulators if there is any doubt about compliance.

Risk 12: A business operated by one of the MP tenants may fail, leaving MP with several months of unpaid rent.

Action: MP should choose tenants carefully (by checking references and general reputation) and avoid long-term leases with unproven tenants. MP should also be aware of how tenants are using their property and be on the lookout for any signs of financial difficulty (such as decreased business traffic or employee layoffs).

To create this kind of plan, management needs to analyze business activities, develop practices to minimize risks, and know when to seek assistance outside the business, whether through securing insurance or retaining professionals for advice.

The management of legal risks can be an even greater challenge in the international arena. The box on the next page describes some of the risks of doing business in the global marketplace.

Interacting with the Legal Environment

Reacting when Prevention Fails

Prevention of loss is the primary goal of a risk management plan, but some risks cannot be avoided. Disputes inevitably arise. Products and services sometimes fail. The business climate, the attitude of government toward business, or the marketplace can change. The value of a risk management plan is that when a risk does materialize, the business already has in place an effective way of dealing with it and can more readily assess when legal advice may be necessary.

In the MP example, a potential risk involves the serious problem of computer **hackers**, who spend their time probing computer systems in order to gain unauthorized access. MP is a distributor of computer hardware and software and therefore relies on the manufacturers to build security into those products. An MP customer whose computer system and data are compromised by a hacker could allege that MP recommended and sold a system that was especially vulnerable to hackers because it lacked the most current security protection. When MP investigates the complaint, it may discover that several other customers have bought a similar system and are also vulnerable. MP could view this problem as one that the manufacturer is responsible

hacker
A person who attempts to gain unauthorized access to computers.

Managing Risks when Going Global

The emerging economies of the countries in the former Soviet Union, Eastern Europe, Central and South America, Asia, and Africa provide tremendous opportunities for investment. Although the rewards from doing business in these countries can be great, so can the risks. Consider, for example, the problems that could face a manufacturer who sets up a manufacturing facility in a foreign country:

INTERNATIONAL PERSPECTIVE

- The foreign government might confiscate the entire investment.
- The local currency could become inconvertible and prohibit repatriation of anticipated profits or dividends.
- A civil war could break out, destroying the foreign country's infrastructure.

If the project is to go ahead and succeed, these potential risks need to be evaluated and managed. However, forecasting political risk is extremely difficult. Furthermore, the scope of the loss if the political risk materializes can be catastrophic. There are, however, steps that business can take to manage risks:

- Plan early, keeping in mind that the foreign legal environment may be different not only in terms of its laws, but also in terms of enforcement of its laws.
- Access all available sources of information, including the Department of Foreign Affairs, business associations, consultants, and people who have experience with the foreign country.
- Determine how competitors are handling these risks.
- Consider relying on local partners in managing indigenous issues before they become a problem.
- Seek the assistance of the political risk insurance market to put the risks into context and quantify the costs of transferring them. Find out the available coverage and the costs.

Critical Analysis: How should the legal risk management model be adapted for conducting international business? Which steps are most important?

---

for, but since the customer also relied on MP for advice, MP may have considerable legal risk. In the meantime, the customer is contacting other businesses and disparaging MP's products and services. Not surprisingly, MP is worried about damage to its reputation in the business community.

MP's risk management plan will almost certainly have identified customer dissatisfaction as a potentially significant legal risk. The plan would include guidelines as to how employees are to address customer complaints; what kind of investigation, if any, is to take place; how solutions are to be developed; what kind of record is to be made of the complaint; what follow-up is to be done to ensure that the customer is satisfied; and what steps are to be taken to prevent such a problem from recurring. As well, the plan would indicate when senior management should be alerted about a customer concern. In the scenario above, the employee should immediately involve senior managers because the customer's complaint about computer security is serious, ongoing, and potentially wide-reaching. MP's risk management plan will also direct senior managers as to when formal legal advice is required. Ideally, that legal advisor will be someone with intimate knowledge of the organization and the personalities within it.

The current problem that MP is facing requires the help of a lawyer, since it involves issues of breach of contract and defamation. The contract issue relates to the possibility that MP supplied defective equipment. If MP did so, it may be in breach of contract. The second legal issue relates to the possibility that the customer is defaming MP and ruining its business reputation. Management may need specialized legal advice on this issue. Whether MP should take formal steps to stop the customer from denigrating MP's products and services depends on that legal advice, on MP's assessment of the need to restore its reputation, and on the resources necessary to pursue such a claim.

MP's risk management plan should address dispute resolution procedures, which are discussed in Chapter 4.

Managing Legal Services

Lawyers and the Legal Profession

The legal profession is governed by a professional society within each province and territory. The societies control

- the admission of lawyers to the profession
- the standards of competence required of all members
- the discipline of members who fail to meet those standards

Individuals are eligible for membership as practising members of the profession upon completing a degree from a recognized law school, a period of articling (apprenticeship) with a practising member, and the bar admission exams set by the particular society. Admission to a provincial or territorial society qualifies a **lawyer** to engage in the full practice of law in that jurisdiction. In Canada, there is no distinction between barristers (who appear for clients in court) and solicitors (who perform legal tasks apart from litigation), as there is in the British system. As well, there is no formal system of specialization, as there is in the medical profession. Lawyers can be general practitioners or specialists in a few areas of law.

Lawyers are required to be insured for liability to clients arising from professional negligence—that is, a failure to act in a reasonably competent way. In addition, they are subject to discipline by their law society, which can take the form of a reprimand, suspension, or ultimate disbarment. Lawyers are liable to criminal prosecution, like every other citizen, if they engage in illegal activities, such as misappropriation of a client's funds.

Lawyers may choose to be sole practitioners or become members of a firm of lawyers. **Law firms** are partnerships, consisting of two or more partners and perhaps a number of associate lawyers at earlier stages of their careers. In most provinces, members are able to incorporate for tax and other management purposes but cannot escape personal liability to clients and others dealing with the firm. Depending on their size and composition, firms may provide full legal services to their clients. Others may choose to specialize in such areas as tax law, corporate law, employment law, or criminal law.

When to Seek Legal Advice

There is no simple way to approach this issue. In minimizing risk, timing is everything. Consulting lawyers too soon and too often is expensive and cumbersome.

lawyer
A person who is legally qualified to practise law.

law firm
A partnership formed by lawyers.

Consulting them infrequently to save money may be more expensive in the long run. Government regulation is becoming more prevalent and complicated, and penalties for violation are generally on the increase. Seeking advice at the appropriate time is preferable to waiting for problems to develop. A healthy, ongoing relationship with legal professionals will guide the business in this regard.

MP has a comprehensive risk management program and will already have identified the most serious areas of potential liability. Legal advice may be necessary to understand the legal process, especially in regulatory matters. It may be more efficient for a lawyer to clarify sign regulations, waste disposal guidelines, and import requirements than for an ill-informed business to explore such issues on its own. Even if a dispute is unlikely to go to court, the legal issues and options are important in negotiations. Of course, if a formal legal process has begun or is imminent, the business should seek legal advice. Otherwise, it may lose the dispute by failing to respond.

It is important to clarify within the organization who should decide when a matter requires legal advice. Defining responsibility will depend on whether or not the business has its own internal law department.

If there is an internal law department, likely those in that department will make the decisions about whether to go to outside lawyers and which lawyers to consult. To allow other managers to unilaterally approach external lawyers seriously undermines both the credibility and the effectiveness of the law department. Managers and employees will go directly to external lawyers only if they have prior authorization from the internal law department. Employees should understand that legal services involve a cost. They should be discouraged from referring nonlegal or trivial problems to the legal department and distracting it from more serious legal concerns.

If there is no internal law department, there must be clear guidelines as to who has the authority to seek outside counsel and when. If external legal advice is sought, the organization must clearly indicate which services are desired, what authority the lawyer has, and the extent to which the business will continue to be involved in the proceedings. Lawyers may define the boundaries of the relationship if the organization fails to do so. Such an approach could prove both costly and inefficient.

Lawyers can seldom resolve disputes instantly. Their role is to provide assistance. For this reason, the business must remain actively involved.

How to Choose a Lawyer

A lawyer provides expert advice on legal matters of concern to a business. The business should manage legal services in the same way as any other service. The first step is to find the lawyer or firm appropriate to the business's needs in terms of expertise and approach to dealing with clients. The selection will be much easier if the client has a clear idea of the nature and the volume of the advice required, as well as the allocated budget for legal services. Those responsible for engaging legal services need to discuss a legal services agreement with a number of potential legal service providers in order to achieve the right fit.

Not all lawyers are appropriate for all situations. What an organization needs is a lawyer with the expertise for the particular issue. That lawyer may not be part of the law firm the organization typically uses. Good lawyers will recognize the limitations to their firm's expertise and refer clients to other firms when necessary.

There are many sources available for identifying lawyers, although there is no easy way to decide who are the most competent or appropriate for a particular business. Friends, relatives, and business associates of management may be able to recommend lawyers who have served them well. Local and provincial bar associations maintain lists of members by geographical area and preferred type of practice. The *Canadian Law List* is a publication available in libraries or online that includes basic biographical information about most lawyers in private practice.

Some advice follows for choosing from among a group of lawyers or firms:

- Consult with business associates with similar legal problems and needs about the service they have received from any of the prospects.
- Consider meeting with each lawyer or with a representative of each firm to discuss the need of the business for legal advice in general or in relation to a particular legal problem. Lawyers have a strict professional duty to maintain the confidentiality of client affairs.
- Discuss alternative fee structures with the prospects. Lawyers are increasingly willing to provide a fee structure that suits the client, such as billing at an hourly rate, working on an annual retainer, or even setting a percentage fee. The client should expect an itemized billing on a schedule that suits the business's financial cycle. Another option is to put the provision of legal services out to tender, but this requires detailed knowledge of the services required over a period of time.
- Evaluate the prospects according to a predetermined list of criteria that suit the needs of the business in terms of expertise, availability, willingness to understand the business, and willingness to communicate.

The object of the exercise is to develop a productive, long-term relationship between the business and the legal advisor. For this reason, there is also a need to continually monitor and evaluate the relationship, primarily to ensure that the business is receiving the advice and assistance it needs at a cost it can afford.

Businesses must be prepared to change law firms if circumstances warrant. Whatever loyalty may develop between lawyer and manager, a critical evaluation of the value of the law firm's services may identify the need for a move to another firm.

When to Set Up a Corporate Law Department

corporate law department
A group of lawyers hired as in-house counsel to do the legal work of a business.

If the cost of external legal services for a business becomes significant, the business is faced with the difficult decision of whether to set up a **corporate law department** by hiring lawyers as in-house, full-time employees (sometimes referred to as "in-house counsel"). It is important that this decision be approached systematically and that all costs, quantitative and qualitative, be incorporated in the analysis. What level of experience is required of an in-house lawyer? Is there a need for specialization, and will there still be a need to hire externally from time to time, and if so at what cost? In-house counsel should provide enhanced value through their knowledge of the organization, their skill in managing external legal services, and their ability to introduce risk management programs that supplement existing reactive services. It is often inherently attractive to management to pass legal issues to a specialist colleague, but experienced and effective counsel are costly. Moreover, care must be taken to ensure that the lawyer will be effective in the corporate environment.

Legal Departments Add Value

Richard Bailey is vice president of legal and corporate affairs for Kraft Canada Inc. and is co-chair of the Corporate Counsel section of the International Bar Association. He spends a lot of time advising other corporate lawyers of the need to integrate their department's work with the company's business. Otherwise, corporations tend to see a legal department as a necessary expense that deals with legal problems but contributes nothing to the bottom line. In-house counsel must do more than handle lawsuits. They must help the corporation avoid lawsuits, and they can only do so if actively involved in

A BUSINESS PERSPECTIVE

Corporate counsel, like Richard Bailey of Kraft Canada, can identify business opportunities.

management. They can't simply wait to be asked for their advice.

Kraft Canada ships a huge volume of products to the U.S. market and is therefore subject to all the regulations under NAFTA. Many managers at Kraft perceived these regulations as a significant barrier to exporting. Bailey's department did an audit to determine which perceived barriers were real. The lawyers discovered that many barriers had disappeared or were subject to challenge before trade tribunals. The result was that Kraft Canada identified $8 billion in additional export opportunities.

Bailey says, "When I'm asked to show what value our department has added to the bottom line, I'm not going to tell management we successfully challenged regulation such-and-such. I'm going to tell them about the business opportunity we found."

Source: Michael Fitz-James, "Legal Departments Add Value, Counsel Argues" *Financial Times* (11 September 1997) 22.

Business Law in Practice Revisited

1. What are the legal risks arising from MP's business activities?

Manon Sevigny and the team she assembles to assist her can study the Mainplace business in order to identify the legal risks that exist. They can use the three suggested approaches: assess MP's functional areas, assess its business decisions, and assess its business relationships. This process will enable the team to compile a list of risks such as the 12 presented in the box on page 47.

2. How should MP handle these risks?

Manon and her team need to evaluate the identified risks by assessing the probability and the severity of each potential loss. They must then develop a risk management plan by deciding how to address each risk—by avoiding, reducing, retaining, or transferring, or through some combination of those options. The plan must contain specific actions for dealing with each risk and assign responsibility for each action. Figure 3.2 on page 52 presents the outline of a plan that Manon might produce. The plan must be supported by top management, and all affected employees must be familiar with it. Risk management is a continuous process, so Manon or others must monitor the plan to measure its effectiveness in dealing with risks and be prepared to recommend any necessary adjustments.

A key part of the risk management process is managing legal services. Manon should have legal advice as she develops her plan. To be effective, the MP lawyers must be familiar with the business and be involved in all stages of developing and maintaining the plan. MP needs a stable relationship with lawyers outside the business, even if MP decides that the volume and nature of the legal work that MP requires warrants in-house counsel. MP also needs a plan to acquire specialized legal advice as the need arises from unexpected events.

Chapter Summary

It is crucial for a business to actively manage the legal risks arising from its activities in order to avoid and minimize legal claims and expenses. Legal risk management involves a four-step process: identifying legal risks, assessing those risks, and devising a risk management plan, and implementing the plan. A business also must monitor and revise its plan to ensure that it is current and effective.

No risk management plan can anticipate and deal with all possible developments. A business must be prepared to react in a coordinated and timely fashion to unexpected events.

A business also needs to actively manage its legal services, whether it is employing outside lawyers or in-house counsel. This management involves identifying the legal services that are needed and carefully searching out an appropriate lawyer or firm. Every business needs a stable relationship with its legal advisors, whether they are external or internal, and must be prepared to seek specialized advice as needed.

Study Chapter

Questions for Review

1. What steps are involved in a legal risk management plan?

2. What are the approaches for identifying the legal risks arising from business activities?

3. What additional risks are involved in doing business internationally?

4. How can a business keep its risk management plan current and relevant?

5. What are some benefits of employing in-house counsel?

6. How does a business know when hiring its own lawyer is cheaper than continuing to pay outside counsel?

Questions for Discussion

1. Who should be responsible for managing legal risks and legal services?

2. At what point should a business decide to discontinue an activity rather than try to manage the risk involved?

3. How do the benefits of a risk management plan compensate for the time and expense involved in its design and implementation?

4. Why should a business retain lawyers before involvement in litigation absolutely requires it?

5. How can a business evaluate the cost and quality of its legal services?

6. Why should a company's lawyer be familiar with the company's business activities?

Situations for Discussion

1. Sally is the comptroller of a highly aggressive firm in the high-tech industry which specializes in software development. The CEO prides himself on his ability to make fast decisions and doesn't worry about documenting his actions. His favourite sayings are, "If I had wanted red tape, I would have joined the government" and "Why worry? That's why we have insurance." This approach appears to have served him well, at least in the initial years of the business. Sally is concerned, however, because she is often faced with legal bills without having any knowledge of the background. The firm's legal costs are steadily increasing. What recommendation should Sally make to the CEO for developing a legal risk management plan?

2. If Sally's recommendation in Situation 1 is accepted by the CEO, how should she go about identifying the legal risks in the firm's business? Whom should she consult?

3. Sally's review has identified a particular problem with software designers. Their designs are failing at a higher rate than the industry norm when used by customers. The designers are unwilling to go back and correct problems because they prefer to develop new products and are under pressure to do so. The company is faced with legal claims and lost customers. How should Sally evaluate and address this problem in the context of her risk management plan, taking into consideration the software designers and the company's profitability?

4. Pascal comes into work and discovers that Bill, the lead software designer, has announced that he is leaving the company as of today. Pascal discovers that Bill is now employed with the company's main competitor. Pascal fears that in his new job, Bill will use technology developed while at the company and disclose the identities of key customers. How could Pascal and his company have identified and addressed this risk? What should Pascal do now?

5. A routine review of ABC's accounts receivable discloses a recurring problem with collections from one important customer. What factors should ABC examine in its review of this account? How could a risk management plan help ABC in determining its course of action regarding this customer?

6. Birnbaum is the vice president of administration of XYZ Ltd. She notices that a trend has developed in XYZ where managers from the CEO down have started "passing things by the lawyer" when they are not sure whether a legal issue is involved. Birnbaum suspects that this trend flows from the CEO's close acquaintance with the senior partner of the law firm used by the company; they both sit on the board of a local charity and socialize frequently. Birnbaum is concerned that legal costs are getting out of hand. There is no internal law department. How should Birnbaum approach the CEO about the company's management of legal services? What factors should she consider? What recommendations should she make to the CEO?

Four Chapter

Dispute Resolution

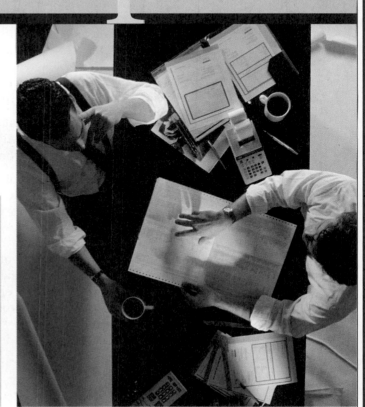

Objectives

AFTER STUDYING THIS CHAPTER, YOU SHOULD HAVE AN
UNDERSTANDING OF:

► HOW BUSINESS ACTIVITIES MAY LEAD TO LEGAL
DISPUTES
► THE OPTIONS FOR RESOLVING A LEGAL DISPUTE
► WHEN AND HOW ALTERNATIVE DISPUTE RESOLUTION
WORKS
► THE LITIGATION PROCESS

Business Law in Practice

Mainplace Stationers Ltd. (MP) developed a risk management plan using the approach outlined in Chapter 3. The basic elements of the plan are presented in Figure 3.2 on page 52. Over the course of a year, a number of events occurred that related to the risks anticipated by MP management, including the following:

■ *The "Slip and Fall."*[1] A customer slipped on a patch of wet floor and suffered a bruised elbow and a strained back.
■ *The Bylaw Change.* The municipal authorities decided to change the bylaw for commercial signs in order to limit their size and preserve the genteel character of the town. The main sign on the MP building exceeded the new size limits.
■ *The Delinquent Customer.* A customer failed to pay its account within the usual 30 days. When MP investigated, it discovered that the customer was in serious financial difficulty.

---

1. A "slip and fall" is an expression lawyers use to refer to an incident in which someone slips on a wet floor, ice, or some other slippery surface and suffers an injury.

65

- *The Dissatisfied Customer.* A customer failed to pay its large account to MP, and when contacted about this matter, informed the company that the computer system that MP recommended, supplied, and installed was not functioning properly and was inadequate to perform the needed tasks.
- *The Damaged Goods.* MP received from a supplier a shipment of office furniture that was seriously dented and scratched. When MP contacted the supplier about this problem, the response was that the damage must have occurred in transit and was therefore the responsibility of MP.
- *The Problem Employee.* Without authorization, a salesperson gave a customer a discount in order to make a sale. The price was so low that MP will incur a loss on the contract.
- *The Motor Vehicle Accident.* An MP delivery truck was involved in a collision with a car. Both vehicles were considerably damaged, but there were no injuries.

1. How well does MP's current risk management plan deal with these events?
2. What approaches should MP use in dealing with these events?
3. What are the possible outcomes?

As emphasized in Chapter 3, business organizations require a risk management plan to minimize the potentially adverse impact of the legal environment and to realize the opportunities that proactive use of the law can produce. Legal problems are not always avoidable, however, and sometimes arise even when sound management practices are in place.

It is not in the best interest of a business to avoid all legal conflict at all costs. For example, if MP is not being paid on a large account, it must risk a legal dispute or face the unpalatable alternative of a substantial write-off. It could spell the end of MP if management were simply to concede defeat any time a legal problem seemed to be developing. Businesses like MP should seek, instead, to manage such disputes with the express goals of

- avoiding time-consuming and expensive court proceedings (known as litigation)
- preserving desirable long-term commercial relationships

Business Activities and Legal Disputes

Business operations—both internal and external—involve numerous interactions that have potential legal consequences. Consider the following analysis of events in the Business Law in Practice scenario.

The "Slip and Fall"

MP must report the incident and possible injuries to its insurer as soon as possible. If MP has arranged for the proper coverage and has kept its policy in good standing, the insurer will deal with any legal claim made by the injured party. MP must provide the insurer with immediate, complete, and accurate information concerning the accident. If the insurance company decides that the injured party is seeking greater compensation than is justified, it may resist paying the injured party, and the matter may ultimately be decided before a judge. In such a case, MP is obliged to cooperate with the legal counsel appointed by the insurer, such as by providing sworn testimony in court.

MP will probably experience an increase in its insurance premiums, particularly if the accident occurred because the company neglected to keep the floors free of water or other hazards. MP management should investigate the accident to determine whether it was caused by a failure to follow maintenance practices or was an isolated and unavoidable incident.

Provided that the insurance company pays the claim, there is an excellent chance that this "slip and fall" will be resolved with minimal involvement of the legal system. A legal dispute is unlikely to emerge. MP's risk management plan has been successful because it calls for comprehensive insurance coverage.

The Bylaw Change

MP may not have properly prepared for this kind of issue in its risk management plan. This would be the case, for example, if MP had been unaware of the proposed amendments to the signage bylaw before those changes went before the municipal council; if prior to the passage of the bylaw, MP had failed to contact the municipality to point out problems with the proposal; or if MP had failed to propose a compromise, such as a "grandfather clause" in the bylaw that would exclude existing signs.

Now that the sign bylaw has been changed, however, MP must observe it and make whatever alterations are required to ensure that its signs comply. Assuming that the municipality was given by the province the power to regulate signs and has done so in the proper exercise of that jurisdiction, there is little point in challenging the bylaw in court, because the chances of success are low. MP could consider approaching the municipal council and asking for an amendment, but it may simply be too late at this point to effect any change.

On this basis, there is little possibility that a legal dispute will arise from this matter, since MP has no other viable option but to comply.

The Delinquent Customer

The customer's refusal to pay its account may indicate that MP has failed in its procedures for extending credit. Management should explore this possibility to prevent recurrences. In the meantime, MP must decide if it should (1) give the customer an opportunity to recover before demanding payment; (2) write off the debt altogether; or (3) take steps to be paid on its account, such as selling the debt to a collection agency at a discount, suing for the debt, or filing a claim if the customer is involved in bankruptcy proceedings.

Setting guidelines for granting credit to customers does not guarantee that every debt will be collectible. If this debt is not large and this customer is in serious financial difficulty, writing it off may be more practical than spending money to try to collect it. The debtor is certain to welcome such a proposal, and therefore no legal dispute will arise from this event.

The Dissatisfied Customer

MP's problem with this customer goes beyond the immediate challenge of collecting what it is owed. If the customer's business has been disrupted by a malfunctioning or inadequate system, the customer may sue MP for compensation. The long-term relationship with this customer is also in jeopardy. MP should consult the contract between them to determine the extent of its liability, if any, and avoid any hasty actions that might harm its ability to resolve this matter amicably. For example, it would be imprudent for MP to acknowledge or deny responsibility without knowing more about the substance of the allegations.

MP may also have a form of commercial liability insurance. This insurance provides coverage should MP be sued by customers who allege that they have been provided with substandard goods or services. If such a policy is in place, MP must immediately notify its insurer of the potential claim.

This matter is now a legal dispute, since the customer is refusing to pay an account that is too large to forgive and, furthermore, is maligning the goods and services MP provided.

The Damaged Goods

MP has received a shipment of furniture that cannot be sold to its customers, except at a discount. MP should review its contract with the supplier—which, it is hoped, is in writing and clearly worded—because this is what should determine who is responsible for damage to goods in transit. If the contract identifies the supplier as being responsible for the damage, a legal conflict may still arise if the supplier is unable or unwilling to pay compensation or does not agree that the damage was as extensive as alleged by MP. If the contract does not specify which party is responsible, the supplier may take the position that MP was responsible and should bear any loss.

This matter may develop into a legal dispute. In the meantime, MP managers should review their practices for negotiating and recording contracts. Specifically, they must be sure that MP contracts state who bears the risk of loss or damage to goods in transit—the buyer or the seller.

The Problem Employee

Generally, MP must honour the terms of the sale to the customer, even though the contract is not to its liking and not one that it authorized.[2] The problem with the employee is an internal matter for which the customer is not responsible.

A risk management plan would ensure that MP's policy manuals, company rules, and the relevant job description already specify the employee's authority, as well as the consequences for exceeding that authority or otherwise being insubordinate. Performance appraisals and discipline records should document any previous infractions by this employee.

This matter will likely develop into a legal dispute if MP decides to fire the employee with no termination pay or with an amount that the employee considers inadequate.[3]

The Motor Vehicle Accident

MP must immediately report this accident to its insurer and cooperate fully in the investigation. Assuming that appropriate insurance coverage is in place, the insurance company will deal with the matter in a similar way to how it dealt with the slip and fall, and a legal dispute is unlikely to arise.

As the foregoing analysis suggests, MP's risk management plan predicted and planned for several events that did in fact occur. As a result, a legal dispute is unlikely to arise from them. For example, the insurance company will likely sort out the slip and fall incident, as well as the motor vehicle accident. Other events will not develop into legal disputes because the company has no other viable option but to

---

2. For more discussion on this point, see Chapter 13.
3. The law concerning wrongful dismissal is discussed in Chapter 22.

live with what has happened. That is, MP will likely write off the delinquent customer's bad debt as an anticipated cost of doing business—MP will not throw away its resources on a lost cause. Similarly, there is little point in launching a legal challenge to the unfavourable sign bylaw because the chances of success are remote. Yet other events probably will give rise to legal conflict, including the problems with the dissatisfied customer, the supplier of damaged furniture, and the discount-granting employee.

MP's challenge with these latter issues is to actively and effectively manage them—just as they would any other aspect of the business's environment. Managing disputes does not mean simply proceeding to court. There are many ways to resolve a dispute that do not involve litigation.

Resolving Disputes through Negotiation

Clarification of the Situation

The first step for a manager faced with an apparent conflict is to investigate the situation to determine the nature and extent of the dispute. The manager should contact the individuals involved in his or her own organization and the appropriate people on the other side of the dispute. The objective is to clarify the situation before formulating an approach to its resolution.

Managers must contend with numerous disputes in the operation of their business organization, and not all are of equal importance. They must set priorities, decide which disputes justify the use of the firm's resources, and determine when professional legal advice is required.

Even if a dispute escalates, the objective is still to resolve the matter as quickly as is reasonably possible. Prolonging legal conflict is expensive, in terms of both dollars spent and managerial hours unproductively consumed. A quick resolution will produce real cost savings for all concerned and a greater chance that relationships between the parties will not be irreparably harmed.

negotiation
A process of deliberation and discussion used to reach a mutually acceptable resolution to a dispute.

Negotiation is a tool that owners and managers can use effectively to assess, evaluate, and develop resolutions to legal disputes on a relatively informal and inexpensive basis. The goal is to reach a fair and acceptable outcome without having to activate the burdensome, costly, and unpredictable machinery associated with formal litigation. The process of negotiation is not governed by technical rules. It can operate in whatever way the parties wish to solve their problem. With a negotiated resolution or settlement, all parties agree to a compromise that is preferable to allowing someone else, such as a judge, to impose a resolution on them.

In fact, although some disputes go to court through the litigation process, the overwhelming majority are resolved through negotiation between the parties involved or through other informal methods of dispute resolution that do not involve judges or even lawyers.

There are some situations where negotiation is not the proper way to proceed, even as a first step, such as when insurance covers the risk that is the subject of the dispute. In such circumstances, the business is required to allow the insurer to conduct settlement negotiations. Any attempt by the business to negotiate privately may jeopardize the coverage.

The Negotiation Process

Assuming that there are no insurance issues, negotiating an end to the dispute should become management's focus once a good understanding of the dispute has been achieved. Whether negotiations will succeed depends on a number of factors, including the following:

- the willingness of the parties to compromise and negotiate in good faith
- the nature and significance of the dispute
- the priority the parties give to its resolution
- the effectiveness of those involved in the negotiations

The parties choose their own negotiators. They could be employees, lawyers, or professionals who specialize in bringing parties together.

MP has three legal disputes that it may well be able to resolve through negotiations.

The Dissatisfied Customer

In order to get negotiations off on the right foot, MP must assure its dissatisfied customer that it is looking into its concerns; it must also quickly choose the appropriate MP manager to investigate the matter internally. The investigation will involve a review of documentation, as well as consultation with the MP employees who provided the advice and computer products. The customer should then be contacted for its full version of events.

MP's problems with the dissatisfied customer may appear to be exclusively about money, owing to the unpaid account and the financial losses—present and future—that the customer may claim as a result of the allegedly substandard service and products MP supplied. Also at risk, however, is the opportunity for future dealings with this customer, as well as the reputation of MP in the marketplace.

MP will need to negotiate with the dissatisfied customer, as the situation is complicated and the stakes appear to be high. Negotiation should occur at the senior management level in both organizations, and legal advice will be needed. Perhaps the customer's complaints are a means to get MP to reduce its account, or perhaps there is some merit to the allegations. To try to end the dispute and also to test the customer's reaction, MP could offer to compromise by making a small reduction in its account. However, MP must be prepared for its compromise to be rejected; if it is, MP must then reconsider its options.

The Damaged Goods

MP could use a similar approach to manage the situation involving the supply of damaged goods. It must designate an MP manager to determine the background to the problem. This would include checking documentation and consulting with the MP employees who were involved in the transaction. MP can then contact the supplier for clarification of its position.

While any conflict with the supplier of damaged office furniture is primarily financial, the trading relationship between the parties is an important factor in the dispute and its possible resolution. For example, if MP is a major customer of the supplier, MP can use this fact as leverage to achieve a favourable compromise with respect to this transaction or, perhaps, to secure concessions with respect to future orders.

MP has a good chance of informally negotiating a settlement with the supplier. The stakes (financial and otherwise) appear to be relatively low and are unlikely to justify taking the matter to litigation, particularly if the supplier shows some flexibility.

The Problem Employee

Resolving issues related to the problem employee should involve less investigation, particularly if MP's general policies are documented and this salesperson's performance record and job responsibilities have been clearly established and documented. MP may decide to simply discuss with the employee the problems she has caused by the money-losing contract and ask her to respect the limits on her authority in the future. The employee may have a viable explanation for her conduct and should be given an opportunity to provide her side of the story. In the end, MP may decide not to discipline the employee but to simply remind her to clear discounts with her supervisor before agreeing to provide them to customers under any circumstances. She should be warned that further incidents of this kind may lead to her being dismissed from the company.

When Negotiations Fail

In the majority of disputes, such as the ones explored here, settlement is reached informally between the parties, often without the involvement of lawyers. Other times, an impasse is reached where neither party is prepared to compromise further. If the damaged goods problem is settled through negotiation, the legal issues remaining from the Business Law in Practice scenario are reduced to two: the dissatisfied customer and the problem employee.

MP's negotiations with the dissatisfied customer have been disappointing. The customer is unwilling to pay anything on MP's account of $100 000 and is insisting that MP compensate it for a loss of $250 000. MP is not prepared to accept responsibility for any loss and considers this an unreasonable claim.

MP's employee has failed on three more occasions to follow company policies and other limitations on her authority to provide discounts. At the same time, she wants to remain employed by MP. Management is disturbed by her attitude but is reluctant to fire her because of the sales she has generated for MP.

When impasses such as these are reached, the business is faced with a difficult choice: concede or fight, cut its losses or risk the expenditure of more time and money. MP can abandon its claim against the customer or become more aggressive in its efforts to collect, knowing that the customer must decide what to do about its claim for business disruption losses. In dealing with its employee, MP can tolerate the employee's behaviour and realize that it is likely to persist, or begin the termination process.

Whether MP should continue or abandon these legal conflicts depends on an analysis of what is in the best interests of the organization in the long term.

If MP decides to pursue the matter with the employee—perhaps culminating in that employee's termination—MP could end up being sued for wrongful dismissal. If MP decides to continue its dispute with the customer, it faces the possibility of having to sue that customer or being sued by it. In both situations, however, the parties have a strong incentive to avoid litigation because it is a cumbersome, expensive, and uncertain process.

The alternatives to litigation are known collectively as **alternative dispute resolution (ADR)**.

alternative dispute resolution (ADR)
A range of options for resolving disputes as an alternative to litigation.

To Proceed or Not to Proceed

Consider these questions when deciding whether to proceed with a legal conflict:

- How long will the next step take, and what further steps or events are likely to follow?
- How much of its resources should the business devote to the dispute, in terms of both the commitment and the time of business personnel? Does it have these resources available?
- Will a lengthy dispute affect the public profile and reputation of the business?
- Is the relationship with the other side valuable?

- Will that relationship be harmed, whatever the outcome?
- What is the likely cost in terms of legal fees and company time?
- Are there principles at stake that go beyond the particular dispute?
- What are those principles worth?
- If the dispute goes to court, what are the chances of winning?
- If the court decides in favour of the business, does the other side have the assets to pay the claim?

BUSINESS APPLICATION OF THE LAW

Alternative Dispute Resolution

How ADR Works

ADR refers to a broad range of options for resolving disputes that are often considered alternatives to litigation, but it also includes ways to avoid disputes entirely as part of a risk management approach to resolving disputes as quickly and as efficiently as possible.

The most common forms of ADR are mediation and arbitration. Both involve a person who is independent of the parties and who has expertise in resolving disputes. The function of a **mediator** is to help the parties reach their own compromise. The mediator brings the parties together to clarify the situation and to assist them in appreciating the validity of the other's position. A mediator normally refrains from evaluating positions or in any way judging the parties or deciding the outcome.

An **arbitrator** fulfills a more formal role by hearing from the various sides their desired outcome of the dispute. The role is also more formal than in mediation in that the arbitrator makes a definite ruling after considering the submissions of the parties. This ruling is in the form of a decision that is usually **binding** on the parties (depending on the arbitrator's terms of reference). Binding means that the decision is final—it generally cannot be appealed, and it is enforceable in the courts. Arbitration is ordinarily chosen by the parties before a dispute arises, through a term in the contract providing that disagreements arising from the contract are to proceed to arbitration in accordance with the terms of the *Arbitration Act* in the relevant jurisdiction.

mediator
A person who helps the parties to a dispute reach a compromise.

arbitrator
A person who listens to both sides of a dispute and makes a ruling that is binding on the parties.

binding
Final and enforceable in the courts.

ADR in Big Business

A BUSINESS PERSPECTIVE

Major corporate battles involving Molson Breweries, Maple Leaf Gardens Ltd., Groupe Videotron Ltée, and McCain Foods Ltd. have been resolved outside the regular court system through private mediation or arbitration. Mediation is often completed in a single day and arbitration in a matter of weeks, while complicated litigation can drag on for years. "If you're running a business, you've got to find out sooner or later if you're going to get clobbered," says Robert Nelson, an Ottawa lawyer at Gowling Strathy & Henderson, who also heads the Arbitration and Mediation Institute of Canada.

ADR is most popular in disputes between companies that wish to continue a business relationship, such as a franchise agreement. It is less effective when one party decides to delay rather than settle quickly—for example, when there is a claim for one side to pay out a large sum, says Samuel Rickett, a lawyer at Fasken Campbell Godfrey in Toronto.

The ADR mechanisms are private and fast, and the parties involved pick their own facilitator. As Mr. Rickett says, "You get to select an arbitrator or a panel who is acceptable to you, instead of taking your chances with a judge who may or may not be familiar with the business area under dispute."

There is a cost involved because ADR is not publicly financed in the same way as the courts are. The parties pay the fee charged by the facilitator, usually based on the time spent. However such fees are moderate compared to the expenses of litigation.

Source: Janet McFarland, "Companies Move Away from Courtroom Battles" *The Globe and Mail* (22 November 1996).

A major attraction of ADR is that the parties are entitled to choose the process they wish to use and the individuals they wish to have assist them. They are not constricted by predetermined formal rules and structures, as they are in the litigation process. At any stage of the dispute, they can opt for a mediator to assist or for an arbitrator to make a final decision.

There are no mandatory qualifications for ADR practitioners as there are for professionals such as lawyers, but there are many training programs available through universities[4] and the private sector. Mediators and arbitrators are often lawyers or retired judges, but anyone is eligible to become a full- or part-time practitioner. Success depends on securing referrals from satisfied clients, which in turn depends on building a reputation for achieving results. The practitioner builds a reputation by demonstrating the qualities needed in an impartial, respected facilitator. Although mediators are primarily facilitators and arbitrators are decision makers, both need to be good at listening, adapting, grasping situations quickly, and gaining the trust of the participants. There are provincial and national associations[5] that maintain directories of those available for service and make referrals for interested clients.

---

4. For example, the Centre for Conflict Resolution Studies at the University of Prince Edward Island and the John V. Decore Centre for Alternative Dispute Resolution at the University of Alberta.

5. Such as the Arbitration and Mediation Institute of Canada.

ADR has many positive features, including the following:

- The parties control the process, the timing, and the selection of the facilitator.
- The process is usually faster and cheaper than litigation.
- The parties are directly involved in the process and better able to express their views and emotions than in litigation.
- The process can be made confidential.
- The parties have access to expert assistance.

There are also some negative features:

- The process does not always produce a resolution, so time and money may be invested, only to have the matter proceed to litigation.
- There is a long-term concern that widespread use of ADR will result in diminished openness and accountability of the legal system. Awareness of the law depends on its public nature. ADR is usually a private process; thus, those not directly involved in the dispute have no access to the process or the results. The outcomes of ADR do not provide the guidance to the business community that court decisions do.

When ADR Works

Every dispute is theoretically capable of being resolved through one or more forms of ADR, but the nature of the relationship between those involved and the particular circumstances of the disagreement will affect the suitability of ADR and its chance of success (see Figure 4.1).

Figure 4.1

DECIDING WHEN TO USE ADR

When ADR Is Appropriate	When ADR Is Inappropriate
The parties are interested in considering each other's position with the goal of achieving a compromise and settling the dispute.	One or both of the parties is unwilling to consider the other's position and has no wish to compromise or settle.
The parties wish to maintain their commercial relationship.	One or both of the parties does not care about the commercial relationship.
The parties need a quick resolution of minor problems as they arise in an ongoing transaction.	One or both of the parties has no desire to resolve problems as they arise and, in fact, may wish to terminate the ongoing transaction.
The dispute is complicated, meaning that litigation is likely to be costly.	One or more of the parties does not respond to cost incentives.
The dispute involves sensitive or emotionally charged issues that the parties wish to keep private or confidential.	One or both of the parties is unconcerned about privacy or confidentiality and may, in fact, wish for the other to be publicly sanctioned by a judge.
The parties are acting in good faith (i.e., the goal is to resolve the dispute in a manner acceptable to both).	One or both of the parties is acting in bad faith or values its own position more than the goal of reaching a resolution.
The parties wish to avoid setting a precedent.	One or both of the parties wishes to create a precedent and therefore wants to proceed to court.

Note: Where a situation displays a mix of factors found on both sides of this chart, management must assess the relative weight of each in determining the feasibility of ADR.

The suitability of disputes for ADR is not dependent on the type of law involved. ADR can work well whatever the nature of the legal rules that apply. ADR can work effectively in these types of legal disputes:

- commercial or contract matters (disputes about payment for goods or the quality of goods)
- personal injuries (claims by a customer who slips and falls or who is injured by a defective product)
- employment matters (claims of improper dismissal or discrimination)
- regulatory matters (a dispute about signs)
- environmental protection (application of waste storage regulations)
- trade matters (difficulty with import documentation)
- intellectual property (claims of copyright infringement)
- professional/client matters (an accountant's difficulty collecting fees or a client's complaint about the quality of service)
- partnerships (disagreement by partners on contributions of work or compensation)
- real estate (dispute among adjoining landowners about a common boundary)
- franchising (a dispute arising from a franchise agreement)

MP's two outstanding matters—involving the dissatisfied customer and the problem employee—are types of disputes in which ADR has been successfully employed. A key factor in the customer dispute is the need to preserve the relationship and come to a fair resolution. The employee problem may benefit from the involvement of an objective outsider who can help each party appreciate the other's view of the matter.

Both disputes are candidates for mediation. The employee problem, as an internal situation, is especially appropriate. A mediator might, for example, help MP and the employee agree that the relationship cannot survive. The mediator would also be able to assist the parties in devising a termination package that would provide the employee with time-limited financial assistance while she seeks a new job; finally, it would enable MP to avoid a lengthy wrongful dismissal action.

The situation with the customer involves a contract between the two parties that may specify a process for resolving disputes arising from the transaction. For example, if the contract calls for arbitration, it will preempt litigation and likely result in a binding decision. If the contract is silent, the parties could try mediation or agree at any time to resort to arbitration. If they fail to agree on anything, the only option available is litigation.

ADR Sources

There are several ways in which a form of ADR may become the means of resolving a dispute. Business people should anticipate the possibility of a dispute arising in the course of a particular transaction or a longer-term relationship. They may include a dispute resolution process as part of their agreement for the purpose of diverting potential disputes away from litigation and into a process that they define and control. The agreement between MP and its customer may contain such a clause.

If parties do not agree in advance on ADR, they can do so at any later time. They are always free to agree on a process of dispute resolution that serves their mutual needs. MP should suggest ADR to the customer and the employee and attempt to agree on an appropriate process. As litigation looms or progresses, the incentive to agree on an alternative process becomes greater. ADR by agreement is especially prevalent in international transactions, where litigation is complicated by competing sets of rules and procedures.

ADR Is the Norm in International Transactions

INTERNATIONAL PERSPECTIVE

Litigation of a business dispute in a domestic transaction can be a time-consuming, damaging, and expensive process. If the dispute arises in an international transaction, these problems are compounded by questions of which country's law applies, which country's courts will hear the case, and whether the courts of one country will recognize and enforce a judgment obtained in another country. There is no international court for the resolution of commercial disputes, nor is there a comprehensive international system for the enforcement of awards obtained in domestic courts of other countries. Individual countries may have agreements with other countries that provide for the reciprocal enforcement of judgments. For example, there is a convention between Canada and the United Kingdom that each country will recognize and enforce judgments from the other in civil and commercial matters. Such a convention is the exception rather than the norm, however.

For these reasons, ADR mechanisms are extremely popular for settling international commercial disagreements. In international commercial contracts, arbitration has emerged as the favoured form of settlement and arbitration clauses are the norm. The arbitration process has been greatly enhanced by the adoption in many countries of standardized rules and procedures and provisions for the reciprocal recognition and enforcement of the arbitral award. In Canada, the federal government and each province have implemented the 1958 New York Convention on the Recognition and Enforcement of Foreign Arbitral Awards. This convention established rules for the recognition of arbitration clauses in contracts and has been adopted by more than 70 countries. As well, all jurisdictions in Canada have enacted legislation modelled after the UNCITRAL Model Law, an international convention that deals with international arbitration procedures and enforcement. The adoption of this legislation has markedly increased the effectiveness of the international commercial arbitration system in Canada, particularly with respect to the courts' recognition of arbitral awards. Canadian courts have become receptive to the process and tend to limit their judicial review to questions of jurisdiction. This attitude is illustrated by the words of Mr. Justice Gibbs of the B.C. Court of Appeal in *Quintette Coal.* v. *Nippon Steel:* "[T]here is a worldwide trend toward restricting judicial control over international arbitration awards.... The concerns of international comity, respect for the capacities of foreign and transnational tribunals, and sensitivity to the need of the international commercial system for predictability in the resolution of disputes ... are as compelling in this jurisdiction as they are in the United States or elsewhere." [6]

Critical Analysis: Do you agree with Justice Gibbs' attitude toward arbitration? Why is commercial arbitration not used more in domestic business arrangements?

Source: Mary Jo Nicholson, *Legal Aspects of International Business* (Scarborough: Prentice-Hall, 1997) at 226–233.

Some industries have recognized the need to provide customers with a means of submitting and resolving complaints about the quality of goods or services provided. For example, the Canadian Bankers Association has a code of conduct governing credit disputes between its members and small business customers. This code requires commercial banks to have their own systems for mediating these disputes. The Canadian Motor Vehicle Arbitration Plan is available to consumers and vehicle

---

6. *Quintette Coal Ltd.* v. *Nippon Steel Corp,* [1991] 1 W.W.R. 219.

manufacturers to settle differences over alleged defects or warranties for purchased or leased vehicles.

The Investment Dealers Association of Canada has an arbitration system to deal with complaints by clients against their brokers. The system was first used in British Columbia in 1992 and is now available to clients in most provinces. The system can be accessed by phone and the Internet. Cases are decided by independent arbitrators, through a designated dispute resolution body in each province. Clients pay an administration fee for the service. This type of industry-related ADR is a competitive tool for increasing customer satisfaction.

Many regulatory bodies now have an ADR element for the purpose of attempting to resolve disputes without the cumbersome process of a tribunal proceeding. For example, human rights complaints go through a mediation stage, and the Competition Bureau has a process for attempting to resolve allegations of misleading advertising.

The Litigation Process

If Mainplace Stationers succeeds in resolving its employee dispute through mediation, only the dispute with the dissatisfied customer remains. If the parties tried mediation but were unable to agree on a settlement amount, or if MP proposed referring the dispute to arbitration and the customer refused, then litigation is the last option.

Litigation should not be undertaken without an understanding of its potentially adverse consequences. Court backlogs have made the system slower to access and can seriously harm commercial relationships by prolonging disputes for years. There is no guarantee of success, either in obtaining a favourable decision from the court or in collecting a judgment from the defendant. When and if success is achieved, it comes only after a significant investment of money, time, and commitment. In particular, complicated litigation can be a significant drain on corporate resources, an unproductive diversion from profitable business activities, and a source of stress for those involved in the process. Litigation is a slow, expensive, and risk-ridden process. It must be considered as the last resort for resolving disputes and should be deployed only when all other feasible methods have failed and the claim cannot realistically be abandoned.

Commercial litigation arises when one business makes a deliberate decision to take legal action against another. The legal foundation and outcome of the claim are governed by the legal rules contained in relevant common law and statute law. MP could sue (initiate legal action, known as a lawsuit or litigation) to recover money owed by the dissatisfied customer. If the dispute with the problem employee had not been resolved through mediation, the employee could have sued MP to secure compensation for being wrongfully dismissed. The common law and statute law are the substantive rules applicable to the matter. How the claim is carried through the civil justice system is dictated by the procedural rules—that is, the rules that mandate such matters as what documents are to be filed with the court, what the process leading up to the trial will be, and how the trial will proceed.

limitation period
The time period specified by legislation for commencing legal action.

A crucial set of rules affects litigation in each province by establishing specific time periods for commencing legal action. **Limitation periods** vary widely, depending on the nature of the lawsuit and the province in which the litigation will occur. For example, in most provinces[7] an action based on breach of contract (such

---

7. See *Limitations Act*, R.S.O. 1990, c. L-15; *Limitation of Actions Act*, R.S.N.S. 1989, c. 258.

as failure to pay money owing) must begin within six years of the time when the right to collect arises. Other limits are much shorter. In some provinces,[8] the courts can permit actions to proceed after the limitation has expired if there is a reasonable explanation for the delay, but the general rule is that the right to sue is lost after the specific period of time ends. The rationale for these limits is that there is a need to bring closure to legal disputes by preventing claimants from indefinitely delaying the initiation of lawsuits. These rules are an important reason why legal advice should be sought at an early stage in disputes with significant financial consequences. Lawyers in such cases must be aware of the relevant limitation period and ensure that litigation is commenced if settlement does not occur within that period.

Commercial litigation is known as private, or civil, litigation. The costs of bringing a matter through the judicial system are borne by the litigants, and any recovery of compensation comes from the losing party. The only involvement of government in the process is through the provision of the administrative structure, the court facilities, the judges, and other court officials. There is no government funding for the private litigants themselves, with the limited exception of legal aid programs, which assist in certain civil matters, such as divorce and custody lawsuits.

Every province and territory has its own system of courts and rules for civil litigation. This section describes those features generically, largely from the viewpoint of the key elements that are relevant to business.

A business may become involved in litigation by starting a lawsuit as a **plaintiff** or being sued as a **defendant**. In the MP–customer dispute, the likely scenario is that MP will be the plaintiff and begin the suit for the unpaid account.

The System of Courts

Each provincial and territorial system of courts has three basic levels: trial, intermediate appeal, and final appeal. The ultimate appeal is from the highest court of each system to the **Supreme Court of Canada** and is available only after permission or "leave" to appeal has been received from the Supreme Court itself. Such leave is granted only when the legal question under appeal is of national concern or significance.

The trial level is the point of entry into the system and consists of courts organized by type of case, such as criminal, family, and commercial. In a lawsuit in which one business is suing another for nonpayment, the amount of the claim determines the relevant court. Relatively small claims can be processed in the local equivalent of a **small claims court**. The name and monetary limit vary from province to province, but a common limit is between $5000 and $10 000. These claims can be litigated with minimal legal advice and assistance, in part because less is at stake. The process is designed to be simpler, quicker, and less expensive than mainstream litigation. Parties often appear in this court without a lawyer. Claims in excess of the designated "small claim" must be pursued in the local equivalent of the **superior court**, which has unlimited monetary jurisdiction. Since MP is claiming that there is an outstanding account of $100 000 with the dissatisfied customer, the MP claim must be brought to superior court.

Figure 4. 2 indicates the hierarchy of courts relevant to commercial disputes. The **Federal Court of Canada** has special authority to deal with cases in which one of the parties is the federal government or one of its agencies.

plaintiff
The party that initiates a lawsuit against another party.

defendant
The party being sued.

Supreme Court of Canada
The final court for appeals in the country.

small claims court
A court that deals with claims up to a specified amount.

superior court
A court with unlimited financial jurisdiction.

Federal Court of Canada
The court that deals with litigation involving the federal government.

---

8. For example, N.S., s. 3.

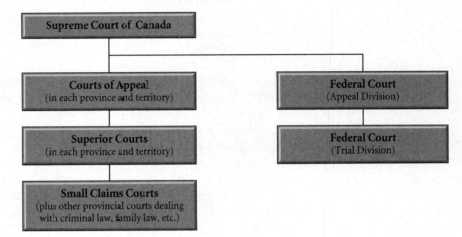

Figure 4.2

COURTS DEALING WITH COMMERCIAL DISPUTES

Stages of a Lawsuit

settlement out of court
A negotiated resolution of a lawsuit after litigation begins, but before going to trial.

There are four formal stages in a lawsuit that goes through the full court process. The majority are settled informally by the parties at some stage in the process. **Settlement out of court** after litigation begins is generally preferable to going to trial, for many reasons:

- It saves time, legal expenses, and effort by company personnel.
- It provides a better chance of preserving a commercial relationship.
- It offers a certain result, rather than the unpredictable decision of a trial judge.
- It keeps the outcome private by avoiding the publicity of a public trial.

Litigation, other than small claims, is ordinarily conducted by a lawyer in consultation with the client. It is technically permissible but inadvisable for a business to attempt to meet the many formal requirements of the litigation system without the benefit of legal advice. The litigation process is governed by complicated and technical rules of court in each province.

Pleadings

pleadings
The formal documents concerning the basis for a lawsuit.

The first stage is known as **pleadings** and involves the exchange of the formal documents outlining the basis of the suit. The plaintiff initiates the action by preparing a document that contains the allegations supporting the claim. For example, in MP's claim for payment of goods and services, the initial document would describe the contract; state that MP had provided the goods and services pursuant to the contract; and observe that in breach of contract, the customer had not yet paid the account. This document is a notice of the claim and is registered, or "filed," with the appropriate court office. It is then delivered to the party being sued (the defendant), through a process known as service. If the defendant has retained a lawyer, that lawyer may accept service of the documents on the defendant's behalf.

This first stage does not include evidence, but instead outlines the key points that the plaintiff needs to prove at trial in order to succeed. The defendant has a short period of time (for example, 10 days in Nova Scotia) in which to respond to the allegations. Failure to respond within the allowed time is equivalent to admitting the claim. If the amount claimed is not in dispute and the reason for nonpayment is financial, the defendant will likely choose not to incur legal expenses to contest the claim. Instead, the defendant will concede responsibility and allow the plaintiff to "win" the case. The plaintiff, in turn, simply explains to the judge that the defendant has conceded the case. The court gives judgment to the plaintiff, who is then free to move to the collection stage.

counterclaim
A claim by the defendant against the plaintiff.

If there are matters in dispute, the defendant will likely seek legal advice and prepare a formal response to the claim, known as a defence. The lawyers may agree to allow the defendant longer than the minimum period in which to prepare the defence. This document might allege, for example, that the goods and services provided by the plaintiff were inadequate or of no value at all. The defence is then filed with the court and delivered to the plaintiff. The defendant may also consider suing the plaintiff by preparing a document known as a **counterclaim**. In this counterclaim, the MP customer can seek to recover compensation for its business disruption losses caused by MP's deficient goods and services (in this case $250 000). It is also at this stage that the parties may consider expanding the suit to include other parties. For example, if the defendant alleges that the computers delivered under the contract were defective, MP may decide to sue the manufacturer and supplier of the computer, on the theory that these are the people who caused all the problems in the first place.

Discovery

discovery
The process of disclosing evidence to support both claims in a lawsuit.

Once the basic claims and allegations have been made and clarified, the suit proceeds to the second stage, commonly known as **discovery**. Both parties must now reveal and demonstrate the facts that support their allegations. These facts are found in documents, in the oral testimony of those directly involved in the situation, and in expert reports. The time frame for this stage is undefined and depends largely on the degree of complexity of the case. The purpose of this stage is to test the strength of the opposing positions, so that the parties will be encouraged to reach a compromise, based on their greater appreciation of the strengths and weaknesses in both sides of the case. In the MP case, the key information for discovery will be the contract and other documentation supporting the MP claim for $100 000, the testimony of personnel on both sides who were involved in the original deal and in the subsequent events, and the details of the basis of the customer's claim for $250 000. Computer technology can help track the numerous documents in complicated cases.

At this stage, several initiatives in the various provinces come into play for the purpose of clearing the backlogs in the courts and streamlining the litigation process. Generally, these initiatives require the parties involved in litigation to engage in a formal attempt to resolve their dispute before it actually goes to court. These attempts may require the parties to engage in a process of mediation, whereby a facilitator, who may be a judge, helps them reach a compromise and avoid a trial. For example, Ontario began a program in Toronto and Ottawa in 1999 that requires mediation to be scheduled within 90 days of the filing of the defence to the plaintiff's claim. There are strict time frames for such dispute resolution initiatives, and only when this process is completed without successful resolution can the parties proceed to trial. Besides these mandatory dispute resolution methods, the parties are required to participate in a pretrial conference, the purpose of which is to narrow the issues in dispute and make the actual trial as short as possible in the event that it does occur.

Should ADR Be Mandatory?

ETHICAL CONSIDERATIONS

It is a matter of debate whether it is fair or ethical to impose some form of mandatory ADR in all lawsuits. For example, mandatory mediation before trial requires the parties to attempt to end their dispute through facilitated negotiation before they are permitted to proceed through the steps of the litigation process.

One of the parties may be much stronger than the other in terms of size and resources to devote to the litigation. This economic advantage can be used to produce a settlement that may not be in the best interest of the weaker party, if the stronger makes it clear that protracted litigation is the only other option. Conversely, the stronger party may exhibit little interest in a mediated settlement if it is confident of its ability to outlast the other party in litigation.

Another factor is the chance that the mandatory ADR will succeed. Perhaps one party has already proposed ADR to the other and been rejected. Perhaps the parties have already used one or more forms of ADR and failed to resolve their dispute. The ongoing dispute between MP and its customer is an example of this sort of situation. To require ADR in such cases may further prolong the dispute and act as a diversion from the litigation process.

The challenge is to find a means to identify those lawsuits that could benefit from ADR and provide a means of getting them out of the litigation backlog. The matters under litigation must be suitable for ADR, and the parties must be made to appreciate its utility.

Critical Analysis: Can mandatory ADR serve two purposes: easing the backlog in the courts and producing settlements that are fair to the parties? Is there any logical way to identify suitable disputes for ADR as an alternative to a blanket requirement for all? Is it desirable or possible to develop a mechanism that makes it difficult for the stronger party to exploit the weaker?

Trial

trial
A formal hearing before a judge that results in a binding decision.

burden of proof
The obligation of the plaintiff to prove its case.

evidence
Proof presented in court to support a claim.

If no settlement is reached at the discovery stage, the plaintiff can proceed to **trial**. The timing will depend on the availability of the courts and on how long it takes the parties to prepare for the formalities of the trial. Most trials proceed with a single judge and no jury. Jury trials are available for commercial matters, but a jury trial can be opposed if, for example, the case is deemed too complex for a jury to understand. At trial, the **burden of proof** falls on the plaintiff. The plaintiff must formally introduce **evidence** according to established rules to prove that its version of events is more likely true than not, known as "proving the case on the balance of probabilities." Expressed numerically, the plaintiff must prove that there is a better than 50 percent chance that the circumstances of the contract are as it contends they are and that, furthermore, these circumstances entitle it to receive what it claimed. The defendant has the opportunity to challenge the plaintiff's witnesses and documents and to introduce its own account of events to oppose the claim. The judge is required to decide what happened between the parties and what the nature of their contract, if any, was. This is not generally a straightforward task, as the parties typically have widely differing versions of events. Once the facts have been established, the judge is then in a position to consider and apply the relevant case law.

The parties make submissions about the legal rules and precedents that support their desired conclusion. The judge then applies relevant legal rules to those factual findings to produce a decision. When the judge takes this second step, she is applying precedent. Locating and interpreting the common law rules that govern contract law is generally not a simple process, for several reasons. First, the principles themselves have been developed over time on a case-by-case basis; they are scattered through the law reports over hundreds of years. Second, common law principles are unavoidably derived from cases that have defied out-of-court settlement or informal resolution. This fact frequently makes case law difficult, less than routine, and at times even quirky. Third, since not all judgments are complete or clearly written, those reading them can be left confused and unenlightened. The decision may be given by the judge immediately at the end of the trial or reserved until a later time, to allow her some time for deliberation.

The Mainplace trial is likely to proceed before a judge without a jury, unless one side feels that a jury might be more sympathetic to its position than a judge. In a commercial matter such as this, that is unlikely to be the case. MP will present its evidence to support its claim and oppose the customer's counterclaim. The customer will produce evidence in opposition to the MP claim and in support of its counterclaim. In this case, the crucial issues are likely to be the quality of the goods and services provided, the interpretation of the terms of the contract, the effect of any statements MP personnel may have made to the customer concerning the application of those terms, and the actions of the customer following its identification of the problems with the system, including steps to limit its losses for any disruption of business that might have occurred.

Decision

decision
The judgment of the court that specifies which party is successful and why.

costs
Legal expenses that a judge orders the loser to pay the winner.

The judge's **decision** contains her resolution of the case—who must pay how much to whom—supported by the appropriate justification and based on the evidence and legal rules. While MP is seeking a monetary award, other remedies are available in exceptional circumstances, such as when the successful party requests an order from the court for the losing party to perform a specific act (e.g., transfer a piece of land) or cease some activity (e.g., trespassing on property).

Any monetary award includes the basic amount of the claim (e.g., the unpaid price of the goods) plus interest, and, in the usual case, the legal **costs** of the successful party. These costs usually fall far short of fully compensating the winning party for all its legal expenses. They are awarded by the judge based on a predetermined scale, combined with her view of the complexity of the case. In any event, these costs provide only a partial recovery, with the result that even successful litigation involves expense. The downside for the losing party is significant: it may be required to pay "costs" to the winner, as well as pay its own legal expenses.

In exceptional cases where the conduct of one of the parties has been seriously objectionable, the court will award against it what are known as solicitor and client costs. These costs come much closer to fully compensating the other party for its legal expenses.

The many possible outcomes to the MP case depend on the evidence presented, the persuasiveness of the lawyers, and the judge's view of the case. For purposes of illustration, here is one possible outcome:

MP v. The Dissatisfied Customer The judge concluded that MP's customer did order and receive the computer system and services in question and that the customer was not misled by MP personnel about the capacity and suitability of the system for the customer's needs. However, there were some significant, but only partial, defects in the system's performance. The judge therefore awarded MP $75 000 ($25 000 less than MP claimed). This reduction was intended to take into account the fact that the system and services provided by MP caused some disruption to the customer's operations and made the system itself less valuable. The customer's counterclaim for $250 000 was disallowed.

In addition, MP was awarded interest on its claim (from the time when payment was due to the date of the decision) of $5000 and legal costs of $20 000, for a total of $100 000. The customer must pay this amount, along with its own legal costs, and absorb the remainder of the cost of the adverse impact on its business. Recovery by MP will be less than complete because the legal expenses of MP are likely to be well above the recovered costs of $20 000.

Enforcement

judgment debtor
The party ordered by the court to pay a specified amount to the winner of a lawsuit.

The winner of the suit must enforce the judgment with the assistance of the court. The judge issues a judgment for a certain amount of money ($100 000 in the MP case), which, in turn, can be enforced against the loser, now known as the **judgment debtor**. Court officials or other designated persons will assist in proceeding against the assets of the judgment debtor, which may include land, vehicles, houses, monthly income, and other assets. Laws in every jurisdiction limit the extent to which the winning party can take assets from the losing party; the point of this is to ensure that the person is not left destitute.

The winner recovers the judgment only to the extent that the loser's assets provide. There is no public fund from which these judgments are paid. Therefore, it is advisable for a prospective plaintiff to investigate the defendant's ability to pay before commencing the suit. MP should not sue the customer without reasonable certainty that the customer is financially healthy. A judgment in any amount is of little value if the customer has insufficient assets to pay, has a large number of other unpaid creditors, or is in bankruptcy proceedings.

Chances are that in a commercial dispute of this sort, the customer will acknowledge the result and pay the debt, if at all possible. Although a judgment is valid for a long period (up to 20 years) and can be renewed, its value is questionable if the judgment debtor's assets are insufficient to pay it.

Appeals

appeal
The process of arguing to a higher court that a court decision is wrong.

A party who is seriously dissatisfied with the trial decision may consider an **appeal** to the next court in the hierarchy. An appeal must be initiated within a specific period of time (such as 30 days). There are several reasons why an appeal should not be undertaken without careful consideration. In addition to the time and commitment required to pursue an appeal, the chances of success are limited. An appeal is not a rehearing of the case, but merely an opportunity to argue that the trial decision contains significant errors in how the law was applied. It is normally not possible to dispute the conclusions regarding what events actually transpired between the parties (i.e., what the trial judge found the "facts" to be), but only to dispute the judge's understanding and application of the law. Appeal courts tend to confirm trial decisions unless serious errors have been demonstrated.

Appeals at higher levels are normally conducted by a panel of at least three judges. No new evidence is presented. The lawyers representing the parties make written and oral submissions to the appeal judges, who then decide whether to confirm the original decision, vary it in some way, reverse the decision, or, in exceptional cases, order that another trial be conducted. In the MP case, it is unlikely that either party will appeal, considering the amount in dispute and the legal costs already incurred. However, if the customer still feels strongly about its counterclaim and legal advice indicates possible serious error by the trial judge, an appeal may be viable. Since the MP action was brought in superior court, the potential appeals would be to the provincial court of appeal and ultimately to the Supreme Court of Canada.

MP appears to be the winner in its case by recovering 75 percent of its claim, but it has incurred significant legal costs and experienced disruption of normal business activities. The relationship with the customer is destroyed, and the reputation of MP has possibly been harmed. It is often difficult to decide whether litigation has been worthwhile, even when it has been successful.

Litigation in the United States

Largely owing to the dominance of the U.S. media in Canada, the public's perception of litigation in Canada is often skewed toward the U.S. system. In fact, there are many differences in attitude, perception, and practice between the two systems:

- Americans tend to be more litigious than Canadians, perhaps because they are more conscious of their civil rights and property rights and are more willing and eager than Canadians to take legal action to protect those rights.
- There are more lawyers per capita in the U.S. system, and Americans tend to make more use of legal services.
- More civil cases are decided by juries in the United States, so that damage awards are less predictable and potentially higher.
- The U.S. system does not provide for partial recovery of costs by the successful party, so there is no risk of being required to pay any legal expenses of the other side.
- The use of contingency fees is more widespread in the United States. Contingency fees are a means for a lawyer to bear the risk that litigation may fail. If it does, the client pays only the actual expenses, not fees. If the suit succeeds, the lawyer receives (by prior agree-

ment) a significant portion of the judgment as compensation for services.

- American juries have more latitude to award punitive damages (to punish the loser) in addition to damages to compensate the victim.[9]
- Class actions are more widely available in the United States. These suits enable individuals with similar claims to unite and pursue their claim as a group, with representation by the same lawyer. For example, consumers who have been harmed by the same defective product can unite to sue the manufacturer.
- American consumers can more easily hold manufacturers liable for defective products based on the principle of strict liability.[10]

Critical Analysis: Class-action suits and contingency fees are becoming increasingly common in Canada as well. Are these positive developments? What do the number of lawyers and the volume of litigation in a country tell us about the business climate in that country? Should government be more active in controlling access to litigation? Is it the role of government to provide courts and facilities to meet the demand from litigation? Is there a maximum period of time that a lawsuit should be in the system?

9. See Part 3.
10. See Part 3.

Figure 4.3

FORMS OF DISPUTE RESOLUTION

	Negotiation	Mediation	Arbitration	Litigation
Who is involved	Parties only	Parties and facilitator	Parties and arbitrator (maybe lawyers)	Parties, lawyers, and a judge
When it is used	Anytime	By negotiation	By negotiation or contract	When one party sues the other
How it works	Parties decide	Mediator helps the parties	A formal hearing is held	The dispute goes through a four-stage process, ending in trial
Outcome	Settlement	Settlement	Binding decision	Court order
Advantages	Quick, cheap, controllable, private, preserves relationships	Quick, cheap, controllable, private, preserves relationships	Avoids litigation, final, preserves relationships	Final
Disadvantages	May fail	May fail	Imposed decision, unpredictable	Imposed decision, unpredictable, public, destroys relationships

Business Law in Practice Revisited

1. How well does MP's current risk management plan deal with these events?

The MP plan had mixed success. While it anticipated several possible events that could give rise to legal consequences, MP failed to always implement the plan effectively. The surprise concerning the change to the signage bylaw is evidence of that failure. In other respects, the plan worked well. MP bought insurance coverage against some risks. As a result, the car accident and slip and fall were expeditiously resolved through the insurer. Other issues, such as the matters involving the problem employee and the dissatisfied customer, were anticipated but proved difficult to manage. These disputes do not mean that MP's risk management plan failed with respect to these more tenacious matters. Some legal conflicts are inherently difficult to resolve.

2. What approaches should MP use in dealing with these events?

This chapter proposed that how MP should deal with each event depends on the particular circumstances. The chapter also made several suggestions on how management might proceed. It is important to emphasize, however, that there is no clear path or set of procedures that the decision makers should follow in every event. The best courses of action depend on

- the nature of the relationship between the parties
- the objectives each party has in relation to the particular dispute
- the attitudes of the parties: Are they more interested in resolution or in making a point to the other side?
- the amount of money at stake

- the resources the parties are prepared to devote to the dispute
- risk analysis and cost-benefit analysis of prolonging the dispute

The key is to adopt and follow a rational approach to dispute resolution and avoid litigation, with all of its pitfalls, if at all possible.

3. What are the possible outcomes?

This chapter presented a hypothetical outcome for each of the events outlined at the beginning. Actual outcomes depend on the circumstances, the other party, the way MP chooses to proceed, and the influence of outside decision makers, such as the courts:

- Insurance covered the slip and fall and the motor vehicle accident.
- MP complied with the bylaw changes and considered attempting to have them reconsidered.
- MP wrote off the delinquent customer's account as a bad debt.
- MP resolved the damaged goods problem through negotiation with the supplier.
- Mediation resolved the dispute with the problem employee.
- MP sued the disgruntled customer and was partly successful.

To improve its management of legal risk, MP must review each resolution and decide whether its plan needs adjustment in order to prevent or deal more effectively with similar events in the future.

Chapter Summary

This chapter has explored a range of disputes in which a business such as Mainplace Stationers might become involved. A risk management plan that is well developed and carefully implemented can minimize the number of disputes that arise and provide guidance for dealing with those that do. Legal disputes should be approached with a view to achieving an acceptable resolution, rather than winning at all costs.

There are a wide variety of techniques for resolving disputes that avoid litigation altogether or enable the parties to minimize damage to the businesses and their commercial relationships. The parties can negotiate their own resolution, or involve another person as a mediator to assist them or as an arbitrator to make a decision for them. When the parties resort to litigation, they are involving themselves in a lengthy, costly, public, and risky process. They are giving up some control over the process and the final result if the case goes to trial. The winner must collect the amount awarded by the court. That amount usually does not include full recovery of the legal expenses incurred to win the lawsuit.

Study Chapter

Questions for Review

1. What are scme potential business law disputes arising from the operation of a fast-food restaurant?

2. What is the process for attempting to resolve disputes informally?

3. What are three reasons for using ADR?

4. What are the differences between mediation and arbitration?

5. What are the major steps in the litigation process?

6. Who provides the funds to finance a lawsuit?

Questions for Discussion

1. How should management deal with the disputes you identified in question 1, above?

2. When should a dispute be litigated?

3. Who ultimately pays the "costs" in litigation?

4. Are Canadians moving closer to American attitudes toward litigation?

5. Is mandatory ADR likely to be more effective than voluntary ADR?

6. How can the various processes for resolving disputes be improved?

Situations for Discussion

1. Manon Blanchard is told that her company has just received a shipment of important inventory from a supplier who has been reliable in the past. Not only is the shipment significantly short, but the quality is poor and about 20 percent is of no use. Identify the informal steps Manon could take to address this problem.

2. The supplier company in Situation 1 above insists on full payment of $50 000. The company is under new management, and the managers are unwilling to concede anything. Manon's company is seeking a reduction in price of $15 000. What critical factors should Manon consider in deciding whether to pursue this dispute further?

3. The supplier sues Manon's company for $50 000. Manon's CEO is puzzled and upset about the supplier's attitude. He is about to advise outside counsel to "take them to the Supreme Court, if necessary." What arguments could Manon use to persuade him that this is not a particularly sound approach to a legal dispute?

4. The Loewen Group, based in Burnaby, B.C., and founded by Ray Loewen in the 1960s, is one of the largest owners of funeral homes in North America. Throughout the 1980s and 1990s, the company pursued a strategy of growth through the aggressive acquisition of U.S. funeral homes.

   In 1990, Loewen purchased Wright & Ferguson, the largest funeral operation in Jackson, Mississippi. Several years prior to the purchase, Wright & Ferguson had sold its insurance division to Gulf National Insurance Co., owned by J.J. O'Keefe. Gulf sells insurance policies through funeral homes to people who use this as a way to pay future funeral expenses. As part of the agreement between

Wright & Ferguson and Gulf, Wright & Ferguson agreed that they would sell only Gulf insurance policies. O'Keefe alleged that after Loewen purchased Wright & Ferguson, this clause was breached. He alleged that Loewen offered for sale and sold other insurance policies.

Gulf and O'Keefe sued for breach of contract. In 1991 an initial settlement of the suit was reached. Gulf agreed to sell two funeral homes and related assets to Loewen, in return for Loewen's agreeing to sell an insurance company to them. The deal, worth US$8.5 million to Gulf, was not completed. Gulf alleged that Loewen refused to complete, knowing that Gulf was having financial difficulties and that the failure of the sale would sorely damage Gulf's position.

Gulf amended its original breach of contract suit to include charges of fraud, breach of good faith, and malicious monopoly. Gulf and O'Keefe asked for damages of US$107 million. Loewen defended the charges. In 1995 a Jackson jury awarded the plaintiffs US$100 million in compensation and US$400 million in punitive damages. The award equaled almost half the value of Loewen's assets and almost 13 times its 1994 profit of $38.5 million. Jury foreman Glenn Miller told the *New York Times*: "[Ray Loewen] was a rich, dumb Canadian politician who thought he could come down and pull the wool over the eyes of a good ole Mississippi boy. It didn't work."

The jury award was subsequently upheld by a Mississippi judge. Ray Loewen expressed outrage at the award and vowed to appeal. However, under Mississippi law, Loewen was required to post a bond of 125 percent of the award—US$625 million—while appeals were pending. Rather than face several years of uncertainty, the company agreed to pay the plaintiffs $50 million immediately, to issue them 1.5 million shares in Loewen, and to pay them $4 million a year for the next 20 years.[11]

What does this case illustrate about the uncertainties of litigation? How could Loewen have tried to avoid these uncertainties?

5. The volume of electronic business (e-business) is rapidly increasing. In transactions between consumers and business, consumers are buying such items as books, food, and clothing on the Internet. Consumers are not always satisfied with every aspect of their purchases. Their complaints concern delivery of the wrong items, failure of items to meet statements and descriptions made on business Web sites, late delivery, refusal of returns, and problems with warranties. Consumers sometimes have difficulty contacting sellers and getting them to deal effectively with complaints. The value of individual sales is small, so legal action through small claims court is impractical. Consumers, government, and business are all concerned about the volume of complaints and are interested in devising a system to deal with them.

Who should take responsibility for developing a dispute resolution mechanism for these complaints? What should be the goals of the mechanism? How could it work?

11. Based on *O'Keefe* v. *Loewen Group* (1995), online: The National Law Journal <www.ljx.com/nlj> (11 December 1995).

Part Two

Contracts

BUSINESS RELIES ON CONTRACT LAW—MORE THAN any other area of law—as a way of facilitating commerce. Contract law provides a structure through which individuals and organizations are able to create legally binding, commercial commitments. Essentially, parties must keep their contractual promises or pay damages to the other side for breach.

A working knowledge of contract law is essential to anyone involved in business. This knowledge is crucial because the law advances commercial activities and can be used to build productive and cooperative business relationships. In fact, contract law forms the basis of many commercial relationships, including employment, credit, property, and insurance dealings, as well as the sale of goods and services.

Chapter 5 Contract Law Defined

► Chapter 5 introduces contract law and sets the stage for a more detailed consideration of the rules in the four chapters that follow. It defines a contract and presents some key factors in the contractual relationship, such as communication, bargaining power, and dispute resolution. In addition, Chapter 5 discusses the context of contract law formed by business relationships and the economic realities of the marketplace.

Chapter 6 Forming Contractual Relationships

► Chapter 6 deals with the formation of a contract as a voluntary agreement that must contain several basic elements: offer, acceptance, consideration, and intention to form a contract.

Chapter 7 The Terms of a Contract

► Chapter 7 focuses on the content of the contract, known as its "terms." Terms of a contract specify the rights and obligations of the parties and allocate risks. This chapter explains how judges determine and interpret the content of a contract and describes some common commercial contracts.

Chapter 8 Nonenforcement of Contracts

► Chapter 8 looks at the rare situations in which contracts are not enforced because of unequal relationships, illegality, misrepresentations, and mistakes. It also explores the types of contacts that must be in writing in order to be enforced by a court.

Chapter 9 Termination and Enforcement of Contracts

► Chapter 9 discusses the termination of contracts through performance, agreement, or frustration and looks at the requirements for enforcing a contract: privity, breach of promise, and entitlement to a remedy. The most common remedy for breach of contract is compensation for financial loss.

Five Chapter

Contract Law Defined

Objectives

AFTER STUDYING THIS CHAPTER, YOU SHOULD HAVE AN UNDERSTANDING OF:

► THE CONCEPT OF A CONTRACT
► THE KEY FACTORS IN THE CONTRACTUAL RELA- TIONSHIP
► CONTRACT LAW IN THE CONTEXT OF BUSINESS RELATIONSHIPS

Business Law in Practice

Amritha Singh is a middle manager with Coasters Plus Ltd. (Coasters), a company that designs and manufactures roller coasters for amusement parks across North America. She has been appointed one of the project managers for the design and delivery of a special roller coaster for the Ultimate Park Ltd., a customer in Florida. A major component of the project is the steel tracking, and one possible source is Trackers Canada Ltd. (Trackers). Amritha's supervisor has asked her to negotiate the necessary contract. This task causes Amritha some concern, since she has never been solely responsible for contractual negotiations before. She does know, however, that

The agreement to acquire the tracking is only one piece of a project to design and install a roller coaster in an amusement park.

Coasters needs a reliable supplier who can deliver high-quality tracking for under $2 million, and in good time for installation at the Ultimate Park's site.

1. How should Amritha approach her task of securing the necessary tracking?
2. How can the law facilitate Amritha's acquisition task?
3. What rules apply to a commercial relationship between a manufacturer (such as Coasters) and a supplier (such as Trackers), and how are disputes resolved?
4. What are the legal consequences to Coasters of assigning the negotiation task to Amritha?
5. What is the business context of the proposed legal agreement?

Defining Contract Law

contract
An agreement between two parties that is enforceable in a court of law.

A **contract** is an agreement between two or more parties that is enforceable in a court of law. Under the agreement, each party makes *binding* commitments or promises to the others. For example, to ensure that the Florida project comes in on budget and on time, Amritha wants guarantees from a supplier, such as Trackers, that quality tracking will be provided in the amount agreed upon and by the date specified (see Figure 5.1). For its part, Trackers wants a guarantee from Coasters that the established purchase price will be paid. These guarantees or promises are known as **terms of the contract**.

terms of the contract
Binding commitments that form part of a contract.

Figure 5.1

A CONTRACT CONTAINS BINDING PROMISES

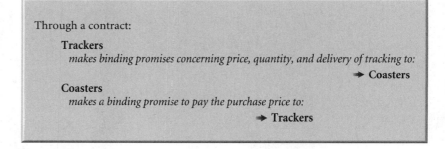

Through a contract:

Trackers
makes binding promises concerning price, quantity, and delivery of tracking to:
➤ **Coasters**

Coasters
makes a binding promise to pay the purchase price to:
➤ **Trackers**

The genius of contract law is that it permits both parties to *rely* on the terms they have negotiated and plan their business affairs accordingly. If one of them fails to keep its word and breaches a term, the court will award damages for whatever losses the innocent party has sustained. In short, contract law ensures that each party gets what it bargained for—namely, performance of the promises made to it or monetary compensation in its place.

Contracts are the legal cornerstone of any commercial operation. Through a contract, the business enterprise can sell a product or service, hire employees, rent office space, borrow money, purchase supplies, and enter into any other kind of binding agreement it chooses. In this way, contract law is *facilitative*: it allows participants to create their own rights and duties within a framework of rules that a judge will later enforce, if called upon to do so.

Contracts come in a wide variety of forms. A contract for the purchase and sale of a box of pens from the corner store, for example, is casually conducted and instantly completed. The only document that will be produced is the sales receipt. Other contracts, such as for the purchase and sale of high-quality steel tracking, will require lengthy negotiations, considerable documentation, and time to perform. Some contracts are one-shot deals, in that the parties are unlikely to do business with each other again. Other contracts are part of a long-standing and valued commercial relationship, as one might find between supplier and retailer. Regardless of the context, however, every contract is subject to the same set of *mandatory* legal rules. This means that contract law principles will be applied by a judge to resolve a contractual dispute between the parties, whether the parties were aware of those principles or not.

Amritha's attention is currently focused on one transaction: her company's acquisition of tracking from a suitable supplier. Her goal should be to enter into a *contract* with a supplier like Trackers, because Coasters requires legally enforceable assurances that its supplier will fulfill its commitments. The alternative to a contract—in the form of a casual understanding—makes little business sense, even if Trackers is highly reputable and trustworthy, because cooperation and goodwill between parties can suddenly evaporate when an unforseen conflict or problem arises. Personnel can change. Memories may become selective and self-serving. Genuine differences of opinion may arise. At this point, Amritha's company needs the protection of a well-constructed contract—including the right to commence a lawsuit based upon it—not the vague assurances she may have received from Trackers personnel sometime in the past.

This is not to say that informal business arrangements never succeed, but only that there is no remedy in contract law should one of the parties fail to keep its word. This is a risk that a business should ordinarily not be prepared to run.

In discussing contracts, it is easy to become entangled in the legal details. The aim of this chapter is to introduce important aspects of contract law, while highlighting their application to the business world. These essentials are more fully developed in Chapters 6 to 9.

Key Factors in Contractual Relationships

Communication

Every contractual relationship begins with communication. The contractual relationship may originate in a number of ways—through informal contact between individuals in different businesses who recognize mutual needs, or perhaps through a preliminary inquiry made to a supplier concerning price and availability of materials. Amritha will likely approach existing suppliers first to see if they can meet Coasters' special requirements for this project. She may initiate contact with other potential tracking suppliers by obtaining recommendations from others in her company who have purchasing experience, from colleagues in the industry, or from industry organizations. And, of course, Coasters may be approached periodically by suppliers in the industry. Regardless of who makes the first move, Amritha will likely negotiate with a number of suppliers in order to determine who can give her company the most favourable terms.

Some negotiations fail, while others succeed in creating a contract. Whether a contract exists between the parties does not depend on their subjective opinion of the matter. For practical reasons, contract law concerns itself with what the negotiators say and do, not with what they think or imagine. In the event of a dispute as to whether or not a contract exists, a judge will apply the **objective standard test**. This test asks whether the reasonable person, observing the communication that has occurred between the negotiators, would conclude that a legal agreement had been reached. Amritha needs to be clear in her dealings with potential suppliers so that no one is misled into thinking a contract is in place when, according to the objective standard, it is not. This important matter will be explored further in Chapter 6.

Individuals who communicate and negotiate in the commercial world are usually acting not on their own behalf, but on behalf of the business that employs them. Therefore, the business organization becomes bound by the negotiated contract and gains rights and liabilities according to its terms. For example, Amritha will be negotiating on behalf of Coasters, and the supplier's representative will be negotiating on the supplier's behalf. If a contract is made, the parties will be Coasters and the supplier company. Amritha and the representative will not be parties and will therefore have no personal rights or obligations under the contract. Put in legal language, Amritha and the representative do not have **privity of contract**. This matter is discussed more extensively in Chapter 9.

objective standard test The test applied in dealing with a contractual dispute based on how a "reasonable person" would view the conduct of the parties.

privity of contract A doctrine providing that only parties to a contract have rights and obligations under the contract.

Bargaining Power

equality of bargaining power
The legal assumption that parties to a contract are able to look out for their own interests.

Contract law is constructed on the basic assumption that those who negotiate and enter into contracts have **equal bargaining power**, meaning that they are capable of looking out for themselves and will work to maximize their own self-interest. As a result, courts are normally not entitled to assess the fairness or reasonableness of the contractual terms the parties have chosen. Courts will almost invariably assume that the parties had their eyes open, considered all the relevant factors, evaluated the risks, and were prepared to accept both the costs and benefits of the contract.

The law will assume equality of bargaining power even though, in almost every situation, one party will have some distinct advantage over the other. A seller of goods in limited supply has more power in bargaining than the buyer; a person who is more knowledgeable about an industry is in a stronger position than the less informed party he or she is negotiating with. Likewise, there will normally be differences in the size and financial strength of businesses entering into a contract. These imbalances, however, are insufficient to result in the contract being set aside or cancelled by a judge. The rationale is that parties should be able to rely on contractual commitments. Though one party may have agreed to a price she or he now considers too high or, in fact, may have made a bad deal, none of this is justification for securing the court's assistance and intervention. People are simply expected to take care of themselves.

Occasionally, however, circumstances favour one party over the other to such an extent that the court will come to the assistance of the weaker party and set the contract aside.

Case

Atlas Supply v. *Yarmouth Equipment* (1991), 103 N.S.R. (2d) 1 (S.C.A.D.)

The Business Context: Businesses are expected to obtain necessary information and refrain from agreeing to terms until they have an agreement they can live with. This case is an exception to the general rule that courts will not interfere with a bargain freely made.

Factual Background: Atlas was a subsidiary of Esso that supplied parts and accessories to Esso auto service stations. Atlas decided to franchise its operations because its profits were declining. Mr. Murphy's company, Yarmouth Equipment, was interested in purchasing the franchise for a particular area. Atlas prepared two sets of financial projections for the business in that area. The projections given to Murphy portrayed a viable operation. The other set showed a more realistic and much less profitable picture. Yarmouth bought the franchise, but the business failed and closed in less than a year. Murphy was called upon to pay a substantial sum under his personal guarantee of Yarmouth's debt to Atlas. The trial judge found in Murphy's favour and set aside the contract by characterizing the projections as terms of the contract that were broken and not covered by other clauses that exempted Atlas from responsibility. Atlas appealed.

The Legal Question: Should Murphy be held to the promises he made based on the projections supplied by Atlas?

Resolution: The appeal court ruled 2 to 1 in favour of Murphy. Justice Matthews focused on the misleading information given to Murphy and the contrary information withheld. Justice Matthews found that the agreement "was entered into on the one hand by a national company with international connections through its parent, Imperial Oil, and on the other by a small businessman who, though no neophyte, had little or no retail experience." In a similar vein, Justice Freeman ruled that "Atlas sold Mr. Murphy and Yarmouth Equipment on an enterprise that it should have known had no reasonable chance of success."

Justice Hallett, the dissenting judge, took a more traditional view. He found that Murphy was an experienced business person who was aware of the basis for the financial projections and was not compelled to agree to the terms, which were clearly expressed. He cautioned that the courts should be very reluctant to set aside business deals such as this one.

Critical Analysis: Should a large business with the advantage in information (such as Atlas) be allowed to take advantage of a small, relatively uninformed one (such as Yarmouth)? Which of the judges do you find to be the most persuasive?

The *Atlas* case is unusual in the disparity in bargaining power between the parties and the extent of the manipulation, which led the court to set the contract aside. As Chapter 8 will show, only in extreme circumstances—as when a person takes gross advantage of another person's pronounced weakness or vulnerability—does the innocent party have any legal recourse.

For this reason, Amritha must ensure that she is fully aware of her company's needs and the supplier's capabilities. Coasters is unlikely to succeed in having its contract set aside because Amritha was an inexperienced negotiator or because the supplier was a relatively bigger, more powerful company.

Completeness

To arrive at an enforceable contract, it is essential that the agreement between the parties be complete. Amritha must make it her objective to achieve consensus with the other side on such terms as price, quantity of tracking, quality of tracking, payment schedule, and delivery dates. If she creates an **incomplete agreement**, she may find that the supplier's obligations are not part of an enforceable agreement, much to the disappointment of her employer.

incomplete agreement
An agreement that is not contractual because its content is not sufficiently comprehensive.

This does not mean that the contract must be crystal clear to be enforceable, though that would be helpful. As a last resort, the courts can be called upon to decide what the terms mean in relation to the words used and the apparent intentions of the parties, but there must be some expression of what was agreed. Therefore, the negotiators must communicate clearly and understand their mutual desires. The courts will not ordinarily provide missing content for an agreement but will find, instead, that the contract has failed because it is too uncertain. Should this happen in Amritha's case, Coasters may find that it has no contract to enforce whatsoever.

Form

It is generally of no importance to its enforceability whether a contract is written down or not, though there are significant exceptions to this rule (discussed in Chapter 8). Even so, it is preferable for negotiators to create a record of their agreement and have the agreement signed by the appropriate personnel on both sides of the contract. Not only does a written contract generate a more definite and clear structure for the business relationship between the parties, but it is also evidence of the contract's existence and contents, should a legal dispute arise.

A contract may take many forms.

Dispute Resolution

If a dispute arises between two parties to a contract, there are various stages and options for dispute resolution, outlined in Chapter 4.

For the most part, the rules governing contractual disputes are based on the common law. The common law, as discussed

Inequality of Bargaining and the Standard Form Contract

An important, practical, and modern form of inequality of bargaining is found in the proliferation of the standard form contract. Sales and rental businesses frequently require their customers (consumer and commercial) to consent to a standard set of terms that have been developed by the business over years of operation. Such

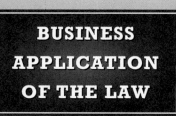

BUSINESS APPLICATION OF THE LAW

terms often heavily favour the business that created them and normally are not open to negotiation. For this reason, such contracts are known colloquially as "take it or leave it" contracts.

Many businesses use a standard form contract for all customers.

A car rental agreement is a good example of a standard form contract. There are two types of information in the contract. One type is unique to the particular transaction and is inserted in the blanks of the contract. This is the part of the contract that would record the customer's name and address; licence plate number and model of car supplied; dates for rental; rental charges (per day or kilometre); and insurance charges.

The other type of information consists of standard terms that apply to every transaction with this rental company. The major purpose of these terms is to impose responsibility for risk on the customer. Some typical terms could be as follows:

This is an agreement between you, the customer, and the company to rent a motor vehicle.

You, the customer, are renting the vehicle from the company and entering into a contract with the company for the use of the company's vehicle.

You are agreeing to pay on demand the rental charges. By entering into this contract, you are subject to the following terms and conditions:

Authorized Use. The vehicle may be used only by an authorized driver. An authorized driver is:

- you, the customer, if you are a licensed driver
- a licensed driver who has signed this agreement and has been accepted by the company as an additional driver
- a licensed driver who assumes the responsibility of an authorized driver and has your permission to use the vehicle and who is at least 21 years old and is either a member of your immediate family (and residing in the same household) or your business associate (partner, employer, employee, fellow employee)

Prohibited Use. You, the customer, agree that the vehicle shall not be used:

- for carrying persons or property for hire
- for propelling or towing any vehicle, trailer, or other object
- in any race, speed test, or contest
- by any person who is under the influence of alcohol, intoxicants, narcotics, or other substances to an extent prohibited by law

- in the commission of any crime or for any illegal trade or transport

- in a reckless or abusive manner or for any abnormal use of the vehicle

- by anyone for whom the company has been given a false name, age, address, or other information

Vehicle Condition and Return. The vehicle is delivered to you in good operating condition. You agree to return the vehicle in the same condition in which you received it (except for ordinary wear and tear) to the company's location at the place and on the date specified.

You will pay to the company on demand all loss or damage to the vehicle and related expenses, including loss of use while rented under this agreement.

Even in the circumstances such as these, where bargaining is not contemplated, the law expects people to take care of themselves. While there is provincial consumer protection legislation that may be of assistance in certain consumer transactions, the better course is to read and understand the standard form contract before signing it.

in Chapter 2, refers to judge-made laws, as opposed to laws made by elected governments. This means that a judge resolving a contractual conflict is usually relying not on statute law to guide deliberations, but rather on what other judges have said in past cases that resemble the current case. As noted in Part 1, these past cases are known as precedents because they contain a legal principle found in a past situation similar to the one being litigated. The judge will hear evidence from the two parties in support of their respective positions and then determine which common law rules of contract are applicable to the situation and what the outcome should be. Depending on the nature of the dispute between Coasters and its supplier, legislation such as the *Sale of Goods Act* may also be relevant. Chapter 9 deals with the enforcement of contracts.

Contract Law in Context

Although contract law is significant, it is not the only relevant factor in a commercial transaction. The business person must also take into account

- business relationships
- economic reality
- public relations

Business Relationships

Contract law is narrow in scope: its emphasis is often on a specific transaction, such as a single sale, and is not traditionally concerned with longer-term business relationships. Because contract law does not focus on the longer-term relationship, business and law students alike may be misled into thinking that if someone has suffered a legal wrong, they should automatically sue the wrongdoer. This approach can be counterproductive in many circumstances, however. For example, if Coasters' supplier is late in delivering its tracking, the supplier is in breach of contract, and

Coasters will be entitled to compensation for any resulting loss, such as that caused by late completion of the project for the Ultimate Park, in Florida. However, if Coasters insists on that compensation, the relationship with that supplier may be irreparably harmed. Absorbing the loss in this instance may be a small price to pay in the long term, particularly if the supplier is otherwise reliable and Coasters is not interested in investing time and money in finding a replacement. Put another way, insisting on one's strict legal rights may not be the best business option.

The expense and uncertainty of litigation are also reasons to avoid a full-blown legal conflict.

Economic Reality

Though contract law exists to create legally binding commitments, it is not always the best economic decision for a party to keep that commitment. The law has some built-in flexibility, since all it requires is for contractual obligations to be performed *or* for compensation to be paid for nonperformance. Accordingly, there may be situations where the cost of compensation is a perfectly acceptable price to pay for release from obligations. For example, a business whose production is committed to a one-year contract may be quite willing to pay what is necessary to be relieved of the one-year obligation if a more profitable, long-term deal becomes available for the same production. This idea is explained further below.

Public Relations

If a given contract stands in the way of a better opportunity, the business organization may choose to disregard its contractual obligation and accept, instead, the financial consequences that come with breach of contract. A business that makes a practice of breaching contracts and paying damages instead will certainly be within its legal rights but is also likely to acquire a reputation in the industry as an unreliable and undependable company. Although a business organization may gain in the short term, its long-term viability may be compromised if customers, suppliers, and employees grow reluctant to deal with it.

Similarly, a business that insists on strict observance of its legal rights may damage its reputation in the marketplace. Although a manufacturer may have a valid defence for having produced a defective product that injures a customer, for example, it may be better, in the end, to compensate the customer voluntarily rather than fight out a lawsuit. A lawsuit in the circumstances of this example may result in a public relations disaster.

Business Law in Practice Revisited

1. How should Amritha approach her task of securing the necessary tracking?

Given the size and expense of the proposed acquisition of tracking, Amritha should make it a priority to enter into a *contract* with a supplier such as Trackers. Nothing less than a contract will do, since Coasters must be able to exercise the legal right to sue, should Trackers fail to perform as promised.

2. How can the law facilitate Amritha's acquisition task?

Legal knowledge will help Amritha ensure that her negotiations produce an enforceable contract that meets her employer's needs and protects its interests. If Amritha

Economic Breach

Suppose Trackers signs a contract to deliver 900 metres of tracking to Coasters for $2 million, in two equal installments. After Trackers has delivered half the order, Thriller Rides Ltd. (a competitor of Coasters) contacts Trackers and explains that, owing to an emergency, it desperately needs 450 metres of track to complete a major project. Thriller offers Trackers $2 million to supply the necessary tracking—double the price Trackers would receive from Coasters for the same amount of tracking. Trackers has several options in response to Thriller's request:

BUSINESS APPLICATION OF THE LAW

- *Option 1:* Complete delivery to Coasters as agreed and decline Thriller's request.
- *Option 2:* Try to persuade Coasters to accept late delivery of the remainder of their order and offer a price break as an incentive.
- *Option 3:* Abandon the balance of Coasters' contract and fill Thriller's order.

Each option has its own economic and legal consequences:

- *Option 1* respects the Coasters contract and maintains good relations with Coasters but concedes the extra profit and the potential relationship to be gained from filling Thriller's order.
- *Option 2* has the potential to satisfy both customers and to gain from Thriller (less some portion for Coasters as compensation).

- *Option 3* generates extra profit and a potential long-term relationship with Thriller, but it destroys any relationship with Coasters and likely will lead to a claim for compensation from Coasters for their extra tracking cost and potential losses from late delivery to the Ultimate Park. Before accepting the Thriller order, Trackers needs to assure itself that the extra profit generated from Thriller will offset the damages it will have to pay to Coasters for breach of contract. Those damages could be quite high, depending on the circumstances, and difficult for Trackers to assess.

There is no question that Trackers has a legal obligation to Coasters, but that does not preclude Trackers from considering other opportunities. If Trackers chooses to breach the contract, there are also nonfinancial factors to be considered, such as future relations with Coasters; but in legal terms, a business that is prepared to pay damages for breach of contract can always refuse to perform its contractual obligations. Contract law provides compensation for breach, rather than punishment. There are no criminal consequences to breach of contract, and the law has traditionally refrained from making moral judgments about business activities.[1]

does not know what a contract is, how it is formed, and what its legal significance might be, she is not competent to accomplish the task her employer has set for her.

3. What rules apply to a commercial relationship between a manufacturer (such as Coasters) and a supplier (such as Trackers), and how are disputes resolved?

The rules governing contracts are found in the common law (which develops through the decisions of the courts on a case-by-case basis), and to a lesser extent in statute law. If a dispute arises between Coasters and Trackers, there are several

---

1. For further discussion of economic breach, see Richard Posner, Economic Analysis of Law, 5th ed. (New York: Aspen Law & Business, 1998).

options available for attempting to resolve the dispute, including mediation and arbitration. Litigation is a last resort and will bring the matter to court. A judge will evaluate the terms of the contract and the conduct of the parties, apply the relevant law, and then come to a determination.

4. What are the legal consequences to Coasters of assigning the negotiation task to Amritha?

Amritha is representing her employer in negotiations. She will therefore need to appreciate at what point legal commitments are being made by both sides. Coasters should consider its relative bargaining position with available suppliers and ensure that Amritha has adequate support in her negotiations. Her inexperience and Coasters' size and expertise in contract negotiations will not relieve Coasters of its obligations. The contract itself will be between Coasters and the supplier (as the parties privy to the contract). They are the only parties able to enforce rights and the only parties who are subject to the obligations in the contract.

5. What is the business context of the proposed legal agreement?

If Coasters has a good working relationship with companies that can supply the required tracking, those suppliers are the logical candidates for Amritha's project. Their business practices and reliability will be known to Coasters, and negotiating a contract with them is likely to be more efficient than with a new supplier. Even a significant price advantage from a new supplier may not justify endangering long-term relationships with others.

Although both parties are obligated by the terms of any contract they make, there may be developments in the market or in the situation relating to the operations of Coasters or Trackers. The request to Trackers from a competitor of Coasters for the supply of tracking is only one example of an event that may cause these companies to reconsider their business and legal relationship. They must weigh all factors, including long-term business dealings and their reputation in the industry, when they are faced with a decision about whether to honour the contract, seek adjustment, or consider breaching the contract.

Chapter Summary

Through an awareness of contract law, business organizations are better able to protect themselves in both the formation and the enforcement of contracts. Contracts generally are not required to be in a particular form, but clear agreement on all essential terms is necessary. Those involved in negotiating contracts should be aware of the legal impact of their communication with each other, and they should realize that they are largely responsible for protecting their own interests before agreeing to terms. Contract rules are understood best when assessed in the broader business context, which includes the impact that any given legal decision by a business may have on its reputation with other businesses, with its customers, and in the community at large. A business must also assess its legal options in light of the business relationship at issue, the need to generate a profit, the uncertainty of the marketplace, and the importance of conducting operations with a sense of commercial morality, honesty, and good faith.

Study Chapter

Key Terms and Concepts

contract (p. 93)
equality of bargaining power (p. 96)
incomplete agreement (p. 97)
objective standard test (p. 95)
privity of contract (p. 95)
terms of the contract (p. 93)

Questions for Review

1. What is a contract?

2. What are the purposes of contract law?

3. How do the courts resolve disputes about contracts?

4. Is it necessary for contracts to be in writing?

5. What are some important factors in a contractual relationship?

6. Why was the result in *Atlas Supply* v. *Yarmouth Equipment* unusual?

7. What is meant by privity of contract?

8. What is the role of public relations in contracts?

Questions for Discussion

1. Is there a better way to resolve disputes about contracts than by applying common law rules in litigation?

2. Is the assumption of equal bargaining power a reasonable one?

3. Why will the courts not change the terms of a contract except under extraordinary circumstances?

4. Why is it important to place contract law in a business context?

Situations for Discussion

1. Trackers is a manufacturer of steel tracking, which is used by customers in a variety of applications, including rides for amusement parks. Trackers' business is booming, and its scheduling is tight for meeting delivery commitments. Trackers is contacted by a representative of Coasters, who inquires whether Trackers is capable of providing track for a special roller coaster in Florida, and if so, what price Trackers could offer and when it could deliver. Trackers knows that Coasters is a coming leader in the industry and would be a valuable customer. What factors should Trackers consider before responding to the Coasters inquiry? What are the risks and benefits of agreeing to fill Coasters' order?

2. Representatives of Trackers and Coasters discuss the key terms of their agreement over several weeks. Finally, in a meeting they agree on price, quality, delivery, and terms of payment. Trackers representatives volunteer to draw up the formal contract, based on the results of the meeting. When Coasters receives the contract the following week, it contains the key terms as agreed, but it also includes several complex terms that appear to protect Trackers if they fail to deliver, and it places responsibility on Coasters for shifts in the market or transportation difficulties. When Coasters inquires about the "extra" terms, Trackers replies that these terms are standard for all of their customers. How should Coasters deal with the standard terms? What role does bargaining power play in these negotiations?

3. Systems Unlimited (SU) is a well-established and successful retailer of computer systems. Mega Computers (MC) has been a major supplier to SU for many years. MC is having difficulty meeting the demand from all of its customers and decides that it needs to focus on a number of key customers, which do not include SU. The loss of MC as a supplier will be a major blow to SU's business. Does MC have any legal obligation to continue supplying SU? How should MC approach SU with its policy change? Could SU have prevented this situation from arising?

Six Chapter

Forming Contractual Relationships

Objectives

AFTER STUDYING THIS CHAPTER, YOU SHOULD HAVE AN
UNDERSTANDING OF:

► HOW NEGOTIATIONS LEAD TO A CONTRACTUAL RELATIONSHIP
► HOW NEGOTIATIONS CAN BE TERMINATED
► WHAT THE LEGAL INGREDIENTS OF A CONTRACT ARE
► HOW CONTRACTS CAN BE AMENDED OR CHANGED

Business Law in Practice

Amritha, introduced in Chapter 5, began negotiations with Jason. Jason is a representative of Trackers, the steel tracking manufacturer willing to supply tracking to Coasters, Amritha's employer. Amritha provided Jason with the plans and specifications for the roller coaster, and they negotiated on a number of points, including price, delivery dates, and tracking quality. A short time later, Jason offered to sell Coasters a total of 900 metres of track in accordance with the plans and specifications provided. Among other matters contained in Jason's offer were the purchase price ($1.5 million); delivery date; terms of payment; insurance obligations concerning the track; and a series of warranties related to the quality and performance of the tracking to be supplied. There was also a clause in the offer that stated:

"Trackers will use its best efforts to secure insurance from the insurer named by Coasters." Another clause, inserted at Amritha's express request, required Trackers to pay $5000 to Coasters for every day it was late in delivering the tracking.

After reviewing the offer for several days, Amritha contacted Jason and said: "You drive a hard bargain, and there are aspects of your offer that I'm not entirely happy with. However, I accept your offer on behalf of my company. I'm looking forward to doing business with you."

Within a month, Trackers faced a 20 percent increase in manufacturing costs owing to an unexpected shortage in steel. Jason contacted Amritha to explain this development and worried aloud that without an agreement from Coasters to pay 20 percent more for the tracking, Trackers would be unable to make its delivery date. Amritha received instructions from her supervisor to agree to the increased purchase price in order to ensure timely delivery. Amritha communicated this news to Jason, who thanked her profusely for being so cooperative and understanding.

Jason kept his word and the tracking was delivered on time. However, Coasters has now determined that its profit margin on the Florida deal is lower than expected, and it is looking for ways to cut costs. Amritha is told by her boss to let Jason know that Coasters would not be paying the 20 percent price increase and would remit payment only in the amount set out in the contract. Jason and Trackers are stunned by this development.

1. At what point did the negotiations between Jason and Amritha begin to have legal consequences?
2. In what ways could negotiations have been terminated prior to the formation of the contract?
3. Can Coasters commit itself to the price increase and then change its mind with no adverse consequences?
4. How could Trackers have avoided from the outset this situation related to cost increases?

The Contract

Chapter 5 defined a contract as an agreement between two or more parties that is enforceable in a court of law. This chapter expands on that definition by identifying the building blocks of a contract. It sets out the legal ingredients that transform a simple agreement—which either party can break with impunity—into an enforceable contract.

A contract is composed of the following:

- an offer
- an acceptance
- consideration
- an intention to create legal relations

These basic components are generally present in every contract, whether it is for a $5 stapler or for million-dollar roller coaster tracking.

Definition of Offer

offer
A promise to perform specified acts on certain terms.

An **offer** is a promise to enter into a contract, on specified terms, as soon as the offer is accepted. This happened in negotiations between Amritha and Jason when Jason committed to provide tracking to Coasters in the concrete terms noted above: he named his price, terms of payments, delivery date, and other essential matters. At this point, negotiations have taken an important turn because Amritha is entitled to accept that offer, and upon her doing so, Trackers is obligated to supply its product exactly as Jason proposed, assuming that the other ingredients of a contract are established.

An offer is different from showing a general interest to do business with someone else. When Amritha provided Jason with the plans for the roller coaster, she was not offering to buy tracking from Jason at that point but merely indicating her interest in receiving an offer from him. Similarly, if Jason had offered to sell tracking to Coasters during negotiations but provided no other detail, he would simply be demonstrating his wish to do business with Coasters. Such expressions of interest have no legal consequences because, at bottom, they have no content. How can vague commitments to buy or sell tracking amount to offers when they fail to specify the terms or scope of the proposed arrangement? In short, an offer must be reasonably complete before it counts as an offer that is open for acceptance.

invitation to treat
An expression of willingness to do business.

A communication lacking specificity is seen as a mere expression of wishing to do business and has no legal repercussions whatsoever. In law, such a communication is called an **invitation to treat**.

The common law has devised a number of rules that determine when an offer has been made and when the matter at hand is simply an invitation to treat. A rule of particular significance to business relates to the advertising and display of goods for sale in a store.

Enterprises such as retail outlets prosper by attracting customers to their premises. They do this through advertising their existence, as well as describing the products they sell and prices they charge, especially when those prices have been reduced. For practical reasons, these advertisements are normally not classified as offers.[1] If advertisements were offers, then the store owner would be potentially liable for breach of contract if the store ran out of an advertised item that a customer wished to purchase. By classifying the advertisement as in invitation to treat, the law ensures that it is the customer who makes the offer to purchase the advertised goods. The owner is then in a position to simply refuse the offer if the product is no longer in supply. As a result of this refusal, no contract could arise.[2]

Similarly, the display of a product in the store is not an offer by the store to sell. The display is simply an indication that a product is available and can be purchased. In short, it is an invitation to treat and, by definition, is not capable of being accepted. In this way, the store maintains the option of refusing to complete the transaction at the till[3] (see Figure 6.1).

---

1. An exception to this general rule occurs when the advertisement is so clear and definite that there is nothing left to negotiate. See *Lefkowitz* v. *Great Minneapolis Surplus Store, Inc.*, 251 Minn. 188, 86 N.W. 2d. 689 (1957).

2. A store owner may have other legal problems if he or she runs out of an advertised sale product. For example, the "bait and switch selling" provision of *The Competition Act*, R.S.C. 1985, c. c-34, s. 57(2) provides:

   No person shall advertise at a bargain price a product that he does not supply in reasonable quantities having regard to the nature of the market in which he carries on the business, the nature and the size of the business carried on by him and the nature of the advertisement.

   Subsection (3) provides defences for contravening (2). Note that s. 57(4) provides for a punishment of a fine not exceeding $25 000, imprisonment for a term not exceeding one year, or both.

3. Human rights legislation across the country prohibits a business owner from refusing to serve a customer on the basis of race, gender, and other discriminatory grounds.

Figure 6.1

LEGAL ANALYSIS OF THE RETAIL PURCHASE

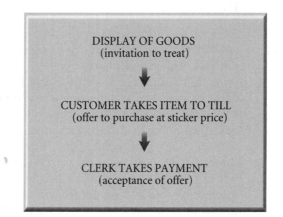

DISPLAY OF GOODS
(invitation to treat)

↓

CUSTOMER TAKES ITEM TO TILL
(offer to purchase at sticker price)

↓

CLERK TAKES PAYMENT
(acceptance of offer)

In the end, there is no definitive explanation as to why the law generally regards the display of goods as being invitations to treat. To a large extent, this characterization simply arises as a result of a historical approach established by precedent.

Some contracts, like the purchase of photocopying paper from an office supply store, are formed without any negotiations whatsoever. The customer simply takes the purchase to the cashier—thereby offering to purchase the item at its sticker price—and the cashier accepts the offer by receiving payment. Other contracts arise only after protracted discussions.

When negotiations are complicated, it is important for the parties to know *when* an offer has been made, since at that moment significant legal consequences arise, whether the parties intend them to or not. A fundamental rule is that a contract is formed only when a *complete* offer is unconditionally accepted by the other side. The key factor in deciding whether an offer has been made is this: if the purported offer is sufficiently comprehensive that it can be accepted without further elaboration or clarification, it is an offer in law. Jason's proposal to Amritha, outlined in the opening scenario, contains the requisite certainty and completeness. On this basis, the first building block to a contract between Trackers and Coasters is in place.

The person who makes an offer is known as the **offeror**. The person to whom an offer is made is known as the **offeree**. In the Business Law in Practice scenario, Jason is the offeror and Amritha is the offeree.

Some contracts are easily concluded, as when a consumer makes a retail purchase, while others are the result of lengthy negotiations.

offeror
The person who makes an offer.

offeree
The person to whom an offer is made.

Termination of Offer

An offer can be accepted only if it is "alive," meaning that it is available to be accepted. If the offer has been legally terminated, no contract can come into existence, since one of its essential ingredients—the offer itself—is missing.

An offer can be terminated or taken "off the table" by any of the following events:

- revocation
- lapse
- rejection
- counteroffer

Revocation

revocation
The withdrawal of an offer.

The offeror can **revoke** his or her offer at any time before acceptance simply by notifying the offeree of its withdrawal. An offer that has been revoked does not exist anymore and therefore cannot be accepted.

In the opening scenario, there were several days between the communication of Tracker's offer and Amritha's acceptance of that offer. During this time, Jason would have been legally entitled to revoke his offer by simply advising Amritha of that fact. Amritha's alternatives would then be reduced, since she cannot accept an offer that has been revoked, nor can she make Trackers do business with her if it is no longer interested.

As the following case illustrates, the law even permits offerors to revoke their offers despite a promise to leave the offer open for a set period of time. In short, such a promise is enforceable only if the other party has *purchased* it or otherwise has given the offeror something in return for the commitment. Accordingly, if Jason had promised to leave his offer to sell tracking open for 30 days, but Amritha did

Landmark Case

Dickinson v. *Dodds,* [1876] 2 Ch.D. 463 (C.A.)

The Historical Context: This case is the leading decision—valid even today—on whether an offeror can renege on a commitment to hold an offer open for a specified period of time.

Factual Background: On Wednesday, June 10, Dodds delivered to Dickinson a written offer to sell his property to Dickinson for £800. The offer stated that it would be open for acceptance until 9 a.m. on Friday, June 12. On Thursday, Dickinson heard that Dodds had been offering or was agreeing to sell the property to Mr. Allan. That evening, Dickinson delivered an acceptance to the place where Dodds was staying, and at 7 a.m. on Friday morning—a full two hours before the deadline—he personally delivered an acceptance to Dodds. Dodds declined the acceptance, stating: "You are too late. I have sold the property." Dickinson sued Dodds, alleging there was a contract between them.

The Legal Question: To determine whether Dickinson's action should succeed, the court had to decide whether

Dodds was entitled to revoke his offer prior to the deadline he had sent. This decision was necessary because if the offer had been properly revoked, it was not capable of being accepted, and, accordingly, there could be no contract between the two men.

Resolution: The court decided that what Dodds did was permissible: "[I]t is a perfectly clear rule of law ... that, although it is said that the offer is to be left open until Friday morning at 9 o'clock, that did not bind Dodds. He was not in point of law bound to hold the offer over until 9 o'clock on Friday morning."

Furthermore, the court held that Dodds' offer had been effectively revoked when Dickinson learned that Dodds would be selling the property to someone else: "When once the person to whom the offer was made knows that the property has been sold to someone else, it is too late for him to accept the offer...."

Critical Analysis: Being guided primarily by legal principles is certainly an acceptable way of doing business. However, what might be the impact on your business reputation of "going back on your word" and revoking an offer sooner than you had promised you would?

not provide something in return for this promise—like the payment of a sum of money—she would have no legal recourse if Jason were to break his word and revoke his offer the next day.

Dickinson v. *Dodds* also demonstrates that an offer does not have to be directly revoked by the offeror. It is enough that the offeree learns of the revocation through a reliable source.

The way to avoid application of the rule in *Dickinson* v. *Dodds* is for the parties to form an **option agreement**, whereby the offeree pays the offeror to keep the offer open for the specified time. An option agreement is a separate contract that may or may not lead to the acceptance of the offer and a resulting agreement of purchase and sale. Its purpose is simply to give the offeree a guaranteed period of time within which to deliberate whether to accept the offer or not. If the offeror withdraws the offer before the option agreement permits, he or she has committed a breach of contract, and the offeree can sue for damages.

Option agreements are commonly found in real estate developments—the developer will buy a number of options to purchase land from owners in the development area. The developer can choose whether to exercise the options and knows that during the option period, the owners are contractually bound to not withdraw their offers to sell at the specified price.

option agreement
An agreement where, in exchange for payment, an offeror is obligated to keep an offer open for a specified time.

Lapse

An offer **lapses** in one of two ways. It may contain a date upon which it expires. After this date, it is no longer "alive" and therefore cannot be accepted. If the offer contains no expiry date, it will remain open for a reasonable period of time, which, in turn, will depend on all the circumstances of the case, including the nature of the transaction at issue. For example, an offer to sell a piece of woodland that is sitting idle would probably remain open longer than an offer to sell a piece of property that is about to be commercially developed. A judge will bring as much precision as possible to the question of when an offer lapses, but the whole exercise is inherently speculative.

With this in mind, an offeror should consider specifying an expiry date for her or his offer and thereby avoid the debate altogether. For its part, the offeree should act promptly, because of the principle in *Dickinson* v. *Dodds* permitting revocation prior to the expiry date, or at least keep in contact with the offeror to ensure that the status of the offer is known.

lapse
The expiration of an offer after a specified or reasonable period.

Rejection

It is important for those involved in contractual negotiations to know that an offer is automatically terminated when it is **rejected** by the offeree. The offer can be accepted only if the offeror revives it by offering it anew or if the offeree presents it as his or her own offer, which can then be accepted or rejected by the original offeror. The risk in rejecting an offer is that it may never be renewed by the other side.

rejection
The refusal to accept an offer.

Counteroffer

A **counteroffer** is a form of rejection. Through a counteroffer, the offeree is turning down the offer *and* proposing a new offer in its place. The distinction between an acceptance and a counteroffer is not always readily apparent. For example, suppose that a seller offers 100 widgets to the buyer at $10 per widget, and the buyer responds, "Great, I'll take 800." Or suppose a seller offers a car for $10 000, and the buyer says,

counteroffer
The rejection of one offer and proposal of a new one.

"I'll take it. I'll give you $5000 today and the balance next week." In both situations, it looks like the buyer has accepted, but in law he or she has made a counteroffer. Any change to a term of an offer, whether it be price, quantity, time of delivery, or method of payment, is a counteroffer. Because a counteroffer is a rejection, the original offer is automatically terminated and can be accepted only if is renewed by one of the parties. Whenever a party makes an counteroffer, she or he jeopardizes the chance of being able to accept the original offer.

Acceptance

Definition of Acceptance

acceptance
An unqualified willingness to enter into a contract on the terms in the offer.

When an offer made by one party is unconditionally and unequivocally accepted by the other party, a contract is formed. To be effective, the **acceptance** must manifest an unqualified willingness to enter into the contract on the precise terms proposed. If the purported acceptance does not mirror the offer by agreeing to *all* its content, it is a counteroffer and no contract has been formed.

In the opening scenario, Amritha clearly accepted Jason's offer—she did not propose modifications or alterations to his proposal. While she expressed some reservations, saying that she was not entirely happy with the offer, this was not a rejection. Rather, she went on to fully and completely accept his offer. At this point, two of the building blocks of a contract between Coasters and Trackers are in place—namely, offer and acceptance.

An immediate need can bypass the requirements for forming a contract.

Communication of Acceptance

In order to effect legal acceptance, the offeree must communicate an unconditional assent to the offer in its entirety. This message of acceptance can be conveyed in any number of ways: in person, in writing, by mail, by fax, through e-mail, or by telephone. In fact, any manner of communication that is reasonable in the circumstances ordinarily will do. However, the offer must be scrutinized to determine if it requires a specific method of communicating an acceptance. If it does, and by the terms of the offer that method of communication is mandatory, then the offeree must follow that method of communication in order to ensure legal acceptance. For example, if a company offers, by telephone, to sell a given item but specifies that acceptance must be in writing, then the offeree's calling back with a purported acceptance will be ineffective. The offeror is entitled to insist on written acceptance before it is bound.

Since entering a contract is about assent, the law determines that the offer is effective only when it has been communicated to the offeree. In this way, the offeree becomes aware of its terms and can respond. Similarly, the acceptance, if any, must be communicated to the offeror so that the offeror is aware of the unqualified acceptance. Acceptance is achieved expressly, as when the offeree accepts in person or sends a message through some medium to the offeror. Occasionally, however, acceptance can be indicated by conduct, as the following case illustrates.

Case

Lowe (D. J.) (1980) Ltd. v. *Upper Clements Family Theme Park Ltd.* (1990), 95 N.S.R. (2d) 397 (S.C.T.D.)

The Business Context: Businesses often have to act quickly to address a problem that has developed. In such circumstances, there is a risk that proper attention will not be given to the legal requirements of contract formation. This lack of focus can lead to disappointed expectations.

Factual Background: Mr. Bougie, Construction Manager of Upper Clements Family Theme Park, was under a tight construction schedule and quickly needed a crane to complete construction of a theme park. He discussed leasing a crane from Mr. Lowe's company, but the two men could not come to an agreement. Lowe insisted that the crane be leased for a minimum period of two months, whereas Bougie did not want to commit to that length of a term, preferring to prorate[4] charges based on a monthly rental. The next day, however, Bougie delivered the following letter to Lowe from Mr. Buxton, the general manager of Family Theme Park:

November 24, 1988

D. J. Lowe (1980) Limited
Deep Brook
Anna Co., Nova Scotia
B0S 1J0

Dear Sirs:

Further to your verbal agreement with our Construction Manager, I can confirm the following arrangements with respect to the hiring of a crane for the erection of steel to the flume ride:

1. The Upper Clements Family Theme Park Limited agrees to pay the sum of $10,000 (ten thousand dollars) per month, pro rated for partial months for crane hire.

2. The Upper Clements Family Theme Park Limited agrees to supply the crane operator.

3. D.J. Lowe (1980) Limited agrees to supply fuel and maintenance for the above crane.

If you are in agreement with these conditions, kindly sign one copy of this letter and return to me.

Yours truly,

(Signed)
PAUL G. BUXTON, P.Eng.

GENERAL MANAGER
SIGNATURE OF AGREEMENT
D.J. LOWE (1980) LIMITED

This letter did not, in fact, reflect the parties' agreement and was never signed by the Lowe company, but Lowe did send a crane to the construction site. Lowe apparently believed that he and the Theme Park personnel could come to an agreement on price, and within two days of delivering the crane, approached Bougie with a draft agreement setting out a monthly rate for a two-month term. Bougie said that he had no authority to deal with the document, and it would have to wait for Buxton's return from an out-of-town trip. In the end, the Theme Park had the crane on-site for four days and then immediately returned it, along with payment of $1250. Lowe's company sued for the balance, claiming that it was owed a total of $20 000.

The Legal Question:
Did delivery of the crane constitute an acceptance of Buxton's offer contained in the letter of November 24?

Resolution: The trial judge determined that there was a contract between the parties for the rental of the crane. Whether Buxton's letter was classified as an acceptance or a counteroffer,

> it was the serious expression of an intention by the Theme park to enter into a contract with the Lowe company.... Having received that letter, Mr. Lowe had his company go ahead with delivery of the crane, knowing it was essential that the Theme Park have it at the earliest possible moment. Rather than risk losing the contract, Lowe accepted the offer by delivering the crane and acquiescing in the Theme Park's use of it.

> In doing so Mr. Lowe was not intentionally capitulating to an unfavourable counter-offer. Based upon his experience in the industry and his previous dealings with the Theme Park, Mr. Lowe was taking a calculated risk that even though his company was entering into a contract, he could later negotiate more satisfactory terms.... His expectations were not unreasonable. However they were frustrated first by Mr. Buxton's absence and then by his own..... The two-month term [set forth in the draft lease that Lowe subsequently presented to Bougie] was not part of the contract that was entered into. The governing provision is in Mr. Buxton's letter of November 24th.... That is the provision of the counter-offer Mr. Lowe wished to avoid, but it is the one that governs. The Theme Park is entitled to return the crane for the monthly rental pro rated for the partial month when it had possession of the crane.... The amount to be paid

---

4. When a sum is prorated, it means that what is charged is determined in relation to a certain rate. In this example, the monthly rate is $10 000. Based on a 30-day month, the prorated daily charge would be $10 000 divided by 30, or $333.

was calculated at $1,250.00 by the Theme Park and previously tendered to the Plaintiff. I accept that calculation and award the Plaintiff damages.

Critical Analysis: How can a business avoid unwanted obligations when there is insufficient time to properly negotiate a contract? Is it reasonable for the judge to decide the case based on the terms of one letter?

It is also possible—though less than usual—for the offer to be expressed in such a way that no communication of acceptance is needed.

Landmark Case

Carlill v. *Carbolic Smoke Ball Co.*, [1893] 1 Q.B. 256 (C.A.)

The Historical Context: This case was decided at a time when Victorian England was being inundated with quack cures. Examples of "miracle" cures included Epps Glycerine Jube Jubes and a product called Pepsolic, which claimed to prevent marriage breakups because it prevented indigestion. The ad for this product noted that indigestion "Causes Bad Temper, Irritability, Peppery Disposition, Domestic Quarrels, Separation and—the Divorce Court."[5]

Factual Context: This case considers the legal obligations that resulted from the advertisement placed by the Carbolic Smoke Ball Co. in a London newspaper at the turn of the 19th century.

Figure 6.2

CARBOLIC SMOKE BALL ADVERTISEMENT

> **£100 REWARD**
> WILL BE PAID BY THE
> **CARBOLIC SMOKE BALL CO.**
> To any person who contracts the increasing Epidemic,
> **INFLUENZA**
> Colds, or any diseases caused by taking cold, AFTER HAVING USED the BALL
> 3 times daily for two weeks according to the printed directions supplied with each Ball.
> **£1000**
> Is deposited with the ALLIANCE BANK, REGENT STREET, showing our sincerity in the matter.
> During the last epidemic of Influenza many of our CARBOLIC SMOKE BALLS were sold as Preventives against this Disease, and in no ascertained case was the disease contracted by those using the CARBOLIC SMOKE BALL.

Mrs. Carlill used the Smoke Ball as directed for two weeks but caught influenza anyway. When the company refused to pay her the advertised reward, she commenced an action for breach of contract.

Legal Question: Was there a contract between the parties, even though Mrs. Carlill did not communicate her acceptance of the Carbolic Smoke Ball Company's offer?

Resolution: While communication of acceptance is generally required, this is not always the case. Because the Carbolic Smoke Ball Company—the offeror—had chosen to dispense with the necessity of notice, it could not complain about Mrs. Carlill's failure to communicate acceptance now. In the end, the court found that Mrs. Carlill had accepted the company's offer of a reward by using the smoke ball as requested and that, upon becoming sick, she was contractually entitled to the £100.

Critical Analysis: This case is an example of an offer of a unilateral contract, though the court did not identify it as such. Through such an offer, the offeror promises to pay the offeree a sum of money *if* the offeree performs the requested act. For example, a company might offer a $200 reward to anyone who finds a missing laptop computer. Unlike the ordinary business contract, where both parties have obligations, in the unilateral contract only the offeror is bound because the offeree can perform the requested act—find the laptop—or not. He has no obligation even to try. If he does find the computer and returns it, the contract is complete, and the offeror is contractually required to pay. For obvious reasons, this kind of offer typically does not require people who decide to look for the computer to advise the company of their intention to do so. From the company's perspective, it is enough to hear from the person who actually finds the computer.

---

5. A.W.B. Simpson, "Quackery and Contract Law: The Case of the Carbolic Smoke Ball" in (1985) 14 J. of Legal Studies 345 at 356. The historical information contained in this box draws heavily on Simpson's analysis.

Ordinarily, however, communication of acceptance is expected and required. In practical terms, the offeror needs to be aware of the acceptance in order to appreciate that the contract exists and that performance of the obligations in it should proceed.

A problem arises if the offeree sends an acceptance that for some reason never reaches the offeror. Perhaps a letter gets lost in the mail, an e-mail message goes astray, or a fax gets sent to the wrong number. Has there been acceptance or not? Normally, the answer would be that no acceptance has occurred until actually received. Put another way, acceptance is effective only when communicated—it is at this moment that a contract comes into existence.

A specific exception to this general rule is the "postbox rule," also called the "postal rule." If it is clear that the offeror intends the postbox rule to apply to his offer, then acceptance is effective at the time of mailing the acceptance, rather than the time of delivery. Even if the letter containing the acceptance is never delivered to the offeror, a contract has been formed. Since application of the postbox rule means that an offeror could end up being in a contract without even knowing it, that person is best advised to avoid application of the postbox rule by making it clear in the offer that actual communication or notice of acceptance is absolutely required.

The practical application of the rules governing offer and acceptance is affected by the requirement of proof that the necessary events occurred. Someone who seeks to enforce a contract that the other party denies exists must be able to prove that offer and acceptance occurred. While ideally this proof is created through documentary evidence, documents are not always available. In such circumstances, the individual seeking to rely on the contract must convince the court of its existence without the benefit of extraneous proof. Oral agreements are very difficult to prove without some independent verification or corroboration—by a witness to the negotiations, for example—of what was said.

Developments in technology have created new methods of doing business that test the relevance and applicability of the older common law rules already alluded to.

Contract Formation in Electronic Business

Electronic business—commercial transactions conducted via electronic data interchange (EDI) systems or over the Internet—is increasing. Such contracts are governed by the same rules as all contracts. There must be an offer, an acceptance, and communication of the acceptance. Technology, however, creates uncertainty as to what constitutes an offer and acceptance in a digital environment. In most commercial relationships, the issues can be covered in an agreement between electronic trading partners, just as they are in the paper world. However, in a situation where there is no continuing business relationship and therefore no underlying agreement, the potential for disputes increases.

TECHNOLOGY AND THE LAW

For example, is an electronic advertisement considered an offer or an invitation to treat? Generally, advertisements have not been viewed as offers, so presumably the same result would apply in a digital environment. By entering his or her name in an electronic order form on the homepage or equivalent, a prospective purchaser would normally be making an offer. A contract would then be formed when the seller communicates the acceptance back to the offeror. In other words, only when the offeror receives confirmation that the offer has been accepted is there a contract in place. This raises the question of whether the automated acknowledgment of the offer is an acceptance or whether there must be a more formal acceptance or purchase acknowledgment.

Uncertainties concerning offer and acceptance are particularly complicated in international transactions. The sequence of offer and acceptance is important in determining where a contract is formed and, consequently, whose law applies to the transaction. Generally, the law of the country where the contract is concluded will govern the contract, and a contract is concluded where the acceptance becomes effective. Ordinarily, in the case of instantaneous communications, such as the telephone, telex, or fax, acceptance is effective not at the offeree's location, but at the place where the offeror receives the acceptance.

How these rules will apply in the international electronic commerce environment in the absence of an agreement is uncertain. A seller may be dealing with potential buyers from around the world using a network of electronic communications that crosses many national boundaries. If the rule is the same as it is in other forms of instantaneous communications, then potentially a seller may have hundreds or thousands of contracts governed by the law of different countries. The situation becomes even more complicated when trading partners from different countries use the services of third-party value-added networks (VANS) based in different countries for receiving messages. In this situation, it is unclear whether receipt of an acceptance by a VAN (in country A) constitutes receipt by the offeror, or whether receipt of the acceptance is effective only when it is received by the offeror (in country B).

The need for legislation to govern electronic commerce has been the subject of international consideration. In 1996 the UN approved the United Nations Commission on International Trade Law (UNCITRAL) Model Law on Electronic Commerce, which covers a broad range of electronic commerce issues, including formation of contracts, electronic signatures, and the like. The Act is meant to serve as a model for countries in enacting legislation to accommodate electronic commercial practices. However, until appropriate statutory revisions are adopted by the world's trading nations, an important strategy for ensuring the validity and predictability of electronic transactions is the implementation of a trading partner agreement. In Canada, the Electronic Data Interchange Council of Canada (EDICC) has developed a model agreement (EDICC trading partner agreement) that addresses, among other issues, contract law.

In 2000, Ontario became the first province to bring e-commerce legislation into effect. The *Electronic Commerce Act*, S.O. 2000, c. 17, lends some legal clarity to the e-commerce regime by providing rules as to when, for example, an electronic document is presumed to have been received by the addressee.

Critical Analysis: Are the rules of offer and acceptance adaptable to electronic contracts? Can business afford to wait for the courts to apply the rules to these transactions? Can legislation remove all the uncertainties?

Sources: Michael Erdle, *Legal Issues in Electronic Commerce* (1996), 12 C.I.P.R. 251; United Nations Commission on International Trade Law, online: <http://www.un.or.at/uncitral>; Task Force on ECommerce, online: <http://e-com.ic.gc.ca/>; and "E-signatures, Contracts Now Legal in Ontario" *The Toronto Star* (17 October 2000) C6.

Certainty of Offer and Acceptance

A contract is formed only when a *complete* offer is unconditionally accepted. This means that all essential terms must be set out in the offer and clearly agreed upon. If not, one of the parties can ask a court to set the alleged contract aside and declare it to be of no force or effect.

An offer does not have to meet the standard of perfection in how it is expressed. If the parties intend to have a contract, the courts will endeavour to interpret the contract in as reasonable a fashion as possible and thereby resolve ambiguities. For example, Jason's offer promised that "Trackers will use its best efforts to secure insurance from the insurer named by Coasters." Is the idea of using "best efforts" so vague that the offer lacks sufficient certainty? A court would likely say no and conclude that such a promise was enforceable—"best efforts" in this context would require

Trackers to take conscientious and reasonable steps to secure insurance from the company Coasters named.[6] In this way, a court is prepared to resolve some vagueness in an offer.

An offer can achieve the requisite standard of certainty even if it leaves certain matters to be decided in the future. For example, Jason's offer could have made the final price for the tracking contingent on the market price of steel, as determined by a given formula. Though the price is not set out in the offer, a workable mechanism for determining price has been established, and a contract can be entered into on that basis. What a court will not do is speculate on what the parties would have agreed had they completed their negotiations, as the following case illustrates.

Case

Courtney v. *Tolaini Brothers (Hotels) Ltd.*, [1975] 1 All E.R. 716 (C.A.)

The Business Context: Parties may wish to enter into a contractual relationship but leave essential terms to be decided in the future, such as when there are time constraints or contingencies that cannot be addressed immediately. If the parties leave too much undetermined, however, they run the risk of there being no contract at all.

Factual Background: Mr. Tolaini asked Mr. Courtney to help him find financing for the development of a hotel, motel, and gas station. Courtney agreed on the following terms, contained in a letter from Courtney to Tolaini.

Re: Thatched Barn Hotel

... I am now in a position to introduce you to those who: (a) are interested in your proposals, (b) have access to the necessary finance.... I think I should mention, at this point, that my commercial interest in this matter is that of a Building Contractor.... I work for a number of large investing and development concerns, and thought it possible that I might be in a position to be of service to you.

You will understand, therefore, that in addition to making myself useful to you, my objective is to build the three projects mentioned, namely, the Motel, the Filling Station, and the future hotel.... Accordingly I would be very happy to know that, if my discussions and arrangements with interested parties lead to an introductory meeting, which in turn leads to a financial arrangement acceptable to both parties you will be prepared to ... negotiate fair and reasonable contract sums in respect of each of the three projects as they arise....

Courtney was successful in securing the financing, but he and Tolaini could not agree on a price for the construction work. Courtney sued for breach of contract.

The Legal Question: Is Courtney's letter a sufficiently complete offer to form the basis of a contract?

Resolution: Though Tolaini received a benefit from Courtney, there was no contract between them. The main problem was that there was no agreement on the price that Tolaini would pay for Courtney's building work, nor was there agreement on the method by which the price would be established. The parties had simply agreed to negotiate "fair and reasonable contract sums." As the court observed,

> All was left to be agreed in the future. It was to be agreed between the parties themselves. If they had left the price to be as agreed by a third person such as an arbitrator, it would have been different. But here it was to be agreed between the parties themselves.
>
> Now the price in a building contract is of fundamental importance. It is so essential a term that there is no contract unless the price is agreed or there is an agreed method of ascertaining it, not dependent on the negotiations of the two parties themselves....
>
> [The law] cannot recognise a contract to negotiate. The reason is because it is too uncertain to have any binding force. No court could estimate the damages because no one can tell whether the negotiations would be successful or would fall through; or if successful, what the result would be.... I think that we must apply the general principle that when there is a fundamental matter left undecided and to be the subject of negotiation, there is no contract. So I would hold that there was not any enforceable agreement in the letters between the plaintiff and the defendants....

Critical Analysis: How can parties in such a situation preserve flexibility and yet create an enforceable contract? Should the courts be prepared to create a contract between the parties in order to protect someone like Mr. Courtney?

---

6. For a discussion of what "best efforts" means, see *CAE Industries Ltd.* v. *R.* (1985), 20 D.L.R. (4th) 347 (C.A.), leave to appeal to S.C.C. refused (1985), 20 D.L.R. (4th) 347n.

Finally, a court will not enforce an agreement that the parties have decided will not be effective until the exact wording of the contract has been agreed upon and the contract has been written and signed. This kind of intention is signalled by phrases like "this agreement is subject to formal contract." Unless and until the formal contract comes into existence, there are generally no enforceable obligations between the parties.

Conclusion of Acceptance

The basis of a contract is the voluntary *agreement* by two or more people or organizations. This agreement takes the form of a complete offer and an unqualified acceptance. The agreement is reached as a result of consensus between or among all parties on the package of rights and obligations (benefits and costs) to which they are willing to commit. This consensus results from communications or negotiations that may be directly and speedily concluded or that may emerge only as a result of long and protracted bargaining.

If parties disagree about whether an agreement has been reached, the matter will be decided by a judge. As noted in Chapter 5, the judge will consider all the circumstances surrounding the negotiations and assess the matter from an objective perspective. The subjective intent of the parties is of no legal relevance. What matters is how the parties have conducted themselves.

Consideration

The Nature of Consideration

A contract is a set of commitments or promises. It therefore entails a bargain or an exchange between the parties. Each party must give up something of value *in exchange* for receiving something of value from the other contracting party. In the example of the agreement between Jason and Amritha, it is clear that there is consideration on both sides of the transaction: the *buyer* promises to pay the purchase price in exchange for the *seller's* promise to provide tracking of the specified quality and quantity. Seen from the other perspective, the *seller* promises to provide tracking of the specified quality and quantity in exchange for the *buyer's* promise to pay the purchase price (see Figure 6.3). This bargain, or exchange of promises, is a classic example of the legal requirement of **consideration**.

consideration
The price paid for a promise.

Consideration is a key ingredient that distinguishes a legally enforceable promise from one that is not legally enforceable. If Trackers *promises* to provide tracking to

Figure 6.3

CONSIDERATION AS AN EXCHANGE OF PROMISES

Coasters

→ promises to pay in consideration for Trackers' promise to supply

Trackers

→ promises to supply in consideration for Coasters' promise to pay

Coasters at no charge and later changes its mind, Coasters cannot sue for breach of contract. Coasters has not given something back to Trackers in order to *purchase* Tracker's promise; accordingly, there is no contract in place, and any lawsuit by Coasters will fail. In law, Trackers has made a **gratuitous promise**—that is, a promise unsupported by consideration. Such promises can be broken with legal impunity. Conversely, if the parties have exchanged promises or something else of value, their obligations are contractual and therefore enforceable.

gratuitous promise
A promise for which no consideration is given.

As the above examples illustrate, a "price" must be paid for a promise before a party can sue when it is broken. Most commonly, the price for a promise to supply goods or services takes the form of another promise—including a promise to pay an agreed-upon sum in the future—or immediate payment of money. However, the consideration need not be monetary. The only requirement is that something of value be given up by the party seeking to purchase the promise of another. Furthermore, that item of value may be conferred on a third party and still amount to consideration, provided it was conferred at the request of the other side. For example, if Jason requested that the purchase price of the tracking be paid to a creditor of Trackers, Coasters' agreement to do so would support Trackers' promise to supply the tracking.

The requirement for consideration is strongly linked to the idea of freedom of bargaining. Although the law requires that consideration be present on both sides of the transaction, it is up to the parties to negotiate a deal that is mutually acceptable. *They* decide what is a fair and reasonable price, not a judge. Therefore, the *adequacy* of consideration is normally not open to challenge. If Amritha has agreed to pay a price for the tracking that turns out to be well above its market value, that is her choice. She cannot later go to a judge and ask that the price be lowered on that basis alone. The law will generally enforce a contract even where one party has agreed to pay too much because the parties are responsible for being fully informed of all aspects of the transaction and for evaluating the risks involved. If Amritha is concerned that she may end up paying too much for tracking, she should consult experts in the field and seek competing bids to help her establish a fair market price before accepting Jason's offer. Similarly, if one or both of the parties is concerned that the value of the goods or services contracted for may change between the time of agreement and the time of performance, a clause allowing the contract price to be adjusted for market fluctuations should be included in the contract. In short, parties are expected to take care of themselves and plan for contingencies.

Pre-existing Legal Duty

Just as a contract can be viewed as a set of promises, it can also be viewed as a set of duties. The consideration for each party's duties is the other party's duties. Once those duties or promises have been finalized, the contract is concluded. If the parties agree to alter the contract in a way that benefits only one of them, that alteration is unenforceable. In other words, a new promise needs new or fresh consideration. For example, if a contract provides that a project is to be completed on a particular date, a promise by the owner to pay an additional sum of money, say $2000, to ensure completion on that date is unenforceable. The promise to pay an additional $2000 is not supported by fresh consideration because completion on a particular date is already required under a contract. In short, it is a **pre-existing legal duty**.

pre-existing legal duty
A legal obligation that a person already owes.

Case

Gilbert Steel Ltd. v. *University Construction Ltd.*
(1976), 12 O.R. (2d) 19 (C.A.)

The Business Context: A business may enter into a contract that suddenly becomes unfavourable because of changes in the market. If it secures a concession from the other side in response to these changes, without regard to legal requirements, the concession may prove to be unenforceable.

Factual Background: Gilbert Steel (Gilbert) and University Construction (University) were in a contract that required Gilbert to supply a set amount of fabricated steel at an agreed-upon price. When steel prices rose dramatically, Gilbert asked University if it would pay more for the steel. University agreed but later refused to pay the increase and sent only payment for the originally agreed-upon price. Gilbert sued for breach of contract.

The Legal Question: Is there consideration supporting University's promise (i.e., what is Gilbert doing in return for University's promise to pay more for the steel)?

Resolution: There is no consideration from Gilbert for University's promise, and it is therefore unenforceable. Gilbert is doing only what it is already contractually obliged to do—namely, supply steel to University. Put another way, Gilbert has a *pre-existing legal duty* to provide the steel and, accordingly, is giving nothing "extra" to University to support University's promise to pay more. The promise is therefore unenforceable, even though University made the second promise in good faith, possibly with a full intention to pay the higher price. Gilbert's action for breach of contract therefore fails.

Gilbert should have contemplated a rise in the cost of steel when setting the original price and built into the contract a formula permitting an increase in the contract price. Alternatively, it could have provided something in return for the higher price, such as earlier delivery or any other benefit that University requested. A final option would have been to get University's promise under seal.

Critical Analysis: Does this rule concerning performance of a pre-existing legal duty reflect the reasonable expectations of both the parties involved and the broader business community?[7]

Variation of Contracts

The rule that performance of a pre-existing legal duty is not good consideration for a new promise also finds expression in the rule that all variations of a contract must be supported by "fresh"consideration. As *Gilbert Steel Ltd.* v. *University Construction Ltd.* illustrates, just as a contract needs to reflect a two-sided bargain, so must variations or changes to that contract. This is why University's promise to pay more for the steel is worthless without some corresponding concession from Gilbert.

If parties decide to terminate their contract and replace it with a new agreement altogether, consideration is automatically present because *both* sides have given something up—namely, the old contract. However, a judge will consider the substance of the transaction. If in reality only one side has given something up, then a variation has occurred, and a court will insist on evidence of fresh consideration to support it.

When Trackers, through Jason, asked Amritha's company to pay more for the steel, it was seeking a variation of the contract. Because Trackers did not provide anything new to Coasters in return, Coasters' commitment to pay an increased price was a gratuitous promise. The fact that Trackers supplied the steel on time does not count as consideration because Trackers had a pre-existing duty to do just that. On this basis, Coasters is not bound by its promise to pay more. Its only obligation is to pay the price recited in the contract that Amritha first negotiated. From a business perspective, however, its refusal to abide by its own promise will almost certainly destroy any possibility of Coasters and Trackers ever doing business together again.

---

7. In England, the law appears to be changing on this point. In *Williams* v. *Roffey Bros. & Nicholls (Contractors) Ltd.,* [1990] 1 All E.R. 512 (C.A.), the court held that variations of a contract do not always require legal consideration to be enforceable; a factual benefit is sufficient.

Consideration is not always necessary for a contract or contractual variation to be enforceable. Important exceptions to the consideration requirement are promises under seal, promissory estoppel, and, in some jurisdictions, partial payment of a debt.

Promise under Seal

Before commercial negotiations became as commonplace and sophisticated as they are today, and before the rules of contract were fully developed, a practice originated to authenticate written agreements by putting hot wax beside the signature on a document and placing an imprint in the wax, unique to the person who signed. The use of a seal has evolved so that today the seal takes the form of a red gummed circle or wafer attached to the document beside the signature of the party making the promise. The legal effect is the same, however. If the document containing the promise is signed and the seal affixed, the fact that there may not be consideration for the promise is irrelevant. The seal is taken as evidence of serious intent by the promisor and amounts to an acknowledgment that the promise is enforceable, even if it is gratuitous. Contracts of guarantee, for example, typically have seals attached.[8]

Promissory Estoppel

Without a seal, a gratuitous promise is simply not enforceable at common law, even if made with great deliberation, and regardless of the adverse consequences to the person who relied on the promise. In response to the harshness that this common law rule could sometimes generate, courts began to assist parties through the equitable doctrine of **promissory estoppel**.

promissory estoppel
A principle whereby someone who relies on a gratuitous promise may be able to enforce it.

Promissory estoppel focuses on the idea of fairness, but since fairness is relatively subjective and courts are reluctant to stray too far from the doctrine of consideration, the party seeking to rely on the doctrine (Party A) must show that a number of distinct factors also exist in relation to the promise made by Party B, as listed below:

- Party B has, by words or conduct, made a promise or an assurance to Party A that was intended to affect their legal relationship and to be acted on.
- In reliance on the representation, Party A acted on it or in some way changed its position.[9]
- Party A's own conduct has been above reproach and, in this way, Party A is deserving of the court's assistance.

A final requirement is that promissory estoppel can be used only as a defence to legal claims made by the promise-breaker.[10]

Assume, for example, that Jason contacts Amritha one month before the delivery date specified in their contract. Jason tells her that Trackers is having minor production difficulties and so there is a chance that the tracking will be delivered three days

---

8. Guarantees are discussed in detail in Chapter 26.

9. *Maracle* v. *Travellers Indemnity Co. of Canada*, [1991] 2 S.C.R. 50.

10. Most Canadian courts insist that promissory estoppel can be used only as a defence, though there is some case law to the contrary. See, for example, *Robichaud c. Caisse Populaire de Pokemouche Ltee* (1990), 69 D.L.R. (4th) 589 (N.B.C.A.). Note that the doctrine of promissory estoppel cannot be used by Trackers to enforce Coasters' promise to pay more for the tracking. Trackers cannot sue on the promise—it can use it only as a defence.

late. He asks Amritha if this will be a problem for Coasters. He also wants to know if Coasters will insist on enforcing the late delivery clause in their contract obligating Trackers to pay $5000 per day for every day it is late. After securing instructions from her supervisor, Amritha gets back to Jason and tells him not to worry: "Jason, it poses no problem for us if you are up to one week late, and no, we won't come after you for late charges. We just want our tracking in good time." In the end, the tracking is delivered three days late, and Coasters is suddenly taking the position that it is owed $15 000.

Coasters' promise not to rely on the late charges clause is unenforceable at common law because there is no consideration supporting it. Trackers is giving nothing back to Coasters in exchange for Coasters' promise to accept late delivery without complaint. For this reason, the common law would allow Coasters to go back on its word and collect the $15 000. However, there is an excellent chance that the doctrine of promissory estoppel would be applied by a judge to prevent this outcome because

- Coasters promised not to rely on its contractual right to collect late charges.
- Trackers relied on this promise and changed its position by scheduling production accordingly and taking no additional steps to speed up its schedule.
- Trackers' conduct throughout has been beyond reproach—it did not threaten Coasters or otherwise place undue pressure on it to accept late delivery.
- Trackers is using the doctrine to *defend* itself from a claim by Coasters for the late charges.

For these kinds of reasons, Coasters would be estopped from relying on the late charges clause, and its action for $15 000 would fail.

Promissory estoppel is a relatively complicated doctrine and cannot be fully detailed here. The foregoing analysis is offered only as an introductory account of how the doctrine might arise in a business context.

Partial Payment of a Debt

A common difficulty encountered by a business arises when the customer cannot pay its account but offers a smaller amount to settle the debt in full. Can the business agree to the customer's proposal, accept the smaller amount, and then sue for the balance? Put another way, does the compromise on a bill amount to a binding contract, or is it simply a gratuitous promise by the creditor to accept a lesser amount? This matter is explored further on page 122, "Settling a Bad Debt."

Intention to Contract

The last important ingredient in a contract is the intention to contract. In order for one party to enforce the promise of another, the promise at issue must have been *intended* to be a contractual one, that is, one that would be enforceable by a court of law. Absent such an intention, there is no contract between the parties.

Business Agreements

Most agreements in the commercial world, such as the one between Trackers and Coasters, are quite obviously intended to be contractual. The common law recognizes this reality through the rule stating that in the marketplace, the intention to

Settling a Bad Debt

BUSINESS APPLICATION OF THE LAW

Assume that Coasters has fallen on hard times and has been able to pay only $1 million on its account with Trackers. Therefore, $500 000 is outstanding. Trackers agrees to accept $300 000 from Coasters and write off the balance.

At common law, Trackers can go back on its word and sue for the remaining $200 000 because its promise to accept a smaller sum is gratuitous. There is no consideration from Coasters supporting Trackers' promise to accept less than what is owed. Since Coasters has a pre-existing legal duty to pay $500 000, paying $300 000 is not consideration for Trackers' promise to forgive the balance. Put another way, Coasters is not giving Trackers anything in return for Trackers' promise, except a $300 000 payment that it was obligated to make in any event, and then some. The common law rule that the creditor can therefore sue for the balance is known as the rule in *Pinnel's case*, and it dates back to 1602.

The rule in *Pinnel's case* has been altered by legislation in several provinces, including Alberta, so as to prevent the creditor from later claiming the full amount once a lesser amount has been agreed upon and paid.[11] Similar provisions are in effect in British Columbia (*Law and Equity Act*, R.S.B.C. 1996, c. 253, s. 43); Manitoba (*Merchantile Law Amendment Act*, C.C.S.M., M-120, s. 6 as amended by the *Law Reform (Miscellaneous Amendments) Act*, S.M. 1992, c. 32, s. 10); Ontario (*Mercantile Law Amendment Act*, R.S.O. 1990, c. M.10, s. 16); and Saskatchewan (*Queen's Bench Act*, S.S. 1998, c. Q-1.01, s. 64); as well as the Northwest Territories and the Yukon. A policy rationale of the legislation is to promote settlement of debts on a final basis. In the remaining provinces, the consideration rule remains in force, so that in order for the promise to be enforced, the creditor must give the promise under seal or receive something in return for his or her promise to accept less (such as payment earlier than required). Another alternative for the debtor seeking to enforce the creditor's promise is to rely on promissory estoppel, if circumstances permit.

The varying status of the rule in *Pinnel's case* illustrates two important aspects of contract law. First, provincial legislatures may intervene at any time to alter or override a common law rule governing contracts. Second, though largely uniform across the country, contract law is under provincial control and is therefore subject to important provincial variations.

Critical Analysis: Why have the legislatures chosen to change this particular common law rule?

---

contract is *presumed*. Therefore, if Trackers ends up suing Coasters for breach of contract, it will not have to prove that the agreement between them was intended to be a contractual one. The court will assume that this was the intention and, instead, place the onus on Coasters to prove a lack of intent to contract—a truly uphill battle, given the circumstances of its relationship with Trackers.

Family Agreements

Agreements between family members are regarded differently in law because of the personal nature of the underlying relationship. In fact, the common law presumes that promises between family members are noncontractual. Therefore, people who

---

11. For example, the *Judicature Act*, R.S.A. 1980, c. J-1, s. 13(1) provides:

    (1) Part performance of an obligation either before or after a breach thereof shall be held to extinguish the obligation

        (a) when expressly accepted by a creditor in satisfaction, or

        (b) when rendered pursuant to an agreement for that purpose though without any new consideration.

Case

Rose & Frank Co. v. *Crompton and Bros. Ltd.,* [1923] 2 K.B. 261 (C.A.)

The Business Context: Business people sometimes want to create a formal record of what has transpired between them, with the intention that the record not generate legal rights of any description.

Factual Background: The parties signed a document containing the following clause:

This arrangement is not entered into ... as a formal or legal agreement, and shall not be subject to ... the Law Courts ... but it is only a definite expression and record of the purpose and intention of the ... parties concerned to which they each honourably pledge themselves with the fullest confidence, based upon past business with each other, that it will be carried through by each of the parties with mutual loyalty and friendly co-operation.

The Legal Question: Does this clause demonstrate intention to contract?

Resolution: The Court of Appeal ruled that the clause showed the absence of intention: "The particular clause in question shows a clear intention by the parties that the rest of their arrangement or agreement shall not affect their legal relations, or be enforceable in a court of law...."

Critical Analysis: What is the point of such a document if it has no legal consequences?

want to enforce an alleged contract against their parents or siblings, for example, must demonstrate to a court that there was an intention to contract. If they cannot positively prove that intent, their action will fail.

Business Law in Practice Revisited

1. At what point did the negotiations between Jason and Amritha begin to have legal consequences?

When Jason made an offer to sell tracking on specific terms, his negotiations with Amritha took a legal turn. At this point, Amritha is in a position to accept Jason's offer, and if she does, Trackers will be obligated to supply tracking on precisely those terms.

2. In what ways could negotiations have been terminated prior to the formation of the contract?

Amritha could have ended her negotiations by rejecting Jason's offer and telling him that Coasters would be looking elsewhere for its tracking. Though Amritha is not legally obligated to reject an offer, it is helpful to do so to ensure clarity and to avoid misunderstandings and disappointed expectations later on. Amritha should also withdraw any offer she may have made on behalf of Coasters to prevent Jason from accepting it sometime down the road. While the doctrine of lapse will prevent Jason from accepting after a certain point in time, it is difficult to predict how long a court would consider the offer to be open. It is preferable to simply withdraw the offer and avoid the debate altogether.

3. Can Coasters commit itself to the price increase and then change its mind with no adverse consequences?

Trackers has a pre-existing legal duty to supply the tracking at the price stated in the contract. Since it has given Coasters nothing in return for its promise to pay more, Coasters has no legal obligation to pay the increase. Put another way, the promise is gratuitous. Any change to a contract—known in law as a "variation"—must be supported by consideration or under seal in order to be enforceable.

There is, however, a significant consequence to Coasters' decision from a business perspective: its relationship with Trackers will be seriously harmed and possibly destroyed. If Coasters ever needs tracking again, it is unlikely that Trackers will agree to be its supplier.

4. How could Trackers have avoided from the outset this situation related to cost increases?

Trackers should have negotiated a clause in the contract that included a formula for varying the price according to prevailing market conditions, as established by a third party, trade journal, or other source. Other possibilities include negotiating a "cost plus contract," meaning the contract price would comprise the tracking manufacturer's actual costs, plus a set percentage of profit. Another alternative would have been to charge a higher price to begin with to cover unexpected cost escalations.

If Trackers were unsuccessful in getting such price adjustment mechanisms into the contract, it would assume the full risk of unanticipated cost increases. If Coasters did subsequently agree to pay more for the steel, Trackers should provide consideration for that promise or get it under seal.

Chapter Summary

A contract comprises four essential elements: an offer, an acceptance, consideration, and an intention. Before a contract can be formed, one party must make on offer on a complete set of certain terms, and the other party must unconditionally accept all the terms of the offer. Each party must give something (called consideration) in exchange for the promise or performance of the other. The parties must intend their bargain to be a contractual one. If any one of these elements is missing, then the relationship is noncontractual by definition.

There are rare occasions, however, when the law will enforce a promise that is not supported by consideration. In short, if the promise is under seal, meets the requirements of promissory estoppel, or is subject to a specialized statutory scheme, such as the partial payment of debt, it will be enforceable. Aside from these exceptions, a gratuitous promise is not binding, no matter how seriously it was intended and no matter how much the other party may have relied on it. This legal reality is particularly important when varying a term in an existing contract. The variation must be supported by fresh consideration, be under seal, or fit the requirements of promissory estoppel—otherwise, it will not be enforced by a court of law.

While the conditions for creating legal agreement may seem stringent, they serve an important purpose. Contract law is about creating voluntary agreements and is therefore facilitative. In sum, it helps those in the marketplace to determine—in advance of litigation—the legal enforceability of commitments they have received, and thereby lets them do business more effectively.

Study Chapter

Questions for Review

1. What must an offer contain?

2. Is an advertisement an offer or an invitation to treat? Why?

3. Does the acceptance of an offer have to mirror it exactly, or are slight variations permissible?

4. When must an offeree communicate acceptance to the offeror in a specific form?

5. What is the effect of a counteroffer?

6. When can an offeror revoke or withdraw an offer?

7. What is consideration?

8. What is the key question relating to consideration in the enforceability of a promise?

9. What is a pre-existing legal duty? Why is a promise to pay more for its performance generally not enforceable?

10. What is a gratuitous promise? Give an example.

11. How does the relationship between the parties affect presumptions concerning their contractual intent?

Questions for Discussion

1. Is the consideration requirement reasonable, or should all promises be legally enforceable if they were seriously intended?

2. Why should the relationship between the parties affect the enforceability of their promises?

3. Are the traditional rules of contract formation appropriate for modern methods of communication?

4. How does lack of knowledge of the rules of contract formation create risks for negotiators?

Situations for Discussion

1. Mr. Gaff made the following written offer to Ms. Paulo:

MEMO FROM: J. Gaff

TO: R. Paulo

DATE: June 7, 2000

I hereby agree to sell to R. Paulo my entire fleet of Rolls-Royce automobiles for the sum of $1 million.

This offer is open until Friday, June 9, 2000, at 9:00 a.m.

On Thursday, June 8, Gaff decided to sell the cars to his well-to-do neighbour instead. Paulo heard about the alleged sale later that same day and rushed over to Gaff's house, stating that she wished to accept Gaff's offer. Gaff smiled and said, "Sorry, you're too late. I've sold to someone else."

Is Gaff obligated to keep the offer open until the specified time? What could Paulo have done to better protect her position?

2. An advertisement similar to the following appeared in a popular Canadian business magazine. What legal obligations does it create for Star?

At ☆Star☆ We try harder!!

Any car rental company will reserve you a car.
Only ☆Star☆ tries harder to get you where you're going.

3. Greedy Cablevision provided various packages of cable television channels to its customers. When the regulatory authority approved five new channels, Greedy provided the new channels free of charge for one month. Greedy informed their customers in a letter included with their regular monthly bills that unless customers notified Greedy by a specific date that they did not want the extra channels, a $5 monthly charge would be added to each bill.

   Does Greedy's policy on the new channels fit the rules of offer and acceptance? Are customers obligated to pay if they fail to notify Greedy? What other methods could Greedy use to persuade customers to order the new channels?

4. Page developed accounting software and sold it in North America and abroad. A company known as DIS Ltd. wanted to acquire exclusive distribution rights for the Page accounting system in the United Kingdom. The two companies corresponded and eventually signed a "memorandum of understanding," which outlined their progress and expressed their desire and intention to finalize the deal. DIS had difficulty with their financing and asked for a delay of further commitments. Page agreed in a letter to extend negotiations, but the terms in the letter were much different from those in the memorandum of understanding and were unacceptable to DIS. Have the dealings between DIS and Page resulted in a contract? Is there a better way to negotiate a deal as complicated as this one? Who will suffer loss if the deal falls through?[12]

5. Cogan was a long-standing season ticket holder to Toronto Blue Jay baseball games and had made a practice of allowing his friends and business associates—Sherman and Fingold—to purchase some of those tickets. It was agreed that Cogan would provide them with a total of six tickets per season. After 10 years, Cogan decided to discontinue this practice, since he no longer had any social or business dealings with these individuals and his children had expressed the wish to have additional baseball tickets. Do Cogan and his friends have a contractual relationship? Which of the four requirements for a contract is in doubt?[13]

6. Jawa supplied a product to Luke but Luke has yet to pay Jawa's account of $1,000. Luke has told Jawa that he cannot and will not pay the full amount and that Jawa had just better be satisfied with a cheque for $500. "Take it or leave it," said Luke. Jawa took the cheque and cashed it, feeling that he had no choice in the matter. He would now like to go after Luke for the balance. Can he do so?

---

12. Based, in part, on *DIS, Datawhiz Information Systems Inc.* v. *Q.W. Page Associates Inc.* (1995), 20 B.L.R. (2d) 1 (Ont. Gen. Div.); leave to appeal refused 1998 CarswellOnt 4071.

13. Based, in part, on *Fobasco Ltd.* v. *Cogan* (1990), 72 O.R. (2d) 254 (H.C.J.).

Seven

The Terms of a Contract

Objectives

AFTER STUDYING THIS CHAPTER, YOU SHOULD HAVE AN
UNDERSTANDING OF:

▶ THE DIFFERENCE BETWEEN IMPLIED AND EXPRESS TERMS
▶ HOW JUDGES DETERMINE AND INTERPRET THE CONTENT
  OF A CONTRACT
▶ HOW A PARTY CAN INCLUDE TERMS TO PROTECT ITSELF
  FROM LIABILITY
▶ SOME COMMON COMMERCIAL CONTRACTS

Business Law in Practice

The dispute discussed in Chapter 6 between Coasters and Trackers over the purchase price was resolved reasonably amicably—the parties agreed to split the increased cost of the steel required to manufacture the tracking and thereby avoid the expense and disruption of litigation. All the tracking has been delivered, and the new purchase price has been paid. Jason is tremendously relieved but also wants to improve his performance as a negotiator, since matters did not proceed entirely smoothly. He is reviewing the Coasters–Trackers contract to determine whether it did, in fact, contain the terms Trackers needed to protect itself.

The contract between Coasters and Trackers covered a number of terms already discussed in the previous chapter, including price ($1.5 million); quantity (900 metres); delivery dates; and late delivery charges ($5000 a day). Other significant clauses are excerpted below.

Excerpt from the contract between Trackers (the "Seller") and Coasters (the "Buyer") for the purchase and sale of tracking (the "Goods")

...

12. Warranties—Guarantees.

Seller warrants that the goods shall be free from defect in material, workmanship, and title and shall conform in all respects to the design specifications provided by Buyer and attached as Appendix A to this contract. Where no quality is specified, the quality shall be of the best quality.

If it appears within one year from the date of placing the goods into service for the purpose for which they were purchased that the Goods, or any part thereof, does not conform to these warranties, Buyer, at its election and within a reasonable time after its discovery, may notify Seller. If notified, Seller shall thereupon promptly correct such nonconformity at its sole expense.

...

13.   Limitation of Seller's Liability.

Except as otherwise provided in this contract, Seller's liability shall extend to all damages proximately caused by the breach of any of the foregoing warranties or guarantees, but such liability shall in no event exceed unit price of defective Goods and in no event include loss of profit or loss of use.

...

14. Exclusion of Seller's Liability.

Seller is exempted from all liability in respect to losses, damages, costs, or claims relating to design of Goods.

...

20. Entire Contract.

This is the entire agreement between the parties, covering everything agreed upon or understood in connection with the subject matter of this transaction. There are no oral promises, conditions, representations, understandings, interpretations, or terms of any nature or kind, statutory or otherwise, as conditions or inducements to the execution hereof or in effect between the parties or upon which the parties are relying relating to this agreement or otherwise.

1. How is the scope of Trackers' and Coasters' obligations determined?
2. Are there any ambiguous or unclear terms in the contract?
3. Are there any additional terms that Jason should have tried to have included?
4. Does the contract relieve the parties from responsibility for inadequate performance?

Terms

A contract is an agreement that is enforceable, *according to its terms*, in a court of law. The terms of a contract simply refer to promises made by one party to another by virtue of offer and acceptance. In this way, contractual terms provide a blueprint of what the parties have obligated themselves to do.

Express Terms

express term
A provision of a contract that states a promise explicitly.

An **express term** is a provision of the contract that states or makes *explicit* one party's promise to another. In the Trackers–Coasters contract, for example, a number of terms are express, including the price, quantity, and warranties associated with the tracking. It is important that the essential terms of a contract be express so that each party knows its obligations and the obligations of the other side. Parties negotiating a contract should be very careful not to make assumptions about any aspect of the transaction, as only terms, not assumptions, have legal weight.

When parties fail to address an important aspect of their contractual relationship, the law may help to "fill in the blanks" through implied terms, discussed below. The assistance that implied terms can provide, however, is sporadic and cannot be relied on with any certainty.

Implied Terms

implied term
A provision that is not expressly included in a contract but that is necessary to give effect to the parties' intention.

When an event arises that is not addressed in the contract through express terms, courts may be asked to **imply a term** in order to give effect to the parties' intention. A judge will do so if satisfied that not all of the terms that the parties intended to include in the contract were in fact included. In the classic scenario, the plaintiff argues to include an implied term but the defendant asserts that no such term was intended. Since the plaintiff carries the burden of proof, she will lose unless she can demonstrate that the term exists based on the balance of probabilities (i.e., she needs to prove that it is more likely than not that the parties intended such a term to be included). Courts will imply terms based on a number of grounds, such as those listed below.

Business Efficacy

Through the doctrine of business efficacy[1] a judge is entitled to imply terms necessary to make the contract workable. For example, if Trackers promised to use a certain grade of steel, "providing it is available," a court will almost certainly imply a promise by Trackers to put reasonable effort into trying to find that grade of steel. Though Trackers has not expressly committed itself to make systematic efforts in this regard, business efficacy makes the obligation implicit. Were it otherwise, the express term in relation to the quality of steel would mean next to nothing.[2]

A term that courts are increasingly willing to imply as part of commercial contracts is that of good faith, owing, in large part, to the influence of the following case.

---

1. G.H.L. Fridman, *The Law of Contract*, 4th ed. (Scarborough: Carswell, 1999) at 502.
2. For a case that follows this analysis, see *Dawson* v. *Helicopter Exploration Co.*, [1955] S.C.R. 868.

Landmark Case

Gateway v. *Arton Holdings Ltd.* (1991), 106 N.S.R. (2d) 180 (S.C), aff'd (1992), 112 N.S.R. (2d) 180 (C.A.)

The Business Context: Business people may assume that the only obligations they owe the other party are those recited in the contract between them. This assumption may prove to be unfounded, particularly in the situation where one party is in a position to adversely affect the interests of the other.

Factual Background: Gateway owned a shopping mall in which Zellers was the anchor tenant. The lease permitted Zellers to occupy the premises, leave them vacant, or assign them to a third party without any obligation to secure the consent of the landlord. After being approached by Arton, a competitor of Gateway, Zellers agreed to locate in Arton's mall. As part of this arrangement, Arton agreed to take an assignment of Zeller's lease with Gateway, meaning that Zellers would legally drop out of the lease with Gateway and Arton would takes its place as the new tenant. As a result, a large part of Gateway's mall had been assigned to its competitor. Pursuant to a subsequent contract between Gateway and Arton, the companies agreed to use their best efforts to get a tenant for the space formerly occupied by Zellers. Arton, however, rejected all prospective tenants. Gateway then sued, alleging that Arton was in breach of contract for declining prospective tenants. From Gateway's perspective, Arton was simply trying to undermine the economic viability of the mall by letting a large portion of it remain unoccupied.

The Legal Question: Is there an implied obligation of good faith on Arton's part to take reasonable steps to sublet the premises?

Resolution: The court found that Arton breached the express obligation to use its "best efforts" to find a tenant, as well as an *implied term to act in good faith*. According to the court,

> The law requires that parties to a contract exercise their rights under that agreement honestly, fairly and in good faith. This standard is breached when a party acts in a bad faith manner in the performance of its rights and obligations under the contract. "Good faith" conduct is the guide to the manner in which the parties should pursue their mutual contractual objectives. Such conduct is breached when a party acts in "bad faith"—a conduct that is contrary to community standards of honesty, reasonableness or fairness.

The court went on to say,

> In most cases, bad faith can be said to occur when one party, without reasonable justification, acts in relation to the contract in a manner where the result would be to substantially nullify the bargained objective or benefit contracted for by the other, or to cause significant harm to the other, contrary to the original purpose and expectation of the parties.

Critical Analysis: Gateway's case has been followed or cited with approval by numerous Canadian courts, but the case has not yet been expressly considered by the Supreme Court of Canada. Other courts have determined that a good-faith clause is not an automatic term of every contract and can be implied only when it is consistent with the parties' intentions. Should all parties to a commercial deal be bound by a duty to act in good faith, or should parties be expected to take care of themselves?

Source: Shannon Kathleen O'Byrne, "Good Faith in Contractual Performance: Recent Developments" (1995) 74 Can. Bar Rev. 70.

Customs in the Trade of the Transaction

Relying on trade customs to imply a term is rarely successful, since it must be proved that the custom is so notorious that the contract in question must be presumed to contain such an implied term.[3] The more prudent course is to ensure that all important terms in a contract are expressly recited.

---

3. See Fridman, *supra* note 1 at 512.

Previous Dealings between the Parties

If parties have contracted in the past, it may be possible to imply that their current contract contains the same terms.[4] A risk management perspective would suggest, however, that the parties clarify the basis of their contractual relationship each time they do business with each other.

Statutory Requirements

An important source of terms implied by statute[5] is found in provincial sale-of-goods legislation, which is largely uniform across the country. This legislation provides that certain terms are a mandatory part of every contract for the sale of goods unless specifically excluded by the parties.[6] Specialized rules governing the sale of goods and the extent to which consumer transactions can exclude their application are discussed in more detail in Chapter 24.

If Trackers delivers too much tracking to Coasters under its contract, the *Ontario Sale of Goods Act,*[7] for example, would resolve the situation according to the following rule:

> **29. –(2)** Where the seller delivers to the buyer a quantity of goods larger than the seller contracted to sell, the buyer may accept the goods included in the contract and reject the rest, or may reject the whole, and if the buyer accepts the whole of the goods so delivered, the buyer shall pay for them at the contract rate.[8]

---

4. *Ibid.* at 510.

5. For discussion, see *ibid.* at 514.

6. For a discussion of Sale of Goods legislation, see G.H.L. Fridman, *Sale of Goods in Canada,* 4th ed. (Scarborough: Carswell, 1995).

7. R.S.O. 1990, c. S-1.

8. Sale of Goods legislation imports a number of other rules governing a contract for the sale of goods, discussed further in Chapters 24 and 25.

A Request for Goods or Services

When someone requests the supply of goods or services, the law—be it through common law or by applicable legislation such as the *Sale of Goods Act*—will imply a promise to pay a reasonable price for those goods or services. The law draws this conclusion because, in a business situation, it is the intention of the parties that goods or services are not to be provided for free, but rather are to be purchased. Implying such a term reflects what can only be the reasonable expectation of the parties—especially that of the seller—and is needed to give purpose and effect to

BUSINESS APPLICATION OF THE LAW

the rest of the contract. If the goods or services have already been provided but there has been no agreement on price, a term must be implied to require payment. The obligation on the customer is not to pay whatever the supplier chooses to charge or whatever the customer is willing to pay, but to pay a *reasonable* amount, as determined by the judge.

Given the expense and uncertainty of judicial proceedings, it is in the interests of both parties to agree on the price, in advance, as an express term. The objective is to avoid the surprises and misunderstandings that may lead to a legal dispute.

In general, terms are not easily implied except in routine transactions or unless the *Sale of Goods Act* applies. It must be clear that *both* parties would have included the term in question, had they addressed the matter.

Similarly, courts ordinarily will not imply terms when the parties have agreed that their contract is complete as written. The clearest way parties can signal this intention is through an **entire contract clause** like the one in the Coasters–Trackers contract excerpted earlier in this chapter. The function of this clause is to require a court to determine the parties' obligations based only on what is recited in the contract itself. Such a clause is not essential to exclude implied terms, however, as the case on page 135 illustrates.

entire contract clause
A term in a contract in which the parties agree that their contract is complete as written.

Judicial Interpretation of Terms

How Courts Interpret Contracts

As already emphasized, contract negotiators should make contractual terms as express and as clear as possible. The reality is that time and resources may not permit such detail. Another difficulty in achieving the goal of clarity is that language, by nature, is ambiguous. Despite best intentions, disagreements may arise about

- whether a given term should be implied, as discussed above
- the meaning and application of an express contractual term

rules of construction
Guiding principles for interpreting the terms of a contract.

It can be very difficult to predict how a court will interpret any given contract because **rules of construction**—or guiding principles—are often conflicting. For example, on the one hand, courts are required to enforce the contract as it is written and to rely primarily on the plain, ordinary meaning of the words that the parties

Case

Solar U.S.A. Inc. v. *Saskatchewan Minerals,* [1992] 3 W.W.R. 15 (Sask. Q.B.)

The Business Context: When a business enterprise relies on a producer to supply it with essential components, the results can be disastrous if that producer decides that it cannot or will not continue with the relationship. Whether such a decision amounts to a breach of contract, however, depends on the circumstances.

Factual Background: Solar U.S.A. Inc. ("Solar") had developed a mechanism that harnessed heat from the sun, called a "collector." Solar did not, however, have a method for adequately storing the heat until it was needed. Solar learned that Saskatchewan Minerals ("Sask.") had developed a unique tray, which appeared to solve the storage problem. The parties entered into negotiations, whereby it was agreed that Sask. would sell solar trays to Solar at a set unit price per tray, for a term of one year, to be renewed automatically unless terminated upon 30 days' notice prior to the anniversary date. No particular volume for the year was agreed upon.

The trays were produced, but owing to a design flaw that Sask. could not fix, they leaked and were unable to hold any solar heat. For this reason, Sask. refused to fill orders for the trays placed by Solar. Solar sued for breach of contract, claiming that Sask. failed to deliver trays pursuant to an implied term in the contract that Sask. would make trays available to Solar as required.

The Legal Question: Was there an implied term in the contract between Solar and Sask. requiring Sask. to supply trays as ordered?

Resolution: The court noted that various tests exist to determine whether such a term should be implied into the Solar–Sask. contract. For example, Lord Pearson in *Trollope & Colls Ltd.* v. *North West Metropolitan Regional Hospital Board*[9] provides

> An unexpressed term can be implied if and only if the court finds that the parties must have intended that term to form part of their contract: it is not enough for the court to find that such a term would have been adopted by the parties as reasonable men[10] if it had been suggested to them: it must have been a term that went without saying, a term necessary to give business efficacy to the contract, a term which, although tacit, formed part of the contract which the parties made for themselves.

The court found that business efficacy did *not* require it to imply a term that Sask. would make the product available to Solar as required. Furthermore, such an implied term would directly contradict the agreement that the parties had reached—namely, that the contract was not to guarantee any sales volume whatsoever.

Critical Analysis: What is the theoretical basis for implying terms into a contract? How can a business avoid having terms implied into a contract?

have chosen. The court simply asks how a reasonable person would regard the term in question and can refer to dictionaries, legal reference materials, and cases that have considered such terms in the past. On the other hand, courts are to give effect to the parties' intentions. Both of these rules make sense standing alone, but they do not provide a solution to the situation in which the parties' intentions may be inadequately reflected in the written contract itself. Should the court apply the plain meaning rule or give effect to the parties intentions? Which rule should prevail?

In the Coasters–Trackers contract, for example, Trackers promised to pay $5000 to Coasters for every day it was late in delivering the tracking. The intent of the parties, objectively assessed, may have been to motivate Trackers to do everything in its power to provide the tracking by the contractual delivery date. On this basis, if Trackers were late delivering because of a mechanical problem in its plant, the clause would apply. It would be more contentious to apply the clause if late delivery were caused by an event completely outside of Trackers' control—such as a severe light-

---

9. *Trollope & Colls Ltd.* v. *North West Metropolitan Regional Hospital Board,* [1973] 2 All E.R. 260 (H.L.) at 268.

10. Regrettably, it is only recently that the judiciary has begun to use inclusive language.

ning strike disrupting electricity to its plant for several days. Trackers might advance the position that to apply the clause in such circumstances would be contrary to the parties' intention.

In response, Coasters would ask that the court apply the plain meaning rule and disregard evidence of the parties' intention. On the basis of the plain meaning rule, a court could easily conclude that the late delivery clause speaks for itself and is unconditional: if Trackers delivers late, it has to pay $5000 per day. Whether a court would use the plain meaning rule standing alone or allow the clause's plain meaning to be tempered with evidence of what the parties *intended* the term to mean is impossible to predict—another inherent risk of litigation.

Trackers could face further problems in convincing a court of its interpretation of the late-delivery clause based on the parties' intention. Two possible sources of problems are the parol evidence rule and the fact that the Trackers–Coasters contract contains what is known as an entire contract clause. Both matters are discussed in the next section.

The Parol Evidence Rule

Contracts may be oral, written, or partly oral and partly written. Except in a few specialized instances discussed in Chapter 8, the form a contract takes does not affect its enforceability. So long as the party claiming that there is a contract can prove it—through witnesses, for example—the fact that the parties only "shook hands" on the deal is not an impediment.

parol evidence rule
A rule that limits the evidence a party can introduce concerning the contents of the contract.

When a contract has been reduced to writing in a document intended to be the whole contract, the **parol evidence rule** applies. This rule limits the kind of evidence a party is able to introduce concerning the contents of the contract. In short, if the language of the written contract is clear and the document is intended to be the sole source of contractual content, then no evidence outside the contract can be used to change or add to the contract. Entire contract clauses, like the one in the Trackers–Coasters contract, are used to ensure application of the parol evidence rule to the contract in question. As noted earlier, such clauses generally operate to prevent a party from arguing that the terms of the agreement were found not just in the written document, but also in oral form.

The parol evidence rule emphasizes the sanctity of the written agreement and means that the parties should, before agreeing to a written contract, ensure provision of all terms important to them. Failure to do so may mean that the rule is invoked against the party that cannot support its interpretation of the contract without leading evidence "outside" of the contract.

The parol evidence rule has itself become the subject of judicial consideration, which in turn has justifiably limited its operation. Indeed, there are several situations where evidence outside the contract is important and is considered:

- If there is an alleged problem going to the *formation* of the contract—because one party alleges fraud at the hands of the other, for example—a party may bring to the court evidence to establish that allegation. Chapter 8 considers problems going to the formation of a contract in more detail.
- If the contract is intended to be partly oral and partly in writing, the rule has no application. The rule applies only when the parties intended the document to be the whole contract.

- If the promise to be enforced is contained in a separate (collateral) agreement that happens to be oral, the rule does not apply. For example, an agreement to sell for a set price a building with all the equipment in it may not include the equipment if the written agreement fails to mention it. If there is a separate agreement and a separate price for the equipment, however, the fact that the agreement for the building says nothing about the equipment is likely not a concern. The difference in the two situations is in the matter of there being separate consideration for the building and the equipment. If there is only one agreement and one price, the rule likely applies to the detriment of the party seeking to enforce the purchase and sale of the equipment.

The following case demonstrates how even an entire contract clause may not prevent a court from considering parol evidence.

Case

Corey Developments Inc. v. *Eastbridge Developments (Waterloo) Ltd.* (1997), 34 O.R. (3d) 73, aff'd (1999) 44 O.R. (3d) 95 (C.A.)

The Business Context: The parol evidence rule in its absolute form may cause manifest injustice and defeat the true intentions of the parties. Thus, almost from its inception, it has been made the subject of many exceptions. In recent times, the rule has also received disapproval from various law reform commissions. As well, several provinces have abolished the rule altogether in consumer situations. Consumer protection legislation in these provinces effectively makes oral precontractual statements supersede written terms.

In commercial transactions, however, the parol evidence rule has generally prevented the introduction of extrinsic evidence in challenging the written document (usually a standard form contract) and establishing the existence of oral promises. This treatment of the parol evidence rule as an absolute bar in commercial transactions has recently come under attack.

Factual Background: Corey Developments Inc. ("Corey") signed an agreement of purchase and sale with Eastbridge Developments Ltd. ("Eastbridge"), which was controlled by Mr. Ghermezian ("Ghermezian"), a well-known Alberta developer. Corey gave a deposit of $201 500 to Eastbridge. According to Corey, as the money was to be used by Eastbridge to fund the costs of obtaining subdivision approval, Ghermezian said he would give his per-sonal guarantee for the return of the deposit if the agreement did not close. The agreement of purchase and sale, however, made no mention of the personal guarantee, and Ghermezian denied ever having made such a promise. Evidence, including various letters between the parties, established the existence of the promise. The agreement of purchase and sale, however, contained an entire contract clause indicating that the agreement was intended to be the whole agreement. Therefore, by strict application of the parol evidence rule, the judge could not admit the oral evidence of Corey or the other documentary evidence.

The Legal Question: Was Ghermezian's personal guarantee to return the deposit a part of the contract?

Resolution: Justice MacDonald referred to *Gallen* v. *Allstate Grain Ltd.,*[11] in which Mr. Justice Lambert found that the parol evidence rule provided only a presumption that the written terms should govern and allowed the extrinsic evidence. Justice MacDonald went on to state, "The court must not allow the rule to be used to cause obvious injustice by providing a tool for one party to dupe another."

Applying the principle from *Gallen,* Justice MacDonald ruled that Ghermezian's personal guarantee was part of the contract between the parties, notwithstanding the entire contract clause and the parol evidence rule.

Critical Analysis: Is the *Corey* decision a welcome development? What are the justifications, if any, for abolishing the parol evidence rule in a commercial context?

Source: Jan Weir, "The Death of the Absolute Parol Rule" *The Lawyers Weekly* (6 February 1998) 3.

---

11. *Gallen* v. *Allstate Grain Ltd.* (1984), 9 D.L.R. (4th) 496 (B.C.C.A.).

re vague claus.
on a exception
root

Vague or Ambiguous Language

If the existence of the contract is not in doubt, the court assigns as reasonable a meaning as possible to vague or ambiguous terms.[12] As well, if the contract has been drafted by one of the parties, any ambiguity in language will be construed against that party in favour of the other.[13] The policy rationale for this rule is that the drafter should bear the risk of unclear language.

The reference to "best quality" in clause 12 of the Coasters–Trackers contract is somewhat nebulous, as it introduces an express element of subjectivity: What, exactly, is "best quality"? If faced with such a question, a court would conclude that "best quality" refers to the highest quality available, which, in turn, is a matter that expert evidence would establish. A court would not set the contract aside for uncertainty because some meaning can be assigned to the phrase "best quality."

There is a point, however, at which language is so ambiguous that the contract cannot be understood. In such cases, the contract will fail for uncertainty, and none of the promises it contains will be enforceable.

Proof of the Contract

Those who seek to enforce a contract must be able to prove that the contract was formed and that its terms support the claim that is made. Traditionally, that proof takes the form of witness testimony and documents that are submitted to the court as evidence. With the growth of electronic business, contracts are increasingly negotiated online and the terms are recorded electronically, without a paper version. This

Evidence of Electronic Contracts

TECHNOLOGY AND THE LAW

In 1997, the Uniform Law Conference of Canada produced a draft *Uniform Electronic Evidence Act*, which proposes to replace the emphasis on original documents with reliance on the integrity of the computerized records system that is used to record and preserve the data. The legislation would support the admissibility of electronic evidence in court, while allowing for challenges to the reliability of the system that produced the electronic records.

Until this legislation is adopted, parties are left to make their own agreement on evidence as part of their contracts. They can agree on how records of their electronic communication will be kept, such as by maintaining an electronic transaction log.

Ontario's *Electronic Commerce Act*, S.O. 2000, c. 17, provides for legal recognition of electronic information and documents, with certain exceptions. So far, it is the only province to enact such legislation. John Wetmore, president of IBM Canada Ltd., is reported as welcoming the legislation. He states, "By ensuring that electronic signatures and documents are legally recognized, it will facilitate speedy business transactions."

Critical Analysis: Can electronic records ever truly replace formal signed contracts? What are some practical problems with the emphasis on computer systems?

Sources: "E-signature, Contracts Now Legal in Ontario" *The Toronto Star* (17 October 2000) C6; and George Takach, *Computer Law* (Toronto: Irwin Law, 1998) at 380–381.

---

12. Christine Boyle & David Percy, eds., *Contracts: Cases and Materials,* 6th ed. (Scarborough: Carswell, 1999) at 125.

13. *Ibid.* at 542.

method of doing business creates difficulty if it becomes necessary to produce the "original" contract in court. In response, draft legislation has been proposed to make the proof of electronic contracts subject to a uniform set of rules.

Managing the Risk of Uncertainties

Changed Circumstances

Numerous circumstances may arise that prevent a party from performing its contractual obligations or that make performance much more expensive than anticipated. The rule, however, is that the terms of a contract are settled at the time of acceptance. Therefore, if disaster strikes—such as when a plant burns, railways go on strike or are closed, trade regulations change, or an entire manufacturing process becomes obsolete—the obligations in a contract are enforceable, unless a clause to the contrary is included. Though the legal doctrine of "frustration" occasionally relieves parties from their obligations (see Chapter 9), it operates in very limited circumstances and cannot be counted on to provide an avenue of escape.

It is therefore particularly important in longer-term contracts that negotiators evaluate risks, speculate on possible changes in the business environment, and be wary of making inflexible commitments. Taking these precautions is essential because changed circumstances may render a contract extremely disadvantageous to one party. For example, the price for the steel that Trackers needed to fill Coasters' order for tracking dramatically increased, making it very expensive for Trackers to fulfill its end of the bargain. Rather than run such a risk, Trackers could have negotiated for a term that would permit the contract price for the tracking to rise should the price of steel increase. A contractual term could

Well-drafted contracts will anticipate events that can affect performance.

- provide a formula setting the price of the goods supplied, in a manner that is tied to market value
- set the price according to the cost of materials, plus a specific percentage for profit
- allow the parties to reopen negotiations or terminate the contract altogether if specified events occur, such as a commodity price reaching a certain level

Instead of having to go to Coasters for some kind of accommodation, Trackers could have included a clause protecting its interests. Though the approach of voluntarily altering the agreement as the need arises can be successful, the parties must recognize that *legally* there is no obligation on either party to reach agreement. Furthermore, as discussed in Chapter 6, the voluntary agreement is unenforceable unless fresh consideration is given, promissory estoppel applies, or the document is put under seal.

In every situation, parties must try to build some flexibility into their agreements, while avoiding creating a document that is so loose and vague that they run the risk of having no contract at all. When a customer like Coasters refuses to accept a price variation clause of any description, the supplier must then choose between risking an adverse change in market conditions and losing the order altogether.

Conditional Agreements

Conditional agreements are essential when one party wants to incur contractual obligations *but only under certain circumstances.* For example, a business enterprise may be interested in buying a warehouse but only if it is able to secure financing from the bank. If the business simply agrees to purchase the warehouse without making its agreement conditional on securing financing, it will be obligated to complete the transaction even if the bank refuses the request for a loan. This outcome could have devastating financial consequences for the business in question. Conversely, if the business makes an offer to purchase the property *subject to financing,*[14] and that offer is accepted by the vendor, then the business is only obligated to complete if and when the financing is approved.

From a business perspective, it is important that the law provide a mechanism not only for making the contractual obligation conditional on a certain event happening, but also for binding the parties in some way during the time set aside for that condition to occur. If the vendor of the warehouse were entitled to sell to someone else while the business enterprise was trying to secure necessary financing, the whole arrangement would be somewhat futile.

To bind the other side during the time set aside for the condition's fulfillment, the law provides two mechanisms: the condition subsequent and the condition precedent. **Conditions subsequent** will always bind the parties to a contract pending the fulfillment of the condition. The occurrence of a condition subsequent operates to terminate the contract between the parties—that is, it must, by definition, relate to an existing contract. For example, parties to an employment contract may agree that an employee is to work for an organization until her sales drop below a certain amount. This is a contract subject to a condition subsequent. If the condition occurs—that is, if the employee's sales fall below the threshold—the contract automatically comes to an end.

For the most part, **conditions precedent** work in the same way—that is, there is a contract between the parties.[15] Unlike the condition subsequent situation, where parties perform their contractual obligations *until* the condition occurs, the condition precedent situation means that the parties' obligations to perform are *not triggered* pending fulfillment of the condition. That is, a contract exists between the parties, but the obligation to perform the contract is held in abeyance pending the occurrence of the event. Because there is a contract between the parties, the law is able to imply certain terms binding on the parties in the meantime. In the real estate situation, for example, a court would imply a term that the vendor must wait until the time for fulfilling the condition has passed before it can sell to someone else. Similarly, a court would imply a term on the purchaser to make good-faith efforts to secure the necessary financing. Without a contract between the parties, these kinds of terms could not be implied, because without a contract, there are no terms whatsoever.[16]

condition subsequent
A condition that, when it occurs, brings an existing contract to an end.

condition precedent
A condition that, until it occurs, suspends the parties' obligation to *perform* their contractual obligations.

---

14. Such a clause must contain sufficient detail; otherwise, it will be unenforceable owing to uncertainty. For discussion of such clauses, see Gwilym Davies, "Some Thoughts on the Drafting of Conditions in Contracts for the Sale of Land" (1977) 15 Alta. L. Rev. 422.

15. Not all conditions precedent operate within the context of a contract, however, and this is where the law can become somewhat confusing. As a rule of thumb, conditions precedent will bind the parties to a contract if the condition itself is reasonably certain and objective. Conditions that are tied to whim, fancy, or extreme subjectivity—as in, "I'll buy your house if I decide that I like it"—do not bind the parties because they essentially have no objective content. These are known as illusory conditions precedent and leave the parties free to do as they please, since there is no contract between them. For obvious reasons, illusory conditions precedent are rare. For discussion and case law on this point, see Christine Boyle & David Percy, *supra* note 12 at 345-382.

16. It is beyond the scope of this text to discuss the issue of waiver of conditions precedent. For an assessment of this particularly thorny problem, see Gwilym Davies, "Conditional Contracts for the Sale of Land in Canada" (1977) 55 Can. Bar Rev. 289.

Case

Wiebe v. *Bobsien* (1985), 14 D.L.R. (4th) 754
(B.C.S.C.) aff'd (1986) 20 D.L.R. (4th) 475 (C.A.),
leave to appeal refused (1985), 64 N.R. 394 (S.C.C.)

The Business Context: Because the purchase of real estate
can involve a large expense, businesses and individuals
alike often require time to either borrow the money necessary to make the purchase or divest themselves of an
existing property, the proceeds of which can be applied to
the contemplated purchase. Such a process can take weeks
or months, during which time the freedom of the vendor
to deal with other buyers or back out of the arrangement
altogether can become an issue.

Factual Context: Dr. Wiebe made an offer to purchase a
house owned by Mr. Bobsien. This offer was made conditional on Wiebe being able to sell his current residence on
or before August 18, 1984. Wiebe's offer was accepted by
Bobsien. However, on July 22, 1984, Bobsien changed his
mind and informed Wiebe that their agreement was "cancelled." Wiebe did not accept this cancellation and on
August 18, he informed Bobsien that he had obtained a

buyer for his current house and that, since the condition
had been fulfilled, the main transaction had to go
through. Bobsien refused to complete the sale, saying that
he had no contractual obligation to do so.

The Legal Question: Was there a contract between Wiebe
and Bobsein such that Bobsein was obligated to wait until
August 18 to see whether Wiebe could fulfill the condition?

Resolution: The court ruled that the condition precedent
merely suspended the obligation to perform the contract
pending occurrence of the event—in this case, the sale of
Wiebe's current residence. On this basis, Wiebe had a
contractual obligation to take all reasonable steps to sell
his house, and if he failed to take those reasonable steps,
he would be in breach of contract and liable in damages
to Bobsien. As for Bobsien, he was contractually bound to
wait and see if Wiebe would be successful in selling his
current residence and did not have the legal right to
"cancel" the contract on July 22. Since Wiebe fulfilled the
condition within the time provided in the contract,
Bobsein was contractually bound to sell to him. Bobsien's
failure to do so was a breach of contract.

Critical Analysis: Do conditions precedent introduce too
much uncertainty into contracts?

Purchasers of real estate, for example, frequently rely on the conditional agreement
by making the contractual obligation to buy and sell subject to

- rezoning
- subdivision approval
- annex of the property by a municipality
- mortgage financing
- provision of adequate water and sanitary sewer services to the property

Conditional agreements might also arise in other contexts. For example, a business
may be willing to commit to perform a contract provided it can

- access a certain source of supply
- engage people with the necessary expertise
- obtain a licence to use certain intellectual property

Conditional agreements would permit such an enterprise to contract with the other
side but would provide an established reason to escape the obligation to perform.

Managing Liability

Parties obviously do not enter into contracts if they expect the other party to breach
the contract, but circumstances change and relationships can deteriorate. Like all
other aspects of a transaction, a clear indication of what is to happen upon default

ensures that both parties know where they stand, should they become unwilling or unable to perform. Managing liability is an important aspect of terms of contractual negotiations.

Limitation of Liability Clause

When a party fails to meet its contractual obligations, it is liable for breach of contract and is responsible to the other side for any reasonably foreseeable damages the breach may have caused.[17] For example, in the Trackers–Coasters contract, a failure by Trackers to deliver adequate tracking may result in Coasters losing its contract with the Florida amusement park, the ultimate purchaser of the ride.

Figure 7.1

TRACKERS' LIABILITY TO COASTERS

> 1. **Trackers ➔ ➔ ➔ ➔ to Coasters**
>   *breaches contract by*
>   *supplying substandard tracking*
> 2. **Coasters ➔ ➔ ➔ ➔ to Florida customer**
>   *breaches contract by*
>   *failing to deliver tracking*
> 3. **Florida customer finds an alternative supplier and terminates contract with Coasters.**
> 4. **Coasters loses $1 million in profit on contract with Florida customer.**

On the basis of this scenario, Coasters could recover from Trackers its loss of profit, particularly since Trackers knew very well that Coasters needed the tracking to fulfill contractual obligations to a Florida amusement park. However, since contracts are about consensus and choice, parties can agree to limit liability for breach to something less than would otherwise be recoverable. This is precisely what the parties to the Trackers–Coasters contract accomplished. Clause 13 of the contract (set out in the opening scenario) is a **limitation of liability clause**. It provides that Trackers' liability shall in no event exceed the unit price of the tracking, and in no event shall it include loss of profit. Therefore, by the clear words of the contract, any loss of profit that Coasters may suffer from Trackers' breach is not recoverable. Since the parties agreed to place such a limit on damages when they entered into the contract, Coasters is bound.

Exemption Clause

Through an **exemption clause**, a party to a contract can identify events or circumstances causing loss for which it has *no liability whatsoever*. Clause 14 in the Trackers–Coasters contract achieves such an end, since it exempts Trackers from all

limitation of liability clause
A term of a contract that limits liability for breach to something less than would otherwise be recoverable.

exemption clause
A term of a contract that identifies events causing loss for which there is no liability.

---

17. The classic test for foreseeability in contract, discussed further in Chapter 9, is stated in *Hadley* v. *Baxendale* (1854), 9 Exch. 341:
> Where two parties have made a contract which one of them has broken, the damages which the other party ought to receive in respect of such breach of contract should be such as may fairly and reasonably be considered either arising naturally, i.e., ... such as may reasonably be supposed to have been in the contemplation of both parties, at the time they made the contract, as the probable result of the breach of it. Now, if the special circumstances under which the contract was made were communicated by the plaintiffs to the defendants , and thus known to both parties, the damages resulting from the breach of such a contract, which they would reasonably contemplate, would be the amount of injury which would ordinarily follow from a breach of contract under these special circumstances so known and communicated.

liability in respect to losses, damages, costs, or claims relating to design of tracking. This means that if there is a problem with the design, Coasters cannot sue Trackers for any loss it might sustain to replace or alter the tracking, for example.

Liquidated Damages Clause

liquidated damages clause

A term of a contract that specifies how much one party must pay the other in the event of breach.

A **liquidated damages clause** sets out—in advance—what one party must pay to the other in the event of breach. Through such clauses, the parties themselves decide before a breach has even happened what that breach would be worth by way of compensation. Provided that the clause is a genuine pre-estimate of the damages that the innocent party will suffer, it is enforceable.[18] The clause will not be enforceable, however, if it sets an exorbitant amount as a remedy for the innocent party. If so, the clause is a penalty clause—it intends to punish, not compensate—and a court will simply disregard it in assessing damages for the breach in question.

Standard Form Contracts

Standard form contracts are an extremely common feature of the modern commercial world and pose a set of unique problems.

Nature of the Standard Form Contract

The rules of contract law assume that the parties fully understand the terms of a contract before entering into it. This basic premise is at odds with the reality of business, in which tremendous numbers of transactions are completed every day through standard form contracts. A standard form contract is one in which the main terms cannot be changed through negotiation. The terms are offered to the other side on a "take it or leave it" basis. Such contracts save transaction costs because resources are not put into negotiating fresh terms with each new customer. Furthermore, in many situations, such as renting a video, neither party has the time or the inclination to negotiate.

Standard form contracts are also common for more significant agreements, such as obtaining a credit card, renting a car, buying insurance, or signing a guarantee of another's debt. Key terms, such as price, terms of payment, and basic obligations, are likely to be discussed, but these items are often used to fill in the blank spaces on standard form agreements. The remaining terms in these agreements are common to every transaction and are not subject to negotiation. For example, car rental agreements (see Chapter 5) are well known for containing standard terms. Only the name of the person renting the car, the kind of car being rented, the rental charges, and the duration of the rental agreement will ordinarily vary from one customer to the next. Most transactions proceed smoothly (the supplier provides the goods or services, and the customer pays), so that the standard terms do not come into play. However, if a transaction does not go as planned and the parties resort to the agreement to sort out the situation, the standard terms may be a problem. The customer may have agreed to the terms without reading them, understanding them, or even being aware that they form part of the contract. The terms are often expressed in very legalistic language because suppliers develop and refine the language over time to achieve their goals. These goals often involve maximum protection for the supplier at the expense of the customer. The supplier's liability may be severely limited, to the consternation of the customer.

---

18. See Harvey McGregor, *McGregor on Damages*, 16th ed. (London: Sweet & Maxwell, 1997) at para. 491.

Given the prevalence of standard form contracts, one might be tempted to simply advise customers to know and understand what the terms of the agreement are, and if any are unacceptable, to reject them before the agreement is made. The first part of the advice is valid, subject to the time the customer is able to spend on the exercise. The second part may be impractical because suppliers are seldom willing to negotiate the standard terms—if they did so, the advantages of convenience and consistency would be weakened. In fact, standard form contracts are known as "take it or leave it" contracts for this very reason.

Judicial Interpretation

The law dealing with standard form contracts begins with the proposition that parties negotiating a contract must protect their own interests and ensure they understand the terms before accepting them. If someone agrees to terms without fully investigating, that person ought to be the one who suffers the consequences. The rule is even more stringently applied if the customer signs a contract, since signing is evidence that the customer has agreed to its terms. However, the law places some responsibility on the supplier who creates the standard form agreement. There is, for example, an obligation on suppliers to make customers aware of the restrictive, unexpected terms in the agreement, including limitation clauses and exclusion clauses. The more restrictive the terms, the greater the duty of the suppliers to bring terms to the customer's attention. Perhaps even more so than in the customized contract, courts are apt to construe ambiguous language in a standard form contract against its maker.

Landmark Case

Tilden Rent-A-Car Co. v. *Clendenning* (1978), 83 D.L.R. (3d) 400 (Ont. C.A.)

The Business Context: Standard form contracts are a feature of many businesses, including the car rental industry. Unless the business does a proper job of explaining to the consumer the consequences of the standard form contract in question, it runs the risk of a court taking the customer's side and disallowing a term that would otherwise protect the business.

Factual Background: Mr. Clendenning rented a car from Tilden at the Vancouver airport. At the time of entering into the agreement, he was asked if he wanted additional insurance, which involved a higher fee but did provide full, nondeductible coverage. Thinking that this would protect him if the car were damaged in his possession, he agreed. As he was in a hurry, he signed the long and complicated rental agreement without reading it. An exemption clause, on the back of the agreement and in very small type, provided that the insurance would be inoper-

ative if the driver had consumed *any alcohol whatsoever* at the time the damage occurred. Clendenning was unaware of the clause. When the car was damaged—Clendenning drove into a pole after consuming some alcohol—Tilden sued to recover the full cost of repairing the vehicle.

The Legal Question: Can Clendenning rely on the clause providing him with full, nondeductible coverage, or is that clause inoperative because Clendenning had consumed some alcohol?

Resolution: The Court of Appeal held that Clendenning's signature on the contract was not a true assent to the terms of the contract and, therefore, Tilden could not rely on the exemption clause denying insurance cover to Clendenning. According to Justice of Appeal Dubin,

In modern commercial practice, many standard form printed documents are signed without being read or understood. In many cases, the parties seeking to rely on the terms of the contract know or ought to know that the signature of a party to the contract does not represent the true intention of the signer, and that the party signing is unaware of the stringent and onerous provisions which the standard form contains. Under such circumstances, I am of the opinion that the party seeking to rely on such terms should not be able to do so in the absence of first having taken reasonable measures to draw such terms to the attention of the other party....

Tilden Rent-A-Car took no steps to alert Mr. Clendenning to the onerous provisions in the standard form of contract presented by it. The clerk could not help but have known that Mr. Clendenning had not in fact read the contract before signing it. Indeed, the form of the contract itself with the important provisions on the reverse side and in very small type would discourage even the most cautious customer from endeavouring to read and understand it. Mr. Clendenning was in fact unaware of the exempting provisions. Under such circumstances, it was not open to Tilden Rent-A-Car to rely on those clauses....

Since the trial judge had accepted that Clendenning was capable of proper control of a motor vehicle at the time of the accident, and since Clendenning had paid the premium, he was not liable for any damage to the vehicle.

Critical Analysis: Courts may be less helpful to the customer in a nonconsumer context, since parties are expected to look after the own interests. In a recent decision from the Ontario Court of Appeal, for example, the court emphasized that inadequate notice of the kind complained of in the *Tilden* case will not be grounds for attacking an exemption clause in a commercial situation. The court affirmed the rule that a person will be assumed to have read and understood any contract that he or she signs.[19] Should consumer and commercial contracts be treated differently?

Common Contracts

A wide variety of contracts are found in the business world. The specialized rules relating to these common commercial contracts are discussed in more detail in later chapters.

Employment Contracts

Virtually every business has employees. Many employment contracts are informal, with little or no documentation. Written contracts, however, are becoming more common. In addition to terms put in place by statute, the key aspects of the agreement are the duties and responsibilities of the employee and the compensation package provided by the employer. The agreement may also restrict the activities of the employee during employment and sometimes after the contract ends, in terms of competing with the employer or misusing trade secrets or confidential information. Employment contracts with no fixed term have some important implied terms: either party can terminate by giving reasonable notice, and the employer can terminate immediately for just cause (such as misconduct or incompetence). As well, employment standards legislation will have application in certain cases. Employment contracts are considered in detail in Chapters 21 and 22.

Inequality of bargaining power may be an issue in enforcing the agreement, since the employer is normally in a superior bargaining position. This matter is considered in Chapter 8.

Purchase and Sale of Goods

A business is frequently involved in purchasing supplies that are used in various activities of the business. The business will, in turn, sell finished products to its customers.

---

19. See *Fraser Jewellers (1982) Ltd.* v. *Dominion Electric Protection Co. et al.* (1997), 34 O.R. (3d) 1 (C.A.).

All of these transactions involve the sale of goods. Common terms included in these contracts deal with price; terms of payment; description and quantity of the goods; quality and special features of the goods; time and place for delivery; definition of when ownership moves from the seller to the buyer; and the remedies for each party if the other defaults on the obligations in the contract. Each province has a comprehensive statute called the *Sale of Goods Act* that provides for implied terms related to these aspects of the contract, unless the parties include express terms in their contract. For further discussion of this kind of contract, see Chapters 24 and 25.

Equipment Leases

A business's purchase of equipment involves a sale through which the purchaser becomes the new owner of the goods in question. A lease is a much different sort of agreement. The owner of the equipment (the lessor) retains ownership throughout the term of the contract. The business using the equipment (the lessee) agrees to pay for the use based on the length of the lease or the extent to which the equipment is used. The lease deals with responsibility for repairs, maintenance, and damage and outlines any restrictions on use. The lease may provide for periodic replacement of the equipment. It may also give the lessee the option of buying the equipment when the lease ends (see Chapter 17).

Real Estate Agreement

A business may choose to buy land for its own use, for development, or for leasing to other businesses. The purchase of land is often facilitated by real estate agents acting for the two parties. The agreement includes the price, method of payment, description of the property, description of the building's contents that are included, and a specific date on which the transaction will be closed (i.e., when final payment is due, when the buyer takes possession, and when transfer documents are delivered). Buying land is very much a "buyer beware" situation. The buyer must verify the size and boundaries of the land, check for outstanding mortgages or other claims, verify any existing leases, and ensure that the land can be legally used for the buyer's intended purpose. The buyer acquires the land subject to existing claims or defects, so the buyer must be careful to protect itself in the agreement.

Real estate transactions are discussed further in Chapter 19.

Credit Agreement

There are a variety of ways that a business can be financed through credit. All involve some form of credit agreement between the borrowing business (the debtor) and the lending financial institution (the creditor). These credit agreements contain common basic features, such as the amount of the loan, interest rate, repayment schedule, provision for refinancing, security (known as collateral) in the event of default by the debtor, and remedies available to the creditor to recover payment. Normally, the creditor will acquire the right to seize and sell the collateral and to file a claim against the debtor to recover any outstanding balance. All provinces have a system for public registration of these agreements in order to provide notice to other potential creditors and to secure the claim of the creditor against the specified assets. The agreements are normally in standard form. They are created by the creditor institutions to give them maximum protection in the event of default by the debtor. Credit agreements are discussed in Chapter 27.

Professional Services Agreement

A business may engage a range of professionals to provide periodic or ongoing expert advice; accountants, lawyers, engineers, and architects are just a few examples. Agreements between professionals and their client businesses may be informal—the client simply requests advice when needed, and the professional charges the going rate. Alternatively, there may be in place a relatively formal retainer agreement through which the professional undertakes specific duties and time commitments. The arrangement for calculation and payment of fees may be quite detailed. Clients normally have the bargaining advantage in these arrangements, since they are in the position of choosing the particular professional or firm, of which there are many. The client can also expect a certain level of competence based on the standards established by the various professions. For analysis of professional services agreements, see Chapter 23.

Insurance

A business will normally have a range of insurance protection appropriate for the risks of its activities. Determining the range and extent of coverage needed and acquiring the coverage at a cost that the business can absorb are major challenges. Insurance contracts, called "policies," are some of the most difficult standard form agreements to grasp. They contain many terms dictated by legislation. The other terms are a product of the industry and are designed primarily to limit the insurance company's liability. A business needs expert advice to interpret the fine print included in the policy so that the customer knows what is included and excluded at the time of purchase. Reading this fine print at the time of filing a claim is too late. Insurance contracts are analyzed further in Chapter 20.

Business Law in Practice Revisited

1. **How was the scope of Trackers' and Coasters' obligations determined?**

If the parties cannot resolve a dispute concerning obligations by themselves, a judge will determine whether there is a contract between the parties, and if so, what its content is. Every contract must cover certain essentials in order to be enforceable. If key terms are missing, the court may conclude that the parties were still at the point of negotiating and had not actually entered into a contract yet. The other possibility is that the court will imply a term that one or the other party finds unsatisfactory or contrary to expectations.

   The Coasters–Trackers contract was complete because it contained all the terms that the circumstances of the case would identify to be essential, as well as some clauses that defined the relationship in more detail. For example, the contract identified the following terms:

   Parties: Coasters and Trackers
   Price: $1.5 million
   Delivery dates: as specified
   Product: tracking
   Quantity: 900 metres
   Quality: as per specifications and where no specifications, of the best quality

Guarantees: tracking to be free from defect for one year
Limitations on/exclusions of liability: liability not to exceed unit price; no liability for design defects; no liability for defects after one year
Insurance: vendor to insure tracking

2. Are there any ambiguous or unclear terms in the contract?

While certain aspects of the contract were somewhat ambiguous, such as the term specifying that the quality was to be of the best quality, a court would have been able to assign meaning to the term because there was a contract between the parties and expert evidence would have been available to establish what the phrase meant.

3. Were there any additional terms that Jason should have tried to have included?

Jason managed to negotiate a reasonably complete contract, as noted above. He included a number of clauses to limit the liability of Trackers, which was prudent, but he should have gone further and included a clause expressly eliminating application of the *Sale of Goods Act*. This term would have ensured that the Act would have no application in a contractual dispute with Coasters sometime down the road. It was wise from Trackers' perspective to include, as it did, an entire contract clause, as this would have helped forestall any arguments from Coasters that there were additional warranties or guarantees not expressly recited in the contract.

Jason probably should have included a price variation clause to deal with the problems that arose when the price of steel rose dramatically. In addition, an arbitration or mediation clause might have proven useful to deal with conflicts, although, as it turns out, the parties negotiated their own resolution to the pricing dispute that arose.

4. Did the contract relieve the parties from responsibility for inadequate performance?

The contract limited Trackers' liability for defective tracking for one year and to an amount not exceeding the unit price. Trackers had no liability for problems in the design of the tracking.

Coasters' obligation to pay the purchase price was not qualified by the express terms of the contract. Of course, if Trackers had failed to deliver, Coasters would not have had to pay. If Trackers had delivered seriously defective goods, Coasters would have had the option to refuse delivery. If the defect had been less significant, Coasters probably would have remitted payment in a reduced amount, to reflect the track's lesser value or the cost of repairing the defects in the tracking. Clauses to this effect are not necessary and probably do not help in establishing certainty, in any event. Whether the tracking was seriously defective or only somewhat so would had been a question of fact and therefore a matter of debate, which no clause in a contract can resolve. If the parties cannot resolve that question informally, it will be determined by a judge in an action by Trackers against Coasters for the purchase price set out in the contract.

Chapter Summary

The nature, scope, and extent of the obligations of the parties to a contract are known as the terms of the contract. The terms may be express, as when they have been specifically mentioned and agreed upon by the parties, or they may be implied. Since the court has considerable discretion to imply a term or not, parties are best advised to make their agreement as clear and explicit as possible.

How courts will resolve a contractual dispute over terms is an open question, as is any matter that proceeds to litigation. An important evidential rule that guides a judge is known as the parol evidence rule. It prevents the introduction of evidence that varies or adds to the terms of a written contract when the contract is clear and intended to be the sole source of the parties' obligations. Entire contracts clauses are used to propel a court to apply the parol evidence rule in any given case.

An important planning function of contract law lies in the fact that it permits parties to establish, in advance, the extent of responsibility for breach through limitation clauses and exclusion clauses. In addition, parties can bargain for what will be payable in the event of breach. Such an express term will be enforceable, provided the amount is a genuine pre-estimate of damages and not a penalty.

Standard form contracts are a fixture of modern business practice. Courts may refuse to apply a clause that disadvantages a consumer if the business in question failed to take reasonable steps to ensure that the consumer was alerted to the clause in question. Courts are less likely to assist the commercial or industrial customer, however, on the basis that sophisticated business interests should be left to take care of themselves.

The chapter concluded with a brief introduction to some common commercial contracts.

Study Chapter

Questions for Review

1. What is the difference between an express and an implied term?

2. Who decides the content of a contract?

3. What are four sources that the court can rely on to imply terms?

4. Why are express terms preferable to implied terms?

5. How do the courts deal with ambiguities in the contract?

6. What are three ways that a party can control its exposure to liability for breach of contract?

7. Why are conditional agreements important?

8. What is the parol evidence rule?

9. What is a collateral agreement?

10. Why does business make extensive use of standard form agreements?

11. What assumptions do the courts make about how contract terms relate to changing circumstances?

Questions for Discussion

1. What are some factors a business should consider before negotiating a contract?

2. How should a business formulate its negotiating strategy?

3. How should a business deal with the risk factor in contracts?

4. Should the use of standard form agreements be regulated by legislation?

5. A shrink-wrapped computer software package contains the following notice on the outside of the package:

When you open this package, you accept
the terms of the enclosed agreement.

If the customer opens the package, are the enclosed terms part of the contract, whatever the enclosed agreement says?

Situations for Discussion

1. Laba Karl owned two adjacent businesses: a grocery store and a bakery. Both were served by the same parking lot. Laba agreed to sell the grocery store to Azar. The agreement of purchase and sale contained this clause:

   The premises shall include use of the parking located at the rear of the store for customers, on the understanding that such parking shall be shared with the vendor with regards to his operation of the bakery.

   A disagreement developed about the use of the parking. Azar's position was that she was to have full use of the lot for herself and her customers, subject only to Laba's right to park two delivery vehicles. Laba argued that it was intended that he be able to use the lot for his bakery business, his employees, and his tenants.[20]
   What is the most reasonable meaning of the clause? How could the language be better expressed?

2. Shibamoto Ltd. had a contract to buy fish from Western Fish Producers on an ongoing basis. The price for the fish was to be "the prevailing market price for processed fish." A clause in the contract gave Shibamoto the right to terminate the contract if the fishing grounds price reached a level that would result in no profit on resale by Shibamoto. The market turned out to be extremely volatile

---

20. Based, in part, on *Azar* v. *Fancy Pastry Shop Ltd.* (1984), 63 N.S.R. (2d) 124 (S.C.T.D.).

and almost impossible to predict.[21] How well is this agreement likely to work? What must Shibamoto show if it wishes to terminate?

3. In 1985 Howard MacDonald was hired as chairman of Dome Petroleum. At that time, Dome was heavily in debt and showed little prospect of being profitable. MacDonald was hired to turn Dome around. MacDonald's employment contract provided that he would receive a lump sum payment of US$1.5 million if either he or the company decided to terminate the contract before the end of its five-year term. The termination required 30 days' notice and was triggered if any group bought more than 20 percent of Dome's voting shares, if Dome merged with an unaffiliated company, or if Dome disposed of substantially all of its assets. Dome's financial position improved over the next two years, and in 1987 Dome was taken over by Amoco Corp. MacDonald chose to terminate and received $1.5 million.

    Evaluate the advisability of this 1985 agreement for both parties.

4. Weir was engaged by Canada Post to deliver ad flyers for a five-year term. She was entitled to payment on a per piece basis. The contract provided that Canada Post could terminate the agreement on 60 days' notice if it changed its ad flyer distribution system and "alternatively, Canada Post may in its sole discretion terminate this agreement immediately on giving written notice to the Contractor." Payment per piece became costly for Canada Post, and two years later it instituted a new payment system based on packages (containing several pieces).[22]

    Is Canada Post entitled to terminate the contract with Weir? What evidence is relevant? Is it a contract at all when one party has so much discretion?

5. Jolly Games Ltd. and Yahoo College signed a two-year agreement stating that Jolly would supply and maintain electronic videogames for the college. The contract included insurance, a machine rotation plan, and a payment schedule for commission on receipts to be paid to the college (including a guaranteed minimum payment). Shortly after the machines were installed, Jolly began to experience problems with vandalism. Machines were upset, glass broken, cords and plugs removed, cash boxes broken into, and drinks poured into the machines. Jolly employees serviced most of their machine sites once a week. They had to service the college sites every day. Jolly requested that the college provide security for the machines, but the vandalism continued. Jolly earned no commissions and refused to make any payments to the college, claiming that security was the college's responsibility as an implied term.[23]

    Is this the sort of situation where a term should be implied? How could the issue have been resolved through an express term?

6. In July, Zola saw an advertisement for a Celtic Twilight Holiday from Gougemaster Tours Ltd. Zola went to her local travel agent and picked up a brochure that contained six glossy, colourful pages of print with several photos of hotels, villages, and beaches with sunbathers.

    Zola booked her 14-day holiday over the Christmas period for $1899. She paid the full amount and received tickets that detailed her flight schedules, seven-day coach tour, and seven nights in the Water Spirit Hotel in Dublin. The travel agent did not discuss with Zola the terms of the contract, other than noting that half the price was nonrefundable if Zola changed her mind.

21. Based, in part, on *Shibamoto & Co. Ltd.* v. *Western Fish Producers Inc. (Bankrupt)* (1992), 145 N.R. 91 (F.C.A.).

22. Based, in part, on *Weir* v. *Canada Post Corp.* (1995), 142 N.S.R. (2d) 198 (S.C.). See also the Federal Court of Appeal analysis in *Shibamoto & Co.* v. *Western Fish Producers Inc.*, ibid., that "even the broadest form of contractual discretion must be exercised with well recognized limits" at 102.

23. Monique Conrad, "Security for Games Is Implied Term of Contract" *Lawyers Weekly* (3 May 1991) 2. See too *Algonquin College* v. *Regent Vending and Amusements Ltd.* (Ont. Gen. Div.).

Zola was dissatisfied with her holiday from the beginning. The seven-day coach tour was unguided and appeared to Zola to consist of endless wandering through boring villages and countryside. The bus was hot, dirty, and slow. Because there was no guide, Zola could find no one to whom she could complain. In Dublin, Zola was escorted to the El Sleezo Hotel because the Water Spirit Hotel was full. The El Sleezo had a small, unremarkable restaurant and lounge. There was no swimming pool, and Zola's room contained only a bed, bureau, and chair. She shared a bathroom with three other guests. She was three kilometres from the city centre. Zola would have flown home in the second week, but she could not afford to buy a new ticket.

Zola was depressed for months afterwards and could think only of getting compensation from Gougemaster Tours. She finally sued. In response, Gougemaster Tours pointed out to Zola several paragraphs in the holiday brochure, including the following:

Hotel Changes: Gougemaster Tours has contracted with the hotels shown in this brochure to supply accommodation. From time to time the accommodation reserved is unavailable and a substitute hotel is provided. There are several reasons why this may occur, including unexpected maintenance problems, guest stayovers, and hotel overbookings. The chances of a hotel change are remote, but we would like you to be aware that the possibility exists.

Gougemaster's Responsibility: Gougemaster Tours Ltd. does not assume responsibility for any claims, losses, damages, costs, or expenses arising out of loss of enjoyment, upset, disappointment, distress, or frustration, whether physical or mental, resulting from the following:

(a) the need for us to change itineraries or substitute accommodation, hotels, or services, provided that every effort is made to supply the most comparable service and accommodation available

(b) cancellation of a tour by Gougemaster, provided that full refund of all monies paid is made to the passenger

It appeared that the hotel change in the second week was caused by Gougemaster's policy of overbooking. To what extent has Gougemaster limited its liability? Is the brochure part of the contract? Is Zola subject to the terms if she hasn't read them?

Eight Chapter

Non-enforcement of Contracts

Objectives

AFTER STUDYING THIS CHAPTER, YOU SHOULD HAVE AN UNDER-STANDING OF:

► WHY ENFORCEMENT OF CONTRACTS IS THE NORM

► THE EXCEPTIONAL CIRCUMSTANCES IN WHICH CON-TRACTS ARE NOT ENFORCED

► WHICH CONTRACTS MUST BE IN WRITING, AND WHY

[handwritten margin notes:]
- Bi-polar
- Manic depression
- not enforceable for whom who lack capacity
- the other party must know of incompetance in order for it not to be enforceable
- Repudiate (revoke)

Business Law in Practice

Martha Smith bought a fitness club in downtown Toronto and renamed it "Martha's Gym." She invested $50 000 of her own money and financed the remainder through a business loan from the local bank. Martha tried to attract a large clientele to the facility, but the volume of business failed to meet her expectations. She began to run short of cash and fell behind in her monthly loan payments to the bank. Eventually, the bank called the loan, which had an outstanding balance of $20 000. The bank told Martha that unless she paid off the entire balance in two weeks, it would start seizing assets from the fitness club.

Martha convinced her elderly parents, Mr. and Mrs. Smith, to help her by bor-rowing $40 000 from the same bank. She explained that through such a cash infu-sion, she would be able to retire her own loan with the bank and use the balance as operating capital for her business. Martha assured her parents that the problems at the fitness club were temporary and that by hiring a new trainer, she would be able to quickly turn the business around.

Martha and her parents went to meet Jones, the branch manager, who had handled Mr. and Mrs. Smith's banking for over 35 years. Jones said that he would give the Smiths an attractive interest rate on the loan—namely, 8 percent—but insisted that the loan be secured by a mortgage on their home. Since the Smiths had no other means of paying back the loan and the house was their only asset, they were nervous about the proposal, which they did not fully understand. However, they did not want Martha to go through the humiliation of having her fitness equipment seized and sold at auction.

For his part, Jones was tremendously relieved that the Smiths had come in to see him. Jones was the one who had approved Martha's ill-fated business loan in the first place, and he had failed to ensure that it was properly secured. He saw this as an opportunity to correct his own error and get Martha's loan off his books altogether.

Jones had the mortgage documents prepared and strongly encouraged the Smiths to sign, saying that this would protect Martha's assets from seizure. He also told them that to a large extent, signing the mortgage was just a formality and that he was confident that nothing would come of it.

In the end, the Smiths decided to put their trust in Jones that he would not let them enter into a contract that could bring about their financial ruin. They simply signed the mortgage. Immediately, $20 000 went to the bank to pay the outstanding balance on Martha's loan. The remaining $20 000 was paid directly to Martha.

Figure 8.1

MARTHA'S AND HER PARENTS' FINANCIAL ARRANGEMENTS WITH THE BANK

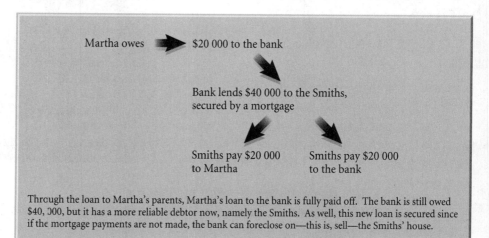

Martha owes → $20 000 to the bank

Bank lends $40 000 to the Smiths, secured by a mortgage

Smiths pay $20 000 to Martha

Smiths pay $20 000 to the bank

Through the loan to Martha's parents, Martha's loan to the bank is fully paid off. The bank is still owed $40, 000, but it has a more reliable debtor now, namely the Smiths. As well, this new loan is secured since if the mortgage payments are not made, the bank can foreclose on—this is, sell—the Smiths' house.

Martha's business continued to operate until the additional capital was completely expended. Its prospects failed to improve, as Martha was still unable to attract customers and the new trainer quit. Eventually, neither Martha nor her parents could make the payments on the mortgage, and the bank began to foreclose on the Smiths' home. Mr. and Mrs. Smith are in shock—they never believed that it would come to this.[1]

---

1. This Business Law in Practice scenario is based on *Morrison* v. *Coast Finance Ltd.* (1965), 55 W.W.R. 257 (B.C.C.A.) and *Lloyds Bank* v. *Bundy*, [1975] Q.B. 326 (C.A.).

1. Did Jones manipulate or pressure the Smiths into signing the mortgage? If so, what legal remedies do the Smiths have?
2. Did Mr. and Mrs. Smith enter into the contract on the basis of mistake or misrepresentation? If so, what legal remedies do they have?
3. How could Jones have managed this transaction better?

The Importance of Enforcing Contracts

Once negotiators reach an agreement that appears to contain their consensus on the essential elements of a bargain, a contract is formed. The law then focuses on enforcing that agreement in order to preserve the integrity, reliability, and predictability of contractual relationships. Were it otherwise, the business world would be unable to predict with any certainty which agreements would be binding.

At the same time, the Canadian legal system recognizes the injustice of enforcing contracts without any provision for exceptional circumstances. Accordingly, the law endeavours to achieve a balance between two competing goals. On the one hand, it must prevent people from pulling out of deals because they have found better opportunities elsewhere or have failed to conduct diligent negotiations. On the other hand, it must remedy situations where an apparently valid contract fails to reflect the real agreement of both parties or is fundamentally unjust.

This chapter presents a number of legal doctrines—developed through common law and statute—that are exceptions to the general rule that a contract, once formed, is enforceable. It categorizes these doctrines on the basis of there being

■ an unequal relationship between the two parties
■ misrepresentation or important mistakes concerning the contract
■ a defect within the contract itself.

If the aggrieved party can bring itself within one of the doctrines discussed in this chapter, there are two possible outcomes. In certain circumstances, he or she may *elect* whether to keep the contract in force or have it brought to an end. Where this option is available, the contract is said to be **voidable**. In other, more limited instances, the legal problem is so serious that the aggrieved party has no choice in the matter: a court must declare the contract to be *null and void*. In other words, because of some tremendously substantial defect, the contract is considered never to have existed at all and, for that reason, to be of no force or effect. This is known as a **void contract**.

Contracts Based on Unequal Relationships

Legal Capacity

In general, the law assumes that individuals and properly constituted organizations have the **legal capacity** to form contracts. Contract law also emphasizes the importance of consent and voluntariness. Because they may be unable to give true consent to their agreements, certain kinds of people—namely, children and those with mental incapacities—are given the benefit of special legal protection.

voidable contract
A contract that in certain circumstances an aggrieved party can choose to keep in force or bring to an end.

void contract
A contract involving a defect so substantial that it is of no force or effect.

legal capacity
The ability to make binding contracts.

Minors

age of majority
The age at which a
person becomes an
adult for legal purposes.

[handwritten: not liable]

[handwritten: necessaries - legal category]
[handwritten: - Food]
[handwritten: - shelter]
[handwritten: = clothing]
[handwritten: - (education) ← free until of the High school]
[handwritten: - (medical care) ← medical insurance]
[handwritten: - transportation to + from work]
[handwritten: Minors are liable for necessaries and necessities]

[handwritten: enforceable]
[handwritten: executory]
[handwritten: every that has to be done is done]
[handwritten: Beneficial contract of Service]
[handwritten: - you are an employee]
[handwritten: - over and above payment]
[handwritten: → cannot repudiate unless not non-beneficial]
[handwritten: - ii: apprenticeship contracts]

The **age of majority** is the age at which a person is recognized as an adult for legal purposes. Those under the age of majority (minors or infants) are in a very different position concerning their ability to enter contracts than are those who have attained the age of majority. To protect minors from the enforcement of contracts that may not be in their best interests, the general rule is that minors are not obligated by the contracts they make.

However, since the goal of the law in this area is to protect the underaged, minors have the option to fulfill their contractual commitments, and can enforce a contract against the other party should that party be in breach. In this way, contracts with a minor are usually voidable, at the option of the minor alone.[2]

The age of majority—which defines who is not a minor—is within provincial control and is set at 18 or 19 years of age, depending on the province.[3] For example, the Ontario *Age of Majority and Accountability Act*[4] states,

> **s. 1** Every person attains the age of majority and ceases to be a minor on attaining the age of eighteen years.

Because minors may have to provide for their own welfare in certain circumstances, there are exceptions to the general common law rule of immunity from liability. Minors are obligated by contracts for essentials, known in law as "necessaries," and are required to pay a reasonable price for them. The definition of necessaries varies from one minor to another, since what amounts to a necessity in a given case is legally determined in relation to two questions:

1. Is the item being acquired necessary, given the socioeconomic circumstances of the minor in question?
2. Does the minor already have an adequate supply of the item?[5]

While food, shelter, and clothing are the most common categories of necessaries, the two-step test must still be satisfied in order for the supplier to be able to enforce the specific contract. Suppliers should also be aware that even when the contract is one for necessaries, problems of enforcement can arise. Suppliers may be faced with the presumption that a minor who lives with a parent or guardian is already adequately provided for and has no outstanding needs.[6]

Contracts known as beneficial contracts of service are also binding if they are considered largely for the benefit of the minor. For example, an employment contract with a minor is enforceable if the employer can show that the contract involves a significant element of training and career development, such as one would expect in a program required to enter or progress through a trade or profession. Enforceability in this context means that the employer can be awarded damages for breach of contract.

[handwritten: - Might not accept the wrecked car b/c can put on record (credit rating)]
[handwritten: - if they did something criminal (lie about age)]

2. It is beyond the scope of this chapter to discuss whether there is a category of void minor's contracts. For discussion see G.H.L. Fridman, *The Law of Contract*, 4th ed. (Scarborough: Carswell, 1999) at 162 and following.

3. Fridman, *ibid.* at 152.

4. R.S.O. 1990, c. A.7.

5. Fridman, *supra* note 2 at 155. This common law rule has been codified in Sale of Goods legislation in Canada. For example, s. 4 of the Alberta legislation, R.S.A. 1980, c. S-2 states:

   > 4(2) When necessaries are sold and delivered to a minor ... he must pay a reasonable price therefor.
   >
   > (3) In this section "necessaries" means goods suitable to the condition in life of the minor ... and to his actual requirements at the time of the sale and delivery.

6. See David Percy (Institute of Law Research and Reform), *Minor's Contracts*—Report #14 (Edmonton: Institute of Law Research and Reform, 1975) at 5.

Case

Toronto Marlboro Major Junior 'A' Hockey Club v. *Tonelli* (1979), 96 D.L.R. (3d) 135 (Ont. C.A.).

The Business Context: When a business hires an infant as an apprentice or a trainee, it must be prepared to demonstrate how the contract benefits the infant. In the absence of such evidence, the infant may be able to walk away from the contract with impunity.

Factual Background: Tonelli was an exceptionally talented young hockey player who, in 1973 at the age of 16, entered into a two-year contract with the Toronto Marlboro Major Junior "A" hockey club, a team in the Ontario Major Junior "A" Hockey League. The Junior league had an agreement with the NHL (National Hockey League) that prevented the drafting of underage players and that called for the payment of certain fees once a player was drafted at the end of his junior career. When a similar agreement could not be reached with the newly formed WHA (World Hockey Association), Tonelli—like all other Junior hockey players of his time—was forced to sign a new contract as a condition of continuing to play in the Junior league. This new contract essentially bound him to play three years longer than his earlier contract with the Toronto Marlboros; moreover, it imposed monetary penalties if he signed with a professional team within that time frame, or within a period of three years after he ceased to be eligible to play in the Junior league. As soon as he attained the age of majority (18), Tonelli abandoned the contract with the Toronto Marlboros and signed with the Houston Aeros, a professional team. The Marlboros sued for breach of his employment contract.

The Legal Question: Was Tonelli's contract enforceable against him?

Resolution: Since Tonelli signed this service contract when he was a minor, it could be enforced against him only if it was for his benefit when he signed it. It was up to the Marlboros to establish that benefit. They were unable to do so, owing to the economic disadvantages of the contract in terms of money and time. While the salary and expenses provided were not intended to represent a normal or reasonable income to an amateur player, the effect was to prevent him from earning a normal income as a professional player. Furthermore, Tonelli simply did not require a full three years of instruction and experience before he was capable of playing professionally. In short, the contract was preventing him from realizing his full potential.

Critical Analysis: Should Tonelli be able to sign a contract and then disregard it?

The common law generally provides that when a minor reaches the age of majority, there is no impact on contracts formed when underage. They remain unenforceable against the minor unless they involve necessaries or beneficial service contracts. Only if the person—now of legal age—expressly adopts or ratifies the agreement does it become enforceable. The one exception to this rule is where the agreement is of a permanent or continuous nature, such as a partnership agreement. In such a case, the minor, upon attaining the age of majority, must reject (repudiate) this obligation, even if it is for non-necessaries. If he or she fails to do so, liability will be imposed from the time the minor becomes of age.[7]

In all Canadian jurisdictions except British Columbia, the common law governs the contractual capacity of minors.[8] In British Columbia, a different set of rules applies, as set out in the *Infants Act*.[9] This legislation provides even more protection for the infant than is present at common law, since generally, even contracts for necessities and beneficial contracts of service are unenforceable at the election of the minor.[10] However, a court has a number of powers under the legislation and can order, for example, that compensation be paid by or to any of the parties to the contract. See section 20(1)(2).

---

7. See Fridman, *supra* note 2 at 158 and following.

8. *Ibid.* at 153 and following.

9. See Part 3 of the *Infants Act*, R.S.B.C. 1996, c. 223.

10. Fridman, *supra* note 2 at 169, describes the operation of B.C.'s *Infants Act* in the following terms:

   A contract by a minor, *i.e.*, someone who was an infant at the time the contract was made, is unenforceable against him unless: (a) the contract is enforceable against him by some statute; (b) the minor affirms the contract on attaining majority; (c) it is wholly or partially performed by the minor after majority; or (d) was not repudiated by the minor within a year after majority. However, the minor can enforce the contract against the adult party as if the minor had been an adult at the time of contracting. In the case of an unenforceable contract, the minor or another party (if the minor has repudiated the contract or is in breach) can apply to a court for relief.... [footnotes deleted]

Mental Incapacity

In order for a contract to be formed freely and voluntarily by both parties, they must be able to understand the nature and consequences of their agreement. If people are mentally impaired through illness or intoxication by alcohol or drugs, such that they are unable to understand the consequences of their actions, and the other party was aware of their state, they may be able to avoid the contract[11] at their option.[12] And to the extent that the other party has unfairly taken advantage of the party who is lacking capacity, there are additional grounds for attacking the contract's validity—namely, duress, undue influence, and unconscionability. All three are considered below.

The fact that Martha's parents are elderly does not, of itself, mean that they lack mental capacity to enter into financial transactions. Rather, before Martha's parents can avoid paying the mortgage on this ground, a court will have to be satisfied that their advanced age has affected their sanity or mental competence—an unlikely outcome on the facts of this scenario. Though they are old and overly trusting, they are not legally incompetent.

Duress

duress
The threat of physical or economic harm that results in a contract.

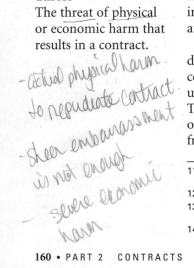
- actual physical harm.
  to repudiate contract.
- sheer embarassment
  is not enough
- severe economic
  harm

Contracts that are made as a result of one of the parties being threatened with physical harm are obviously not enforceable. The presence of this extreme form of **duress** indicates that the threatened party did not freely consent to the terms of the contract and, in fact, was the victim of a crime.

In the more difficult cases—those more likely to arise in commercial dealings—duress takes the form of one party financially pressuring the other. For example, a company might threaten to break a contract that it knows is crucial to the other side unless the other side gives certain financial concessions or payments in return.[13] These concessions will be unenforceable if it is shown that the coercion went beyond ordinary commercial pressure to a force or compulsion that prevented the other side from giving true consent to the proposal.[14]

---

11. Fridman, *ibid.* at 174-75 and G. H. Treitel, *The Law of Contracts,* 10th ed. (London: Sweet & Maxwell, 1999) at 516 and following.

12. Fridman, *ibid.* at 170-74.

13. This was held to amount to duress in *North Ocean Shipping Co. Ltd.* v. *Hyundai Construction Co. Ltd.,* [1978] 3 All E.R. 1170 (Q.B.).

14. The leading case in the area is *Pao On* v. *Lau Yiu Long,* [1979] 3 All E.R. 65 (P.C.).

There is no possibility that Martha's parents can rely on the doctrine of duress to avoid their obligations under the mortgage. Though the bank was going to seize Martha's fitness club equipment and offer it for public sale, this "threat" did not amount to duress. Certainly, her parents may have been very upset and worried by the situation, but this would not force them to borrow $40 000 from the bank. Furthermore, the bank is fully within its legal rights to seize property when a loan has fallen into arrears.

Undue Influence

[handwritten: - have to physical for economic harm.]

Since the basic premise of contract formation is that both parties have chosen to enter into the contract, surrounding circumstances that put in question the ability of one of the parties to exercise free will are of great concern. If these factors are sufficiently strong, then the contract is *voidable* at the option of the party whose free will was lost because of the **undue influence** of the other contracting party.

Undue influence traditionally operates in two circumstances:

undue influence
Unfair manipulation that compromises someone's free will.

- *Actual pressure.* Sometimes a transaction—commercial or otherwise—arises because one party has exerted unfair influence on the other. In such a case, the party who seeks relief from the contract must show that the influence existed, was exercised, and resulted in the agreement in question.[15] If an elderly person is pressured into signing over her estate to caregivers in return for care, such a transaction could be set aside for undue influence.

- *Assumed pressure.* Sometimes the relationship that already exists between the parties gives rise to a *presumption* that the ensuing agreement was brought about by one party's unfair manipulation of the other. For example, when the contract is formed between family members or between a professional and a client/patient, the court is entitled to assume that undue influence has been exerted. It then falls to the more powerful party to prove that no undue influence was present.

There is a chance that the elderly Mr. and Mrs. Smith would succeed in having the $40 000 mortgage set aside as having been procured by undue influence, either actual or presumed. The Smiths could argue that they entered into the mortgage with the bank only because the bank manager insistently preyed on their overwhelming need to help their daughter.[16] If so, they could then win on the grounds of actual pressure. An argument could also be advanced on the grounds of presumed pressure. Though courts will not ordinarily presume that a bank has undue influence over its customers, the Smiths may succeed by proving that they placed themselves entirely in the hands of their long-standing bank manager and had received no qualified outside guidance.[17] It would then fall to the bank to show that the mortgage was freely and independently entered into by the Smiths.[18]

One way of proving that the contract was freely chosen is to arrange for the weaker party—such as the Smiths—to get independent legal advice concerning the transaction *before it is entered into*. The lawyer providing that advice will also produce what is called a "certificate of independent legal advice," which is then

---

15. G.H. Treitel, *supra* note 1 at 378.
16. Whether there must be evidence that the agreement in question was actually unfair or otherwise amounted to a manifest disadvantage to the weaker party remains an open question in Canadian law. See Fridman, *supra* note 2 at 341-42.
17. This argument is based on *Lloyds Bank Ltd.* v. *Bundy*, *supra* note 1.
18. See Treitel, *supra* note 11 at 381.

appended to the mortgage or other document in question. In the certificate, the lawyer attests that

- he or she has explained the proposed transaction to the weaker party
- the weaker party appears to understand the proposed transaction
- the weaker party is proceeding with the transaction on a free and informed basis

Unconscionability

The Traditional Test

unconscionable contract
An unwise contract formed when one party takes advantage of the weakness of another.

Where one party stands in a position of being able to take advantage of someone and causes that person to enter into an unwise or improvident contract, the doctrine of **unconscionability** applies. In this way, unconscionability traditionally requires two elements:

- inequality between the parties
- an unfair or improvident bargain[19]

INEQUALITY BETWEEN THE PARTIES The required inequality may result because one party is unsophisticated, is poorly educated, lacks language facility, or has lower economic standing than the stronger party. Parties to a contract are never on strictly equal bargaining terms; therefore, disparity between them is, on its own, insufficient to upset a contract.

Since the Smiths are inexperienced and unsophisticated senior citizens who received no independent legal advice prior to signing the mortgage, this element could arguably be established, particularly if a court were sympathetic to their plight.

AN UNFAIR BARGAIN The party seeking to have the contract set aside must also be able to demonstrate that its terms greatly advantaged one party over the other. In short, there must be proof of substantial unfairness.

In the case of the Smiths' mortgage to the bank, the rate of interest was set at 8 percent and, from that perspective, was more than reasonable. However, there is a strong argument that the transaction was nonetheless a very unfair bargain for them. Through the mortgage, the Smiths put at risk their only substantial asset, for a loan they could never repay out of their own resources. In fact, while the bank and Martha stood to gain enormously from the transaction, the Smiths stood to lose everything for absolutely no return.

Contracts that appear normal may be challenged on the basis of the relations between the parties or the surrounding circumstances.

---

19. Christine Boyle & David Percy, *Contracts: Cases and Commentaries* (Scarborough: Carswell, 1999) at 727.

Unconscionability Legislation in Canada

There are several pieces of legislation in Canada that rely on unconscionability as a standard against which to assess the fairness of a consumer transaction. For example, the Ontario *Business Practices Act*[20] gives remedies to the consumer who has entered into a contract on the basis of unconscionable representations. In determining whether such a representation has been made, the court is directed by the legislation to consider whether the person making the representation knows or ought to know

LANDMARK
IN
THE LAW

i. that the consumer is not reasonably able to protect his or her interests because of his physical infirmity, ignorance, illiteracy, inability to understand the language, or similar factors,

ii. that the price grossly exceeds the price at which similar goods or services are readily available to like consumers,

iii. that the consumer is unable to receive a substantial benefit from the subject matter of the consumer representation,

iv. that there is no reasonable probability of payment of the obligation in full by the consumer,

v. that the proposed transaction is excessively one-sided in favour of someone other than the consumer,

vi. that the terms or conditions of the proposed transaction are so adverse to the consumer as to be inequitable,

vii. that he or she is making a misleading statement of opinion on which the consumer is likely to rely to his or her detriment,

viii. that he or she is subjecting the consumer to undue pressure to enter into the transaction.[21]

Comparable legislation in other jurisdictions includes the *Fair Trading Act*, S.A. 1998, c. F-1.05 (Alberta); the *Trade Practices Act*, R.S.B.C. 1996, c. 457 (British Columbia); the *Business Practices Act*, S.M. 1990–91 (Manitoba); the *Trade Practices Act*, R.S.N. 1990, c. T-7 (Newfoundland); and the *Business Practices Act*, R.S.P.E.I. 1988, c. B-7 (Prince Edward Island).

Many jurisdictions also have legislation that applies when the cost of the loan is excessive, including the *Unconscionable Transactions Act*, R.S.A. 1980, c. U-2 (Alberta); the *Unconscionable Transactions Relief Act*, R.S.M. 1987, c. U20 (Manitoba); the *Unconscionable Transactions Relief Act*, R.S.N.B. 1973, c. U-1 (New Brunswick); the *Unconscionable Transactions Relief Act*, R.S.N.S. 1989, c. 481 (Nova Scotia); the *Unconscionable Transactions Relief Act*, R.S.N. 1990, c. U-1 (Newfoundland); the *Unconscionable Transactions Relief Act*, R.S.P.E.I. 1988, c. U-2 (Prince Edward Island); the *Unconscionable Transactions Relief Act*, R.S.S.1978, c. U-1 (Saskatchewan); the *Consumer Protection Act*, R.S.B.C. 1996, c. 69, ss. 59-61 (British Columbia—this legislation grants relief from unconscionable mortgages); and the *Unconscionable Transactions Relief Act*, R.S.O. 1990, c. U-2 (Ontario).

Critical Analysis: Does such legislation fill a real need in commercial transactions? Does it unfairly restrict business?

---

20. R.S.O. 1990, c. B.18, s. 2.
21. *Ibid.*, s. 2(2).

very vague & subjective

The Wider Test

The doctrine of unconscionability most certainly applies when the traditional test is met. More controversially, it has been applied when "the transaction, seen as a whole, is sufficiently divergent from community standards of commercial morality."[22] The terminology of this wider test seems to give the courts even more room to set a contract aside,[23] but it has yet to be assessed by the Supreme Court of Canada.

The Smiths have a reasonable chance of having the mortgage set aside on this version of unconscionability, as well. A judge could conclude that unless they have had independent legal advice, senior citizens like the Smiths should not be mortgaging their only asset in exchange for a loan that exposes them to tremendous risk. A judge might then rule that, in taking such a mortgage under these circumstances, the bank acted in a manner that offended community standards of commercial morality.

People seeking to avoid a contract owing to mental capacity, duress, undue influence, or unconscionability must do so as promptly as possible or risk losing their case.

Misrepresentations and Important Mistakes

Misrepresentation of Relevant Facts

Stat can have enormous effect

Parties involved in negotiating a contract are usually not obligated to volunteer information. The basic principle or rule is that both parties are to look out for their own interests. On the other hand, if one party is asked a question, for example, he or she must respond truthfully and completely.

Sometimes parties do owe a duty to disclose information, however.[24] A duty to disclose can arise, for example, in situations involving special relationships, as when someone applies for insurance. The person applying for insurance coverage has a duty to disclose all information that would be relevant to the insurer who is assessing the risk of accepting the application.[25]

The difference between a statement made *in* the contract and one that is made *prior to entering into* the contract is crucial in this area of law.[26] If the statement is made *in* the contract, it is a promise or a term of the contract. If it proves to be untrue, a breach of contract has occurred. However, if the statement is made *prior to entering into* the contract but is not a term, it still can have legal consequences. A statement that meets the conditions set out below is known in law as an actionable **misrepresentation**.

Contract law allows the party who has relied on a misrepresentation to have the contract cancelled. This cancellation is called **rescission** and involves putting the parties back into their precontractual positions. Because rescission is an equitable remedy, the court requires the person seeking such assistance to act promptly in bringing the complaint forward.

misrepresentation
A false statement of fact that causes someone to enter a contract.

rescission
The remedy that results in the parties being returned to their precontractual positions.

---

22. *Harry* v. *Kreutziger* (1978), 95 D.L.R. (3d) 231 (B.C.C.A.) at 241.

23. Christine Boyle & David Percy, *supra* note 19 at 744 and following.

24. There are a number of areas in which a duty to disclose can arise. For discussion of these, see Shannon O'Byrne, "Culpable Silence: Liability for Non-Disclosure in the Contractual Arena" (1998) 30 Can. Bus. L.J. 239.

25. Fridman, *supra* note 2 at 326-27.

26. Consumer protection legislation in some jurisdictions, however, specifies that precontractual representations are part of the contract. The distinction between precontractual representations and terms of the contract, while important in the commercial context, is less important when a business deals with a consumer.

Where rescission is not possible, such as when one party has substantially altered the subject matter of the contract, the courts will endeavour to do what is practically just so that the innocent party gets some redress, including monetary compensation.[27]

Ingredients of an Actionable Misrepresentation

The law provides that a negotiating party must answer inquiries accurately and that any information volunteered must be correct. Whether or not a statement is a misrepresentation that allows the other party a remedy depends on its nature and effect. To count as a misrepresentation, it must be proven that the statement is

- false
- clear and unambiguous
- material to the contract; that is, it must be significant to the decision of whether or not to enter into the contract
- one that actually induces the aggrieved party to enter into the contract
- concerned with a fact and not an opinion, unless the speaker claims to have special knowledge or expertise in relation to an opinion

relied on it

When Jones told the Smiths that signing the mortgage was a formality, this statement amounted to a misrepresentation, since a mortgage is in fact a legal instrument with far-reaching consequences, the most serious being that the bank could foreclose on the Smiths' house. If the Smiths can prove that they relied on that representation in deciding to sign the mortgage, they will probably succeed in establishing an actionable misrepresentation.

When Jones told the Smiths he was confident that nothing would come of their signing the mortgage, this was arguably an expression of opinion—not a statement of fact—and therefore not actionable. A court might find, however, that since Jones is an expert in the area of mortgages and other banking matters, his statement was one of fact, and the court would order the contract rescinded on that basis.

Remedies for Misrepresentation

Besides entitling courts to rescind or set aside a contract, certain kinds of misrepresentations are torts, which provide for remedy in damages. If there was a deliberate intent to mislead, or if the statement was made carelessly without knowing or believing that it was true, the misrepresentation is characterized as *fraudulent*. Since fraudulent misrepresentation is a tort, damages in tort can be awarded *in addition* to the remedy of rescission provided by contract law. Similarly, if the statement was negligently made, damages in tort can be awarded *in addition* to the remedy of rescission provided by contract law. Where the misrepresentation is neither fraudulent nor negligent, an action is still available to set the contract aside based on innocent misrepresentation.

Given the cost of litigation—and the fact that the innocent party may fail to prove his or her case on the balance of probabilities—prevention is the best medicine. It is prudent to insist that important terms be an express part of a written contract, so as to achieve the goal of clarity between the parties. It is generally easier to prove breach of a written term than to establish that an oral statement made during contractual negotiations amounts to a misrepresentation in law. If the other party balks at reciting an important representation as an express, written term, the customer would be best advised to do business elsewhere.

---

27. See, for example, *Kupchak* v. *Dayson Holdings Ltd.* (1965), 53 W.W.R. 65 (B.C.C.A.).

Mistake

The doctrine of legal **mistake** is one of the most difficult aspects of contract law. In the course of its development by the courts, the law of mistake has become so complex and confusing that it presents a major challenge even to seasoned lawyers and judges. In practice, legal mistake is rarely proven.

The central point is that *legal* mistake is much narrower than the everyday idea of a mistake. A simple oversight or error by one negotiating party does not constitute a legal mistake and provides no basis for voiding a contract. As previously noted, negotiators are expected to look after themselves and to exercise appropriate caution before making legal commitments.

Compare the following two examples:

EXAMPLE 1 Kerry intends to make an offer to sell her car for $11 000 and in error sends a written offer to Sean for $10 000. Sean accepts her offer.

EXAMPLE 2 Kerry makes a written offer to sell her car for $1100 rather than $11 000, and Sean promptly accepts. There is no reason to believe that the car, worth approximately $11 000, should be sold at a substantially lower price. Moreover, there is nothing in the relationship that would suggest that Kerry would give Sean a break in price.

In both cases, Kerry has made a mistake according to the common understanding of that word. However, in all likelihood, only in Example 2 would this be interpreted at law as a mistake worthy of a remedy. The error Kerry has made in Example 1 is not one that would surprise Sean. This could be exactly the price for which Kerry intends to sell her car. In contrast, in Example 2, Sean could not reasonably expect that the price would be so low, especially if Kerry and Sean have had earlier discussions about the possible price range. Kerry has made an error, and any reasonable person in Sean's position would realize that. In the latter example, there can be no true agreement for $1100.

A legal mistake may also occur if both parties have made the same error. If Kerry's car appears to be old and relatively worthless, and she and Sean negotiate on that basis for a relatively low price, their agreement is based on a common mistake if the car turns out to be a valuable antique. Only if the error is such that the car purchased is a *totally different thing* from what the parties thought it was, will the contract be set aside on the basis of mistake. For example, if the difference is between low-grade transportation (what the parties thought the car was) and a classic car to be displayed and never driven (what the car actually is), a mistake in law could possibly be established. To the extent that the error is simply a mistaken assumption about the *quality* of the car (i.e., in terms of value), however, no legal mistake has occurred, and the purchaser is entitled to retain what may appear to be a windfall. Needless to say, such distinctions can be subtle.

Under the Business Law in Practice scenario, Martha's parents may have signed the mortgage under the mistaken belief that Martha's business problems were temporary and reversible. This is not a legal mistake, however, and there is no possibility that the mortgage would be set aside on the basis of this misapprehension.

An argument that is often made, though seldom successfully, concerns signed documents. The signor may misunderstand the type or nature of the document. Perhaps the signor thinks he is signing a guarantee of a debt, but the document is

[handwritten margin notes: Snapping up an offer; if for typo. — order rectification — to rectify; must represent genuine agreement of parties; non est factum — deed — when people are unable to read or can read but not a certain language]

actually a mortgage on his residence. Or the document is a transfer of land, and the signor thought she was signing an option to sell the property. The argument is, "I never intended to sign this type of contract." In practice, this argument tends to succeed only when there is a good reason for the signor's failure to more closely examine the document before signing—as when the signor is poorly educated, illiterate, or otherwise dependent on the creator of the document (the other party) for an explanation of what it is. Simple carelessness in signing a document without attention to what it is or to what its consequences might be is not enough to avoid enforceability.[28]

Contracts Based on Defects

Illegality

Under the classical model of illegality, even a freely chosen contract will be unenforceable if it

- is contrary to a specific statute and/or
- violates public policy

These contracts are void and of no effect, unless the court decides that the offending portions of the contract can be deleted, or severed, and the remaining portions saved. In such a case, only some of the contract will remain in effect and be enforceable. What a court will not do, however, is redraft the offending portions to make them comply with the law.

Contracts that are illegal may or may not be criminal. In this context, an **illegal contract** is simply one that violates statute law or public policy.[29]

Illegal by Statute

Numerous kinds of contracts are made illegal by legislation. For example,

- The *Criminal Code* forbids loans at a rate of interest considered "criminal"—defined as a rate exceeding 60 percent per year.[30] The courts may or may not invalidate the entire transaction, depending on whether it is possible to sever the clauses dealing with the criminal rate of interest from the rest of the contract. If the interest rate clause is severed, the debtor will only be obliged to repay the principal.
- The federal *Competition Act*[31] invalidates a range of commercial transactions that unduly restrict competition. For example, resale price maintenance contracts are prohibited because through them, manufacturers attempt to influence retail prices in the stores by keeping them high. Entering into such contracts can lead to criminal sanctions.
- The Ontario *Real Estate and Business Brokers Act* provides that an unlicensed realtor cannot maintain an action for services rendered.[32]

illegal contract
A contract that cannot be enforced because it is contrary to legislation or public policy.

---

28. For an exception to this statement, see the discussion in Chapter 7 concerning *Tilden Rent-A-Car Co.* v. *Clendenning* (1978), 83 D.L.R. (3d) 400 (Ont. C.A.).
29. See Percy & Boyle, *supra* note 19 at 760.
30. *Criminal Code*, R.S.C. 1985, c. C-46, s. 347.
31. *Competition Act*, R.S.C. 1985, c. C-34.
32. *Real Estate and Business Brokers Act*, R.S.O. 1990, c. R.4, s. 22.

Business enterprises should take care to meet their statutory and regulatory obligations lest they be faced with a challenge to the legality of a contract they have entered into. Increasingly, however, the consequences of statutory illegality depend on all the circumstances of the case.[33] As one leading text in this area of law states, "If every statutory illegality, however trivial in the course of performance of a contract, invalidated the agreement, the result would be an unjust and haphazard allocation of loss without regard to any rational principles."[34] This statement signals a more flexible perspective, which may fully eclipse the strict, traditional approach which says that illegal contracts are automatically unenforceable.

Contrary to Public Policy

public policy
The community's common sense and common conscience.

At common law, contracts are contrary to **public policy** when they injure the public interest. For example, employment contracts often contain a noncompetition covenant (or clause) preventing the employee from competing with the employer for a certain period of time after the contract ends. Similarly, noncompetition clauses are often found in an agreement for the purchase and sale of a business. If these clauses are drafted too broadly, the courts will not enforce them because they are contrary to public policy. In short, they unduly interfere with an individual's ability to earn a livelihood, and they reduce competition within a sector.

The enforceability of noncompetition clauses is discussed in the following case.[35]

Case

Elsley v. *J.G. Collins Insurance Agencies Limited,*
[1978] 2 S.C.R. 916

The Business Context: The purchaser of a business often wants to prevent the vendor from competing against him for a specified period of time in order to prevent the vendor from setting up a similar business across the street. If the purchaser hires the vendor to work at the business, the employment contract may also contain a noncompetition covenant for a related reason.

Factual Context: Elsley and Collins entered into a purchase and sale agreement, whereby Collins purchased Elsley's general insurance business. This agreement contained a noncompetition covenant, which stipulated that Elsley was restricted from carrying on or engaging in the business of a general insurance company within a certain geographic area for a period of 10 years. By a separate employment agreement, Elsley worked as a manager for Collins. This agreement also contained a noncompetition covenant covering the same geographic area, whereby

Elsley could not compete with Collins for a period of 5 years after he ceased to work for Collins. After 17 years, Elsley resigned and opened his own general insurance business, which took some of Collins' customers.

The Legal Question: Is the noncompetition covenant in Elsley's employment contract valid?

Resolution: In finding the noncompetition covenant to be valid, the court stated,

A covenant in restraint of trade is enforceable only if it is reasonable between the parties and with reference to the public interest. As with many of the cases which come before the Courts, competing demands must be weighed. There is an important public interest in discouraging restraints of trade, and maintaining free and open competition unencumbered by the fetters of restrictive covenants. On the other hand, the courts have been disinclined to restrict the rights to contract, particularly when the right has been exercised by knowledgeable persons of equal bargaining power. In assessing the opposing interests the word one finds repeated throughout the cases is the word "reasonable." The

---

33. See *Still* v. *M.N.R.,* [1998] 1 F.C. 549 (C.A.).
34. S.M. Waddams, *The Law of Contracts,* 4th ed. (Aurora: Canada Law Book, 1999) at 572.
35. Written and researched by Dion Legge.

test of reasonableness can be applied, however, only in the peculiar circumstances of the particular case....

After stating that noncompetition clauses in employment contracts are to be more strictly interpreted than those contained in an agreement for the sale of a business, the justice provided guidelines for determining whether such clauses are enforceable as being reasonable between the parties. According to the court, the assessment of non-competition clauses involves considering whether:

- the employer has a proprietary interest that he or she is entitled to protect

- the temporal and geographic restrictions are reasonable
- the restrictions are reasonably necessary to protect the employer, given the nature of the business and the nature and character of the employment

Once the reasonableness of a restrictive covenant has been established, it is enforceable unless it runs contrary to the public interest.

Critical Analysis: Why are noncompetition clauses in employment contracts less likely to be enforced than similar clauses in sale of business agreements? What are an employer's "proprietary interests"?

Writing as a Requirement

As a general rule, contracts do not have to be written down in order to be enforceable; however, as set out in the *Statute of Frauds,* there are important exceptions.

The *Statute of Frauds* was imported into Canada from England. Except in Manitoba, where it has been completely repealed,[36] it applies to differing extents in all common law provinces.

The purpose of the *Statute of Frauds* is to prevent fraud and perjury by requiring written proof of certain kinds of contracts. The categories discussed below are of the most relevance to business. A contract falling into these categories must have its essential terms contained in a document or documents signed by the party against whom the contract is to be enforced. Several documents can be combined to meet the requirement if each of the documents can be connected with the others. If the writing requirement cannot be met, however, the contract is generally unenforceable.

Contracts of Guarantee

guarantee
A promise to pay the debt of someone else, should that person default on the obligation.

A **guarantee** is a promise to pay the debt of someone else, should that person default on the obligation. Except in Manitoba, a guarantee must be evidenced in writing.

The province of Alberta has gone even further than the *Statute of Frauds* by requiring additional formalities from noncorporate guarantors, including the requirement that the written guarantee be accompanied by a notary's certificate. In this certificate, the notary attests that the guarantor understands the consequences of entering into the guarantee and that the guarantee is freely given.[37]

Contracts Not to Be Performed within a Year

The rationale for requiring a written record of these kinds of contracts is the difficulty of proving promises, which were possibly made in the distant past. Since the arbitrary cutoff of one year is bound to be unfair in some cases, the courts have been known to interpret the *Statute of Frauds* in such a way as to avoid an injustice.

---

36. *An Act to Repeal the Statute of Frauds,* R.S.M. 1987, C. F-158. British Columbia, has also repealed the *Statute of Frauds* with the *Law Reform Amendment Act,* S.B.C. 1985, c. 10, s. 8. However, s. 59 of the *Law and Equity Act,* R.S.B.C. 1996, c. 253 requires contracts for land or a disposition of land, as well as contracts of guarantee and indemnity, to be in writing in order to be enforced unless the transaction fits with an exception contained in s. 59.

37. See the *Guarantees Acknowledgement Act,* R.S.A. 1980, c. G-12. British Columbia has extended the writing requirement to indemnities owing to the *Law and Equity Act,* R.S.B.C. 1996, c. 253, s. 59(6).

E-Business: Writing in Cyberspace

Commercial contracts are generally enforceable, no matter what form they take, but there are important exceptions. There are writing requirements in numerous statutes, including the *Statute of Frauds* and the *Sale of Goods Act*, as well as in consumer protection legislation and even the *Bank Act*.

Since most of these Acts do not define "in writing," the *Interpretation Act* of the applicable province may provide some guidance. For example, Alberta's *Interpretation Act* defines "writing" to include words represented or reproduced "by any mode of representing or reproducing words in visible form" (section 25(1)(z)). Whether this definition accommodates electronic documents is debatable. An electronic document that is represented in digitized format in computer memory or in a storage means, such as a disk, tape, or CD-ROM, may not constitute "in writing" as it is not in "visible form." On the other hand, a reproduction that is obtained by making a hard copy of the digitized representation in human-readable format may indeed constitute "in writing."

Similar concerns surround signature requirements. A common definition of a signature is a "physical, handwritten mark that authenticates a document." The courts, however, have been quite liberal in applying the signature requirement and have accepted typewritten names, initials, and the like as signatures. Whether an electronic signature, such as a personal identification number, fits the definition of signature is unclear and has not, to date, been the subject of established case law.

Parties intending to transact in cyberspace should adopt trading agreements whereby they specifically agree that their electronic messages will constitute "writings" for purposes of the applicable law or that their electronic agreements will be considered "signed writings" when they are transmitted according to a predetermined format.

Legislators have begun to recognize the need for guidance in this area. Most U.S. states are considering legislation on digital signatures. Ontario's *Electronic Commerce Act*, 2000, also addresses this emerging area. Section 11(1), for example, provides that, with some exceptions, "a legal requirement that a document be signed is satisfied by an electronic signature."

Source: Michael Erdle, "Legal Issues in Electronic Commerce" (1996) 12 C.I.P.R. 251; and Alan Gahtan, Martin Kratz, et al., *Internet Law: A Practical Guide for Legal and Business Professionals* (Scarborough: Carswell, 1998) at 313.

The requirement of writing for this kind of contract has been repealed in Ontario,[38] British Columbia, and, of course, Manitoba.

Contracts Dealing with Land

Except for in Manitoba, contracts concerning land—including leases and sales—generally must be evidenced in writing in order to be enforceable. In the interest of fairness, the courts have also created an exception to the absolute requirement for writing in the case of "part performance." If the person attempting to enforce an oral agreement for purchase and sale of land has performed acts in relation to the land that could be explained by the existence of an agreement, that performance may be accepted in place of a written agreement.[39]

---

38. *Statute of Frauds*, R.S.O. 1990, c. S-19, s. 4, repealed by *Statute Law Amendment Act,* S.O. 1994, c. 27, s. 55.

39. It is beyond the scope of this text to discuss the varying tests for part performance that exist at common law.

The mortgage given by the Smiths to the bank must comply with the *Statute of Frauds,* since it concerns an interest in land. That is, through the mortgage, the bank acquires the right to sell the land and apply the proceeds against the Smiths' loan, should they default on payments. The mortgage prepared by the bank appears to meet the requirements of the *Statute of Frauds* because the agreement is a written contract and has been signed by the Smiths.

Contracts for the Sale of Goods

All provinces have a version of the *Sale of Goods Act,* and most[40] contain a provision that contracts for the sale of goods above a specified amount must be in writing to be enforceable by the courts. The amount is generally set at $50 and is not adjusted to reflect inflation. Thus, it would appear that most sales of goods are caught by the Act. Since written contracts are generally not produced for routine transactions, it is fortunate that sales of goods legislation also contains very broad exceptions that limit the application of the rule. For example, if partial payment is made by the buyer, or if the buyer accepts all or part of the goods, no written evidence is required for the contract to be enforceable.

Conclusion

Even without *Statute of Frauds* requirements, creating a record of an agreement is generally a prudent business decision. Personnel may change and memories may fade, and genuine disagreement as to the terms of a contract can be the result. Through a well-recorded written document, such disagreements—and perhaps the expense of litigation—can be avoided.

That said, businesses and individuals must strike a reasonable balance between the comfort of complete records and the time and effort required to produce them, particularly in small transactions.

Business Law in Practice Revisited

1. Did Jones manipulate or pressure the Smiths into signing the mortgage? If so, what legal remedies do the Smiths have?

While the Smiths have the capacity to contract and were not subject to duress by Jones, the mortgage transaction is probably unconscionable. There was inequality between the parties—namely the bank and the Smiths—because the Smiths were inexperienced senior citizens who had received no prior independent legal advice. As well, the transaction was very unfair, since the Smiths were risking their only substantial asset for a loan they could never repay on their own. In short, only the bank and Martha would benefit from the transaction, while the Smiths stood to lose everything. On this basis, both of the steps necessary to establish unconscionability have been met, and a court will set the mortgage aside. The contract will be unenforceable.

The mortgage transaction is also liable to be set aside at common law on the grounds that it was signed on the basis of undue influence. There is a good argument that the Smiths did not freely enter into the mortgage but did so only because Jones

---

40. The exceptions are New Brunswick, Manitoba, Ontario, and British Columbia. Note that in British Columbia, for example, certain executory contracts must be in writing by virtue of the *Consumer Protection Act,* R.S.B.C. 1996, c. 69, s. 13. See G.H.L. Fridman, *Sale of Goods in Canada,* 4th ed. (Scarborough: Carswell, 1995) at 46.

preyed on their deep need to help Martha, their daughter. As well, it appears that the Smiths put their entire trust in Jones, which is another basis for a court to find undue influence.

2. Did Mr. and Mrs. Smith enter into the contract on the basis of mistake or misrepresentation? If so, what legal remedies do they have?

The Smiths could argue that they did not understand what they were signing and that the whole thing was a "mistake." This may be true from their point of view, but they did sign the mortgage document. The law ordinarily expects people not to sign documents unless they understand them. Accordingly, the mortgage is unlikely to be set aside on the grounds of mistake.

There is a very strong argument, however, that Jones misrepresented the nature of the transaction by telling the Smiths that signing the mortgage was just a formality and that likely nothing would come of it. While it could be argued that this statement was merely an opinion, this defence is unlikely to succeed since the words were spoken by a banker who should and does know better. While it also could be argued that the Smiths did not *rely* on Jones' statement—in other words, that they knew very well that their house could be foreclosed upon if Martha failed to make the payments—a judge is much more likely to take the Smiths' side. There is an excellent chance that the mortgage would be set aside on the basis of Jones' misrepresentation.

3. How could Jones have managed this transaction better?

Since the essence of a contract is the free and voluntary adoption of obligations, Jones should never have asked the Smiths to sign the mortgage until they had secured independent legal advice.

Furthermore, it would probably have been better for Jones not to have been involved in the transaction at all, and instead to have sent the Smiths elsewhere. Most of the legal problems in this scenario arose because Jones was trying to get a bad loan he had given to Martha off his books. This motivation may have interfered with his judgment in how to handle the Smiths from the outset.

Chapter Summary

There is a broad range of doctrines available to cancel all or part of a contract, but they apply only in relatively unusual or extreme circumstances. Moreover, courts are justifiably demanding in what parties must prove in order to be released from their obligations. They expect parties to negotiate carefully and deliberately to ensure that any commitment they make accurately reflects their intentions. If the deal merely turns out to be less desirable than expected, the doctrines in this chapter are unlikely to apply.

With limited exceptions, contracts made by minors are not enforceable against them. At common law, unless the contract is for a necessary or amounts to a beneficial contract of service, it is unenforceable at the election of the minor. In British Columbia, minors have even more protection through legislation. Persons suffering from a mental impairment also do not generally have the capacity to contract when they are incapable of understanding the transaction.

The doctrine of duress permits a court to set aside a contract when one of the parties was subjected to such coercion that true consent to the contract was never given. The doctrine of undue influence permits the same outcome if one party, short of issuing threats, has unfairly influenced or manipulated someone else into entering into a contract. Unconscionability also considers the unequal relationship between the two contracting parties. If both inequality between the parties and an improvident bargain can be established, the contract can be rescinded by the court. Other courts have invoked the doctrine when the transaction has gone against community standards of commercial morality.

Misrepresentation concerns the parties' knowledge of the circumstances underlying a contract. If one party misrepresents a relevant fact and thereby induces the other side to enter into the contract, the innocent party can seek to have the contract set aside or rescinded. If the misrepresentation also counts as a tort, the innocent party is entitled to damages as well.

A party who has entered into a contract based on wrong information can try to have the contract set aside on the basis of mistake, but this strategy will rarely be successful. This is because mistake is an exceedingly narrow legal doctrine.

Contracts that are illegal because they violate a statute or are at odds with public policy can also be rescinded. Courts are increasingly looking at all the circumstances surrounding the contract and will not automatically set them aside.

The *Statute of Frauds*, in its various forms, seeks to prevent fraud and perjury by requiring written proof of certain kinds of contracts.

Study Chapter

Questions for Review

1. Who has the legal capacity to form contracts?

2. What must be proven by someone seeking to avoid a contract based on mental impairment?

3. Describe the doctrine of undue influence.

4. What is an unconscionable transaction?

5. Give an example of economic duress.

6. What is a misrepresentation?

7. How does the concept of a legal mistake differ from its ordinary meaning?

8. What is the role of public policy in contract enforcement?

9. How are noncompetition covenants used in employment contracts?

10. How does the *Statute of Frauds* affect contracts?

11. What four types of contracts relevant to business law are required to be in writing?

Questions for Discussion

1. How important is the sanctity of contracts—the principle that once a contract is made, it should be enforced?

2. Do the courts have too much discretion in deciding whether to enforce contracts?

3. Are there too many ways to avoid a contract? Can the conclusion be drawn that there may always be an argument for avoiding a contract?

4. Should negotiators be required to disclose all information relevant to a transaction to each other?

5. What factors should a business consider in developing a policy on documentation of commercial relationships?

6. Review the contract examples at the end of Chapter 7. What challenges are created in this chapter for the parties to those contracts?

Situations for Discussion

1. Carlsen was sued by Financial Collection Services for outstanding principal and interest on a student loan. He claimed he had no recollection of receiving money from a student loan or of signing loan agreements and that he has been mentally unstable for most of his life. A letter from a psychiatrist indicated that Carlsen had severe mental problems for a long time. Is the loan agreement enforceable? What are the implications for the lending policies of those who grant student loans?[41]

2. Tim Donut Ltd. was founded by Tim Horton, a professional hockey player, in 1964. Ron Joyce, the company's first franchisee, became an equal partner with Horton in 1966. Tim Horton died in 1974, and his wife inherited his share of the business. In 1975 she sold that share to Joyce for $1 million. Mrs. Horton now claims that after the death of her husband, she became addicted to drugs and did not know what she was doing when she sold her share. She says she was unaware for days that she had sold her interest and remembers little from the day of the sale, other than sitting in an office and signing some papers. She now seeks to have the contract cancelled.

    What doctrines in this chapter are relevant to the situation? What further information is needed to apply those doctrines? What are the major challenges that Mrs. Horton faces to succeeding on her claim?

3. Stewart bought a business operating in rented space in a shopping mall. Shortly after she took over the business, the landlord pressured her to sign a lease that made her responsible for the arrears in rent of the previous tenant. She was unso-

---

41. Based, in part, on *Financial Collection Services Ltd.* v. *Carlsen* (1995), 166 A.R. 78 (Q.B.).

phisticated in business dealings and signed the lease without seeking advice. Is she obligated to the lease?[42]

4. Brace was considering the purchase of a mortgaged apartment building. He incorporated a numbered company to be the purchaser. He visited the bank holding the mortgage in order to have the mortgage transferred to him. Brace alleges that the bank employee with whom he spoke assured him that the building was worth more than the purchase price and was an excellent investment in an expanding market but, since a company was buying the building, Brace would be required to give a personal guarantee of the mortgage debt. Brace bought the building, took over the mortgage, and signed the guarantee. In the months following the purchase, the value of the building fell sharply, owing to an economic downturn, deterioration of the building, a high vacancy rate, a glut of similar accommodation, and a lack of investment in property in the area. Brace defaulted on the mortgage, and the bank foreclosed and claimed on the guarantee. Brace now claims that the bank employee misled him and that he did not understand the nature of the guarantee he signed. Can he avoid his obligations?[43]

5. The Craig Agency operates an employment agency business by obtaining orders for job openings from employers, obtaining job applicants, and then trying to match the applicant with the job opening. Bennett and Leek were employed as counsellors with the agency, and their employment contracts included this covenant:

> 8. Non-Competition.... It is understood and agreed that in the event of the cancellation of this Agreement, Counsellor shall not, for a period of three months from the date of said termination, engage in the employment agency business, directly or indirectly, or as an owner, operator, partner, officer, director, shareholder, employee or contractor of another employment agency situated or operated within a radius of 25 miles of Agency. Counsellor warrants and represents to Agency that in the event that the restrictions set forth herein become operative, he will be able to engage in other business or businesses for the purpose of earning a livelihood.

Are Bennett and Leek bound by the noncompetition clause? What are the relevant factors? What should they do if they decide to leave Craig and open their own agency?[44]

6. Wendy and Sam were shareholders of a corporation that built and sold homes. Symphony and Rose were the developers and builders of high-rise condominium projects. They told Wendy and Sam that a penthouse apartment was still available in their project. Wendy and Sam provided Symphony and Rose's real estate agent with information relevant to the purchase and delivered cheques for the various deposits. The agent told them that in a few days they would be required to sign an offer on Symphony and Rose's standard form. They thought they had a deal. A few days later, a senior representative of S&R contacted Wendy and Sam to tell them that the penthouse had already been sold and 40 units were currently available.

Do Wendy and Sam have an enforceable agreement? Should they have done anything differently?

---

42. Based, in part, on *Stewart* v. *Canada Life Assurance Co.* (1994), 132 N.S.R. (2d) 324 (C.A.).

43. Based, in part, on *Toronto Dominion Bank* v. *2047545 Nova Scotia Ltd. and Brace* (1996), 148 N.S.R. (2d) 228 (C.A.).

44. Based, in part, on *Craig Agency of Ontario* v. *Bennett* (1977), 14 O.R. (2d) 740 (H.C.J.).

Nine Chapter

Termination and Enforcement of Contracts

Objectives

AFTER STUDYING THIS CHAPTER, YOU SHOULD HAVE AN UNDERSTANDING OF:

► THE TERMINATION OF A CONTRACT BY PERFORMANCE
► THE TERMINATION OF A CONTRACT BY AGREEMENT
► THE TERMINATION OF A CONTRACT BY FRUSTRATION
► THE METHODS OF ENFORCING CONTRACTS
► THE CONCEPT OF PRIVITY
► REMEDIES FOR BREACH OF CONTRACT

Business Law in Practice

Bridget Murphy hired Carla Seifner, the owner of a wedding supply and catering company, to cater a wedding reception, as well as a small buffet luncheon at a gift-opening party to be held on the day following the wedding reception. Bridget and her groom chose the menu and wine and selected the china and table linens for the reception. Carla was asked to supply flowers, as well. As for the buffet luncheon, Bridget left all the details to Carla, since it was a smaller event and did not require her personal touch.

The breakdown of the costs was as follows:

wedding reception:	$18 000
buffet luncheon:	2000
flowers:	750
TOTAL:	$20 750, including GST

Bridget was particularly anxious about the reception—as she said over and over again, this was to be her perfect day. Carla was experienced in dealing with such pre-wedding jitters. She assured Bridget that she and her staff were professionals and knew what they was doing. Bridget gave Carla a $10 000 deposit and agreed to leave everything in her capable hands.

The big day came, and, unfortunately, there were several problems associated with the reception:

- *The forgotten flowers.* Carla's assistant completely forgot to order the flowers. This oversight was discovered only two hours before the guests were to arrive at the reception hall. The bride was temporarily beside herself but then had the idea of calling a local florist to send over the necessary bouquets on a rush basis. The florist agreed to do so but said she would send only the flowers she had on hand and only for a premium, given the short notice. The bouquets arrived in time, but they were very expensive ($3000) and not in the colours Bridget had originally wanted.
- *The wrong china.* When Carla began to set the tables, she discovered that her assistant had mistakenly sent along low-grade dishes instead of the china that Bridget had specified, and it was too late to change them.
- *Possible food poisoning.* Bridget's grandparents and great uncle began to experience abdominal cramps at the end of the evening. Though she is not 100 percent sure of the cause, Bridget attributes it to the raw egg white that Carla admits to using in the icing on the wedding cake. Carla disagrees and suspects that Bridget's relatives simply overindulged at the reception. Bridget has kept a sample of the icing to be tested for salmonella.

Apart from these significant difficulties, Carla did everything else she had promised to do in the contract, and the evening otherwise went off without a hitch. Bridget was nonetheless furious with Carla, telling her she had ruined the wedding and not to bother catering the buffet luncheon the next day. "You've already poisoned several of my relatives," she said. "I'm not going to give you a chance to finish off the rest of them. " Bridget hired another caterer, who supplied the luncheon for $5000.

Carla waited a week or two for things to settle down. She then sent her account to Bridget for $10 750—the full balance owing under the contract—but Bridget refused to pay. Seeing no alternative, Carla sued Bridget for breach of contract. Bridget responded by suing Carla for the return of her $10 000 deposit, as well as damages for out-of-pocket expenses, including the cost of the replacement caterer, and emotional distress.

1. Can Bridget prove that Carla was in breach of contract?
2. Did Bridget properly mitigate her loss?
3. What damages will Bridget receive, assuming that she can establish breach of contract?
4. Is Bridget in breach of contract for refusing to permit Carla to cater the event on the next day and refusing to pay Carla's account?

A catering contract can raise many issues related to termination and enforcement of contracts.

Termination of Contracts: An Overview

When parties enter into a contract, there are several ways in which it can be brought to an end—known, in law, as "termination":

- *Through performance.* When both parties fulfill their contractual obligations to each other, they have *performed* the contract. This is generally the ideal way of concluding a contractual relationship.
- *Through agreement.* Parties are always free to voluntarily bring their contract to an end. Both parties could agree to simply walk away from their agreement, or one party could pay a sum to the other side by way of settlement in exchange for agreeing to end the contract.
- *Through frustration.* The doctrine of frustration applies when, after the formation of a contract, an important, unforeseen event occurs—such as the destruction of the subject matter of the contract or the death/incapacity of one of the contracting parties. The event must be one that makes performance functionally impossible or illegal.[1] When a contract is frustrated, it is brought to an end.
- *Through breach.* A breach of contract, when it is particularly serious, can release the innocent party from having to continue with the contract if that is his or her wish. Less significant breaches generally entitle such a party to damages only.

What follows is a discussion of these four methods of termination and an outline of the remedies available for breach of contract.

---

1. G.H. Treitel, *The Law of Contract*, 10th ed. (London: Sweet & Maxwell, 1999) at 805-806.

Termination through Performance

What amounts to termination by performance depends on the nature of the contract, as in the following examples:

- A contract to provide an audit of a corporation is performed when the audit is competently completed and the auditor's account for service rendered is paid in full.
- A contract to buy and sell a house is performed when the purchase price is paid and title to the property is transferred to the buyer.
- A contract to provide a custom-designed generator is complete when a generator conforming with contract specifications is delivered and the purchase price paid.

In short, a contract is performed when all of its implied and express promises have been fulfilled. When a contract is terminated through performance, this does not necessarily mean the end of the commercial relationship between the parties, however. They may continue to do business with each other by means of new, continuing, and overlapping contracts.

Performance by Others

The law easily distinguishes between those who have the contractual obligation to perform and those who may actually *do* the necessary work. When a corporation enters into a contract to provide goods or services, for example, it must by necessity work through employees/agents. Even when the contracting party is an individual, employees may still have an important role. In both cases, the employee/agent is ordinarily not a party to the contract. Expressed in legal terms, such an employee/agent lacks privity of contract and therefore cannot sue or be sued *on the contract,* though there may be liability in tort. Privity is discussed in more detail later in this chapter. Agency is discussed in Chapter 13.

vicarious performance
Performance of contractual obligations through others.

It is permissible to use employees to **vicariously perform** a contract in question, as long as *personal* performance by the particular contracting individual is not an express or implied term of a contract. For example, if a client engages an accountant and makes it clear that only that particular accountant is to do the work, performance through other accountants is not permitted. If there is no such term, the accountant is free to delegate the work to others in the firm while remaining contractually responsible for the timing and quality of the work.

In the case of Carla the caterer, there was nothing in the contract requiring Carla to perform the contract unassisted. In fact, it would appear that Bridget fully understood that Carla would use staff members to help her. For this reason, Carla is not in breach of contract simply because she did not perform every aspect of the contract with her own hands. She is, however, in breach of contract because her assistant failed to properly perform aspects of the contract: the assistant forgot to order flowers and sent along the wrong kind of dishes. The law holds Carla responsible for her assistant's incompetence.

Termination by Agreement

By Agreement between Parties

Parties may enter into an agreement that becomes unfavourable for one or both of them. In response, they may decide to

novation
The substitution of parties in a contract or the replacement of one contract with another.

- *Enter into a whole new contract.* This is known as **novation**. Provided both parties benefit from this arrangement, the agreement will be enforceable by the court as a new contract. For example, if Bridget subsequently decides that she wants to provide a more expensive menu to her guests, she and Carla are free to negotiate a new contract and to cancel the old one.
- *Vary certain terms of the contract.* As discussed in Chapter 6, the party benefiting from the variation must provide consideration to the other side. Without consideration, a variation is usually not enforceable.
- *End the contract.* The parties may decide to simply terminate the contract, with both parties agreeing not to enforce their rights or with one party paying the other to bring his or her obligations to an end.
- *Substitute a party.* The law permits a more limited form of novation whereby one party's rights and obligations are transferred to someone else. In short, a new party is substituted, and the old party simply drops out of the contract altogether. For example, if Carla the caterer discovered that she had double-booked herself and could not in fact cater Bridget's wedding reception, she might be able to recommend someone else who would step into her "contractual shoes." This new caterer would assume all of Carla's obligations but also be entitled to payment by Bridget. However, everyone—Bridget, Carla, and the new proposed caterer—must agree to this substitution in order for it to be effective. If Bridget is unhappy with Carla's proposal, for example, she can insist on performance and sue Carla for breach of contract if she fails to perform.[2]

An agreement between the parties is almost always the best way of dealing with events that make the contract disadvantageous in some respect. By taking such a route, the parties are able to avoid the expense and uncertainty of litigation.

Transfer of Contractual Rights

A party who wants to end his or her involvement in a particular contract has the option—in certain circumstances—to transfer it to someone else. In short, while contractual duties or obligations cannot be transferred to someone else without agreement by the other side, contractual *rights* can be transferred without any such permission being required.

This means that Carla cannot unilaterally transfer to another caterer her *obligation* to cater Bridget's wedding reception. Bridget has contracted for performance by Carla and her staff and cannot be forced to deal with a new caterer altogether. However, Carla can transfer her right to be *paid* for the catering job to someone else, and this would not be Bridget's concern.

assignment
The transfer of a contractual right by an assignor to an assignee.

In law, when one party transfers a contractual right to someone else, this is known as an **assignment** (see Figure 9.1). The person who is now or will be entitled to payment from a contract is known as a creditor. The party who is obligated to make the payment is known as a debtor.

---

2. If she chooses this route, Bridget still has a duty to mitigate, as discussed later in this chapter.

The law of assignment of rights permits the creditor (the assignor) to assign the right to collect to another person (the assignee) without the agreement of the debtor. To be effective, the creditor must inform the debtor of the assignment (give notice) so that the debtor knows that he or she should pay the assignee rather than the creditor. The assignee is entitled to collect the debt despite not being involved in the creation of the contract that produced the debt. Conversely, after receiving notice of the assignment, the debtor can perform his or her obligation only by paying the assignee. If the same debt is assigned to more than one assignee, normally the assignee who first notifies the debtor is entitled to payment.[3] Expressed in legal language, the rule is that the assignees who take in good faith rank in the order that they have given notice to the debtor. This means that a later assignee may end up collecting from the debtor ahead of an earlier assignee simply by being the first to give notice to the debtor. In the meantime, the disappointed assignees can sue the assignor for breach of the contract of assignment; however, doing so is usually pointless if the assignor has disappeared or has no resources to pay damages.

The advantage of an assignment for a creditor like Carla is that she can "sell" rights for cash now and let the assignee worry about collecting from Bridget. Of course, Carla will pay a price for this advantage by accepting less than the face value of the debt from the assignee. This discount will reflect the real cost of early receipt, as well as the risk that the debtor cannot or will not pay.

Additionally, the assignee's right to payment is no greater than the right possessed by the assignor. This means, for example, that if Carla breaches her contract with Bridget and becomes entitled to less than the full contract price, Carla's assignor is likewise entitled to less. The objective is to ensure that the debtor—in this case, Bridget—is not disadvantaged by the assignment.[4]

Figure 9.1

THE STEPS IN ASSIGNMENT

Step One: Creditor–Debtor Relationship
C (creditor) ←→ D (debtor)
Contract is entered between C and D, whereby D owes money to C for services rendered.

Step Two: Assignor–Assignee Relationship
C (assignor) ←→ A (assignee)
Contract is entered between C and A, whereby C assigns the debt he or she is owed by D.

Step Three: Assignee–Debtor Relationship
A (assignee) ←→ D (debtor)
A gives notice to D.
D is now obligated to pay debt directly to A.

3. Treitel, *supra* note 1 at 628.
4. *Ibid.* at 635. Note that in certain jurisdictions, there is also legislation related to assignments. These are discussed in G.H. Fridman, *The Law of Contract,* 4th ed. (Scarborough: Carswell, 1999) at 720 and following.

Termination by Frustration

frustration
Termination of a contract by an unexpected event or change that makes performance functionally impossible or illegal.

When a significant, unexpected event or change occurs that makes performance of a contract functionally impossible or illegal, the contract between the parties may be **frustrated**. In such circumstances, both parties are excused from the contract and it comes to an end. Neither side is liable to the other for damages.

Unlike the doctrine of mistake—which relates to severely erroneous assumptions concerning *existing* or *past* circumstances surrounding a contract at its formation—frustration deals with events that occur *after* the contract has been formed. Like mistake, however, the defence of frustration is difficult to establish, given that the purpose of contract law is to enforce voluntarily chosen agreements.

The person claiming frustration must establish that the event or change in circumstances

- was dramatic and unforeseen
- was a matter that neither party had assumed the risk of occurring
- arose without being either party's fault
- makes performance of the contract functionally impossible or illegal[5]

All of these elements must be demonstrated.

Landmark Case

Taylor v. *Caldwell* (1863), 122 E.R. 309 (C.A.)

The Business Context: A common situation giving rise to frustration occurs when the subject matter of the contract is destroyed, as discussed below.

Factual Background: Taylor rented the Surrey Gardens and Music Hall for four days to be used for a series of concerts. Prior to the scheduled concerts, the music hall was destroyed by a fire for which neither party could be faulted, and all of the concerts had to be cancelled. Taylor sued for his expenses related to advertising and other preparations, which were now wasted.

The Legal Question: Was Caldwell in breach of contract for failing to supply the music hall as promised?

Resolution: Since the parties had not expressly or implicitly dealt with who would bear the risk of the music hall being destroyed by fire, the court had to decide whether the contract had been frustrated or not. It reasoned that the existence of the music hall was essential to performance of the contract, or, put another way, its destruction defeated the main purpose of the contract. On this basis, the contract had been frustrated, and Taylor's action failed.

Critical Analysis: Why did the court not simply decide that the owner of the music hall was liable when he failed to supply the promised venue, no matter how extenuating the circumstances?

Many circumstances that may appear to frustrate a contract do not amount to frustration in law. For example, if Carla finds that the food she has contracted to provide at Bridget's wedding has unexpectedly tripled in price, and thus she will suffer a substantial loss on her contract, this circumstance would not amount to frustration. It has become financially disadvantageous to perform the contract, but it is still possible to do so. Similarly, if Carla contracts to provide a certain kind of caviar and no other, which proves to be unavailable at any price, that part of the contract has not been frustrated. Carla has simply made a promise that she cannot keep and is in breach. As a final example, if Carla is unable to perform the catering contract because

5. See Treitel, *supra* note 1 at 805 and following, as well as Fridman, *supra* note 4 at 675 and following.

she has fired her staff at the last minute, the contract may have become impossible to perform, but only owing to Carla's own conduct. Self-induced impossibility does not count as frustration in law.

In those rare cases in which a contract is terminated by frustration—as when the contract expressly states that the goods to be supplied must come from a particular source, which fails[6]—the consequences for the parties are often unsatisfactory. At the moment frustration occurs, any further obligations under the contract cease. If neither party has performed, they are left where they were before the contract was formed. If one party has begun to perform and incurred costs, there is no easy way to compensate that party, the reason being that by definition, the contract has ended through the fault of neither party. Shifting the loss to the other would be no more just than leaving it where it lies. There are complicated and uneven developments in the common law and in the statutes of some provinces that attempt to address these problems, but these are beyond the scope of this book.[7]

Force Majeure Clauses

INTERNATIONAL PERSPECTIVE

The commercial objective of parties to a contract sometimes can be defeated by circumstances beyond their control. Unforeseen events, both natural and human-made, may occur that make performance onerous or even impossible. The risk of unforeseen events is particularly great in international transactions. Storms, earthquakes, and fires may destroy the subject matter of the contract. Wars, blockades, and embargoes may prevent the performance of the contract. Hyperinflation, currency devaluation, and changes in government regulation may create hardship for the parties to the contract.

Legal systems, for the most part, recognize that the occurrence of *some* unforeseen events may be a valid excuse for nonperformance. This notion finds expression in various doctrines, such as commercial impracticality, impossibility, and frustration. The difficulty for traders is that although legal systems recognize this kind of defence, there are varying rules governing when nonperformance is excused without liability on the part of the nonperforming party. It is difficult to predict precisely which events will release a party from contractual obligations. Additionally, exemption from performance is normally restricted to situations where it is impossible to perform—hardship or additional expense involved in performance is usually not an excuse. For these reasons, it is common business practice to include a *force majeure* clause in contracts involving international transactions.

A *force majeure* clause deals with the risk of unforeseen events. It allows a party to delay or terminate a contract in the event of unexpected, disruptive events such as the following:

- fire, flood, tornado, or other natural disaster
- war, invasion, blockade, or other military action
- strike, labour slowdown, walk-out, or other labour problems
- inconvertibility of currency, hyperinflation, currency devaluation, or other monetary changes
- rationing of raw materials, denial of import or export licences, or other governmental action

Critical Analysis: What is the problem with drafting a clause that is very simple, such as, "In the event of a *force majeure*, the affected party may terminate its obligations under a contract"? Similarly, what is the problem with drafting a very specific clause that lists the events that allow a party to terminate the contract?

Source: Mary Jo Nicholson, *Legal Aspects of International Business* (Scarborough: Prentice Hall, 1997) at 175-179.

---

6. *Howell* v. *Coupland* (1876), 1 Q.B.D. 258 (C.A.).
7. For a discussion of statute law applying to frustration, see Fridman, *supra* note 4 at 704 and following.

Enforcement of Contracts

When one party fails to perform its contractual obligations, it is in breach of contract and subject to a lawsuit. To succeed in its action for breach of contract, the plaintiff (the person who initiates the lawsuit) is obligated to demonstrate the following elements to the court's satisfaction, that is, on the **balance of probabilities**:

- *Privity of contract.* The plaintiff has to establish that there is a contract between the parties.
- *Breach of contract.* The plaintiff must prove that the other party (the defendant) has failed to keep one or more promises or terms of the contract.
- *Entitlement to a remedy.* The plaintiff must demonstrate that it has suffered loss as a result of the breach or is otherwise deserving of the court's assistance.

As noted in Chapter 4, the balance of probabilities means that the plaintiff must prove there is a better than 50 percent chance that the circumstances of the contract are as it contends they are and, furthermore, that these circumstances entitle it to receive what is claimed.

Privity of Contract

The concept of privity was introduced in Chapter 5 as a critical ingredient to enforcing a contract. It means that, generally speaking, only those who are parties to a contract can enforce the rights and obligations it contains.[8]

Because a strict application of the doctrine of privity can lead to serious injustices, courts have recently shown a willingness to allow third parties to rely on contractual clauses placed in the contract for their benefit. For example, a contract between a business and a customer may have an exclusion clause protecting employees from liability in the event that the customer suffers a loss. Under a classical approach to privity, employees would not be permitted to rely on such clauses as a defence to any action brought by a disgruntled customer because they are not parties to the contract—only their employer and the customer are. In the case on the next page, however, the Supreme Court of Canada refused to apply privity in this way, choosing instead to create a limited exception to its application.

Carla the caterer could easily establish the first step in a successful breach of contract action against Bridget—namely, privity of contract. Carla and Bridget entered into a contract whereby Carla would supply certain goods and services to Bridget in exchange for a fee. If Carla tried to sue Bridget's groom for breach of contract, however, that action would fail because he is not a party to the contract, though he did help Bridget make the arrangements.

Bridget may well have an action against Carla's assistant, but only for the tort of negligence (discussed in detail in Chapter 11) because she failed to order the flowers and packed the wrong dishes for the reception. There is no action in contract, however, because there is no privity of contract between them.

Similarly, Bridget's relatives who became ill could sue Carla in tort for causing them food poisoning, but not in contract.

---

8. There are a number of ways in which someone who is not a party to a contract may acquire an enforceable benefit, but this chapter discusses only one of them, in the employment context.

Case

London Drugs Limited v. *Kuehne & Nagel International Ltd.* (1992), 97 D.L.R. (4th) 261 (S.C.C.)

The Business Context: Businesses may try to protect their employees from being successfully sued by including clauses in their contracts with customers that shelter employees from liability.

Factual Background: Kuehne & Nagel International Ltd. (K&N) stored a variety of merchandise for London Drugs, including a large transformer. A term in the storage agreement limited K&N's liability on any one item to $40. Owing to the negligence of two K&N employees, the transformer was dropped while it was being moved and sustained over $33 000 in damage. London Drugs brought an action for the full amount of damages against both the employees and K&N. It was acknowledged that K&N's liability was limited to $40.

The Legal Question: Can the employees rely on the clause limiting liability to $40?

Resolution: The trial judge agreed that the negligent employees could be sued by the customers. Expressed in more technical legal language, the court applied the rule that employees are liable for torts they commit in the course of carrying out the services their employer has contracted to provide. Because the K&N employees were negligent in their attempt to lift the transformer, they were liable for the full extent of London Drugs' damages. The employees could not rely on the clause limiting recovery to $40 because this clause was found in a contract to which they were not a party. Put another way, the employees lacked privity to the contract between London Drugs and K&N.

In response to the harshness that the strict doctrine of privity creates in this kind of situation, the Supreme Court of Canada created an exception to its application. As Justice Iacobucci explains,

> This court has recognized ... that in appropriate circumstances, courts have not only the power but the duty to make incremental changes to the common law to see that it reflects the emerging needs and values of our society:... It is my view that the present appeal is an appropriate situation for making such an incremental change to the doctrine of privity of contract in order to allow the ...[employees] to benefit from the limitation of liability clause.

> ... I am of the view that employees may obtain such a benefit if the following requirements are satisfied:

> (1) the limitation of liability clause must, either expressly or impliedly, extend its benefit to the employees (or employee) seeking to rely on it; and

> (2) the employees (or employee) seeking the benefit of the limitation of liability clause must have been acting in the course of their employment *and* must have been performing the very services provided for in the contract between their employer and the plaintiff (customer) when the loss occurred.

The court went on to hold that the employees could rely on the limitation of liability clause. This is because the clause in question did extend its benefit to the employees and, when the transformer was damaged, it was due to the negligence of the employees while doing the very thing contracted for, as employees. Though the negligence of the employees caused London Drugs damages in the amount of $33 955.41, it was entitled to recover only $40 from the employees.

Critical Analysis: Do you agree with Justice Iacobucci's decision? Should employees be able to rely on a clause in a contract to which they are not parties? How could employees protect themselves if they were not permitted to rely on such a clause?

Breach of Contract

Classification of the Breach

Virtually every breach of contract gives the innocent party the right to a remedy. When determining what that remedy should be, the courts will first consider whether the term breached can be classified as a condition or a warranty.

A contractual term will be classified as a condition or warranty only if that is the parties' contractual intention. Courts will consider all the circumstances surrounding

condition
An important term, which, if breached, gives the innocent party the right to terminate the contract and claim damages.

either contract to end or want damages

warranty
A minor term, which, if breached, gives the innocent party the right to claim damages only.

innominate term
A term that cannot easily be classified as either a condition or a warranty.

fundamental breach
A breach of contract that affects the foundation of the contract.

allowed asking for money may get recession

the contract, including the language chosen by the parties in the contract itself, in making this determination.

A **condition** is an important term, which, if breached, gives the innocent party the right not only to sue for damages, but also to treat the contract as ended. This latter right means that, if it so chooses, the nondefaulting party can consider itself to be freed from the balance of the contract and to have no further obligations under it. For example, it would be an implied term of the contract between Bridget and Carla that the food supplied would not cause food poisoning or other illness. This is a significant term, and its breach therefore would permit Bridget to end the contract. On this basis, Carla has breached a condition of the agreement, and Bridget is not obligated to use Carla's services for the buffet luncheon part of the contract. However, Bridget must be prepared to prove—perhaps through the results of a lab test of the icing sample—that the cake was contaminated with an illness-causing toxin. Otherwise, Bridget faces the risk that she herself will be found to have been in breach of contract for not permitting Carla to cater the buffet luncheon.

A term classified as a **warranty** is a promise of less significance or importance. When a warranty is breached, the innocent party is entitled to damages only. Carla's failure to provide the flowers and proper dishes is likely to be regarded as a breach of warranty, entitling Bridget to damages only.

Even after the parties' intentions have been assessed, some terms cannot easily be classified as warranties or conditions and are known in law as **innominate terms**. In such circumstances, the court must look at exactly what has happened in light of the breach before deciding whether the innocent party is entitled to repudiate the contract. For example, it is a term of Bridget's and Carla's contract that Carla supply the menu that Bridget chose. It would be difficult to classify such a term as either a condition or a warranty of the contract on the spot because, presumably, the parties have not done so themselves and, furthermore, it is the kind of term that could be breached in large and small ways. If Carla failed to supply a few of the smaller items Bridget had ordered, this is likely a breach of a warranty-like term, giving rise to a claim for damages only. On the other extreme, if Carla provided nothing from the chosen menu, replacing it with vastly inferior food, that would be a breach of a condition-like term, allowing Bridget to end the contract and cancel Carla's involvement in the buffet luncheon scheduled for the next day.

Exclusion or Limitation of Liability Clause

As already noted, parties are free to include a clause in their contract that limits or excludes liability for breach. This is what the storage company did in the *London Drugs* case discussed earlier. Historically, courts have been reluctant to allow the party in breach to rely on such a clause when the breach in question was severe and undermined the whole foundation of the contract. This is known as a **fundamental breach**. The argument is that such a breach automatically renders the entire contract (including the exclusion clauses) inoperative, and therefore the innocent party should be compensated. While such judicial concern might be helpful in a consumer contract, it is less welcome in a commercial context. The Supreme Court of Canada has therefore weighed in on the issue in *Hunter Engineering Co.* v. *Syncrude Canada Ltd.*, described on the following page, but this case provides limited assistance because the judges split between two competing approaches,[9] making the law in the area unclear.

---

9. As Fridman notes, *supra* note 4 at 634, "Far from resolving ... issues relating to fundamental breach and its effect on exclusion clauses, the decision of the Supreme Court of Canada ... can be said to have left a legacy of more uncertainty. In it two different views were expounded as to the proper method of dealing with such clauses where a fundamental breach occurred, although, in the case in question, no such breach was held to have been involved."

Case

Hunter Engineering Co. v. Syncrude Canada Ltd.
(1989), 57 D.L.R. (4th) 321 (S.C.C.)

The Business Context: Those who provide goods and services frequently include contractual clauses to limit or exclude their liability in the event of breach. Sometimes, these clauses are even intended to cover the situation of fundamental breach.

Factual Background: Syncrude purchased gearboxes, which are used to drive conveyor belts at its oil sands operation in Alberta. These gearboxes were purchased from Hunter Engineering and from Allis-Chalmers. Both the Hunter and Allis-Chalmers gearboxes were designed by Hunter U.S. and manufactured by a subcontractor. Both purchase contracts contained express warranties with time limits. Additionally, the contract between Syncrude and Allis-Chalmers contained a clause expressly excluding any other warranty or condition, "statutory or otherwise."

After the expiry of the express warranties and conditions, the gearboxes failed owing to a design defect in the manner in which the gears were welded. Syncrude repaired the gearboxes at its own considerable expense and brought an action against both Hunter Engineering and Allis-Chalmers for breach of contract.

The Legal Question: What is Hunter's liability under its contract with Syncrude? What is Allis-Chalmers' liability under the doctrine of fundamental breach? Can it rely on the exclusion clause in its contract with Syncrude, given the nature of its breach?

Resolution: The Supreme Court held that the welding design details were the seller's responsibility, and that the failure of the gearboxes constituted a breach of a condition that the gearboxes be fit for the purpose sold. The presence of an express warranty or condition did not exclude the statutorily implied terms. Thus, Hunter was liable to Syncrude on this basis. Allis-Chalmers, however, was not liable because of the express exclusion of statutory warranties and conditions.

The court also discussed the issue of whether an exclusion of liability was effective when there is a fundamental breach of contract. Two judges, including Chief Justice Dickson, held that the breach in this case was not a fundamental breach, and in any event, an exclusion of liability for fundamental breach was enforceable unless it was unconscionable.

As Chief Justice Dickson explained,

> The doctrine of fundamental breach in the context of clauses excluding a party from contractual liability has been confusing at the best of times. Simply put, the doctrine has served to relieve parties from the effects of contractual terms, excluding liability for deficient performance where the effects of these terms have seemed particularly harsh.

> In light of the unnecessary complexities the doctrine of fundamental breach has created, the resulting uncertainty in the law, and the unrefined nature of the doctrine as a tool for averting unfairness, I am inclined to lay the doctrine of fundamental breach to rest, and where necessary and appropriate, to deal explicitly with unconscionability.... It is preferable to interpret the terms of the contract, in an attempt to determine exactly what the parties agreed. If on its true construction the contract excludes liability for the kind of breach that occurred, the party in breach will generally be saved from liability. Only where the contract is unconscionable, as might arise from situations of unequal bargaining power between the parties, should the courts interfere with agreements the parties have freely concluded.

Two other judges, including Madam Justice Wilson, took a different approach and would preserve a role for fundamental breach in certain circumstances, though they agreed that no fundamental breach had occurred in this particular case. For these judges, a fundamental breach would render an exclusion clause inoperative or ineffective if, in light of what happened, it would be unfair and unreasonable to allow the defendant to rely on the clause.

Critical Analysis: A clause that excludes or limits liability even for a profoundly serious breach of contract is enforceable, provided it is not unconscionable or would not be unfair or unreasonable. Would it not be better to simply apply the contract and expect parties to take care of themselves, at the bargaining stage, particularly in a contract involving sophisticated business people?

Timing of the Breach

anticipatory breach
A breach that occurs before the date for performance.

A breach of contract can occur at the time specified for performance—as when Carla used the wrong dishes, failed to supply flowers, and possibly even served poisoned food. A breach can also occur in advance of the date named for performance; this is known as an **anticipatory breach**. Anticipatory breaches are actionable because each party to a contract is entitled to a continuous expectation that the other will perform during the entire period between the date the contract is formed and the time for performance.

Bridget arguably committed an anticipatory breach by telling Carla that she would not be permitted to cater the buffet luncheon scheduled for the following day and, by implication, that she would not be paying Carla for arranging that luncheon. Whether this action amounts to an anticipatory breach of contract depends on whether Carla's breaches of contract were sufficiently serious to allow Bridget to treat the contract as ended. This question puts the innocent party in somewhat of a dilemma, since she will not know for sure whether the contract can legally be treated as at an end unless and until the matter is litigated—an event that will occur months or, more likely, years later.

Entitlement to a Remedy

The final step in an action for breach of contract is for the plaintiff to satisfy a court that he or she is entitled to a remedy. In the usual case, damages—or monetary compensation—are awarded, but in specialized circumstances, a plaintiff is entitled to an equitable remedy.

The Measure of Damages

damages
Monetary compensation for breach of contract.

The purpose of **damages** in contract law is to *compensate* a plaintiff for loss, not to *punish* the defendant for breach. Expressed in legal language, the plaintiff, in this case Bridget, is entitled to compensation that puts her, as much as possible, in the financial position she would have been in had the defendant, Carla, performed her obligations under the contract.

This section will provide the necessary background to assess the kinds of damages that Bridget may have sustained owing to Carla's breaches of contract.

Pecuniary and Nonpecuniary Damages

As will be discussed in detail in Chapter 10, damages in tort can be pecuniary (for financial loss) and nonpecuniary (for loss of enjoyment, mental distress, and other emotional consequences). The same holds true in contract law, except that recovery for nonpecuniary damages is very unusual. In law, a defendant is responsible only for the reasonably foreseeable damages sustained by the plaintiff and not for absolutely every adverse consequence experienced by the innocent party after the contract has been breached.[10] While pain and suffering or other emotional distress is reasonably foreseeable when one person negligently injures another in a car accident, it is not generally anticipated as being the consequence of a breach of contract.

TEST FOR REMOTENESS The kinds of damages recoverable in contract law are determined by the test for remoteness, set out in the following case.

---

10. It is beyond the scope of this book to discuss whether the test for remoteness is stricter in contract than it is in tort.

Landmark Case

Hadley v. *Baxendale* (1854), 9 Exch. 341

The Historical Context: This case represents an important effort by the courts to articulate a test that distinguishes between losses that are attributable to the defendant's breach of contract and those that are simply too far removed from the circumstances of the case to be the defendant's responsibility.

Factual Background: Hadley owned a mill, which experienced a work stoppage because an important shaft broke. A replacement shaft was needed, and Hadley hired Baxendale to transport the shaft to Greenwich so that it could be used as a model. Hadley urged Baxendale to send the shaft immediately, but Baxendale failed to do so. As a result, Hadley did not receive the new shaft for several days and therefore lost profits, since the mill was forced to stand idle during that entire time.

The Legal Question: Is Hadley entitled to damages for loss of profit?

Resolution: In determining whether Hadley could recover damages for loss of profit, the court provided the classic test for remoteness in contract. This test provides

that the damage claimed—in this case, for loss of profit—is recoverable provided

1. the damages could have been anticipated, having "arisen naturally" from the breach, or
2. the damages—although perhaps difficult to anticipate in the ordinary case—are reasonably foreseeable because the unusual circumstances were communicated to the defendant at the time the contract was being formed.[11]

The court found that Hadley's claim for loss of profit was too remote because it could not meet either test. The main reason for this finding was that Baxendale, the transporter, had not been told that the mill would remain shut down until the shaft was replaced. As the court observed, "[I]t is obvious that in the great multitude of cases of millers sending off broken shafts to third persons by a carrier under ordinary circumstances, such consequences [i.e., the mill not being able to run at all] would not, in all probability, have occurred; and these special circumstances were never communicated by the plaintiffs to the defendants."

Critical Analysis: The law requires a party like Hadley to take the initiative and communicate any special circumstances surrounding the contract in question. Why not, instead, put the onus on a transporter like Baxendale to *ask* whether such circumstances exist?

Any claim for damages in contract must pass one of the remoteness tests set out above; otherwise, it is simply not recoverable. The policy rationale of such a rule is the need to ensure that defendants do not face unlimited liability for the consequences of a breach and to allow them, by being informed of special circumstances, the option of turning down the job, charging a higher price to compensate for the increased risk, or, perhaps, purchasing the necessary insurance.

RECOVERY OF NONPECUNIARY DAMAGES As already noted, recovery for nonpecuniary damages—such as for mental distress— is rare in contract law, except in the employment context.[12] However, Bridget stands a reasonable chance of successfully claiming for mental suffering, based on the decision in *Newell* v. *Canadian Pacific Airlines Ltd.*

---

11. The exact wording of the test is as follows:

   Where two parties have made a contract which one of them has broken, the damages which the other party ought to receive in respect of such breach of contract should be such as may fairly and reasonably be considered either arising naturally, i.e., according to the usual course of things, from such breach of contract itself, or such as may reasonably be supposed to have been in the contemplation of both parties, at the time they made the contract, as the probable result of the breach of it. Now, if the special circumstances under which the contract was actually made were communicated by the plaintiffs to the defendants, and thus known to both parties, the damages resulting from the breach of such a contract, which they would reasonably contemplate, would be the amount of injury which would ordinarily follow from a breach of contract under these special circumstances so known and communicated.

12. See Chapter 22.

Case

Newell v. *Canadian Pacific Airlines Ltd.* (1976), 14 O.R. (2d) 752 (Co. Ct.)

The Business Context: There are a few cases in which aggrieved parties have received damages for mental distress caused by breach of contract. The amount of damages has been quite low, as this case illustrates.

Factual Background: Canadian Pacific agreed to carry in a safe manner from Toronto to Mexico City two pet dogs owned by the Newells. When the flight arrived in Mexico, one dog was dead and the other comatose. The Newells sought general damages to compensate them for the "anguish, loss of enjoyment of life and sadness" that they allege resulted from the breach of contract.

The Legal Question: Were the Newells entitled to anything other than compensation for direct financial loss, namely the value of the dogs?

Resolution: Judge Borins concluded,

[T]he question that must be asked is this: Was the contract such that the parties must have contemplated that its breach might entail mental distress, such as frustration, annoyance or disappointment? I would answer the question in the affirmative. The contract was to safely carry the plaintiffs' pet dogs from Toronto to Mexico City. On the evidence it is abundantly clear that the defendant was aware of the plaintiffs' concern for the welfare of their pets. The defendant, through its employees, acknowledged the plaintiffs' concern by reassuring them that the dogs would be safe in the cargo compartment of the aircraft and reported to the plaintiffs before they boarded the aircraft that their dogs had been safely placed in the cargo area. I find that the contract was such that the plaintiffs and the defendant must have contemplated that if injury or death were to befall the dogs this might result in the plaintiffs suffering mental distress. The plaintiffs are therefore entitled to recover general [i.e., nonpecuniary] damages in the sum of $500.

Critical Analysis: Should contract law compensate for mental distress? How can a court put a dollar figure on suffering? How did the court determine that $500 was an adequate amount?

Since mental distress following a totally botched wedding reception "arises naturally," thereby passing the test of remoteness, Bridget will be able to recover for mental distress provided she can also prove that the food Carla served at the reception actually did poison some of Bridget's relatives and that Bridget actually suffered emotional trauma or upset as a result.

RECOVERY OF PECUNIARY DAMAGES Those who have suffered a breach of contract can recover all their resulting pecuniary (or monetary) losses unless a clause is included that limits, excludes, or fixes liability at a set amount.[13] Recovery of pecuniary damages is possible in situations such as the following:

- A purchaser of a warehouse with a leaky roof can recover the cost of repairing the roof provided the roof was warranted to be sound.
- A client who suffers a financial loss owing to negligent legal advice can recover those losses from the lawyer in question.
- A person whose goods are stolen while they are in storage can recover the cost of those items from the warehouse owner.

Similarly, Bridget can recover her losses from Carla. Because Carla supplied a lower grade of dishware in breach of contract, Bridget is entitled to recover the difference

---

13. Liquidation of damages clauses were discussed in Chapter 7.

in value between what the wedding did cost ($20 750) and what it should have cost in light of the lower grade of china. More significant, from a damages perspective, is the possibility that Carla provided food contaminated with salmonella. If Bridget can prove that Carla served unfit food, she may be able to recover the full cost of her deposit and have no liability for the balance, on the theory that she got absolutely nothing for her money. While Carla may argue that Bridget should have to pay for all the food that was not tainted, a judge is just as likely to say that such a benefit is totally negated when even one guest suffers food poisoning. On this basis, a court would order Carla to return Bridget's deposit, as well as dismiss Carla's claim for the balance owing under the contract.

duty to mitigate
The obligation to take reasonable steps to minimize the losses resulting from a breach of contract or other wrong.

DUTY TO MITIGATE Everyone who suffers a breach of contract has a **duty to mitigate**. This means that they must take reasonable steps to minimize losses that might arise from the breach, as in the following examples:

- A person who is fired from his job, in breach of contract, has a duty to mitigate by trying to find replacement employment.
- A landlord whose tenant breaches a lease by moving out before the expiry of its term has a duty to mitigate by trying to find a replacement tenant.
- The disappointed vendor whose purchaser fails to complete a real estate transaction has a duty to mitigate by trying to find a replacement purchaser.

If the plaintiff fails to mitigate, its damage award will be reduced accordingly. For example, if the employee making $100 000 a year had one year left on his contract before he was wrongfully terminated, his damages would be $100 000. However, his duty to mitigate requires him to look for comparable employment. If he immediately does so and secures a job at $80 000, his damages drop to $20 000. If he fails to mitigate—by, for example, refusing such a job—a court will reduce his damages by $80 000, since that loss is more attributable to him than to his former employer.

By the same token, any reasonable costs associated with the mitigation are recoverable from the party in breach. An employee could, in addition to damages related to salary loss, also recover *reasonable* expenses related to the job search.

In Bridget's case, the bride mitigated on two occasions. First, when Carla failed to supply the flowers, Bridget secured bouquets from another florist, at a premium because of the short notice. This extra expense for these flowers is recoverable from Carla on the mitigation principle. Similarly, when Bridget hired a replacement caterer because she believed her relatives had suffered food poisoning from Carla's cake, this too counts as mitigation, and the additional cost should also be recoverable from Carla, provided Bridget can convince a court that the food was the cause of her relatives' illness. Otherwise, Bridget herself is in breach of contract for not permitting Carla to complete her job the next day.

Equitable Remedies

In those relatively rare situations in which damages would be an inadequate remedy for breach of contract, the court may exercise its discretion to grant one of the equitable remedies discussed below.

SPECIFIC PERFORMANCE An order by the court for the equitable remedy of specific performance means that instead of awarding compensation for failing to perform, the court orders the party who breached to do exactly what the contract obligated him or her to do. This remedy is available only when the item in question is unique and cannot be replaced by money. The classic situation for specific performance is a contract for the sale of land, where the particular piece of land covered by the contract is essential to the buyer's plans, perhaps as part of a major development project. Without the remaining piece, the project cannot proceed, so damages would fail to provide a complete remedy.

Because specific performance is an equitable remedy, a court can refuse to order it, at its discretion, as in the following circumstances:

- *Improper behaviour by the plaintiff.* Any improper motive or conduct on the part of the plaintiff may disqualify him from being granted such special assistance. Rules governing equity, like "he who seeks equity must do equity" or "she who comes to equity must come with clean hands," mean that only the deserving plaintiff will succeed. Delay by the plaintiff in bringing the claim, for example, can be grounds for denying him an equitable remedy.[14]
- *Impossibility.* A court will not order a defendant to do something that is impossible, such as convey land she does not own.[15]
- *Severe hardship.* If specific performance would cause a severe hardship to the parties, or to a third party, a court may refuse to order it.
- *Employment contracts.* A court will not, ordinarily, order specific performance of an employment contract because being forced to work for someone else against his wishes would interfere too much with the employee's personal freedom.

INJUNCTION If a contract contains promises *not* to engage in specified activities, disregarding those promises by engaging in the prohibited acts is a breach of contract. The only effective remedy would be a court order requiring the offender to refrain from continued violation of the contract. For example, if the vendor of a business agrees not to compete with the new owner and the relevant clauses are reasonable restrictions (see Chapter 8), damages are an inadequate remedy for breach because they fail to prevent the vendor from competing. Only an order to cease doing business will provide the buyer with a complete remedy.

Like an order of specific performance, an injunction is an equitable remedy and is subject to the court's discretion. However, it is commonly ordered to restrain a party from breaching a promise *not* to do something, as noted above. There are occasions where a court will not order an injunction, however, as when the plaintiff does not have "clean hands" (e.g., is undeserving) or delays in bringing the matter before the court.

interlocutory injunction
An order to refrain from doing something for a limited period of time.

Courts also have the jurisdiction to order an injunction for a limited period of time. This type of injunction, known as an **interlocutory injunction**, requires someone to stop doing something until the whole dispute can be resolved through a trial.

RESCISSION It may be appropriate, in some cases, to restore the parties to the situation they were in before the contract was formed, rather than use compensation to put the innocent party in the position it would have been in had the contract been completed. For example, many of the doctrines in Chapter 8 for avoiding contracts provide rescission as the contractual remedy.

---

14. For a discussion and excerpts of relevant case law concerning equitable remedies and defences thereto, see C. Boyle & D. Percy, *Contracts: Cases and Materials*, 6th ed. (Scarborough: Carswell, 1999) at 934 and following.
15. See *Castle* v. *Wilkinson* (1870), 5 L.R. Ch. App. 534.

As with other equitable remedies, there are bars to receiving rescission of a contract. For example, where parties cannot restore each other to their precontractual positions—because, perhaps, the subject matter of the contract has been altered—the court has the power to do what is practically just, including the power to order that the innocent party be compensated. Another bar to rescission is delay by the plaintiff in seeking the court's assistance.

Business Law in Practice Revisited

1. Can Bridget prove that Carla was in breach of contract?

Bridget can meet all the steps to succeed in an action for breach of contract. She can show privity of contract between Carla and her. She can show that Carla breached at least two terms—namely, the term to provide flowers and the term to provide china. With proper proof, such as a toxicology report on the icing, she may also be able to show that Carla breached the contract by serving contaminated food. Finally, Bridget can show that she is entitled to a remedy, as she has suffered both pecuniary and nonpecuniary damages.

2. Did Bridget properly mitigate her loss?

Bridget secured replacement flowers at a premium in response to Carla's breach of contract. This would appear to be an appropriate step, and assuming that the premium was not unreasonably high, her mitigation is proper.

Bridget's other instance of mitigation was hiring a replacement caterer to handle the buffet luncheon on the following day. As long as Bridget can show that Carla served contaminated food and that the replacement caterer's price was not unreasonably high, this too would be considered reasonable mitigation.

3. What damages will Bridget receive, assuming that she can establish breach of contract?

The damages that Bridget will receive depend largely on whether she can prove that Carla's food caused her relatives to become sick. What follows is an analysis based on Bridget's establishing food poisoning and one based on her being unable to prove that point.

SCENARIO 1: BRIDGET PROVES THAT CARLA CAUSED THE FOOD POISONING

Bridget stands a good chance of receiving considerable pecuniary and nonpecuniary damages.

Pecuniary Damages
- return of Bridget's $10 000 deposit

There is a strong argument that Bridget should get the full amount of her deposit back because a wedding reception that makes the guests ill is worth nothing. Bridget got nothing for her money and should therefore receive a full refund from Carla.

- additional cost of flowers (a mitigation cost)

Bridget was obligated to pay $750 for flowers provided that Carla properly performed the contract and supplied the flowers. Owing to Carla's breach,

Bridget had to pay $3000 for the flowers. She is therefore entitled to the difference, namely $2250, assuming that the mitigation was reasonable.

- additional cost of replacement caterers (a mitigation cost)

Bridget was obligated to pay $2000 for the buffet luncheon provided that Carla properly performed the contract. Because of Carla's breach, she had to pay $5000. She is therefore entitled to the difference, namely $3000, assuming that the mitigation was reasonable.

Nonpecuniary Damages

Bridget may also be able to recover damages for mental distress and suffering because a wedding reception that causes illness to the guests is tremendously upsetting and foreseeably so. A court could easily find that both parties would have considered that Bridget might suffer mental distress if Carla's food made the guests ill. On this basis, Bridget would be able to recover damages, though it is difficult to predict how much.

A judge in this scenario would also dismiss Carla's action for breach of contract against Bridget. Bridget is perfectly within her rights to not permit Carla to cater the luncheon and to refuse to pay Carla's account.

SCENARIO 2: BRIDGET CANNOT PROVE THAT CARLA CAUSED THE FOOD POISONING

In this scenario, Bridget has a very weak case. All the court can do is put a value on the kind of reception Bridget actually received and the kind of reception Bridget had contracted for. Bridget will be awarded the difference in value between them. The court will discount the value of the reception in light of the breaches that Bridget can establish, namely the wrong china and the forgotten flowers. This amount is unlikely to be substantial and is probably not worth pursuing through the courts.

Bridget is also unlikely to get nonpecuniary damages under this scenario, since every wedding will have its minor mishaps. What Bridget seems to have been most upset about was that some of her guests became ill, not that the wrong dishes were being used or that the flowers had been forgotten. As she is now unable to prove that Carla was the cause of the illness, the fact that Bridget became upset is not Carla's responsibility.

Under the heading of mitigation, Bridget will almost certainly be able to recover from Carla the premium she paid for the flowers, namely $2250.

Since Bridget cannot prove food poisoning, a court will find that Bridget herself is in breach of contract for failing to let Carla cater the buffet luncheon. This means that Bridget is liable to Carla for the full amount of the contract price ($20 750), minus the deposit already paid ($10 000) and any other discount a court might order because of Carla's minor breaches.

4. **Is Bridget in breach of contract for refusing to permit Carla to cater the event on the next day and for refusing to pay Carla's account?**

The answer to this question depends entirely on whether Bridget can establish that Carla's food made her relatives ill. Causing food poisoning is a breach of condition and allows Bridget to repudiate the contract. Forgetting the flowers and using the wrong dishes are most likely breaches of warranty, which allow Bridget to sue only for damages.

If Bridget cannot establish food poisoning, all she has is her suspicions. On this basis, a court will find that Bridget herself is in breach of contract for not permitting Carla to cater the buffet luncheon. Bridget will then be liable for the balance of the contract price, less any discount for Carla's relatively minor breaches as discussed above.

Chapter Summary

In the vast majority of situations, a contract terminates or ends when the parties fully perform their obligations. Less common are situations where the contract ends because the parties find it impossible or tremendously difficult to perform their obligations. In such cases, prudent business parties will have addressed such a possibility through a force majeure clause or equivalent.

A more usual and complicated situation, from a business perspective, occurs when one party breaches the contract by failing to perform or by performing inadequately. The innocent party must then make a business decision—as much as a legal one—and decide how it should treat that failure This decision involves evaluating the remedies available, calculating the amount of damages, and determining whether the parties can negotiate a settlement, whether the parties want to preserve a business relationship, and ultimately whether it is worthwhile to pursue a court action.

There are several ways that a contract is terminated: by performance, by agreement, through frustration, and through breach.

When a contract is terminated by performance, the parties have fulfilled all their implied and express promises. The work necessary to achieve performance may be done by the parties personally or through their agents/employees, unless a term to the contrary is included.

Sometimes, parties terminate a contract by agreement. For example, the parties may agree to end the contract entirely or to replace it with a new one. Alternatively, the parties may vary certain terms of the contract or substitute a new party who, in turn, assumes rights and duties under the contract.

Contract law allows one party to assign his or her *right* under a contract but not the liabilities. The law of assignment permits the creditor to assign her or his right to collect under a contract to another (the assignee) without the agreement of the debtor. Once the creditor (assignor) has given notice to the debtor, the latter can only perform the obligation by paying the assignee.

The doctrine of frustration terminates a contract, but only in very limited circumstances. It must be shown that an unanticipated event or change in circumstances is so substantial that performance has become functionally impossible or illegal. Provided the risk of such an event has not been allocated to one party or the other, and provided the event did not arise through either party's fault, the contract has been frustrated.

When one party fails to perform its contractual obligations, it is in breach of contract and subject to a lawsuit. To succeed in its action for beach of contract, the innocent party must establish privity of contract, breach of contract, and entitlement to a remedy.

Privity means that, with limited exceptions, only those who are parties to a contract can enforce the rights and obligations it contains.

When a party to a contract fails to keep its promise, it has committed a breach of contract and is liable for such damages as would restore the innocent party to the position it would have been in had the contract been performed. If there is an exclusion or limitation of liability clause in the contract, the defendant's liability will be reduced or eliminated, depending on the circumstances.

Damages in contract are ordinarily pecuniary, but in limited circumstances the innocent party is entitled to nonpecuniary damages for mental suffering and distress. Nonpecuniary damages are usually not recoverable because they are considered to be too remote in the ordinary commercial context.

When one party suffers a breach of contract, he or she must take reasonable steps to mitigate. If the party fails to do so, the damage award will be reduced accordingly. By the same token, any reasonable costs associated with mitigation are also recoverable from the party in breach.

Contract law also offers equitable remedies, such as specific performance and the injunction, when damages are an inadequate remedy. On occasion, the best solution is to rescind the contract—that is, return the parties to their precontractual positions.

Study Chapter

Questions for Review

1. What is an assignment?
2. What risks does the assignee of a contractual right assume?
3. What is privity of contract?
4. How is vicarious performance used by business?
5. How is a new contract created through novation?
6. When is a contract frustrated?
7. How is the severity of a breach of contract evaluated?
8. What is the purpose of awarding damages for breach of contract?
9. What is specific performance?
10. When will a court grant an injunction?

11. What is the remedy of rescission?

12. When can the innocent party treat the contract as at an end?

Questions for Discussion

1. A contract is considered frustrated only in very unusual situations. Should the doctrine of frustration be applied more often? Would a broader application produce fairer results? What is the downside of such a change in commercial contracts?

2. Damages for breach of contract are meant to compensate the victim for financial loss resulting directly from the breach. Would compensation be more complete if the courts took a broader approach to damages and considered factors such as inconvenience, harm to reputation, or upset of a business caused by the breach? Should the motive or reason for the breach of contract also affect the amount of damages?

3. The privity rule is one of the basic elements of contract law. Is it too restrictive? Is there any reason why a person named in a contract should not be permitted to enforce this rule? On the other hand, is there a danger in creating too many exceptions to the rule?

4. Contract law is intended to facilitate commercial activities and to enable businesses to conduct their affairs so that their legal obligations are certain. Do you think, after considering the material in the last five chapters, that contract law achieves its goals? Can you think of ways to improve the effectiveness of contract law?

5. Most of the rules of contract are found in the common law as developed by the courts. As a result, it is often difficult to find the rules outside the context of particular cases. With the growth in e-business, there is concern that the existing rules are inadequate to enable e-business to reach its full potential. Would contract law be improved if the rules were expressed in legislation?

Situations for Discussion

1. Total Waste Disposal Ltd. (TWD) made a contract with the City of Kingsville for collection of garbage in a growing area of the city. When the contract was made, there were 3000 households in the collection area. The contract was for three years, and TWD estimated that in three years' time there would be 1000 more households in the area. TWD agreed to remove all garbage in the defined area for three years for $400 000 a year. TWD projected a profit of $75 000 on the contract. The area developed more quickly than expected. By the end of the first year, there were 4000 households and more growth appeared likely. TWD broke even in year one, but it now predicts significant losses in years two and three. TWD is considering whether to approach the city for renegotiation of the contract for years two and three.

How does this contract allocate the risk? How else could the risk have been allocated? Should TWD request renegotiation? On what terms? What factors should the city consider in responding to the request? Has the contract been frustrated? Should TWD try to buy its way out of the contract? What is the best strategy for TWD?

2. Action Distributors (AD) and Bonny Toys (BT) had an agreement whereby AD was the sole distributor of BT's toys in Canada. The agreement made no provision for termination. Two years into the contract, BT was bought by AD's major competitor, Entertainment Plus (EP). Shortly after the takeover, BT terminated its contract with AD without notice. By this time, BT's toys made up 75 percent of AD's business. AD was unable to find another supplier and eventually went out of business. AD estimates that as a result of BT's termination, it lost $450 000 in profit and $625 000 in the value of the business as a going concern.[16]

   Was BT entitled to terminate the contract? Should AD have received notice of BT's intention? Can AD hold EP responsible for BT's termination? Are AD's losses the result of the termination? How could this contract have been better designed?

3. Ready Construction (RC) was the successful bidder on a road-building project in British Columbia. RC's bid was based on specifications and drawings prepared by Martin and Short, who were engineers with Martin, Short and Associates, a firm of engineers. RC completed the project but suffered a large loss, owing to the lack of detail and errors in the specs and drawings. Building the road turned out to be more difficult and expensive than RC had expected. The contract between RC and the province contained a clause stating that the province accepted no responsibility for errors in the tender documents (which included the drawings and specifications). RC is now seeking recovery of the lost profit on the project.[17]

   Does the contract protect the province from responsibility? Can the engineers and their firm use the contract between RC and the province to protect them from responsibility? How could RC have better handled the risk of errors in the tender documents?

4. Cartright owned a large house, which he converted into five small apartments. He leased the apartments to tenants for monthly rents ranging from $900 to $1500. Cartright decided to sell the property, and Luxury Developments (LD) agreed to buy it for $500 000. In the agreement, Cartright promised that "the property may continue to be lawfully used as it is presently being used" and that all zoning bylaws had been observed. When LD's lawyer investigated the property, she discovered that the applicable zoning regulation permitted a maximum of three rental units for each property.[18]

   How significant to the contract is the three-unit restriction? Can LD demand that Cartright attempt to have the regulation changed? Can LD demand a reduction in the price? If so, how much? Can LD choose to terminate the contract? How would you advise each party to deal with the situation?

16. Based, in part, on *Cosco Inc.* v. *Cambridge Recreation Products Inc.,* [1995] O.J. No. 717 (Gen. Div.) Online: Q.L. (O.J.).

17. Based, in part, on *Edgeworth Construction Ltd.* v. *N.D. Lea & Associates Ltd. et al.,* (1993) 157 N.R. 241 (S.C.C.).

18. Based, in part, on *Jorian Properties Ltd.* v. *Zellenrath* (1984), 26 B.L.R. 276 (Ont. C.A.).

5. Atlantic Fertilizer (AF) operates a fertilizer plant in New Brunswick. AF made a major sale to the government of Togo in Africa and engaged Pearl Shipping (PS) to transport the fertilizer to Togo for a fee of $60 000. The contract between AF and PS specified that AF would deliver the cargo to PS for loading on its ship between March 25 and 31 and that AF would pay $1000 (in addition to the shipping charges) for each day after March 31 that the cargo was delayed. AF had difficulty in filling the large order in its plant and notified PS that delivery would be sometime after March 31.[19]

   PS is contemplating AF's message and deciding how it should react. Options under consideration are to wait for AF to deliver and add the $1000 daily charge to the bill; give AF a firm date by which it must deliver; or terminate the contract with AF and seek another cargo for its ship. Which options are legally available to PS? Which should PS choose?

6. Pool Construction (PC) agreed to build a swimming pool for Foster at his home. The pool was to be 2.5 metres deep at the deep end, and the price was set at $40 000. The job took longer than expected, and Foster was dissatisfied with the quality of PC's work from the beginning. When the pool was almost finished, the floor cracked and had to be replaced. When the pool was finished, Foster discovered that the deep end was only 2.25 metres deep. Foster and PC are in serious disagreement about payment for the work. PC wants an extra $20 000 as payment for all the extra work. Foster says the pool is unacceptable because of the depth deficiency and that he needs $60 000 to have the pool replaced by another contractor.[20]

   What terms in their contract might have lessened the severity of this disagreement? What is each party entitled to from the contract as agreed? How can their dispute be resolved?

---

19. Based, in part, on *Armada Lines Ltd.* v. *Chaleur Fertilizers Ltd.* (1994), 170 N.R. 372 (F.C.A.); rev'd [1997] 2 S.C.R. 617.
20. Based, in part, on *Ruxley Electronics and Construction Ltd.* v. *Forsyth,* [1996] 1 A.C. 344 (H.L.).

Part Three

Business Torts

TORT LAW IS CONCERNED WITH COMMERCIAL AND human interactions out of which some harm results, be it physical, economic, or both. Tort law plays an important role in many fields of activity. It affects the contractual arena, it will arise where two or more people come into contact because of an accident or other mishap, and it will be called upon if someone intentionally causes harm to another.

Business is exposed to tort risks on a variety of fronts. A paper mill may release toxins into a nearby river and ruin the water downstream. A customer may slip on the floor of a store and suffer serious injury. One business may intentionally seek to drive a competitor out of business by spreading lies. An accountant or lawyer may provide negligent advice that causes the client to lose money. Tort law provides a set of rules through which the innocent party can recover financial compensation for the loss sustained.

While tort law presents significant risk to the business enterprise, this risk can be managed. For example, a business can take action to reduce its risk of legal liability by implementing preventative measures, and it can transfer risk by taking out insurance. In addition, tort law can be used by a business to protect its interests in the face of a loss wrongfully caused by someone else.

The next three chapters consider the risk exposure of business in the context of tort law:

Chapter 10   Tort Law Defined

▶ Chapter 10 provides a general introduction to the law of torts.

Chapter 11   The Tort of Negligence

▶ Chapter 11 is devoted to the tort of negligence, as this is one of the most common sources of tortious liability that a business will face.

Chapter 12   Other Torts

▶ Chapter 12 provides an account of other torts that also play a significant role in the commercial world.

Tort Law Defined

Objectives

AFTER STUDYING THIS CHAPTER, YOU SHOULD HAVE AN UNDERSTANDING OF

► THE BROAD SCOPE OF TORT LAW
► THE DIFFERENCES BETWEEN A CIVIL ACTION AND A CRIMINAL ACTION
► THE PURPOSE OF TORT REMEDIES
► HOW BUSINESS CAN MANAGE ITS POTENTIAL LIABILITY IN TORT

Business Law in Practice

Good Time is a small restaurant and bar operating in Grand Bend, Ontario. Its clients tend to be the young people who come to Grand Bend either to enjoy the beach or to work in the many service industries. Good Time has always hired a bouncer/doorman to handle situations that the wait staff and bartenders cannot handle.

Reggie is a young Nova Scotian who has come to Ontario for work. He visits the Good Time one night with friends and, after several hours, decides to engage in some "slam dancing." Since this kind of dancing involves crashing into others on the dance floor, it is prohibited by Good Time. Mike, the bouncer, cannot persuade Reggie to stop this activity and finally throws Reggie from the premises with such force that Reggie suffers serious spinal injuries and subsequent paralysis.[1]

---

1. Adapted from a true case reported by David Mabell, "It Happened in Banff, but It Could Just as Easily Happen Here..." *The Lethbridge Herald* (20 January 1997).

1. What kinds of tort actions might a business such as Good Time encounter?
2. What potential legal actions result from the altercation between Reggie and Mike?
3. Is Good Time responsible for Mike's actions?
4. What actions could Good Time have taken to prevent this altercation?

What Is Tort Law?

tort
A harm caused by one person to another, other than through breach of contract, and for which the law provides a remedy.

Tort law cannot be defined precisely. The word **tort** describes any harm caused by one person to another, other than through breach of contract, and for which the law provides a remedy.[2] The word *harm* incorporates a broad range of events for which the innocent party can seek compensation. To distinguish between the various kinds of harm that can occur, the law gives each tort its own distinct legal definition, as illustrated in the following examples:

- Parking garage operators might rely on the tort of *trespass* when drivers leave their cars in the lot but fail to purchase the required ticket from the automated ticket dispenser. The driver is responsible for the tort of trespass because he or she has left the vehicle on the property without consent.
- Someone injured during an unsafe lane change by another driver is the victim of the tort of *negligence*. The driver is responsible for the tort of negligence because she has made the unsafe lane change and failed to show the care and attention that the circumstances required.
- The purchaser of a vehicle is the victim of the tort of *deceit* if the vendor intentionally misrepresents the vehicle as having a new engine when, in fact, it does not. The vendor is responsible for the tort of deceit because he made an untrue statement, which the purchaser relied on in deciding to make the purchase.

Each tort comprises an individual legal wrong and therefore has it own legal definition and set of requirements.

Good Time's operation, described in the Business Law in Practice scenario above, exposes it to liability for several different kinds of torts, the most important being negligence. Negligence can take any number of forms:

- Patrons may drink too much and cause injury to themselves or others. Good Time could be found liable in negligence for not preventing such a situation from arising or for failing to reduce its severity.
- Altercations may break out between patrons or between patrons and staff. Good Time could face liability in negligence for failing to train and supervise its staff properly.
- Patrons may slip and fall on beer spilled on the floor or suffer food poisoning from food served on the premises. Good Time may therefore be liable for negligence since it has a legal obligation to keep its facilities safe[3] and serve uncontaminated food.

The law of torts will not automatically provide a remedy when someone has been physically or economically injured. One of the key objectives of tort law is to distinguish between a situation in which the loss suffered by an injured individual should

2. J. Fleming, *The Law of Torts*, 8th ed. (Sydney: Law Book Co., 1992) at 1.
3. This situation can also be treated under occupier's liability; see Chapter 12.

Routine events can be
accidents waiting to happen.

remain uncompensated and one in which responsibility for the loss should be "shifted" to another party considered responsible for causing the loss. Tort law provides an evolving set of rules for making that determination.

To a large extent, tort law seeks to impose liability based on blame, as the following two examples illustrate:

EXAMPLE 1   Susie has set up a ladder in front of her store so that she can climb up and replace the light bulbs in the sign. A truck goes by, shaking the ladder and startling Susie, causing her to fall. She suffers serious fractures of both legs.

Tort or no? Susie has undoubtedly suffered much harm and there will likely be real economic consequences to her. No tort has occurred, however. Although the truck driver was on the scene, he was not sufficiently connected to Susie's injury to be liable for it.

EXAMPLE 2   Susie has set up a ladder in front of her store so that she can climb up and replace the light bulbs in the sign. As she steps on the second to top rung, it breaks away because it is defective. Susie falls and suffers serious fractures of both legs.

Tort or no? Susie has a negligence claim against the retailer for selling an unsafe ladder[4] and against the manufacturer for producing an unsafe ladder.

An important function of tort law is to compensate an injured party when the injury is the result of someone else's blameworthy conduct. While one may feel sympathy for everyone who suffers damages, tort law does not provide a remedy in all circumstances.

How Torts Are Categorized

Although there is no functional definition of the word *tort*, there are very important definitions of individual torts. These definitions signal whether, based on any particular set of facts, a tort has occurred.

Many torts can be categorized as falling into two main groups: torts committed intentionally and torts committed through negligence. The first, called **intentional torts**, are harmful acts that are committed on purpose. For example, if the bouncer at Good Time threatens, punches, or shoves Reggie before removing him from the

intentional tort
A harmful act that is committed on purpose.

---

4. Assuming privity exists, Susie also has an action for breach of contract, since it is a term of her contract with the retailer that the ladder would be fit for climbing and standing on.

assault
The threat of imminent physical harm.

battery
Nonconsensual physical contact that violates an individual's bodily security.

negligence
A careless act or omission that causes harm to another.

premises he has committed the torts of **assault** and **battery**—there have been intentional threats and physical contact with Reggie without his consent. Chapter 12 examines several kinds of business-related torts, most of which are intentional.

Another large group comprises torts committed through **negligence**. The defendant is found responsible for the event that caused damage even though there was no intention to cause that event. For example, assume that Reggie's injuries were caused by his falling down a flight of stairs at Good Time after tripping on a loose step. Under these circumstances, Reggie can sue Good Time in negligence for failing to keep the staircase in good repair. The tort of negligence is assessed in more detail in Chapter 11.

This chapter discusses tort law from a more general perspective in order to lay the foundation for subsequent discussion.

Addressing Multiple Causes for One Event

Circumstances that give rise to a claim based on the tort of negligence are not necessarily simple. In particular, there may be more than one cause of the tortious event and the "victims" may be at least partially responsible for their own injuries. The common law grappled with how to handle these issues but failed to devise resolutions that were perceived to be fair. For example, at one time, if the victim was even slightly responsible for the event, the person who was primarily responsible would have had no legal responsibility whatsoever.[5]

The harshness of these common law rules resulted in the passage of provincial legislation, today known variously as the *Negligence Act* or the *Contributory Negligence Act*.[6] This legislation states that if the negligence of more than one person is responsible for the loss, the victim (plaintiff) can sue any or all of them, and recovery is apportioned between the respective defendants according to their

LANDMARK IN THE LAW

level of responsibility. If the defendant successfully argues that the plaintiff was responsible for at least part of the loss—that is, the defendant uses the defence of **contributory negligence**—the amount of damages the plaintiff is awarded is reduced by the proportion for which the plaintiff is responsible. Contributory negligence is a common defence used in lawsuits involving car accidents. If the plaintiff was not wearing a seat belt at the time of the accident, the defendant may well be able to establish that the injuries sustained were worse than they otherwise would have been. The court will then go on to decrease the plaintiff's damages award in proportion to the plaintiff's degree of contributory negligence. For example, if the plaintiff's damages are set at $100 000 and the court finds the plaintiff to have been 20 percent contributory negligent—that is, responsible for 20 percent of the loss—then the plaintiff's damages award will be reduced to $80 000.

---

5. L.N. Klar, Tort Law, 2d ed. (Toronto: Carswell, 1996) at 365.
6. For example, *Negligence Act*, R.S.O. 1990, c. N.1; *Contributory Negligence Act*, R.S.N.B. 1973, c. C-19; *Contributory Negligence Act*, R.S.N.S. 1989, c. 95; *Negligence Act*, R.S.B.C. 1996, c. 333.

Statutory Changes to Tort Law

workers'
compensation
legislation
Provincial legislation
that provides no-fault
compensation for
injured employees in
lieu of their right to
sue in tort.

Although tort law remains primarily a common law matter, it has also been modified by statute law. **Workers' compensation legislation**, for example, provides monetary compensation to employees for work-related injuries and illnesses. At the same time, it prohibits the employee from suing the employer for any negligence that might have caused the problem. In this way, the statute takes away the employee's common law right to sue but provides compensation no matter who is at fault.

Statute law has also played an important role in the development of the defences to tort claims.

Tort Law and Criminal Law

The same event can give rise to two distinct legal consequences: one in tort and one in criminal law. For example, since Reggie has been seriously attacked by Mike the bouncer, section 268(1) of the *Criminal Code of Canada*[7] likely applies: Everyone commits an offence of aggravated assault "who wounds, maims, disfigures or endangers the life of the complainant." And, if found guilty, section 268(2) "... is guilty of an indictable offence and liable to imprisonment for a term not exceeding fourteen years."

Mike will be charged with aggravated assault by the police *and* be sued by Reggie in tort. Put another way, Mike's behaviour and its consequences give rise to two separate legal actions. This is because, in addition to tort law, the *Criminal Code* prohibits one person from assaulting another, except in self-defence. There are important differences between tort claims and criminal prosecutions.

Purposes of the Actions

The purpose of a criminal prosecution is to *sanction* behaviour, such as the assault that Reggie experienced at the hands of Mike, and secure the punishment of a fine, imprisonment, or both. The action is brought because the Parliament of Canada has determined that anyone who violates the *Criminal Code* should be punished and deterred from such conduct in the future. Prosecution is considered to be critical to maintaining a rights-respecting society.

contributory
negligence
A defence claiming that
the plaintiff is at least
partially responsible for
the harm that has
occurred.

In tort law, on the other hand, the objective is to compensate the victim for the harm suffered due to the culpability of another. It enforces the plaintiff's private right to extract compensation from the party who has caused the loss.[8]

Commencing the Actions

In criminal law, the legal action is called a prosecution and is brought most often by Crown prosecutors employed by the federal or provincial governments. Rarely do

---

7. R.S.C. 1985, c. C-46.

8. Note, in Ontario, for example, victims of crime have access to a fund that allows some compensation for their loss or suffering; *Compensation for Victims of Crime Act,* R.S.O. 1990, c. C-24. In Ontario there is also the *Victims' Bill of Rights,* 1995, S.O. 1995, c. 6 and the *Victims' Right to Proceeds of Crime Act,* 1994, S.O. 1994, c. 39.

the injured parties bring the prosecution, though it is technically possible for them to do so.[9] In a criminal action, Mike, the bouncer, would be known as the "accused" and Reggie, the injured party, as the "complainant."

In tort law, the injured party brings the legal action. This means that Reggie would sue in order to enforce his personal or private right to secure compensation for Mike's attack. His action is called a civil action because it is enforcing a right belonging to an individual. In a civil action, Reggie is known as the "plaintiff" and Mike as the "defendant."

Proving the Actions

To secure a conviction under section 268(1) of the *Criminal Code*, the Crown must prove that force was applied, that it was intentional, and that the actions were so serious as to "wound, maim, disfigure or endanger" Reggie's life. The Crown would have to establish that Reggie was not the aggressor; that even if Reggie were the aggressor, the response from Mike was not reasonable in light of Reggie's actions; that Mike did indeed use excessive force; and that it was this force that caused Reggie's injuries.

The Crown has the burden of proof in a criminal action. This means that the prosecutor must prove all the elements of the offence beyond a reasonable doubt based on "reason and common sense," not on "sympathy or prejudice." It must be a logical deduction from the evidence, and it is not sufficient that the jury or judge believed the accused "probably" committed the act.[10]

In tort, by way of contrast, the injured party, Reggie, must prove that Mike is responsible for the assault and battery, on the balance of probabilities. Put another way, Reggie must establish that it is more likely than not that assault and battery took place. Represented in numerical terms, Reggie must convince the judge that there is a better than 50 percent chance that he was harmed by the defendant.

Given the different burdens, it is obviously easier to prove a civil case than a criminal case, and for good reason (see Figure 10.1). Criminal convictions can result in depriving persons of their liberty. This has always been considered to be far more serious than requiring them to pay damages in a civil action. While the odds are high that the plaintiff will succeed in tort if the defendant has already been convicted under criminal law, this is not a certainty since the definitions of the individual torts and crimes are not always exactly the same. Furthermore, only recently have some courts decided that evidence of a conviction for conduct constituting a crime is relevant to establishing the existence of a related tort.[11]

The scenario between Mike and Reggie is loosely based on an actual incident that occurred in August 1995.[12] In that case, the bouncer was convicted of aggravated assault and sentenced to 18 months, to be served in the community, and prohibited from owning a gun for 10 years. In addition, he was ordered by the judge to

- perform 240 hours of community service
- speak to bouncers about their responsibilities

---

9. Private prosecutions, that is, those brought by the victim or anyone else who is not an agent of the Crown, are uncommon but permissible. Law Reform Commission of Canada, *Private Prosecutions*, Working Paper No. 52 (Ottawa: Law Reform Commission of Canada, 1986) at 51-59.

10. *R. v. D. (W)* (1991), 63 C.C.C. (3d) 397 (S.C.C.); *R. v. Lifchus,* [1997] 3 S.C.R. 320.

11. *Simpson* v. *Geswein,* [1995] 6 W.W.R. 233 (Man. Q.B.). For a further discussion of this point, including relevant statute law, see Klar, *supra* note 5 at 37.

12. *Supra* note 1.

- take anger-management courses
- pay a $1000 victim surcharge

The victim started a civil action against all parties involved, including the bar. The case was settled out of court for an undisclosed amount. The victim was provided with what is known as a "structured settlement." He receives an annuity that provides him with annual, tax-free benefits.

Figure 10.1

DIFFERENCES BETWEEN CIVIL AND CRIMINAL ACTIONS

Type of action	Commencing the action	Proving the action	Outcome
Assault and battery as torts	Reggie files a claim against Mike based on the tort of assault and battery.	Reggie must prove his case on the balance of probabilities.	A court orders Mike to pay Reggie compensation for his injuries.
Aggravated assault as a crime	The Crown prosecutes Mike based on s. 268(1) of the Criminal Code.	The Crown must prove its case beyond a reasonable doubt.	A court orders Mike to be fined, imprisoned, or both.

A Successful Tort Action

compensation in tort
Financial compensation awarded for the harm suffered by the plaintiff.

The primary goal of a tort remedy is to **compensate** the victim for loss caused by the defendant. Generally, this is a monetary judgment. Less common alternatives are equitable remedies, such as an injunction. An injunction would be ordered if money would not suffice—for example, in the case of a recurring trespass where there is little economic harm, but the plaintiff simply wants the trespasser to stop coming onto the land in question.

Financial compensation means the defendant is ordered by the court to pay a sum of money to the successful plaintiff. Such a remedy has obvious limitations. For example, where the plaintiff has suffered serious physical injuries, how can money truly compensate someone for the permanent loss of health? However, in personal injury cases there are no ready alternatives to financial compensation such as in the trespass example above.

Traditionally, only where the damage was something for all to see—a building destroyed by fire or a leg that was broken—was money viewed as an appropriate means of compensation. Gradually, the principle of compensation extended into other, less tangible, fields so that the plaintiff could be compensated for mental pain and suffering and other forms of emotional distress. These latter areas are approached with more caution by the judiciary but are compensable if proven through psychiatric and other expert evidence.

New Products and Liability

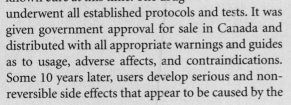

The question of what harm should be compensated raises complex social and moral issues. A case in point is the development of new products that later prove to be unsafe. Assume that Drug Corp. devised a drug that it believed would significantly alleviate the symptoms of Crohn's disease, a serious gastrointestinal complaint with no known cure at this time. The drug underwent all established protocols and tests. It was given government approval for sale in Canada and distributed with all appropriate warnings and guides as to usage, adverse affects, and contraindications. Some 10 years later, users develop serious and non-reversible side effects that appear to be caused by the product. Because of major recent advances in pharmacology, it is discovered that there is, in fact, a direct link between the side effects and the drug. Drug Corp. removes the product from sale immediately and notifies all physicians in Canada of the risks.

Critical Analysis: Should the innocent users be entitled to compensation through tort law for the suffering this drug has caused them? When assessing Drug Corp's liability, what is the relevance of the state of scientific knowledge at the time the product was put on the market? Is it fair to impose liability upon Drug Corp. under these circumstances?

Damages in Tort

The Purpose of Damages

The primary purpose of a damages award is to compensate a plaintiff such as Reggie for loss or injury suffered due to the culpable conduct of the defendant. Because any award or out-of-court settlement is final, a plaintiff's lawyer will not usually settle or bring the case to court until the full extent of damages is known.

Pecuniary and Nonpecuniary Damages

Under Canadian law, the losses for which damages are awarded are categorized as being either pecuniary (that is, monetary) or nonpecuniary.

nonpecuniary damages
Compensation for pain and suffering, loss of enjoyment of life, and loss of life expectancy.

Nonpecuniary losses—sometimes called general damages—are damages that are awarded to compensate the plaintiff for

- pain and suffering
- loss of enjoyment of life
- loss of life expectancy

Because Mike's attack on Reggie caused him severe spinal injuries and subsequent paralysis, Reggie undoubtedly has suffered a considerable amount of general damages. These damages are nonpecuniary in the sense that they are not out-of-pocket, monetary losses, but they are nonetheless both real and devastating. The quality of Reggie's life has been seriously diminished due to a loss of mobility and independence. His life expectancy has likely been reduced. A judge will award damages based on these facts, as well as on expert testimony as to how badly Reggie has been injured.

The more serious and permanent the injury is, the higher the general damages will be. Courts have developed precedents to assist in this process, and the Supreme Court of Canada has set a clear upper limit on what can be awarded for general damages.[13]

Pecuniary losses fall into three main categories:

■ cost of future care
■ loss of future income
■ special damages

pecuniary damages Compensation for out-of-pocket expenses, loss of future income, and cost of future care.

COST OF FUTURE CARE   A plaintiff like Reggie is entitled to an award sufficient to provide him with all the care and assistance his injury will necessitate. This can include the cost of a personal care attendant for the rest of his life, modifications to his living accommodations to increase accessibility, and the costs related to equipment and treatment of his condition. As in other areas of damages, what the plaintiff is ultimately awarded will be based on the testimony of experts, including occupation, rehabilitation, and medical experts.

LOSS OF FUTURE INCOME   A judge will value the plaintiff's diminished earning capacity that has resulted from the injury. This calculation can be complex, involving the input of vocational experts, labour economists, accountants, and actuaries. Since Reggie has suffered paraplegia as a result of Mike's attack and he is a young person, his loss of future income will likely be large.

SPECIAL DAMAGES   These relate to out-of-pocket expenses resulting from the injury-causing event. These expenses may include any number of items, including ambulance costs, medication costs, housekeeping, and yard work. Reggie should keep records and receipts of such costs and expenses in order to prove them in court. In some provinces medical costs must be claimed as special damages, although these will be repaid to the provincial health insurer under the insurance principle of subrogation.[14]

Punitive or Exemplary Damages

punitive damages Compensation awarded to the plaintiff to punish the defendant for particularly offensive behaviour.

Punitive damages—also known as exemplary damages—are an exception to the general rule that damages are intended only to compensate the plaintiff. Punitive damages are awarded to punish the defendant for particularly heinous or callous conduct or where the defendant might otherwise profit from the behaviour.[15] If, for example, the bouncer or the bar refused to call an ambulance for the seriously injured Reggie, punitive damages would almost certainly be awarded. The court would seek to punish such offensive conduct.

Aggravated Damages

aggravated damages Compensation for intangible injuries such as distress and humiliation caused by the defendant's reprehensible conduct.

Aggravated damages compensate the plaintiff for intangible injuries such as distress and humiliation caused by the defendant's reprehensible conduct.[16] For example,

---

13. *Andrews* v. *Grand & Toy Alberta Ltd.,* [1978] 2 S.C.R. 299; *Arnold* v. *Teno,* [1978] 2 S.C.R. 287; and *Thornton* v. *School Dist. No. 57 Bd. of School Trustees,* [1978] 2 S.C.R. 267.
14. See Chapter 20 for more detailed explanation.
15. Klar, *supra* note 5 at 93.
16. *Vorvis* v. *Insurance Corporation of British Columbia,* [1989] 1 S.C.R. 1085.

Punitive Damages in the United States

In general, tort damages awards are higher in the United States than in Canada and any other common law country. One of the reasons for this has been the approach to punitive damages. The actual definition of punitive damages is very similar in the United States and Canada. However, at least until recently, there has been a significant difference in the willingness of courts to make such awards. For the most part, the spectacular U.S. awards that are reported in the Canadian press are a consequence of punitive damages, usually by juries sympathetic to the victim.

This highlights another difference between the two jurisdictions. While there exists a right in both countries to have a jury in civil cases, it is far more common in the United States to do so than in Canada. For example, if the case involves a consumer grievously harmed by the actions of a manufacturer, the request for a jury will be the norm in the United States. The lay person is thought to be more likely than an experienced judge to be swayed by the alleged injustices that have befallen an injured plaintiff.

Concern for the impact of spectacular punitive damages awards has been widespread in the United States. Arguments that multimillion dollar awards representing many times the amount of actual losses are unconstitutional have failed. Attempts to pass federal legislation that would reform this area of the law, particularly in product liability cases, have also been unsuccessful. However, a number of states have now passed tort law reform acts that attack the problem in a variety of ways; for example, some have placed caps on punitive damages, some do not allow any punitive damages in product liability cases, some require "clear and convincing evidence" of the need for punitive damages, and some require part of the punitive damage award to go for public purposes and not to the plaintiff.

Critical Analysis: Should juries be given free rein to assess damages as they see fit? Is it fair for legislative bodies to limit their power in this way?

Source: Roger LeRoy Miller & Gaylord A. Jentz, *Fundamentals of Business Law*, 2d ed. (Minneapolis/St. Paul: West Pub. Co. c. 1993) at 135.

when store detectives unlawfully restrain a customer, they have committed the tort of false imprisonment. If, in restraining the customer, they treat the person in a humiliating or degrading fashion, a court may well award aggravated damages to compensate the plaintiff for the mental distress the whole experience caused.

Vicarious Liability

vicarious liability
The liability of the employer for the tortious acts of an employee committed in the normal course of employment.

The doctrine of **vicarious liability** makes an employer liable for the torts committed by its employees acting in the normal or ordinary course of employment. In the likely event that the employee who caused the loss or injury does not have the resources to pay a judgment awarded against him or her, the plaintiff has another defendant from whom to recover damages. In practice plaintiffs therefore sue both employee and employer.

To determine whether the tort occurred during the course of employment, the court must decide whether the employee's conduct was merely "unauthorized" and something for which his employer is liable or, conversely, conduct so unconnected to his job that the employee alone is responsible for it.[17] For example, Mike's assault and battery of Reggie was an unauthorized manner of discharging his duties as a bouncer. Good Time, his employer, will therefore be vicariously liable for Mike's tortious conduct. By way of contrast, if Mike assaulted one of his friends whom he had invited to the Good Time bar—after hours and without his employer's permission—the doctrine of vicarious liability would, almost certainly, have no application.

The doctrine of vicarious liability has been justified as a means to ensure that

- the person who benefits from a business enterprise (the employer) also bears the associated costs
- the innocent plaintiff has a better chance of being compensated
- the employer has an incentive to try to prevent torts from occurring in the first place[18]

Managing Tort Risk

Chapters 3 and 4 discussed extensively the issues of risk management and dispute resolution. Businesses are exposed to a wide variety of risks related to tort actions, particularly in the area of negligence. In addition, they are vulnerable due to the doctrine of vicarious liability.

No business can eliminate all risk. It must, however, assume active measures to minimize it. This is because ignoring tort risk can result in

- incurring the costs of a tort that could have been avoided, including lawyer's fees, management time devoted to defending the claim, and the amount of the actual judgment awarded to the successful plaintiff
- losing continued insurance because of a poor claims history
- losing a hard-earned business reputation

The risk of liability in tort calls for business operations like Good Time to institute a risk management plan that deploys a variety of strategies. Possibilities include the following:

- reducing risk by hiring employees with care and instituting training programs to help them perform their jobs well
- eliminating the risk of patrons engaging in slam dancing by removing the dance floor altogether
- transferring risk by purchasing insurance to cover the business's liability to patrons who are injured on its premises

On the next page is an account of risk awareness in a very prominent Canadian institution, the Canadian Hockey Association. Much of the analysis it contains would also apply to the for-profit enterprise.

---

17. See discussion by Klar, *supra* note 5 at 483-484.
18. *Ibid.* at 479.

Glen McCurdie, Director, Insurance Programs, for the Canadian Hockey Association

The Canadian Hockey Association (CHA) brings together the main amateur hockey interests in Canada. It is responsible for a number of publications addressing risk management, including *Safety Requires Teamwork* and *Speak Out*. Glen McCurdie was part of the team that put together these publications. He has training in law, as well as experience in the insurance industry.

A BUSINESS PERSPECTIVE

I would like to say that the CHA came into the risk management business purely out of our concern for the safety of hockey players in Canada. While that was in part our motivation, we had always thought we were fulfilling our responsibilities when, for example, we set helmet and other standards. What pushed us into a proactive program was a combination of good intentions, guilt, and economic pressures. The CHA was the self-insurer for most amateur hockey programs around the time in the early 90s when some major cases were decided against hockey teams in Canada. In particular, the *Unrah* v. *Webber*[19] case ended up with a $6 million award being made to a midget player who was checked into the boards from behind and left a quadriplegic.

Our "risk management" approach at that time was to defend this case as far as we could, but ultimately we lost. This made us rethink seriously our approach to safety programs and risk management in particular. Indeed, when we subsequently acquired insurance coverage, this was something that the insurer insisted upon. It is no secret that the cost of our coverage is a function of how good our preventative programs are and how much we minimize the number of claims. The risk of major personal injury claims against the CHA has forced us to do what we no doubt should be doing anyway: making sure the game is as safe as possible for all our players.

More recently, the Sheldon Kennedy disclosures have forced us to address issues that we long preferred to avoid. Again, it is obviously the right thing to do to educate all our players, parents, coaches, and officials, but it also makes good economic sense. If we do not establish a program that encourages the protection of players, we face large potential [tort] lawsuits.

Glen McCurdie

---

19. *Unrah (Guardian ad litem of)* v. *Webber* (1994), 88 B.C.L.R. (2d) 353 (C.A.).

Business Law in Practice Revisited

1. What kinds of tort actions might a business such as Good Time be exposed to?

It is safe to assume that almost every business will find the tort of negligence to be its greatest concern. Since, in general terms, negligence is any careless act that causes harm to another, there are obvious ways in which this might arise in Good Time's business. Good Time serves food and beverages. It must ensure that these are safe for consumers at all times. It must also ensure that its premises are safe. Apart from the tort of negligence, Good Times may face vicarious liability for the torts of its employees, including assault and battery. Good Time also employs staff and will, from time to time, be called upon to provide references. If Good Time makes inaccurate and damaging statements about the former employee—wrongly suggesting that the employee has stolen from the till, for example—then Good Time may face an action in defamation.

2. What potential legal actions result from the altercation between Reggie and Mike?

Mike could be prosecuted for a criminal offence, perhaps that of aggravated assault. If successful this would lead to a fine and/or imprisonment. Mike can also be sued by Reggie, who will be seeking compensation by way of civil action—here a complaint based on the torts of assault and battery—for the damages he has suffered.

3. Is Good Time responsible for Mike's actions?

Reggie will claim that Good Time is responsible for Mike's actions based on the principle of vicarious liability. Since Mike is an employee of Good Time and it appears that Mike was acting in the normal course of his employment when he threw Reggie out of the premises and caused him injury, Good Time will probably be responsible for Mike's tortious actions.

4. What actions could Good Time have taken to prevent this altercation?

Good Time is engaged in a relatively high-risk business. There are two main areas of risk management on which Good Time should focus: hiring and training. Employees should be hired for their good judgment and interpersonal skills and not simply their brawn. They should be instructed as to both the parameters of acceptable behaviour and how to address patrons who threaten to cross the bounds. Employees should learn what they are entitled to do and when they have to call in the police, as much for their own safety as for that of patrons. Finally, it may be appropriate to have employees working in pairs to ensure they have backup and are able to monitor each other's behaviour and well-being.

The second focus should be on the design of the property itself. If slam dancing is becoming a problem, perhaps the dance floor should be eliminated altogether.

Chapter Summary

Tort law has a significant impact on business enterprises, particularly in the area of negligence. Tort law permits someone who has been injured or suffered a loss to sue the responsible person for damages. The objective of a damages award is to compensate the plaintiff, though punitive damages are sometimes available if the defendant's conduct has been particularly egregious. Less commonly, the injured party will seek an injunction or other form of equitable remedy.

The law of torts also makes the employer vicariously liable for the actions of employees acting in the ordinary course of employment. Since a business may have several employees, its exposure in this area can be considerable.

Criminal law also affects a business, though to a lesser degree. As the purpose of a criminal law is to punish the offender—through fines and imprisonment—distinct procedures are in place to help ensure that only guilty people are convicted. For example, in a criminal prosecution the Crown must prove its case beyond a reasonable doubt. By way of contrast, the plaintiff in a tort action need only demonstrate his or her case on the balance of probabilities.

The best response a business can have to its potential liability in tort is to establish a risk management plan that reduces, eliminates, or transfers risk.

Study Chapter

Questions for Review

1. The goals of tort and criminal law are quite distinct, even when they stem from the same event. Explain the differences.

2. Why is it so difficult to find a single, workable definition for *tort*?

3. What does *burden of proof* mean?

4. How does the burden of proof differ between a criminal case and a tort action?

5. What is the difference in the way tort and criminal actions are initiated?

6. What is the purpose of damages in tort?

7. Under what circumstances might an injunction be awarded in tort?

8. Vicarious liability is an essential feature of modern tort law. What is it?

9. What might be a defence to a claim for vicarious liability?

10. Explain the difference between pecuniary and nonpecuniary damages.

11. How are pecuniary damages typically calculated?

12. What are punitive damages?

Questions for Discussion

1. It is increasingly common to see plaintiffs sue in tort, where they believe—because of the difference in burden of proof—that a criminal prosecution would not succeed. For example, victims of childhood sexual assault, crimes for which it is notoriously difficult to obtain criminal convictions, will sometimes turn to the civil courts. Obtaining a verdict in their favour may meet their emotional needs even when there may, in the particular circumstances of the case, be little opportunity for actual recovery. Do these experiences highlight fundamental problems with our judicial system? Is there any justification for the basic legal principle that the standard of proof is higher in a criminal matter than in a civil one?

2. Punitive damages are somewhat controversial even in jurisdictions where they are relatively common. At the same time, there are circumstances in which a person's tortious actions have been particularly callous and calculating, yet the actual loss suffered by the plaintiff is not extensive in monetary terms. In these latter cases, what are the compelling reasons for allowing the plaintiff additional compensation over and above her actual loss? Should the compensation principle of tort law be compromised in this way?

Situations for Discussion

1. It was Samara's turn to drive her three classmates to university, this time for the final exam in the business law course. Unfortunately she had left home late, and by the time she had picked up everyone else, they were in serious risk of arriving at least 10 minutes after the exam began. The weather was not good and the roads were obviously slippery—there were cars off to the side of the road in a number of locations. Samara's friends urged her to speed up, which she did, although as a relatively inexperienced driver she was uncomfortable handling the car under these conditions. As she approached a major intersection the light turned amber and Samara braked. The car began sliding and Samara instinctively braked harder, causing the car to go out of control and enter the intersection into the path of a car proceeding on a green light from the cross street. In the subsequent collision, one of the passengers in Samara's car, Jean-Guy, was seriously injured.

   The police arrived and, after investigating the case, charged Samara with dangerous driving under the *Criminal Code*. In time it became clear that Jean-Guy's injuries had resulted not only in short-term harm—for example, he could not sit his exam and had fallen behind one term in his program—but also permanent damage. In particular, his right arm and wrist were shattered and, being right-handed, he has and will continue to have limited manual dexterity. He was planning a career in IT and finds that these injuries severely affect his ability to perform basic tasks. For which categories of damages will Jean-Guy seek compensation?

2. Discuss the relationship between criminal and civil law in relation to Situation 1. How will each case be proven and by whom?

3. Security Services-R-Us was hired by the Ferry Corporation to provide security for its premises. Mr. Brown, the security guard sent to the site, fell asleep during his watch. A break-in occurred and valuable computer equipment owned by Ferry Corporation was stolen. Later that same night, Brown intentionally destroyed an outbuilding by pouring an accelerant around the periphery of the building and igniting it. The Ferry Corporation is now suing both Brown and his employer, Security Services-R-Us, for damages arising from the theft and Brown's arson.

   Why would Ferry Corporation sue both Brown and his employer? To what extent is the security company responsible for its employee's behaviour?[20]

20. Based, in part, on *British Columbia Ferry Corp.* v. *Invicta Security Corp.* (1998), 167 D.L.R. (4th) 193 (B.C.C.A.).

Eleven Chapter

The Tort of Negligence

Objectives

AFTER STUDYING THIS CHAPTER, YOU SHOULD HAVE AN
UNDERSTANDING OF:

► THE CONDUCT THAT THE LAW OF NEGLIGENCE ADDRESSES
► THE PRINCIPLES OF THE LAW OF NEGLIGENCE
► THE DEFENCES IN A NEGLIGENCE ACTION
► THE COMMON KINDS OF NEGLIGENCE ACTIONS
  BUSINESSES FACE

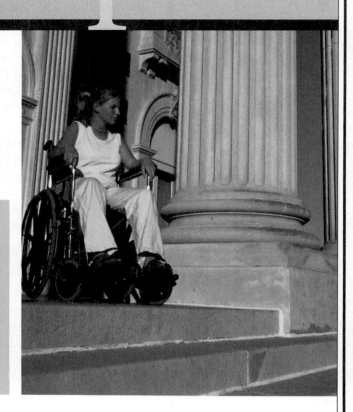

Business Law in Practice

Pierre Bouffard is vice president of operations at Excel-Fibreglass Canada Ltd.
(Excel). Excel produces fibreglass repair kits that are used primarily in auto-body
work. Each kit comes with a piece of fibreglass cloth, a can of liquid resin, and several tubes of liquid hardener. Since the liquid hardener contains corrosive chemicals,
the tube carries the following warning, in small print:

> **Warning**: Flammable material. Store in a cool place away from sunlight and
> other sources of heat. Keep out of reach of children. Can cause skin irritation
> and blindness—not to be taken internally. If swallowed, dilute stomach con-
> tents and induce vomiting. In case of contact with skin or eyes, flush with lib-
> eral quantities of water. For eye contact, get immediate medical attention.
> Composition: 60% methyl Ethyl Ketone Peroxide in Pi-Methyl Phthalate.

Pierre has recently received a disturbing phone call from a lawyer representing Hugh
Thomkins. According to the lawyer, Hugh was seriously injured by Excel's product.
It seems that Hugh had purchased Excel's repair kit from a local retailer and brought
it home to do repairs on his car. Hugh perforated the nib of the tube of the hardener

and pointed the tube downward in order to add a few drops into the bowl of resin. When Hugh squeezed the tube, the seal on the bottom failed, squirting the corrosive product in Hugh's eyes. Hugh experienced tremendous pain, was hospitalized for seven days, and has only recently regained his sight. He was unable to work for four months following the accident and still suffers serious eye irritation.

Pierre is now gathering documents to bring to Excel's lawyer. Included is a memo that outlines Excel's quality control program to check for defects in the sealed tubes of hardener. According to the memo, workers squeeze the tubes by hand at two stages of production. The first occasion is when the tubes are filled with the hardener—one of every six tubes is tested this way. The second occasion for testing the seals is when the tubes are packed into the kit boxes. Nine out of ten tubes are squeezed at this point, but there is no standard as to how much pressure employees should put on each tube nor any way of measuring the pressure exerted, in any event.[1]

1. What kind of legal action is likely to be commenced against Excel by Hugh's lawyer? What will Hugh need to establish to succeed?
2. Will Excel be liable for Hugh's injuries? Is there additional information that would be helpful in answering this question?
3. What should Excel be doing differently?

The Law of Negligence

What Is Negligence?

reasonable care The care a reasonable person would exhibit in a similar situation.	

Chapter 10 defined the tort of negligence as a careless act that causes harm to another. The law understands carelessness as a failure to show **reasonable care**, that is, the care that a reasonable person would have shown in a similar situation.

Negligence is a very common tort action in the commercial world because it covers a broad range of harmful conduct. For example, a negligence action can be brought by someone

- who has been injured by the dangerous driving of a delivery truck driver
- who has suffered loss by relying on poor advice provided by an accountant, lawyer, architect, or engineer
- whose furniture has been damaged in transit by a moving company

The plaintiff need not show that the defendant intended to cause the damage or that there were deliberate acts that gave rise to the damage. Instead, the tort of negligence makes the defendant liable for failing to act reasonably—for driving too fast, for giving unprofessional advice, or for not taking proper care of furniture entrusted to its care.

In the Business Law in Practice scenario above, Hugh has an action in negligence against Excel on two grounds. First, it appears that Excel has failed to use reasonable care in the production and testing of the tubes containing the hardener, since the company's quality control program is probably deficient. As well, the warning on each tube appears inadequate, given that the hardener is corrosive. The warning states that the contents can cause skin irritation and blindness but does not recommend that protective gear, such as safety goggles, be worn while the product is in use.

---

1. Based, in part, on *LeBlanc* v. *Marson Canada Inc.* (1995), 139 N.S.R. (2d) 309 at paras. 17-18, aff'd (1995) 146 N.S.R. (2d) 392 (C.A.).

For both these reasons, it may well be that Excel has been negligent and is therefore liable to Hugh for his damages.

Negligence law—like tort law in general—seeks to compensate victims for their loss or injury. It provides this compensation after applying rules that determine who is liable to compensate another, on what basis, and for how much. Without such limiting rules, business and professional people might be reluctant to produce goods and services because the risk of liability in negligence would be too unknowable. Those goods and services that did reach the market would be relatively more expensive since the price would need to reflect the increased risk flowing from widespread liability.

With these kinds of factors in mind, the courts have the task of balancing competing interests. They must compensate victims of negligence, but without discouraging legitimate activity and without making the legal standards a business must meet unreasonably exacting.

Steps to Negligence Action

The rules that limit when a plaintiff like Hugh will succeed in a negligence action are set out in a series of classic steps, as summarized in Figure 11.1.

Figure 11.1

STEPS TO NEGLIGENCE ACTION

Step 1: Does the defendant owe the plaintiff a duty of care? If yes, proceed to the next step.

Step 2: Did the defendant breach the standard of care? If yes, proceed to the next step.

Step 3: Did the defendant's careless act (or omission) cause the plaintiff's damage? If yes, proceed to the next step.

Step 4: Was the damage suffered by the plaintiff too remote? If not, the plaintiff has proven negligence.

Step 1: Does the defendant owe the plaintiff a duty of care?

duty of care
The responsibility owed to avoid careless acts that cause harm to others.

neighbour
Anyone who might reasonably be affected by another's conduct.

The defendant Excel will only be liable to Hugh if it owes Hugh what is known in law as a **duty of care**. A defendant owes a duty of care to anyone who might reasonably be affected by the defendant's conduct. This is known as the **neighbour** principle, as formulated by the House of Lords in *Donoghue* v. *Stevenson*.[2]

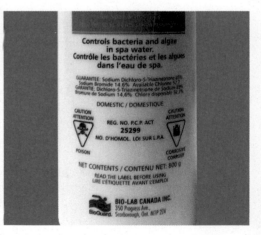

Manufacturers have a duty of care to consumers to warn them of any harm their products might cause.

2. *M'Alister (or Donoghue)* v. *Stevenson*, [1932] A.C. 562 (H.L.).

Landmark Case

M'Alister (or Donoghue) v. *Stevenson,* [1932] A.C. 562 (H.L.)

The Business Context: Before large-scale production, most goods were sold directly from producer/artisan to consumer. By the 20th century, a multistage distribution chain was the norm, which comprised several distinct transactions or contracts—from manufacturer, to supplier, to retailer, to the ultimate consumer.

Factual Background: A customer bought some ice cream and an opaque bottle of ginger beer for her friend, Donoghue. Some of the ginger beer was poured over the ice cream and some was drunk by Donoghue. When the remainder of the beer was being poured into a tumbler, a decomposed snail was discovered in the contents. Donoghue, not surprisingly, became ill and subsequently sued the manufacturer for damages, based on negligence.

The Legal Question: At this time, the extent of the manufacturer's duty of care was severely constricted: the manufacturer was responsible only to those with whom it had a contractual arrangement. Most consumer "victims" were prevented by this from recovering from the manufacturer. There was almost certainly a "middleman" in the transaction and no direct contractual relationship between the manufacturer and consumer.

Resolution: The trial judge summarily dismissed the case based on the existing legal principles, and Donoghue appealed. The House of Lords reversed the decision, ruling that Donoghue had a proper cause of action, and ordered the case tried. The parties then settled out of court. The significance of the decision is in the majority opinion delivered by Lord Atkin, who wrote the following classic statement when discussing how to determine to whom a duty of care is owed in negligence:

> The rule that you are to love your neighbour becomes in law, you must not injure your neighbour, and the lawyer's question, Who is my neighbour? receives a restricted reply. You must take reasonable care to avoid acts or omissions which you can reasonably foresee would be likely to injure your neighbour. Who, then, in law, is my neighbour? The answer seems to be—persons who are so closely and directly affected by my act that I ought reasonably to have them in contemplation as being so affected when I am directing my mind to the acts or omissions which are called in question.

Critical Analysis: Is it reasonable to make manufacturers liable for their products to end users? Would it be enough simply to make the retailer liable for breach of contract and leave the manufacturer out of the equation?

Based in part on *M'Alister* v. *Stevenson*, the Supreme Court of Canada in *Hercules Managements Ltd.* v. *Ernst & Young*[3] has provided a definitive, two-step test for assessing whether a duty of care in negligence is owed by one person to another.

STEP ONE Is there a relationship of proximity between the parties? In the words of Lord Atkin, quoted above, are the parties neighbours? Put another way still, is it reasonably foreseeable that carelessness by one party would adversely affect the other? If the answer is yes, then a duty of care is owed, subject to Step Two.

STEP TWO Are there any considerations that should limit the duty owed or eliminate it entirely?

For a business like Excel, virtually everyone who came into contact with the fibreglass repair kit product would be its neighbour. This is because Excel manufactures a product for mass consumption. It is reasonably foreseeable that carelessness in the production process could injure the ultimate user, whoever that person might be,

---

3. *Hercules Managements Ltd.* v. *Ernst & Young,* [1997] 2 S.C.R. 165.

and wherever he or she might live in the world. For this reason, the manufacturer's duty extends to all purchasers and consumers of the product, not just those with whom the manufacturer has a contract.

To conceptualize how the first step in the test for duty of care is applied, assume that the events leading up to Hugh's injury were captured on film. The defective tube slips through the quality control program undetected. It is packaged into the kit and shipped to the retailer. Hugh purchases the kit, returns home, and begins to use the product. He perforates the nib of the hardener tube, points it downward into a bowl of resin, and squeezes the tube. At this point, imagine stopping the film and asking the audience the following question: Who is reasonably likely to be affected by Excel's defectively produced hardener tube? The answer is clear: Hugh and anyone else who could have come into contact with the product. On this basis, Hugh is Excel's neighbour.

The only difference between the exercise described above and one that might occur in a court of law is that now the audience is a judge and the judge knows the outcome—the tube failed and the hardener injured Hugh. What judges must do is place themselves in the hypothetical position of observing the events as they are about to occur. While this might appear to be a somewhat strained exercise, it is a process with which judges are very familiar.

Once a trial judge has determined that the defendant owes a duty of care to the plaintiff, the judge must go on to Step Two and assess whether there are any considerations that ought to eliminate or reduce that duty.[4] The objective of this important second step is to ensure that businesses and other defendants are not made liable to an unreasonably broad, unknowable, and indeterminate extent. In practice, considerations that eliminate or reduce a defendant's duty of care are more likely to arise in the area of general economic loss, such as loss of profit, than in cases of physical harm. An example of such occurring can be found in the context of negligent misstatement, which is discussed later in this chapter.

In Excel's case, a judge is very unlikely to find that such a consideration exists because of the nature of Excel's business—Excel wants people like Hugh to use its product. If consumers are injured in the process, what possible reason could there be to suggest that Excel should not owe a duty of care to them?

Step 2: Did the defendant breach the standard of care?

Once it is established that Excel owes a duty of care to Hugh, the next formal question is whether there has been a breach of the **standard of care** associated with that duty. In short, did Excel show a lack of reasonable care in the preparation of the fibreglass hardener tube?

In general, the defendant's conduct is judged according to the standards of behaviour that would be observed by the reasonable person in society. In law, a **reasonable person** is regarded as being an ordinary person of normal intelligence who uses caution to guide his conduct. She is a person who thinks about what she is doing and avoids conduct that might present a danger to others. The law does not demand that the reasonable person be perfect.

Where the defendant exercises specialized skills, the standard of the reasonable person described above is not applied. Professionals such as doctors, accountants,

standard of care
The standard by which reasonableness is determined.

reasonable person
The standard used to judge whether a person's conduct in a particular situation is negligent.

4. *Ibid.*

specialized standard
of care
The standard of care
exhibited by average
persons with the
requisite specialized
training.

engineers, and lawyers must meet a higher or **specialized standard of care** because the level of expertise of the average member of society is simply inadequate as a measure of competence. In cases involving specialized tasks, courts introduce the standard of the "reasonable" person with that specialized training—the reasonable electronics engineer, or the reasonable heart surgeon, for example. To determine just what the standard is on the facts before it, the court will hear from expert witnesses who, in turn, will present evidence of what that standard is.

Where the activity or product poses a high risk, the law imposes a higher standard of care. The policy reason for this higher standard is to encourage competence and caution in light of the very serious harm that could result if the task were poorly performed.

In assessing whether Excel breached its duty of care, a court will likely apply a higher standard because of the inherent dangers in the Excel product. A central issue will be Excel's quality control procedures. As noted earlier, these procedures involve employees squeezing the tubes by hand at two separate steps in the production process. This is a factor suggesting that Excel fulfilled its duty of care—the tubes were checked and passed the squeeze test. On the other hand, the quality control measure may itself be inadequate. In fact, the procedure for assessing whether the tube was properly sealed could be described as totally haphazard, unscientific, and uncontrolled[5] since, among other problems, there was no way of measuring the pressure exerted by an employee at any given time. If this second argument prevails, then a court will find that Excel did breach the standard of care it owed to Hugh in how it packaged the fibreglass hardener.

There is another basis upon which Excel may have breached the standard of care. The warning label on the tube noted that the product was flammable and could cause skin irritation and blindness. It did not recommend that any special precautions be taken, such as the wearing of protective gloves and goggles. There was also no warning to the user to exercise caution in applying pressure to the tube. Given the very hazardous quality of the fibreglass hardener, such deficiencies in Excel's warning are likely fatal to its case.

In sum, there is a very strong argument that Excel failed to meet a reasonable standard in packaging its products: its quality control procedures were inadequate, as was the warning on its product.

Excel is not the only kind of plaintiff that is measured against a high standard of care, as the box on the next page illustrates.

Step 3: Did the defendant's careless act (or omission) cause the plaintiff's damage?

causation
The relationship that
must exist between the
defendant's action and
the plaintiff's loss.

While the legal test for **causation** is sometimes debated, courts generally have little difficulty reaching a decision on causation by asking this simple question: Would the harm not have occurred *but for* the defendant's actions?[6]

It seems relatively clear that Excel's failure to use reasonable care in the production process and to provide proper warnings on the product caused Hugh's injury. But for these failures, Hugh would not have been injured.

In order to understand the concept of causation in more detail, compare the following two examples:

---

5. This is how the trial judge described the process in the case upon which the Excel-Hugh scenario is based. See *LeBlanc* v. *Marson Canada Inc.*, supra note 1 at paras. 17-18.

6. L.N. Klar, *Tort Law,* 2d ed. (Toronto: Carswell, 1996) at 321.

Environmental Hazards

Greater understanding of environmental hazards has dramatically increased the risk exposure of business. Since many activities and events pose a serious risk to the environment, the standard of care imposed by a court will be higher than with less dangerous activities.

For example, transporting explosive cargo may be necessary, but extreme care ought to be exercised by those doing so. This expectation is reflected in the statutory law that regulates the transportation of dangerous goods. It is also reflected in the common law rules that hold those who transport such explosives to a higher standard of care than those who transport products that are not inherently dangerous to the public.[7] Similarly, the storage or disposal of toxic substances, and the emission of certain gases, for example, carry a high standard of care. Whenever the state of scientific knowledge expands to include a greater understanding of the inherent risks of an activity, it can be assumed that this knowledge will be incorporated into the standard of care imposed in any subsequent negligence action.

Critical Analysis: Should businesses be subject to the control of the legislature and courts in how they transport goods or dispose of waste? Why not simply let the marketplace discipline businesses that show a disregard for the environment—for example, through consumer-organized boycotts?

EXAMPLE 1 Shannon is walking down a staircase in a mall. Unfortunately, the handrail is not properly attached to the wall and pulls away. Shannon loses her balance, falls down the stairs, and suffers serious injuries.

EXAMPLE 2 Shannon is walking down the staircase in a mall. A group of teenagers on the stairs just above her start jostling each other. Several of them end up tumbling down the stairs, knocking Shannon over. When Shannon grabs for the handrail, it pulls out of the wall. Shannon continues her fall down the stairs and suffers serious injuries.

Both examples involve carelessness by the mall owner, but in the second example, there is a good argument that the extent of causation is insufficient to meet the legal requirements of negligence. In the first instance, "but for" the defective handrail Shannon would not have fallen down the stairs. In contrast, in the second instance, a judge might decline to reach the same conclusion. A court might decide that Shannon would have been knocked down the stairs merely by the impact of the teenagers tumbling into her. Put another way, the judge could well find that the defective handrail had nothing to do with the accident and that it did not *cause* Shannon's injuries.

Step 4: Was the damage suffered by the plaintiff too remote?

At this point in the test for negligence, a court asks, "Even if there is an obligation to take reasonable care and it was breached, how far will the legal liability of the defendant stretch?"[8] The idea is that there must be some limit on the defendant's responsibility for the consequences of his negligence.

---

7. *Canadian Pacific Limited* v. *Jones Estate,* [1989] B.C.J. No. 1241 (S.C.), online: QL (B.C.J.R.).
8. *Ibid.* at 333.

Because Hugh got a corrosive product in his eye due to Excel's negligence, he was unable to work at any job for four months after the injury. His loss of income due to this enforced period of unemployment is foreseeable, and Excel will be ordered to pay damages accordingly. While Excel is not responsible for every negative event in Hugh's life after the accident, it is certainly responsible for his inability to work in the months following his hospitalization.

By way of contrast, assume that Hugh's fiancée—who is involved in a start-up Internet company with a bright future—cannot cope with the stress caused by Hugh's injury. She calls off the wedding. Hugh cannot argue that the injury prevented him from becoming a millionaire because he otherwise would have married his fiancée and reaped the future financial success of her company. Such a claim would fall into the category of **remoteness of damage**.

remoteness of damage
The absence of a sufficiently close relationship between the defendant's action and the plaintiff's loss.

In assessing Excel's responsibility for Hugh's damages, a court need only be satisfied that the type of damage he suffered was foreseeable. It is not necessary, in addition, to foresee the full extent of the damage of any given type. If Hugh is a world famous neurosurgeon whose loss of income claim amounts to millions of dollars, Excel is still liable for the full amount. Provided that it is reasonably foreseeable that someone injured by the fibreglass hardener would have employment income, it is not necessary to foresee that the person injured may work in a particularly lucrative field.

The principle that only the type of the loss must be foreseeable also finds expression in the **thin skull rule**. This rule protects the plaintiff who has an inherent weakness or "thin skull" that makes a given injury more serious than one might otherwise reasonably anticipate. The rule states that such a plaintiff is still entitled to the full extent of the loss. For example, if Hugh's recovery from his eye injury takes a longer period of time than would normally be anticipated because he has an impaired immune system, his damages will not be reduced for that reason. Though the condition impairing the immune system is reasonably rare, Excel cannot use this fact to escape liability for Hugh's entire loss of income claim.

thin skull rule
The principle that a defendant is liable for the full extent of a plaintiff's loss even where a prior vulnerability makes the harm more serious than it otherwise might be.

Hugh is entitled to recover for damages related to the personal injuries caused by a defective product such as the fibreglass hardener, but he cannot sue Excel for any financial or economic loss suffered merely because the product did not work properly. If, for example, Hugh is unable to go through with a contract to sell his car to a neighbour because the failed product meant that he was unable to effect the necessary fibreglass repairs in sufficient time to satisfy his neighbour, Hugh cannot sue Excel for any loss of profit on that contract. One explanation for such a rule is that recovery for this kind of **pure economic loss** is too indirect or remote for Excel to be responsible. A related explanation is that the rule prevents defendants from being overwhelmed with liability. Yet another explanation is that to permit recovery of damages in such cases would lead to a mass of litigation that the courts would have difficulty handling.[9] It is only in a relatively few areas, such as negligent misstatement, that a plaintiff can recover for pure economic loss.

pure economic loss
Financial loss that results from a negligent act where there has been no accompanying property or personal injury damage.

Conclusion

The law requires the plaintiff to prove each and every step in a negligence action. It is not enough to establish half of the steps or even most of them. In short, the plaintiff must show that the defendant owed a duty of care and breached the standard of care associated with that duty. Provided that the breach in question caused the plaintiff's loss and that the loss was not too remote, the plaintiff has won its negligence action.

---

9. *Stevenson* v. *East Ohio Gas Co.* (1946), 73 N.E. 200 (Ohio C.A.). For a general discussion of these points, see Klar, *supra* note 7 at 172.

If proving the tort of negligence appears to be somewhat technical, this may be because the four steps, by design, lack much specificity. Their purpose is to describe general standards or markers that help a court assess whether the defendant in any given case has been negligent.

Defences to a Negligence Action

Though a court may find the defendant to have been negligent, the plaintiff is not automatically entitled to recover all of his or her damages. The defendant may raise defences against the plaintiff in order to place at least some of the responsibility for the loss on that party. This section explores two such defences: the defence of contributory negligence and the defence of *volenti non fit injuria*—that the plaintiff has voluntarily agreed to assume the risk in question.

Contributory Negligence

The defence of contributory negligence was introduced in Chapter 10. It is used to describe unreasonable conduct by the plaintiff that contributed—or partially caused—the injuries that were suffered.[10] This defence recognizes that in many instances, *both* the defendant *and* the plaintiff may have been negligent. For example, Hugh may have partially caused his own injury by squeezing the hardener tube with excessive pressure. Since the tube was clearly marked as containing a corrosive and potentially harmful substance, he should have been more cautious in how he handled it.

If Hugh is found to have been part-author of his own misfortune, Excel has made out its defence of contributory negligence. Provincial legislation[11] will then come into play. It provides that responsibility for the tortious event must be apportioned between or among the respective parties, in this case, Hugh and Excel. Through this mechanism, Hugh's damages award is then reduced in proportion to his own negligence.

Voluntary Assumption of Risk

voluntary assumption of risk
The defence that no liability exists as the plaintiff agreed to accept the risk inherent in the activity.

When the court makes a finding of *volenti non fit injuria* or **voluntary assumption of risk**, it is concluding that the plaintiff consented to accept the risk inherent in the event that gave rise to the loss. *Volenti* is therefore a complete defence to the lawsuit, and the plaintiff will be awarded nothing by a judge even though the defendant had been negligent.

To succeed on the defence, the defendant must show that the plaintiff—knowing of the virtually certain risk of harm—released his right to sue for injuries incurred as a result of any negligence on the defendant's part.[12] In short, both parties must understand that the defendant has assumed no legal responsibility to take care of the plaintiff and that the plaintiff does not expect him to.[13] Since this test is not easy to meet, *volenti* is a very rare defence.

---

10. Klar, *supra* note 7 at 363.
11. *Ibid.* at 365. Each common law province has contributory negligence legislation, which has replaced the common law.
12. *Dube* v. *Labar*, [1986] 1 S.C.R. 649.
13. *Ibid.*

Consider the following:

EXAMPLE 1 Yolanda leaves a party in a car driven by her very best friend, who, like Yolanda, has consumed too much alcohol. Yolanda is aware of the friend's condition but knows that the trip home is short and has seen her friend drive in far worse condition without harm. This time Yolanda's luck runs out. The friend runs a red light and collides with another vehicle, and Yolanda is injured. Later, Yolanda sues her friend in negligence.

Yolanda's friend—the defendant—will argue that the risk of driving with someone who has been drinking is obvious. This will not be sufficient to establish the defence of *volenti*, however. The defendant will have to prove that Yolanda consented not only to the *physical* risk of injury but also to the *legal* risk of not being able to sue her friend, the driver. Only then will the defence prevail. Needless to say, this is unlikely.

For the purposes of comparison, consider the following:

EXAMPLE 2   Yoshi, a seasoned hockey fan, goes to an NHL hockey game and seats himself in prime seats just to the left of the net. A shot on net deflects off the crossbar, glides over the Plexiglas screen, and hits Yoshi, causing a serious head injury.[14]

Rather than just arguing that Yoshi caused his own injury by failing to keep a proper lookout—which is the defence of contributory negligence—the defendant hockey arena owners could rely on *volenti*. The argument is that Yoshi implicitly agreed that the defendant would have no legal responsibility for an injury of this nature. For this defence to succeed, a court would have to find that Yoshi's experience with the game, his familiarity with the location of his seat, and his decision to remain in a seat that provided only limited protection amounted to an implied agreement by the plaintiff to waive any claim for negligence.[15]

Negligence Actions and Business

One of the largest sources of tortious liability for a business is in negligence. Tort actions arising from motor vehicle accidents are routine. For various types of operations, liability arising from negligently produced goods and negligent misstatements may be of major significance.

Product Liability

product liability
The manufacturer's liability for negligently made goods that cause harm to the consumer.

The law imposes a standard of care on manufacturers in relation to the design, manufacture, and marketing of their merchandise.[16] This area of law is known generically as **product liability**. The scenario under discussion in this chapter is a product liability case because Excel breached the standard of care it owed Hugh by manufacturing an unsafe tube. It also failed to exercise proper care in marketing—it did not adequately advise users of the precautions they should take to minimize the risk of harm.

---

14. The facts of this example are based on *Hagerman* v. *City of Niagara Falls* (1980), 29 O.R. (2d) 609 (H.C.J.).
15. The Court in *Hagerman, ibid.,* used this kind of reasoning as an alternative reason to exonerate the defendant.
16. Klar, *supra* note 7 at 276.

Product liability cases often involve contract law as well. Besides being able to sue Excel in negligence, Hugh has an action for breach of contract against the retailer who provided him with the defective fiberglass repair kit. The retailer is in breach of contract because it supplied Hugh with a product that was not fit to be sold. Hugh does not, of course, have a contract action against the manufacturer, since there is no contract between them.

Hugh's contract action against the retailer will probably be more straightforward than his negligence action against Excel. This is because liability for breaching a contractual term is *strict*. Since the retailer's promise to supply a nondefective product is not qualified in any way, there is no defence for breaching that promise. It is no defence to the contract action for the retailer to prove that it purchased from a reputable supplier, for example, or that there was no way of telling that the product was defective apart from opening the package and performing a squeeze test on-site. To succeed in negligence against the *manufacturer*, however, Hugh has to demonstrate all the steps in the action, as outlined earlier in this chapter. It is not enough for Hugh simply to show that the tube seal broke, leading to a serious eye injury. Hugh has to show that the break in the tube was due to Excel's negligence.

Because of the nature of product liability, Hugh has two defendants he can sue and is well advised to proceed against both of them. Having two defendants increases the chances that Hugh will be able to collect at least something on any judgment in his favour. For example, if the retailer is out of business by the time the matter goes to trial, Hugh will still have the manufacturer left as a source of payment of damages.

Strict Liability

Some of Canada's major trading partners, such as members of the European Union (EU), and parts of the United States, use a strict liability rather than a fault-based standard in defective product liability cases.

For example, all EU member states are subject to a directive which requires that manufacturers be strictly liable for their defective products. The directive provides that a product is defective when it does not provide the safety that a person is entitled to expect, taking into consideration all the circumstances. Relevant considerations include the presentation of the product, expectation of use, and the time when the product was put into circulation. The directive also provides for a "state of the art" defence by stating that a product will not be considered defective for the sole

INTERNATIONAL PERSPECTIVE

reason that a better product is subsequently put on the market.

The effect of a strict liability standard is that manufacturers can be held liable for unsafe products even if they were not negligent in any way and exercised due care. This is markedly different from the result under a fault-based standard. In the latter case, if the manufacturer takes due care at all stages of product production—in designing the product, in selecting a production process, in assembling and testing, and in packaging and labelling—then there is no liability regardless of defects. Strict liability, on the other hand is imposed irrespective of fault.[17]

Critical Analysis: Which approach to liability do you prefer and why?

17. EC, Commission Directive 85/374/EEC of 25 July 1985 on the approximation of the laws, regulations and administrative provisions of the Member States concerning liability for defective products, O.J. Legislation (1985) No. L210/29; G. Howells, *Comparative Product Liability* (Aldershot, England: Dartmouth, 1993); S.N. Hurd & F.E. Zollers, "Product Liability in the European Community: Implications for United States Business" (1993) 31 Am. Bus. L.J. 245.

strict liability
The principle that liability will be imposed irrespective of proof of negligence.

In some jurisdictions, the manufacturer is liable for a defective product regardless of whether it has been negligent. This is known as **strict liability** or no-fault liability.

The strict liability or no-fault system compensates victims simply because they have been injured. Chapter 10 introduced such a concept in the context of workers' compensation legislation. Employees injured at the workplace are entitled to compensation whether or not a tort was involved in causing the injury.[18]

Negligent Misstatement

negligent misstatement or negligent misrepresentation
Negligence that arises out of uttering a misleading statement with less than the appropriate standard of care.

When negligence takes the form of words, the tort is known as a **negligent misstatement** or **negligent misrepresentation**. Whether the tort has occured depends on the results of applying the two-step test in *Hercules* to the legal dispute in question. That is, there must be a neighbour relationship (or relationship of proximity) between the parties and there must be no considerations limiting or eliminating any duty of care established under the first step.

It is particularly relevant to the second step of the *Hercules* test whether the misstatement resulted in physical or economic harm. For example, if Excel gave erroneous first aid instructions on the product labelling and these instructions resulted in permanent vision loss to Hugh, Hugh has suffered physical harm. He will easily pass the two-step *Hercules* test because he is Excel's neighbour and there are no considerations that should limit the duty of care that Excel owes to him. Excel's negligent words injured Hugh, and the company should be fully responsible for Hugh's injuries.

When the loss is merely economic—that is, purely monetary—different considerations come into play. Such torts arise most frequently in the context of an advisor, such as an accountant or appraiser, giving a professional opinion. The difficulty with words or representations, in contrast to physical acts, is that once they have been uttered, they are very difficult to retract or contain. The law is legitimately concerned that such professionals could face an untenable level of liability should that advice be passed along to others—known as third parties—and relied on. The problem this poses was most aptly described in the 1932 *Ultramares* case in the United States: imposing liability in this context would expose the auditor to loss "in an indeterminate amount for an indeterminate time to an indeterminate class."[19]

In *Hercules*—discussed further in Chapter 23—the Supreme Court of Canada had to apply the second step of the test to an auditor whose negligent audit of a company had been relied on by several investors. After reviewing all the circumstances of the case, the court found that there was, indeed, a consideration or reason to limit the duty that would otherwise be owed by the auditor to the investors. It held that the purpose of the audit was to allow existing shareholders to assess the performance of management at the time of the annual general meeting. It had no other intended purpose. The extent to which it was used for any other reason—such as to inform investment decisions—was beyond the scope of the auditor's duty, and he should not have to answer for losses associated with such extraneous reliance. On this basis, the auditor did not owe a duty to the investors, and accordingly their action failed.

---

18. For a very helpful account of this area of law, see Douglas Mah, *Workers' Compensation Practice* (Toronto: Carswell, 1996).

19. *Ultramares Corp.* v. *Touche* (1931), 255 N.Y. 170 (C.A.).

The Consequences of *Hercules*

BUSINESS APPLICATION OF THE LAW

The result of the *Hercules* decision has been a significant change in the exposure of the auditing profession, in particular, to third-party liability. Indeed, it is difficult to see after this case how any claim can be successfully made by a third party for investment losses based on negligence where there has been a negligently prepared audit in a public company context. It was suggested by the courts that users could seek a letter from the auditor accepting liability prior to the publication of the audit.[20] This would bring the user within a contractual relationship. To date, however, Canadian accounting firms have been reluctant to provide such letters.

Critical Analysis: What might the consequences be, both good and bad, of a profession having its liability limited in this way? Could the court have found some other way to avoid the *Ultramares* dilemma—that is, unlimited liability—but without these extreme results?

Negligence and the Service of Alcohol

The growing number of successful alcohol-related negligence suits illustrates the flexibility of the law of negligence. As society's intolerance for the harm caused by those who are impaired grows, those who caused this impairment or who failed to prevent the harm from occurring are increasingly being found responsible in negligence.

Case

Stewart v. *Pettie*, [1995] 1 S.C.R. 131

The Business Context: Until the 1970s it was uncommon for providers of alcohol to be held responsible for the conduct of their intoxicated patrons. However, changes in attitudes toward alcohol consumption—fuelled in large part by the widely publicized role of intoxication in highway traffic accidents and by the lobbying efforts of grassroots organizations such as Mothers against Drunk Drivers (MADD)—and changes in various aspects of the law (mandatory breath and blood testing, and provincial liquor laws, for example) have resulted in an expansion of the alcohol provider's duty of care.

Factual Background: Gillian Stewart, her brother Stuart Pettie, and their spouses attended a company party at the Stage West Dinner Theatre at the Mayfield Inn. Over the course of the evening, Pettie drank five to eight double rum and colas. He did not, however, appear to be intoxicated. Stewart and Pettie's wife did not consume any alcohol. When the group left the theatre at around 11 p.m, they discussed whether Pettie was fit to drive. After concluding that he was, they proceeded home. Stewart's husband sat in the front with Pettie, and the two women sat in the back. The roads were slippery that night, but Pettie endeavoured to drive carefully. Despite his careful driving, Pettie lost control of the car. The car hit a light post and a wall. Stewart was thrown across the car and hit her head. Pettie was subsequently given a breath test by the police, and it was determined that his blood-alcohol level was far above the legal limit.

Stewart sued her brother, the City of Edmonton, and Mayfield Investments Ltd. (owner of the Mayfield Inn). The action against the brother and the city was settled out of court. At trial, the judge ruled in favour of Mayfield Investments, but the Alberta Court of Appeal held that the inn was partially responsible because it served too much alcohol to Pettie. Mayfield Investments appealed to the Supreme Court of Canada.

---

20. *Ibid.*; *Caparo Indust. plc* v. *Dickman*, [1990] 1 All E.R. 568 (H.L.), rev'g [1989] Q.B. 653.

The Legal Question: Should a reasonably prudent bar owner have foreseen that the intoxicated guest would be driving and have taken steps to prevent him from so doing?

Resolution: A duty of care is owed by the bar owner to protect against the foreseeable risks of intoxication. The bar owner owes a duty of care to the patron. This duty requires a bar to take reasonable steps to prevent an impaired person from driving when it is apparent that he intends to do so. The duty also extends to people who may be using the roads and who might be expected to come in contact with the patron. Again, this duty would require the bar to take reasonable steps to prevent the patron from driving.

The Supreme Court ruled, however, that the bar had met its responsibility because there was no reason to believe that the intoxicated guest would be driving when he left the bar in the company of two sober individuals.

Although the inn escaped liability, the Supreme Court was quite clear that commercial hosts who sell alcohol owe a duty of care to their patrons and third parties.

Critical Analysis: Do you agree that businesses should bear a portion of the costs of injuries in these kinds of situations? What might businesses be able to do to prevent such incidents?

Businesses would be remiss to think that this growing area of liability applies only to owners of bars or restaurants. The principles established in *Stewart* v. *Pettie* may be applied to any context associated with the provision of alcohol or the hosting of an alcohol-related event.[21]

Business Law in Practice Revisited

1. **What kind of legal action is likely to be commenced against Excel by Hugh's lawyer? What will Hugh need to establish to succeed?**

Hugh's lawyer will commence a negligence action against Excel. Hugh will need to establish that he is owed a duty of care by Excel. This will be straightforward, as manufacturers such as Excel owe a duty of care to consumers. Hugh will also have to establish that Excel breached the standard of care by failing to have an adequate quality control program in place and/or by failing to put an adequate warning on its dangerous product. Hugh will also need to show that these failures caused his injuries—but for the poor quality control and the incomplete warning on the package, he would not have suffered an eye injury. Finally, Hugh will need to establish that his damages—including his claim for loss of future income—were not too remote. This will also be straightforward, as they were entirely foreseeable.

2. **Will Excel be liable for Hugh's injuries? Is there additional information that would be helpful in answering this question?**

Excel provided no instructions about the appropriate manner for opening the tube, minimal warnings about the dangers of the contents, and no first aid instructions. These are basic, minimum requirements when a consumer good has inherent dangers. It would be helpful to know more about the testing procedures at Excel. The evidence does not suggest that they were designed to test for more than leakages. Do the contents of the tube sometimes deteriorate and harden or otherwise block the nib? As such, is it likely that a consumer will need to apply considerable pressure to the tube? Since no warning not to do this was provided, were the tests adequate to determine whether the tube would withstand such pressure?

---

21. *Jacobsen* v. *Nike Canada Ltd.,* [1992] B.C.J. No. 2626 (S.C.) online: QL (B.C.J.).

3. What should Excel be doing differently?

Excel is producing a consumer good with obvious dangers. It must provide all relevant information to users as to appropriate use, and instructions in the event of inadvertent splashing or spills. Since the chemicals are corrosive, extraordinary care should be taken to ensure that tubes can withstand the normal wear and tear derived from average use. Is there a better form of packaging? If not, is this particular packaging adequate?

Chapter Summary

Donoghue v. *Stevenson* is the foundation of the modern negligence law and has allowed for the rapid expansion in its scope. Negligence law is an inherently flexible, expanding legal field. It seeks to provide a remedy to the plaintiff who has suffered a loss or injury due to the culpable though unintentional conduct of the defendant.

The effectiveness of negligence in addressing society's concerns is enhanced by the defences it offers. Most importantly, contributory negligence provides for the complexity of human interaction. Seldom is there only one cause for an event. The principles of vicarious liability likewise ensure that compensation is available not only in principle, but also in fact.

Today, negligence addresses many of the issues that arise in business and the professions and overcomes some of the limitations that result from the privity rule in contract. Consumers have attained considerable protection from carelessly produced products through negligence. Businesses can themselves seek recovery from others in the distribution chain.

Businesses and the professions should remain alert to changes both in statute law and in the common law of negligence. The call for strict liability in consumer goods cases will continue to be heard. The extent to which pure economic loss and economic loss derived from negligent misstatement should be compensated continues to be debated.

Risk management programs addressing negligence must focus on more than minimizing the risk of liability. Firms must monitor for changes to the law and ensure that their interests are considered in any public debate.

Study Chapter

Questions for Review

1. Before *Donoghue* v. *Stevenson*, what was the defence most manufacturers of goods could raise when faced with a claim for negligence brought by an injured user of those goods?

2. How does the foreseeability test help in defining the neighbour principle in negligence?

3. What is the standard of care in negligence?

4. How is causation usually determined in negligence?

5. Does the normal standard of care vary in any specific circumstances? If so, how?

6. What does *contributory negligence* mean and what are the consequences of it being found to exist?

7. What is the consequence of a *volenti non fit injuria* finding? What might be an example of it being applied?

8. Sometimes the contractual notion of exclusion clauses is very relevant to the issue of tort liability for negligence. Describe how they might arise.

9. What is a no-fault system?

10. Give an example of when the no-fault system might be applied and why.

11. What kinds of plaintiffs will be likely to succeed in an action for negligent misstatement against a professional?

12. What second part of the test for duty of care did the Supreme Court of Canada apply in the case of *Hercules Managements* v. *Ernst & Young*?[22]

Questions for Discussion

1. The principles of *volenti non fit injuria* have been restricted to allow the defence to apply only in limited circumstances. Are these circumstances too limited? For example, should the person getting into the car with an impaired driver still be allowed to recover in negligence? Is there not sufficient public knowledge of the dangers of impaired driving for people to understand the risk they assume? What about those who deliberately choose not to wear a seatbelt? Why should they potentially recover?

2. From time to time, it has been proposed that the principles of strict liability be applied to product liability in Canada as they are in certain other jurisdictions. What are the pros and cons of applying this concept in Canada? What changes would result for producers of goods and services, as well as consumers? Are there inherent risks that might arise for society as a whole if strict liability was imposed in certain industries?

3. Exemption clauses are a powerful means of avoiding liability in negligence (and other torts). When is it fair for these clauses to apply and to what extent should they apply? For example, if a spectator at an NHL game was attacked by a player, or if the scoreboard collapsed and injured a spectator, would it be appropriate to exempt the owners of the team (assuming they sold the ticket) from liability for negligence? What bounds would it be reasonable to apply to this concept?

4. One of the areas in which liability for negligence is expanding is in the case of those serving alcohol both as a business and socially. Think of the contexts in which businesses might be exposed to these risks either because they make their money from selling alcohol or because they are conducting a social event. To what extent should the business be held liable for negative outcomes of the overconsumption of liquor? How should the business protect itself?

5. It is relatively new for courts to allow recovery for pure economic loss in negligence, that is, loss unrelated to any physical loss. Some would argue that extending negligence in this regard potentially places an unfair burden on some occupations and service providers. In our society, people should accept that there are some losses for which recovery cannot be obtained. What are the pros and cons of allowing recovery for purely economic loss?

---

22. *Hercules, supra* note 3.

1. A van driver swerves to avoid hitting a large dog that has run onto the highway. The van goes out of control and turns over, and the passengers suffer a serious injury. Is the van driver negligent? What further facts would you be interested in knowing?

2. Klutz won a contest sponsored by a radio station, entitling him to play in a twilight golf tournament. He went to the radio station and signed a form releasing the station from any liability connected with the tournament. The event was held at the Dark Side Country Club, beginning at 11 p.m. Klutz attended a pre-tournament instructional meeting and was told that his team was to tee off on the second hole. While the team headed for that spot, Klutz hurried to his car to get his clubs and golf shoes. As he sprinted down the path to the parking lot, he ran into one of a series of black iron posts embedded in the asphalt path at the point where the walkway and parking lot met. Klutz somersaulted several times, ending up on the driveway with banged knees and a badly bruised elbow. He played seven holes of golf, but could not carry on. Prior to the accident he was a self-employed upholsterer. Following the accident, he was unable to work for three months. After that his production was down 20 percent. His ability to participate in household and leisure activities was also reduced.[23]

    Apply the principles of tort law to this situation. Suggest a result. What further information would be useful?

3. Burger Heaven (BH) is a large chain of restaurants specializing in burgers and fries. In response to customer demand, BH added coffee to its menu. The temperature of the coffee and the style of container and lids were part of BH operating standards to be followed by all restaurant operators and staff. BH restaurants provide counter and drive-through service. Sandra bought coffee at the drive-through for herself and her husband, Morley. Sandra passed both cups of coffee to Morley. The car hit a big bump and the coffee spilled in Morley's lap, burning him severely.

    What should BH do about this particular incident? Is Morley likely to be successful in any claim for negligence? What defences might BH raise?

4. FunTime manufactures children's toys in Winnipeg. It has a new product that is a variation on a bow and arrow: there are suction cups instead of points on the end of arrows. The products are solidly manufactured of plastic in a variety of very attractive fluorescent colours. The product, if correctly used, is completely safe. It is possible, however, for a determined child to remove the suction cup, rendering the arrow dangerous. FunTime, mindful of this potential, takes great pains to ensure that all parts of the packaging are labelled with a warning to consumers that this toy should not be given to children under age 5.

    FunTime embarks on an aggressive pre-Christmas advertising campaign in which the new bow and arrow set is its showcase product. The primary focus of the campaign is children's television cartoons. The most popular advertisement shows a group of small children playing a game of hide and seek in an imaginary location; the advertisement highlights the attractive colours of the product, and the entire ad is bright, loud, and appealing. The marketing strategy has resulted in most of the advertisements being placed in the 9 a.m. to 11 a.m. time slot on

---

23. Based in part on *Poluk* v. *City of Edmonton* (1996), 191 A.R. 301 (Q.B.).

weekdays and weekends. The jingles soon become a favourite theme with young children, the campaign is a great success, and sales increase dramatically.

Ms. Wong, a grandmother, is persuaded by her persistent young grandchildren, age 4 to 7, to buy the product. Unfortunately, the youngest child gets in the habit of chewing on the arrows while watching TV. The suction cups disintegrate, but the children keep playing with the toy. Inevitably one suffers a serious eye injury as a result of the misuse of a damaged arrow.

Assuming that the injured child, through his parents, now sues FunTime for negligence, review the arguments that might be used by both parties in the case. What defences might FunTime raise? Should it consider "joining" any other parties (arguing that they are responsible)?

In light of the litigation, FunTime is engaging in an internal review of its policies to ensure that the risk of this type of suit is minimized. Discuss the failings of corporate practices in the above case, and present a proposal for a risk reduction program.

5. Big Pizza, a province-wide pizza chain, has a new promotional campaign. It guarantees that all pizzas will be delivered within 30 minutes or they will be free. While this promise is readily kept in small cities and towns, it places considerable stress on franchises in large urban areas. Franchisees are required by their franchise agreement to pass on this stress to drivers by fining them half of the cost of any pizza not delivered within the requisite time. To overcome this threat, drivers often are forced to drive well above the speed limit. A driver, attempting to meet the deadline, fails to notice another vehicle in its path and collides with it, seriously injuring the passengers in that vehicle.

Assuming that the issue of negligence by the driver is clear-cut and that the driver is an employee, can the injured persons claim damages from the franchisee for the actions of the employee? Why? Is there any argument that Big Pizza has itself been negligent? Present arguments for both sides of the case, and determine whether liability will be upheld.

6. The Bridge Engineering Company contracted to build a bridge between a suburb and the downtown of a medium-sized town. For years the two communities were joined by a one-lane bridge, and this new four-lane bridge was a major improvement. Indeed, as a result of the new bridge, a local contractor began building a new housing project of 30 homes. Just before the first home sales were made, a major defect was discovered in the bridge design that meant that the bridge would be unusable for at least two years. Residents would be forced to use a lengthy detour that added approximately 30 minutes to the average drive between the suburb and downtown, where the majority of the residents worked. The market for the new housing project immediately collapsed, and the contractor was unable to sell any houses. The contractor is considering litigation but realizes that she has no claim in contract against the engineering company. Are there any alternatives? Explain.

Chapter Twelve

Other Torts

Objectives

AFTER STUDYING THIS CHAPTER, YOU SHOULD HAVE AN UNDERSTANDING OF:

► THE RANGE OF TORTS THAT ARE RELEVANT TO BUSINESS ORGANIZATIONS
► HOW TORTS ARISE FROM THE USE OF PROPERTY
► HOW TORTS ARISE FROM BUSINESS OPERATIONS
► HOW A BUSINESS CAN MANAGE ITS EXPOSURE TO TORT LIABILITY

Business Law in Practice

Ron Smithson owns and operates a small manufacturing business in St. John's, Newfoundland. The business supplies specially crafted items for gift stores, specialty boutiques, and craft shops. Ron sells mostly through trade shows, although online sales are beginning to account for a sizable part of his business. He also has a small factory outlet.

Ron conducts business in a two-storey building that he owns in a historic part of the city. The basement houses a manufacturing facility consisting of pottery wheels, kilns, and a decorating and glazing studio. The main floor is used for warehousing and storage, packing, and shipping. The second floor, with the exception of a small unit devoted to the factory outlet, is leased to a number of other small businesses.

Ron has had a successful year, although there are two situations that have the potential to jeopardize the bottom line:

- Julie Osbourne, a local resident, suffered serious injuries on Ron's premises. Julie had planned to visit the factory outlet to purchase some gifts for visitors "from away." To access the store, she had to use a historic elevator. As she travelled between floors, the steel plate covering the indicator lights above the elevator door became unhinged and fell, hitting her on the head, neck, and shoulders. Apparently, the plate fell off because the elevator maintenance company, Elevator XL Services, which had been hired by Ron to maintain all features of the elevator, had run out of plate clips and instructed its employee to use a broken clip for the time being rather than leave the steel plate off altogether. Ron knew that a broken clip had been used on the steel plate but had also been assured by the elevator maintenance company that a proper clip would be installed on the very next business day.
- While visiting a trade show on the mainland, Ron spied a replica of his best-selling figurine "Old Man of the Sea." The replica was dressed in the same fisher garb as Ron's figurine, was decorated with the same colours, and had the same style of packaging and labelling. The only differences were that the replica was made with a cheap plastic and that it was named "Man of the Sea." Ron is concerned about the impact that sales of this competing figurine will have on his business.[1]

1. What potential legal actions does Julie have against Ron's business?
2. What is the responsibility of Elevator XL Services here?
3. Does Ron have any recourse against the manufacturer of the replica figurine?
4. How can Ron manage his business's potential tort liabilities?

Introduction

Business activity, whether it involves the generation of electricity, the cutting of hair, the filing of tax returns, or the sale of an automobile, involves interactions that may ultimately have a negative impact on others and their property. Consider these examples:

- A customer slips on a lettuce leaf and falls, breaking an ankle.
- A store detective detains a shopper, assuming, incorrectly, that the shopper has taken merchandise.
- A salesperson intentionally overstates an important quality of a product in her anxiety to close a sale.
- A golf course design means players consistently drive balls into an adjacent landowner's yard.

In each of these examples, the business may have interfered with a legitimate interest of another and could, as a result, be subject to a tort action.

The laws that make a business liable for its tortious conduct also operate to *protect* that same business when it is the victim of a tort. Consider these examples:

- A newspaper columnist maligns the environmental record of a business.
- Vandals continually spraypaint graffiti on factory walls.

---

1. Based, in part, on *Sawler* v. *Franklyn Enterprises Ltd.* (1992), 117 N.S.R. (2d) 316, [1992] N.S.J. No. 480 (C.A.).

- A competitor entices a skilled employee to break his employment contract and join the competitor's business.
- A new business creates a logo that is remarkably similar to that of an existing business in the same market.

Tort actions relevant to businesses can be conveniently divided between those that arise because a business occupies a property and those that arise because of actual business operations.

Torts and Property Use

occupier
Any person with a legal right to occupy premises.

Tort actions may arise in relation to property in a number of ways, most commonly when the **occupier** of the property harms others. An occupier is generally defined as someone who has some degree of control over land or buildings on that land. An enterprise conducting business on property is an occupier, whether it is owner, a tenant, or a temporary provider of a service. Following from this definition, it is entirely possible to have more than one occupier of land or a building.

Ron, as owner and user of the building, is an occupier. His tenants on the second floor are occupiers of that space. Elevator XL Services Ltd. was hired to service and maintain the elevator. As such, Elevator XL Services had control of the elevator at a critical time and can also be classified as an occupier, although for a much more fleeting moment in time.

The main tort actions in relation to occupation of property are occupiers' liability, nuisance, and trespass.

Occupiers' Liability

Occupiers' liability describes the liability that occupiers have to anyone who enters onto their land or property. This area of the law varies by jurisdiction. New Brunswick, Newfoundland, Nova Scotia, Quebec, and Saskatchewan retain the common law. Other provinces have occupiers' liability legislation.[2]

Liability at Common Law

The liability of the occupier for mishaps on property is not determined by the ordinary principles of negligence. Rather, liability is determined by classifying the visitor as a trespasser, licensee, invitee, or contractual entrant. Each class is owed a different standard of care, with the trespasser being owed the lowest standard and the contractual entrant being owed the highest. This area of law is often criticized for the difficult distinctions between the different classes of visitors, the blurring of duties owed between the various classes, and the severity of the result when the visitor is classified as a trespasser.

contractual entrant
Any person who has paid (contracted) for the right to enter the premises.

A **contractual entrant** is someone who has contracted and paid for the right to enter the premises.[3] Visitors to the premises who have bought tickets to see a pottery

---

2. *Occupiers Liability Act*, R.S.A. 1980, c. O-3; *Occupiers Liability Act*, R.S.B.C. 1996, c. 337; *Occupiers' Liability Act*. R.S.M. 1987, c. O-8; *Occupiers' Liability Act*, R.S.O. 1990, c. O.2; *Occupiers' Liability Act*, R.S.P.E.I. 1988, c. O-2.

3. A.M. Linden & L.N. Klar, *Canadian Tort Law: Cases, Notes and Materials*, 11th ed. (Toronto: Butterworths, 1999) at 581.

exhibit would be contractual entrants. The duty owed to this class (in the absence of a contract specifying the duty) is akin to the negligence standard—that is, the standard of reasonableness.

An **invitee** is someone whose presence on the property is of benefit to the occupier, such as store customers and delivery or service personnel. The occupier owes a slightly lower duty to the invitee than to the contractual entrant. He must warn the invitee of any "unusual danger, [of] which he knows or ought to know."[4]

Julie is clearly an invitee, and the improperly fastened steel plate would be classified as an "unusual danger." She is therefore entitled to hold the owner and elevator maintenance company liable for injuries suffered as a result of that unusual danger.

A **licensee** is someone who has been permitted by the occupier to enter for the benefit of the licensee.[5] A licensee might include guests invited to the property for a social occasion. Alternatively, if Ron allows people accessing an adjacent business to use his elevator, those users would be licensees.

The general rule is that occupiers are responsible to licensees for any unusual danger of which they are aware or which they have reason to know about. The latter part of the rule is a recent addition and tends to blur the distinction between the duty owed an invitee and the duty owed a licensee.

A **trespasser** is someone who "goes on the land without invitation of any sort and whose presence is either unknown to the occupier, or if known, is practically objected to."[6] A burglar clearly fits the definition of a trespasser.

An occupier still owes some responsibility to a trespasser. In particular, the occupier will be liable for any act done with the deliberate intention of doing harm to the trespasser, or an act done with reckless disregard for the presence of the trespasser.[7]

Suppose that in the opening scenario, John Jackson, a 12-year-old boy, is engaged in the dangerous practice of joy-riding on top of the elevator and is seriously injured. There is a technical defect in the elevator that allows this practice to persist. Ron has seen other boys doing this before and has asked them to leave. What is the duty owed to John?

Technically, John is a trespasser and as such is owed a very low duty. The courts, however, have often mitigated the harshness of this result, particularly when the trespasser is a child. For example, courts have at times reclassified the trespasser as a licensee, interpreted the duty owed the trespasser very generously, and even brought the children's claims under the ordinary law of negligence.

In all probability, if Ron knew that children were playing on the elevator and could have taken steps to prevent it—that is, steps that would actually have removed the defect, as opposed to simply posting signs that were routinely ignored—liability would be imposed.

Liability under Occupiers' Liability Legislation

Alberta, British Columbia, Manitoba, Ontario, and Prince Edward Island have enacted occupiers' liability legislation.[8] Although there are differences in the legislation from one jurisdiction to the next, there is also considerable common ground.

The legislation normally provides for a high duty of care—equivalent to the negligence standard—to be owed to entrants who are legitimately on the property (at

---

invitee
Any person who comes onto the property to provide the occupier with a benefit.

licensee
Any person whose presence is not a benefit to the occupier but to which the occupier has no objection.

trespasser
Any person who is not invited onto property and whose presence is either unknown to the occupier or is objected to by the occupier.

---

4. *Indermaur* v. *Dames* (1867), L.R. 2 C.P. 311 at 313.
5. Lewis N. Klar, *Tort Law*, 2d ed. (Toronto: Carswell, 1996) at 433.
6. *Robert Addie & Sons* v. *Dumbreck*, [1929] A.C. 358 (H.L.).
7. *Ibid.* at 371.
8. *Supra* note 2.

common law, contractual entrants, invitees, licensees). Responsibility to trespassers differs among the various statutes. In general, however, an occupier must not create deliberate harm or danger, and the responsibilities increase where the trespassers are children.[9]

If Ron's business were located, for example, on Prince Edward Island instead of in Newfoundland, the court would likely still find both the elevator company and Ron liable to Julie. Specifically, it would find that the elevator company ought to have foreseen that harm would occur as a result of a defective clip. Likewise, since Ron was aware of the use of the defective clip and was prepared to allow the elevator to remain in service, the subsequent harm was foreseeable. In the alternative scenario of 12-year-old John Jackson, liability would likely also be imposed.

In the context of Ron's business, the outcomes using either statutory or common law applications are, to all intents and purposes, the same. Nonetheless, it remains important to apply the correct principles to the specific provincial context, as responsibilities can and will vary at times.

The Tort of Nuisance — *people interfere with the usage of the property.*

nuisance
Any activity on an occupier's property that unreasonably and substantially interferes with the neighbour's rights to enjoyment of his or her property.

The tort of **nuisance**[10] addresses conflicts between neighbours stemming from land use. It concerns intentional or unintentional actions taken on one neighbour's land that cause harm of some sort on another's, as in these examples:

- Noise from a steel fabricator's 800-ton press seriously interrupts the neighbours' sleep.
- Ashes and unpleasant odours escaping from a rendering company because of dated technology are carried onto neighbouring properties.
- Sophisticated electronic equipment installed on the roof of a taxi company interferes with the television reception of neighbours who do not have cable.

The focus of nuisance is on one's right to enjoy the benefits of land/property uninterrupted by the actions of neighbours. The general test is whether the impugned activity has resulted in "an unreasonable and substantial interference with the use and enjoyment of land."[11] For example, Ron may vent the kiln and the decorating and glazing operation in the direction of the window his neighbour must routinely leave open in the summer for cool air. Conversely, the restaurant/bar in the building next door may begin hiring bands that play so loudly that Ron's tenants are threatening to leave.

Although the test for nuisance sounds straightforward, it forces courts to balance competing interests and has therefore been difficult to apply, particularly as society becomes increasingly urbanized. The following case illustrates these problems.

Locating houses and factories adjacent to each other may lead to claims in nuisance.

---

9. Klar, *supra* note 5 at 443–450.

10. As Klar, *ibid.* at 525, indicates, there are two distinct causes of action in nuisance: public nuisance and private nuisance. Since public nuisance plays only a "peripheral role in contemporary law," this text will focus only on private nuisance.

11. *Ibid.* at 535.

Case

Mandrake Management Consultants Ltd. et al. v. Toronto Transit Commission, [1993] 102 D.L.R. (4th) 12 (Ont. C.A.)

The Business Context: Many of the byproducts of a business's legitimate activity cause harm to those on properties nearby. At what point should legitimate activities be curtailed because of these unavoidable consequences?

Factual Background: Mandrake were owners and occupiers of an office building who complained of noise and vibration coming from the subway system of the Toronto Transit Commission (TTC), although the TTC was operating according to its statutory authority to do so.

The Legal Question: Had a nuisance taken place? In particular, would the ordinary and reasonable resident of that locality view the disturbance as a substantial interference with the enjoyment of land?

Resolution: In forming an opinion, the court had to consider the following:

(a) the nature of the locality in question
(b) the severity of the harm
(c) the sensitivity of the plaintiff
(d) the utility of the defendant's conduct

The court found that the TTC's intrusion on Mandrake's enjoyment of property did cause significant discomfort to the plaintiffs, but that the plaintiff was unusually sensitive and that the TTC's use of its own property was reasonable.

Critical Analysis:

1. If a court has to balance the rights of individual property owners against the wider public interest (through a transit authority) to enjoy a subway system, what actions might be considered sufficient for a successful nuisance action?
2. Is it appropriate to place the onus of making these decisions on the courts? What should be the role of elected officials and the executive arm of government?

In striking a balance between the respective parties, courts have evolved the following guidelines:

- Intrusions must be significant and not reasonable. For example, in the *Mandrake* case, the building owners and occupiers were found to be unusually sensitive, and this was something for which the subway operator should not be responsible.
- Nuisance typically does not arise where the intrusion is only temporary. For example, construction and demolition may be unpleasant, but are likely to be considered temporary and typically will not lead to a remedy in nuisance.
- Not all interests are protected by the tort of nuisance. The most well-known interests for which there is no protection through nuisance are a view from the property[12] and access to natural light.[13]
- In nuisance actions courts will consider trade-offs in interest. For example, in the *Mandrake* case the court ruled that the benefits of the subway, both to the citizens as a whole and to Mandrake in particular, outweighed the impact of the particular nuisance.
- Original and/or prevailing uses are important in deciding competing uses. A person building a home on a site near an existing factory will have few rights to complain about, for example, truck or machinery noise.[14]

A finding of nuisance has serious consequences. Those affected may claim damages, as well as an injunction. The latter could result in not only a curtailment of activities, but also the financial destruction of the business.

---

12. *Becze* v. *Edmonton (City)* (1993), 13 Alta. L.R. (3d) 61, 144 A.R. 321 (Q.B.).

13. *Earl Putnam Organization Ltd.* v. *Macdonald* (1978), 21 O.R. (2d) 815, 91 D.L.R. (3d) 714 (C.A.).

14. In *Mandrake Management Consultants Ltd. et al.* v. *Toronto Transit Commission*, [1993] 102 D.L.R. (4th) 12 (Ont. C.A.) 6 at 21, the court said, "...I think it must follow, similarly, that people operating businesses in a locality which is essentially a commercial area are required to put up with a considerably greater intrusion on their sensibilities than do people living in a locality which is residentially oriented or substantially residential."

Competing Interests

Some of the limitations to the tort of nuisance may seem unfair. For example, why should a home owner who has a magnificent view of, say, English Bay, Vancouver, not have that view protected from a neighbour wishing to build a major addition? In other cases, courts are being asked to make difficult choices when weighing competing interests. Should a factory employing large numbers of people be forced to close because the addition of a third shift, necessary to make it run at economically viable levels, will cause serious noise disturbances to nearby homeowners?

While there is no doubt these issues are complex, it is important to remember the role of statute law.

In modern society, laws and regulations are often enacted to address many of the competing interests surrounding land use. For example, local zoning laws address who can build where and how to protect light and views. Noise bylaws prepared at a local level control the hours during which a factory can engage in noisy operations. Where the issues can be handled in this manner, courts are often reluctant to intrude by way of the common law.

Critical Analysis: Who is in the best position to deal with the underlying causes of nuisance disputes—courts or legislatures? Why?

Trespass to Property

trespass
The act of coming onto another's property without the occupier's express or implied consent.

Trespass arises in one of two ways:

- A person comes onto the property against the occupier's express or implied permission.
- A person comes onto the property with the occupier's express or implied consent but is subsequently asked to leave.[15] Any person who refuses to leave becomes a trespasser.

It is usually easy to prove trespass. However, taking legal action may accomplish little for the occupier because often the "injury" produced by the trespass is simply an annoyance.[16] For example, perhaps Ron is worried about children who take a short cut to school through the alley behind his building, despite notices to "Keep Out." Bringing a claim in trespass against the children may accomplish little. It may be far simpler and certainly cheaper to erect a gate. In serious cases of trespass, an injunction is often the remedy of choice.

Torts from Business Operations

Business operations involve a broad range of activities from which tort action can arise. A useful way of categorizing these torts is to consider separately torts involving customers or clients and those involving competitors.

---

15. It should be noted that there are statutory restrictions on a business person's common law right to do business with whom she or he sees fit. Alberta human rights legislation, for example, prohibits discrimination by those who offer goods or services that are customarily available to the public. This means that if a business person refused to serve a customer because of that customer's ethnicity or gender, for example, and that customer refused to leave, then a trespass has occurred. However, the business person would also be subject to a penalty for violating human rights legislation.

16. In New Brunswick, for example, legislation has been passed that imposes fines against trespassers, particularly in public places; *Trespass Act*, R.S.N.B. 1973, c. T-11.2.

Torts Involving Customers

Chapter 11 considered the most important tort arising in this context: negligence. Product liability, motor vehicle accidents, alcohol-related liability, and negligent misrepresentations are all examples of negligence affecting the business/consumer relationship.

In this section additional torts will be considered.

False Imprisonment

false imprisonment
Unlawful detention or physical restraint or the perception thereof.

False imprisonment occurs most often in retail selling. It arises where any person detains another without lawful justification.

In order for a false imprisonment to have occurred, the victim must have been prevented from going where he or she has a lawful right to be. The tort includes both actual physical restraint and the perception that restraint exists.

For example, assume that Ron has been experiencing major losses through theft from his factory outlet. Instead of applying his usual honour system with customers (they bring the items downstairs to him), he hires a salesperson for the three-week period before the holidays. The salesperson believes that a customer has hidden a valuable item in his bag, so she takes his arm and asks him to come downstairs to Ron. It turns out that the customer has nothing in the bag and has only agreed to go downstairs as he feared an embarrassing scene would otherwise ensue. In this case, a false imprisonment has likely occurred since the customer's liberty has been constrained without any lawful justification.

The tort of false imprisonment clearly presents retailers in particular with a real dilemma. In order to defend against the tort of false imprisonment, the retailer and its employees must prove that they actually saw the person being detained commit a crime. In short, they must have seen the customer taking an item from the store without having paid for it. A suspicion or even a "reasonable belief" that someone committed a crime is not justification for restraint. This is in contrast to the rights of the police, who may detain when there are reasonable grounds to believe a crime has taken place. Whatever the predicament of storekeepers facing serious shoplifting problems, it is clear that neither they nor their store detectives have any greater rights to detain than does any other citizen.[17] When in doubt, they should call the police.

False imprisonment can arise in other contexts, although these are not common. Ron may have had a recurring problem with children riding his elevator and hitting the emergency button between floors. Ron is angry about the cost to him of this practice, and one day, when the elevator accidentally stops between floors confining some children, he decides to teach them a lesson by leaving them there for an hour

Stores can take preventive action to minimize the risk of shoplifting.

---

17. *Kovacs* v. *Ontario Jockey Club,* [1995] O.J. No. 2181, 126 D.L.R. (4th) 576 (Ont. Gen. Div.).

or so before summoning a repair person to assist. The confined children may well succeed in a claim based on the tort of false imprisonment. Ron has no right to detain them in this manner.

Assault and Battery

The torts of assault and battery (introduced in Chapter 10) are not common in a business or professional context although they may occur, as illustrated in these examples:

- A security firm hires a physically intimidating employee to evict tenants. The employee's practice is to advise the tenant that she can leave voluntarily or with the help of his friends and that he strongly recommends the former.
- A physician performs non-emergency surgery, competently but without appropriate informed consent.

The torts of assault and battery often occur consecutively but can also occur independently. An assault is the act of threatening someone with physical harm by disturbing his or her sense of security. Battery is the actual physical contact or violation of that bodily security. The contact need not cause actual harm. Any form of contact is sufficient to meet the definition of the tort.[18] Where the torts are proven, the most common remedy is damages.

Deceit

deceit
Fraudulent misrepresentation that induces another to enter a contract.

The tort of **deceit** arises out of misrepresentations that are made either fraudulently or with reckless disregard for their truth. If fraud or reckless disregard is proven, the person harmed may be released from the contract (see Chapter 8). The commercial implications are immense.

---

18. Klar, *supra* note 5 at 39, 41.

Business to Business Torts

Passing Off

passing off
Presenting another's
goods or services as
one's own.

The tort of **passing off** occurs when one person represents her goods or services as being those of another. While it may be common to think of the tort in terms of the "dirty tricks" some businesses might adopt to compete unfairly with others, the tort can also be committed inadvertently or innocently.

The tort of passing off arises, for example, when a business name is used that is so similar to an existing business name that the public is misled into thinking that the businesses are somehow related. It also may occur where a competing company markets a product that is similar in presentation or overall look to a product already established on the market.

Ron's discovery of the "Man of the Sea" replica product at a trade show presents a classic passing off scenario.

To prove passing off, Ron will need to establish the following:[19]

1. Goodwill or a reputation is attached to his product.

   Ron's "Old Man of the Sea" product already has a well-established and valuable reputation among the relevant buying public. In other words, he holds goodwill[20] in the product, and that goodwill, or ability to attract buyers, flows either from the look of the product or from its name, or from both.

2. A misrepresentation—express or implied—by the maker of the cheap replica has led or is likely to lead members of the public into believing that it is Ron's product or a product authorized by Ron.

   Whether the competitor actually intended to confuse the public does not matter. Given the similarity of the two figurines, the competitor will make many of its sales by falsely associating itself with the established reputation of Ron's "Old Man of the Sea" product.

3. He has or will likely suffer damages.

   Ron does not necessarily have to show monetary loss—his action will succeed if he is able to show loss of control over his business reputation.

The following case illustrates the tort of passing off.

While the award of damages is one remedy for a passing off action, businesses claiming they are being harmed in this way will likely first seek an injunction forbidding the defendant from continuing the deceptive copying. In the case of *Walt Disney Productions* v. *Triple Five,* for example, Walt Disney Productions secured a permanent injunction prohibiting the use of the name Fantasyland at West Edmonton Mall's amusement park.

The *Trade-marks Act*[21] contains a statutory form of action that bears a strong resemblance to the tort of passing off. Such legislation will be considered more thoroughly in Chapter 18. Where the legislation is not relevant, as in the *Walt Disney Productions* v. *Triple Five* case, the plaintiff is entitled to pursue her action for passing off at common law.

---

19. *Walt Disney Productions* v. *Triple Five Corp. et al.,* [1994] 113 D.L.R. (4th) 229 (Alta. C.A.).
20. Goodwill refers to the reputation of the business and its expectation of patronage in the future.
21. R.S.C. 1985, c. T-13, s 7.

Case

Walt Disney Productions v. *Triple Five Corp. et al.*,
[1994] 113 D.L.R. (4th) 229 (Alta. C.A.)

The Business Context: Businesses take a good deal of care in selecting names that they believe best capture the nature of their activity. The question is, to what extent can this name be protected?

Factual Background: Disney has operated Disneyland, an outdoor amusement park in Anaheim, California, since 1955 and Walt Disney World in Florida since 1971. It also owns amusement parks in Europe and Japan. Each amusement park contains three theme parks. One of these parks is Fantasyland, a name that Disney created and has used in its international promotions. Since 1981 Triple Five has owned and operated the West Edmonton Mall, a retail shopping mall. In 1983 it opened in the mall an indoor amusement park called Fantasyland.

Surveys conducted on behalf of Disney revealed that the majority of people in the Edmonton area associated the name Fantasyland with the West Edmonton Mall. However, in other areas of Canada, excluding Calgary, most people associated the name Fantasyland with Disney's theme parks.

The Legal Question: Had Triple Five, by using the name Fantasyland, deprived Disney of the right to control that name and the reputation and goodwill associated with it?

Resolution: Judge Thomas McCarthy accepted Disney's expert evidence and used it, along with other evidence, in finding the existence of goodwill and confusion about actual ownership of the name:

> Of significance is the fact that the name adopted by the appellants [Triple Five] is identical to that in respect of which the respondent [Disney] has established goodwill. Both facilities are amusement parks with many similar features. In these circumstances, confusion on the part of the ordinary member of the public using ordinary care is difficult to avoid....

The judge also found that these actions diminished Disney's property rights and their potential value in the Edmonton area. The judge stated,

> The control over the reputation, image or goodwill which it has carefully nurtured and developed has passed into other hands.... [Because] an appreciable number of people believe that there is a business relationship between Fantasyland at West Edmonton Mall and the Disney amusement parks, or are uncertain about it, there exists a real risk of harm to the reputation or image which the respondent has carefully built. A likelihood exists that any lack or deficiency in the entertainment, service, or safety, provided by the appellants [Triple Five] at its amusement park will reflect in the minds of members of the public on the reputation of the respondent [Disney] and its facilities.

Critical Analysis: Is there a problem with obtaining a business advantage in this way? Businesses compete aggressively in all kinds of ways; why not this way as well?

Interference with Contractual Relations

interference with
contractual relations
Incitement to break the
contractual obligations
of another.

The tort of **interference with contractual relations** is known by a variety of names, including interference with contract, inducement of breach of contract, and procuring a breach of contract.[22] It has its origins in the relationship of master and servant. The common law made it actionable if one master attempted to "poach" the servant of another. In legal terms, the "poacher" was seen as enticing the servant to break his existing contract of employment, which, in turn, caused economic harm to the master. Over time, this tort extended beyond master/servant relations to any form of contractual relationship.

---

22. P. Burns, "Tort Injury to Economic Interests: Some Facets of Legal Response" (1980) 38 Can. Bar Rev. 103 at 103.

The tort prohibits a variety of conduct, including conduct whereby the defendant directly induces another to breach its contract with the plaintiff.

In Ron's business, the tort could be important in at least two different contexts:

- Ron employs a skilled potter who makes the "Old Man of the Sea" product. The potter has a three-year employment contract. A competitor approaches the potter in the second year of the contract and encourages the potter to work for him with promises of higher wages and better conditions. The competitor's conduct is tortious because he knew about the contract and acted with the objective of convincing the potter to join him. Since this could only happen if the potter were to breach his contract with Ron, the tort has been made out.
- Ron's largest and most lucrative supply contract is with one of the leading tourism organizations in Nova Scotia. The owner of the competing business making "Man of the Sea" products approaches the tourism organization and suggests that if it breaks the contract with Ron and buys from her, she can offer larger profit margins and the final product can sell for less, thus increasing the volume of sales. This scenario also has all the ingredients of this tort.

In both cases, then, Ron could likely make out the tort of interference with contractual relations. While he will sue for damages, he may also seek an injunction to prevent a breach of contract occurring if he finds out in time. A court would never order the potter to work for Ron—courts will not award specific performance with contracts of personal service—but it can order damages against the potter for breach of contract and damages and/or an injunction against the competitor for the tort of interference with contractual relations.

An example of a successful tort action is *Ernst & Young* v. *Stuart*.[23] A partner left the accounting firm of Ernst & Young to join the firm of Arthur Andersen. In so doing, the partner violated a term of the partnership agreement requiring one year's notice of intention to retire from the partnership. Ernst & Young sued both the partner and the new firm, the latter for interfering with contractual relations. Both actions were successful.

Defamation   ← intensional tort.

The categorization of torts between those affecting customers and those that are business to business does not work particularly well with defamation. A business can defame or be defamed by any person with whom it comes in contact.

defamation
The public utterance of a false statement of fact or opinion that harms another's reputation.

the person is intended.

The tort of **defamation** seeks to "protect the reputation of individuals against unfounded and unjustified attacks."[24] Though all jurisdictions in Canada have legislation modifying the common law of defamation to some extent, the fundamentals of the common law action remain.[25]

Common terms for defamation are *slander* (typically for the oral form) and *libel* (usually the print form). These terms are not always consistently applied, and the correct legal usage for either is defamation.[26]

---

23. (1997), 144 D.L.R. (4th) 328, 92 B.C.L.R. (2d) 335 (B.C.C.A.).

24. Klar, *supra* note 5 at 551.

25. *Ibid.*

26. The distinction between libel and slander has been abolished by statute in a number of provinces—namely, Alberta, Manitoba, New Brunswick, Newfoundland, Prince Edward Island, and Nova Scotia; *ibid.* at 552.

The key ingredients to the tort are as follows:

- *has to be false*
- The defendant has made a statement about the plaintiff;
- *defence on defamation* The statement presents the defendant in an uncomplimentary light;
- The statement would have had the effect of lowering the plaintiff's reputation in the mind of a reasonable person hearing it;
- *- fair comment* The statement has been communicated to at least one person who is not the person being defamed.[27]
- *- truth*

The plaintiff will then succeed if the defendant is unable to establish a defence to the action. If, for example, the defendant can show that the statement is true, he has a complete defence.[28]

While defamation is most common in the print or broadcasting industries, it can occur in other contexts. Whenever anyone expresses a negative opinion about another, whether it be in casual conversation or by formal reference, there is the potential for a defamation suit. In Ron's case, for example, Ron might become so irritated by the actions of his "Man of the Sea" competitor that he falsely accuses her of operating a sweatshop. In *Moores* v. *Salter*,[29] a letter of reprimand stated that the employees who were involved in a fight showed violent tempers and used language "not conducive to civilized human beings." This was found to be a defamatory statement by the Newfoundland court.[30]

A particular problem today is the ability to defame by electronic means, as is illustrated in the following box.

Injurious Falsehood or Product Defamation

injurious or malicious falsehood
The utterance of a false statement about another's goods or services that is harmful to the reputation of those goods or services.

Injurious or malicious falsehood concerns false statements made not about a person but about the goods or services produced by that person. Sometimes the distinction between injurious falsehood and defamation is subtle; for example, if the

E-Business Applications

TECHNOLOGY AND THE LAW

A growing objective for business is to guard against defamation via electronic media. The danger of e-mails, in particular, is that once they are sent they cannot be retrieved, yet they can be instantaneously transmitted to an enormous audience. There is likely no one who has not hit the Send key and then realized they were transmitting to unintended recipients. Similar risks arise on the Internet. Since the legal process allows for the discovery or tracing of electronic words to their author, electronic defamation can most certainly be established even long after a defamatory message has apparently been deleted.

Critical Analysis: What practical steps can a business implement to minimize the risk of its employees or managers defaming others? Where does the line lie between protecting the business from this harm and protecting the privacy of employees?

---

27. *Ibid.* at 554-555.
28. *Ibid.* at 564.
29. (1982), 37 Nfld. & P.E.I.R. 128, 104 A.P.R. 128 (Nfld. Dist. Ct.).
30. *Ibid.* at 134-135.

statement is made that a particular company routinely provides shoddy maintenance, is this a negative reflection on the quality of the people doing the work or on the company's services? In such a situation, the complainant would sue in both defamation and injurious falsehood.

Injurious falsehood requires the plaintiff to establish that the statement about the goods or services was false and was published (uttered) with malice or improper motive. For example, if Ron told others that the material used in the "Man of the Sea" product was cheap and inferior when he knew that the product was actually made with high-quality wood, malice would be established.

Injurious falsehood can be particularly problematic in the context of comparative and negative advertising, as the following case shows.

Case

Mead Johnson Canada v. *Ross Pediatrics* (1997), 31 O.R. (3d) 237 (Gen. Div.)

The Business Context: It is relatively common for sellers to engage in comparative advertising. In this case, Mead Johnson Canada (Mead), was claiming that Ross Pediatrics (Ross) uttered a false statement (injurious falsehood) in its promotional materials. Here it sought an interim injunction to prevent the continued distribution of the material.

Factual Background: Ross began selling a new infant formula, Similac Advance, using promotional materials that included many representations to which Mead, the maker of a competing infant formula, Enfalac, objected.

Mead representatives obtained samples of the professional brochure and some of the consumer materials. Research Management Group conducted market studies for Mead, which suggested that 81 to 91 percent of new parents, having seen the promotional materials, would choose the new product.

Mead argued that the Similac Advance materials were false and misleading in claiming that Similac was

- superior to other formulas
- similar to breast milk
- clinically proven to strengthen infants' immune systems

The Legal Question: Had injurious falsehood occurred? Ross argued that Mead and Enfalac were not identified by the Ross promotional materials. No injurious falsehood could be established where there was no identification of the injured party.

Resolution: While it was true that Enfalac was not identified in the brochure materials, Enfalac was identified as a target in the materials distributed to the Ross sales force. It was also true that Enfalac, being the other major competitor in this marketplace, would be identified by implication. On this basis, the court held that all of Ross's competitors, including Mead, might have a cause of action if the representations were false and misleading.

Critical Analysis:
1. Many companies engage in comparative advertising. What could Ross have done that would have avoided any suggestion of injurious falsehood?
2. If the injunction continued, what would be the business implications for Ross? What recommendations might you have for senior management in order to avoid a similar episode in the future?

Managing Risk for Diverse Commercial Torts

Each of the torts discussed in this chapter exposes a business to liability. A risk management analysis should address the fundamental issues that may arise, always taking into account that business activities are usually engaged in by employees in the course of employment. As discussed in Chapter 10, an employer is responsible under the doctrine of vicarious liability for the torts of their employees committed in the course of employment

An occupier's liability risk management plan would ask the following questions:

- Are there dangers on the property? Are adequate warnings and protections given to visitors?
- Are there known trespassers, in particular children, who come onto the property?
- What could be done to reduce the risk flowing from the dangers?
- Has the occupier complied with all legislative obligations? Examples include provincial legislation concerning workers' health and safety, as well as municipal bylaws providing for snow and ice removal.

Although the classification of entrants under the common law of occupiers' liability is a useful exercise after an incident occurs (it helps determine liability), from a risk management perspective the process is not particularly helpful since the business that occupies property cannot easily predict what class of entrant will be injured on its property. Maintaining safe premises as a preventative measure is much better than having to debate, after the fact, what class of entrant the injured plaintiff is and what standard is owed.

For each additional tort, a similar list of questions could be generated. For example, if the business designs and creates consumer goods,

- Do staff understand that they cannot innovate by copying the ideas of others?
- Is a program in place to review new product ideas, including all aspects of design, to ensure there can be no accusation of passing off?
- Is a climate in place that allows a manager to step in and say, "This cannot be done because I believe we have crossed the line"?

Tort law evolves to reflect changing social values. What at one time might have been acceptable behaviour may no longer be considered appropriate. This can be seen, for example, in the changing approach to the environmental effects of commercial activities. When a business is assessing its tort exposure, it cannot assume that existing legal rules will apply in perpetuity. Also, it must consider how it can influence public opinion and social values, as it is these that will determine the bounds of future tort liability.

One business's approach to risk management is described in the box below.

McCurdy: The *Record*

A BUSINESS PERSPECTIVE

I am the managing editor of the *Record*, a daily regional newspaper in southwestern Ontario with a circulation of about 75 000 weekdays and 100 000 Saturdays. I am the person with primary responsibility for ensuring our paper avoids legal difficulties, which includes acting as the intermediary between lawyers and reporters.

As a newspaper, we must always be aware of legal risks, mainly defamation (libel) law and issues of contempt of court. The latter arise primarily in the context of reporting police charges and court cases and, occasionally, the protection of story sources. Because defamation is a constant concern, all our senior editors and some copy-editors are trained to identify potential problems. If any problem comes up, they bring it to the editor or me. If we know we have a contentious issue, our overriding rule is to proceed with caution. The editor works closely with the reporter from the beginning of the story, and the monitoring continues through to the final proofing and headline writing.

We do not have in-house counsel at the *Record*. We have a local law firm and a specialized Toronto firm on 24-hour call. Our paper is edited overnight, so lawyers have to be available when we need them. The key to the protection of our business from defamation suits is prevention. All senior editors

and some reporters are obliged to attend an annual seminar on recent legal developments run by our Toronto law firm. We also belong to the Canadian Newspaper Association, which puts out a regular bulletin, *Press in the Courts*, alerting us to current legal issues.

Part of our strategy in protecting our business involves how we handle complaints when they first arise. We are self-insured and, as such, have a certain amount of freedom in developing this strategy. Complaints, or potential lawsuits, fall into two categories: nuisance complaints and genuine errors on our part causing harm. However good we are at protecting ourselves, we will always face complaints in both groupings. We have long ago developed the strategy of defending vigorously the nuisance claims. We cannot afford to be seen as a soft target—word gets around too quickly. On the other hand, as soon as we are notified of a genuine error, our approach is to do everything we can to minimize the harm done and address the complainant's concerns. It has been our experience that if we acknowledge our errors candidly and with courtesy and even compassion, most complainants are satisfied with our corrective actions. The way in which we manage our initial response is critical to the final resolution of the complaint.

The ultimate defence for libel is the truth. However, proving truth in a courtroom isn't always that easy. That's why documentation is so important. Reporters and editors must keep their notes and tapes to prove a story is fair and accurate.

I have a word of advice to anyone who has a defamation complaint. This is a very technical area of the law. There are perhaps only a handful of law firms across Canada handling highly specialized defamation cases, and they are expensive. From our experience, you get what you pay for.

McCurdy, managing editor of the *Record*.

Business Law in Practice Revisited

1. What potential legal actions does Julie have against Ron's business?

Ron is the occupier of the building. As such, he is responsible to different classes of people who come onto his property both lawfully and unlawfully. The extent of the responsibility varies depending on why the person is on the premises and whether this is in a common law or statutory jurisdiction.

In Newfoundland, common law principles apply. Julie is clearly an invitee and, as such, Ron owes a duty to warn of "any unusual danger [of] which he knows or ought to know." In this case, it appears he was aware of the inadequate, temporary repair job on the elevator, and therefore had the requisite knowledge.

If these events occurred in a jurisdiction where statute law has replaced the common law of occupier's liability, the responsibility to Julie, a person on the property legitimately, would be very similar to that of the tort of negligence. In all likelihood Ron would be equally responsible.

2. What is the responsibility of Elevator XL Services here?

Elevator XL Services is an occupier, since it had control over the elevator in order to conduct the repairs. This was also the time when the harm occurred. Following the same analysis as used in question 1 above, Elevator XL Services will be liable to Julie under both common and statute law, since she was on the property lawfully and, at common law, was an invitee.

3. Does Ron have any recourse against the manufacturer of the replica figurine?

Ron can take action based on the tort of passing off. He can claim that the actions of the competitor met the conditions of the tort of passing off, and as such he will either seek an injunction to stop any further action by the competitor, or damages, or both. He will need to prove that his "Old Man of the Sea" figurine existed prior to the "Man of the Sea" product, that it had an established reputation that was of value, that the products' names and appearances were similar enough to result in genuine confusion in the minds of the potential purchasers, and that the confusion will result in loss of sales or harm to Ron's business.

4. How can Ron manage his business's potential tort liabilities?

Ron, as owner/occupier of premises, should do a safety audit of all parts of the building to ensure that neither his tenants nor his visitors (lawful or otherwise) could be harmed by any hazards. Ron should consider all aspects of his business operations, including the building itself, obvious hazards such as the kiln, maintenance of elevators, clearing of sidewalks, hiring and training of all employees, and insurance coverage.

In terms of Ron's products, Ron must

- monitor the activity of competitors and potential competitors to ensure that there is no inappropriate copying of his designs.
- ensure that the glazes and materials he uses are lead-free and otherwise harmless.
- hire staff who know how to treat customers well and are trained (or will be trained) as to their obligations should they have to handle shoplifters

Chapter Summary

While negligence is the most common tort a business will encounter, various other commercially relevant torts merit analysis. These torts can be categorized and assessed according to whether they would arise because the business is an occupier of property or because it provides a product or service. Furthermore, torts that could be committed against a competitor can be grouped separately from those more likely to involve a consumer. Though these distinctions are not definitive, they provide a useful way of organizing the variety of torts that affect the commercial world.

As an occupier, a business must be sure to keep its property safe so that people coming on site are not injured. Otherwise it faces occupiers' liability according to a regime that classifies the entrant in question. To avoid committing the tort of nuisance, a business must not unreasonably and substantially interfere with the right of its neighbours to enjoy their property. The law governing trespass gives occupiers a right to exert control over who comes onto their premises, subject to human rights codes.

Torts arising from business operations in relation to customers are false imprisonment, assault and battery, and deceit. Through these torts, the law seeks to ensure people's right to move about as they please, to have their bodily integrity respected, and not to be misled about the quality of a product or service.

Torts more likely to be committed against a competitor include passing off, inference with contractual relations, defamation, and injurious falsehood or product defamation. These torts endeavour to protect a business's property in its own reputation. This means that one business cannot falsely represent its goods or services as being someone else's, nor can it malign the reputation of another business or the product or service it sells.

Given the diverse and wide-ranging nature of a business's potential liability in tort, preventing torts from ever occurring should be one of management's top priorities.

Study Chapter

Key Terms and Concepts

contractual entrant (p. 243)
deceit (p. 249)
defamation (p. 252)
false imprisonment (p. 248)
injurious or malicious falsehood (p. 253)
interference with contractual relations (p. 251)
invitee (p. 244)
licensee (p. 244)
nuisance (p. 245)
occupier (p. 243)
passing off (p. 250)
trespass (p. 247)
trespasser (p. 244)

Questions for Review

1. How does the law define the occupier of property?

2. What is the major change made by legislation in many provinces of Canada to the common law of occupiers' liability?

3. What is a nuisance in tort law?

4. The courts have developed pragmatic rules for resolving inherent conflicts that arise in applying the tort of nuisance. Give two examples of these rules.

5. Under what conditions can trespass arise?

6. What are the limitations to the ability of a store detective to detain a customer who is suspected of shoplifting?

7. Describe how a false imprisonment claim might arise, other than by a person being physically restrained.

8. Most tort claims against doctors fall within negligence. What other tort might be relevant and why?

9. What is passing off and what practices was this tort created to prevent?

10. What are the two forms of defamation, how do they arise, and what is a complete defence to this tort?

11. Identify what must be established to prove deceit.

12. Give a practical example of injurious falsehood.

Questions for Discussion

1. One of the controversial aspects of the tort of occupiers' liability and its more recent statutory form arises out of the rights afforded trespassers. One possible change to the law would be to eliminate all rights. What would be the consequences of this approach? Are there some trespassers and some circumstances that you would feel uncomfortable leaving without protection? Is it right that property owners should have absolutely no responsibilities whatsoever to those coming onto their property, even for improper purposes?

2. The classic example of a modern nuisance claim involves a couple who realize their rural dream by buying land 30 kilometres outside of town. Unfortunately, this is an active agricultural area and the local farmers engage in the practice of spreading liquid manure over their fields each spring. Not surprisingly, this is not a welcome addition to the lifestyle of the newcomers to the area. In this example of competing interests, what issues do you think it is relevant for courts to consider? Would it make any difference if it was the offending farmer who broke up the land to sell as building lots? Are these issues relevant to the common law?

3. Retailers suffer extensive losses due to "inventory shrinkage" or shoplifting. This is a very real cost that is passed on to all virtuous shoppers who have no intention of engaging in theft. The tort of false imprisonment places serious limitations on any action the retailer can take to detain suspected shoplifters. What are the pros and cons of these limitations? Are they fair? What are the countervailing interests at stake here?

4. The tort of interference with contractual relations has its origins in the ancient master/servant relationship. Today, however, there is greater recognition of mobility rights, and those in business are generally used to competing in an aggressive marketplace. Given that the aggrieved party has the right to sue for breach of contract, should this tort be retained? What rights might not be protected if it were to be abolished? Are these important?

Situations for Discussion

1. A convenience store owner has suffered several burglaries in the past few months. He is very concerned, as he believes this trend means he will likely lose his livelihood. He elects to arm himself with a shotgun for self-protection: the most recent break-in was by armed thieves. One evening, three thieves enter the premises. He shouts at them to leave as they approach the till and he brings out his shotgun. The thieves immediately start running out of the store. The store owner shoots one of them as he is leaving. Has the injured thief any right to compensation?

2. A customer fell in a puddle of dishwashing soap that had dripped onto the floor of a supermarket. She was wearing high heeled shoes and, although she saw the puddle, she was reasonably confident that she could walk through it safely. Instead, she fell and sustained serious injury. She is now suing for compensation for her injuries. What are the chances of her suit succeeding?[31]

3. Gum Company manufactures the dominant brand of sugarless peppermint gum in Canada. Chewing Company wants to compete by introducing a new product. Chewing sells gum in a package that looks very similar to Gum's product: both products are white with red lettering, each has red on the end of the packages, and the packages are soft foil and paper combinations. A closer analysis of other sugarless and sugar-containing peppermint gum products shows that all packages are some combination of white and red and that the majority are made of similar types of materials. What action can Gum pursue, and what are the chances of success?

4. The Kumar family are long-time residents of an older neighbourhood of a major city. They inherited their home from Ms. Kumar's parents. Their own family is now grown up and gone, and Mr. and Ms. Kumar enjoy the pleasures of the quiet and beautifully maintained back garden—that is, until the past few months. The neighbours on one side of the Kumars sold their property about a year ago, and the new owners have shown the Kumars their plans for the property. The plans involve demolishing the home and building a much larger house, very close to the boundaries of the property. Because the building will be three storeys high and because of its size and location, all afternoon sun will effectively be blocked from the Kumars' garden. Moreover, they will lose their privacy. The Kumars are distraught about this. They are also very concerned about the noise and disruption from the demolition and construction. Finally, they have noticed that large and noisy air-conditioning and heating units will be placed adjacent to their property, right beside their bedroom wall. Assuming that all these changes are within the local planning rules, what are the Kumars' rights?

5. The Happy Bar operates in Fergus, Ontario. The bar routinely attracts large numbers of students from the local universities. Because of its location, students have to drive at least 20 kilometres. The owners of the bar are acutely aware of their responsibilities both to ensure that no underage students drink and that all patrons leave the bar in a vehicle driven by a designated driver. On peak nights the bar brings in additional staff to ensure that its policies are complied with. On

---

31. Based on *Westfair Foods Ltd.* v. *Derby Holdings, Ltd.* [1996] S.J. No. 733, 150 Sask. R. 71 (Q.B.).

one particular Saturday night, a regular staff member calls in sick, but recommends his friend, who is a law and security student at the local community college. He assures the manager that this friend is familiar with the appropriate practices and guidelines and is fully responsible. The friend is hired for the night and appears to the manager to be capable. Around 11:30 p.m., a group of young people become particularly rowdy, and one moves toward the door, car keys in hand and shouting to her friends to get into the car quickly so they can find a "really good party." The new staff member is the only employee nearby and able to intervene. He rushes to the young woman, pins her arms behind her with one hand, and puts a choke hold around her neck. He demands she throw down her keys. Unfortunately, the woman suffers from epilepsy. This action precipitates a seizure, and in the course of the seizure, perhaps in part because of the amount of alcohol consumed, the woman chokes. She is unconscious for 10 minutes and suffers serious brain damage. Discuss the tort principles that arise in this case. Who will be sued and for what? What are the merits of the case?

6. The *Newspaper for Smart Readers (NSR)* has a long and proud history as the dominant paper in a major city in Canada. Recently a new, province-wide paper has started up whose business plan includes becoming the primary print news source in this particular city. It intends to capture this market with an aggressive negative advertising campaign, using the primary slogan "Smart Is Not Enough." In different ads, the new paper includes direct attacks on *NSR*. The most recent states that foreign news coverage in *NSR* contains more material taken directly from press agencies than any other major paper in Canada. *NSR* believes this is an inaccurate and highly damaging statement, although there is some ambiguity in exactly what is meant by "press agencies." *NSR* is part of a news group that shares foreign coverage. What tort action might *NSR* take? What chance will it have of success? What are the risks of litigation here even if *NSR* succeeds?

   NSR has a second concern. The new paper has begun approaching the leading columnists at *NSR* and is attempting to persuade them to move to the new paper. Is there any relevant tort action for *NSR*, and if so, what evidence will it need in order to succeed?

Part Four

Structuring Business Activity

AN ENTREPRENEUR WITH A QUALITY SERVICE OR product ready for market needs to select a business vehicle—or ownership structure—through which to offer those goods and services. This choice has broad legal consequences because each kind of business vehicle has a specific set of rights and liabilities to go along with it.

Although methods of ownership can run from the simple to the complex, the choice is essentially limited to three basic forms:

▶ A *sole proprietorship* refers to an individual carrying on business alone. The actual business activity may be conducted by others, such as agents or employees, but ownership remains the responsibility of one person.

▶ A *partnership* involves two or more persons carrying on business together. Ownership responsibilities are shared either equally or in some proportion among the partners.

▶ A *corporation* is a separate legal entity that is owned by one or more individuals called shareholders.

The choice of the business ownership structure is often confused with the choice of business technique or the arrangements made for carrying on the business activity. There are numerous options such as distributorship, franchise, joint venture, and sales agency. However, any arrangement that is entered into is a separate matter from how the business is to be owned.

Regardless of the form the business takes, it will almost certainly rely on agency and employment rela-

tionships for its day-to-day operations. An agency relationship involves the business relying on someone else to act on its behalf. The choice of whether and when to use an agent is important because the actions of the agent are often treated in law as the actions of the business itself.

Chapter 13   The Agency Relationship

▶ Chapter 13 introduces the agency relationship and explores its relevance to business activity and the different forms of business organizations.

Chapter 14   Business Forms and Arrangements

▶ Chapter 14 compares the major forms of business organizations and provides detailed coverage of the partnership form. Also, several methods or arrangements of carrying on business are defined.

Chapter 15   Corporate Form: Organizational Matters

▶ Chapter 15 describes how a corporation is formed and owned and concludes with an examination of corporate securities.

Chapter 16 The Corporate Form: Operational Matters

▶ Chapter 16 deals with corporate liabilities and the rights and duties of directors and shareholders.

Thirteen Chapter

The Agency Relationship

Objectives

AFTER STUDYING THIS CHAPTER, YOU SHOULD HAVE AN UNDERSTANDING OF

► THE AGENCY RELATIONSHIP AND ITS RELEVANCE TO BUSINESS

► HOW AN AGENCY RELATIONSHIP COMES INTO BEING

► AGENCY DUTIES AND LIABILITIES

► HOW THE AGENCY RELATIONSHIP ENDS

Business Law in Practice

Lisa Jamieson owned and operated a high-end women's clothing store in Vancouver. Every year she made numerous trips to Europe and eastern Canada to purchase clothing to sell in her store. As Lisa's business became increasingly successful, she found it hard to find the time to make these journeys herself. Lisa therefore began sending Leonard VanWart, her marketing manager, to do the job.

Leonard became well known in the fashion industry as Lisa's utterly amazing buyer who had developed an unfailing eye for what would sell in Lisa's store. Eventually, Lisa left all purchasing decisions up to Leonard, since his judgment was sound and he had built up considerable expertise in the area.

While in Toronto recently on a buying trip for Lisa, Leonard uncharacteristically became involved in two unfortunate contracts:

- *The ugly clothes contract.* Leonard purchased $90 000 of clothing from a line that, to Lisa, amounted to the ugliest, most bizarre and impractical clothes she had ever seen. Lisa wants to return the clothes to the Toronto manufacturer for a full refund because she is reasonably sure that she will only be able to sell them in her store at a loss.
- *The atrociously expensive contract.* Leonard agreed to pay $200 000 to a Montreal fashion house to supply Lisa's business with a variety of women's business suits. Lisa likes the suits but is sure that Leonard has agreed to pay too much. She wants to renegotiate the contract herself. She is also particularly annoyed with Leonard since she expressly told him he could not enter into any contracts on her behalf in excess of $100 000 without getting her permission first.

1. What is the nature of the legal relationship between Lisa and Leonard?
2. Is Lisa bound by the two contracts Leonard entered into during his Toronto buying trip?
3. How should Lisa have handled this agency relationship from the outset?

The Nature of Agency

agency
A relationship that exists when one party represents another party in the formation of legal relations.

agent
A person who is authorized to act on behalf of another.

principal
A person who has permitted another to act on her or his behalf.

Agency is the relationship between two persons that permits one person, the **agent**, to affect the legal relations of another, known in law as the **principal**.[1] These legal relationships are as binding on the principal as if that person had directly entered them himself or herself.

Agency is about one person representing another in such a way as to affect the latter's relationships with the outside world. In business, agency is a common relationship, as is shown in the following examples:

- A sports agent negotiates a multimillion dollar deal on behalf of a basketball player.
- An insurance agent sells fire and theft insurance on behalf of several insurance companies.
- A travel agent sells tickets, cruises, and vacation packages on behalf of carriers and hotels.
- A booking agent negotiates fees and dates on behalf of entertainers.
- A stockbroker buys and sells shares on behalf of individuals and companies.

In each case, the agent is acting for someone else (the principal) and is doing business on that person's behalf. This kind of relationship is essential to the success of the principal, who may not necessarily have the expertise to handle the given matter—as may be the case with an athlete or an investor—or who cannot manage and promote his or her business single-handedly. For this latter reason, insurance companies, hotels, carriers, and entertainers rely on agents regularly.

In the Business Law in Practice scenario, Leonard was needed for just these kinds of reasons. He had acquired expertise in the area of buying that outmatched Lisa's, and she also required his assistance because she could not run her business alone. Consequently, Leonard became Lisa's purchasing agent.

---

1. G.H.L. Fridman, *Fridman's Law of Agency,* 7th ed. (Toronto: Butterworths, 1996) at 11.

Real Estate Agents

The real estate agent is one of the most familiar and common types of agents. Most sales of property, especially those involving residential property, involve the services of a real estate agent. The real estate agent, however, is somewhat of an anomaly in agency law. Unlike most other agents, usually a real estate agent has no authority to make a binding contract of sale on behalf of his principal, the homeowner. Normally a real estate agent's role is limited to listing and advertising the property, showing the property to perspective purchasers, and introducing and bringing together the parties. He does not enter a contract on behalf of the seller.

The case of real estate agents illustrates an important point. The term *agent* is often used very loosely to refer to anyone who represents another, and is not always restricted to relationships where the agent enters into contracts on behalf of the

BUSINESS APPLICATION OF THE LAW

principal. It is always necessary to look at the essence of a relationship rather than merely relying on what the parties call themselves. Just as agents are not always agents in the strict legal sense, so too there may be an agency relationship even though the parties have not labelled it as such.

Agency has many business applications.

Many of the examples of agency given so far are familiar because they involve businesses engaging external specialists or experts to act on their behalf in various transactions. The scope of agency, however, is considerably broader than these examples would suggest.

In fact, in almost every business transaction, at least one of the parties is acting as an agent. A corporation enters into a contract through the agency of one of its directors or employees. A partnership is likewise bound to a contract through the agency of one of its partners or a firm employee. Even in a sole proprietorship, the owner may hire others, such as office managers and sales clerks, to carry out critical tasks on his behalf. In short, the agency relationship—which formally recognizes the delegation of authority from one party to another—is a cornerstone of business activity. It is a relationship that makes it possible for businesses to conduct a wide array of transactions, both nationally and internationally.

Using a Foreign Agent

Many Canadian firms begin their entry into the international marketplace by using the services of a foreign agent. The agent, who may be a private individual or an independent firm, acts on behalf of the domestic firm or principal either to sell the principal's goods or services or to buy goods or procure services for the principal. The agent operates in a manner similar to an agent in the domestic market.

The use of an agent in another country, however, is not without potential hazards. Each nation's legal system has its own rules defining the relationship and the obligations between the principal and the agent. Significantly, in most instances these regulations will supersede any written contract between the parties. Some countries totally ban the use of agents for foreign sellers. Other countries require an agent to be a citizen. Some countries require all commercial agency relationships to be registered with the government.[2]

Because of the difficulties created for international traders by the variations in national laws in this area, the International Chamber of Commerce (ICC) has developed a model agency form.[3] The form is an attempt to find balanced solutions to the conflicting rules in national states and incorporates many of the prevailing practices in international trade. Two of the major areas dealt with by the form are termination provisions and international arbitration in the event of a dispute.

Critical Analysis: How do the issues dealt with in an international agency agreement differ from those dealt with in an a domestic agency agreement?

Agency Defined

Agency relationships, like contractual relationships in general, operate for the most part with few difficulties—agents simply represent principals in transactions with others. This is not to say, however, that problems cannot occur. The fact that parties use agents instead of dealing with each other face to face can result in complications and questions.

There are two key relationships at play in an agency situation. The first is the relationship between the agent and the principal (see Figure 13.1).

Figure 13.1

THE AGENT–PRINCIPAL RELATIONSHIP

---

2. For further information on using a foreign agent, see Carolyn Hotchkiss, *International Law for Business* (New York: McGraw-Hill, 1994) at 258-261; Mary Jo Nicholson, *Legal Aspects of International Business* (Scarborough: Prentice Hall, 1997) at 261-268.

3. The model agency form may be purchased through the homepage for the ICC <http://www.iccwbo.org/>.

This aspect of agency raises numerous questions, such as the following:

- How does A become an agent? When is one person considered to be an agent for another?
- What is the authority of A? What types of transactions can A enter on behalf of P?
- What are A's duties?
- What are P's obligations?

The second relationship that figures in agency is between the principal and the party with whom the agent does business (see Figure 13.2). Such parties are known as **outsiders** because they are "outside" of the agency relationship between principal and agent. The outsider is also sometimes called the third party.[4]

Figure 13.2

THE OUTSIDER–PRINCIPAL RELATIONSHIP

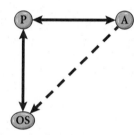

(Outsider or Third Party)

This relationship raises questions, including these:

- When is the principal liable to the outsider?
- When is the agent himself liable to the outsider?

The complications resulting from these relationships have necessitated rules of law to regulate and resolve them. These rules are known as the **law of agency**, which, in turn, is derived largely from tort and contract law. There is very little legislation pertaining to agency as such, other than special statutes that govern the duties and responsibilities of specific kinds of agents.[5]

The remainder of this chapter will explore how the common law of agency has dealt with the kinds of questions and problems posed above.

Creation of Agency

Agency relationships are created in a variety of ways. Most often, particularly in a business context, the relationship arises by contract between the parties. At other times, the relationship arises by conduct. The parties do not specifically agree to an agency relationship, but by words or actions outsiders are led to believe the relationship is one of agency.

---

4. The principal and agent are the first and second parties.

5. For example, insurance brokers, mortgage brokers, and mercantile and real estate agents are regulated by legislation that provides for their registration, their training, the regulation of their conduct, and so forth. See, for example, *Real Estate and Business Brokers Act,* R.S.O. 1990, c. R4.

Agency by Agreement

An agency relationship created by contract normally involves the principal authorizing an agent to act on her behalf and the agent agreeing to do so in return for some fee or other remuneration. This often occurs through a contract created expressly and only for that single purpose, as illustrated in this example:

■ A retired public figure who wishes to earn income by speaking about his experiences in office may engage an agent to contact organizations, negotiate fees, and book engagements on his behalf. In return the public figure will pay the agent a certain sum, perhaps a percentage of his fee.

In other situations, the agency relationship may arise as part of another, broader contract:

■ An employment contract may provide for a person to be paid a salary in return for carrying out certain duties *including* entering into contracts on behalf of the employer. For example, a sales clerk, besides greeting and assisting customers and stocking shelves, would have the authority to enter into sales transactions—at least at the sticker price—on behalf of his employer. Similarly, it was through his employment contract as Lisa's marketing manager that Leonard also came to be her buying agent.

Of course, not all employees are agents for the businesses that employ them. Often it depends upon the circumstances. A clerk/typist is not normally an agent, but, if asked to take money from petty cash and purchase a gift for a departing employee, then in this situation and for this purpose, the clerk/typist is an agent for the employer.

The Concept of Authority

The authority of the agent is a key aspect of the agency relationship. It determines whether there is a contract between the principal and the outsider. When an agent acts within the scope of her authority and negotiates a contract for the principal, the principal is bound by the contract, whether the principal likes it or not. However, even when the agent has acted outside the scope of her authority in entering into the contract—that is, by exceeding the powers she has been given—the contract may still bind the principal.

The principal will be obligated by the contract when the agent has actual authority or when the agent has apparent authority.

actual authority
The power of an agent that derives from either express or implied agreement.

ACTUAL AUTHORITY An agent's **actual authority** can be both express and implied. Express authority is the written or oral authority granted by the principal to the agent and is an authority that the agent *actually* has. Implied authority is also an authority that the agent *actually* has, but it is present by *implication* only. An agent will have implied authority when that authority

■ inferred from the position the agent occupies
■ is reasonably necessary to carry out or otherwise implement the agent's express authority
■ arises by virtue of a well-recognized custom in a particular trade, industry, or profession

Purchasing agents are part of the fashion industry scene.

Like other contracts, then, the agency contract can contain implied terms concerning the nature and extent of the agent's authority. It is important to remember that these terms are not any less "real" than express terms are. They just exist in another, less tangible form.

In the Business Law in Practice scenario, it is clear that Lisa's agent, Leonard, has the *actual* authority to buy clothes on Lisa's behalf, but she has limited this authority to $100 000 per contract. Above that amount, he is required to secure Lisa's approval before proceeding. What kind of implied authority might Leonard have? This is always a fact-specific inquiry, but since Leonard is empowered to purchase clothes, he almost certainly has the power to arrange for their transportation to Vancouver. This, in turn, would also include the power to acquire insurance to cover any loss or damage to the goods while in transit. For this reason, transportation and insurance contracts will be binding on Lisa.

In a similar vein, the manager of a business may have aspects of his authority expressly recited in his employment contract or job description. To the extent that these documents are not exhaustive on the subject, other components of his authority exist due to the nature of his position and as a result of what is reasonably necessary to manage the business. For example, if he were the general manager of an automotive dealership, he presumably would have the implied power to purchase merchandise, order office supplies, arrange for appropriate advertising of the business, and hire and fire employees. A manager of another kind of business—a fast food outlet or a convenience store—would have less implied power.

The nature of the authority given to the agent is inherently flexible and easily customized. For example, it can be

- very broad or very narrow
- for only one transaction or for several
- for a short, long, or indefinite period of time
- very formal, as in the case of a power of attorney, or very informal, in that it is included in the job description of an employee or merely consists of oral instructions

Leonard has entered into two contracts on behalf of Lisa. Were they within his actual authority, thereby binding Lisa?

- *The ugly clothes contract.* This contract is almost certainly binding on Lisa because it was concluded within Leonard's actual authority. It is a contract for clothes that was within his allowable monetary range. That he may have exercised poor taste on this occasion is no reason why Lisa should be able to renege and send the clothes back to the manufacturer for a refund. Lisa is bound by this contract, whether she wants to be or not.

A Power of Attorney

A power of attorney is a written document in which the principal gives authority to an agent to act in relation to his property and financial affairs. The person receiving the power to act is called the "attorney." The person giving the power is called the "donor."

The power of attorney can be general in that the agent has *full* authority to exercise all the principal's rights in relation to her property and financial affairs, or it can be a *specific* power of attorney in that it limits the authority of the agent to act for the principal in relation to certain matters or in certain specified circumstances.

Powers of attorney are commonly used to allow the agent to do the following kinds of things:

- cash or deposit cheques, pay bills, withdraw money from bank accounts, or make payments on loans
- purchase, sell, or deal with stocks or bonds
- collect rents, profits, or commissions
  - manage, buy, and sell real estate
  - conduct business operations

At common law, a power of attorney ends on the death or incompetency of the donor. All provinces have enacted legislation providing for an "enduring" power of attorney. This allows for the power of attorney to operate when the donor becomes incapacitated and unable to manage his or her business.[6]

A power of attorney can be a useful tool for conducting business in the event of incapacity. However, it also presents an obvious potential for abuse. An attorney with unlimited power over a donor's affairs can easily take advantage of the situation. A donor needs to understand the nature and extent of the power given to the attorney.

■ *The atrociously expensive contract.* The facts surrounding this contract establish that Leonard acted outside of his actual authority because the contract is worth more than $100 000. As his principal, is Lisa bound by the contract anyway? Or can she use this as an opportunity to negotiate a better price with the fashion house?

The answer to these questions depends on whether Leonard has the apparent authority to enter into contracts over that monetary limit.

apparent authority
The power that an agent appears to have because of conduct or statements of the principal.

APPARENT AUTHORITY   Sometimes called ostensible authority, **apparent authority** is the authority that a third party or outsider would reasonably believe the agent has, given the conduct of the principal. For example, as Leonard is acting as Lisa's purchasing agent, it would be reasonable for the outsider to infer that he had the usual authority of someone in such a position. It would not be reasonable to expect clothing manufacturers and suppliers to guess that Leonard's authority to contract on Lisa's behalf had been limited to contracts for less than $100 000. Lisa is sending Leonard off into the fashion world as her buying agent without telling outsiders that his authority is in any way limited. She must bear the risk of Leonard exceeding the monetary limit she has privately set for him.

---

6. Law Reform Commission of Nova Scotia, *Enduring Powers of Attorney in Nova Scotia* (Halifax: Law Reform Commission of Nova Scotia, 1999) at 6.

In sum, so long as an agent is acting within his apparent authority the principal will be bound by the transaction unless the third party knew or ought reasonably to have known of the limitation on the agent's authority.

Case

Panorama Developments (Guildford) Ltd. v. Fidelis Furnishing Fabrics Ltd., [1971] 2 Q.B. 711 (C.A.)

The Business Context: A director is an agent of a corporation and usually has broad actual authority to transact business on behalf of the corporation. Even in situations where the director's authority has been limited, the director still has broad apparent authority to act on behalf of the corporation. Whether officers of a company—the company secretary and the company treasurer, for example—are agents with apparent authority, however, has not always been clear.

Factual Background: Fidelis appointed Mr. Bayne as its company secretary. Bayne rented cars from Panorama, who ran a car rental business. The rental agreements named Bayne as hirer, and he signed the agreements describing himself as company secretary. Bayne, however, used the cars himself and not for company business. Fidelis refused to pay the charges. Panorama sued Fidelis, alleging that Bayne was the agent of Fidelis and therefore it was liable to pay the charges. Fidelis argued that Bayne had no authority to enter contracts on its behalf and therefore Fidelis had no responsibility for the bill.

The Legal Question: Was Fidelis liable to pay the car rental charges?

Resolution: The court held that a company secretary had apparent or ostensible authority to enter into contracts for the hire of cars on behalf of the company. A company secretary is an important person in the organization, with extensive duties and responsibilities. He is not a mere clerk. He can make representations on behalf of the company and he can enter into contracts dealing with the administrative side of the company's business, such as employing staff and hiring cars. He has the apparent authority to do so. Fidelis was therefore bound by the hiring agreement made by the company secretary even though Bayne used the cars for his own purposes.

Critical Analysis: How is the apparent authority of an agent determined? Why is this question important?

Agency by Estoppel

agency by estoppel
An agency relationship created when the principal acts such that third parties reasonably conclude that an agency relationship exists.

In the preceding section, one of the risks of agency was illustrated: an agent may exceed his actual authority but act within his apparent authority and thereby bind a principal to a contract against her wishes. Lisa was bound to pay for the expensive clothes even though the contract was for an amount above Leonard's authority. This was because the contract was within Leonard's apparent authority and the clothing manufacturer was unaware of the limitation on Leonard's authority. This is an application of what is known in law as **agency by estoppel**. The relationship between Lisa and Leonard has been broadened or extended, not through their mutual consent but by conduct. Lisa is not entitled to deny Leonard's apparent authority unless she actually informs the outsider in advance that Leonard's authority is limited.

A less common situation in which an agency relationship can be created by estoppel involves one in which the principal indicates that another is his agent when, in fact, no agency relationship exists. For example, suppose that the owner of a business—in a burst of effusiveness—introduces a prospective employee to a customer, saying, "I want you to meet Terrence, my new vice president of marketing." It would be usual and reasonable for the customer to infer that Terrence has the authority to act on behalf of the owner with respect to selling, promotions, and advertising. Suppose, however, that ultimately Terrence is not hired and, unfortunately, the owner forgets all about having introduced him as the new vice president of marketing. Terrence—now sorely disappointed and wishing to extract some revenge—contacts the customer and enters into a transaction with him, pretending to act on behalf of the owner. Is the owner liable? Assuming the contract is marketing- or sales-related and assuming the customer was unaware of the truth, then the owner probably will be liable.

In such a situation, the principal's actions (introducing his "new vice president of marketing") created the appearance of an agency relationship. The principal will therefore be estopped from denying the relationship and be bound by the contract with the customer. Put another way, the principal is not permitted to avoid the contract by claiming—albeit truthfully—that no agency relationship existed, because he gave every appearance that one did.

Is it fair to place all responsibility on the owner like this? The difficulty is that someone—either the owner of the business or the customer—is going to end up being adversely affected by the conduct of Terrence. That is, either the owner will be stuck with a contract that he never wanted or the customer is going to be denied the benefit of a contract that he negotiated in good faith. Between these two competing claims, the law sides with the customer through estoppel. In theory, at least, the owner can sue Terrence for misrepresenting himself as an agent, but this can be of little value if Terrence has few assets.

A third situation in which agency by estoppel may operate to bind a principal is that in which an agency relationship has been terminated or an agent's authority has been curtailed. In both situations the agent had at one time the actual authority to bind the principal, but now the authority has been taken away or reduced.

Case

Rockland Industries Inc. v. Amerada Minerals Corporation of Canada (1978), 108 D.L.R (3d) 513 (S.C.C.), rev'g 95 D.L.R (3d) 64 (Alta. C.A.)

The Business Context: This case concerns an agent whose authority has been reduced. The same general principles will apply where the agency relationship has been completely severed.

Factual Background: Rockland was a textile manufacturer that also engaged in the purchase and resale of sulphur. Amerada was a producer of natural gas. One of the by-products of the gas processing procedure is sulphur. Mr. Kurtz was the manager of Amerada's petrochemical products with responsibility for domestic and foreign sales and the marketing of petrochemicals, including sulphur. He reported to Mr. Deverin, a senior vice president and a member of the executive operating committee.

After protracted negotiations between Amerada represented by Kurtz, and representatives of Rockland, an agreement was reached for the sale by Amerada to Rockland of 50 000 tons of sulphur at $8 per ton. This agreement was concluded by telephone on September 5, 1974. In the meantime, on September 3, 1974, Deverin informed Kurtz that he would need to get the approval of the executive operating committee for the sale to Rockland. In other words, he no longer had the authority to conclude the sale on behalf of Amerada.

The agreement, concluded on September 5, was not performed by Amerada, and Rockland sued for breach of contract. Amerada argued that there was no contract between the parties as Kurtz did not have the authority to act on Amerada's behalf.

The Legal Question: Was Amerada bound by the contract negotiated by Kurtz?

Resolution: The court determined that Kurtz had actual authority to act on behalf of Amerada in negotiating and entering the contract with Rockland up until September 3. At that time his actual authority was curtailed. This limitation on Kurtz' authority, however, was not communicated to Rockland. The court held that the onus was on Amerada to notify Rockland of the limitation—it was not up to Rockland to inquire as to Kurtz's authority.

Amerada, by permitting Kurtz to act in its business by conducting negotiations, had represented to Rockland that he had permission to act. In short, there was a representation of authority by Amerada on which Rockland relied.

Critical Analysis: How could Amerada have prevented this situation?

The situations described in this section illustrate several of the risks associated with agency. The onus is on the principals to inform outsiders when a person ceases to be their agent; otherwise the principals run the risk of continuing to be liable for the agent's actions. Similarly, the principals have a responsibility to inform outsiders of any limitation on their agent's usual authority; otherwise the principals run the risk of being bound if the agent exceeds his actual authority but acts within his apparent authority. A principal can inform outsiders by actually contacting them by letter, telephone, or other means; by taking out advertisements in trade publications and newspapers; by clearly indicating on company forms what constitutes necessary approvals; and by otherwise indicating that only properly documented transactions will be binding.

Agency by Ratification

agency by ratification
An agency relationship created when one party adopts a contract entered into on his or her behalf by another who at the time acted without authority.

Agency by ratification occurs when a person represents himself as another's agent even though he is not, and when the purported principal *adopts* the acts of the agent. For example, suppose Ahmed is keenly interested in obtaining a franchise for a certain fast-food restaurant, and his friend Frank is aware of this interest. An opportunity comes on the market, but Frank cannot reach Ahmed to tell him about it. Feeling pretty sure of himself, Frank goes ahead and purchases the franchise on Ahmed's behalf although he does not have any authority to do so. Though Frank acted with good intentions, Ahmed has no responsibilities unless he chooses to adopt the contract. When and if he does adopt the transaction, an agency relationship will be created between Frank and him. The result is that Ahmed's rights and duties under the franchise contract are absolutely identical to what they would have been had Frank been properly authorized to act as Ahmed's agent all along.

In both agency by estoppel and agency by ratification, the agent has no authority to do what he does. What distinguishes the two doctrines is whether the principal has conducted himself in a misleading way. Agency by estoppel forces the principal to be bound by the unauthorized contract because the principal has represented someone as his agent and must live with the consequences when that agent purports to act on his behalf. Under agency by ratification, the agent is perhaps equally out of line but not due to any fault of or misrepresentation by the principal. For this reason, the law does not force the principal to adopt the contract, but rather permits him to make that decision for himself, according to his own best interests.

Duties of the Agent

An agency relationship created by contract imposes on an agent certain duties to perform. If the agent fails to perform these duties, then the agent is in breach of the contract. An agent is required to perform in accordance with the principal's instructions. In the event that the principal has not given any instructions as to how the performance is to be carried out, then the performance must meet the standard of the particular trade or industry.

Case

Fine's Flowers Ltd. et al. v. General Accident Assurance Co. et al. (1978), 2 B.L.R. 257 (Ont. C.A.)

The Business Context: An insurance agent acts on behalf of the insurance company and as such owes duties to it. An insurance agent, however, is also seen to owe a duty to the insured. The standard of performance required in this context is the subject of this case.

Factual Background: Fine's Flowers operated a greenhouse in Ottawa. Over the years, it had established a close and continuing relationship with Mr. Ault, an insurance agent. Fine's relied on Ault to keep it insured against all foreseeable and normal risks to its business. One of these risks was the loss of heat in the winter. Ault placed insurance for Fine's boilers but not for its water pumps, which were part of the heating system. The water pumps seized, causing the heating system to shut down. As a result, the greenhouse crops were destroyed. Fine's brought action against Ault for failure to arrange insurance to protect against this event.

The Legal Question: Was Ault liable for Fine's losses?

Resolution: Ault was held liable for failing to provide proper coverage. The court described Ault's obligations in the following way:

> An insurance agent's duty when asked to obtain a specific type of coverage is to use a reasonable degree of skill and care in doing so and to inform the principal promptly if such coverage is not available. If the principal gives no specific instructions, but relies on the agent to see that he is protected, then the agent, if he agrees to act on such terms, must inform himself of the principal's business in order to assess the foreseeable risks and to insure his client against them. If such coverage is not available, the principal must be informed.

Critical Analysis: How are the duties of particular agents ascertained?

Normally, it is expected that the agent will personally perform the obligations. However, there may be express or implied provision for delegation—that is, the agent may be permitted to "download" responsibility for performance onto someone else. For example, it may be that Leonard and Lisa have an understanding that Leonard can send his assistant on less important buying trips to act in his place.

fiduciary duty
A duty imposed on a person who has a special relationship of trust with another.

An agent also owes a **fiduciary duty** to the principal. A fiduciary duty is not unique to the law of agency. This duty is found in many other relationships. This duty requires the agent to show what the law describes as "utmost good faith to the principal." For example, it would be a breach of his fiduciary duty for Leonard to go on a buying trip for Lisa and acquire clothes for a store that he was secretly running on the side. Lisa, as his principal, is entitled to his full attention, and any good deals he may find must go her way, not his.

Generally, utmost good faith imposes a duty on the agent to

- fully disclose all information regarding transactions involving the principal
- act for only one party in a given transaction
- avoid any conflict of interest that affects the interests of the principal
- not use the principal's property to secure personal gain

A Fallen Agent

ETHICAL CONSIDERATIONS

The career of hockey great Bobby Orr is well known to sports fans. What is probably not as well known is that Orr was the first superstar to use an agent to negotiate a contract with a team in the National Hockey League. In 1966, Orr hired an unknown Toronto lawyer, Alan Eagleson, to represent him in negotiations with the Boston Bruins.

From that initial contact with Orr, Eagleson rose to become one of the most influential people in hockey. In addition to acting as agent for over 200 players, he was instrumental in founding the National Hockey League Players Association (NHLPA) in 1967. He served as its executive director from 1967 to 1991. He played a significant role in organizing the 1972 Canada–Russia series and subsequently became Canada's chief negotiator for international hockey and the ensuing Canada Cups. In this capacity he was co-worker with the NHL owners in negotiating tournaments with teams outside the NHL and selling the associated products, most notably advertising rights. He also acted as the organizer and director of the numerous international tournaments that he helped negotiate. He was also a close personal friend of the then NHL president, John Ziegler. The president of the NHL is chosen by the NHL board of governors, composed of owners of the teams that compete in the NHL.

Eagleson's rise to power can only be matched by his fall from grace. By 1996, he faced over 40 fraud-related charges in Canada and the United States. The charges included racketeering, embezzlement, and theft from the players that he represented. It was alleged that he diverted to his own use profits from the Canada Cup tournaments in the 1980s that were supposed to go to the hockey players' pension funds; that he defrauded Labatt's of their rink-board advertising rights; that he dipped into NHLPA funds to pay personal expenses for himself, family, friends, and associates; and that he kept insurance payments that should have gone to injured players.

In 1998, as a result of an international plea bargain, Eagleson was convicted on six of the lesser charges. In the United States he was ordered to pay CDN$1 million in restitution for the money he stole from the players. In Canada, he was sentenced to 18 months in jail. His legal difficulties did not end there, however. He also faced a number of civil suits, including these: a $500- to $800-million class-action suit by five former NHL players on behalf of 1200 more who said Eagleson and former NHL president John Ziegler conspired to suppress their salaries; a $100 000 racketeering lawsuit by player Andre Savard over disability payments; and an appeal from a 1996 case in which former player Mike Gillis was awarded over $570 000 for insurance-related fees, punitive damages and costs. The conspiracy suit was dismissed on the basis of the statute of limitations. The plaintiffs are considering an appeal. Mr. Eagleson served four months in prison and than was paroled. He spent his parole working as an office manager. Other cases are in various stages of litigation.

Critical Analysis: How did Eagleson's various positions in hockey conflict with his role as a player's agent? In other words, what agency duties were breached? How far should the law go in protecting the player/principal from the actions of the agent?

Source: Jane O'Hara, "In the Name of Greed" *Maclean's* 111:3 (19 January 1998) 22.

Athletes often use the services of a sport's agents.

Duties of the Principal

A principal's duties usually are not as onerous as an agent's and normally are set out in the contract creating the agency relationship. Such contracts usually obligate the principal to

- pay the agent a specified fee or percentage for services rendered
- assist the agent in the manner described in the contract
- reimburse the agent for reasonable expenses associated with carrying out his agency duties
- indemnify against losses incurred in carrying out the agency business

In the example involving Lisa and her buying agent Leonard, it may be that Leonard has had to fly to Toronto to make the necessary purchases. In the absence of any agreement to the contrary, Lisa would be required to reimburse Leonard for his airfare. This is a cost that rightfully belongs to Lisa since Leonard incurred it on a buying trip she herself instigated and sent him on. Similarly, she has an obligation—either express or implied—to reimburse him for meals and hotel and other reasonable expenses associated with the buying trip.

Liability in the Agency Relationship

Liability of the Principal to the Outsider

The most significant result of an agency relationship is that when an agent enters into a contract on behalf of a principal with a third party, it is the principal, not the agent, who ordinarily is liable on the contract. To a large extent, discussion of this point is simply the flip side of a discussion regarding an agent's actual and apparent authority. Put another way, the principal's liability to the third party depends on the nature of the agent's authority.

As we have already seen under the discussion of an agent's authority above, Lisa is liable on the ugly clothes contract—even though she does not much like the deal—because Leonard was acting within his actual authority. Leonard did exceed his actual authority on the second contract because it went over the monetary limit his principal had placed on him, but the doctrine of apparent authority likely applies. The outsider did not know about the limitation on Leonard's authority, so on this basis, Lisa is bound. She will not have an opportunity to renegotiate this contract in order to get a lower price.

Liability of the Agent to the Outsider

An agent will be personally liable on a contract with an outsider when he exceeds his actual or apparent authority.[7]

For example, Lisa would not be bound by a contract Leonard enters into on her behalf to purchase a private jet. She could adopt, that is, ratify, such a contract, but otherwise she is not bound because such a contract is not within Leonard's actual or apparent authority. Leonard would be personally liable on the contract.

An agent may also be bound when he contracts on his own behalf to be a party to the contract along with his principal.[8]

---

7. *Supra* note 1 at 217.
8. F.M.B. Reynolds, *Bowstead & Reynolds on Agency,* 16th ed. (London: Sweet & Maxwell, 1996) at 552.

For example, if Leonard negotiated the contract such that both he *and* his principal were ordering the clothes and promising to pay for them, then he has as much liability to the outsider as Lisa. They are both parties to the contract—Leonard is contracting on his own behalf as well as on Lisa's behalf.

Liability of an Undisclosed Principal

undisclosed principal
A principal whose identity is unknown to a third party, who has no knowledge that the agent is acting in an agency capacity.

An agent may incur liability when he contracts on behalf of an **undisclosed principal**. A principal is said to be "undisclosed" when the third party does not know that she is dealing with an agent at all and assumes that the party she is face to face with is acting only on his own behalf. From the perspective of the outsider, there is no principal waiting in the background.

When the agent is acting for an undisclosed principal, the general rule is that the principal is still liable on the contract so long as the agent is acting within his authority.[9] The agent has no liability, however.

For example, assume that in negotiations with outsiders Leonard represents himself neither as an agent nor as a principal and that he could be acting in either capacity. In such circumstances, Lisa will generally be liable on the contract, but not Leonard. This is a simple application of the general rule stated above.

The general rule, however, has been subject to qualification that may operate to render the agent liable on the contract in certain circumstances.[10] One such qualification relates to representations made by the agent.

Suppose that for the purposes of a buying trip to a small clothing manufacturer overseas, Lisa wishes to keep her identity a secret. She thinks that Leonard, her purchasing agent, will get a better price if the seller (the outsider) is unaware of her identity.[11]

If Leonard *pretends* to be the principal—representing to the outsider that he is actually the owner or proprietor of the clothing business—and does not disclose the existence of Lisa, his principal, then Leonard runs the risk of being personally liable on the contract that is concluded. For example, if the written contract expressly indicates that Leonard is the principal, the parol evidence rule[12] may operate to prevent the admission of evidence of an undisclosed principal.[13] In such circumstances, Leonard is liable.

A variation on the undisclosed principal is the *unnamed*[14] *principal*. If Leonard tells the seller that he is acting for a principal but that he is not at liberty to reveal that person's identity, then Lisa will be liable on any contract he enters into with the seller. In such circumstances, Leonard himself has no liability on the contact because the outsider was fully aware of his status. The outsider did not know the identity of his principal but decided to enter into a contract anyway. If the outsider did not want to deal with an unnamed principal, the outsider could simply have refused to enter the contract in the first place.

Liability of the Agent to the Principal

When an agent exceeds his or her authority, the principal can sue the agent for breach of contract—assuming that there is a contract in place—or for negligence.

---

9. *Supra* note 1 at 253. This rule has been subject to heavy criticism as being inconsistent with the general principles of contract law.

10. *Supra* note 1 at 258-264.

11. This is a not uncommon practice in the real estate industry, particularly when a developer wishes to purchase several tracts of land.

12. The parol evidence rule is discussed in Chapter 7.

13. *Supra* note 1 at 258-263. The law is unsettled in this area: it is unclear when the law will permit evidence of an undisclosed principal.

14. *Supra* note 8 at 30. As Bowstead notes, terminology in this area is not consistently employed by the judiciary and legal writers.

The idea is that if the agent does not meet the standard of the reasonably prudent and competent agent, the principal must be reimbursed for associated damages. If the agent breaches the fiduciary duty owed to the principal, that too is actionable.

Because Leonard exceeded his authority on the second contract, Lisa could sue him for breaching his agency or employment contract. It is unlikely that she could successfully sue him on the first contract for buying what she considered to be ugly clothes, because it seems in this particular instance that he and Lisa simply have a difference of opinion as to what will sell in her store.

Figure 13.3

SUMMARY OF LIABILITY IN AGENCY

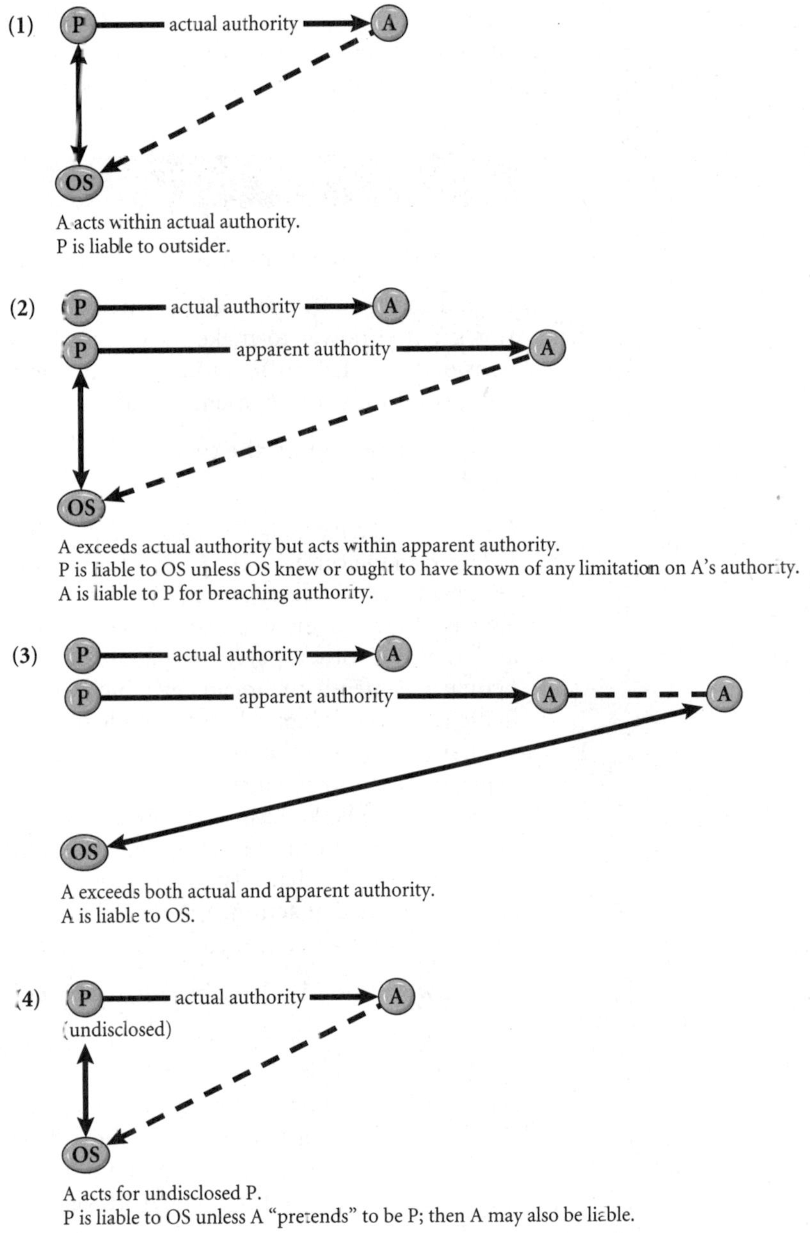
(1)
P
actual authority
A
OS
A acts within actual authority.
P is liable to outsider.
(2)
P
actual authority
A
P
apparent authority
A
OS
A exceeds actual authority but acts within apparent authority.
P is liable to OS unless OS knew or ought to have known of any limitation on A's authority.
A is liable to P for breaching authority.
(3)
P
actual authority
A
P
apparent authority
A
A
OS
A exceeds both actual and apparent authority.
A is liable to OS.
(4)
P
actual authority
A
(undisclosed)
OS
A acts for undisclosed P.
P is liable to OS unless A "pretends" to be P; then A may also be liable.

Termination of Agency Agreements

An agency agreement can come to an end in a number of ways:

- The parties may agree to bring their relationship to an end. For example, Lisa and Leonard may simply agree to end their relationship.
- One party may give notice of termination to the other.[15]
- An agency relationship can cease by operation of the law. Most commonly this occurs due to the death, dissolution (in the case of a corporate agent), insanity, or bankruptcy of one of the parties.

When an agency agreement is terminated by the parties, the principal should give notice to third parties so that customers do not assume that the relationship is continuing. In the absence of such notice, the principal may face liability to outsiders, based on his agent's apparent authority.

Business Law in Practice Revisited

1. What is the nature of the legal relationship between Lisa and Leonard?

Leonard is an employee of Lisa's business. In his position of marketing manager, he was granted power to make purchasing decisions on Lisa's behalf. Therefore, he is considered in law to be an agent, and the relationship between Lisa and Leonard comprises both employment and agency.

2. Is Lisa bound by the two contracts Leonard entered into during his Toronto buying trip?

Much of this chapter has been devoted to Lisa's liability on the unfortunate contracts Leonard made on her behalf. It has been emphasized that if Leonard makes poor or reckless purchase decisions, Lisa will normally be obligated to pay for the purchases. This is because agency law states that the principal, Lisa, is one party to the contract and that the other party is the outsider, the clothing manufacturer. The agent, Leonard, is merely the means by which the parties enter the contract. Lisa will not be liable for Leonard's purchases if the manufacturer knew or ought to have known that Leonard was not authorized to make the purchases he did. But a manufacturer is not expected to know or suspect that Leonard was limited to entering into contracts not exceeding $100 000. Lisa is bound, but she can hold Leonard liable for breaching his agency agreement in that he exceeded his authority. As noted, however, this will not relieve Lisa of her liability to the clothing manufacturer, and it is probably not an attractive course of action, as Leonard may not have the means of satisfying the debt. As well, suing one's agent can create a lot of adverse publicity.

3. How should Lisa have handled this agency relationship from the outset?

Lisa should have expressly granted Leonard the authority to enter contracts on her behalf either orally or in writing. The latter would have been the best course of action as it would have provided Leonard with proof of the relationship and clarifies exactly what his authority is (i.e., how much he can contract for), any limits on whom he can contract with, and so on. It would also have assisted Lisa if one day she was required to prove that Leonard exceeded his actual authority.

---

15. As Leonard is Lisa's employee, the rules of notice in employment relationships are applicable. These rules are discussed in Chapter 22.

It is also incumbent on Lisa to monitor the activities of those who act on her behalf. Proper supervision may prevent an employee from acting in a manner that detracts from the achievement of business goals and objectives.

Chapter Summary

This chapter introduced one of the cornerstone relationships in business. Agency is a relationship that allows one person's actions to be attributable to another. In this way, agency permits one party to represent and bind another in contractual matters. Thus a business may use agents in many facets of its operations, such as buying, selling, leasing, and hiring. As a practical matter, without the advantage of agency relationships, business could not be conducted on any significant scale.

The agency relationship most commonly comes into existence when a principal grants authority to the agent to act on her behalf. The law, however, recognizes an agency relationship when the principal represents to another that he is represented by an agent—agency by estoppel—or when the principal adopts a contract made on his behalf by someone who is not his agent—agency by ratification. In this area, it is the substance of the relationship that is important, not what parties call their relationship.

An agent's authority to act on behalf of a principal varies. An agent may have *actual* authority. This is the authority that she is actually given by the principal or that is implied from her position. Alternatively, an agent may have *apparent* authority. This is the authority that a third party would reasonably believe the agent to have. The scope of an agent's apparent authority is fact-specific and therefore varies with the circumstances.

An agent has both express and implied duties to her principal. Most importantly, an agent has a fiduciary duty to act in the best interests of the principal. The principal also has express and implied duties, particularly the duty to compensate the agent for services rendered and for costs associated with the agency relationship.

Agency operates in such a way that the principal is generally liable on contracts entered into by the agent on her behalf. A contract is formed between the principal and the outsider, and the agent drops out of the transaction. Though there are a number of potential problems, the agency relationship generally functions well and according to plan. However, it is possible that agency can operate in ways not desired. For example, the principal may be liable on contracts not desired, as when the agent negotiates a poor contract, or exceeds her actual authority but not her apparent authority. Thus, ironically, the same person who can help a business to grow and prosper can lead that same enterprise to financial loss. The key point is that agency, like other aspects of a business, needs to be managed and monitored: choose your agent wisely, instruct your agent carefully, and review the agent's work regularly.

Study Chapter

Questions for Review

1. What is agency? Give an example.

2. Is a real estate agent a typical agent? Explain.

3. How is an agency relationship entered into?

4. What is meant by agency by estoppel?

5. What is the difference between the actual and apparent authority of an agent?

6. Explain what a power of attorney is. What is it commonly used for?

7. What are the duties of the agent?

8. What are the duties of the principal?

9. When can an agent be personally liable on a contract entered into on behalf of a principal?

10. Describe how an agent can be liable to the principal.

11. What is an undisclosed principal?

12. How may an agency relationship be terminated?

Questions for Discussion

1. In the insurance industry, the agent acts primarily for the insurance company, which is the principal. Typically, the insurance agent also advises the client on the needed coverage and the meaning of the insurance policy. Do you see any potential problems with this situation? Should insurance companies be responsible for the conduct of insurance agents?

2. Consider the following employees of MNO Corp.: risk manager, sales manager, director of safety, employment equity officer, and administrative clerk. Would the individuals who occupy these positions have any authority to act on behalf of MNO Corp.?

3. Is it reasonable to hold principals responsible for contracts formed with only apparent authority? What are the tradeoffs?

4. In some real estate transactions, the agent advises both the vendor and the purchaser. Is this a violation of the real estate agent's duties? Why or why not?

Situations for Discussion

1. Kerry is interested in selling her convenience store for approximately $250 000 to $300 000. As Kerry is unfamiliar with the commercial real estate market in Red Deer, she engages a real estate agent, Patrick. The engagement is a standard form listing agreement. Patrick shows the building to a young couple, Paul and Rick, who seem to be quite interested. In fact, they make an offer in writing to purchase the building for $250 000. They also indicate that they need a reply immediately. Patrick calls Kerry but is unable to reach her. Patrick is in a quandary, but knowing that Paul and Rick's offer is in Kerry's range, albeit at the bottom, Patrick accepts the offer on Kerry's behalf (he signs the written offer). Upon learning of Patrick's actions, Kerry is quite upset and wonders whether she must sell the building to Paul and Rick. Advise Kerry.

2. Mattie and Rajiv were interested in taking a dream vacation to celebrate their 10th wedding anniversary. They contacted Windemere Travel Agency and informed the proprietor of their needs—a seven-day, luxury Caribbean cruise with several stops at various resorts. The travel agent quoted a price of $1900 per person. Mattie and Rajiv paid the price in full. The cruise, however, turned out to be more of a nightmare than a dream—the ship was a refurbished oil tanker, it stopped at several resorts but only at night, and Mattie found a mouse in the bathroom. Unfortunately, Mattie and Rajiv were unsuccessful in obtaining a refund from the cruise line as it had gone out of business. Do they have any recourse against the travel agent?

3. Raoul Inc. entered into a contract with Pavel Manufacturing whereby Pavel agreed to manufacture air compressors for Raoul. The parties agreed orally that the compressors would not be assembled until Pavel received instructions as to the type of wiring configuration to be used. While at Pavel's offices, Raoul, the president of Raoul Inc. telephoned Eli, a supplier of electrical equipment, to make inquiries that would lead to a decision respecting the wiring. Pavel was advised by Raoul that Eli would be phoning back at a later date. While Raoul was

out of the country, Eli called and advised Pavel that Raoul had decided on a particular configuration, and Pavel proceeded to assemble the compressors. Raoul had in fact chosen another configuration. Pavel refused to rewire the compressors and Raoul refused to pay for them.[16]

Should Raoul be required to pay? If so, on what basis? How could this problem have been avoided?

4. Cesare was an experienced and knowledgeable stock market investor who maintained a substantial retirement savings fund with Dominion Trust. The fund was managed by Scott, an employee of Milan, Fraser & Reilly (MFR), a firm of stockbrokers. Cesare heard about a volatile and speculative stock called Bleakwater Resources, which was trading on the Vancouver Stock Exchange. On the morning of February 8, he placed an order with Scott to purchase 13 000 shares for his RRSP account. At about 4:30 p.m. on the same day, he telephoned the offices of MRF to place an additional order for 11 000 shares of the same stock. Scott had left for the day, so the order was placed with another salesman, George. Cesare requested that the purchase take place "at the market price first thing in the morning." George undertook to do so. The next day, George arrived at the office at 7:00 o'clock, but he did not place Cesare's order as he was concerned about the wisdom of the order. Instead he waited for Scott's arrival, which occurred between 8:30 and 9:00 a.m., at which time George referred the order to Scott. Trading in the shares was suspended at 8:45 a.m. that day and Cesare's order was never placed. When trading resumed the shares had more than doubled in price.[17]

Does Cesare have an action against George or Scott? On what basis? Would your answer be the same if, when trading resumed, the shares had dropped in price by half?

5. Doby, a landowner, hired a contractor, Josh, to erect a grain-handling plant on her land. Most of the equipment, bins, machinery, and the like were to come from Westisle Inc. Westisle's agriproducts manager Morgan was very experienced in this area and helped prepare the contract between Doby and Josh.

After a time Doby had paid Josh a lot of money and Westisle had supplied a lot of supplies, but the project was moving very slowly. In fact, it appeared as if Josh was in financial difficulty, and Westisle refused to supply any more goods without payment. Doby complained to Morgan, who said that Josh needed more money. Doby was skeptical, but Morgan assured him that money on account would solve the problem. Doby was still skeptical and asked for a guarantee of completion. Morgan said he would consult his superiors.

A couple of days later he gave Doby a letter of guarantee by Westisle, typed on their letterhead and signed by him as agriproducts manager. In exchange, Doby gave Morgan a $60 000 cheque payable to Westisle and another large cheque payable to Josh. One of Morgan's superiors deposited the Westisle cheque.

The contractor later stopped work, and Doby wrote a demand calling on the guarantee. Morgan pocketed the demand letter without revealing it to anyone. Doby contacted Morgan's superiors and the truth came out. Westisle denied any contractual dealings with Doby and disclaimed the guarantee. Almost a year later, and after proceedings had been commenced by Doby against Westisle, Westisle alleged that Morgan had no authority to enter into the guarantee transaction.[18]

What principal of agency law is important in this situation? Is Westisle liable for Morgan's actions? Should it be?

16. Based on *Lyon Developments Ltd* v. *Airways Compressor Sales Ltd.* (1985), 37 Alta. L.R. (2d) 80 (Q.B).

17. Based on *Volkers* v. *Midland Doherty Ltd. et al.* (1985), 17 D.L.R. (4th) 343 (B.C.C.A.).

18. Based on *Great Nor. Grain Terminals Ltd.* v. *Axley Agricultural Installations Ltd. (1990),* 76 Alta. L.R. (2d) 156 (C.A.).

Fourteen

Business Forms and Arrangements

Objectives

AFTER STUDYING THIS CHAPTER, YOU SHOULD HAVE AN
UNDERSTANDING OF

► THE CHARACTERISTICS OF THE MAJOR FORMS OF BUSINESS
ORGANIZATIONS
► THE ADVANTAGES AND DISADVANTAGES OF THE MAJOR FORMS OF
BUSINESS ORGANIZATIONS
► THE LEGAL CONSEQUENCES OF A PARTNERSHIP
► METHODS OF ARRANGING BUSINESS ACTIVITY

Business Law in Practice

Adam is young, energetic, smart, and largely broke. In fact, Adam has only two possessions to his name: a second-hand BMW worth under $10 000 and a 1974 vintage Corvette worth over $15 000. Both vehicles were gifts from his father.

Adam has spent the last year experimenting and thinks that he has come up with an improved voice recognition system for computers. He wants to contract out the manufacture of his product and set up an organization for its distribution and sale. He already has a name in mind: "I-know-that-it's-you Enterprises," or IK Enterprises for short.

Adam's father, Cameron, is retired and reasonably well off. He has $100 000 that he is willing to invest in IK Enterprises, but he does not wish to risk his position and that of Adam's young brother by having any greater commitment to the business.

Adam has also found Diane, a manufacturer's agent for many products, who is willing to advise Adam on setting up IK Enterprises and to assist in marketing the product. Diane is willing to invest $20 000 and to devote some of her time and expertise to the new business. The bank is also willing to lend some start-up capital.

1. What forms of business organization are available for carrying on Adam's business?
2. What are the major considerations in choosing a particular form?
3. Which form is best for Adam's business?

Forms of Business Organization

Choosing *how* to own a business is a critical decision because it determines in large part who

- is financially liable for the business
- shares in business profits and other assets
- makes and is accountable for management decisions

The Sole Proprietorship

sole proprietorship
A business organization that has only one owner.

The **sole proprietorship** is the oldest form of business organization and the one most often used by small business. It is a particularly popular choice for the home-based enterprise. From a legal perspective, it also represents the simplest form of business organization because there is no legislation pertaining to the sole proprietorship as such. A discussion of the legal consequences of this form of business is really a discussion of the rights and liabilities of an individual.

Financial liability

The financial consequences to Adam should he conduct his computer business as a sole proprietorship are both straightforward and significant: any obligation of the business is Adam's personal obligation. Consider the following examples:

An entrepreneur may begin as a sole proprietorship.

- *The bank loan.* If Adam decides to borrow start-up capital from the bank, it is Adam who promises to repay the loan, not his business. This is because a sole proprietorship is not legally capable of borrowing money on its own, unlike a corporation. Adam *is* the business. Adam is the debtor and is responsible for the debt.

Suppose that IK Enterprises, Adam's sole proprietorship, begins to falter and the loan cannot be repaid. The bank will take the appropriate legal steps—discussed in more detail in Chapter 26—to recover as much as it can on the loan. All of Adam's business and personal assets are subject to the debts of the business.

Also, any judgment against him can be kept alive indefinitely. This means that his creditors can bide their time until he comes into some money, even if this is decades down the road. Adam's personal credit rating will also be adversely affected now and in the future. This may make it next to impossible to start another venture in the future that would depend on Adam's creditworthiness.

■ *The breach of contract.* If at some point IK Enterprises supplies defective computers to a customer, Adam, not IK Enterprises, is in breach of contract. This is because, as noted above, IK Enterprises cannot enter into a contract. As in the preceding example, Adam is the one who will be sued, and it is Adam's assets that are at risk.

In short, a sole proprietor has what is known in law as **unlimited liability**. Regardless of what the owner has invested in his business, his personal assets—and not just the business assets—may be seized to pay the outstanding debts of the business. Unfortunately, these debts can far exceed anything anticipated when the business was started.

unlimited liability
Unrestricted responsibility for obligations.

Profit Sharing

The sole proprietor bears the risk of failure, but also enjoys this advantage: all the profits after taxes accrue to the sole proprietor alone. If IK Enterprises is a runaway success, Adam reaps all the benefits. The profit motive can be a strong incentive for the sole proprietor to seek to ensure the success of the business.

Decision Making

The sole proprietor, having no partners and no board of directors to report to, can make business decisions very quickly and independently. He has a lot of personal freedom to do exactly as he pleases concerning all aspects of the business, even if it means deciding to discontinue business activities altogether. Should the owner die, the business is terminated—in other words, the proprietorship has a limited life span.

There are, of course, disadvantages to working alone in this way: few people are good at everything, yet the sole proprietor is responsible for every aspect of the business, from buying and selling to financing and advertising. Another serious consideration is that the sole proprietor's absence through illness or incapacity can adversely affect the business because so much of the enterprise revolves around this one individual. Though the sole proprietor may hire employees, they have limited opportunities for advancement, since by definition a sole proprietorship is a one-person show. As a result, these workers may not be particularly motivated or able to provide a high level of commitment.

Sources of Capital

A major difficulty with "going it alone" is that the sole proprietor has limited access to capital. Since the proprietor has no business partners, he is limited to his own assets and to whatever credit he can draw on to finance the operation. Usually this is less than what would be available if more than one person was involved, as in a partnership, for example.

Taxation

Because a sole proprietorship is not a legal entity separate from the owner, there are no formal or specialized tax rules governing it. Profits and losses are simply reported on the owner's personal income tax return. This may be favourable or unfavourable depending on the taxpayer's circumstances, including whether the owner's marginal tax rate is higher or lower than the applicable corporate tax rate.

Transferability

A sole proprietorship cannot be transferred or sold to another because it has no legal status. There is, in effect, nothing to transfer. However, the assets associated with the proprietorship—such as inventory—are transferable.

Regulations

The legal requirements for establishing and conducting this form of business organization are minimal—one simply commences business activity. There is no general need to incur legal fees to create the business vehicle. In short, doing business through the sole proprietorship is simple and inexpensive.

This is not to say that sole proprietorships are unregulated. They are subject to the same general legislation as any other business form. One important requirement is the registration or licensing of the business. Requirements vary from province to province, but generally persons who offer specialized services to the public must be licensed to practise their particular skill. Thus, lawyers, doctors, dentists, and electricians, for example, are required to follow provincial legislation governing their activity before providing services. Some businesses, such as those involving interprovincial trucking, require a federal licence to operate. Other types of business, such as door-to-door selling and the transportation of goods, are subject to specialized rules. The fees associated with licensing and registration are generally not substantial.

In addition to the regulations put in place by the federal and provincial governments, municipalities often impose their own registration or licensing requirements. For example, taxi businesses frequently require municipal licences to operate within municipal boundaries.

A sole proprietor who wishes to use a name other than his or her own for conducting the business must register the name at the local registry office or other government office designated by the province, where such records are kept and made available to the public.[1] The objective is to enable a person who deals with such a business to determine the identity of the proprietor of the business. Failure to register may result in a fine or other penalty.

Aside from these requirements, the sole proprietor is subject to laws of general application. Local zoning bylaws may require sole proprietors to locate in certain areas, provincial tax laws may require them to obtain a permit to act as a collector of sales tax, and health legislation may require them to maintain a high degree of cleanliness where food service or processing is involved. As well, a sole proprietor who hires employees must comply with all applicable legislation, such as that regulating employment standards, employment insurance, workers' compensation, and occupational health and safety.

A sole proprietor (unlike a public corporation) is not required to publish the business's financial statements. Success or failure in the business is a private matter, restricted to the proprietor, the business's accountant, Revenue Canada, and perhaps the local bank manager.

---

1. The use of trade or business names is discussed in Chapter 18.

Figure 14.1

PROS AND CONS OF THE SOLE PROPRIETORSHIP

Pros

Simplicity: There are few licensing and registration requirements. The sole proprietor just starts doing business and is free to discontinue business activities at any time.

Speed and independence: Since the sole proprietor has no partners and is not answerable to a board of directors, he or she can make decisions quickly and independently.

Profit motive: Any after-tax profit or other assets that accrue go entirely to the sole proprietor.

Lower costs: The fees for provincial and municipal licences are relatively small, varying according to the nature and size of the business and the municipality in which it is located. Generally, there is no need to incur legal fees.

Tax benefits: Profits and losses are reported on the owner's personal income tax return. This may be favourable or unfavourable depending on the taxpayer's circumstances.

Cons

Unlimited personal liability: The sole proprietor carries the risk of the business failing and losing both business and personal assets.

Working alone: The sole proprietor is responsible for all aspects of the business operation. Though a sole proprietor can hire employees, it is difficult to retain high-calibre people because of the limited opportunities available to them in a sole proprietorship.

Limited access to capital: The capital available to the business is limited to the assets of the proprietor and the extent of his or her credit.

Limited life span: The owner's death terminates the business. The proprietorship cannot be transferred.

Tax disadvantages: See tax benefits.

The Partnership

partnership
A business carried on by two or more persons that is not a corporation.

When two or more persons want to pool their resources and carry on business together, the most common option is to form a **partnership** or create a corporation.[2] A partnership is much like a sole proprietorship, in that neither has a legal personality—or legal existence—separate from the people who make them up. There are no special steps to create a partnership. It is simply the legal relationship of two or more people doing business together with the objective of making a profit.

The rules governing partnerships come from three sources: partnership legislation (in place in every province), contract law, and agency law. Later in the chapter, these sources will be analyzed in some depth. What follows is a general account of the basic principles that govern partnerships.

Many professionals practise as partners.

2. There can be restrictions on professionals, such as accountants and lawyers, incorporating companies. See Chapter 23 for detail.

Financial Liability

If Adam, his father, and Diane (the manufacturer's agent) decide to join forces and bring Adam's product to market through a partnership, each of them has *unlimited liability* for partnership debts and other obligations. Consider the following examples:

■ *The bank loan.* If the partners borrow start-up money from the bank (say $100 000 plus interest) and fail to repay it, Cameron, Adam, and Diane are liable for the full amount outstanding. This is because—like a sole proprietorship but unlike a corporation—a partnership is not legally capable of borrowing money on its own. The partners *are* the partnership. The partners are the debtors and are responsible for the debt.

A very important feature of partnership law is that each partner is *fully* responsible for *all* the liabilities of the partnership and not just for some appropriate proportion. Accordingly, the bank can proceed against the partner with the most assets—perhaps Adam's father, Cameron—and collect from that one individual the entire amount owing on the debt. In law, this is known as **joint liability**.[3] The liability is considered to be joint because responsibility is not in relation to the partner's share in the partnership; rather, each one of the partners has full and complete exposure on each and every obligation incurred. If the bank proceeds only against Cameron for repayment of the bank loan, however, Cameron is entitled to be reimbursed by his partners for their share of the debt. Of course, if the other partners have no assets, Cameron will end up bearing the partnership debts himself.

■ *The breach of contract.* If the partnership supplies defective computers to a customer, each of the partners is liable for the entire amount of the damages. The contract is between the customer, on one hand, and *all* the partners, on the other.

The key point from a liability perspective is that each partner's personal assets can be seized and sold through the judicial process if the partnership assets are insufficient to satisfy partnership obligations. This legal reality should give Adam's father, Cameron, some particular cause for concern. Since Cameron wants to limit his financial exposure to $100 000—in part because he has a young son whom he supports—Cameron will probably not find the partnership to be a feasible business vehicle through which to bring Adam's product to market. This is because a partnership, like a sole proprietorship, puts all of Cameron's assets at risk, not just his capital contribution. Adam and Diane also have cause for concern. Though they may have less at risk they still need to consider the impact of a judgment on their assets and their future.

Profit Sharing

It is the partners themselves who decide how profits and other firm assets are to be divided. If they fail to agree on this point, partnership legislation requires them to share profits equally.

Adam, Cameron, and Diane may decide to divide the partnership into unequal interests because the contribution of each partner varies. Since Adam has come up

joint liability
Full responsibility for all debts.

---

3. See, for example *Partnership Act,* R.S.N.B. 1990, c. P-4, s. 10: Every partner in a firm is liable jointly with the other partners for all debts and obligations of the firm while he is a partner.

with the product and presumably will be working full-time at the business, the partners may decide that he should hold a majority interest in the firm, for example, 60 percent. Diane will be contributing her expertise as well as some cash, so she may end up with 30 percent. Since Cameron is unlikely to have much involvement in the day-to-day operations and primarily will be contributing capital, his interest in the firm may be set at 10 percent. The point is that the relationship among the partners themselves—including profit sharing—is something they are free to define in any way they see fit.

Decision Making

Because a partnership is made up of two or more persons pooling their resources, the management base is potentially strong. Adam's product knowledge, Diane's marketing savvy, and Cameron's general life experience will all assist in making IK Enterprises a viable operation. If one of the partners becomes sick or otherwise unable to devote sufficient attention to the business, the other partners are in place to carry on.

The downside is that managing the business will require consultation among the partners, and they may not always achieve consensus. A dispute or disagreement between the partners can be extremely disruptive. Even though the partners may have agreed in advance—through a partnership agreement—on a method of dispute resolution, such clauses can be subject to varying interpretations and can be the source of ill-feeling among the partners.

Just as there is the danger of disagreement, there is also the danger of divided authority, which may impede decision making. Although the partners may have determined that they will have authority in different areas, instances are bound to arise in which responsibility overlaps. This too can result in conflict and delayed decision making.

Sources of Capital

Because a partnership is composed of two or more persons, it provides more sources of capital than the sole proprietorship does. The partnership looks to each partner for a capital contribution and can rely on the creditworthiness of each one to secure financing from other sources, including the bank.

Taxation

The partnership is not a separate legal entity, and therefore any income from the partnership business is allocated to the partners—on the basis of their interest in the partnership—and they must, in turn, include it on their individual tax returns.[4]

Transferability

The partnership does not provide for the ready transfer of interest from one owner to another. Partners do not individually own or have a share in specific partnership property. Each partner has an interest in *all* partnership property, from the photocopier to the filing cabinets to its intellectual property.

---

4.   J. Anthony VanDuzer, *The Law of Partnerships and Corporations* (Concord, Ont.: Irwin Law, 1997) at 26.

Agency and the Partnership Act

Partnership law is based in large part on contracts law, agency law, and provincial partnership legislation, known in every jurisdiction as the *Partnership Act*.[5] The acts in place in the common law provinces provide mandatory rules with respect to

- when a partnership exists
- what the relationship of partners is to outsiders

These acts have optional rules (i.e., the rules are subject to an agreement to the contrary) with respect to

- what the relationship of partners is to one another
- how and why a partnership ends

Some of these partnership concepts have already been introduced to give a sketch of how partnerships operate relative to other business vehicles. The following section describes partnerships from a more technical and detailed perspective.

WHEN A PARTNERSHIP EXISTS   According to the *Partnership Act*, a partnership exists when two or more people "carry on business in common with a view towards profit." The definition excludes charitable and not-for-profit endeavours. It does not, however, exclude unprofitable ventures that otherwise meet the definition of partnership so long as an *intention* to make a profit is present.

The statutory definition of partnership covers people who expressly intend to be partners as well as people who may not necessarily intend to be partners but act as if they were. That is, a person who conducts himself *as if* he were a partner—by sharing in profits, by managing the business, by contributing capital to establish a business— *is* a partner in the eyes of the law. Such a person, therefore, has all the rights and liabilities of a partner.

The *Partnership Act* also sets out a number of circumstances that point toward there being a partnership but not conclusively so. For example, if two or more persons own property together, this does not of itself make them partners. However, if in addition to owning property together, the persons share profits associated with that property and restrict their ability to sell unilaterally their interest in the property, a court is likely to conclude that a partnership exists.[6] This would likely be the result even though the parties have indicated in their written agreement that their relationship is a "joint venture" and not a "partnership."[7] The court will look to the essence of the relationship rather than the labels used by the parties.

This means, for example, that if Cameron wants to take an active part in the management of the partnership and share in the profits yet simultaneously avoid the joint, unlimited personal liability that goes with partnership, he is unlikely to succeed. If the business runs into financial difficulties, creditors can come after Cameron for the liabilities, even if Cameron has a document—signed by Diane and Adam—stating that Cameron is *not* a partner. In classifying Cameron's status, what matters is what Cameron actually does in relation to the business, not what a document says.

THE RELATIONSHIP OF PARTNERS TO ONE ANOTHER   If Adam, Cameron, and Diane become partners, the *Partnership Act* provides that they also become one another's

---

5. Legislation is virtually identical across the common law provinces.
6. For a discussion of the difference between partnership and mere co-ownership, see *A.E. LePage Ltd.* v. *Kamex Developments Ltd.* (1977), 78 D.L.R (3d) 223 (Ont. C.A.), aff'd (1979), 105 D.L.R. (3d) 84*n*.
7. *Lansing Building Supply (Ontario) Ltd.* v. *Ierullo* (1990), 71 O.R. (2d) 173 (Dist. Ct.).

agents as well as the agents of the firm in matters relating to the partnership's business. This is significant because it imports the law concerning agency discussed in Chapter 13. It also means that the partners owe fiduciary duties to one another, which require a partner to put the interests of her partners above her own interests.

Accordingly, Adam cannot set up a secret business that competes with the partnership he has formed with Diane and Cameron. He cannot tell a client of the firm to buy its computer equipment from him "on the side" and then proceed to pocket the profits, or use the firm photocopier at night to run a duplicating service without his partners' permission. In short, the law does not allow a partner to make personal profit from the partnership property, to compete against the partnership, or to use a partnership opportunity for exclusive personal gain. Adam is required by law to put the interests of the partnership ahead of his own.

Persons who wish to be associated in partnership should have a partnership agreement, preferably one drafted by a lawyer; Figure 14.2 summarizes the issues that the agreement should address. An agreement will not change the fiduciary duties of the partners to one another, but it can specify the rights and obligations of each partner. For example, a partnership agreement can provide for the division of profits among Cameron, Adam, and Diane in any proportion they see fit. If there is no agreement, the *Partnership Act* will dictate that Cameron, Adam, and Diane will share in profits equally—a result that may not be wanted nor intended.

Figure 14.2

PARTNERSHIP AGREEMENT CHECKLIST

A partnership has been described as a "marriage without love" because many of the concerns that partners face are similar to the ones faced by spouses—sharing of work, financial matters, authority to make decisions, and resolution of disputes.[8] And just as many marriages end in divorce, so too many partnerships fail. Just as a marriage contract cannot save a bad marriage, a partnership agreement cannot guarantee a successful partnership. An agreement can, however, help in avoiding costly litigation and personal animosity if a "divorce" proves necessary.

A partnership agreement should address the following issues:

Creation of the partnership—name and address of partners; partnership name; term of partnership, if any; description of firm's business

Capital contribution—description of contribution by each partner, how shortfalls are handled, how the accounts are managed

Decision making—description of the partners' duties, any limits on authority, dispute resolution mechanism

Profit distribution—description of how profits are to be shared, how and when they are to be distributed, rights of withdrawal

Changes to partnership—rules for changing the relationship, admission of new partners, retirement of partners, option to purchase partner's interest, valuation of interests

Dissolution of partnership—description of what events trigger dissolution, how it will be handled, valuation of assets

A partnership agreement should also be reviewed and updated periodically to reflect changes in circumstances.

As already noted, if the partners do not have a contract or if they have a contract that is silent on some points, then the *Partnership Act* of the province in which the partners are residing will govern the relationship.

---

8. For a discussion of concerns in partnership agreements among accounting professionals, see Mort Shapiro, "Get It in Writing" *CA Magazine* (August 1996) 39.

The *Partnership Act*

All of the common law provinces have a *Partnership Act* modelled on the British act of the same name.

These acts are substantially similar from province to province and have been subject to little change since their original enactments.

The acts have both mandatory and optional provisions. The rules with respect to the relationship between partners are optional, meaning that they are only applicable if the parties do not otherwise have a contract. In each province, the *Partnership Act* provides for the following:

1. All partners are to share equally in the capital and profits of the business and must contribute equally to the losses.

2. Property acquired for the partnership shall be used exclusively for the partnership and not for the private purposes of individual partners. Property purchased with partnership money is deemed to be partnership property.

3. A partner shall be indemnified by the other partners for any liability incurred on behalf of the partnership. This means that all partners are liable for partnership liabilities and that a partner who pays a debt is entitled to reimbursement from her partners.

4. A payment made by a partner for the purposes of the partnership in excess of his agreed subscription shall earn interest.

5. Each partner may take part in the management of the business.

6. No partner is entitled to remuneration for acting in the partnership business.

7. No new member shall be admitted to the partnership without the consent of all the partners.

8. Disputes regarding the partnership business may be decided by a majority, but the nature of the partnership may not be changed without the consent of all the members.

9. Partnership books shall be kept at the partnership's place of business, and all partners shall have access to them.

10. No simple majority may expel any partner.

Source: *Partnership Act*, R.S.N.B. 1990, c. P-4.

RELATIONSHIP OF PARTNERS TO OUTSIDERS   While partners are free to enter into a partnership agreement in order to set out the rights and obligations between them, this will not modify the relationship between partners and outsiders, which is governed specifically by the *Partnership Act* and generally by partnership law, including agency law.

First and foremost, a partner is an agent of the firm. She acts for herself as well as for her partners, who from the perspective of the agency relationship are her principals. For this reason, the firm is responsible on contracts she enters into with actual or apparent authority. For example, assume that Diane enters into a long-term contract for a cell phone to be used for partnership business. Assume further that Cameron and Adam are appalled, since it is not clear that a cell phone is needed at this point, let alone for an extended period of time. They are still bound, however, because Diane—as a partner and therefore as their agent—has the apparent authority to lease phones for the purpose of the partnership. Between the disappointed principals (Cameron and Adam) and a cell-phone company that had no idea that Diane was entering into a contract unpopular with her partners, the law protects the cell-phone company. This is because Diane's partners are in a better position to monitor and restrict her ability to do business on behalf of the firm, even to the point of voting her out of the partnership altogether. They must, therefore, absorb the risk of her "going astray."

Indeed, because the relationship between partners is based on agreement, Diane's authority to enter into contracts on behalf of the firm can be restricted. The parties can enter into an agreement whereby Diane promises not to enter into any long-term contract without first securing her partners' approval. Diane will presumably respect and abide by this restriction, and should she enter into a contract that exceeds her actual authority, the firm will not be bound if the outsider knows or should know that her authority has been limited in this way. Otherwise, the firm is obligated by virtue of the doctrine of apparent authority.

The *Partnership Act* and agency law also make partners responsible for one another's mistakes. For example, if Adam gives poor advice to a client as to its computer systems needs and is sued for the tort of negligence, all the partners, not just Adam, are liable for any damages that result. This is because Adam was acting in the course of firm business and incurred a liability by committing a tort. He and his partners have **joint and several liability**.[9] They are individually and collectively responsible for the liability.

joint and several liability
Responsibility together and individually.

Case

McDonic v. Hetherington (1997), 142 D.L.R. (4th) 648 (Ont. C.A.), leave to appeal to S.C.C. dismissed [1997] S.C.C.A. No. 119

The Business Context: A partner's obligation is not limited to the ordinary debts of the partnership. Partners can also be responsible for each other's misconduct.

Factual Background: Robert Watt was one of six partners in a Toronto law firm. Between May 1985 and December 1989, he made various investments in mortgages on behalf of two elderly sisters. The investments were mainly either unsecured or undersecured and resulted in losses in excess of $250 000. The sisters sued Watt and his partners, claiming negligence and breach of fiduciary duty. Watt, who was disbarred for unrelated reasons, did not defend the action and was deemed to have admitted liability.

The Legal Question: Were Watt's former partners liable for his misconduct?

Resolution: The *Partnership Act* provides that partners are liable for the wrongful acts or omissions of a partner committed in the course of the business of the firm. The former partners argued that they should not be liable as Watt was acting outside the normal scope of the law firm's business—the firm was in the business of providing legal advice, not advising on investments. The court disagreed. Although Watt did not have the express authority of his partners—indeed, the partners were unaware of his activities—his activities fell within the scope of his implied authority. The law firm had invested funds on behalf of clients in the past, which meant that the firm was in the business of advising on investments. In short, Watt's activities fell within the scope of the firm's ordinary business. The partners were liable on this basis.

The court went on to say that even if Watt's actions had fallen outside the ordinary course of the law firm's business, the partners would still be liable as Watt had "apparent authority" to act on behalf of the firm. Any reasonable person in the position of the sisters would not have doubted that they were dealing with Watt as a partner of the law firm. The sisters were clients of the firm, correspondence came on the firm's letterhead, cheques came from the firm, and investment records were kept at the firm's offices. In short, there was nothing to suggest to the sisters that Watt was acting in any capacity other than as a partner in the law firm.

Critical Analysis: What kind of precautions could the partners have taken in this situation to prevent liability?

---

9. See, for example, *Partnership Act*, R.S.N.B., 1990, c. P-4, s. 13, which provides that every partner is liable jointly with co-partners and also severally for wrongful acts or omissions of a partner acting within the course of employment.

HOW AND WHY A PARTNERSHIP ENDS The *Partnership Act* provides for the termination of a partnership under certain circumstances:

- if entered into for a fixed term, by the expiration of the term
- if entered into for a single venture or undertaking, by the termination of that venture or undertaking
- by any partner giving notice to the others of her intention to dissolve the partnership
- following the death, insanity, or bankruptcy of a partner

These provisions apply only if the partners have not agreed on the duration of the partnership.[10] Many partnership agreements do in fact provide for the continuation of the business by the remaining partners even if the particular partnership entity is dissolved. For example, large professional partnerships—such as accounting firms and law firms—have partners joining or leaving every year. Their carefully drafted agreements generally call for an immediate transfer of all assets and liabilities from the old partnership to the new one.

Regulations

As with sole proprietorships, there are no legal requirements for the establishment and conduct of a partnership. The partners simply begin their business activity. While a lawyer may be required to assist in the preparation of a partnership agreement, doing business through a partnership is reasonably simple and inexpensive.

Figure 14.3

PROS AND CONS OF THE PARTNERSHIP

Pros

Simplicity: There are few licensing and registration requirements for partnerships.

Lower costs: The fees for provincial and municipal licences tend to be small. However, a lawyer may be required to assist in drafting the partnership agreement.

Greater access to capital: The capital available to the business includes the assets of each partner and the extent of *each* partner's credit.

Profit motive: Any after-tax profits or other assets accrue to the partners, according to their partnership interest.

Tax benefits: Profits and losses are reported on each partner's personal income tax return, according to that person's share in the partnership. This may be favourable or unfavourable, depending on the taxpayer's circumstances.

Cons

Unlimited personal liability: Each partner carries the entire risk of the business failing. If it does, both the partnership assets and each partner's personal assets are at risk.

Loss of speed and independence: The partners must work together, and a consensus is not always achievable.

Limitations on transferability: The partner's interest in the partnership is not freely transferable.

Profit sharing: The partners must share profits equally or according to their partnership agreement.

Tax disadvantages: See tax benefits.

---

10. See Figure 14.2, Partnership Agreement Checklist.

Partnerships are bound by all rules of general application, including the obligation to comply with laws concerning licensing, employment, tax collection, and public health, for example. Additionally, most provinces require the filing of a declaration of partnership that contains information on the partners, the partnership name, and the duration of the partnership. Failure to file a declaration is not fatal, but it can impede legal actions filed in the name of the partnership and can result in fines.[11]

Partnership Variations

There are two variations on the partnership: the limited partnership, which is available in all provinces, and the limited liability partnership, which is available in only a few provinces.[12]

Limited Partnership

limited partnership
A partnership in which the liability of some partners is limited to their capital contribution.

A **limited partnership** is a partnership in which at least one partner has unlimited liability while others have limited liability. General partners have unlimited liability whereas the limited partners have a liability limited to the amount that they have contributed to the partnership capital.

This vehicle has mostly been used as an investment device. Limited partners put money into a business, such as health care (Health First Doctors Offices) or real estate (Journey's End motels), in return for tax breaks and profits. The general partner manages the investment for a fee and carries the responsibility—assuming that the limited partners have not made guarantees or commitments beyond their investment.[13]

This type of business entity cannot be created informally. A limited partnership requires a written agreement that must be registered with the appropriate provincial body. The registration of the agreement is important because it provides public notice of the capital contribution of the limited partners and identifies the general partners. This, in effect, allows members of the public to decide whether they want to do business with the limited partnership.

General partners have substantially the same rights and powers as partners in ordinary partnerships; limited partners have more narrowly defined rights. They have the right to share in profits and the right to have their contribution returned on dissolution, but they cannot take part in the management of the partnership. If they do, they lose their status of limited partners and become general partners. This is a significant consequence, since it puts all their assets, not just the amount of their capital contribution, at risk should the enterprise fail. Furthermore, what constitutes partaking in management can be a contentious issue and is difficult to define. In the end, the question is resolved by courts assessing the extent and the nature of the limited partner's involvement and deciding whether, on the balance, the limited partner should lose protected status.

Because Cameron wants to protect his assets, he might want to suggest that Adam's product be marketed through a limited partnership. The advantage is that Cameron's losses as a limited partner will be restricted to his capital investment. For example, creditors will not be able to come after his personal assets. The disadvantage is that Cameron must not take part in management or he risks unlimited personal liability.

---

11. There are variations from province to province in this area.

12. See Chapter 23.

13. For a discussion of problems with investing in limited partnerships, see Dan Westell, "When Limited Partnerships Go Sour" *The Financial Post* (27 January 1996) 5.

Limited Liability Partnership

limited liability partnership (LLP)
A partnership in which the partners have unlimited liability for their own malpractice but limited liability for other partners' malpractice.

A **limited liability partnership (LLP)** is a variation on the partnership that is designed to address the liability concerns of professionals who are not permitted to incorporate.[14] The LLP is similar to an ordinary partnership in that members continue to have unlimited liability for negligence and malpractice attributable to their own actions. They are not, however, liable for the negligence or malpractice of their partners unless they are in some way personally involved.

The Corporation

The corporation is the most important form of business organization today. For this reason, Chapters 15 and 16 explore the corporation in detail, including its formation, operation, and termination. The purpose of this section is to provide a brief account of the corporation for the purpose of contrasting it with the other business vehicles already discussed.

Financial Liability

shareholder
A person who has an ownership interest in a corporation.

director
A person elected by shareholders to manage a corporation.

The corporation is the safest vehicle that Adam, Cameron, and Diane could choose to conduct their business. This is because a corporation is a distinct legal entity in law and is therefore capable of assuming its own obligations. Adam, Cameron, and Diane can participate in the profits of the corporation as **shareholders** and manage its operations as **directors**.

Consider the following examples:

- *The bank loan.* If Adam, Cameron, and Diane form a corporation, the corporation has the legal capacity to borrow the necessary start-up capital. This means that the corporation promises to repay the loan with interest, making the corporation, and no other entity, the debtor.

  If the corporation cannot repay the loan, the bank will take the necessary steps to recover as much as it can from the corporation to make up the full amount owing. The bank will be in a position to seize anything owned by the corporation. What the bank will not be able to do is seize assets belonging to Adam, Cameron, and Diane. Even though they have a close relationship to the corporation as its three shareholders, they did not promise to repay the loan. That commitment came from the corporation alone. Put another way, the corporation is the debtor, not the shareholders.

  There is an important proviso to this analysis, which concerns guarantees.[15] When a corporation does not have an established track record of creditworthiness and perhaps holds few assets, the bank will seek personal guarantees from those involved in the corporation, such as the shareholders. There is a very strong possibility that when Diane, Cameron, and Adam approach the bank for a loan to the corporation, the bank will agree only if the three provide personal guarantees. A personal guarantee means that if the corporation fails to meet its obligation to the bank, Diane, Cameron, and Adam will be held responsible for that default. Then, as with a partnership or sole proprietorship, all their personal assets will be at risk. At such a point, it becomes irrelevant that a corporation is a separate legal entity capable of assuming its own obligations. Diane, Cameron, and Adam have no more protection than if they had proceeded by way of a partnership.

---

14. Alberta Law Reform Institute, *Limited Liability Partnerships*, Report 77 (Edmonton: The Alberta Law Reform Institute, 1999) at 5.

15. See Chapter 25 for a discussion of guarantees.

limited liability
Responsibility for obligations restricted to the amount of investment.

- *The breach of contract.* If the corporation supplies defective computers to a customer, it is the corporation and no other entity that is in breach of contract. It is the corporation that will be sued, and it is the corporate assets that are at risk.[16]

  Again, recall the discussion of guarantees. Any entity that deals with a corporation may demand the personal guarantee of the corporation's shareholders or directors.

The key characteristic of a corporation is that it provides **limited liability** to its shareholders. That is, should the corporation's financial health take a bad turn, the shareholder's loss is limited to what she paid to purchase shares in the corporation. Unless, in addition, the shareholder provided a personal guarantee, she has absolutely no liability for the corporation's obligations, however they were incurred.[17]

Profit Sharing

dividend
A division of profits payable to shareholders.

Profits of the corporation are distributed to shareholders through **dividends**. That is, shareholders are paid a return on their investment in the corporation, but only if there is profit, and only if the directors declare a dividend.

The corporate form of business organization is inherently flexible from an investment perspective, because it permits varying degrees of ownership and various means for sharing profits.

Decision Making

The corporation is managed by a board of directors, which in turn is elected by the shareholders.

In addition, officers—that is, high-ranking corporate employees—can be hired by the board to assist in running the corporation. This provides a broad management base that allows the corporation to benefit from specialized and high-level expertise. However, it can also result in layers of authority that can delay decision making.

Sources of Capital

A corporation can get its capital in two ways: it can borrow, or its directors can issue shares. The purchase price of the shares is an important and potentially large source of capital for the corporation. A share represents an equity position in the corporation and provides the shareholder with the chance of making a profit through the declaration of dividends, which it is hoped will be greater than the interest rate the shareholder would have received had she simply lent the money. The disadvantage is that if the corporation fails, the shareholder is left with nothing while the creditor technically retains the right to be repaid. However, if the corporation is insolvent, that right is of little value.

Because the principle of limited liability protects investors against unlimited losses, the corporation is well-suited to raise large amounts of capital.

Corporations that offer their shares to the public must publish information concerning their finances; this makes the corporation subject to greater outside scrutiny than the partnership or sole proprietorship.

---

16. Of course, if an employee of the corporation misrepresented the product or committed a tort of some description, that employee would be liable. This is a matter distinct from the contractual liability of the corporation. See Chapter 16.

17. Only in rare situations, such as fraud on the creditors, will the courts hold the shareholders personally responsible for the corporation's actions. See Chapter 16.

Taxation

Because it is a separate legal entity, a corporation pays its own taxes. In other words, the income of the corporation is subject to taxation quite apart from the taxation of its owners. A shareholder of a corporation will be taxed if she earns a salary from the corporation, receives a dividend from it, or realizes a capital gain from the sale of her shares. Advantages in the form of reduced or deferred taxes may sometimes be gained through the appropriate splitting of distributions to shareholders between dividend and salary payments. For example, Cameron could take a salary from the corporation and his son could receive income through dividends. This may produce a more favourable tax treatment than if Cameron took *both* a salary *and* dividend payments himself. The ultimate effect of this kind of income splitting depends on a variety of factors, including the corporate tax rate and the marginal tax rate of the shareholder and employee. It is significant that the partnership and sole proprietorship enjoy no such options, since all income from the business is taxed at personal rates.

Transferability

The fact that a corporation has a separate legal identity often allows for easy transference of an ownership interest represented by shares. A shareholder can sell or bequeath her shares with no interference from corporate creditors because the shareholder has no liability for corporate debts. The shares belong to her and she can do what she wants with them. Transferability is, however, subject to restrictions in the corporation's incorporating documents and may also be restricted by a shareholders' agreement.

Perpetual Existence

Because the corporation exists independently of its shareholders, the death or bankruptcy of one or more shareholders does not affect the existence of the corporation. The corporation continues in existence perpetually unless it is dissolved by order of a court, for failure to comply with statutory regulations, or through a voluntary surrender of its legal status to the government.

Regulations

Like sole proprietorships and partnerships, a corporation must comply with laws of general application.

Unlike other kinds of business vehicles, however, the corporation comes into existence only if proper documents are submitted to the government and it issues, in return, a certificate of incorporation. Thus, it can be more expensive to organize a corporation than a sole proprietorship or partnership because there tend to be legal bills and additional filing fees to pay. As well, there are extensive rules contained in corporations statutes that govern many corporate decisions and result in the need for considerable record keeping. These extra requirements and expenses, however, can be more than offset by the protection provided to investors by the principle of limited liability.

Figure 14.4

PROS AND CONS OF THE CORPORATION

Pros

Limited liability: Because it is a separate legal entity, a corporation can assume its own liabilities. The shareholder stands to lose the amount he invested in the corporation, but no more.

Flexibility: A corporation permits differing degrees of ownership and sharing in profits.

Greater access to capital: Limited liability makes the corporation a very suitable vehicle through which to raise capital.

Continuous existence: The life span of a corporation is not tied to its shareholders.

Tax benefits: Though this is a fact-specific issue, a corporation can facilitate greater tax planning, for example, by permitting income splitting.

Transferability: Ownership in a corporation is more easily transferable through shares.

Potentially broad management base: A corporation is managed by directors and officers, who can provide a level of specialized expertise to the corporation.

Cons

Higher costs: Creating a corporation incurs filing fees and legal costs.

Public disclosure: When a corporation offers shares to the public, the corporation must comply with strict disclosure and reporting requirements.

Greater regulation: Corporation statutes govern many decisions, which limits management options and required specific kinds of record keeping.

Dissolution: Ending a corporation's life can be complicated.

Tax disadvantages: A corporation may be subject to double taxation, depending on the circumstances. This is a fact-specific issue.

Possible loss of control: A corporation has diminished control because it issues shares with voting rights.

Potential bureaucracy: The many levels of authority in a corporation may impede decision making.

Figure 14.5

A COMPARISON OF MAJOR FORMS OF ORGANIZATIONS*

Characteristic	Sole Proprietorship	Partnership	Corporation
Creation	• at will of owner	• by agreement of the parties	• by incorporation documents
Duration	• limited by life of owner	• terminated by agreement, death	• perpetual unless dissolved
Liability of owners	• unlimited	• unlimited	• limited
Taxation	• net income taxed at personal rate	• net income at personal rate	• income taxed to the corporation; dividends and salary taxed to shareholders
Transferability	• only assets may be transferred	• transferable by agreement	• transferable unless incorporating documents restrict transferability
Management	• owner manages	• all partners manage equally unless otherwise specified in agreement	• shareholders elect a board to manage the affairs of the corporation; officers can also be hired

* These are the legal differences between the major business forms. In practice, however, there are ways of minimizing the consequences of these differences. Whether one form of business organization or another is chosen will depend on individual circumstances. As with all other legal concerns, legal, accounting, and management advice should be sought in order to make an informed decision.

The preceding sections introduced the basic forms of business organizations. Subject to some specialized exceptions, such as real estate investment trusts and mutual funds, every business will use one of these forms.

There are additional ways to carry on the business activity itself. These ways are not distinct business organizations but are, for the lack of a more accurate term, *arrangements*. These arrangements do not have any strict legal meaning as such; most commonly they refer to some sort of contractual commitment between two or more business organizations.

Adam, for example, may at some point want to expand his business. One option is to grow internally by opening new branches, expanding existing branches, and hiring new employees. He may, however, for many reasons decide to enter an arrangement with another entity. Adam may want to capitalize on the goodwill he has developed in his business, or another organization may more easily be able to penetrate a market, or he may simply feel that he does not have the time and expertise needed to handle an internal expansion. The following section explores the range of options open to entrepreneurs like Adam.

The Franchise

franchise
An agreement whereby an owner of a trademark or trade name permits another to sell a product or service under that trademark or name.

A **franchise** is a contractual arrangement between a manufacturer, wholesaler, or service organization (franchisor) and an independent business (franchisee), who buys the right to own and operate one or more units of the franchise system. Franchise organizations are normally based on some unique product, service, or method of doing business; on a trade name or patent; or on goodwill that the franchisor has developed.

Almost every kind of business has been franchised—motels, fast-food restaurants, dental centres, hair salons, maid services, and fitness centres, to name a few. Some familiar examples are Pizza Hut, 7-Eleven, McDonald's, Subway, Molly Maid, Magicuts, and Weight Watchers.

Franchising involves a contract between the franchisor and the franchisee. Wide variations exist in franchise agreements, but generally they cover arrangements regarding such matters as how the business is to be run, where supplies may or must be purchased, royalty levels to be paid to the franchisor for sharing its business operation plan and other benefits, and charges for management, advertising, and other corporate services. The agreement negotiated depends on the relative bargaining power of the parties and the issues brought to the table. Usually, however, the franchisor, having a great deal more information about the business, is in the better position to negotiate an advantageous agreement or to insist on the use of a standard form contract.[18] This has often led to litigation.

The Franchise Relationship

As illustrated in the Pizza Pizza case, the relationship between a franchisor and a franchisee is one of contract. The relationship does not normally create fiduciary obligations,[19] but there are a few cases that suggest there is a duty of fair dealing and

---

18. See Part 2 for a discussion on the role of bargaining power and standard form contracts.
19. *Jirna Limited* v. *Mister Donut of Canada Ltd.,* [1975] 1 S.C.R. 2.

Case

887574 Ont. v. *Pizza Pizza Ltd.* (1995), 23 B.L.R. (2d) 259 (Ont. Gen. Div.)

The Business Context: Pizza Pizza Ltd. (PP) is one of the oldest and most successful franchise operations in Canadian history. In the early 1990s, however, the relationship between PP and its franchisees soured. A group of 50 franchisees commenced action against PP, alleging breach of contract and fraud. By agreement, all issues were referred to private commercial arbitration. The discussion below relates to an appeal from the arbitrator's decision regarding rental and advertising "pools."

Factual Background: The relationship between PP and its franchisees is governed by a series of standard form agreements—the franchise agreement, a sublease for premises rented from PP, and a general security agreement. The franchise agreement provides for a series of pools of money, funded by the franchisees and managed by PP. The pools pay for the costs incurred by PP for advertising, central telephone ordering, rent, and delivery of product. Franchise owners contribute a specified amount to the pool, and if at the end of the year there is a deficit in the pool, it must be paid by the franchisees in proportion to their net sales.

Each franchisee leases premises from PP. The sublease (PP leases premises and in turn sublets to the franchisees) sets out the actual rent payment for premises. A franchisee's payment is calculated as a percentage of net sales and is capped at a percentage of net sales. The percentage ranges from 5.5 to 8 percent.

By the late 1980s, there was not enough money in the pool to pay all of PP's expenses. PP unilaterally increased the percentage rates for rent to 7 percent and then to 10 percent regardless of the terms of the subleases. PP argued that by the terms of the franchise agreement, all deficits are to be paid by the franchisees and therefore it was entitled to increase the rent payments. It further argued that if there is a conflict between the franchise agreement and the lease, the agreement takes precedence. The franchisees contended that PP could not increase rent above the ceilings set in the sublease agreements.

The Legal Question: Whose interpretation of the contractual arrangements was correct?

Resolution: The dispute between the parties involves the construction of their contractual arrangements. First, the issue of rent is dealt with by both the franchise agreement and the sublease; therefore it is essential to look at the whole package of agreements to ascertain the intention of the parties. Second, the percentage of net sales payable as rent was a fundamental part of the agreement. In short, the court did not consider it to be consistent with the parties' intentions that PP have a unilateral power "through the side door of the rental pool deficit provision, to increase by massive amounts the rents payable by the franchisees." Third, the paramountcy of the franchise agreement could only be triggered if there were an inconsistency between the two documents, but no such inconsistency existed. In conclusion, the court determined that the proper interpretation was that the franchisees were to fund the deficit in the pool only up to a maximum amount of rent specified in the sublease.

Critical Analysis: When sales and profits are high, both the franchisor and franchisee are happy. Problems arise when sales decline and losses are incurred. Was the court's decision a fair way of handling franchise deficits?

---

good faith in the franchise relationship. For example, in *McKinlay Motors Ltd.* v. *Honda Canada Inc.*,[20] Honda did not allocate a reasonable share of cars to McKinlay Motors, intending to force the dealer to terminate. In response to this tactic, the court stated the following:

> I find that Honda acted in bad faith under the agreement. It is obviously an implied term of any agreement that the parties act toward each other in their business dealings in good faith.[21]

---

20. (1989), 46 B.L.R. 62 (Nfld. S.C.T.D.).
21. *Ibid.* at 80.

Franchise Law

There is not a distinct body of law in Canada called franchise law. As in the Pizza Pizza case, courts apply contract law principles to the relationship. The exception is jurisdictions that have enacted franchise legislation. The legislation is designed to provide greater protection to franchisees who are entering franchise relationships.

The *Alberta Franchise Act*

LANDMARK IN THE LAW

Alberta enacted franchising legislation in 1970. Ontario has passed franchise legislation,[22] and other provinces continue to study the issue. The *Alberta Franchise Act* and its regulations were thoroughly revised in 1995. Two of the more salient features of the revised Alberta act are the definition of franchise and the disclosure requirements:

1. The definition of franchise is extremely broad and encompasses virtually every entity that engages in distribution, dealership, or franchising.

2. The 1995 act removes the requirement for franchisors to file documents or register with the Alberta Securities Commission or other government agency. However, franchisors must obey the continuing requirement to give prospective franchisees a disclosure document. The disclosure guidelines set out in the regulations require the franchisor to disclose all material facts relating to the franchise trade, including but not limited to the following:
   - the background of the franchise and its officers and directors
   - previous convictions and pending charges in the last 10 years against the franchisor, associates, and officers and directors with management responsibilities for indictable franchise-related offences
   - civil litigation and liabilities (details as above)
   - details of bankruptcy or insolvency proceedings in the last six years involving the franchisor and its associates, officers, and directors
   - nature of the business—the retail concept, target market, and competition of the franchise, and any identified trends
   - terms and conditions of any financing arrangements, including lease and sublease arrangements
   - names, addresses, and telephone numbers of existing franchise outlets
   - description of all franchise closures in the last three years
   - exclusive territory provisions;
   - financial statements from last fiscal year

The franchise agreement may be rescinded if the disclosure document is not produced by the time specified in the act. In such a case, the franchisor must pay for any net losses incurred in setting up the business.

Critical Analysis: Is legislation such as this necessary? Why?

Source: *Alberta Franchise Act*, S.A. 1995, c. F-17.1.

---

22. *Arthur Wishart Act (Franchise Disclosure), 2000,* S.O. 2000, c. 3. The Act received Royal Assent June 8, 2000, and was partially proclaimed in force July 1, 2000.

Joint Venture

A **joint venture** is an association of business entities—corporations, individuals, or partnerships—that unite for the purpose of carrying on a business venture. Normally the parties agree to share profits and losses and management of the project. The key feature of a joint venture is that it is usually limited to a specific project. For example, several oil and gas companies may join for offshore exploration in a certain region, or a steel fabricator may combine with a construction company to refurbish a nuclear plant.

The joint venture itself can take a variety of forms. The joint venture may be a partnership, in which case all the legal consequences associated with a partnership apply. It may also be what is known as an equity joint venture. This is when the parties incorporate a separate corporation for the project and each party holds shares in that corporation. A joint venture also may be simply a contractual arrangement between the parties. However, the law can impose duties on the parties beyond those specified in the contract.[23] Most significantly, parties to a joint venture owe fiduciary duties to one another.

Strategic Alliance

A strategic alliance is a cooperative arrangement among businesses. It is an arrangement that may involve joint research, technology sharing, or joint use of production, for example.[24] Toshiba, a Japanese electronics company, has alliances with many companies to develop new products, such as mobile telecommunications equipment and computer chips.

Like a joint venture, a strategic alliance does not have a precise legal meaning. The underlying relationship between the parties is normally contractual. The contract or a series of contracts will spell out the parties' rights and obligations.

Distributorship or Dealership

A product or service distributorship is very much like a franchise. A contract is entered into whereby a manufacturer agrees to provide products and the distributor or dealer agrees to carry products or perform services prescribed by the manufacturer. This kind of arrangement is often encountered in the automotive and computer industries.

The relationship between the parties is governed by the contract. There are no fiduciary obligations owed by the parties to each other beyond those that are spelled out in the contract.

Sales Agency

A sales agency relationship is usually an arrangement whereby a manufacturer or distributor contracts with an agent to sell goods or services supplied by the manufacturer or distributor on a principal/agent basis.[25] The agent is not the actual vendor but acts on behalf of a principal, who is the owner of the goods or services. As this relationship is one of agency, fiduciary obligations are owed. This arrangement is often encountered in the travel and insurance industries.

---

23. *Supra* note 4 at 57.
24. The term *strategic alliance* is sometimes used to include joint ventures. There is little precision in terminology in this area. The key point is that terms usually describe a contractual arrangement between two or more parties.
25. See Chapter 13.

Establishing a Foreign Presence

In recent years, the development of international and regional trade agreements and the trend to market-oriented economies have offered new opportunities to business.

To take advantage of the opportunities in the international marketplace, companies often need to establish a presence in other countries. Such a presence can take many forms. A business may begin by employing the services of an agent to act on its behalf. Other options that fall short of actually having a business in the foreign jurisdiction are a distributorship, a franchising agreement, and a licensing agreement. A business may opt to create a subordinate entity in a foreign country, such as a branch—a unit of the parent company or a subsidiary—an independently organized and incorporated company controlled by the company. Another alternative is a joint venture with one or more other businesses.

Which option is chosen will be influenced by many factors similar to the factors that influence which business form is chosen in the domestic market, such as degree of control, degree of participation in management, tax rates, and limited liability. A unique factor, however, influencing the choice of form in the international market is that many developing countries require a business to recruit local participants before allowing it to invest or expand in their territories. This means that a joint venture is a particularly popular method of expanding into a foreign market, as it can readily accommodate the requirement of local participation by having a local partner.

Critical Analysis: Why would a country require that a foreign business have local participation? Can you think of any legal reasons?

Source: Ray August, *International Business Law,* 2d ed. (New Jersey: Prentice-Hall, 1997) at 167-171; Carolyn Hotchkiss, *International Law for Business* (New York: McGraw-Hill, 1994) at 275-277.

Product Licensing

In this arrangement, the licensee is granted the right to manufacture and distribute products associated with the licensor's trademarks or other proprietary rights. Licensing is common for many consumer goods such as clothing, sporting goods, and merchandise connected to the entertainment industry. This arrangement is explored in more depth in Chapter 18.

Business Law in Practice Revisited

1. **What forms of business organization are available for carrying on Adam's business?**

Adam may carry on his business as a sole proprietorship, in partnership with others, or through a corporation.

2. What are the major considerations in choosing a particular form?

Adam's father, Cameron, is willing to invest in the business but is unwilling to accept risk beyond his investment. This consideration eliminates an ordinary partnership, as it would expose him to additional risk. A limited partnership is a possibility. However, Cameron would not be able to partake in the management of the organization. If he did, he may lose his limited liability status. As Adam is young and presumably inexperienced, he might want to be able to seek the assistance of his father. A sole proprietorship exposes only Adam to unlimited liability; however, if Cameron participates in profits and management, there is a risk of an "unintended" partnership. Thus, it would seem that the most viable alternative is a corporation with Cameron investing his money in shares. This alternative limits his exposure to risk and also allows for his potential participation in profits.

Diane is interested in taking a role in the management of the venture, as well as in investing a sum of money. These considerations could be accommodated within a partnership agreement, although it may be difficult to agree on the valuation of her time and expertise, as she will not be working full-time on the project. As well, she may be averse to the risks associated with a partnership. The other option is a corporation with Diane investing in shares. This would allow her to participate in profits as a means of compensation for her services. A contractual arrangement to compensate her for her services may not be viable, as Adam probably does not have the means to pay her.

3. Which form is best for Adam's business?

For the reasons given above, a corporation may be the most appropriate, but the success of Adam's business is not dependent on the form chosen. Much more important is the viability of his idea and his ability to bring it to fruition.

Chapter Summary

Most businesses are carried on using one of the basic forms—sole proprietorship, partnership (or one of its variations), or corporation. These forms have varying characteristics, most notably with respect to the exposure to liability. Sole proprietorships and partnerships expose their owners to personal liability for the business obligations. A corporation, on the other hand, has the attraction of limited liability for the owners—their liability is limited to the amount of their investment. This characteristic however can be neutralized. For example, a sole proprietor can escape the effects of unlimited liability by transferring assets to a relative prior to commencing business. As well, the advantage of limited liability in the corporate form can become meaningless if creditors insist on a personal guarantee from the owners of the corporation.

Each form has other advantages and disadvantages. The form chosen for a business enterprise depends on an evaluation of numerous factors such as investors' aversion to risk, their desire to earn profits, and their wish to participate in decision making. In short, the best form for a particular situation depends on all the circumstances.

A partnership is the form most often found in the professions. This is due, in part, to prohibitions against some professionals incorporating. A partnership subjects the partners to unlimited liability. The other defining feature of a partnership is agency—a partner is an agent for other partners and for the partnership. The effects of agency between the partners can be modified by a partnership agreement; however, the effects of agency in relation to outsiders cannot, and are governed by the *Partnership Act.*

A business may also at some point enter into an arrangement with another entity for carrying out business activities. The various arrangements are all based on a contract negotiated between the parties. Regardless of the arrangement entered into, the business still needs to be carried on using one of the basic business forms.

It is important to remember that it is the viability of the business itself that is critical, not necessarily the form of the business or the particular arrangements made. Put another way, a business does not succeed because it chooses a franchise arrangement over a distributorship. The key to a successful business is having a solid business plan that is well executed.

Study Chapter

Questions for Review

1. Define sole proprietorship, partnership, and corporation.

2. What is the difference between a general and limited partner?

3. What are the advantages and disadvantages of a partnership?

4. How can a partnership come into existence?

5. How can a partnership come to an end?

6. Explain the difference between a limited partnership and a limited liability partnership.

7. What are the advantages and disadvantages of the corporate form?

8. What is the difference between a business form and a business arrangement?

9. What is the basis of a franchise?

10. Is a joint venture a partnership? Explain.

Questions for Discussion

1. What kinds of business activities are particularly well suited to the following arrangements: franchise, joint venture, strategic alliance, distributorship, product licensing agreement, and sales agency? What are the legal considerations in entering into these arrangements?

2. Many people think of franchising as a quick and easy way to start their own business. Indeed, some buyers have experienced almost instant success, but far more have experienced dismal failure. It is estimated that about 20 percent of all franchises fail within the first three to five years. The key to success is often the choice of franchise and the franchise package, or contractual arrangement. What should the franchise contract contain? What issues should it address?

3. Some professionals are prohibited from incorporating companies with limited liability. What do you think might be the reasons for this prohibition? Do you think that increased incidents of professional liability are a good reason for granting professionals limited liability status?

4. What are the circumstances in which a partnership may be found to exist? What steps can be taken to avoid a finding of partnership? How can the consequences of being found a partner be minimized?

5. The three basic business forms are sole proprietorship, partnership, and corporation. How is each of these formed? How is each owned? How does each form allocate the risk associated with doing business?

Situations for Discussion

1. While vacationing in the United States, George, an avid horse enthusiast, met an experienced horse trader, Keith, who had worldwide experience in the buying and selling of horses. George and Keith took an immediate liking to each other and decided to enter into an agreement to carry on the business of purchasing horses in the Middle East and reselling them for a profit in Canada. Under their oral agreement, George provided $100 000 as the only working capital in the business, but he was to take no active part in the business. The money was put in a joint account operable under their joint signatures. Keith was to do all the work but provide no capital.

    A horse was bought in Iran and shipped to Canada. It was resold for a tidy profit of $5000. Despite their initial success, differences arose between George and Keith and they decided to terminate their arrangement.

    The total assets of the business were $104 000 after deducting all expenses. On settlement, Keith claimed he was entitled to $52 000. Is he correct?

2. Colleen, Timothy, and James formed a limited partnership to operate a Saint John River boat cruise. Colleen and Timothy were general partners and James was a limited partner. The necessary documentation was prepared and filed in the appropriate government. The endeavour was wildly successful in the summer, and James would occasionally go on the boat to give commentary to the passengers. Once winter came and the river froze, however, business went downhill. One of the creditors sued the partnership and James. Is James liable?

3. Roj and Maki purchased a fast-food franchise located in a shopping mall. They signed a standard form contract and paid a $50 000 initiation fee. After they took possession, problems developed; sales were well below what Roj and Maki thought they would be and well below what the franchisor implied they would be.[26] Do they have any cause of action against the franchisor? What additional information would be useful?

4. Ken, a recent graduate of a professional accounting program, formed a partnership with a classmate, Lloyd, to provide various accounting services to small and medium-sized businesses. Lloyd made a serious error in the preparation and presentation of a cash budget to a client. Ken is wondering about his responsibility for Lloyd's mistakes.[27] In particular, if Ken compensates the client for all losses, can he claim reimbursement from Lloyd? Would the answer be the same if Ken and Lloyd had several other partners? How should losses between partners be dealt with?

5. Thomas, a young entrepreneur, started a construction business. Ari, who owned and operated an ethnic radio station, agreed to run some advertisements for him. Unfortunately, Thomas was unable to pay Ari for the services. In the hopes of making the business profitable so that he could get payment under the broadcasting contract, Ari, without remuneration, assisted Thomas in his business. In fact, Ari signed a contract with Lopez on behalf of Thomas for plumbing and heating supplies. When payment for the supplies was not forthcoming, Lopez sued Ari, claiming that Ari was a partner of Thomas and was therefore responsible for the debt. Ari claimed that when he signed he was acting as Thomas' agent. What difference does it make whether Ari is considered to be Thomas' agent or his partner? What factors are important in determining the nature of a relationship between individuals?

26. Based, in part, on *447927 Ontario Inc.* v. *Pizza Pizza Ltd.* (1987), 62 O.R. (2d) 114 (H.C.).
27. Based, in part, on *MacDonald* v. *Schmidt*, [1992] B.C.J. No. 230, (S.C.) Online: QL (B.C.J.).

Fifteen

The Corporate Form: Organizational Matters

Objectives

AFTER STUDYING THIS CHAPTER, YOU SHOULD HAVE AN UNDERSTANDING OF

► A CORPORATION AS A LEGAL PERSON

► THE VARIOUS METHODS OF INCORPORATION

► HOW A CORPORATION IS CREATED

► HOW THE CORPORATION IS CAPITALIZED

Business Law in Practice

Adam (introduced in Chapter 14) is still young, energetic, and smart but not quite as broke. He has received glowing industry feedback on his voice recognition system for computers, and Diane has made a definite commitment to help market it. Adam is thinking seriously of incorporating a company. He thinks that the best approach is to start with a small local operation. However, as the product has great national and international sales potential, he projects a fairly rapid expansion of operations.

Adam plans to hold half the shares in the company as he will be the manager. Half the shares will be held by Diane to compensate her for her advice and expertise in marketing. Adam's father, Cameron, is still committed to investing $100 000 in the company. Adam wants Cameron to simply lend the money to the company as he thinks that this is the only way to protect Cameron from unlimited liability should the business venture fail.

The other matter he has been considering concerns capitalization—the company will need more than $100 000 to finance its initial operations. "Simple," says Adam, "I will sell some shares to a bunch of friends."

1. Has Adam considered all the issues in forming a corporation?
2. Does Adam appear to understand the concept of limited liability adequately?
3. What other financing options are available, in addition to Cameron lending money to the corporation?
4. What factors should Adam consider in seeking to raise capital by selling shares?

The Corporation Defined

The corporation[1] is the predominant business vehicle in modern commerce because it is a separate legal entity. For this reason, it is able to remedy many of the shortcomings associated with the other prevalent business forms—the sole proprietorship and the partnership.

The notion that the corporation possesses a legal identity separate and distinct from its owners has fundamental repercussions. It means that the corporation alone is responsible for its own debts and other liabilities. Should the corporation fail to make good on its obligations, the shareholders[2] are not responsible for the default. The most that they stand to lose is the purchase price of their shares.

If Adam decides to run his computer business as a sole proprietorship, he is gambling his personal assets if the venture proves to be a financial disaster. Yet if he decides to run the identical business through a corporation, none of Adam's assets is at risk.

The law recognizes this different outcome as being perfectly legitimate and eminently just. As indicated in Chapter 14, the key question is this: *Who* has incurred the obligation in question? Liability falls on that entity—be it an individual or a corporation—and that entity alone. Put another way, the creditor must decide with whom she is doing business and live with the consequences of that decision.

The concept of a corporation being a separate legal entity is complex. It was established in 1897 in a case that remains at the centre of modern corporations law. Since *Salomon,* the separate legal existence of the corporation has not been seriously challenged. Corporations, with few exceptions, continue to be treated as entities separate from their shareholders. The cornerstone of corporations law—limited liability—is secure.

---

1. In some jurisdictions, such as British Columbia, a corporation is called a "company." Although, strictly speaking, the terms are not synonymous, they are used interchangeably in this text.
2. In some jurisdictions, such as British Columbia, a shareholder is called a "member."

Landmark Case

Salomon v. *Salomon Ltd.* (1897) A.C. 22 (H.L.)

The Historical Context: When Salomon was decided, the corporate form was just coming into wider usage. At the time, it was unclear whether companies with few shareholders would be recognized as separate legal entities.

Factual Background: Aron Salomon carried on a profitable shoe manufacturing business for many years as a sole proprietor. He decided to form an incorporated company—Aron Salomon and Company, Limited—as the vehicle through which to run his business. The *Companies Act,* which set out the rules for creating a company, required that a company have a minimum of seven shareholders. Therefore, Aron took one share and members of his family took the remaining six shares. Aron became the managing director. Practically speaking, Aron Salomon and Company, Limited was a "one-person company" since Aron entirely controlled the company. Put another way, the other participants in the company had no involvement in operations: any decision the company took was only because Aron wanted it to follow that particular course of action.

Next, Aron Salomon and Company, Limited, agreed to purchase the assets of Aron's sole proprietorship. As the corporation had little cash, Aron was issued 20 000 shares and a mortgage secured by the shoe business assets. In this way, Aron became a highly protected creditor of his own company.

The business suffered financial problems due to a series of strikes and the loss of government contracts. The company became insolvent, and a trustee was appointed to deal with its creditors and close down the business. Many creditors of Aron Salomon and Company, Limited—including Aron himself—lined up for payment. As a secured creditor, Aron was at the head of the line, but payment of his debt would leave nothing for the unsecured creditors. In response, the trustee refused to recognize Aron as a legitimate creditor and, furthermore, took the position that Aron was personally responsible for all his company's debts.

The Legal Question: Was Aron liable for the debts of Aron Salomon and Company, Limited? Was Aron a legitimate creditor of the company?

Resolution: A corporation—large or small—is a separate legal entity and, as such, is totally responsible for its own obligations. Indeed, one of the main reasons for creating a company is to limit liability in the event of bankruptcy. The court rejected the argument that there was something essentially improper about an individual conducting his business through a one-person corporation to secure the protection of limited liability. If a number of persons can limit their liability in this way, then why shouldn't a single person be able to do the same thing? After all, it should not make any difference to a creditor whether one or several shareholders limit their liability.

The House of Lords also confirmed that there is nothing wrong with a shareholder being a creditor of the corporation, even when that shareholder essentially controls the company in question. The result was that Salomon was entitled to be paid ahead of the other creditors and was not responsible for the corporation's debts. The creditors had chosen to deal with Aron's *company*—not with Aron, the *individual*—and, furthermore, had done so on an unsecured basis. They, in turn, would have to live with the adverse outcome of that business decision.

Critical Analysis: Do you think that the court went too far in giving independent existence to the corporation, especially when the interests of Aron and his company were virtually identical? Should the shareholder of a one-person company be entitled to limited liability? How could the creditors, other than Aron, have better protected themselves in this situation?

Stakeholders in the Corporation

The corporation has a legal existence, but it is an artificial entity whose activities are controlled entirely by human beings. Although itself invisible, the corporation has a very real legal impact on those with whom it deals. Put another way, a contract with a corporation is just as real as a contract with a human being.

stakeholder
One who has an interest in a corporation.

Not surprisingly, those who have an interest in the corporation—its **stakeholders**—may come into conflict with one another, as well as with the corporation itself. The bulk of corporations law seeks to regulate the relationships among the corporation's main stakeholders (see Figure 15.1).

Figure 15.1

CORPORATE RELATIONSHIPS

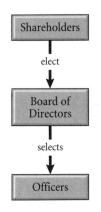

Internal stakeholders are those who have a role—either directly or indirectly—in determining the corporation's mission and how it will be achieved. *Shareholders* are those persons who have invested in the corporation by buying shares in return for a potential share of the corporate profits and other benefits. Shareholders do not have any direct authority to manage the corporation.[3] However, they do have the power to elect the *board of directors* and therefore can have a strong influence on the direction of the corporation. The board of directors is charged with management functions—including policy development—and is answerable to the shareholders since, should it perform poorly, the board runs the risk of being voted out of office. *Corporate officers,* such as the president, secretary, and treasurer, are another important internal group. They are hired by the board of directors and are charged with managing the day-to-day operations of the corporation.

External stakeholders are people who have dealings with or are affected by the corporation but are otherwise on the "outside." They do not have the same power or authority to control the corporation that the internal stakeholders wield. Examples are government, the general public, customers, and creditors. In corporations law, the most important are the creditors.

Chapter 16 will provide a more detailed account of corporate stakeholders. The concept is introduced here to establish some of the basic vocabulary associated with the corporate form, as well to as identify its central players.

Creation of a Corporation

Provincial and Federal Incorporation

Assuming that Adam decides to do business through a company, he must choose between incorporating federally and incorporating provincially. He has this choice because jurisdiction over the incorporation of companies is divided between the federal government and the provincial governments. Federally incorporated corporations

---

3. Federally and in jurisdictions such as Ontario and Alberta, directors are given the power to manage by virtue of statute. The same holds true in British Columbia (see the *Company Act,* R.S.B.C. 1996 c. 62, s. 117.) In Nova Scotia, this end is achieved through a shareholders' delegation of powers set out in the articles of association; see Bruce Welling, Wesley B. Rayner, Cally Jordan, & Lionel D. Smith, *Canadian Corporate Law: Cases, Notes & Materials* (Toronto: Butterworths, 1996) at 52.

have a right to carry on business in each province, whereas provincially incorporated corporations have the right to carry on business only in the province in which they are incorporated.[4] This difference has little practical significance because each province has straightforward licensing procedures through which corporations incorporated in other provinces can do business in that province.[5]

One of the most practical differences between federal and provincial corporations concerns the legislation that governs their creation and operation. Federally created corporations are regulated by the *Canada Business Corporations Act.* Provincially created corporations are regulated by provincial legislation, such as the P.E.I. *Companies Act.*

When, then, should a business incorporate federally, and when would it be best advised to incorporate provincially? There is no hard and fast answer to this question. For corporations that intend to operate in more than two provinces, federal incorporation may result in lower administrative costs. For corporations that intend to operate in only one or two provinces, the administrative costs are usually lower with a provincial incorporation.[6] Since Adam intends to operate nationally and even internationally, he should seriously consider incorporating under federal legislation.

Both the federal and provincial governments also permit the incorporation of not-for-profit or nonshare capital organizations. The purpose of these organizations is not business oriented, but rather to promote cultural, religious, social, or charitable goals.[7]

Methods of Incorporation

royal charter
An official document that established a corporation as a separate legal entity.

Historically, corporations came into existence through the Crown granting a **royal charter**: this took the form of an official document establishing the company as a separate legal entity that could own property, enter into contracts, and sue in its own right. A charter company was deemed to have all the powers of a natural person.[8]

The system of incorporation by royal charter has not been in use since the 19th century, but some well-known corporations created by this method are still in existence. The Hudson's Bay Company is probably the most famous Canadian example of a company created by royal charter.[9]

The Hudson's Bay Company became a federal corporation under the *Canada Business Corporations Act* in 1978.

---

4. More specifically, federal jurisdiction is derived from its residual power known as "peace, order, and good government."

5. Peter Hogg, *Constitutional Law of Canada,* 4th ed. vol. 1 (Scarborough: Carswell, 1997) at 23–27.

6. Kevin Patrick McGuinness, *The Law and Practice of Canadian Business Corporations* (Toronto: Butterworths, 1999) at 108-109.

7. This text is predominantly about business law; therefore, it is beyond its scope to discuss the creation of organizations whose purposes are other than business.

8. *Communities Economic Development Fund* v. *Canadian Pickles Corp.,* [1991] 3 S.C.R. 388. In law, a charter company is created through the exercise of the Crown's royal prerogative. This term refers to powers that historically were vested in the Crown.

9. See Welling, *Cases and Materials, supra* note 3 at 48.

Business corporations in Canada now come into existence through either special acts of incorporation or general acts of incorporation.

Special acts of incorporation are used by the federal and provincial governments to create corporations for specific purposes. Canadian National Railways used to exist by virtue of the *Canadian National Railways Act*,[10] and telephone companies, banks, universities, and Crown corporations have also been created pursuant to special acts. These corporations are created for distinctly identified purposes and, as such, may act only for those purposes. As well, they have only the powers granted under the special act in question. For this reason, Canadian National Railways always had to remain in the railway business and could not diversify.

This method of incorporation is rare and not available to the ordinary business person.

General acts of incorporation are generic in the sense that they are used to create corporations that engage in business of all kinds and descriptions. In contrast to the special act corporation, the *type* of business that the general act corporation conducts is not usually of any concern. All the general act company must do is abide by a global set of rules that the legislation imposes on it and every other corporation created through the general act in question. Not surprisingly, virtually all business corporations are created through general acts of incorporation.

The federal and all provincial governments have passed general acts of incorporation that embody different models or prototypes as to how the corporation comes into existence and what its powers are. The different models presently in use in Canada are letters patent, memorandum of association, and the articles of incorporation.

The Letters Patent Company

The **letters patent** method of incorporation is a direct descendant of the royal charter form and involves an application being made to the Crown's representative (namely, a government bureaucrat), who in turn has the power to issue an incorporating document known as the letters patent.

The letters patent is the constitution of the new company and contains information such as the name of the company, its business purpose, and its ownership or share structure. The rules governing the day-to-day operations of the company—called **bylaws**—are contained in a separate document.

Although at one time this method of incorporation prevailed in the majority of the provinces, today it applies only to business corporations created in Prince Edward Island and Quebec.[11] However, some jurisdictions, including the federal government, retain the letters patent method for incorporating not-for-profit organizations.[12]

The Memorandum of Association Company

This method is patterned after the English general act system. Aspects of the model remain in effect in Nova Scotia[13] and British Columbia.[14] Other jurisdictions, such as Alberta, use the model only for creating not-for-profit corporations.[15]

letters patent
The incorporating document and constitution of a corporation in Quebec and Prince Edward Island.

bylaws
Rules specifying day-to-day operating procedures of a company in letters patent and articles of incorporation jurisdictions.

---

10. R.S.C. 1985, c. C-19, as rep. by S.C. 1995 c. 24, s. 19, deemed effective 24 August 1995. CNR now exists under the *Canadian Business Corporations Act.*

11. See the *Companies Act,* R.S.P.E.I. 1988, c. C-14 and the *Companies Act,* R.S.Q. 1977, c. C-38.

12. See the *Canada Corporations Act,* R.S.C. 1970, c. C-32, as well as Welling's discussion, *supra* note 3 at 49.

13. See the *Companies Act,* R.S.N.S. 1989, c. 81.

14. *Company Act,* R.S.B C. 1996, c. 62.

15. *Companies Act,* R.S.A. 1980, c. C-20, Part 9.

memorandum of association
The incorporating document and constitution of a corporation in Nova Scotia and British Columbia.

articles of association
Rules specifying day-to-day operating procedures of a company in memorandum of association jurisdictions.

articles of incorporation
The incorporating document and constitution of a corporation in Newfoundland, New Brunswick, Ontario, Manitoba, Saskatchewan, Alberta, and the federal jurisdiction.

Incorporation is achieved by registering a **memorandum of association** and **articles of association** with the registrar of the appropriate government office. The memorandum is a brief document that sets out the constitution of the company, including the name of the company, its share capital, and restrictions, if any, on the power of the company.[16] The articles set out the day-to-day operating rules of the corporation and are generally quite extensive. They regulate such internal matters as the constitution of the board of directors, meetings, voting, issuance and transference of shares, and other matters related to the company's internal governance.

The Articles of Incorporation Corporation

The majority of the provinces—Ontario, Alberta, Saskatchewan, Newfoundland, New Brunswick, and Manitoba[17]—as well as the federal government,[18] have some version of an incorporating system patterned after the United States model.

In this system, **articles of incorporation** are filed with the appropriate government body, which issues a certificate of incorporation. The articles of incorporation serve the same function as the memorandum of association and the application for letters patent; they recite the corporation's name, purpose, and capital structure and similarly general matters. The day-to-day operating rules are set out in bylaws, which—though they are not filed with a government office—are nonetheless binding on the shareholders, directors, and officers until amendment or repeal. Bylaws relate primarily to internal stakeholders—directors, officers, and shareholders—and provide for routine matters such as what procedure is to be followed at shareholders' and directors' meetings and how the chair of the meeting will be selected. Bylaws operate at a general level and are directed at internal governance.

Methods of Incorporation Compared

The various models of incorporation have much in common. All methods allow for the creation of an entity that is recognized as a legal person, is owned by shareholders or members who enjoy limited liability for the debts of the entity, and is managed by directors who owe fiduciary duties to the entity.

Historically, the distinctions between entities created by the different methods of incorporation were quite pronounced. Corporations created pursuant to letters patent and articles of incorporation had all the powers of a natural person, whereas the memorandum jurisdiction company had only the powers granted under the act and the objects for which the company was created.[19] This distinction, however, has been virtually abolished by amendments in the memorandum jurisdictions, which provide that a company now has the power and capacity of a natural person.[20]

---

16. Form 1 of the B.C. *Company Act,* which is the form used to create the memorandum itself, requires the incorporators to list the restrictions that the company is under (i.e., the businesses the company is *not* to carry on and the powers that the company is *not* to exercise). Section 10 of the Nova Scotia *Companies Act* provides that the memorandum must state, inter alia, the restrictions, if any, on the objects and powers of the company.

17. See Ontario (*Business Corporations Act,* R.S.O. 1990, c. B.16); Alberta (*Business Corporations Act,* S.A. 1981, c. B-15); Saskatchewan (*Business Corporations Act,* R.S.S. 1978, c. B-10); Newfoundland (*Corporations Act,* R.S.N. 1990, c. C-36); New Brunswick (*Business Corporations Act,* S.N.B. 1981, B-9.1); Manitoba (*Corporations Act,* R.S.M. 1987, C.C.S.M. c. C-225).

18. *Canada Business Corporations Act,* R.S.C. 1985, c. C-44.

19. This meant that any act outside the confines of its powers was *ultra vires*—in other words, a total and complete nullity. This, in turn, meant that any contract entered into in violation of the objects clause could not be enforced against it. This kind of unpalatable result led to the reform of the *ultra vires.* It has been virtually abolished. See Barry Slutsky, "*Ultra Vires*—The British Columbia Solution," (1973) 8 U.B.C. L. Rev. 1.

20. In Nova Scotia, a company incorporated on or after 1 September 1982, will have the status of a natural person: see s. 30 of the NS *Companies Act.* The BCCA s. 21(1) provides that a company has the power and capacity of a natural person of full capacity. The memorandum, however, may set out restrictions on the power of the company.

Incorporating a Business Entity Abroad

At some stages of its development, a business working in the global market may decide that its strategic objectives are best served by a long-term presence in a particular foreign market. There are many ways to achieve this objective—acquire an existing company, establish a branch operation, start a joint venture, or establish a separately organized subsidiary. The establishment of a particular business form in a particular country is, however, very much a matter of the company law of that country. Countries authorize or forbid different forms, based on political ideology and economic and social needs. Historically, some countries were relatively open to foreign presences whereas others, such as those in eastern Europe and Latin America, limited or barred altogether foreign presences. Today, however, there are few restrictions on foreign investment, and borders are increasingly open to international business.

Almost every country whose legal system derives from common law or a civil law system permits some variation of the corporate form. Most permit limited liability for the owners. There are, however, wide variations in terms of what is permitted or required in other areas, such as the issuance of securities, public disclosure, capitalization, registration and government permit requirements, and organizational structure.

Given this range, a prudent business investor planning to organize a firm abroad will investigate in detail the company laws of the country involved.

Critical Analysis: What are the advantages from both a legal and a business perspective of forming a subsidiary in a foreign country?

Source: Carolyn Hotchkiss, *International Law for Business* (New York: McGraw-Hill, 1994) at 271–274.

Today the differences between the methods of incorporation relate mainly to how the internal governance of the entity operates. In short, corporations formed under different methods have different constitutions.

There are considerable variations in details, particularly as they relate to official forms, regulations, and incorporation fees, for example.

Figure 15.2

SUMMARY OF GENERAL ACTS OF INCORPORATION

Jurisdiction	Model	Name of incorporating document	Name of documents containing "in-house" rules
Alberta, Manitoba, New Brunswick, Newfoundland, Saskatchewan, Ontario, and federal jurisdiction	Articles of Incorporation	Articles of Incorporation	Bylaws
British Columbia, Nova Scotia	Memorandum of association	Memorandum of association	Articles of association
Prince Edward Island, Quebec	Letters patent	Letters patent	Bylaws

The Process of Incorporation

incorporator
The person who sets
the incorporation
process in motion.

All jurisdictions follow a similar procedure for the creation of a corporation, though precise requirements do vary. Furthermore, while **incorporators** are often able to handle certain aspects of the incorporation process without legal assistance, legal advice may be required on other matters, such as the capital structure, choosing a corporate name, and the resolution of disputes.

Figure 15.3

ARTICLES OF INCORPORATION FOR FEDERAL INCORPORATION

In all jurisdictions, the creation of a corporation begins with the filing of an application for incorporation. Federally, this application is known as Articles of Incorporation and it requires the following items of information:
* *name of corporation*
* *the place in Canada where the registered office is to be situated*
* *the classes and any maximum number of shares that the corporation is authorized to issue*
* *restrictions, if any, on share transfers*
* *number (or minimum and maximum) of directors*
* *restrictions, if any, on business the corporation may carry on*
* *other provisions, if any*
* *incorporators*

Assuming that Adam wants to incorporate federally, he must send the following[21] to the federal corporate registry in Ottawa:

■ Articles of Incorporation
■ Notice of Registered Office
■ Notice of Directors
■ Newly Upgraded Automated Name Search (NUANS) report
■ the filing fee, payable to the Receiver General of Canada.

Articles of Incorporation

Corporate Name

All jurisdictions require a company to be identified by a name or designated number. The selection and use of corporate names is subject to regulation by trademarks law,[22] torts law,[23] and corporations law.

Regulations passed pursuant to the companies acts specify numerous basic requirements for a name. The name chosen by the incorporators must not be in use by another business. As well, a name may be rejected if, for example, it is obscene, too long, too descriptive, denotes a connection with the Crown, uses another person's family name without permission, or is confusingly similar to the name of another company. The last word in the name must identify the entity as a corporation, for example Limited or Ltd., Incorporated or Inc., or Corporation or Corp. (or the French equivalent). The purpose of the word is to distinguish a corporation from a partnership and a sole proprietorship and to signal to the public the fact of limited liability.

---

21. Discussion of these forms is based on the Canada Business Corporations Act Incorporation Kit and Policy Statements. See Fasken Campbell Godfry, *1999/2000 Consolidation of the Canada Business Corporations Act* (Toronto: Butterworths, 1999) at 363 and following.
22. See Chapter 18.
23. The tort of passing off.

In choosing a name for their corporation, entrepreneurs like Adam are advised to be particularly careful. If the corporate registry inadvertently approves a name that is confusingly similar to the name of another business, Adam can be sued for trademark infringement and the tort of passing off.[24] He will be liable for any damages that the other business has suffered and, perhaps even more problematic, be ordered to change the name of his corporation. This will require Adam to reestablish a corporate identity and reputation in the marketplace, as well as replace letterhead, invoices, business signs, and anything else bearing his former corporate name. This is obviously costly. *Paws Pet Food & Accessories Ltd.* v. *Paws & Shop Inc.* illustrates how such a dispute can arise.

Case

Paws Pet Food & Accessories Ltd. v. *Paws & Shop Inc.* (1992), 6 Alta. L.R. (3d) 22 (Q.B.)

The Business Context: A name is an important and valuable asset to a business. It is what helps distinguish one business from another.

The Factual Background: Paws Pet Food & Accessories Ltd. (Paws Pet Food) was incorporated in 1987 under the Alberta *Business Corporations Act*. Three years later, Paws & Shop Inc. (Paws & Shop) was created under the same piece of legislation. Both corporations operated in Calgary, and both were in the business of retailing pet food and accessories. Paws Pet Food took the position that the registrar should not have allowed the second company to incorporate under a name that was so confusingly similar to its own. It went to court for an order directing the second company to change its name.

The Legal Questions: Is Paws & Shop Inc.—the second company—confusingly similar to Paws Pet Food & Accessories?

Resolution: The court decided that the registrar had made an error in permitting the second corporation to incorporate under the name of Paws & Shop. There was evidence that customers of Paws Pet Food mistakenly believed that it was associated or affiliated with Paws & Shop. The registration of Paws & Shop was therefore contrary to the Alberta *Business Corporations Act* and related regulations because it was leading to public confusion. On this basis, Paws & Shop was forced to change its name.

Critical Analysis: This case illustrates that there is no inherent protection in the fact that the registrar has approved a corporate name for use. A judge can overrule the registrar and, furthermore, since the tort of passing off can be committed unintentionally, a company with a name that is confusingly similar to that of another company can end up paying damages even though the registrar had approved the name to begin with. Is this fair? Who should bear the risk of a mistake being made—the business itself or the taxpayers?

NUANS report
A document that shows the result of a search for business names.

Assuming that Adam wants to incorporate federally, he will have to send his proposed name—IK Enterprises Ltd.—to the federal corporate registry for approval. He will also have to submit to that same office a Newly Upgraded Automated Name Search or **NUANS report**. This is a document that lists those business names and trademarks—if any—that are similar to the name being proposed. A NUANS report is prepared using a database containing existing and reserved business names, as well as trademarks.[25] If some other business is using the name IK Enterprises Ltd. or a name similar to it—such as IK Investments Inc.—then the NUANS report would

---

24. This is because Adam would be representing to the public—either intentionally or not—that there is a relationship between his and the other business when no such relationship exists.

25. *Supra* note 18, see Policy Statement 1.1A, para. 1.4.

presumably contain such information. Adam should avoid the name and come up with an alternative name for his fledgling business.

It is common for companies legislation to permit incorporators to request that the corporation be assigned a numbered name. Under the federal legislation, for example, the corporation is issued a designating number, followed by the word *Canada* and then a legal element—such as *Limited* or *Incorporated*. A numbered company is useful when a corporation must be created quickly, when the incorporators are having difficulty coming up with a suitable name, or when there is a wish to create a **shelf company**. Shelf companies are often incorporated by law firms for the future use of their clients. The company does not engage in any active business. It simply sits "on the shelf" until a firm's client needs it.

shelf company
A company that does not engage in active business.

Place of Registered Office

Every company must have a registered office in the jurisdiction in which it is incorporated. It is usually best to simply identify the municipality in which the corporation will be located. This way, if the corporation moves its registered office to another street address in the same municipality, it will not be necessary to amend the articles and pay another filing fee.

Share Structure

The application for incorporation must define the corporation's **share structure**,[26] which can be very simple or very complex, depending on the wishes of the incorporators. Incorporators must specify capital structure, including the class or classes of shares authorized for issuance or sale. Specifics as to share structure are difficult to change once incorporation is granted, so most applicants build in considerable flexibility.

share structure
The shares that a corporation is permitted to issue by its constitution.

Figure 15.4

SAMPLE SHARE STRUCTURE

The corporation is authorized to issue Class A and Class B shares with the following rights, privileges, restrictions, and conditions:

Class A shares with the right to
- *vote at all meetings of shareholders*
- *receive property of the corporation upon its dissolution*
- *receive dividends as declared by the directors*

Class B shares with the right to
- *receive a dividend as fixed by the board of directors*
- *receive repayment of the amount paid for shares upon dissolution of the corporation*

The type of share structure shown in Figure 15.4 allows varying degrees of shareholder participation and involvement. For example, if Adam's father simply wants to be a passive investor in Adam's business while requiring some qualified assurance of the return of his share capital when and if IK Enterprises Ltd. winds down, the incorporators may want to follow the share structure along the lines set out above. Adam, as the "hands-on" shareholder, would hold Class A shares, which carry the right to vote for the directors. His father, who wants to remain more in the background, would hold Class B shares, which do not carry voting rights.

---

26. The characteristics of shares are discussed in greater detail in Chapter 16.

Restrictions on Share Transfers

An application for incorporation may or may not contain restrictions on the transfer of shares. If the corporation intends to offer its shares to the public—which is Adam's plan—then restrictions on the transfer of the shares are forbidden. On the other hand, if the shares are not intended for public sale, then restrictions may be placed on their transfer in order to control who can become a shareholder in the company in the future. The actual restrictions may take a variety of forms, as shown in this example:

> No shares of the capital of the Corporation shall be transferred without either
>
> (a) the sanction of a majority of the directors of the corporation or alternatively
>
> (b) the sanction of the majority of the shareholders of the corporation.[27]

Other provisions might include "a right of first refusal" for directors or shareholders. When a right of first refusal is in place, it means that the shareholder wishing to sell must first offer her shares to the directors (or shareholders, as the case may be) at the same price she has negotiated with the outsider. This gives the insiders one last chance to acquire the shares for themselves instead of having to welcome a new investor to the company.

Number of Directors

Canadian statutes normally require only one director, leaving the corporate constitution to specify more or to set maximum and minimum numbers. At least three directors are usually required for corporations offering securities to the public.[28] As well, legislation puts into place some basic qualifications for directors. Under the *Canadian Business Corporations Act*, for example, certain people are disqualified from being a director. These are

- anyone who is less than 18 years of age
- anyone who is of unsound mind and has been so found by a court in Canada or elsewhere
- a person who is not an individual (i.e., a corporation is not allowed to be a director; only human beings can)
- a person who is bankrupt

The duties and liabilities of the corporate director are discussed in Chapter 16.

Restrictions on Business

The incorporation application may contain restrictions on the nature of the business. The usual practice, however, is for there to be no restrictions. In such a case, Adam simply has to state "None" at this point on the form.

Other provisions

Incorporators are permitted to further customize their corporation for a variety of reasons. For example, incorporators may include provisions that require directors to own at least one share in the corporation or provisions proscribing how shareholders will fill a vacancy in the board of directors.

---

27. *Supra* note 21 at 369.
28. *Supra* note 3 at 195.

Incorporators

The names of the incorporators must be provided in the appropriate place on the Articles of Incorporation. Two copies of the Articles of Incorporation are required, and each must contain the original signatures of the incorporators.

Notice of Registered Office

The Notice of Registered Office form is very brief because it has only one purpose: to provide a public record of the corporation's official address. This is the address that those having dealings with the company can use to communicate with the corporation, particularly with respect to formal matters, including lawsuits.

Notice of Directors

The Notice of Directors form contains the names and residential addresses of the directors and must correspond with the number of directors given in the Articles of Incorporation.

The completed forms, along with the requisite fee, are then submitted to the appropriate government office—the Corporations Directorate of Industry Canada. If the forms are in order, then the directorate will issue a "birth certificate" for the corporation, known as the "certificate of incorporation."

Organizing the Corporation

Following incorporation, the first directors will ordinarily undertake a number of tasks. Under federal legislation, for example, the directors are required to call an organizational meeting to

- make bylaws[30]
- adopt forms of share certificates and corporate records

Electronic Registration

In Alberta, the registration of documents necessary to create a corporation is now done electronically.[29] Persons authorized by the government—often, employees of law firms—prepare the necessary documents for electronic transmission to the corporate registry, after having ensured that the documents comply with the requirements of the Alberta *Business Corporations Act*. The corporate registry then issues the appropriate certificate electronically. The certificate can then be printed by the person making the application right at his or her office. This means that instead of having to wait days for the paperwork to be processed manually by employees of the corporate registry, people wishing to incorporate can receive their certificate of incorporation almost instantaneously.

Critical Analysis: What are the advantages, other than speed, of electronic filing?

---

29. Other provinces, such as Ontario, are following Alberta's lead in this area.

30. Recall that, in the memorandum of association jurisdictions, the articles of association—the equivalent of bylaws—are included in the application for incorporation, so this would not be an item for the first directors to attend to in British Columbia and Nova Scotia, for example.

- authorize the issue of shares and other securities
- appoint officers
- appoint an auditor to hold office until the first annual meeting of shareholders
- make banking arrangements
- transact any other business[31]

Federal legislation also specifies that the directors named in the Articles of Incorporation hold office until the first meeting of the shareholders. That meeting must be called within 18 months of incorporation.[32] At that first meeting, shareholders elect the permanent directors, who hold office for the specified term.[33] The directors carry on the management of the corporation until the next annual meeting, at which time they report to the shareholders on the corporation's performance.

Provincial incorporations legislation has its own requirements, which parallel but are not necessarily identical to the requirements and procedures under the Canada *Business Corporations Act.*

Capitalizing the Corporation

Adam needs to capitalize his company to have the funds to operate. He has two basic means of doing so: IK Enterprises Ltd. can issue shares or it can borrow money.

Shares

A share represents an ownership interest in the issuing corporation. It is, however, a unique kind of ownership interest. It does not give to the owner or holder any right to use the assets of the corporation or any right to directly control or manage the corporation. It may, however, depending on whether the share has voting rights, give the owner the right to elect those who are responsible for managing the corporation. A share gives to the holder the right to participate in the earnings of the corporation in the form of dividends if and when they are declared by the directors. The shareholders also have the right to share in the proceeds on dissolution of the corporation, after the creditors have been paid. The potentially diverse rights attaching to shares are discussed in more detail in Chapter 16.

Shares are most frequently used to raise money for the use of the corporation. This is done by issuing shares to investors in exchange for a purchase price. *How* shares are issued depends on whether the shares are going to members of the public. If the shares are being issued to the public, then **securities legislation** governs, and the company must follow a complicated and potentially costly procedure. Securities legislation, which seeks to ensure that the potential purchasers know what they are getting into before they make any decision, is discussed in more detail below.

A company that offers shares for sale to the public is known as a **widely held corporation** or public corporation, depending on the jurisdiction. In contrast, a **closely held corporation**, or private corporation, does not sell shares to the public; rather, it issues them to selected persons in a manner consistent with securities legislation. A closely held corporation must limit the number of shareholders and restrict the right to transfer its shares. The vast majority of corporations in Canada fall within this category, including some very large enterprises, such as McCain's and Irving in New Brunswick, N.M. Paterson and Son Ltd. in Manitoba, and Holt Renfrew in Ontario.

securities legislation
Laws designed to regulate transactions involving shares and bonds of a corporation.

widely held corporation
A corporation whose shares are normally traded on a stock exchange.

closely held corporation
A corporation that does not sell its shares to the public.

---

31. *Supra* note 18 at s. 104.
32. *Supra* note 18 at s. 133(a).
33. *Supra* note 18 at s. 106(3). This section limits the term.

Debt

bond
A document evidencing a debt owed by the corporation, often used to refer to a secured debt.

debenture
A document evidencing a debt owed by the corporation, often used to refer to an unsecured debt.

securities
Shares and bonds issued by a corporation.

conversion right
The right to convert one type of security into another type.

A corporation may also raise money by borrowing. The company may obtain a loan from a lending institution or issue **bonds** or **debentures**. The terms *bond* and *debenture* are often used interchangeably and refer to a corporate IOU, which is either secured or unsecured. Note that the word *bond* is sometimes used to describe a *secured* debt and *debenture* to refer to an *unsecured* debt,[34] but the only way to know what is actually involved is to read the debt instrument itself.

A bond or debenture does not represent any ownership interest in the corporation, and the holder does not have any right to participate in the management of the corporation.[35] However, these debts are often secured by a charge on the assets of the corporation; this means that if the debt is not repaid, the assets can be sold to repay the debt and the bondholder has a better chance of recovering his investment. Bonds and debentures—like shares—may have any number of features and are freely transferable, creating a secondary market for their purchase and sale.

The advantage of raising cash by issuing bonds is that Adam does not have to relinquish formal control. That is, he can raise money to run his operation without having to give management rights to his lenders. On the other hand, there is a requirement that the interest on the bonds be paid regardless of whether a profit is earned. In fact, if the interest is not paid on the debt, then the corporation faces bankruptcy unless it can reach a new agreement with the bondholders.

Shares and bonds represent two very different ways of raising money for corporate activities. There are, however, many combinations of these two types of **securities**. Much depends on the features that investors are interested in purchasing. Most businesses, particularly large ones, use some combination of these various methods of raising funds, maintaining a reasonable balance between them. Furthermore, shares and bonds can come with **conversion rights**. A convertible bondholder, for example, is entitled to convert his debt interest into shares and thereby assume an equity position in the company instead of being a creditor.

Figure 15.5
SECURITIES COMPARED

	Shareholder	Bondholder
Status of holder	Investor/owner	Investor/creditor
Participation in management	Elects directors; approves major activities	Does not participate (except in special circumstances)
Rights to income	Dividends, if declared	Interest payments
Security for the holder on insolvency of corporation	Entitled to share in proceeds after all creditors paid	Entitled to payment from proceeds before general creditors, if secured, and before shareholders

Securities Legislation

All provinces have enacted securities acts. In very general terms, the aim of all securities legislation is to

■ provide the mechanism for the transfer of securities

---

34. *Supra* note 6 at 462.
35. It is possible, however, for bondholders to obtain management rights if the company defaults on the loan. This depends on the terms of issuance.

- ensure that all investors have the ability to access adequate information in order to make informed decisions
- ensure that the system is such that the public has confidence in the marketplace
- regulate those engaged in the trading of securities
- remove or punish those participants not complying with established rules

With these objectives at the forefront, all securities regimes have three basic requirements: registration, disclosure, and insider trading restrictions.

Registration

Any company intending to sell securities to the public in a given province must be registered to do so with the relevant provincial securities commission. Furthermore, all persons engaged in advising on and selling securities to the public must be registered with the relevant securities commission. The definitions of those covered by the various statutes vary between provinces but generally extend to advisers, underwriters, dealers, salespeople, brokers, and securities issuers.

Disclosure

prospectus
The document a corporation must publish when offering securities to the public.

The company must comply with disclosure or **prospectus** provisions set forth in the securities legislation. With limited exceptions, this means that any sale or distribution of a security—in this case, meaning either debt (bonds) or equity (shares)—must be preceded by a prospectus that is accepted and approved by the appropriate securities commission. A prospectus is the statement by the issuing company of prescribed information. The list of information required to be in the prospectus is lengthy and ranges from financial information to biographical information about the directors. The overriding requirement is for "full, true, and plain" disclosure of all material facts, that is, facts that are likely to affect the price of the securities. The legislation assumes that prospective investors will rely on the prospectus in making investment decisions.

The issuer of securities has an obligation to continue to keep the public informed of its activities. In general terms, this means that it must notify the public of any material change in its affairs, first by issuing a press release and second by filing a report with the securities commission within ten days of the change. A material change is defined as one that is likely to have a significant effect on the market value of the securities and is not known to the public in general.

Insider Trading Restrictions

insider
A person who has a special relationship with a corporation.

The objective of these provisions is to ensure that trading in securities takes place only on the basis of information available to the public at large. Legislation achieves this aim in two primary ways: first, it requires **insiders** to report any trading that they have engaged in, and second, it prohibits trading by certain insiders—such as directors, senior officers, employees, and the corporation itself—on the basis of information not publicly available.

tippee
A person who acquires confidential information from an insider.

The reason insiders must report trades is simple: if someone in this capacity is either buying or selling large blocks of securities, this is critical information for the investing public. Even small trades can be relevant. Insiders are prohibited not only from trading on material information not publically disclosed but also from passing on this information to a third party or **tippee**. This person is similarly prohibited from trading on such information.

insider trading
Transactions in shares
based on confidential
information of a
material nature.

Those who engage in **insider trading** are subject to both criminal and civil liability under securities legislation and under corporations legislation.[36]

In considering whether to offer shares to the public through a stock exchange, Adam has a number of factors to consider. Although a means of obtaining funds from a wide group of investors, selling shares entails diminished control and public disclosure of information that would otherwise not be known to competitors, and certainly requires costly compliance with regulations.[37]

Business Law in Practice Revisited

1. Has Adam considered all of the issues in forming a corporation?

Adam has received favourable reviews on the product he has developed. This kind of endorsement by industry is probably a much more important consideration in the viability of his business than the actual business vehicle chosen to carry on the business. The choice of the corporate form requires the consideration of a number of issues, including the cost of incorporation and where the corporation will conduct its business. Adam wishes to start small but foresees rapid expansion nationally and internationally; thus a federal incorporation would probably be the logical choice.

Adam also needs to consider such factors as whether the name he has chosen is already in use, what sort of capital structure he will employ, and how the corporation will be capitalized. In particular, Adam needs to recognize that his proposed share structure—half the shares to himself and half to Diane—may result in shareholder deadlock.

2. Does Adam appear to understand the concept of limited liability adequately?

Adam appears to be under a misconception concerning the nature of limited liability. He suggests that Cameron lend the money to the company as this will protect him from unlimited liability. Cameron would be protected from unlimited liability both as a creditor and as a shareholder. A shareholder is not, except in rare situations, responsible for the debts of the corporation beyond the original investment. Thus, whether Cameron invests in debt or shares has little effect on the liability issue.

3. What other options are available in addition to Cameron lending money to the corporation?

Cameron could invest as a shareholder, but a loan would give him priority over shareholders in the event of dissolution; a loan provides little opportunity to participate in profits unless the interest rate is tied to the profitability of the corporation. Shares offer profit opportunities but have greater risks of loss of investment should the company fail. Cameron's investment—whether in shares or debt—can be tailored to address Cameron's desire to participate in profits while avoiding risk.

4. What factors should Adam consider in seeking to raise capital by selling shares?

In attempting to raise money by issuing shares, Adam needs to consider a number of factors. Most importantly, both public and private sales involve a consideration from a financial perspective as to whether there is a market for the corporation's shares. As well, any issuance or sale of shares involves an assessment of the impact on the con-

---

36. See CBCA s. 131(4).
37. Edmund M.A. Kwaw, *The Law of Corporate Finance in Canada* (Toronto: Butterworths, 1997) at 121-122.

trol of the corporation. Sales on the public market also involve requirements as specified by the relevant securities legislation. These requirements can be significant and costly.

Chapter Summary

The corporate form is prevalent and widespread. The characteristic that distinguishes it from the other basic forms for carrying on business is its separate legal status. This means that the owners are not liable for the debts and obligations of the corporation. It also means that those who are dealing with a corporation need to understand that the owner's risk is limited. Thus, if security is important, they should demand a personal guarantee.

Jurisdiction over the incorporation of companies is divided between the federal and provincial governments. Hence, it is not surprising that different methods—letters patent, memorandum of association, and articles of incorporation—for the incorporation of companies have evolved. From a business perspective, however, the distinction between the various methods has little practical significance.

The actual process of establishing a corporation is relatively simple. A corporation may be incorporated federally or provincially, but essentially the same format is followed in all jurisdictions. It is a matter of filling in and filing the correct forms with the appropriate government body. That said, the incorporation process is not without risks, such as the risk of choosing a name that is similar to that of another business. This risk can be substantially reduced by obtaining legal advice.

Much more complex are decisions as to how the corporation will be capitalized. There are two basic choices: shares and debt. Shares represent ownership interests in the corporation and are often strictly controlled through securities legislation. Debt represents an obligation of the corporation.

Study Chapter

Questions for Review

1. What does the term *limited liability* mean?
2. What is the relationship between a shareholder and a director of a corporation?

3. What is the difference between a corporation incorporated under federal law and a corporation created under provincial laws?

4. What kinds of corporations are created pursuant to special acts?

5. What are the differences between the letters patent, memorandum of association, and articles of incorporation methods of incorporation?

6. Are the distinctions between the different methods of incorporation relevant today? Explain.

7. How would you describe the capacity of a corporation?

8. Describe the process for incorporating a company.

9. Compare shares to bonds. Which is the more advantageous method of raising money?

10. What is meant by the term *insider trading*?

Questions for Discussion

1. *Salomon* v. *Salomon* stands for the proposition that the corporation has a separate existence from its shareholders. This means that creditors of a corporation do not have recourse against the shareholders' assets. Is this fair? Is it fair that creditors of a sole proprietorship can go after the sole proprietor's personal assets? What is the justification for the difference in treatment?

2. Is the name S. O'Byrne's Fashions Inc. confusing with O'Byrne's Warehousing Ltd.? What is the problem with confusing business names? What if O'Byrne's Fashions Inc. was a manufacturer of women's clothing with a factory outlet and O'Byrne's Warehousing Ltd. was a bulk sales outlet specializing in women's clothing?

3. The primary function of an organization's constitution is to prescribe how the internal government of the organization is to operate. Describe the constitution of a corporation. How does the government of a corporation operate? What do you think are its guiding principles?

4. A stakeholder is defined as someone who has an interest in the corporation. The general public and government are considered to be external stakeholders. What is the general public's interest in a corporation? What is the government's interest in a corporation?

5. In 1995, Bre-X Minerals burst from the ranks of Canada's junior mining companies to become the toast of markets across North America. It was considered a "can't miss" by gold analysts at many of the top brokerage firms on the strength of reports that it had discovered the biggest gold find the world had ever seen. One short year later, the fiction went up in flames when a development partner did some independent drilling and found insignificant amounts of gold. Billions of dollars in stock market value evaporated; shares that traded at about $286 fell to pennies and were delisted, leaving many people with huge losses.

   What should be the role of securities legislation in preventing frauds such as this? Should anyone be held accountable for the investors' losses?

Situations for Discussion

1. Jemson and Smithson have established a corporation for the manufacture and distribution of laser instruments used in the health care industry. They need to raise about $500 000 in working capital to finance the acquisition of inventory. How could this be done? What would be the advantages and disadvantages of the different alternatives?

2. Steering Clear Ltd. is a manufacturer of an expensive automatic helmsman that is used to navigate ocean cruisers. Mr. Jones ordered such a helmsman on behalf of a company called Cruisin' Ltd. The helmsman was supplied, but Cruisin' Ltd. did not pay its account. Because of this delinquency, Steering Clear Ltd. decided to investigate the background of Cruisin' Ltd. and discovered that it has a grand total of two issued shares—one held by Mr. Jones and the other by his wife. Mr. Jones has advised Steering Clear Ltd. that the debtor company has only $5 in the bank and may have to go out of business soon. Steering Clear Ltd. wants to sue Mr. Jones personally for the debt.[38] Will Steering Clear Ltd. be successful? On what basis? What is the largest obstacle facing Steering Clear Ltd.'s potential action against Mr. Jones? What should Steering Clear Ltd. have done differently from a business perspective?

3. Robert Merchant has been in the commercial real estate business for over 15 years. He wants to start his own real estate business under the name Merchant Commercial Real Estate Services Inc. He is well known in the industry and believes that by using his surname as the distinctive element in his corporate name, he will best be able to capitalize on the goodwill he has built up over the years. He expects, however, that a local competitor, Mr. Larry Wasyliw, would object since Mr. Wasyliw operates under the name and style of Merchant Realty Ltd. and has been doing for a number of years.[39] Is it permissible for Mr. Merchant to incorporate under the name Merchant Commercial Real Estate? What are the objections to the name? What is the test that the court would apply in determining the permissibility of the proposed name?

4. Homer, Raddison, and Bloke are friends who wish to incorporate an enterprise to carry on a small-business consulting, bookkeeping, and accounting business. Each wants to receive profits from the venture in proportion to the amount of effort expended on the business. Homer will spend all of his time; Raddison will spend one-half of his time; and Bloke will spend one-third of his time. What are the potential problems with the proposed venture? What share structure would you recommend to accommodate their profit-sharing goals?

---

38. Based on *Henry Browne & Sons Ltd.* v. *Smith*, [1964] 2 Lloyd's Rep. 477 (Q.B.).
39. Based on *Merchant Commercial Real Estate Services Inc.* v. *Alberta (Registrar of Corporations)* (1997), 199 A.R. 72 (Q.B.).

The Corporate Form: Operational Matters

Objectives

AFTER STUDYING THIS CHAPTER, YOU SHOULD HAVE AN
UNDERSTANDING OF

- ► THE LIABILITIES OF A CORPORATION
- ► THE DUTIES AND LIABILITIES OF CORPORATE DIRECTORS AND OFFICERS
- ► THE RIGHTS AND LIABILITIES OF SHAREHOLDERS AND CREDITORS
- ► HOW THE CORPORATION IS TERMINATED

Business Law in Practice

IK Enterprises Ltd., incorporated by Adam, has been in operation for a little over a
year. Adam owns 50 percent of the common shares and Diane the remaining 50 percent. Adam's father, Cameron, was issued a number of preferred shares. Both Adam
and Diane are directors of the corporation and Cameron is an officer.

The company has had fairly favourable results with marketing and selling its
enhanced voice-recognition system for computers. There is, however, a major
problem confronting the company.

Diane has come across a product that translates computer output into several languages and that she thinks would be quite compatible with the company's present product. She is interested in buying the rights to the translation product for IK Enterprises. Adam, however, is not interested in expansion and wants to continue to operate with a limited product line. Diane is contemplating forming another company to take advantage of this opportunity if the disagreement between her and Adam cannot be resolved. Cameron does not want to get involved in the dispute and is quite annoyed with both Adam and Diane.

1. What obligations do Cameron, Diane, and Adam have as corporate officers and directors?
2. How can the disagreement between Adam and Diane be resolved?
3. Are there any problems with Diane forming her own company to take advantage of the translation product opportunity?
4. What are Cameron's rights as a shareholder if he does not like how Diane and Adam are managing the company?

Corporate Liability

A corporation is a legal person in the eyes of the law. The corollary is that the corporation is responsible for its own actions. To illustrate the impact of corporate responsibility in the business world, a discussion of the corporation's liability for torts and contracts and for criminal and regulatory offences follows.

Liability in Tort

A corporation can experience two distinct kinds of liability in tort: primary liability and vicarious liability.

A corporation has primary liability for a tort when, in law, it is regarded as the entity that actually committed the tort in question. The idea of a corporation having primary liability is inherently problematic since a corporation can only work through human agents. How can a corporation commit a tort when it does not have a mind of its own and does not have a physical existence?

identification theory
A theory specifying that a corporation is liable when the person committing the wrong is the corporation's directing mind.

The courts have overcome this hurdle by developing what is known as the **identification theory** of corporate liability.[1] A corporation has liability—and could therefore be described as directly "at fault"—when the person committing the wrong was the corporation's "directing mind and will."

The theory seeks to determine which person or persons are the directing mind of the corporation. When that person (or persons) commits a tort related to the business enterprise, this conduct is *identified* with or attributed to the corporation itself. The liability of the corporation is thereby made *direct*—not vicarious—because in law, the conduct of the directing mind *is* the conduct of the corporation.

Generally, highly placed corporate officers are seen to be "directing" minds while low-level employees are not. Whether a mid-range employee would be a directing mind is a more complicated and fact-specific inquiry.

A corporation has vicarious liability[2] when the tort has been committed by an agent or employee who is not otherwise a directing mind. The law of vicarious lia-

---

1. *Lennard's Carrying Co.* v. *Asiatic Petroleum Co.*, [1915] A.C. 705.
2. Vicarious liability is discussed in chapters 10 and 21.

bility does not distinguish between the *natural* employer/principal—that is, a living, breathing human being—and the *artificial* employer/principal—that is, a corporation. Instead, the same principle applies to both.

Liability in Contract

While there is no reason why the identification theory could not be used as a way of assessing a corporation's liability in contract, the courts generally have not followed this approach. Instead, agency law largely determines when a corporation is liable on a contract and when it is not.

A corporation is bound by the actions of the agent only if the agent is acting within his actual or apparent authority. Historically, an agent's apparent authority could be limited by filing with the incorporation documents a specific limitation of the agent's authority. As these documents were publicly filed, outsiders were deemed to have notice of them and to have read their contents. This was known as the **doctrine of constructive notice** and produced commercial inconvenience, since the only way that an outsider could fully protect himself would be to go down to the registry office and take a look at what the company had filed there. The doctrine has been abolished,[3] meaning that outsiders can now generally rely on the apparent authority of agents. In such a case, the corporation would be liable on the contract.

To avoid personal liability, the person signing a document on behalf of a corporation should ensure that the document contains a clause clearly indicating that the person is signing on behalf of the corporation and is not signing in her personal capacity. This precaution is equally important in the case of pre-incorporation contracts.

Pre-incorporation contracts are contracts that have been entered into by the company's promoters[4] on behalf of the corporation *before it has even been created*. Such contracts are governed by federal and provincial corporate law statutes, which permit the company to adopt the contract—something that was impossible to do at common law.[5] When adoption occurs, the corporation assumes liability on the contract. The promoter can avoid liability so long as the pre-incorporation contract *expressly* indicates that the promoter was acting on behalf of the corporation.[6] Pre-incorporation contracts can be problematic if they do not indicate clearly who is intended to be liable[7] and if the corporation fails to come into existence.

People would probably do well to avoid pre-incorporation contracts altogether. Although such contracts are sometimes necessary in order to take advantage of a valuable business opportunity that just cannot wait, it is usually possible to find a corporate vehicle quickly—such as through the purchase of a shelf company. In this way the corporation is immediately in place and can enter the contemplated contract directly.

doctrine of constructive notice Deemed notice of publicly filed documents.

---

3. See, for example, *Canada Business Corporations Act*, R.S.C. 1985, c. C-44, s. 17.

4. A promoter is someone who participates in setting up a corporation.

5. There is some debate in the case law as to whether the standard pre-incorporation provisions in corporations legislation are effective in bringing about the desired changes to the common law. This topic is beyond the scope of this text. See, for example, *Westcom Radio Group Ltd.* v. *MacIsaac* (1989), 70 O.R. (2d) 591 (Div. Ct.) and *Sherwood Design Services Inc.* v. *872935 Ontario Ltd.* (1998), 39 O.R. (3d) 576 (C.A.).

6. Supra note 3; see, for example, s. 14(4):

   Exemption from personal liability—If expressly so provided in the written contract, a person who purported to act in the name of or on behalf of the corporation before it came into existence is not ... bound by the contract.

7. The legislative provisions protecting the promoter from personal liability have been strictly construed by the courts. For example, in *Landmark Inns of Canada Ltd.* v. *Horeak* (1982), 18 Sask.R. 30 (Q.B.), the court held that merely naming the yet-to-be incorporated corporation as a party to the contract was insufficient to relieve the promoter of personal liability. The *contract* must also contain an express provision that specifically relieves him of liability.

Criminal and Regulatory Liability

Criminal Liability

The criminal liability of a corporation poses the same conceptual problems as tort liability. As Baron Thurlow, L.C., observed in the 18th century, "Did you ever expect a corporation to have a conscience, when it has no soul to be damned and no body to be kicked?"

The judiciary solved this problem by adapting the identification theory to the criminal law scenario. The theory maintains that a corporation has committed a crime if one of its senior representatives did so in the course of her duties and did so mostly for the benefit of the corporation. The following case illustrates how this principle has been applied in Canada.

Case

Rhône (The) v. *Peter A.B. Widener* (1993), 1 S.C.R. 497

The Business Context:
In the course of carrying on business activity, it is possible to commit a crime such as fraud, bribery, conspiracy, and criminal negligence causing bodily harm. Corporations have been convicted of major criminal offences on the basis of the identification theory.

Factual Background: The defendant vessel was involved in a shipping accident that was attributable to the fault of its captain. The vessel was under the command of Captain Kelch, who worked for the corporation that owned the vessel. The corporation sought to limit its liability under the Canada *Shipping Act,* which provided for a limitation of liability if the damage was caused *without the actual fault* of the owner of the ship. Though the *Shipping Act* is not considered to be criminal law legislation in the way that the *Criminal Code of Canada* fits that description, it requires proof of "fault," a criminal law concept.

The corporation sought protection of the *Shipping Act* provision in question by claiming that although the captain was at fault, the corporation was not. According to the corporation, the captain was not the directing mind of the corporation; therefore his acts were not the corporation's acts.

The Legal Question: Was Captain Kelch the directing mind of the corporation?

Resolution: The court stated that to hold the corporation liable for the accident, the acts of the individual at fault must be attributable to the corporation. In order for the corporation to be responsible, the employee who committed the offence must be the "ego," the "centre" of the corporate personality, the "vital organ" of the body corporate, or its "directing mind." There may be more than one directing mind of the corporation. However, to be considered a directing mind, "the employee must have the express or implied delegation of executive authority to design and supervise the implementation of corporate policy rather than simply to carry out such policy." In other words, he must have "decision-making power in the relevant sphere of activity." Applying this principle to the facts at hand, the court did not attribute Captain Kelch's actions to the corporation. Although he had certain decision-making responsibilities on navigational matters, governing authority over the management and operation of the tug lay elsewhere. "The key factor which distinguishes directing minds from normal employees is the capacity to exercise decision-making authority on matters of corporate policy, rather than merely give effect to such policy on an operational basis, whether at head office or across the sea."

Critical Analysis: On the basis of this decision, what is required to convict a corporation of a criminal offence? What are the justifications for the criminal prosecution of corporations?

Regulatory Offences

In addition to criminal liability under the *Criminal Code of Canada,* a corporation faces liability pursuant to a wide range of statutory enactments related to human rights, pay equity, employment standards, consumer protection, unfair or anticompetitive business practices, occupational health and safety, and environmental protection, to name a few. The relevant legislation often imposes penalties on the corporation, and sometimes even its directors, including civil liability for damages.

The offences alluded to above are known as **regulatory offences**. They have a criminal aspect because they involve forbidding some kind of conduct that is contrary to the public interest, such as polluting streams, and providing a punishment for those who discbey.

Owing to the large number of regulatory offences affecting business, as well as the expense and public relations problems associated with their commission, corporations have become increasingly concerned with assessing and managing their exposure. Although it is difficult to gauge the extent to which corporate liability in this area has increased, there have been dramatic examples of corporations being subjected to regulatory penalties. Consider, for example, the following:

regulatory offence
An offence contrary to the public interest.

The November 1979 Mississauga train derailment and accompanying spill of toxic chemicals sparked a large number of claims, most of which were settled out of court. The total exposure for Canadian Pacific was about $14 million, $5 million of which was covered by insurance.[12]

- Mining giant Inco was fined $750 000 pursuant to Ontario's *Occupational Health and Safety Act* as a result of a mining death.[8]
- Union Carbide Canada Ltd. was fined $1.7 million after pleading guilty to conspiring to fix prices of compressed gases; Canadian Oxygen Ltd., which had a smaller share of the $200 million bulk gas market, received a fine of $700 000.[9]
- A company was ordered to pay damages for infringement of vinyl floor covering patent in the amount of $4 822 000.[10]
- Imperial Oil was fined $4000 on each of 27 different counts arising from a single gasoline spill from a bulk plant into the sewers of the City of Timmins.[11]

IK Enterprises operations may be affected by a host of legislative provisions. Since the corporation is not manufacturing the voice-recognition system itself but has the manufacturing outsourced, statutes concerning waste disposal and related environmental regulation are not likely to have much impact on the corporation. By way of contrast, legislation concerning employment, pensions, workers' compensation, consumer protection, intellectual property, and health and safety, to name a few examples, are likely to affect the corporation.

8. Bill Rogers, "Court Lowers Boom on Inco, Slams Company with Record $750 000 Fine" *The Lawyers Weekly* (1 May 1998) 1.

9. *Calgary Herald* (7 September 1991) F5.

10. *Domco Industries Ltd.* v. *Armstrong Cork Canada Ltd.* (1986), 10 C.P.R. (3d) 53 (F.C.T.D.).

11. Dianne Saxe, "Fines Go Up Dramatically in Environmental Cases" (1989) 3 Can. Env. L.R. (N.S.) 104 at 110.

12. E. David D. Tavender, Catherine M. Poyer, & Donna M. Hallet, "Developments in Corporate Liability: Is the Sky the Limit?" (1993) 22 Can. Bus. L.J. 258.

The directors, who are elected by shareholders, manage or supervise the management of the business and the affairs of the corporation.[13] In addition to this general authority, directors have specific powers and obligations set out in legislation. For example, directors can declare dividends, call shareholder meetings, adopt bylaws, and issue shares. Directors are, however, not usually in a position to carry out the actual management themselves; generally they are authorized to appoint officers to carry out many of their duties and exercise most of their powers.[14] This power of delegation does not, however, relieve the directors of ultimate responsibility for the management of the corporation.

Duties of Directors and Officers

In exercising their management function, directors and officers have obligations contained in two broad categories: a duty of competence and a fiduciary duty.[15]

The Duty of Competence

This duty requires directors and officers to exercise the care, diligence, and skill that a reasonably prudent person would exercise in comparable circumstances. Put more informally, directors and officers must meet a general standard of competence.

At one time, directors had very minimal obligations to act with care in exercising their responsibilities. In *Re City Equitable Fire Insurance Co.*,[16] for example, the court held that "a director need not exhibit in the performance of his duties a greater degree of skill than may reasonably be expected from a person of his knowledge and experience." This meant if the director were ill-informed and foolish, then little could be expected of her; she was only required to display the competence of an ill-informed and foolish person. The unfortunate outcome at common law was that the less qualified a director was for office, and the less time and attention she devoted to her duties, and the greater the reliance she placed on others, the lower was the standard that she was required to meet in managing the business and affairs of the company.

Recognizing that the common law standard of care was unduly low, legislatures began to codify and upgrade what was expected of directors. The present standard contained in corporations legislation requires directors and officers to display the care, diligence, and skill that a reasonably prudent person would exercise in comparable circumstances. There has been little judicial pronouncement on the interpretation of this section, so it is difficult to discern the full extent to which directors' duties have been upgraded. However, by importing the standard of prudence and diligence, the legislation presumably is requiring a higher degree of effort than in days gone by.

The Fiduciary Duty

This duty requires directors and officers to act honestly and in good faith with a view to the best interests of the corporation. They cannot allow themselves to be held to ransom by one particular group of shareholders, for example, because their duty is

---

13. This general power may be circumscribed by the bylaws or by a unanimous shareholder agreement.

14. Note that some matters, such as declaring dividends and approving the annual financial statements, may not be delegated.

15. Corporate legislation in articles of incorporation jurisidictions, as well as in British Columbia, recite these duties right in the statute. For Nova Scotian companies, these duties are owed by virtue of fiduciary law.

16. (1925), 1 Ch. 407 at 428.

not to that group but rather to the corporation as a whole. One of the central principles informing fiduciary duties in corporate law can be summarized as follows: directors and officers must not allow their personal interest to conflict with their duty to the corporation. Not surprisingly, then, the fiduciary principle arises in multiple circumstances, two of which are explored below.

self-dealing contract
A contract in which a fiduciary has a conflict of interest.

THE SELF-DEALING CONTRACT To understand how a **self-dealing contract** works, assume the following scenario. IK Enterprises requires some office furniture, which Adam just so happens to be in a position to supply. He has several reasonably nice executive desks stored in his basement and is willing to sell them to the corporation. Adam is now in a conflict of interest situation.

As director of IK Enterprises Ltd., Adam is obligated to try to buy the furniture at as *low* a price as possible. As vendor of the furniture, however, Adam may be motivated by self-interest to sell the furniture at as *high* a price as possible. In this way, his duty to the corporation and his self-interest may collide because Adam is on both sides of the contract.

Figure 16.1

SELF-DEALING CONTRACT

Adam (the corporate director) → buys from → Adam (the individual)

In law, Adam is said to be in a self-dealing contract: he is dealing with himself in the purchase and sale of the office furniture.
Many jurisdictions have enacted procedures through which self-dealing contracts are permissible. The idea is to ensure that the corporation is not "ripped off" and, at the same time, to avoid a blanket prohibition on self-dealing contracts since some of them could be beneficial to the company. Under the Canada *Business Corporations Act*, for example, Adam's contract to sell furniture to his own company will be enforceable provided that

- Adam discloses the contract to the corporation in writing
- Adam does not participate in any vote of the directors approving the contract
- the contract is fair and reasonable to the corporation[17]

Failure to follow these statutory provisions gives the corporation the right to rescind, that is, "undo," the contract, or alternatively require the director to account for any profits made on the transaction.

corporate opportunity
A business opportunity in which the corporation has an interest.

CORPORATE OPPORTUNITIES Another area in which conflicts of interest frequently arise concerns **corporate opportunities**. Directors and officers are often required to assess any number of projects in which their corporation could become involved. These projects are known in law as "corporate opportunities"—they are opportunities to do business that the company can pursue or decline. If the directors and officers were permitted to take up any of these opportunities for themselves, problems very much like the ones present in the self-dealing contract scenario would arise.

---

17. See section 120 of the Canada *Business Corporations Act*. Welling notes that the following jurisdictions have similar procedures: A.B.C.A., S.B.C.A. and M.C.A. s. 115(7); B.C.C.A. s. 146 and the O.B.C.A. s. 132(7).

Assume that IK Enterprises has been approached by an Ontario company that is in the business of educating executives in the latest technology available for the workplace. That company would like to work with IK Enterprises to create a course on voice-recognition systems, the revenue potential of which appears to be very high. Adam is in a conflict of interest situation. As a director, he is required to assess the corporate opportunity on its own merits. As an individual, however, because he is interested in the contract for himself, he is motivated by self-interest. Put another way, if Adam were permitted to pursue the opportunity himself, he would be tempted—in his capacity as director—to turn down the project, not because it was in the best interests of the corporation to do so but because he wanted to take the opportunity for himself.

Given her fiduciary duty as director, Diane must proceed cautiously if she is still determined to pursue the translation product opportunity. Provided that Diane secures Adam's consent, perhaps in the form of a director's resolution, there is no

Case

Canadian Aero Service Ltd. v. *O'Malley*, [1974] S.C.R. 592

The Business Context: Directors are often presented with opportunities, and it is not always easy to predict whether they can pursue the opportunities in their personal capacity or must decline because of their duties to the corporation.

Factual Background: On behalf of their company Canadian Aero Service Ltd. (Canaero), the president and executive vice president had been negotiating to win an aerial mapping contract in Guyana. Subsequently, both officers left Canaero and set up their own company, Terra Surveys Limited. Terra began to pursue the very same line of work as Canaero and successfully bid on the aerial mapping contract in Guyana. Canaero brought an action against Terra and its former executives for improperly taking Canaero's corporate opportunity.

The Legal Question: Were the former executives in breach of their fiduciary duty to Canaero? Did the fact that the two had resigned and then, some time later, acquired the opportunity for themselves mean that there was no liability?

Resolution: The former executives were held liable to account to Canaero for the profits they made under the contract. They had breached their fiduciary duties by taking something that belonged to the corporation. In determining whether the appropriation of an opportu-

nity is a breach of fiduciary duty, the court suggested an examination of factors such as these:

- the position or office held by the directors and officers (the higher they are in the organization, the higher their duty)
- the nature of the corporate opportunity (how clearly was the opportunity identified by the corporation and how close was the corporation to acquiring the opportunity?)
- the director's or managerial officer's relation to the opportunity (was the opportunity one that the fiduciary worked on or had responsibility for?)
- the amount of knowledge the directors and officers possessed and the circumstances in which it was obtained
- the time between when the opportunity arose and when the officers took the opportunity for themselves
- the circumstances under which the employment relationship between the officers and the company terminated (was termination due to retirement, resignation, or discharge?)

Because the former officers violated their fiduciary duty, any profit gained—even if it was not at the expense of their former company—had to be given to the company. That they had resigned before pursing the opportunity did not change the analysis.

Critical Analysis: When do you think a director of a corporation should be able to take advantage of a business opportunity? In other words, when is a business opportunity her own and when does it belong to the company she serves as director?

obvious legal impediment to her proceeding to develop the translation product. She is being above-board and acting fairly vis-à-vis IK Enterprises. Since IK Enterprises does not want to pursue the opportunity, it would be highly unlikely that a court would decide that Diane was in breach of her fiduciary duty to IK Enterprises by taking the opportunity for herself.

On Directors' Duties

ETHICAL CONSIDERATIONS

A director has a fiduciary duty. This duty not only requires directors to place the corporate interest above their personal interests, but also requires them to act in the best interests of the corporation as a whole. Traditionally, this meant maximizing corporate profitability and share value. Put another way, the test for determining whether directors are fulfilling their duties to act in the best interests of the corporation is whether their decisions maximize profits.

In this context, corporations do not have any social responsibilities. They have no obligation to pursue policies that are desirable in terms of the objectives and values of society, nor do they have an obligation to consider interests other than those of the shareholders. This philosophy is expressed by Milton Friedman when he states that "the social responsibility of business is to increase its profits."[18]

Corporate legislation reflects this traditional approach in that it gives little recognition to outsiders, such as employees and the community within which the company is located, who may have an interest in corporate decisions. A limited exception is found, for example, in the Alberta *Business Corporations Act*, section 117(4), which provides as follows:

In determining whether a particular transaction or course of action is in the best interests of the corporation, a director, if he is elected or appointed ... by employees or creditors ... may give special, but not exclusive, consideration to the interests of those who elected or appointed him.

Courts, too, have occasionally taken a broader view. In *Teck Corporation* v. *Millar*,[19] for example, Mr. Justice Berger stated the following:

I appreciate that it would be a breach of their duty for directors to disregard entirely the interests of a company's shareholders in order to confer a benefit on its employees ... But if they observe a decent respect for other interests lying beyond those of the company's shareholders in the strict sense, that will not, in my view, leave directors open to the charge that they have failed in their fiduciary duty to the company.

These are very much the exceptions, however, and the classic approach—maximizing return to the shareholders—continues to carry the day.

Increasingly, such a limited corporate vision is being challenged by a variety of public-interest organizations, including environmentalists, peace activists, groups opposing child labour, and groups opposing "sweatshop" working conditions.

Critical Analysis: Does a corporation have social responsibilities? Can it be in the best interests of the corporation that directors consider the impact of their decisions on outside stakeholders? What might be the consequences for a corporation that did not act in a socially responsible way?

---

18. Milton Friedman, "The Social Responsibility of Business Is to Increase Its Profits" *New York Times Magazine*, Section 6 (13 September 1970) at 32.

19. (1972), 33 D.L.R. (3d) 288 (B.C.S.C.).

Liabilities of Directors and Officers

Directors and officers are exposed to a broad range of liabilities relating to the business of the corporation, including liability for torts and contracts and for statutory offences.

This section will discuss such liabilities in relation to directors, while recognizing that the same analysis applies to officers.

Liability in Tort and Contract

When a director is acting on behalf of a corporation and commits a tort, his actions may be attributed to the corporation itself by virtue of the identification theory. Similarly, when the director enters into a contract, as agent for his corporation, his actions make the corporation the other party to that contract and the director slips out of the equation altogether. There are times, however, when a director has *personal* liability for a tort he may have committed or a contract he may have entered into.

LIABILITY IN TORT

Traditionally, courts have been reluctant to say that a director or officer is *automatically* liable just because he commits a tort on company time. The idea is to permit the director to conduct company business without risking personal, unlimited liability at every turn. Think of it this way: if Adam were personally liable for any tort he committed during the course of his business day, then there would really be no benefit in incorporating IK Enterprises from his perspective as a director. His liability would be the same whether he was running his business through a corporation or as a sole proprietorship, and the principle in *Salomon* v. *Salomon* would fall by the wayside.

In line with this approach, some courts have ruled that directors are not personally liable provided that they were acting in furtherance of their duties to the corporation and their conduct was justifiable.[20] Recent case law from Ontario takes a step back from such a perspective. It suggests that directors and officers *will almost always* be responsible for their own tortious conduct even if they were acting in the best interests of the corporation.[21] With this in mind, prudent directors will take care not to commit torts, and thereby avoid having to establish what the law concerning the matter is in their jurisdiction.

Where the director's conduct is extreme, he or she will be found liable for committing a tort regardless of the approach taken by the court in question. For example, assume that Adam is meeting in his office with a customer who has not paid his bill to IK Enterprises Ltd. Things get a little out of hand and Adam bars the door for several hours, saying to the customer, "You're not getting out of here until you write a cheque for what you owe us." On these facts, Adam would face *personal* liability no matter what the legal test applied might be.

LIABILITY IN CONTRACT

The director does not generally attract liability for the corporation's contracts—the principles of agency operate in such a way that the corporation is liable to the outsider and the director who has acted as agent for the corporation drops out of the transaction.

---

20. *McFadden* v. *481782 Ontario Ltd.* (1984), 47 O.R. (2d) 134 (H.C.).
21. See, for example, *ADGA Systems International Ltd.* v. *Valcom Ltd.* (1999), 43 O.R. (3d) 101 (C.A.), leave to appeal to S.C.C. refused [1999] S.C.C.A. No. 124.

Nonetheless, a director faces personal liability on a contract if the facts indicate that the director intended to assume personal liability, as when

- the director contracts on his own behalf, as well as on behalf of the company
- the director guarantees the contractual performance of the company

Liability by Statute

In addition to the exposure that directors face for breaching their general management duties, dozens of other pieces of legislation place obligations on them. These statutes impose potentially serious penalties for failure to comply, including fines of up to $1 million and imprisonment for up to two years.[22]

As Figure 16.2 illustrates, legislation affecting directors covers a wide range of circumstances and relates to a broad range of constituents.

Figure 16.2

DIRECTORS' STATUTORY LIABILITIES: A SAMPLING

Statutory breach	Type of statute	Nature of penalty
Failure to pay employee wages	Federal and provincial incorporation statutes	Liability for wages
Directing, authorizing, or permitting the release of a toxic substance into the environment	Federal and provincial environmental protection statutes	Fines and/or imprisonment
Failure to remit required taxes	Provincial and federal revenue acts	Liability for amount outstanding and interest or penalties
Failure to maintain health and safety standards	Provincial workplace health and safety legislation	Fines and/or imprisonment
Insider trading—using confidential information in buying and selling shares	Provincial securities Act, federal and provincial incorporation statutes	Fines and/or imprisonment
Engaging in anticompetitive behaviour	Federal *Competition Act*	Criminal and civil liabilities
Paying a dividend when company is insolvent	Federal and provincial incorporation statutes	Personal repayment
Misrepresentation in a prospectus	Provincial securities legislation	Damages
Improperly transporting dangerous goods	Federal and provincial transportation of dangerous goods legislation	Fines and/or imprisonment

The imposition of environmental liability on directors and officers pursuant to environmental legislation is a relatively recent development. *R. v. Bata* illustrates this liability.

Case

R. v. Bata Industries Ltd. (1992), 9 O.R. (3d) 329 (Prov. Div.); aff'd in (1993), 14 O.R. (3d) 354 (Gen. Div.); varied in (1995), 25 O.R. (3d) 321 (C.A.)

The Business Context: Canadian environmental legislation often imposes liability directly on corporate directors.

The *R. v. Bata* decision was the first Canadian decision on the personal environmental liability of the board of directors of a large corporation. Although Canadian directors had been prosecuted in the past for environmental offences, all involved small, single-location companies.

Factual Background: Bata Industries manufactured shoes at a factory in Batawa, Ontario. The company was experiencing financial difficulties and in an effort to reduce

---

22. See, for example, the federal *Hazardous Products Act*, R.S.C. 1985, c. H-3.

costs, waste chemicals were stored on-site in drums rather than being disposed of properly. The storage containers were in poor condition and some of the chemical contents leaked into the soil. As a result, the corporation was charged with (and convicted of) offences under environmental protection legislation, and three of its directors were charged for failing to take all reasonable care to prevent discharge of contaminants into the environment.

The Legal Question: Were the directors liable under the legislation?

Resolution: The three directors charged were the chairman of the board, the plant manager (who was a director), and the latter's superior, the company president. The chairman was acquitted as he visited the plant only once or twice a year and had no knowledge of the storage problems. He had placed an experienced director on-site and was entitled to rely on that director to address environmental concerns.

By way of contrast, the plant manager/ director had a "hands-on" role. He had experience in production, the authority to act, and the knowledge that toxic chemicals were present on the site. As he failed to take steps to rectify the problem, he was found liable. The president visited the plant once a month and had personal knowledge of the storage problems and yet took no steps to rectify them. It was not sufficient to simply give verbal instructions to plant staff, who were overworked, without following up on the instructions to see that the problem was solved. He too was convicted. In short, the plant manager and the president had failed to take all reasonable care to prevent the discharge of contaminants.

Critical Analysis: What do you think the rationale is for prosecuting the directors personally, as well as prosecuting the corporation, for environmental offences?

---

indemnification

The corporate practice of paying litigation expenses of officers and directors for lawsuits related to corporate affairs.

Avoiding Liability

Directors have onerous duties to the corporation, and no one should agree to become a director without a sound understanding of the obligations involved. Willingness, enthusiasm, and ability are not enough: "the job may well require a considerable and unforeseen time commitment with ultimately limited compensation and considerable exposure of one's own personal assets."[23] The exposure to risk suggests that a risk management plan as discussed in Chapter 3 is warranted. The basis for such a plan is provided in the Business Application of the Law box.

Avoiding Personal Liability

Directors can reduce their exposure to personal liability by exercising care, diligence, and skill in the performance of their duties.

Directors can meet the statutory standard of care by being attentive, active, and informed. In this regard, directors should

- make all their decisions informed decisions
- do what is necessary to learn about matters affecting the company
- identify possible problems within the company
- stay apprised of and alert to the corporation's financial and other affairs
- regularly attend directors' meetings
- ensure that they receive reliable professional advice

BUSINESS APPLICATION OF THE LAW

Directors may also protect themselves by ensuring that an **indemnification** agreement with their company is in place. The purpose of such an agreement is to ensure that the corporation pays any costs or expenses that a director faces as a result of being sued because he is a director.

Directors should also ensure that the corporation carries adequate insurance. Directors' and officers' liability insurance provides coverage to the director who has a judgment or other claim against him. Directors should carefully review the policy's exclusion clauses to ensure that maximum protection is provided.

Source: Johanne Ingram (Edmonton, Legal Education Society of Alberta, 1999).

---

23. David Ross, "Director's Obligations" in *Fiduciary Obligations—1995* (Vancouver: The Continuing Legal Education Society of B.C., 1995) at 5.1.01.

Shareholders

A shareholder is someone who invests in a company by buying shares. As soon as IK Enterprises was created, for example, the company—through the directors—issued shares in the company to Adam, Cameron, and Diane. Another way of becoming a shareholder is by buying the shares from an existing shareholder or receiving the shares as a gift.

Regardless of how the shares are obtained, the shareholder has few responsibilities with respect to the corporation. Unlike directors and officers, the shareholder has no duty to act in the best interests of the corporation.[24] She can freely compete with the corporation in which she holds a share. She is not obligated to attend shareholder meetings, cast her vote, read the corporation's financial reports, or take any interest whatever in the progress of the corporation. And, of course, she is not generally liable for the debts and obligations of the corporation because of the principle in *Salomon*. There are exceptions to this immunity, however, as the following section explores.

Shareholder Liability

piercing the corporate veil
Holding the owners of a corporation personally liable for the corporation's acts.

Owners of the corporation are occasionally held responsible for debts and liabilities incurred by the corporation. This is known as **piercing** or **lifting the corporate veil**. Due to the *Salomon* principle, courts are generally reluctant to lift the corporate veil except when they are satisfied that a company is a "mere facade" concealing the true facts.[25] It must be shown that there is complete domination and control by the person or entity sought to be made liable, and that the corporate form must have been used as a shield for conduct akin to fraud that deprives claimants of their rights.[26]

Case

B.G. Preeco I (Pac. Coast) Ltd. v. *Bon Street Hldg Ltd.* (1989), 37 B.C.L.R. (2d) 258 (C.A.).

The Business Context: This case illustrates the difficulties in lifting the corporate veil. The purchaser incorporated a shell company to sign an agreement of purchase and sale. This allowed the purchasers to renege on the deal without incurring liability because they were not a party to the contract, the shell company was. Furthermore, since a shell company—by definition—has no assets, the vendor would not ordinarily sue for breach of contract because any judgment against a shell company would be worthless.

Factual Background: Preeco received an offer on its property from Bon Street Developments Ltd., an active company with assets and favourable financial records. One month prior to the signing of the agreement of purchase and sale of Preeco's property, the shareholders of Bon Street Developments changed the name of the corporation to Bon Street Holdings. The same shareholders incorporated a shell company and gave it the name Bon Street Developments. The corporation that actually signed the deed was the assetless shell company. It backed out of the deal, and Preeco sued both companies and their shareholders.

The Legal Question: Were the shareholders liable?

Resolution: The court refused to lift the corporate veil and treat the shareholders as the company. The court stated that

---

24. There is an exception in some jurisdictions where an obligation can be imposed on shareholders if they hold enough shares to be classified as insiders, in which case they must not use insider information to their own benefit.

25. Kevin Patrick McGuiness, *The Law and Practice of Canadian Business Corporations* (Toronto: Butterworths, 1999) at 31-32 points out a number of other situations where the veil will be pierced, including when it is required by statute, contract, or other documents and when it can be established that the company is the agent of its controllers or shareholders.

26. *Gregorio* v. *Intrans-Corp.* (1994), 18 O.R. (3d) 527 (C.A.).

corporations are often used to avoid unlimited personal liability, and there is nothing wrong with that. However, what was wrong was the fraudulent misrepresentation by the directors in representing the new Bon Street as the old Bon Street. The court gave relief to Preeco because the directors of the other company had been fraudulent.

This case is a perfect example of how courts approach problems of this nature. Rather than lifting the corporate veil, the courts prefer to assess the conduct of those behind the corporation on its own terms. If these people are guilty of their own wrongdoing—such as fraud—they can be held liable to Preeco and no veils have to be lifted.

Critical Analysis: Can you think of situations in which it would be appropriate to lift the corporate veil?

Shareholder Rights

Shareholder rights fall into three broad categories: the right to vote, the right to information, and financial rights. How directors decide to allocate these rights when issuing different classes of shares is largely up to them, as there are few requirements in this area. One kind of share can have all three rights, while another kind of share may have only one of these rights. All that is normally required, in this regard, is that *all* of the rights referred to above be allocated to at least one class of shares; however, all those rights are not required to be attached to one class.

The idea behind having different classes of shares is to permit different levels of participation in the corporation. As noted earlier, if Cameron (Adam's father) does not want much of a role in the company, he may be content with nonvoting shares. These are often called **preferred shares**.[27] Voting shares are usually called **common shares**. Although nonvoting shares are normally called preferred and voting shares are normally called common, this is not always the case. The only way to know for certain what rights are attached to shares is to review the share certificate itself, as well as the articles of incorporation.

preferred share
A share or stock that has a preference in the distribution of dividends and the proceeds on dissolution.

common share
A share that generally has a right to vote, to share in dividends, and to share in proceeds on dissolution.

RIGHT TO VOTE Corporations legislation requires that there be at least one class of voting shareholders in a corporation. The most significant voting right traditionally attached to common shares is the right to vote for the board of directors. Note that the number of votes that a particular shareholder may cast depends on the number of shares he holds. If Adam holds one thousand common shares, he has one thousand votes. If he holds a majority of the shares, he therefore controls the company and will be in a position to elect at least a majority of the board of directors.

As well, voting shareholders have the right to approve or disapprove of directors' actions since the last general meeting. This is because the right to vote brings with it other rights, including the right to

- hold a shareholder general meeting each year
- be given notice of the meeting
- attend the meeting
- ask questions
- introduce motions

proxy
A person who acts for another in a meeting or a public body.

A shareholder who cannot attend a meeting can exercise her voting power through a **proxy**. This means granting formal permission to someone else to vote her shares on her behalf. The use of a proxy is important, particularly in large corporations when

---

27. They are called preferred shares because ordinarily, the holders of preferred shares get priority—or have a "preference"—on taking a slice of the corporation's assets if it is liquidated.

there is a dispute between competing groups of shareholders. Whichever group does the best job of soliciting proxies is most likely to carry the day.

Nonvoting shareholders—usually preferred shareholders—have the right to vote in certain specialized matters. Under the Canadian *Business Corporations Act,* for example, Cameron—as the holder of preferred shares in IK Enterprises Ltd.—would have the right to vote on any proposal to sell all the corporation's assets.[28] The rationale is that even nonvoting shareholders should have a say when such a fundamental change in corporate direction is being put forward.

RIGHT TO INFORMATION   Shareholders have the right to certain fundamental information concerning the corporation. This includes the right to

- inspect the annual financial statement for the corporation
- apply to the court to have an inspector appointed to look into the affairs of the corporation if it can be shown that there is a serious concern about mismanagement
- inspect certain records, including minute books, the register of share transfers, incorporating documents, bylaws and special resolutions, and the registry of shareholders and directors
- know whether directors have been purchasing shares of the corporation. This is to permit shareholders to determine whether directors have been using confidential information to make personal profits[29]

FINANCIAL RIGHTS   Shareholders generally buy shares with the hope or expectation that the corporation will prosper and generate financial rewards, in terms of either capital gains or income for them. In this respect, one of the fundamental rights of the shareholder is the right to receive any dividend declared by the corporation. The shareholder has no right to have dividends just because the corporation has earned large profits, since the declaration of dividends is within the discretion of the board of directors. However, if the shareholder can show that the directors are abusing their discretion, they can consider bringing an oppression action, which is discussed later in this chapter.

Preferred shares usually have **cumulative dividend rights**. This means that any dividend either not declared or not paid in the full amount of the annual preferred dividend carries over into the next year.

Once dividends are declared, directors are bound to pay them in order of preference assigned to the classes of shares. As well, there cannot be any discrimination among shareholders belonging to the same class. If Diane and Cameron both own Class B shares, for example, it is illegal for the directors to declare that Diane gets a certain dividend but Cameron does not.

Shareholders have a right to share in the assets of a corporation on dissolution after creditors are paid. Again, the right is dependent on the priorities of each class of shares. Preferred shareholders are often given the right to be first in line for corporate assets once all the creditors have been paid.

Additionally, shareholders may have what are known as **preemptive rights**. When this right exists, it requires the corporation to offer existing shareholders the chance to purchase a new issue of shares before these shares are offered to outsiders. This gives existing shareholders a chance to maintain their level of control or power in the corporation. For example, assume that Adam has one thousand common shares in IK Enterprises Ltd, and, because of other entrepreneurial interests, he has

cumulative dividend right
The right of the holder of a preferred share to be paid arrears.

preemptive right
A shareholder's right to maintain a proportionate share of ownership by purchasing a proportionate share of any new stock issue.

---

28. *Supra* note 3, see s. 189(3).
29. See, for example, *Securities Act,* R.S.O. 1990, c. s-5, ss. 106-109.

unwisely resigned as a director in the company for the time being. Diane is the only corporate director left. Assume further that she resolves to issue 2000 common shares to Cameron. This issue would transform Adam's position from being an equal shareholder—with Diane—of common shares to being in the minority, but his pre-emptive right would allow him to maintain his proportional interest in the company if he could afford to purchase further shares.

Shareholder Remedies

A shareholder who is dissatisfied with a corporation's performance or management has a number of remedies available to her.

SELLING THE SHARES   Often the simplest and least costly remedy for a shareholder who is dissatisfied with the operation or performance of a corporation is to simply sell her shares. This, of course, is an easily viable remedy only in the widely held or public corporation, where shares are traded on the stock exchange and there are no restrictions on their transferability.

The situation is quite different in the closely held or private corporation. In this case, there are usually restrictions on the transference of shares and—even where the restrictions are minimal—it may be difficult to find someone willing to buy such shares. Historically, this reality put the minority shareholder in the unenviable position of having little input into the operation of the corporation and no easy way to extricate her investment. In response, both the common law and the legislatures developed a number of remedies to protect a minority shareholder from abuse by the majority. Two of the most important are the derivative action and the oppression remedy.[30]

BRINGING A DERIVATIVE ACTION   Because of their managerial control, directors are well placed to rob the very corporation that they are charged with serving. For example, they could take a corporate opportunity and develop it for their own personal gain; they could vote that the corporation sell corporate assets to one of them at a price ridiculously below market; or they could vote themselves outrageously high compensation packages. What can a minority shareholder do when the directors are breaching their duty to the corporation and causing it injury?

At common law, courts permitted minority shareholders to take action on behalf of the corporation against the directors, but the system was far from adequate. In response, corporate law statutes have created what is called the statutory **derivative action**.[31] This permits a shareholder to obtain leave from the court to bring an action on behalf of the corporation, where he can establish that

- directors will not bring an action
- he is acting in good faith
- it appears to be in the interests of the corporation that the action proceed

This action means that directors cannot treat the corporation as their own personal fiefdom with impunity. They owe strict duties to the corporation. Even if they breach those duties with the support of the majority of the shareholders, the minority has recourse to the courts and can secure any number of remedies on behalf of the cor-

derivative action
A suit by a shareholder on behalf of the corporation to enforce a corporate cause of action.

---

30. Other remedies include appraisal, which is a procedure for having shares bought by the corporation, and winding-up, which involves dissolution of the corporation and the return of surplus assets to the shareholders. The former remedy is quite complicated, and the latter is quite drastic; thus, the use of these remedies is uncommon.

31. For a discussion of the jurisdictions that provide for such an action, see Bruce Welling, *Corporate Law in Canada: The Governing Principles*, 2d ed. (Toronto: Butterworths, 1991) at 525 and following.

poration. By virtue of the derivative action, if the directors have stolen a corporate opportunity, they can be forced by the court to account for that profit. If they have disposed of corporate assets at below market value, the court can order them to account for the difference between what the asset is actually worth and what was paid for it. If they have voted to overpay themselves, the court can order them to return their ill-gotten gains. The court even has the power to remove the directors from office and replace them. In fact, the legislation empowers the court to make any order it sees fit.

BRINGING AN OPPRESSION ACTION The most widely used remedy by shareholders in Canada is called the **oppression remedy**. A shareholder who has been treated unfairly or "oppressively" may apply to a court for relief. Conduct that the courts have found to be oppressive usually falls into the following categories:

oppression remedy
A statutory remedy available to shareholders and other stakeholders to protect their corporate interests.

- lack of a valid corporate purpose for the conduct
- transactions that are not at arm's length
- lack of good faith on the part of the directors of the corporation
- discrimination between shareholders with the effect of benefiting the majority shareholder to the exclusion or the detriment of the minority shareholder
- lack of adequate and proper disclosure of material information to minority shareholders
- a plan or design to eliminate minority shareholders[32]

The court is entitled to make such order as it deems just and appropriate, including ordering the corporation to purchase the complainant's shares, ordering the improper conduct to cease, and, in extreme circumstances, ordering the company to be dissolved. The remedy is extremely flexible and has few attendant technicalities. Unlike a derivative action, which is brought on behalf of the corporation, the oppression remedy is a personal action, which can be brought by shareholders and specified stakeholders—security holders, creditors, directors, or officers.

Case

Tilley v. *Hails* (1992), 7 O.R. (3d) 257; varied (1992), 8 O.R. (3d) 169 (Gen. Div.); aff'd (1992) 9 O.R. (3d) 255 (C.A.)

The Business Context: This case concerns the use of the oppression remedy. The remedy is often used to break a deadlock when it becomes apparent that the shareholders can no longer cooperate and the business cannot continue without some intervention.

Factual Background: In 1980, Alexander J. Tilley founded Tilley Endurables Inc. The company was established to market a hat designed by Tilley. The hat soon became very popular, and the product line was expanded to include a range of sports clothes for men and women.

The products were sold in the company's retail outlets in several cities, as well as by mail order.

All of Tilley's products were closely connected with Alex Tilley. He was very much identified with the products—catalogues and advertisements featured photographs of Tilley and members of his family wearing Tilley products, the Tilley logo bears Tilley's likeness, and he and the company have been the subject of many newspaper and magazine articles.

Tilley became involved with Dennis Hails when Hails undertook to do some interior work on Tilley's stores and residence. At this time, Tilley was in financial difficulty, which was further exacerbated by Hails' bill. Hails offered to lend some assistance in managing the financial end of the business. He eventually lent the company in excess of $1 million.

Tilley was initially very grateful to Hails and offered to give him half of the shares in his company. By doing so he relinquished control in his company, and from that

---

32. M. Patricia Richardson, *McCarthy, Tetrault: Directors' and Officers' Duties and Liabilities in Canada* (Toronto: Butterworths, 1997) at 78-79.

point on decisions could be made only by agreement between Tilley and Hails. The two entered into a shareholder agreement that transferred half of the shares to Hails and provided for the board of directors to be composed of Tilley and Hails, with Tilley as president and Hails as vice president. In practice, Tilley looked after product design and Hails oversaw the financial management of the company. The shareholder agreement provided for the sale of shares but only on the death or disability of the parties; there were, for example, no provisions for sale pursuant to disagreements between the shareholders.

Eventually Tilley and Hails found out that they were incompatible and their relationship became hostile. Hails took several actions designed to get rid of Tilley, including causing him to be charged with the unsafe storage of an unregistered handgun (the charges were eventually dropped) and publishing a catalogue without pictures of Tilley or his family. In turn, Tilley told both employees and the bank that Hails was leaving, the latter causing the bank to reduce Tilley Endurables' line of credit.

Tilley and Hails both applied for the shareholder oppression remedy pursuant to the company legislation.

The Legal Question: Did the remedy apply, and if so who would have to sell their shares to the other?

Resolution: A private corporation is somewhat like a small partnership in that whenever the shareholders cannot cooperate, the court can make an order requiring one shareholder to sell his shares to the other. The court found that Hails was responsible for the deadlock. In particular, his conduct in having Tilley charged with a criminal offence was intended to remove him from the management of the corporation. This was contrary to the intent of the shareholder agreement and was a clear case of oppression. Tilley's conduct, although not in the best interests of the company, was in retaliation for Hails's conduct. Hails was ordered to sell his shares to Tilley at a value to be established by a arbitrator. He could, however, still claim for the money he had lent to the company.

Critical Analysis: What are other examples of treatment that could be considered unfair or oppressive?

Like all litigation, however, the process in securing a shareholder remedy is time-consuming, costly, and unpredictable. Furthermore, the courts historically have been less than enthusiastic about getting involved in the internal affairs of corporations. Put another way, it is often a heavy and onerous burden to convince the court that the majority is in the wrong and has been oppressive.

As a way of avoiding litigation, shareholders may decide to enter into an agreement at the very beginning of their association in order to deal with potentially contentious areas and to streamline the procedure leading to the resolution of any conflict. Depending on the jurisdiction, there are two possibilities in this regard: a shareholder agreement and a unanimous shareholder agreement, also called a USA. Of course, such agreements do not *guarantee* that litigation will be avoided, since the meaning and enforceability of these agreements can themselves become the subject matter of litigation.

shareholder agreement
An agreement that defines the relationship among people who have an ownership interest in a corporation.

unanimous shareholder agreement (USA)
An agreement among all shareholders that restricts the powers of the directors to manage the corporation.

ASSERTING A REMEDY UNDER SHAREHOLDER AGREEMENT OR USA   **Shareholder agreements** are common, particularly in small, closely held corporations. They serve a multitude of purposes, but in particular they allow shareholders to define their relationship by setting out the expectations and obligations of the parties. Such agreements also can provide mechanisms for resolving disputes, and they can provide protection for shareholders by monitoring shareholder participation and regulating the transfer of shares.

A **unanimous shareholder agreement (USA)** is a specialized kind of shareholder agreement found in articles of association jurisdictions. It is an agreement among all shareholders that restricts, in whole or part, the powers of the directors to manage the corporation. The agreement exists to deal with major issues facing a corporation, such as corporate structure, issuance of shares, declaration of dividends, and the appointment of officers. The purpose of a USA is to ensure that control over matters dealt with in the USA remains with the shareholders. When shareholders, through a USA, take management powers away from directors, those directors are relieved of their duties *and* liabilities to the same extent. This means that if the shareholders improperly manage the corporation, they may be successfully sued for negligence or breach of fiduciary duty, for example.

A USA or an ordinary shareholder agreement is not always appropriate, however. These kinds of arrangements are most useful in the smaller corporations whose shares have a limited market, whose shareholders are strongly committed to the enterprise, and whose management will be supplied largely or entirely by the shareholders.[33]

Shareholder Agreements

BUSINESS APPLICATION OF THE LAW

A shareholder agreement allows the shareholders to define their relationship, now and in the future. It should, as well, provide mechanisms and procedures that can be employed when the relationship encounters difficulties, and means for undoing the relationship if the need to do so arises. An agreement must be tailored to meet the requirements of the particular situation and should address the following issues:

1. *Management of the company.* Who will be responsible for management? What will their rights and obligations be? How will they be appointed or elected or hired? How will they be paid?

2. *Protection for the minority shareholder.* How will the minority be protected from domination by the majority? How will representation on the board of directors be achieved? How will fundamental issues, such as dividends, sale of assets, and the like, be handled?

3. *Control over who will be the other shareholders.* What are the qualifications needed for being a shareholder? What happens in the event of a shareholder's death, retirement, disability, or simple loss of interest in the company?

4. *Provision of a market for shares.* What are the circumstances that require a shareholder to sell her shares? What happens if a shareholder dies? Who will buy the shares and for how much? How will the purchase be funded?

5. *Capital contribution.* What happens if the corporation needs more cash? Who will provide it and how much? How will payment be compelled?

6. *Buy-sell arrangements in the event of a dispute.* What (e.g., death, retirement, insolvency) triggers a sale? How will the shares will valued? What method will be chosen for their valuation (i.e., independent third party, formula, value fixed in advance and updated annually)?

7. *Mechanism for terminating the agreement.* How can the agreement be terminated? Can it be terminated on notice? How much notice?

Source: James W. Carr, "Shareholder Agreements" in *Advising the Business Client* (Edmonton: The Legal Education Society of Alberta, 1995) at 14-16.

---

33. For further analysis on this point, see James W. Carr, "Shareholder Agreements" in *Advising the Business Client* (Edmonton: The Legal Education Society of Alberta, 1995).

The objective of a shareholder agreement is to comprehensively set out—by agreement and in advance of any conflict—what the shareholder's expectations are, how the company is to be managed, and how disputes will be addressed. Shareholder agreements seek to confront the reality that disagreements are largely inevitable and can be resolved according to mechanisms set up during the "honeymoon" phase of a business relationship.

Diane, Cameron, and Adam most definitely need a shareholder agreement for the reasons given above.

Creditor Protection

A corporation is responsible for its own liabilities, including its debts. As such, the shareholders/owners may be tempted to strip the entity of its assets in an attempt to defeat creditors, but doing so would be illegal. For example, if IK Enterprises Ltd. falls on hard financial times, Adam cannot clean out all the computer inventory and bring it home with him to sell later. This is because the inventory belongs to the *corporation,* not to Adam, and the corporation's creditors have a prior claim on such property.

To help prevent abuses by shareholders, a number of legislative provisions have been enacted. For example, section 42 of the CBCA forbids the corporation to pay a dividend to shareholders if doing so would jeopardize its ability to pay its own debts as they fall due (the liquidity test). The same section forbids such a dividend if that would make the company **insolvent**—that is, leave it without enough assets to cover its liabilities.[34] Under section 44, financial assistance to shareholders is also forbidden if such assistance would render the company insolvent or illiquid. Directors who consent to a dividend or financial assistance under such circumstances are personally liable to restore to the corporation any amounts so paid. As a final example, when a corporation ceases operations, it must pay creditors first. Only if there are any assets remaining are the shareholders entitled to share in the proceeds.

insolvent
Unable to pay debts or having liabilities in excess of assets.

Termination of the Corporation

When and if the time comes for IK Enterprises to shut down, it can be dissolved in several ways. In most jurisdictions, provisions in the companies act or a separate **winding up** act set out a process. The steps involved can be somewhat complicated, so in many instances it is more feasible simply to let the company lapse. This is particularly the case with a small, closely held corporation. The principals may simply neglect to file their annual report or follow other reporting requirements; this will ultimately result in the company being struck from the corporate register.

A court has the authority to order a company to be terminated when a shareholder has been wrongfully treated and this is the only way to do justice between the parties. As well, a corporation whose debts exceed its assets may eventually go bankrupt. The result of bankruptcy is usually the dissolution of the corporation.

winding up
The process of dissolving a corporation.

---

34. Insolvency is discussed in Chapter 28.

Business Law in Practice Revisited

1. What obligations are Cameron, Diane, and Adam assuming as corporate officers and directors?

As corporate officers and directors, Cameron, Adam, and Diane are obliged to competently manage the corporation and to act in the best interests of the corporation. This means, in effect, that they must not only apply their skills and knowledge to the operations of the corporation but also put the corporation's interests above their own personal interests.

2. How can the disagreement between Adam and Cameron be resolved?

The dispute between Adam and Diane is problematic. Each owns 50 percent of the common shares of the corporation, and thus each has an equal voice in the management of the corporation. Their situation is the classic one of shareholder deadlock. In hindsight, the potential for deadlock should have been addressed in the decision to issue shares, or in a shareholder agreement, or both. An agreement could have provided for a mechanism such as Cameron or an independent person casting a deciding vote. In the absence of an agreement, the parties could still agree to pursue an alternative dispute resolution mechanism. If one party is unwilling, then there is little that can be done to resolve the dispute, short of litigation.

3. Are there any problems with Diane forming her own company to take advantage of the translation product opportunity?

If Diane decides to incorporate a company to pursue the translation product opportunity, she needs to be mindful of her fiduciary obligations to IK Enterprises. The law is somewhat unclear as to when a director may pursue an opportunity that came to her as a result of her position as director. However, as the company has rejected the opportunity, it would seem that Diane in the circumstances (she was in favour of IK Enterprises pursuing the opportunity) is free to take it up on her own.

4. What are Cameron's rights as a shareholder if he doesn't like how Diane and Adam are managing the company?

Cameron could simply sell his shares, if he is permitted to do so and if he can find a buyer. The companies legislation also provides for shareholder remedies; however, the remedies are not usually available simply because a shareholder dislikes how the corporation is being managed. There must be something more, such as oppressive conduct by the directors. Even if oppression can be proved, litigation can be costly and time-consuming. Again, this issue should have been considered in advance, and a remedy or alternative courses of action built into a shareholder agreement.

Chapter Summary

Of particular concern to anyone launching a corporation is the potential liability, both civil and criminal, that the corporation and its stakeholders are exposed to. A corporation, as a distinct legal entity, may be liable in tort, in contract, and for criminal and regulatory offences. Likewise, directors and officers also may be liable both in criminal and civil law for actions relating to the business of the corporation.

Directors and officers who are charged with the management of the corporation owe duties of competence and fiduciary duties to the corporation, and they may be liable to the corporation for breach of these duties.

Shareholders generally face few liabilities with respect to the actions of the corporation. There are, however, limited exceptions to this general rule—most importantly when the corporate form is being used to commit a fraud. Shareholders do, however, have certain statutory rights with respect to the operations of the corporation—the right to vote, the right to information, and financial rights. They also have remedies to enforce their rights. Shareholders can enter into agreements that define their relationships with one another, and that provide mechanisms for resolving disputes and means for protecting their interests.

Creditors have few rights, other than those specifically negotiated, but they do have limited statutory protection.

A corporation can enjoy perpetual existence; however, it can also be dissolved. The most common methods of dissolution are winding-up procedures and simply letting the corporation lapse.

Study Chapter

Key Terms and Concepts

common share (p. 350)
corporate opportunity (p. 343)
cumulative dividend right (p. 351)
derivative action (p. 352)
doctrine of constructive notice (p. 339)
identification theory (p. 338)
indemnification (p. 348)
insolvent (p. 356)
oppression remedy (p. 353)
piercing the corporate veil (p. 349)
preemptive right (p. 351)
preferred share (p. 350)
proxy (p. 350)
regulatory offence (p. 341)
self-dealing contract (p. 343)
shareholder agreement (p. 354)
unanimous shareholder agreement (p. 354)
winding up (p. 356)

Questions for Review

1. How do the courts determine the criminal liability of a corporation?

2. When is a director personally liable for committing a tort?

3. To whom do directors owe duties?

4. What are the duties of directors and officers?

5. How may a director avoid personal liability?

6. What is meant by the term *lifting the corporate veil*?

7. What three main rights do shareholders have?

8. What rights to dividends do shareholders have?

9. What is the difference between a derivative action and an oppression action?

10. When is a shareholder agreement appropriate?

11. What protection do creditors have from shareholders stripping the corporation of its assets?

12. How is a corporation terminated?

Questions for Discussion

1. Some commentators have suggested that the rules for determining corporate criminal liability should be revised to reflect the structure of the modern corporation. These commentators have suggested that corporations be criminally liable for the collective acts of the organization's representatives, even though no one person committed an offence individually; or that corporations be held liable when senior representatives of the corporation created a climate that encouraged employers to disobey the law.[35]

    Can you identify any problems with the currently used identification theory of corporate criminal liability? What are the shortcomings of the proposed alternatives?

2. Directors are to exercise their duties in the "best interests of the corporation." How should that term be defined? Should it be defined at all? What are the advantages and disadvantages of having more specific guidelines for directors?

3. Directors are subject to more and more liabilities. Why do you think that this has occurred? What are the problems associated with holding directors to higher standards? How can directors protect themselves in an increasingly litigious environment?

4. Directors face onerous environmental responsibilities. They are, however, entitled to argue that they took "all reasonable care." What factors should be considered in developing a risk management plan that addresses the environmental liabilities of directors?

5. Should a professional, such as a lawyer or chartered accountant, accept an invitation to act as a director for a corporate client? What are the advantages for the professional? What are the advantages for the corporation? What problems could arise?

Situations for Discussion

1. Catherine held one-third of the shares in a corporation that operated a small retail business. She was also the manager of the one store that the corporation

---

35. Howard Burshtein, "Opinion Divided on Extending Corporate Liability" *The Lawyers Weekly* (1 September 1995) 11.

owned until the other directors voted to terminate her position. What courses of action are available to her?

2. Alicia, the president and CEO of a computer software company, broke into the offices of a competitor late one night in order to see what kinds of products they were in the process of designing. She was caught in the act by the police, who brought to her attention the following provision from the *Criminal Code:*

    s.348 (1) Every one who

    breaks and enters a place with intent to commit an indictable offence therein ... is guilty of an offence ...

    Has Alicia's computer software company committed the crime of break and enter?

3. Lois is the president and CEO of a shoe manufacturing company that produces much of its product line in a low-wage country. Lois is concerned both that her company will become the subject of an international boycott for this reason and that she will not be maximizing shareholder return if she agrees to raise the wages of the company's offshore employees. Furthermore, in her view, the wages the company is paying those employees are competitive with the wages other companies are paying their workers in the same country. Does Lois's company have a social responsibility to pay its workers a living wage?

4. Ryan and Sean are shareholders and directors of Springfield Meadows Ltd. (Springfield), a company that has developed land for a large trailer park. Springfield has 20 other shareholders. Ryan and Sean are approached by Louise, who wants to create a company whose business it will be to lease trailers. Ryan and Sean are interested in participating as directors and shareholders in this new company, since this would be a good way to fill up some of the vacant sites at Springfield's trailer park. The new company is a big success, and Sean and Ryan receive impressively high dividends on a regular basis. Eventually, the other shareholders in Springfield learn about Sean and Ryan's new company and sue them for breach of their fiduciary duty. The shareholders contend that Sean and Ryan should have developed the opportunity to get into the trailer-leasing business for the benefit of Springfield and should not have taken that opportunity for themselves. Are Sean and Ryan in breach of their duty to act in the best interest of Springfield?

5. Peter sold his barbershop business to Andy for $25 000. As part of the agreement of purchase and sale, Peter agreed to a restrictive covenant that prohibited him from providing barbering services in an area within a 10-mile radius of his former shop for a period of one year. Within a month of the sale, Peter incorporated a company and commenced cutting hair in violation of the restrictive covenant.[36] Can Andy do anything about this situation? Should he do anything?

6. Condelle Systems and Marcodious Ltd. were competitors in the security systems industry. For a number of years, Condelle had a substantial contract with Correctional Services of Canada for technical support and maintenance of security systems in federal prisons. On a call for tenders on renewal of the contract, Correctional Services required all tendering parties to submit a list of senior technicians and their qualifications.

---

36. Based in part on *Gilford Motors Co.* v. *Horne,* [1933] Ch. 935 (C.A.).

Marcodious did not have any employees of this nature, so Belding, one of Macrodious's two directors, approached a number of Condelle's employees. He was able to convince them to allow their names to be put on Marcodious's tender and to agree to come to work for Marcodious if it was successful in getting the contract with Correctional Services. As it turned out, Marcodious was successful even though its tender contained the same names as Condelle's tender.[37]

Does Condelle have a cause of action? On what basis? Against whom? What is the likely outcome?

7. Gallino Ltd. and MKX Ltd. were shareholders in a major Canadian steel company, Steel Inc. Gallino owned 55 percent of the shares and MKX owned the balance. Under a shareholder agreement, each shareholder had granted the other a right of first refusal should either wish to sell its shares.

Eventually Gallino decided to sell its shares, and MKX was interested in purchasing them. MKX made an offer, which Gallino considered to be inadequate. Gallino then entered into negotiations with a third party, Prendor Inc. It was agreed between them that Gallino would transfer its shares of Steel Inc. to one of its subsidiaries and that the shares would then be distributed to Gallino's own shareholders. Prendor would then make an offer to Gallino shareholders for the Steel Inc. shares.

Does MKX have any cause of action against Gallino? On what basis?

---

37. Based in part on *ADGA Systems International Ltd.* v. *Valcom Ltd.* (1999), 43 O.R. (3d) 101 (C.A.), leave to appeal to S.C.C. refused [1999] S.C.C.A. No. 124.

Part Five

Property

PROPERTY CONSISTS OF RIGHTS AND INTERESTS IN anything of value that can be owned. The law of property provides for the protection of those rights and interests.

Real property refers to land and anything attached to it. All other forms of property are included under the heading of personal property, which consists of tangible and intangible items. Tangible personal property has a physical substance from which it derives its value. Examples are trucks and appliances, which are sometimes called goods or chattels. Intangible personal property derives its value from legal rights rather than its physical form. Examples are the right to enforce a contract and copyright in a published work. A business is likely to own an interest in many different forms of property that are of crucial importance to its operation and value. An appreciation of the distinctions is useful for applying the different rules that govern ownership and possession of the various forms and for understanding the legal options for using property and generating value from it. As the economy becomes more knowledge based, there is growing emphasis on intellectual property and its value. The value of a business is increasingly found in the form of intangible property (especially intellectual property).

Chapter 17   Personal Property

▶ Chapter 17 provides an overview of personal property and focuses on the law of bailment, which governs situations where someone other than the owner has possession of personal property.

Chapter 18   Intellectual Property

▶ Chapter 18 deals with the most specialized and complicated form of personal property—intellectual property. It includes patents, confidential information, trade secrets, trademarks, industrial designs, and copyright. Many of these are governed by separate legislation, so the law is technical and complex.

Chapter 19   Real Property

▶ Chapter 19 explores the complex law of real property with its ancient origins. Sometimes called land law, it includes the various forms of ownership of land and its use. Of particular interest are the concepts of the mortgage and the lease. The mortgage is a vehicle for using land to secure credit. A lease enables a landowner to give up control of the land for a defined period.

Chapter 20   Insurance

▶ Chapter 20 presents a survey of the types of insurance and the relevant principles. It is included in Part 5 because a primary use of insurance is to provide protection against loss or damage to various forms of property. This chapter also discusses other types of insurance available for other aspects of the operation of a business.

Seventeen

Personal Property

Objectives

AFTER STUDYING THIS CHAPTER, YOU SHOULD HAVE AN UNDERSTANDING OF

► THE DIFFERENT FORMS OF PERSONAL PROPERTY
► HOW OWNERSHIP AND POSSESSION OF PERSONAL PROPERTY ARE ACQUIRED
► THE OBLIGATIONS AND RIGHTS ASSOCIATED WITH PERSONAL PROPERTY
► THE NATURE OF THE BAILMENT RELATIONSHIP
► VARIOUS TYPES OF BAILMENT FOR REWARD

Business Law in Practice

Safe With Us Ltd. (SWUL) operates a large warehouse facility in Moncton, New Brunswick, where it provides storage and safekeeping of customers' property. The customers are commercial enterprises and they store a wide variety of property with SWUL, including surplus equipment, inventory, and supplies.

SWUL owns the land on which the warehouse facility is located. Because storage requirements vary according to customer need, the warehouse contains extensive dividers, containers, and shelving. SWUL leases its delivery vehicles and forklifts from a local dealer. Other property owned by SWUL includes accounts receivable, bank accounts, and investments. Of considerable value is the goodwill associated with the SWUL business name, which has been recognized and respected in the community for 30 years.

1. What property does SWUL own?
2. What property does SWUL possess?
3. How did SWUL acquire these various forms of property?
4. Is SWUL responsible for damage to its customers' property?
5. How can SWUL collect from customers should they fail to pay their bills?
6. Who is responsible for the vehicles leased by SWUL?

Overview of Personal Property

Description

personal property
All property other than land.

tangible property
Personal property, the value of which comes from its physical form.

intangible property
Personal property, the value of which comes from legal rights.

Personal property includes everything except land and whatever is attached to land. Personal property falls into two major categories—tangible and intangible. **Tangible property** refers to property that is concrete or material and includes cars, furniture, office supplies, and anything of substance that is not attached to land or a building and is therefore portable. In law, these kinds of personal property are known as "chattels."

Intangible property derives its value from the legal rights it includes, rather than from its concrete, physical qualities. Examples of intangible property are insurance policies, accounts receivable, bank accounts, and goodwill, as well as the various forms of intellectual property. For example, the value of the fire insurance that SWUL may have on its warehouse is not based on the piece of paper itself, which describes the terms of the insurance coverage. Rather, the value inherent in the fire insurance is the *right* that the policy creates, namely, the right to be compensated in the event that a fire destroys the warehouse. Seen in this light, intangible property is no less real or significant than tangible property—in fact, it drives much of our modern economy.

There are two key aspects of involvement with personal property—ownership and possession. Quite often the two aspects reside in the same party. For example, SWUL owns *and* possesses the dividers and containers in its warehouse. However, it is also common for one person to be in *possession* of property *owned* by someone else. For example, SWUL is only in possession of its leased equipment—the equipment is owned by the dealer. Similarly, it is only in possession of its customers' property, which it holds for safekeeping in exchange for a fee. The property that SWUL stores is *owned* by SWUL customers, who are entitled to retrieve their property at any time.

Acquisition of Ownership

Ownership of property is acquired in a variety of ways:

- The ownership of goods is acquired by purchasing or manufacturing them.[1]
- Insurance coverage is bought by paying premiums and is described in the insurance policy, which gives the customer the right to recover losses in specified circumstances.[2]

---

1. See the sale of goods in Chapter 24. Ownership can also be created by gift or inheritance.
2. See Chapter 20.

- Accounts receivable are created by delivering goods or services to customers, who must make payment at a later date. The supplier acquires the right to collect the accounts, which can be sold to other businesses.[3]
- Certain kinds of intellectual property, such as copyright, are owned as a result of being created. Ownership of other forms—such as trademark—is established through simple use, or registration, or both. Intellectual property can also be bought from other owners.[4]

There is no comprehensive system of publicly registering title to personal property as there is with real property, although there are some specialized registries for items such as motor vehicles, patents, and trademarks. One reason for the difference concerns the mobility of personal property. There is little utility in having a provincial registration system for most personal property when goods are so easily transported to another province. In addition, the value of individual items of personal property may not justify the cost of administering a registration system or the cost to owners of registering.

Interests in chattels are registered, however, when that property is used as security in its purchase on credit or later as collateral for a loan. Registration is considered economical because it protects the creditor's rights to the pledged property.[5]

Acquisition without Ownership

When one party gains possession of the personal property of another with the intent that possession ultimately be returned to the owner, a relationship of bailment has been established. In short, bailment involves possession without ownership. In the SWUL scenario, there are examples of bailment, which are common in a business environment:

- SWUL has chosen to *lease* trucks and forklifts rather than buy them.
- SWUL's customers are using its facilities to *store* their property temporarily. There is no intention for SWUL to become the owner of the stored property.

What most often drives the temporary split of ownership and possession that a bailment creates is that it meets the business needs of both parties in each situation. For instance, by leasing, SWUL gets the benefit of using vehicles and equipment without a large capital outlay. By storing equipment with SWUL, customers get the benefit of a valuable service without having to purchase or lease a building themselves for that purpose.

Obligations Arising from Ownership and Possession

The law of bailment related to leases provides that the lessee of property—the party in possession—must take reasonable care of it and pay the charges for use of the property. Similarly, when the bailee of property is providing a service to the owner, such as storage or repair, the service must be performed as agreed and reasonable care must be taken of the property until it is returned to the owner. This requirement to take reasonable care applies whether the arrangement is contractual or not:

- SWUL, the lessee, must take good care of the leased equipment.
- SWUL, the bailee, must return its customers' property in the same basic condition it was delivered in.

---

3. Known as assignments of contractual rights (see Chapter 9).
4. See Chapter 18.
5. This system of registration is governed by legislation in each province and is discussed in Chapter 27.

If the chattels in SWUL's possession have been lost, damaged, mishandled, dropped, or exposed to water, smoke, fire, or any number of other hazards, then SWUL is in breach of its promise to take reasonable care. It will have to pay damages to the owners by way of compensation. Damages will be awarded in the amount necessary to restore the customer to the position it would have been in had the contract been properly performed.

The owner of personal property is the one who ordinarily bears the risk of loss from its damage or destruction. This risk may cause the owner to take steps to shift the risk to another business by such means as an insurance contract. When such a contract is in place, the insurance company agrees to reimburse the insured for its loss in return for payment of premiums.

In bailment situations, the question of *who* will purchase insurance should be addressed, since there is no utility in *both* the bailor *and* bailee insuring the same property. For example, SWUL and its customers should agree on which of them is responsible if a customer's property is damaged or lost while in SWUL's facilities. Whoever bears the risk of loss should place the insurance policy and keep it in good standing by paying the premiums. In the same manner, the lease agreement between SWUL and the equipment dealer should specify who is responsible for damage to or malfunction of the vehicles. That party, in turn, should insure the property.

Rights Arising from Ownership and Possession

The owner of property who is also in possession is entitled to deal with it essentially as she sees fit. Her options include these:

- selling the property and transferring ownership and possession to the buyer
- leasing the property to another business with the intent of regaining possession or selling it when the lease expires
- using the property as security for a loan, thereby giving the lender the right to seize or sell the property if the borrower defaults on the loan
- transferring possession to another business for storage, repair, or transport with the corresponding right to regain possession

The possessor of property has the right to keep the property for the period of time provided for in the agreement with the property's owner. For example, SWUL has possession of the trucks and forklifts for the duration of time set forth in the lease document. In terms of storage of customers' property, SWUL has the right to be paid the agreed storage charges and generally is not required to relinquish possession until those charges are paid.

Principles of Bailment

Overview

A **bailment** is a *temporary* transfer of possession of personal property from the owner, known as a **bailor**, to another party, known as a **bailee**. Ownership remains with the bailor. Possession, however, is transferred to the bailee. This is what distinguishes bailment from a contract of purchase and sale.

---

bailment
Temporary transfer of possession of personal property.

bailor
The owner of property in a bailment.

bailee
The person who gains possession in a bailment.

There are many examples of bailment in commercial transactions, including the following:

- the short-term rental of a vehicle[6]
- the long-term lease of a vehicle (e.g., SWUL's leases of trucks and forklifts)
- the delivery of property for repair
- the transport of property by a commercial carrier
- the storage of property in a warehouse (i.e., the main business of SWUL)
- the shipping of an envelope by courier

Bailments are also common in the consumer context, as shown in these examples:

- renting videos
- leaving clothing at the dry-cleaning shop
- depositing cars at a garage for servicing
- storing furniture
- borrowing library books

Any transaction that meets the definition of bailment—whether commercial, consumer, or simply personal—is covered by the general discussion in this section. For purposes of identifying the rights and obligations of bailments and better understanding their variations, bailments can be classified in a number of different ways:

Is Payment Involved?

From this perspective, there are two kinds of bailments:

- Most commercial bailments are based on a contract requiring payment for the use of the property or as compensation for storage or another service provided. These are known as **bailments for value**.
- Possession of property may also be transferred without payment by virtue of a loan or a free service. This would occur when, for example, a prospective buyer tries out a vehicle for a few days or someone parks his car in his neighbour's garage for the winter. Because there is no compensation involved in such arrangements, such instances are known as **gratuitous bailment** in the sense of being free or "without reward." The prospective car buyer is a gratuitous bailee because he is not required to pay for use of the vehicle. The person who temporarily stores his neighbour's car is not being paid for the service and is therefore also a gratuitous bailee.

For Whose Benefit Is the Bailment?

From this perspective, there are three kinds of bailment.

- *Gratuitous bailments that benefit the bailor.* This kind of bailment is involved when someone stores his car in his neighbour's garage for the winter, for example. The bailee—the person who owns the garage—derives no advantage from the relationship, while the bailor—the person who owns the car—can now protect his vehicle from harsh weather. It is the bailor, therefore, who gains from the bailment.

bailment for value
Bailment involving payment for use or a service.

gratuitous bailment
Bailment that involves no payment.

---

6. See *Tilden Rent-A-Car Co.* v. *Clendenning* (1978), 83 D.L.R. (3d) 400 (Ont. C.A.) in Chapter 7 and the car rental agreement in Chapter 5.

- *Gratuitous bailments that benefit the bailee.* This kind of bailment arises when, for example, a person borrows his neighbour's lawnmower. The owner of the lawnmower—the bailor—is simply doing a favour and does not derive any tangible benefit from the bailment. The borrower—the bailee—can now cut his grass without having to buy or lease a lawnmower from someone else and is therefore the party who profits from the relationship.
- *Bailments that benefit both the bailor and the bailee.* This kind of bailment is most common in the commercial world and usually involves bailments for value—that is, bailments in which one of the parties is paid for the provision of a service or other benefit. For example, the owner of the vehicles and forklifts leased by SWUL benefits from the relationship since it is paid by SWUL. SWUL also benefits since it gains possession of delivery vehicles and forklifts. Similarly, SWUL benefits from storing the property of its customers since it is paid to provide the service. SWUL's customers benefit because their property is stored and protected by SWUL. There can also be gratuitous bailments that benefit both bailor and bailee, though these are less common in the business world. An example would be a car dealership relinquishing possession of a luxury vehicle so that a serious potential buyer can test it out for a few days. The car dealership benefits since allowing the bailment may close the sale. The customer benefits since he gets to drive a nice car for a few days and gets an enhanced opportunity to make an informed consumer choice. The question of who benefits from a gratuitous bailment is particularly important, since the answer helps later in the chapter to determine the bailee's responsibility for the property.

What Is the Object of the Transaction?

From this perspective, a bailment would be described in relation to its key focus, such as storage, repair, transport, or temporary use. This classification is important because of the special rules that apply to these types of bailment.

The Contract of Bailment

In bailments for value, the contract between the bailor and the bailee is central. The parties are free to negotiate the details of their own agreement. Their contract will normally include a description of these aspects:

- the services to be provided by the bailee
- the bailor's price and payment requirements
- the extent to which the bailee is liable for damage or loss
- the remedies of the parties for failure to perform

In a storage contract, for example, the focus is on the bailee's liability for loss to the chattels in question and the bailee's remedies for collecting storage charges. Because a warehouse operator deals with the property of many customers in similar circumstances and is under pressure to keep prices competitive, a business such as SWUL is likely to have a standard form agreement that all customers are expected to sign. The main object from SWUL's perspective is to minimize its responsibility for damage caused to property in its possession in order to keep costs down. At the same time, it is important for SWUL to maintain a reputation in the industry. Limiting liability through standard form agreements is common in the storage industry, as in the following clause:

(a) The responsibility of a warehouseman in the absence of written provisions is the reasonable care and diligence required by the law.

(b) The warehouseman's liability on any one package is limited to $40 unless the holder has declared in writing a valuation in excess of $40 and paid the additional charge specified to cover warehouse liability.[7]

While clause (b) may seem unfair—after all, if the warehouseman's negligence causes more than $40 in damage, should it not have to pay the full tab?—its function is to signal which party should buy insurance on the item being stored, the bailor or the bailee. In this case, the onus is on the bailor (as the owner who is limited to a claim for $40) to purchase insurance, since the item being stored is likely worth much more than that amount.

The other focus of a bailment contract is on the remedies that the bailee can use to obtain payment from delinquent customers. For example, the contract may provide that SWUL is entitled to retain possession of the chattel until payment is received and may also give SWUL the right to sell the chattel, after the passage of a prescribed period of time, in order to apply the proceeds to the outstanding account. Of course, SWUL's prime interest is timely payment from customers. It is only interested in the right to keep customers' property as a backup remedy.

The terms of SWUL's bailment agreement for the leasing of vehicles are likely to be written by the owner of the vehicles, called the "lessor," who is interested in protecting its property while that property is in SWUL's possession. This is accomplished by inserting a clause in the contract making SWUL responsible for any damage and by imposing limits on the extent to which SWUL can use the vehicles (such as distance for the trucks and time for the forklifts). Again, insurance should be purchased to cover loss or damage, in this case by SWUL. The owner of the vehicles should consider making it a term of the contract that it be named in the insurance policy as the party who is paid in event of loss.

Who is responsible for property damaged during delivery? Who is responsible for damage to a leased truck?

Liability of Bailees

Liability issues arise when some mishap occurs in relation to the property while it is in the possession of the bailee.[8] For example, the property of SWUL's customers might be lost, damaged, or even destroyed while in SWUL's warehouse; employees

7. *London Drugs Limited* v. *Kuehne & Nagel International Ltd.* (1992), 97 D.L.R. (4th) 261 (S.C.C.).
8. The work of Professor Moe Litman of the Faculty of Law, University of Alberta, in this section is gratefully acknowledged.

might drop valuable equipment while moving it around; a forklift might run into items in its path; property could be stolen from the warehouse; there might be damage from water or a fire in the warehouse; if the property is perishable, it could spoil if not properly stored or if kept too long.[9]

Ideally, the contract between SWUL and its customers will specify the extent of SWUL's liability for these events. SWUL is likely to place significant limits on its legal liability through exclusion or limitation of liability clauses. If there is no formal agreement, the common-law rules of bailment will apply.

The obligations of bailees to care for the goods of their bailors have evolved through three distinct stages. Initially, bailees were 100 percent liable for the return of bailed chattels as well as for any damage, whether the bailee was responsible for the damage or not and even where the bailee exercised reasonable or even extreme diligence. Currently, there are remnants of this strict regime. Common carriers such as railways, as well as innkeepers, are caught by this old law; however, statutes have lessened and in some instances displaced the strict obligations of the early common law.

In the second stage of development, the burden of the bailee to care for the goods of the bailor was determined by the concept of "benefit of the relationship." If a bailment benefited the bailor exclusively, the bailee was required to exercise slight care and was therefore liable for "gross neglect." If the bailment benefited the bailee exclusively, the bailee was required to exercise great care and was liable for "slight negligence." If there was reciprocal benefit, the bailee was required to exercise ordinary diligence and was liable for "ordinary neglect."

Today, bailees are expected to exercise reasonable care in all the circumstances. Their standard falls somewhere on a spectrum, as illustrated in Figure 17.1.

Figure 17.1

SPECTRUM OF A BAILEE'S LIABILITY

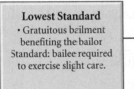

Lowest Standard	**Middle Standard**	**Highest Standard**
• Gratuitous bailment benefiting the bailor Standard: bailee required to exercise slight care.	• Both bailor and bailee benefit Standard: bailee required to exercise ordinary diligence.	• Gratuitous bailment benefiting the bailee • Common carriers • Innkeepers standard Standard: bailee to exercise great care.

The factors that determine the standard include the following:

- *Who benefits from the bailment.* If the bailment is gratuitous and for the benefit of the bailor, the standard is very low. If the bailment is gratuitous and for the benefit of the bailee, the standard is very high.
- *The nature and value of the property.* The bailee's standard is higher for more valuable property and should be appropriate for the type of property. This means that the bailee must show greater care when storing perishables as opposed to commodities like wood products.
- *Whether payment is involved.* A bailee for reward must show ordinary care and diligence.

---

9. Note that employers who are bailees are vicariously liable for the acts of their employees.

- *The terms of the contract.* The contract may raise or lower the standard of care owed by the bailee.
- *The limits on liability.* The contract may set the standard at ordinary care and diligence but limit the amount of damages for which the bailee may be held liable.
- *Special regulations for the type of bailment that may set out the standard of care.* Contracts to transport goods, for example, are subject to standard statutory terms.
- *Special circumstances in the transaction.* Where the bailee is instructed by the bailor as to the value of the goods or special storage requirements, for example, this increases the standard of care that the bailee must meet.
- *The expertise of the bailee.* A bailee who specializes in a certain type of bailment (such as storage) is expected to take greater care than an ordinary person.

Bailees may not escape their responsibilities by turning over a bailed chattel to employees. If the chattel is damaged, lost, or stolen as a result of employees' negligence, the employer as bailee is vicariously liable so long as the employees were acting within the scope of their employment, that is, the employees were engaged in an activity that was reasonably incidental to the discharge of their employment duties. In addition, bailees are liable for the intentional wrongdoing of their employees. A bailee who entrusts bailed goods to an employee is personally (not vicariously) liable for the theft of the goods by the employee. Another basis of liability of a bailee for theft by an employee is the law of negligence. The employer has a duty to hire honest, responsible people. Accordingly, failure to engage in proper hiring practices may result in liability for the employer.

Liability of Bailors

In contractual bailments, bailors warrant that the goods used by their bailees are fit for the purpose for which they were bailed.[10] If the goods are unfit and a bailee is injured while using a bailed chattel, the bailor may be liable. For example, if a SWUL employee is hurt when the wheel falls off the forklift she is operating, the lessor will face liability.[11] This high obligation on the bailor can be reduced in the contract between the parties, however. In any event, insurance is likely to be in place to take care of the loss.

The standard of care of a bailor in a gratuitous bailment focuses on personal misconduct. Gratuitous bailors must exercise reasonable care to ensure that they are aware of defects and must inform their bailees of the existence of such defects.

Remedies

Remedies for failure to perform obligations arising in a bailment relationship arise in two contexts:

- They arise when a bailee is attempting to recover a fee for services performed in relation to the property.

---

10. The work of Professor Moe Litman of the Faculty of Law, University of Alberta, in this section is gratefully acknowledged.

11. In *Matheson* v. *Watt* (1956), 19 W.W.R. (N.S.) 425 (B.C.C.A.), the owner of a roller-skating rink was held liable for injuries sustained by the plaintiff when a wheel came off the roller skate the plaintiff had leased from the rink. In this type of litigation, if a bailee establishes that goods were used in a reasonable manner, the onus then shifts to the bailor to prove that the defect could not have been prevented by reasonable care and skill *from anyone* in the distribution chain, beginning at the manufacturer and ending at the bailor. It is only when the defect is one that no one in this chain could reasonably have foreseen (a "latent defect") that the bailor escapes liability for injury to the bailee. From the perspective of a bailor, this warranty is extremely burdensome.

- They arise when a bailor is trying to recover for damage done to the property while it is in the bailee's possession. This, in turn, usually involves two issues: first, has the bailee met the relevant standard of care, and second, does the agreement cancel or limit the bailee's liability?

Case

Punch v. *Savoy's Jewellers Ltd.* (1986), 33 B.L.R. 147 (Ont. C.A.)

The Business Context: This case explores a claim for lost property in a bailment, as well as the complications that result when property is handled by several businesses acting as bailees in the course of a transaction.

Factual Background: Punch owned a diamond ring for which the appraised value was $11 000. She took it to Savoy's in Sault Ste. Marie for repairs. Savoy's mailed it to Walker's in Toronto to have the repairs done. Savoy's followed normal practice by using registered mail and listing the value for insurance purposes as $100. By the time Walker's had completed the repairs, a postal strike was on. Walker's decided to use CN Rapidex (a courier service) to return the ring to Savoy's. CN's standard clause limited liability to $50 or the declared value if higher. Walker's declared the value to be $100. The ring was never delivered, and there seemed a strong possibility it had been stolen by the CN driver. There was no evidence to indicate that anything other than theft accounted for the loss of the ring. Punch claimed compensation from Savoy's, Walker's, and CN. CN attempted to limit its liability to $100.

The Legal Questions: What duties did the three defendants owe to Punch? Did they perform their obligations to Punch? What protection did CN's limitation clause provide to the three defendants?

Resolution: Justice Cory summarized his ruling as follows:

> Both Savoy and Walker are liable to Lenore Punch for breach of their duty as bailees.

They breached this duty by failing to obtain instructions from the owner as to the means of carriage in light of the postal strike; by failure to give a proper evaluation of the ring to the carrier; and by failure to stipulate as a term of the carriage insurance coverage for the true value of the ring itself. CN also is liable to the owner for the unexplained loss of the ring. Savoy and Walker are to be indemnified by CN for any loss which they must make good to the owner.

The standard of care to which all the defendants were held as bailees for value was to "exercise due care for the safety of the article entrusted to [them] by taking such care of the goods as would a prudent man of his own possessions." Their actions were evaluated according to what someone in Punch's situation as owner would have done.

In terms of the CN limitation clause, Punch knew nothing about CN or the clause, so she was not affected by it. Savoy's knew that CN was being engaged by Walker's, but knew nothing of the terms of engagement. It was not limited by the terms of the agreement. Even Walker's, which made the contract with CN, was not bound because the clause did not specifically cover theft and because the totally unexplained failure of CN to deliver the ring was judged to be a fundamental breach that undermined CN's attempt to limit its liability.

Critical Analysis: Should owners like Punch or bailees like Savoy's or Walker's be able to routinely declare a nominal value for property being shipped and later expect to be fully compensated by a business like CN? Should a business such as Savoy's, acting as bailee, send valuable property to another bailee without the consent of the owner?

Bailees' Ability to Limit Their Obligations

The issues in a dispute about damage to property in a bailment are the standard of care and the clauses in the contract that limit damages. The standard of care depends on the particular circumstances. Limits on damages depend on the language in the contract and on the extent to which the bailor is affected by those limits. The resolution of both issues can be complicated and difficult to predict.

In the United Kingdom, a statute regulates limitations.[12] For example, bailees in rental agreements cannot exclude or restrict liability for failure of the goods to correspond with their description or in respect to their quality or fitness for a particular purpose.[13] If SWUL leased forklifts to move heavy pallets and they were inadequate to the task, under this legislation the lessor would be responsible even if the contract said the opposite. Other terms limiting or excluding liability must be reasonable.[14] If SWUL were responsible to pay the full rental even if the equipment completely failed to function, such a clause in the contract would be unenforceable because of the requirement of reasonableness.

ETHICAL CONSIDERATIONS

Critical Analysis: Should bailment contracts in Canada be regulated so that the standard of care and the substance and form of limitations are defined by statute? Should there be different rules for consumer and commercial transactions? Would a clause limiting damages to $40 be considered reasonable?

Types of Bailment for Reward

The Lease

There are important legal distinctions between *buying* and *leasing* property. The most obvious one is that a lessee of property is not the owner and has possession subject to any limitations in the lease. In addition, because a lease is not a sale, it is not covered by the large number of terms implied through legislation governing the sale of goods.[15] There is an implied term that leased property will be reasonably fit for its intended use. For example, it would be implied that the forklifts leased by SWUL are suitable for the tasks normally performed with forklifts. The lessee must take reasonable care of the property while that property is in its possession and return it in the state that would be expected, subject to the normal wear and tear involved in its use. Of course, it is more prudent to address these issues of suitability, quality, and responsibility expressly in the lease agreement.

There is no legislation dealing specifically with **chattel leases**, so the rules come mainly from the general law of contract. The parties negotiate their own agreement as they see fit, subject to the few terms implied by the common law. These are some of the issues addressed in a typical lease:

chattel lease
A contract where a lessee pays for the use of a lessor's personal property.

---

12. *Unfair Contract Terms Act,* 1977, c. 50.
13. *Ibid.* at s. 1(3).
14. *Ibid.* at s. 3.
15. See Chapter 24.

- the risk that the lessee will remove the property from the district or province
- limits on the use of the property by the lessee in terms of the type and extent of work done with the equipment
- suitability of the equipment for its intended or typical uses
- responsibility for maintenance
- responsibility for damage
- state in which the property must be returned at the end of the lease
- period of time for which the lease runs
- amount and schedule of payments
- termination of the lease
- remedies for breach by either party

operating lease
A lease where the property is returned to the lessor when the term is up.

The short-term lease or rental of property is an attractive way for a business to acquire the use of equipment for a particular task or period of time. It makes little sense to purchase something that is not needed for a long period, unless, of course, the rental charges approach the cost of buying. At the end of a short-term rental, the property is returned to the owner (the lessor). This is known as an **operating lease**. Examples of this type of lease are the crane rental, which was the subject of the *D.J. Lowe* case,[16] and the car rental agreement discussed in Chapter 5. Lowe only needed the crane for a few days. A customer normally rents a car for a short time, such as a day, a weekend, or a week.

Leasing is also a means to acquire property needed on a permanent basis and is an alternative to purchasing. For example, the trucks and forklifts leased by SWUL are needed as part of the ongoing operation, and SWUL has made the financial decision to lease rather than buy. The lease is a means of financing SWUL's acquisition of the equipment, through payment of rent over a defined period of time. SWUL may lease the equipment directly from the dealer, in which case the dealer remains the owner and the lessor. In a more complicated version of the transaction, the dealer sells the equipment to a financial company, who in turn leases it to SWUL. Both variations are known as **financing leases**, but they involve quite different rights and obligations. A feature of both is the possibility that SWUL may buy the equipment at the end of the lease, rather than return it to the lessor.

financing lease
A lease that enables the lessee to finance the acquisition of personal property.

The contractual arrangements are more complicated if the lessor is a financial business rather than the original owner. In such a transaction there are two contracts—one of sale between the dealer and the financier, and the other the lease between the financier and the lessee. The difficulty for the lessee is that the dealer is not a party to the lease and therefore has no rights or obligations connected with it. The only parties to the contract for the purchase of the car are the dealer and the financier. If the lessee has relied on statements or assurances from the dealer in deciding to lease the property from the financier, it is difficult to hold the financier responsible for those statements.

SWUL should know who the lessor is and ensure that the lease adequately protects it if the arrangement fails to go as planned. For example, SWUL should ensure that its obligation to make payments is tied to the suitability and performance of the equipment. This will be the case if SWUL is leasing from the dealer, but likely will not be the case if the other party to the lease is a finance company, because the lease will likely protect the financier from the normal rights of the buyer in a sale. Each type of transaction involves different risks to be managed.

---

16. *Lowe (D...) (1980) Ltd.* v. *Upper Clements Family Theme Park Ltd.* (1990), 95 N.S.R. (2d) 397 (S.C.T.D.).

Figure 17.2

FORMS OF A CHATTEL LEASE

A. Two-party leasing arrangement

Result: One contract—SWUL has remedies against the dealer for problems with the property.

B. Three-party leasing arrangement

Result: Two contracts—dealer sells to financier, who leases to SWUL. SWUL has no contract with the dealer.

Storage

This type of bailment forms the core of SWUL's business—storage of customers' property. Customers entrust their property to SWUL and have limited means for monitoring SWUL's treatment of their property. As a result, the law imposes a high level of accountability on SWUL for the treatment of customers' property. SWUL's standard of care is toward the high end of the spectrum. Of particular importance are any limits on what SWUL can do with the property in terms of the type of storage or the possibility of moving it to other locations. For example, SWUL must keep items that would be harmed by cold temperatures in adequately heated space. SWUL may need permission from customers to store property in any facilities other than its own. Customers expect their property to be returned in the same condition in which it was delivered, unlike in the case of SWUL's leased vehicles, where the intent is for SWUL to use them. If the property is lost, damaged, or destroyed, customers will look to SWUL for compensation. The main concern from SWUL's perspective is payment of the storage fees by customers and its ability to collect.

SWUL's general responsibility toward its customers' property is to treat it as a "skilled storekeeper" would deal with its own property.[17] This imposes a standard of reasonableness that includes responsibility for all foreseeable risks. Because the standard is high and the potential losses are high, SWUL is likely to limit its liability to its customers in its standard form agreements with them. A typical limitation clause is the one shown on page 372, where the contract limits the bailee's liability to $40.

warehouseman
A bailee who stores personal property.

The remedies of a storage bailee, known as a **warehouseman**, are contained in legislation in each province.[18] The bailee has a lien over the property until the owner pays the storage fees. This means that SWUL can keep its customers' property until payment is complete. If payment is not forthcoming, SWUL also has the right to sell the property in a public auction and apply the proceeds to the outstanding charges. Any surplus proceeds of the sale go to the owner. The legislation contains safeguards for the owner in that notice of the intended sale must be given and the bailee must deal with the property in a reasonable manner—for example, not sell valuable property for the amount of a relatively small storage bill.

17. See *Punch* v. *Savoy's* on page 375.
18. See, for example, *Warehouse Lien Act,* R.S.B.C. 1996, c. 480; *Warehouser's Lien Act,* R.S.N. 1990, c. C-2; *Repair and Storage Liens Act,* R.S.O. 1009, c. R-25.

These rights and responsibilities relating to a storage bailment apply only if the arrangement meets the definition of a bailment—there must be a transfer of possession and control from the owner to another person. Otherwise the responsibility for the property is much less and the remedies for collection are less effective. For example, leaving a vehicle in a parking lot and paying a parking fee does not amount to a bailment unless the keys are delivered to an attendant, thereby transferring control of the vehicle. If the owner keeps the keys, the parking lot is not in control of the vehicle and the transaction is likely one for the use of the parking space, with minimal responsibility for what is in the space.[19] Operators of parking space commonly issue tickets that are meant to define the relationship (use of space rather than bailment) and either exclude liability completely or limit it to a small amount. As with any standard form contract, the customer must receive adequate notice of onerous and unexpected terms.

Repairs

When the owner of property takes it to a repair shop, the main purpose of the transaction is the repairs. If the property is left at the shop, then a storage bailment, which is incidental to the main purpose of the arrangement, is also created. At the appointed time for pickup, the owner—the bailor—expects to receive the property in a good state of repair and otherwise in the condition in which it was delivered. The bailee must provide reasonable safekeeping for the property and complete the repairs in a workmanlike manner, as a reasonably competent repairer of that sort of property would.

From a business perspective, it makes sense to agree on a price in advance, but if the parties do not agree on the price for storage and repairs at the outset, the repairer's compensation will be a reasonable amount for the service provided. The repairer cannot charge more than is reasonable, nor can the owner refuse to pay anything, just because no price was agreed in advance. An example of a repair bailment and the complications that can arise is found in *Punch* v. *Savoy's,* which is discussed on page 375.

lien
The right to retain possession of personal property until payment for service is received.

Most provinces have legislation[20] giving the bailee a **lien** against the property for the value of the repairs as long as the bailee has possession of the property. As with the storage situation, the bailee also has the right to sell the property (subject to procedural requirements) to recover the repair charges.

Transportation

carrier
A bailee who transports personal property.

Bailees who receive property and transport it according to the owner's instructions are called **carriers.** There are several categories of carriers, each with different obligations toward the property. The most relevant in business are common carriers—those who represent themselves to the public as carriers for reward, meaning they are prepared to transport any property for any owner so long as their facilities permit and they are paid for the service. Common carriers are held to a very high standard of care regarding the property they carry. They are described as being "insurers" of the property, not in the formal sense of an insurance policy but in the sense that if property is lost or damaged while in their possession, it is presumed that the carrier is liable. The owner is not required to prove fault by the carrier, mainly because it is difficult for the owner to know what happened to the property during the transport.

---

19. Bruce H. Z ff, *Principles of Property Law* (Scarborough: Carswell, 1996) at 279.
20. See, for example, *Mechanics Lien Act,* R.S.N. 1990, c. M-3, R.S.N.S. 1989, c. 277; *Repairers' Lien Act,* R.S.B.C. 1996, c 404; *Repair and Storage Liens Act,* R.S.O. 1990, c. R-25.

It is more practical for the carrier to account for the treatment of the property. Therefore, carriers have very limited legal defences, which mainly relate to circumstances within the control of the owner or beyond the control of the carrier. For example, if the owner fails to pack fragile goods adequately or the goods are destroyed in a natural disaster, the carrier could be excused from liability.

As a result of this heavy responsibility based on legislation and the common law, carriers normally include provisions in their standard form agreements with customers that the carriers' liability will be severely limited should mishap occur with the property. These clauses typically limit liability to a low dollar amount. Customers are protected by legislation covering each form of transport—rail, road, sea, and air. Clauses used in contracts on international or interprovincial routes must be approved by the Canadian Transport Commission.

Case

Carling O'Keefe Breweries of Canada Ltd. v. *CN Marine Inc.* (1989), 104 N.R. 166 (F.C.A.)

The Business Context: Deciding who is responsible for damaged goods and for how much requires a full investigation of the events that occurred and a detailed examination of the terms of the contract, any legislation, and applicable international rules.

Factual Background: Carling engaged CN to ship 4240 cases of beer from St. John's to Goose Bay. CN arranged shipping aboard a ship owned by Labrador Shipping. The beer was placed in three large containers and stowed on the deck of the ship with the edges of the containers protruding over the sides of the ship. The containers were washed overboard in heavy seas. Carling claimed the value of the beer ($32 000) from CN and the owners of the ship. At trial, Carling was successful. The ship was later lost at sea and the shipowners became insolvent, meaning that they would have difficulty paying a judgment. CN appealed on the basis that it was acting only as agent for the shipowners and therefore had no liability, and that in any event its liability should be limited to $500 per container (a total of $1500) by virtue of the federal legislation.

The Legal Question: Did the contract relieve CN from liability as carrier and limit damages to $500 for each container? Did the $500 limit apply to each of the large shipping containers or to each of the 4240 cases of beer?

Resolution: The contract and the bill of lading were governed by federal legislation (the *Carriage of Goods by Water Act*), which incorporated the Hague Rules (an international convention providing for standardized terms in such transactions). The Hague Rules prevented a carrier from avoiding liability for improper storage of goods but also limited claims to $500 "per package." The appeal court confirmed the ruling of the trial judge on both questions. CN was the carrier because it had signed the contract in its personal capacity (becoming a "carrier" as defined in the Hague Rules) and because it had acted as a carrier in the loading and stowage of the cargo on board the vessel.

The Hague Rules prevented CN as carrier from avoiding liability for improper stowage (deemed to be the main cause of the loss). In terms of the number of "packages" on which Carling O'Keefe could recover up to $500, the court looked to the intention of the parties as revealed by the language of the documents, what they said, and what they did. The shipping documents listed 4240 packages. It was also noted that "it is common knowledge that beer is shipped in cases." On this basis, Carling recovered its full loss from CN.

Critical Analysis: Does it make sense to subject a domestic contract such as this one to a set of international rules? Should a carrier be able to avoid liability for careless stowage of goods? How could CN have limited its liability to $1500 instead of $32 000? Where would that leave Carling?

Transportation of goods involves many parties, contracts, and risks.

Carriers do not have the same legislative remedies as those who repair or store property. Carriers have a common-law lien against the property for transport charges, but enjoy no corresponding right to sell the property if the owner fails to pay.

Lodging

Those who offer meals and rooms to the public are known as "innkeepers." At common law, their responsibility for guests' property is similar to that of common carriers. They must take great care of guests' property and are virtual insurers for loss or theft of guests' property. There is an important practical distinction in the degree of control between carriers and innkeepers. Carriers have total control of the property when it is delivered for shipment, while guests share control over their property through their occupation of rooms.

Innkeepers are permitted by legislation[21] to limit their liability to a specific amount ($40 to $150, depending on the province) if they post the legislated limits in the rooms of the establishment. Their protection is lost if the loss to property is due to a negligent or deliberate act of the innkeeper (or the inn's employees) or if the property has been deposited with the inn for safekeeping.

Figure 17.3

SUMMARY OF BAILMENT

Type of bailment	Lease	Storage	Repair	Transport	Lodging
Specialized designation for the bailor	Lessor	Customer	Customer	Shipper	Guest
Specialized designation for the bailee	Lessee	Warehouse	Repairer	Carrier	Innkeeper
Bailee's standard of care	Reasonable	Reasonable	Reasonable	High	High
Liability normally limited	Wear and tear	Contract	Contract	Contract	Legislation
Who gets paid for a service	Bailor	Bailee	Bailee	Bailee	Bailee
Remedies for nonpayment	Possession, damages	Lien, sale	Lien, sale	Lien	Lien
Applicable legislation?	No	Yes	Yes	No	Yes

21. See, for example, *Innkeepers' Act*, R.S.O. 1990, c. I-7, R.S.N.S. 1989, c. 229; *Hotel Keepers Act*, R.S.M. 1987, c. H-150.

Business Law in Practice Revisited

1. What types of property does SWUL possess?

SWUL possesses real property (land, buildings, and whatever is attached to them), tangible personal property (shelving, dividers, vehicles, customers' property), and intangible personal property (goodwill, accounts receivable).

2. Which of these does SWUL own?

SWUL owns everything except the vehicles and customers' property.

3. How did SWUL acquire these various forms of property?

SWUL acquired its property by purchase (land, warehouse furnishings), lease (vehicles), bailment (customers' property), creation and use (business name), and dealing with customers (accounts receivable).

4. Is SWUL responsible for damage to its customers' property?

SWUL has a duty to treat customers' property as a reasonably competent warehouse proprietor would treat its own property, subject to the protection for SWUL contained in its standard form customer contracts. This protection will relate to SWUL's conduct and its level of liability in dollar terms.

5. What remedies can SWUL use to collect from customers?

SWUL has the right (according to legislation) to hold customers' property until they pay the agreed storage fees. If customers don't pay, SWUL can sell their property at public auction to recover the outstanding fees.

6. Who is responsible for the vehicles leased by SWUL?

SWUL must take reasonable care of the leased vehicles subject to normal wear and tear. The leases will likely set out SWUL's obligations in considerable detail.

Chapter Summary

There are two categories of personal property: tangible, which includes goods or chattels, and intangible, which includes various contractual and statutory rights.

Ownership is acquired by purchase or manufacture (goods), creation and registration or purchase (intellectual property), or trading (accounts receivable). Possession can be acquired along with ownership or through a bailment.

The owner of property has full responsibility for it and bears the risk of loss. The owner also has the right to deal with the property in whatever way he chooses.

A bailment is the temporary transfer of possession with no change in ownership. A commercial bailment (bailment for value) benefits both the bailor (owner) and bailee (possessor). Key issues in bailment are the standard of care that the bailee must observe in relation to the property and the remedies that the parties have for recovering fees. Standard form contracts are a common feature of bailments.

The most common types of bailments are leasing, storage, repairs, transportation, and lodging. Each has somewhat different rules for liability and remedies.

Study Chapter

Key Terms and Concepts

bailee (p. 369)
bailment (p. 369)
bailment for value (p. 370)
bailor (p. 369)
carrier (p. 379)
chattel lease (p. 376)
financing lease (p. 377)
gratuitous bailment (p. 370)
intangible property (p. 367)
lien (p. 379)
operating lease (p. 377)
personal property (p. 367)
tangible property (p. 367)
warehouseman (p. 378)

Questions for Review

1. How is personal property different from real property?
2. How is tangible property different from intangible property?
3. How can the owner and possessor of personal property be different people?
4. Who bears the risk of loss to personal property?
5. How is ownership of personal property acquired?
6. What can the owner of personal property do with it?
7. What is a bailment?
8. What are some examples of bailments?
9. How can a bailee for value collect fees?

10. What is the liability of a bailee for damage to the goods?

11. How can a bailee limit the liability for damage to the goods?

12. What are two legal issues arising from chattel leases?

Questions for Discussion

1. Personal property in the form of chattels is portable. Intangible personal property consists of legal rights. What legal challenges do these forms of property entail?

2. How should a business assess its risk in relation to personal property?

3. How can a business deal with risk to its personal property?

4. The standard of care in a bailment depends on the particular circumstances. Is there an easier way to set the standard?

5. What issues should a bailment agreement address? What factors should be considered?

6. Should a bailee always try to minimize its liability in a standard form contract?

Situations for Discussion

1. ABC has a large fleet of company cars. The entire fleet is aging and needs replacement in the next couple of years. ABC has a long-standing relationship with a local dealer and has purchased vehicles there for many years. Clancy, the acquisitions manager of ABC, is considering the possibility of leasing rather than buying the new vehicles. One factor Clancy must consider is pressure on ABC's cash flow. Apart from the financial considerations, what legal issues should ABC take into account? Is Clancy in the best position to evaluate these legal issues? Who should he consult?

2. Clancy is the acquisitions manager of ABC. He has an appointment at a local car dealer to explore the possibility of leasing some vehicles for ABC. Clancy parks his company car at the rear of the dealer's showroom and leaves his laptop computer in the back seat. When he returns to get his vehicle about an hour later, it is gone (and his computer with it). How should Clancy, ABC, and the car dealer handle this situation? What are the key legal issues?

3. Young leased a machine to haul large logs in her lumbering business. The lease required Young to keep the machine in good repair and fully insured, and to return it at the end of the lease in its original condition, subject to "normal wear and tear." The machine never worked very well. Young ran up large repair bills and began to suspect the machine was not heavy enough for the needs of her business. When she contacted the leasing company, she was informed that she was responsible for all of her problems. Young is thinking about stopping her lease payments and insurance premiums and leasing a better machine from another dealer. She needs that better machine to maintain profitable levels of

production. What factors should she consider? What would you advise her to do?

4. Young took her logging machine in for repairs. A week later she got a call from the shop to tell her that the machine was fixed and the bill was $4500. Young had left strict instructions with the shop that she must approve all work before it was done. Is Young obligated to pay the bill? If she refuses, what are the shop's remedies? What safeguards and risks are involved in those remedies for Young?

5. Roach owned a truck with a large crane attached. Roach took the truck to Vern's Auto to have the crane removed with the intention of mounting it on another vehicle in the future. Vern's allowed Roach to leave the crane in their yard, assuring him it would be safe. A few months later, Roach decided to sell the crane. When he went to get the crane, it was gone. Vern's had no idea what had happened to it, and because they had charged nothing for storing it, did not seem to care.[22] Is Vern's responsible for the missing crane? What are the determining factors? What information is missing? What steps should Roach and Vern's have taken to safeguard the crane?

6. Seaway Distributors hired Chet's Transport to move a load of carrots from Boston to Newfoundland with instructions to keep the temperature of the carrots between 2 and 6 degrees Celsius. The carrots were five days late when delivered in Newfoundland, and when unloaded they were heating and beginning to spoil. They were sold at a loss of $5000. Evidence showed that the truck was at the proper temperature when it left Boston. Seaway wants to recover its loss of $5000. Chet's is seeking the freight charges of $4000.[23] What must each claimant prove? Which claim is more likely to be valid?

22. Based on *Lowe (D.J.) (1980) Ltd.* v. *Roach* (1994), 131 N.S.R. (2d) 268 (S.C.), aff'd (1995) 138 N.S.R. (2d) 79 (C.A.).
23. Based on *Chet's Transport Inc.* v. *Seaway Distributors Ltd.* (1987), 81 N.S.R. (2d) 299 (N.S.S.C.).

Chapter Eighteen

Intellectual Property

Objectives

AFTER STUDYING THIS CHAPTER, YOU SHOULD HAVE AN UNDERSTANDING OF

► THE NATURE OF INTELLECTUAL PROPERTY
► THE RIGHTS THAT ATTACH TO INTELLECTUAL PROPERTY
► HOW INTELLECTUAL PROPERTY IS ACQUIRED
► HOW TO PROTECT THE INTELLECTUAL PROPERTY ASSETS OF AN ORGANIZATION

Business Law in Practice

Andrea Charlebois is certain she has invented a revolutionary contact-lens case that ensures that soft contact lenses are stored right side out, thereby preventing the contact-lens user from accidentally inserting lenses inside out. Andrea believes this is such a tremendous advantage that the world will beat a path to her door. She has also developed a unique configuration for her revolutionary case. The case is oval-shaped like a pair of eyes and the cover slides back, not unlike the way an eyelid does. Andrea has also fashioned a particularly attractive design—a replica of an eye—that can be applied to the finished case, and she has even come up with possible names for her invention—Easy Eyes or ECIs.

Andrea is willing to spend considerable time and effort in further developing and marketing the product. Not only will she prepare a detailed business plan, but she will also have brochures and other promotional materials designed. However, she is concerned that as soon as she gets to the market, her product and promotional materials will be copied by competitors and her investment will be worthless.

Andrea also knows that she needs considerable financial support to proceed with further development. She has a drawing of the case with specifications, as well as a prototype, which she keeps under lock and key, to show prospective lenders or investors. But she is very concerned that anyone she contacts may steal her idea.

1. How can Andrea's ideas be protected against encroachment by competitors?
2. How can Andrea's ideas be protected against theft by potential lenders and investors she approaches to back her product?

Figure 18.1

ANDREA'S CONTACT-LENS CASE IS INTELLECTUAL PROPERTY.

Introduction

intellectual property
The results of the creative process.

Intellectual property is a term often used to describe the results of intellectual or creative processes.[1] Put another way, the term is used for describing ideas or ways of expressing ideas. Some common business examples of intellectual property are

- recipes and formulas for making products
- manufacturing processes
- methods of extracting minerals
- advertising jingles
- business and marketing plans
- the distinctive name given to a product or service

Andrea's idea for an improved and attractive contact-lens case and the names she is considering adopting for the product are examples too.

The term *intellectual property* is also used to describe the "bundle of rights" that people have in their ideas or the ways in which they are expressed. These rights are rewards or incentives for creating and developing ideas. There are differing rights in intellectual property as the law gives varying types of protection to its many forms. The main categories of intellectual property laws are patents, trademarks, copyrights, industrial designs, and confidential (business) information.[2] There are other laws, however, that provide protection for specific types of intellectual property. For

---

1. The suggestions of Professor Peter Lown, director of the Alberta Law Reform Institute, in writing this chapter are gratefully acknowledged.
2. The term *confidential information* includes a broad range of information, such as government secrets and private personal information. In this text, the term *confidential business information* is used to distinguish information of a commercial nature from other types of information.

example, there are laws that protect plant varieties,[3] integrated circuit topographies,[4] and personality rights.[5]

Intellectual property is a necessary and critical asset in many industries, as illustrated in these examples:

- Patents protect inventions and are essential to businesses in the pharmaceutical, electronics, chemical, and manufacturing industries, as patents may be used to exclude others from using new technology.
- Industrial designs protect the appearance of useful articles against copying and are relevant to businesses that offer goods to consumers.
- Trademarks serve to distinguish the goods or services of one provider from those of another and are essential to all businesses that sell goods or services to the public.
- Copyright prevents the copying of certain works and is the basis for businesses involved in art, publishing, music, communications, and software, as copyright provides the basis for a saleable product.
- The law governing confidentiality is the means of protecting such information as marketing plans, customer lists, databases, and price lists, and is crucial to all businesses.[6]

Intellectual property offers both opportunities and challenges to business. Businesses can gain a competitive advantage by developing new products, innovative business methods, and creative brand names. Also, they can exploit these things by assigning or licensing their use to other businesses. However, the development of various technologies, such as photocopiers, tape recorders, video cameras, and computers, has made it easier for others to "take" intellectual property. In short, it is often difficult to police and protect intellectual property.[7]

This chapter explores the creation, acquisition, and protection of intellectual property.

Creation of Intellectual Property Rights

Andrea's intellectual property comprises a method for storing contact lenses so that it is difficult for the user to insert a lens into the eye inside out, a unique configuration for the case, a design to be applied to the case, and a name for the product. Various aspects of her intellectual property may qualify for protection under different legal regimes.

patent
A monopoly to make, use, or sell an invention.

Patents

Andrea's method of storing contact lenses may qualify for **patent** protection. A patent is a statutory right[8] that provides protection for inventions.

---

3. *Plant Breeders' Rights Act*, S.C. 1990, c. 20. This Act provides 18-year patent-like protection for distinct new plant varieties.
4. *Integrated Circuit Topography Act*, S.C. 1990, c. 37. This Act provides 10-year protection for layout designs embedded in computer semiconductor chips or circuit boards.
5. Rights in personality are protected under tort actions, trademark legislation, and privacy legislation, such as British Columbia's *Privacy Act*, R.S.B.C. 1996, c. 373.
6. Sheldon Eurshtein, "Executives Remain Unaware of the Value of Intellectual Property Assets" *The Lawyers Weekly* (27 June 1997) 23.
7. For example, in recognition of the difficulties in policing copyright infringement of music, a levy on blank tapes has been introduced. See *Copyright Act*, R.S.C. 1985, c. C-42, as am. by S.C. 1997, c. 24, s. 50.
8. The federal government has jurisdiction to make laws concerning patents, copyrights, and trademarks. See *Constitution Act, 1867*, s. 91.

Patents Defined

The *Patent Act* defines an invention as "any new and useful art, process, machine, manufacture or composition of matter or any new and useful improvement in any art, process, machine, manufacture or composition of matter."[9] The definition is very broad and encompasses a number of different kinds of inventions such as

- processes or methods (e.g., a pay-per-use billing system, a system for applying a selective herbicide to improve crop yield, a method of cleaning carpets)
- machines or apparatuses (e.g., computer hardware, a hay rake, a vacuum cleaner)
- products or compositions of matter (e.g., pharmaceuticals, chemical compounds, microorganisms)

Substances intended for food or medicine were not patentable until recently, although the processes for producing them were. The question of whether new life forms created as the result of genetic engineering should be patentable has been the subject of much controversy.

Patentability of Life Forms

In a landmark Canadian patent case, the Federal Court of Appeal ruled that nonhuman mammals can be patented. In a 2 to 1 decision, the majority overturned a 1995 decision of the Federal Court Trial Division, which had upheld the decision of the Commissioner of Patents not to issue a patent for Harvard's controversial "oncomouse," a cancer-prone lab mouse that is useful in cancer research. The mouse is the product of manipulation of mouse genes at the embryonic stage. The commissioner had granted Harvard a patent for its process of genetically engineering the oncomouse, but denied a patent for the mouse itself. The basis for denial was that animals are created primarily by nature and not by humans. Put another way, the animals were not "inventions" by humans, as the inventors had insufficient control over the process. The Federal Court of Appeal disagreed with this reasoning. The court stated that the oncomouse involved the application of inventive ingenuity and, furthermore, that the *Patent Act* does not exclude the patenting of animals.

This decision marks the first time a Canadian court has ruled that higher, complex life forms can be patented. The decision also brings Canada's patent law into line with that of its major trading partners—the United States, Europe, and Japan. In the United States, for example, patents have been granted for a wide range of life forms, including not only the oncomouse but also sheep, worms, birds, fish, and pigs.

Critical Analysis: Judge Rothstein of the Federal Court of Apeal stated that there may be reasons why so-called higher life forms should not be patented, but these reasons have not been written into the law. What are the reasons for not patenting higher life forms? Should patent law be concerned with morals or ethics? What is the likely impact of this decision on the biotechnology industry?

Source: *Presidents and Fellows of Harvard College* v. *Canada* (*Commissioner of Patents*), [2000] F.C.J. No. 1213 (F.C.A.D.).

---

9. R.S.C. 1985, c. P-4, s. 2. The *Patent Act* was substantially amended in 1987, R.S.C. 1987, c. 33 (3d Supp.) and became effective 1 October 1989. Patents issued prior to this date remain subject to the earlier law. Substantial amendments, notably in respect to pharmaceuticals, were also effected by the *Intellectual Property Law Improvement Act,* S.C. 1993, c. 15.

EXCLUSIONS FROM PATENT PROTECTION   There are also exclusions or exceptions to what may be patented. The most common are the following:

- *Things that receive protection under other areas of the law.* For example, computer programs (i.e., software) are not patentable, as they receive protection under copyright law. They could, however, receive patent protection as part of a broader patent, as for example, a computerized method of controlling the operation of a plant.[10]
- *Things that do not meet the definition of a patent.* For example, scientific principles, natural phenomena, and abstract theorems are "discoveries" as opposed to inventions and are therefore not patentable. A practical application of a theory could, however, qualify for protection.
- *Things that are, for policy reasons, not patentable.* For example, methods of medical or surgical treatment, illicit objects, and business plans and methods are not patentable. The reason why many of these things are excluded from patent protection appears to be the perception that it is unfair to grant monopolies in these areas of endeavour.[11]

The Patenting of Business Methods

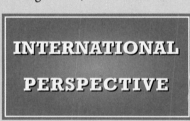

INTERNATIONAL PERSPECTIVE

In both Canada and the United States, business methods such as franchising arrangements, accounting methods, insurance schemes, tax loopholes, and ways of beating the stock exchange have not been patentable. There are two main reasons why these are excluded from protection: business methods are not "technical," and a market monopoly might result.

This exclusion of business methods from patent protection has recently been called into question in the U.S. case *State Street Bank & Trust* v. *Signature Financial Group*.

In this case, Signature, a company that administers mutual funds, was an assignee of a patent, titled "data processing system for Hub and Spoke Financial Services Configuration." The patent claimed a data processing system used to operate an investment structure, known as "Hub and Spoke." Under the investment structure, mutual funds ("Spokes") pooled their assets in an investment portfolio ("the Hub") organized as a partnership.

This arrangement offered tax advantages and economies of scale. The patent was not on the investment structure itself but rather on a system for using computer software to calculate the value of the mutual funds in the scheme at any given time. The patent claimed a data processing system consisting of a machine—a computer running software doing the calculations necessary to operate the Hub and Spoke business scheme.

State Street, which was in the same line of business as Signature, had been negotiating for the use of the patent. After negotiations broke down, State Street brought an action claiming that the patent was invalid.

The lower court found for State Street on the basis of a judge-made exception to patentability. The exception was that business methods are not a proper subject matter for patenting. The U.S. Federal Court of Appeals overturned. The court held that the business methods exception to patentability was ill conceived and unsupported by

10. David Vaver, *Intellectual Property Law* (Concord, Ont.: Irwin Law, 1997) at 129.
11. See W.R. Cornish, *Intellectual Property: Patents, Copyright, Trade Marks and Allied Rights* (London: Sweet & Maxwell, 1981) at 171.

the *Patent Act*. Methods of doing business should be treated like any other process claim. The fact that it involves "business" should not be relevant.

The case has opened the door for banks, brokerage companies, and other financial institutions in the United States to apply for patents relating to such practices as securities trading, insurance underwriting, banking, and Internet commerce.

Critical Analysis: What are the advantages of allowing patents for business methods? What is the down-side of allowing business patents?

Source: *State Street Bank & Trust Co.* v. *Signature Financial Group Inc.*, 149 F. 3d 1368 (Fed. Cir. 1998).

Requirements for Patentability

Not all inventions, however wonderful, are patentable. A patent will only be granted for an invention that is new, useful, and unobvious.

NEW   The invention must be new or novel. This means that any public disclosure, public use, or sale of the invention prior to filing for a patent is a bar to obtaining a patent. The fact that there is not an existing patent for the invention is not conclusive of the invention being new or novel.[12] Any previous public disclosure, such as displaying the new product at a trade show, distributing marketing brochures that describe or display the product, or advertising the product in a way that reveals the invention,[13] is a disclosure and a bar to obtaining a patent.

There is, however, a one-year grace period. If the inventor or someone who derived knowledge from the inventor makes a disclosure within the year preceding the filing of the application, this will not operate as public disclosure.

Andrea needs to determine whether her invention has already been disclosed to the public in some manner. A search of relevant patent literature is conducted by a firm of patent agents so that an opinion can be formed as to whether the invention is novel.

USEFUL   An invention must solve some practical problem and it must actually work—that is, do what it purports to do. An invention that does not work is useless and unpatentable. The invention must have industrial value, although it need not be commercially successful. The invention must have practical use as opposed to being a mere scientific curiosity. For example, a perpetual motion machine[14] lacks utility as it does not have a practical use.

Andrea's case addresses the problem of users mixing up their lenses and inserting them into the eyes inside out; it also provides a solution through the method of storage. Andrea has developed a prototype that presumably works, so this requirement appears to be satisfied.

UNOBVIOUS   The third requirement relates to "inventiveness." It means that there must be some ingenuity or inventive step involved in the invention. Changes to

---

12. Also of relevance to the issue of novelty are *applications* for patents filed in other countries. Canada is a signatory to both the *Paris Convention for the Protection of Industrial Property* and the *Patent Co-Operation Treaty*. An applicant, by filing in a member country, can claim this date in other countries so long as the corresponding applications are filed within one year. This means that the earlier date becomes the disclosure date for purposes of establishing novelty.

13. Ronald Dimock, *Canadian Marketing Law* (Toronto: Richard DeBoo, 1991) at 3-4.

14. *Supra* note 10 at 128.

something that would be obvious to someone skilled in the art to which the invention pertains would not be patentable. For example, simply using a different material for making a product would not be patentable as it does not involve an inventive step.

The test is difficult to apply in practice as it involves ascertaining the state of the art or knowledge prior to the invention and analyzing whether the invention was merely the obvious, next step in the state of the knowledge or instead involves an inventive step.

The question of whether Andrea's invention is unobvious can be answered only by asking someone knowledgeable in the field of contact-lens cases. The patent agent who searches the literature to determine whether an invention is novel will also express an opinion on whether the invention is obvious.

Patent Protection and Application

Patent protection, unlike some other intellectual property rights, does not arise automatically. An application for a patent must be filed with the Canadian patent office.[15] Timing of the application is a critical concern because the patent regime is based on a first-to-file system.[16] This means, for example, that if more than one person has independently invented the same process, method, or machine, the patent office gives priority to the first person to file the application.

The inventor is generally the first owner of the invention and thus the person entitled to apply for a patent. The *Patent Act* does not contain specific provisions for the ownership of inventions created by employees in the course of employment; generally, however, an employee will be the owner unless specifically hired to produce the invention or a contract precludes the employee from claiming ownership of inventions relating to and developed in the course of employment.[17]

patent agent
A professional trained in patent law and practice who can assist in the preparation of a patent application.

specifications
The description of an invention contained in a patent.

claims
What a patented invention can do.

The preparation of a patent application is a highly complex matter and is normally done by a **patent agent**, who has particular expertise in this area. The application has two main parts: one part describes how the product is made or the best way to perform the process or method. This is known as the **specifications**. The other part is known as the **claims**. This part in effect defines the boundaries of the invention. In short, the specifications tell the reader how to put the invention into practice after the patent expires. The claims tell the reader what cannot be done prior to the expiry of the patent.

The application is examined[18] by the patent office to ensure that the invention has not already been invented and that the application complies with the *Patent Act*. If the application is successful, a patent is issued upon the payment of the required fee. The word *patented* and the patent number may be put on all manufactured goods, but there is no requirement that this be done. Often manufacturers will put the term *patent pending* or *patent applied for* on their products before the patent is issued. This has no legal effect other than to warn others that a patent may eventually be issued in respect of these products.

---

15. The Canadian Intellectual Property Office's database is online and can be accessed at <strategis.ic.gc.ca/sc_mrksv/cipo/welcome/welcom-e.html>.

16. Up until 1989, Canada's patent regime was based on a first-to-invent system.

17. *Supra* note 10 at 147-148.

18. *Supra* note 9 at s. 35(1). An application for a patent is not automatically examined. The applicant must specifically request that an examination be done. Requests must be made within five years of filing the application, or the application will be deemed abandoned. The delay for requesting examination gives the applicant a period of time to test the market for the invention.

A patent gives to the inventor the right to exclude others from making, selling, or using the invention to which the patent relates for a period of 20 years from the date of filing the application[19] so long as the appropriate maintenance fees are paid.

Patents are national in nature in that they exist only in the country in which the applications are made and granted.[20] The rights under a Canadian patent do not apply elsewhere. For example, an owner of a Canadian patent cannot stop the use or sale of the invention in the United States, unless the owner also has a U.S. patent.

Andrea's idea may qualify for patent protection if the case that embodies the method of storage is considered to be new, useful, and unobvious. If it is patentable, she will need to apply for a patent and pay the requisite fee. The patent process requires her to disclose her discovery to the world; in return, she receives a monopoly over the invention for 20 years. The patent process is costly and time-consuming, so Andrea needs to evaluate the costs and benefits of pursuing this route.

Industrial Designs

The shape of Andrea's contact-lens case as well as the eye design applied to it may qualify for protection under the *Industrial Design Act*.[21] This act provides protection for the *appearance* of mass-produced (i.e., numbering more than 50) useful articles or objects.[22]

Industrial Designs Defined

industrial design
Ornamentation or shape of functional objects.

The term **industrial design** is not defined in the act. An industrial design is usually taken to mean a feature of shape, configuration, pattern, or ornament, or any combination of these, that in a finished article appeals to and is judged solely by the eye.[23] Put another way, an industrial design protects the shapes or ornamental aspects of a product but does not protect the functional aspect.

Typical examples of industrial designs are the shape and ornamentations applied to toys, vehicles, furniture, household utensils, and the patterns applied to wallpaper or fabric. The shape of Andrea's contact-lens case is an industrial design if the shape relates to asthetics as opposed to function. The eye design applied to the case is unrelated to function. It is merely ornamental, and therefore qualifies as an industrial design.

The unique design of consumer goods receives protection under the *Industrial Design Act*.

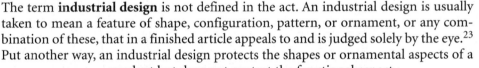

19. *Ibid.*, s. 44. Patent applications filed before October 1, 1989, carry a term of 17 years from the date the patent was granted.

20. There is no such thing as an international patent. International treaties, however, have simplified the procedures for obtaining patents in different countries.

21. R.S.C. 1985, c. I-9.

22. Works that qualify as industrial designs may also qualify for protection under the *Copyright Act*. To address the overlap, copyright protection is not given to designs applied to useful articles that are produced in quantities of more than 50. See *Copyright Act*, R.S.C. 1985, c. C-42, s. 64(2) as am. by *An Act to Amend the Copyright Act and Other Acts in Consequence Therof*, S.C. 1988, c. 65.

23. Martin P.J. Kratz, *Canada's Intellectual Property Law in a Nutshell* (Scarborough: Carswell, 1998) at 63.

Requirements for Registration

To be registered, an industrial design must be original and novel. The originality standard is lower than the standard of inventiveness found in patents. A high degree of ingenuity or creativity is not necessary. The design may be entirely new, or it may be an old design that had not previously been applied for the purpose of ornamenting the article in question.

An industrial design must also be novel. Disclosure or use of the industrial design or of articles displaying, bearing, or embodying the industrial design is a bar to registration unless it was within the year prior to filing the application.[24]

Registration Process and Protection

As with patents, industrial design protection does not arise automatically. An application, usually drafted by a patent agent, must be submitted to the industrial design office.

The owner of the rights in the design is entitled to make the application. The basic principle is that the designer is the owner unless the design was ordered and paid for by another.

The application normally consists of a written description and a graphic depiction, photograph, or drawing. If the application meets the requirements of the act, a certificate of registration will be issued.

The registration gives to the owner the exclusive right to make, import, or sell any article in respect to which the design is registered. As well, the owner of the design can stop competitors from manufacturing and selling a design that looks confusingly similar. An industrial design registration lasts for 10 years.

The rights of the owner of the industrial design may be maintained and enhanced by proper use and placement of markings on articles to which the design is applied. The marking is normally

"Rd" (or the French equivalent, "Enr."), year of registration

Andrea needs to determine whether her design qualifies for industrial design protection and evaluate the costs and benefits of applying.

Trademarks

Andrea's intellectual property also comprises her proposed names for the product (i.e., Easy Eyes or ECIs). This aspect of her intellectual property may qualify for protection under trademark law.

Trademark Defined

trademark
A mark used to distinguish the source of goods or services.

A **trademark**[25] is a mark used to distinguish a person's products or services from those of others. Its function is to indicate the source or origin of the goods or services.

---

24. *Supra* note 10. International conventions also apply to the application for industrial designs. Foreign applications filed up to six months before the Canadian filing may have priority to obtain a patent.

25. In addition to the type of trademark used by a business to identify goods or services, another category of trademark is the *certification mark*. It is a mark used to indicate that a product or service conforms to a particular standard. For example, "Wool Mark," which is a certification mark of the Wool Bureau of Canada, is used to identify garments made from pure wool. Also, the Canadian Standards Council uses "CSA Approved" to indicate products of a certain standard. Certification marks are not owned by producers; thus, they are not used to distinguish one producer from another. Instead, the mark distinguishes products or services of a defined standard from others.

Trademarks are valuable intellectual property.

Theoretically, a trademark could be anything, but it is usually one of the following:

- a word (e.g., EXXON, XEROX, LEGO)
- words (e.g., THE BODY SHOP, THE PINK PANTHER)
- a slogan (e.g., "Just Do It," "Mr. Christie, You Make Good Cookies")
- a design (e.g., McDonald's golden arches, Disney's cartoon characters)
- letters (e.g., ABC for laundry detergent, BMW for a car)
- numbers (e.g., 6/49 for lottery services, 900 Service for telephone operations)
- a symbol (e.g., Chinese characters, NIKE's "swoosh")
- **distinguishing guise** (e.g., Coca-Cola bottle, Perrier bottle)
- any combination of the above (e.g., LONDON FOG with the depiction of the Big Ben Clock Tower for clothing)

distinguishing guise
A shaping of wares or their container, or a mode of wrapping or packaging wares.

Colour[26] (such as pink for insulation) may be claimed as part of the mark as well.

Andrea's proposed names, Easy Eyes or ECIs, are also examples of words and letters that are commonly used as trademarks.

trade name
The name under which a sole proprietorship, a partnership, or a corporation does business.

TRADE NAMES Closely related to trademarks are **trade names**, which also receive protection under trademark law. A trade name is the name under which a business is carried on. It may be the name of a corporation, a partnership, or a sole proprietorship. For example, Andrea may decide to incorporate a business to develop and market her product. To incorporate a company she is required by companies or business corporations legislation to provide an identifier for the corporation.[27] The identifier could be Easy Eyes Inc[28] *if* the name is not being used by another corporation

---

26. *Supra* note 10 at 188–189. The validity of registering sounds and smells as trademarks is uncertain.
27. For a discussion of business names see Chapter 15.
28. Shortened versions of trade or business names may be registered as trademarks.

and the name does not infringe on the trademark of another entity. An important connection between trade names and trademarks is that the adoption of a trademark may prevent the use of an identical or similar trade name, and vice versa—that is, the adoption of a trade name can prevent the adoption of a trademark. For example, Andrea's adoption of Easy Eyes as a trade name prevents others from using the name or a similar one as a trademark. As well, if someone else is using Easy Eyes or a name closely related as either a trade name or a trademark, Andrea will not be able to use the name. Thus, in effect, the law of trademarks has become a means of protecting the names of corporations, partnerships, and sole proprietorships.

COMMON LAW TRADEMARKS   Trademarks may be registered or unregistered. If unregistered, they are often referred to as *common law trademarks*. Whether registered or unregistered, trademarks receive protection under both the common law and the *Trade-marks Act*.[29]

A common law trademark comes into existence when a business simply adopts and uses it. Such a trademark is considered to be part of the goodwill of a company, and rights attach to it in much the same manner as they do to registered trademarks. Infringement of the trademark by a competitor using the same or similar trademark can be addressed through the tort of passing off.[30]

The rights that attach to common law trademarks, however, tend to be more restrictive, and there are certain advantages associated with registration. A common law trademark has rights only in the geographic areas in which it has been used and in areas in which the reputation of the owner has spread. A registered trademark enjoys protection throughout the country. Registration is also advantageous in that it creates a presumption of ownership and validity.

Requirements for Registration

To register a trademark, an applicant must demonstrate that he has title to the trademark (this requirement is sometimes simply referred to as use), that the trademark is distinctive or capable of becoming distinctive, and that the trademark is registrable.

TITLE   An applicant may only register a trademark that he owns. Ownership or title is not established by inventing or selecting a mark. It comes from

- use of the trademark
- filing an application to register a proposed trademark
- making it known in Canada

A trademark is deemed to be in "use" in Canada if the trademark is on the goods or the packaging at the time of any transfer in the ordinary course of business. With respect to services, a trademark is deemed to be in use if it is used or displayed in the performance or advertising of the services. If an applicant has used a mark in this manner, then normally he has title to the mark and can apply to register it. A distinguishing guise is only registrable on this basis.

A trademark can be registered if it is not yet in use, as long as use commences before the registration is actually issued. Thus, Andrea could register the names as trademarks on this basis, as she is not yet in business and using the marks.

---

29. R.S.C. 1985, c. T-13.
30. The tort of passing off is discussed in Chapter 12.

An application to register can be made on the basis that the mark, although not in use in Canada, is nonetheless well known in Canada. An applicant would need to demonstrate that the mark is, in fact, well known in Canada, that knowledge of the mark arose from advertisements that circulated in Canada, and that the applicant used the mark in another country.[31]

DISTINCTIVENESS The second general requirement goes to the heart of trademark law. The mark must be distinctive—in other words, it must actually distinguish the goods or services in association with which it is used. Invented words like *LEGO*, *EXXON*, and *KODAK* are distinctive and are ideal candidates, particularly with respect to applications based on proposed use. Other, more descriptive words, such as *pleasant, sudsy,* and *easy eyes* do not have the same quality of distinctiveness. They may gain this quality only through use in business and advertising.

REGISTRABILITY The *Trade-marks Act* specifies that a mark must be "registrable." To be registrable, the trademark must not be

- primarily the name or surname of an individual who is living or has died within the preceding 30 years (e.g., "Smith" or "Enman")
- descriptive or deceptively misdescriptive of the character or quality of the wares or services, or their place of origin (e.g., "Saint John" for oil that comes from Saint John or "all-silk" for cotton blouses)
- the name in any language of any ware or service in connection with which it is used or proposed to be used (e.g., "avion" for airplanes, or "shredded wheat" for cereal[32])
- confusing with another registered trademark (e.g., "Mego" for children's plastic building blocks; "Devlon" for hair care products)
- an official[33] or prohibited[34] mark

Andrea's proposed trademarks, Easy Eyes or ECIs, may be registrable depending on the above factors. A key concern will be whether the same or a similar trademark has been registered in relation to eye products and whether the mark is considered sufficiently distinctive.

Registration Process and Protection

The first person who uses or makes a trademark known in Canada is entitled to trademark registration. In the absence of use, the first to file a trademark application is entitled to registration.[35]

Prior to applying for registration there is a search of the trademarks office[36] to ensure that the trademark or a similar one is not registered. Federal and provincial

---

31. The foreign country must have been a country that is a member of the Paris Convention or the World Trade Organization.

32. *Canadian Shredded Wheat Co. Ltd.* v. *Kellogg Co. of Canada Ltd.* (1938), 55 R.P.C. 125 (P.C.).

33. Public authorities have the right to adopt an official mark and use that mark in respect of its wares or services. For example THE OFFICIAL ISLAND STORE is an official mark of the Gateway Village Development Inc. of Prince Edward Island.

34. Prohibited marks include marks that are likely to be mistaken for symbols or emblems of royalty, the governor general, the Red Cross, the Red Crescent, and the Royal Canadian Mounted Police. Also prohibited are scandalous and obscene words and anything that suggests a connection with a living or recently deceased individual.

35. Canada is a signatory to the *Paris Convention,* which means that applicants from member countries have reciprocal rights with respect to filing in member countries. The date of filing in a convention country becomes the Canadian filing date, so long as the Canadian application is filed within six months of the date of the first filing in a convention country.

36. The Canadian Intellectual Property Office's trademark database is online and can be accessed at <strategis.ic.gc.ca/sc_mrksv/cipo/welcome/welcom-e.html>.

business name registries and other sources, such as trade journals, telephone directories, and specialty magazines, are also consulted to determine whether there are common law rights.

The application must comply with all the provisions of the Act. In particular, a comprehensive list of products or services associated with the trademark must be provided. An examiner will review the application, and if it is acceptable the trademarks office will advertise the trademark in the trademark journal. Any interested members of the public can object to the registration on the grounds that they have a better title, that the trademark is not distinctive, or that the trademark does not meet the requirements of registrability. If, on the other hand, there is no opposition or the opposition is overcome, then the registration will be issued on payment of the appropriate fee.

A trademark registration gives to the owner the exclusive right to use the trademark in association with the wares and services specified in the registration. It also provides a right to prevent others from using a confusingly similar trademark. A trademark owner should clearly indicate its ownership of a trademark with the following marks:

® for registered trademarks
™ for unregistered trademarks

Registration provides protection across Canada for a period of 15 years. The registration can be renewed for further 15-year terms as long as the renewal fee is paid and the trademark continues in use.

Copyright

copyright
The right to prevent others from copying or modifying certain works.

Andrea's intellectual property will eventually include promotional brochures, business plans, and other written material[37] that may qualify for **copyright** protection.

Copyright is governed entirely by the *Copyright Act*.[38] Copyright is intended to provide a right of exploitation to authors of certain works. As its name suggests, copyright is intended to prevent copying. It does not protect the underlying ideas. For example, no one has copyright in the life story of Ken Thomson or K.C. Irving, but once the story is written, copyright resides in the written word.

Copyright Defined

Copyright applies to both traditional and nontraditional works. Copyright applies to every original literary, dramatic, musical, and artistic work, such as the following:

- *literary works*—books, pamphlets, compilations, translations, and computer programs
- *dramatic works*—any piece for recitation, choreographic works, scenic arrangements, and cinematography productions, such as plays, operas, mime, films, and videos
- *musical works*—any combination of melody and harmony, including sheet music
- *artistic works*—paintings, drawings, maps, charts, plans, photographs, engravings, sculptures, works of artistic craftsmanship, architectural works of art

---

37. *Supra,* note 21. Copyright in the design of the contact lens case is unenforceable when the design is applied to an article that is reproduced in a quantity of more than 50.
38. R.S.C. 1985, c. C-42.

In essence, copyright extends to almost anything written, composed, drawn, or shaped. As well, the examples of works included in each category are nonexhaustive, which means the categories can encompass new technologies and new forms of expression. Copyright also applies to nontraditional works such as sound recordings, performances, and broadcasts.

There are many business examples of these various kinds of works. In fact, whole industries are founded on works of this nature, particularly the entertainment and publishing industries. Businesses that are not so directly affected still create many works that may attract copyright protection, such as advertising copy, photographs, manuals, memorandums, plans, sketches, and computer programs, to name a few common examples. Andrea's proposed business and marketing plans and documents are protected by copyright.

Requirements for Protection

To attract copyright protection, a work must meet requirements of originality and fixation.[39] Originality means that the work must "originate" from the author, not be copied from another, and involve some effort on the part of the author. Unlike in patent law, there is no requirement in copyright law that the work created involve ingenuity or creativity. Thus, while books such as Peter C. Newman's *The Canadian Establishment* are protected, so too is the very common and ordinary book.

A work must also meet the requirement of fixation, that is, be expressed in some fixed form such as paper or diskette. Works such as speeches, luncheon addresses, and lectures, which do not exist in a fixed form, do not attract copyright. The fixation requirement provides a means of comparison for judging whether copyright has been infringed.

Registration Process and Protection

Copyright protection arises automatically on the creation of a work. There is an optional registration process that has an evidentiary advantage in that registration provides a presumption of ownership. The owner of copyright may mark a work; however there is no requirement to do so to enforce copyright in Canada. The mark can, however, enhance international protection of the work. The following is the typical form of a copyright notice:

© year of publication; name of owner

Under the *Copyright Act*, the author of a work is the copyright owner unless there is an agreement to the contrary. The major exception is for works created in the course of employment, in which case the employer is the owner. A further exception relates to photographs, engravings, and portraits that are ordered and paid for by another; in the absence of an agreement to the contrary, the customer is the first owner of the copyright.

Copyright protection is generally for the life of the author or composer plus 50 years.[40]

---

39. The nationality requirement is no longer very important, as Canada has implemented the Agreement on Trade-Related Aspects of Intellectual Property Rights (TRIPS). This agreement means that virtually every work qualifies for protection, regardless of the author's nationality.

40. For some works, such as sound recordings, the term of protection is 50 years.

RIGHTS UNDER COPYRIGHT Copyright gives certain rights to the owner of the copyright (the rights may vary somewhat depending on the type of work). These rights include

- *reproduction*—the right to reproduce the work or a substantial part of it in material form
- *public performance*—the right to perform the work or a substantial part of it
- *publication*—the right, if the work is unpublished, to publish the work
- *translation*—the right to produce, reproduce, perform, or publish any translation of the work
- *adaptation*—the right to convert works into other formats (e.g., a book into a movie)
- *mechanical reproduction*—the right to make sound recording or cinematographic recording
- *cinematographic presentation*—the right to reproduce, adapt, and publicly present the work by cinematograph
- *communication*—the right to communicate the work to the public by telecommunication
- *exhibition*—the right to present in public, for purposes other than sale or hire, an artistic work[41]
- *rental*—the right to rent out sound recordings and computer programs
- *authorization*—the right to "authorize" any of the other rights

Copyright is infringed when anyone does, *without the consent* of the owner, anything only the owner can do. This includes, for example, copying *all or a substantial part* of a work. The question of what is substantial is vexing. It is generally thought that *substantial* has both a qualitative and a quantitative aspect. The test seems to be whether the part that is taken is a key or distinctive part.[42]

The enforcement of such rights has been problematic, particularly the collection of fees and royalties for the use of copyrighted works. These problems have been addressed by provisions in the *Copyright Act* for the establishment of collectives, which negotiate agreements with users on royalties and use. For example, the Canadian Reprography Collective (CanCopy) represents numerous publishers and authors and negotiates agreements with institutions, such as universities, libraries, and copy shops, providing for the payment of royalties for photocopying from books. Similar collectives operate in the music industry.

moral rights
The author's rights to have work properly attributed and not prejudicially modified or associated with products.

MORAL RIGHTS The author of a work has what are known as **moral rights**. Moral rights exist independently of copyright and provide authors with some control over how their works are used and exploited. Moral rights include the following:

- *Paternity.* The author has the right to be associated with the work as its author by name or under a pseudonym and the right to remain anonymous if reasonable in the circumstances.
- *Integrity.* The author has the right to object to dealings or uses of the work if they are prejudicial to the author's reputation or honour.
- *Association.* The author has the right to object to the work being used in association with a product, service, cause, or institution.

---

41. This applies only to works created after June 7, 1988, and does not apply to charts, maps, and plans.
42. *Supra* note 10 at 81-82.

Case

Snow v. The Eaton Centre Ltd. (1982), 70 C.P.R. (2d) 105 (Ont. H.C.)

The Business Context: Many works that receive copyright protection are created for the purpose of making a profit through a sale. However, the sale of a work does not extinguish all of the author's or creator's rights.

Factual Background: Michael Snow created a sculpture of geese known as "Flight Stop," which was sold to the owners of the Eaton Centre. In connection with a Christmas display, the Eaton Centre attached red ribbons to the necks of the 60 geese forming the sculpture. Snow claimed that his naturalistic composition had been made

to look ridiculous by the addition. In short, he alleged that his moral rights in the sculpture had been infringed.

The Legal Question: Were the acts of the Eaton Centre a distortion or modification of Snow's work that would be prejudicial to his honour and reputation?

Resolution: The court held that the ribbons distorted and modified Snow's work and that Snow's concern that this was prejudicial to his honour and reputation was reasonable in the circumstances. The Eaton Centre was required to remove the ribbons.

Critical Analysis: Since the Eaton Centre paid for the sculpture, why should it not be able to do as it wants with the sculpture? Would the outcome have been the same if the sculpture had been sent to the dump or otherwise destroyed?

Exemptions

There are a large number of exceptions or defences under the *Copyright Act*. Many—among them the exemption for home copying, the exemption for libraries, museums, and archives, the exemption for the disabled, and the exemption for educational use—apply to specific situations and have little business application. The exemptions that are particularly relevant to business are the following:

fair dealing
A defence to copyright infringement.

- *Fair dealing.* The **fair dealing** exemption permits the copying of works for the purposes of private study, research, criticism, or review. The copying must not only be "fair," but must also be for one of the enumerated purposes. Generally, the amount and extent of the copying, as well as the impact of the copying on the copyright owner's economic return from the work, are relevant considerations.
- *Computer software.* The exemption relating to computer programs is quite specific. It permits the owner of the program to make a copy for adaptation for use on another computer and a copy for backup purposes.

Confidential Business Information

Andrea needs to be able to disclose her ideas and plans to potential lenders and investors without fear that they will steal them. Andrea may be protected by the law of confidential information.

confidential business information
Information that provides a business advantage as a result of the fact that it is kept secret.

There is no specific statutory protection for **confidential business information**[43] and therefore no statutory definition for the term. Generally, however, the term refers to information that is used in a business or commercial context and is private or secret.

---

43. The term *trade secrets* is also sometimes used either interchangeably with *confidential business information* or as a subset of *confidential information*. The terms are used interchangeably in this text.

E-Business: Copyright on the Internet

There is a prevalent attitude that on the Internet anything goes and that somehow copyright law does not apply in a digitized environment. This is incorrect. Copyright does apply to the Internet, and the issues there are not that different from the issues anywhere else. Take, for example, the case of a business that establishes a promotional site on the World Wide Web that contains material on the company and has links to similar or related Web sites. The copyright issues here relate to the *uploading* of company material onto the site, the *linking* to other sites, and the *downloading* of materials by users of the Internet.

- *Uploading*. A company may want to upload—that is, place on its Web site—materials such as text, pictures, graphs, and pieces of music. The process of uploading involves making a copy of these works. The owner may make copies of works that he has created and owns the copyright to, material that is in the public domain, material that does not attract copyright protection, and material for which he has obtained the copyright owner's permission to upload the material onto the company's Web site. If the work uploaded falls outside these exemptions or the fair dealing defence, then the creator of the Web site is violating copyright. There is no exemption just because the medium is the Internet.
- *Linking*. A company may link its Web site to others. The process of providing links to other sites is akin to writing an address on a piece of paper. It does not involve copying material other than the address of the linked site, so there are no copyright issues.
- *Downloading*. A user may merely browse a Web site or may actually download materials

onto a hard drive or disk. Do these practices infringe copyright in the materials on the Web site? Both acts involve making a copy, and only the copyright owner has the right to do this. There is debate, however, about whether browsing should actually be considered "copying." Some argue that browsing on the Internet is like browsing in a bookstore and hence should not be considered copying. Others argue that browsing on the Internet involves copying an image, at least temporarily, and therefore should be treated like any other type of copying. Assuming that browsing and downloading are copying, the question then becomes one of permission and fair dealing. Does the browser or downloader have permission to do this? The argument is that although there may not be express permission to do these acts, there is implied permission. In short, the act of establishing a site on the Internet, which is open to the public, amounts to extending permission to browse and download. A second argument is that in the absence of permission, browsing—and perhaps even downloading—may fall within the fair dealing exemption. This might be the case particularly if the acts do not harm the commercial interests of the copyright holder.

The Internet, like many technologies, has made copying exceedingly easy, but it has not done away with the principles of copyright law.

Critical Analysis: Whose interests are harmed by copying from the Internet? How should copying from the Internet be addressed?

TECHNOLOGY AND THE LAW

The general categories of business information that is used or capable of use in business are these:

- strategic business information (e.g., customer lists, price lists, book keeping methods, presentation programs, advertising campaign)
- products (e.g., recipes, formulas)
- compilations (e.g., databases)
- technological secrets (e.g., scientific processes, know-how)

Requirements for Protection

A key requirement for protection is the secrecy or confidentiality of the information. A number of factors are considered in ascertaining whether the information is "confidential":

- *Economic value as a result of not being generally known.* The information must have some commercial value to the company or its competitors. An indication of the commercial value of the information may be the efforts by others to obtain it. The value of the information derives in large measure from the fact that it is not known by some or is not generally known.
- *Subject to efforts to keep it secret.* There must be efforts to keep the information secret. Thus, if a company is careless about information or fails to take steps to protect the confidentiality of information, then the information may indeed lose its status of "confidential."
- *Not generally known in the industry.* Information does not have to be absolutely confidential; it can be a compilation of readily available information from various sources. As well, information can be known by some and still maintain its status. In this regard, the extent to which the information is known within the company, as well as outside the company, is relevant.

Process and Scope of Protection

Confidential business information may be protected forever so long as the information is not disclosed to the general public. Recipes for well-known products such as Coke, Listerine, and Kentucky Fried Chicken have been "secret" for many years. There are no application procedures for protection. Information receives protection through claims for breach of express terms, for breach of confidence, or through implied obligations.

Parties may have express obligations to keep information confidential. Nondisclosure agreements require recipients of information to respect its confidentiality by agreeing not to discuss, disclose, or use it. Andrea, for example, could require potential financiers of her project to sign such an agreement. Employees are often required by the terms of their employment contracts to keep certain information confidential.

In the absence of an express provision regarding confidence, an obligation of confidence may be implied in a contract or arise by virtue of a fiduciary relationship. This is the case in the employment context, particularly in industries in which there is a lot of confidential information and the importance of confidentiality is stressed.

Finally, an obligation of confidence can exist when information was conveyed in circumstances suggesting a relationship of confidence. The following case is a leading decision on receipt of confidential information in circumstances of confidentiality.

Case

LAC Minerals Ltd. v. *International Corona Resources Ltd.* (1989), 61 D.L.R. (4th) 14 (S.C.C.)

The Business Context: In the negotiations preceding a contract, the parties may divulge a great deal of information, some of which is sensitive and confidential. This is often necessary in order to reach contractual consensus.

Factual Background: Corona was the owner of a group of mining claims that it was exploring. Being a junior company, it was eager to attract investors and had publicized certain information about its property. LAC Minerals, a major mining corporation, became interested, and a site visit was arranged. The LAC geologists were shown core samples and sections, and the parties discussed the geology of Corona's site, as well as the property to the west known as the Williams property. Another meeting was held a couple of days later in Toronto, during which it was again mentioned that Corona was attempting to purchase the Williams property. No mention was made of confidentiality. Following this meeting, there were further discussions and an exchange of joint venture ideas, as well as a full presentation by Corona of its results and its interest in the Williams property. A short time after these meetings, negotiations between LAC and Corona broke down. Subsequently, LAC made an offer to purchase the Williams property. The offer was accepted, and LAC proceeded to develop the property on its own. It turned out to be the biggest gold mine in Canada, and LAC made huge profits. Corona sued for breach of confidence and breach of fiduciary duty.

The Legal Question: Was LAC liable for breach of confidence or fiduciary duty?

Resolution: The Supreme Court of Canada unanimously found LAC liable on the grounds of breach of confidence. The court confirmed that there are three elements that must be established to impose liability on this ground:
- The information conveyed was confidential.
- It was communicated in circumstances in which a duty of confidence arises.
- It was misused by the party to whom it was communicated.

Although some of the information conveyed by Corona was not confidential, clearly most of it was, and LAC used it to acquire the Williams property. The court said the information was communicated with the mutual understanding that the parties were working toward a joint venture or some other arrangement. A reasonable person in the position of LAC would know that the information was being given in confidence. LAC used the information to its gain and at the expense of Corona. Although the court did not go so far as to find a breach of a fiduciary duty, there was a violation of confidence.

Critical Analysis: What is the importance of this case for business? How can a business determine whether information is confidential? Would it have been easier for Corona simply to have had LAC sign an express confidentiality agreement at the outset?

Limitations on Protection

Confidential business information loses the protection of the law when the information is no longer secret either because the information has been divulged or because the information has been discovered by independent development through using publicly available information or by reverse engineering.

Information is also no longer confidential when it becomes part of the employee's personal knowledge, skill, or expertise (i.e., trade information). In distinguishing between information that is "confidential" and trade information, the courts attempt to strike a balance between the employee's right to use the skills, knowledge, and experience gained during the course of employment and the employer's right to protect its information.

Case

Physique Health Club Ltd. v. *Carlsen* (1996), 141
D.L.R. (4th) 64 (Alta. C.A.); leave to appeal dismissed [1997] S.C.C. No. 40.

The Business Context: It is not uncommon for employees, after gaining knowledge and experience, to leave their employer to start their own business. When the employee engages in a business in the same industry as the former employer and uses the same general know-how and customer connections, the question is often whether the employee has used that which legitimately belongs to the employer.

Factual Background: Glenn Carlsen worked at Physique Health Club as its manager from November 1987 until March 1992, when he left following a pay dispute with the owner, his uncle. A few weeks later, he opened his own store just 18 blocks from his uncle's site. He sold the same exercise equipment to the same market and featured an almost identical sign. His business was instantly successful, and had a serious impact on Physique's operations. Physique sued.

The Legal Question: Did Carlsen breach his fiduciary duty to his former employer? Did Carlsen use confidential information in the operation of his business?

Resolution: Physique argued that pricing policies, marketing techniques, and store layout, although not confidential on their own, eventually take on an economic value that makes them confidential. Carlsen agreed that he was a better business person as a result of running his uncle's store but argued that that was the result of his own hard work and initiative. He also said that if general knowledge about a store's operations were confidential, then employees would never be able to leave and start their own businesses. The trial judge agreed but added that the right of an employer to protect his or her investment takes precedence over the rights of employees who want to start their own businesses.

The Court of Appeal, however, was not of the same opinion. General knowledge about a business is not confidential. As there was no suggestion that Carlsen took customer lists or acquired any special or unique knowledge that belonged to Physique, he was not liable for breach of confidence. Carlsen had not breached any fiduciary duty as he did not actively solicit specific customers of his former employer, nor did he take a maturing business opportunity from Physique.

Critical Analysis: What is the distinction between confidential business information and trade information? How could the uncle have protected his business from competition from his nephew?

Figure 18.2

A COMPARISON OF MAJOR FORMS OF INTELLECTUAL PROPERTY

	Patents	Industrial designs	Trademarks	Copyrights	Confidential business information[1]
Subject matter	Inventions	Shape, configuration, pattern, ornamentation	Word, symbol, design	Literary, dramatic, musical, and artistic works, sound recordings, performances, broadcasts	Business information (e.g., technology, product recipes, databases)
Requirements	New, useful, unobvious	Original, novel	Title, distinctiveness, registrable	Original, fixed	Economic value, efforts to keep secret, generally not known
Protects against	Use, sale, manufacture	Use, sale, manufacture	Use	Copying, modifying	Disclosure, use
Term of protection	20 years	10 years	15+15+15+ years	Life + 50 years	Indefinite (until disclosure)
First owner[2]	Inventor	Designer	First person to use or apply	Author	Creator
Application Process	Mandatory	Mandatory	Mandatory[3]	Optional	Not applicable

1. The term confidential business information is used interchangeably with trade secrets.

2. Ownership rights are subject to contracts that may specify other owners. This is particularly the case in employment.

3. Registration is required for protection under the *Trade-marks Act.* Unregistered trademarks receive protection under the common law.

Intellectual property rights can be extremely valuable to a business. Intellectual property is often created within the business in much the same manner as Andrea created her ideas. The process of doing so is time-consuming and costly. This suggests that an effective intellectual property program should be put in place to ensure that time and money are not wasted.

Assignments and Licences

assignment
The voluntary transfer of ownership rights.

licence
Consent given by the owner of rights to someone to do something that only the owner can do.

Although intellectual property may be created in-house, it is also possible to purchase or receive an **assignment** of intellectual property rights or to receive a **licence** to use the intellectual property. By the same token, it is possible for a business to exploit its rights by assigning them or licensing their use.

An assignment involves a change of ownership from the assignor to the assignee. As a general rule, all intellectual property rights are assignable in whole or part. An exception to the general rule is that moral rights cannot be assigned, although they may be waived.

A business may also obtain a licence to use another's intellectual property. A licence is consent or permission to use the right on the terms specified in the licence. All intellectual property rights are capable of being licensed.

The process of getting an assignment or licence of intellectual property is not always easy. The process is often complicated by technological developments. Consider, for example, multimedia works that integrate text, graphics, still images, sounds, music, animation, or video and with which the user can interact. The product involves various forms of media working together and may rely on literally thousands of sources, including copyrighted text, images, and music, for its content. The developer of the multimedia work has to ensure that all the relevant rights to

Intellectual Property Program

An effective intellectual property program involves the following:

BUSINESS APPLICATION OF THE LAW

- Inventorying intellectual property. It is important to identify and assess the value of inventions, even though they may not be used right away.
- Knowing others' intellectual property. This ensures that resources will not be expended on reinventing the wheel.
- Avoiding infringement of others' intellectual property, with the goal of saving time, money, and energy that would otherwise

have to be devoted to legal challenges by owners.

- Protecting intellectual property early, not when it is too late. Identify at the outset what parts or elements of developments need protection.
- Including intellectual property in the company's planning. Doing so will help ensure that the intellectual property is exploited and protected. In short, recognize that intellectual property is a business asset.

these copyrighted works have been obtained, either through ownership or some form of licence or other permission.

Intellectual rights are often subject to compulsory licencing. For example, a compulsory licence without the consent of the patent holder may be ordered by the patent office if the exclusive rights under a patent are deemed to be "abused." Examples of abuses are refusal to grant a licence on reasonable terms, thereby prejudicing trade or industry, and failure to meet local demand for a patented article.

Protection of Intellectual Property

Intellectual property is an asset in the same manner as other business assets. Just as an organization takes measures to protect its buildings, land, equipment, and personnel, so too must it take steps to protect its intellectual property. It is not sufficient for Andrea to simply "create" intellectual property rights. Her rights require continuous monitoring and protection.

Use

Intellectual property rights are subject to loss if they are not properly used and maintained, as is shown in the following examples:

- A patent may be considered abused if, among other things, insufficient quantities of the patented item are produced to meet demand. As a result, a licence to use the patent may be granted to another, or the patent may even be revoked.
- Industrial design rights may be substantially reduced if the goods are not properly marked. A defence of innocent infringement is available unless proper notice (i.e., capital D in a circle) is used on articles or their containers. The defence has the effect of limiting the owner's remedy for infringement to injunctive relief.
- A trademark can be subject to attacks for non-use or abandonment if it is not used continuously in association with the goods or services for which it is registered. A trademark may also be lost if it loses its distinctiveness, as when it slips into everyday usage. For example, Nylon and Kleenex, once trademarks, lost their distinctiveness and thus their status as trademarks by falling into everyday usage and becoming generic terms.
- Confidential business information is lost once it is disclosed. A business needs to be particularly vigilant in protecting it.

Litigation

At some point it may be necessary to engage in litigation in order to protect intellectual property rights. Intellectual property litigation is complex and expensive, often requiring the services of experts. The most common intellectual property actions are as follows:

- *Patent infringement.* Infringement is not defined in the *Patent Act,* but it is generally taken to mean an unlicenced intrusion on the patent holder's rights (i.e., making, selling, using, or constructing something that comes within the scope of the patent claims). There is no requirement to show that the infringer *intended* to infringe on the patent, nor is it a requirement that the infringer's action come within the precise language of the claims. So long as the infringer is taking the substance of the invention, that will suffice. A successful action for patent

infringement may result in the infringer having to pay damages or turn profits over to the patent holder, also known as the *patentee*. The patentee may also be entitled to an injunction prior to trial or after trial to prevent further infringement and a "delivering-up" of the infringing product.

- *Copyright infringement.* Copyright is infringed whenever anyone, without the consent of the owner of the copyright, does anything that only the owner has the right to do. As noted above, this could involve various activities—copying, publishing, performing, translating, and the like. The copyright owner has a full range of remedies. An owner may also elect statutory damages of up to $20 000 instead of damages and profits. As well, the infringer is subject to criminal sanctions of fines up to $1 million and/or five years in jail.
- *Industrial design infringement.* The *Industrial Design Act* prohibits anyone from applying a registered industrial design to the ornamentation of any article without the permission of the owner. The prohibition also includes applying a confusingly similar design. The traditional remedies for infringement are an injunction to restrain further use of the design, damages, and an accounting of profits made by the defendant in using the design. The act also provides for nominal criminal sanctions.
- *Trademark infringement.* Infringement of trademark is protected by both the *Trade-marks Act* and the tort of passing off. The action can be brought against a trader who misrepresents the source of goods or services so as to deceive the public. This may be done by using the same or a similar trademark. Remedies

for trademark infringement include injunctions, damages or an accounting of profits, and the destruction or delivery of the offending goods or the means to produce them.

■ *Confidential business information.* There is no statutory cause of action related to the misappropriation of confidential business information. There are, however, common law actions for breach of express and implied terms and breach of confidence, as discussed above. It must be shown that the information was confidential, that the information was disclosed under circumstances of confidence, and that the recipient misused the information to the detriment of the owner. Remedies available include injunctions, damages, and an accounting and/or a declaration of the entitlement to the information.

Protecting Intellectual Property Abroad

It is difficult to protect intellectual property in a domestic setting. It is even more difficult to protect it in an international setting as, unlike tangible property, intellectual property is not bound by borders or geography. Protection is not just a question of designing and implementing rules for protection. There are very different perspectives on whether intellectual property should receive protection. The developing countries have little incentive to provide protection, as they need intellectual property in order to grow and prosper. The developed countries have a somewhat different perspective, as they consider intellectual property a valuable investment and worthy of protection.

Canada is a signatory to a number of treaties that give a measure of international protection to intellectual property rights. The major international conventions are these:

• *Paris Convention for the Protection of Industrial Property.* This convention provides national treatment and foreign filing priorities for patents, trademarks, and industrial designs.
• *Patent Co-operation Treaty.* This treaty applies to patent applications and assists an applicant in managing foreign filings.
• *Berne Convention.* This convention, which applies to literary and artistic works, provides for automatic copyright protection to nationals of member states without any requirement for formalities.

• *Universal Copyright Convention.* This convention provides national treatment for foreign copyrighted works provided the copyright symbol, the name of the copyright owner, and the date of publication are on the work.
• *Agreement on Trade-Related Aspects of Intellectual Property (TRIPS).* This is an agreement of the World Trade Organization (WTO) that establishes certain minimum standards of intellectual property protection for patents, trademarks, and copyrights. The agreement provides that a country should treat foreign nationals no less favourably than its own nationals with respect to intellectual property rights. Developing countries have a transition period for implementing it.

The broad intent of the international agreements is to provide protection for foreign intellectual property. For example, works that have copyright protection in Canada have protection in countries that are signatories to the Berne Convention. By the same token, an author who is a citizen of a convention country receives copyright protection in Canada.

Critical Analysis: What is the justification for providing protection for foreign intellectual property? When intellectual property protection is extended in this manner, whose interests are curtailed?

Business Law in Practice Revisited

1. How can Andrea protect her ideas from encroachment by competitors?

Andrea has a number of options available for protecting her ideas. Her invention of a contact lens case may be patentable if she can demonstrate that it is new, useful, and unobvious. The configuration of the case and the design applied to it may qualify as an industrial design if the design is original and novel. The proposed names for the product can be protected by trademark law if they meet requirements of use, distinctiveness, and registrability. Marketing plans, brochures, and other written materials that are original and fixed in some form receive protection against copying pursuant to the *Copyright Act*.

The protection afforded intellectual property may in some cases—industrial designs, patents, and (registered) trademarks—require registration. In other cases, —copyright, confidential business information, and (common law) trademarks—no formal steps are required as protection may arise automatically.

Different rights attach to different categories of intellectual property. In general, the rights encompass the right to prevent others from using the protected work. The length of protection varies: 20 years for patents; 10 years for industrial designs; life of author plus 50 years for copyright; and an indefinite period for trademarks and confidential business information.

There can be significant costs involved in creating and maintaining the various categories of rights. Andrea needs to evaluate the costs and benefits of each type of protection. It is conceivable but unlikely (after an examination of the patents registry) that her contact lens case is patentable. Also of concern is the high cost of patent protection for a relatively low-priced item. Andrea could try to keep her process confidential; however, this would not enable her to exploit it, as it is probable that reverse engineering will reveal how the case works. Andrea's most feasible alternative is to protect the configuration and the eye design through an industrial design registration, if the projected return on sales of the product justifies the expenditure. The name may be protectable, but a search of the trademarks registry would be necessary to make that evaluation.

The relationships between the various categories suggest that Andrea needs to consider the alternatives in her strategic decision making. There are advantages and disadvantages to each alternative regarding type of protection afforded, costs of application and registration, and opportunities to exploit rights. This is an area in which the law affords protection; it is up to business to take advantage of the opportunities.

2. How can Andrea's ideas be protected from encroachment by investors or lenders?

Various aspects of Andrea's ideas can be classified as confidential business information until public disclosure. In the process of developing and exploiting her ideas, particularly as she attempts to attract investors, she can ask to have confidentiality agreements signed that prohibit potential investors and lenders from revealing or using Andrea's ideas. In the absence of a specific agreement, the duty of confidentiality may still arise. However, Andrea should not be content to rely on an implied obligation.

Chapter Summary

The term *intellectual property* is used to describe the results of an intellectual or creative process. The term is also used to describe the rights people have or acquire in ideas and in the ways they express those ideas.

The main categories of intellectual property rights are patents, industrial designs, trademarks, copyrights, and confidential information. The rights that attach to each category vary but generally encompass the right to use and the right to exclude others from using.

There is considerable overlap between the various categories of intellectual property. It is possible for more than one area of intellectual property law to protect different aspects of a single product or process. As well, there may be alternatives for protecting a single product. For example, an invention may qualify for patent protection, or the invention can be kept secret through the mechanism of a trade secret. Patent protection provides a monopoly for a period of time, but the price of the monopoly is the requirement to disclose the invention. A trade secret is just that—a secret! Once disclosure occurs, there is no protection. The ornamentation of a product subject to patent protection may receive industrial design protection.

Businesses acquire intellectual property in a number of ways. A lot of intellectual property is created in-house by employees, but it can also be bought or acquired through a licensing agreement.

Intellectual property, like other business assets, must be protected. An effective intellectual property policy should encompass its acquisition and proper use. Failure to acquire and maintain intellectual property rights may result in missed opportunities and losses for the business. In some cases, intellectual property rights ultimately may need to be protected by bringing legal action against infringers.

Study Chapter

Questions for Review

1. What is intellectual property?

2. What are the major forms of intellectual property rights?

3. What is a patent? Give an example.

4. Are life forms patentable in Canada?

5. How long does patent protection last?

6. What is an industrial design? What are the requirements for industrial design registration?

7. What is the relationship between trademarks and trade names?

8. Must trademarks be registered to receive legal protection? Explain.

9. Who owns the copyright in a book? How long does copyright last?

10. What are the requirements for the protection of confidential business information?

11. What is the difference between an intellectual property assignment and a licence?

12. Why should companies develop an intellectual property program?

Questions for Discussion

1. What role should intellectual property rights play in business plans and goals? How can the creation or acquisition of intellectual property rights enhance or facilitate the advancement of business goals?

2. In some instances, intellectual property rights give a monopoly over certain technologies. What is the justification for the monopoly? Do you think intellectual property rights should be strictly enforced in underdeveloped or developing countries?

3. It is well known that copying infringes on copyright to a great degree. For example, there is widespread copying of music from the Internet, without permission and in violation of the legislation. Can these actions be justified? Can they be prevented? What are the arguments put forward by the infringers?

4. A trademark may be lost if it is not properly used. How should a trademark be properly used? What are the critical elements of a trademark use policy for employees?

Situations for Discussion

1. Harry is an engineer employed by LMN Gas company. Recently he was working in a group designing the natural gas pipeline used for distributing natural gas from offshore to various parts of eastern Canada. Interested in gas in general, Harry did a lot of experimenting and he actually came up with two innovations:

   • a carburetor that greatly improves the efficiency of gas when used in cars and furnaces
   • a method of sealing the pipes used in transporting the gas so that the likelihood of a leak is greatly reduced

   Is Harry entitled to apply for patents for his inventions? What are the considerations in the decision to apply for a patent?

2. Meredith opened a restaurant called Checkers in St. John's, Newfoundland. After about six months, she received a phone call informing her that "Checkers" is the name of a restaurant in Vancouver, British Columbia, and that she must immediately cease using the same name. Must she comply? Why or why not? How can Meredith obtain rights in the name?

3. Hannah attended a seminar put on by the local chamber of commerce on how to successfully market a home-based business. At the seminar, she received a number of printed handouts from the facilitator. Hannah wants to use portions of the material in her business. Is she entitled to do so? Explain.

4. Anne recently returned from a holiday in Ottawa. While there, she visited the National Gallery and was most impressed by a landscape painting by one of the Group of Seven artists. Anne believes that the scene depicted in the painting would provide a wonderful design for her housewares business. She would like to use it for wallpaper, dishes, and other bric-a-brac. Does her plan have any implications in terms of intellectual property? Explain.

5. Daniel is a carpenter who has designed a unique dog house. He has sold a few houses at a local craft show and is now in full production to keep up with demand. Another business has copied Daniel's design and is selling a dog house very much like Daniel's.

   Can Daniel do anything to prevent the competitor from selling dog houses that are almost identical to his? Should he pursue any action?

6. Mechanical engineer Vladislav Ircha was hired by Seanix Technology Inc. in March 1995 to design chassis and cases for computers. For the first few months, Ircha spent most of his time meeting with a subcontractor who was developing a case for Seanix's newest motherboard. Ircha soon realized, however, that the subcontractor's design was flawed, so he began working on a design of his own. Lacking proper design facilities at Seanix's office, he did most of the work at home, and was able to produce a completed mockup of a new "swing-out" case in early 1996. Ircha's design was so impressive that the president of Seanix offered him a 30 percent salary increase and a bonus for a European vacation. Ircha, however, refused the president's offer, left the company, and claimed rights in the case. Seanix brought action for rights in the case. What legal issue(s) must be resolved? Outline the law that governs them.

7. In 1985, photographer Jim Allen took a picture of the then deputy prime minister (Sheila Copps), an opposition MP at the time, sitting on a motorcycle clothed in leather garb. The photograph appeared on the cover of the November issue of *Saturday Night*. A dispute arose when the cover was republished in the *Toronto Star* in 1990 without further compensation to the photographer. What area of the law does this dispute involve? What legal issue(s) must be resolved?

8. Inspector Clouseau is the bumbling Parisian detective in the *Pink Panther* movies that starred the late Peter Sellers. Despite his bungling, Clouseau always solved the crime. In the inaugural film, Clouseau was called on to investigate the theft of a fabulous gemstone with one small flaw. When held to the light, the gemstone resembled a pink panther. Hence, the name.

   The name Pink Panther lives on, not only in films but also in a cartoon series and in the movie's theme music, which won an Academy Award for Henry Mancini. A cosmetics company that operates beauty salons wants to use the name Pink Panther Beauty Corp. in its business. United Artists, the producer of the films, objects.

   Is the cosmetics company permitted to use the name? Why or why not?

Chapter Nineteen

Real Property

Objectives

AFTER STUDYING THIS CHAPTER, YOU SHOULD HAVE AN UNDERSTANDING OF

► THE NATURE AND OWNERSHIP OF REAL PROPERTY
► THE VARIOUS WAYS TO ACQUIRE AND TRANSFER OWNERSHIP
► HOW A MORTGAGE WORKS
► THE RIGHTS AND DUTIES OF LANDLORDS AND TENANTS

Business Law in Practice

Universal Furniture Ltd. (Universal), located in Halifax, Nova Scotia, manufactures and sells custom-made furniture. The consistently high quality of Universal's products has earned it a reputation beyond Nova Scotia so that orders are now coming from several other provinces, as well as from the state of Maine. Universal's current facility, which is leased, is not large enough to accommodate its growing business. This space shortage means that Universal has several business decisions to make. The first is an investment matter regarding *how* expansion ought to proceed: Should Universal lease a larger space, purchase land with an existing building, or buy land on which to construct a building? A related matter concerns size: Should Universal acquire a space just adequate for its immediate needs or large enough to allow for future growth? A final matter is the need for financing if Universal decides to buy or build.

1. What are the legal features of the various real estate options available to Universal?
2. What factors should Universal consider in deciding how to expand?
3. How can Universal use a mortgage to finance the expansion?

Ownership

real property
Land or real estate.

The legal concept of **real property** refers to land or real estate.[1] When people own real property, they own a defined piece of land that includes not only the *surface* of the land but also everything above and below it—expressed in law as "the earth beneath and the air above." In practice, however, these broad ownership rights are limited by legal rules facilitating air travel, mining, and oil and gas production, to name a few examples. The term *real estate* also includes structures on the land, such as fences and buildings, as well as anything attached to those structures. Items so attached are known as **fixtures** and include heating ducts, lights, and plumbing—any item permanently attached to the land through screws, nails, bolts, or similar means.[2]

fixtures
Anything permanently attached to land.

Land has always been a valuable commodity, and therefore the rules governing real property have deep historical roots. The value of land results from two key attributes. First, land is permanent and immoveable, so it is easier to track and control than other, more portable forms of property, such as cars and furniture. Second, the quantity is limited, so the value is determined by the market for a particular type of land.

Real property is largely governed by common law, and traditionally, the law is devoted to protecting rights to property, such as determining who owns the same piece of land when more than one person is making a claim. Nowadays, however, public policy—in the areas of conservation and environmental protection, for example—means that statute law is an increasingly significant factor.

Interests in Land

fee simple
The highest level of land ownership.

The highest and most comprehensive level of ownership of land possible under our system of law is known as a **fee simple**.[3] An owner in fee simple owns the land unconditionally and can dispose of it in any way he or she sees fit. Ownership of land does not, however, have to be concentrated in one person or remain with that person in an uninterrupted fashion. In fact, ownership of land is easily divisible.

Division of Ownership

One piece of land can be owned by several people at once. For instance, if Universal cannot afford a building on its own, it may strike an arrangement with its majority shareholder so that *both* of them buy the building and split the cost equally. Both co-owners have an *undivided* half-interest in the *entire* building. Each of them owns 50 percent of the whole, but their respective halves cannot be singled out or identified in any distinct way.

Though Universal and its shareholders are the owners of the real estate, they are called *tenants* in this context. In ordinary usage, a tenant generally refers to someone

---

1. Bruce H. Ziff, *Principles of Property Law,* 2d ed. (Scarborough: Carswell, 1996) at 81.
2. Hentry Campbell Black, *Black's Law Dictionary,* 6th ed. (St. Paul, Minn.: West, 1990) at 638.
3. *Supra* note 1 at 148.

who leases space rather than owns it outright: however, the legal use of the word *tenant* is much broader and includes someone who has *any* kind of right or title in land at all.

In the time leading up to purchase, Universal and its shareholder can negotiate either **tenancy in common** or joint tenancy. If they choose to be tenants in common, they each have an undivided interest in the land, meaning they can deal with their own interest in any way they see fit and without having to consult the other co-owner.[4] In a related fashion, if one of the tenants in common dies—the shareholder, in our example—his undivided half-interest in the real estate forms part of his personal estate and goes to his heirs.[5]

A **joint tenancy** is also a form of undivided co-ownership but is distinguished by the right of survivorship. Should one of the joint tenants die, his undivided half-interest goes directly and automatically to the other joint tenant.[6] The heirs of the deceased shareholder would have no claim on the land co-owned with Universal. Both forms of co-ownership require cooperation among the owners in order to use or sell the property.

tenancy in common
Co-ownership whereby each owner of an undivided interest can dispose of that interest.

joint tenancy
Co-ownership whereby the survivor inherits the undivided interest of the deceased.

Division of Ownership in Time

Ownership in land can also be divided in time. The most common example is a lease. If Universal buys a building that has more space than Universal needs at the moment, it may decide to find a tenant to use the extra space for a time. Through the mechanism of a lease, the owner—or landlord—gives a tenant exclusive possession of the building (or a portion thereof, depending on the agreement) for a period of time in exchange for rent. When the lease terminates at the end of the defined period, the landlord resumes control.

Limits on Ownership

There are numerous restrictions on land any use imposed by statute law and common law:

- Municipal governments have the authority to control land use through planning schemes and zoning regulations. For example, if an area of a town is zoned for residential use, it is normally not available for commercial development.
- Environmental regulations affect the use of land by limiting or prohibiting the discharge of harmful substances.
- The common law of nuisance limits any use of land that unduly interferes with other owners' enjoyment of their land. A landowner who produces smoke or noise is subject to being sued for the tort of nuisance.[7]
- Many government agencies have the authority to expropriate land for particular purposes. For example, if a new highway is to be built, the government can assume ownership of the portions of land along the route after providing compensation to the owners according to specified procedures.

---

4. The parties can, of course, enter into a contract whereby they agree not to deal with their respective interests freely but to offer the other a right of first refusal, for example.

5. Corporations do not die, but they do wind up. If Universal winds up, its half-interest forms part of the assets used to pay out creditors and shareholders. To facilitate liquidation, the shareholder may offer to buy the land outright or the co-owners may decide to sell. Alternatively, if the shareholder is uncooperative, Universal can seek an order of partition and sale. This would permit the real estate to be sold and the proceeds to be divided between the owners.

6. Most married couples own property as joint tenants because of this right of survivorship.

7. See Chapter 12.

- In a similar fashion, government agencies can use land for a particular purpose, such as a pipeline.
- Ownership of land in a foreign country can be limited by that country's governmental policy. For example, foreign governments may nationalize whole industries without compensation to landowners from other countries. Foreign governments may also impose limits on the quantity of land that can be owned by nonresidents.

Other limits on ownership result from contracts made by the landowner. In short, the landowner has the option to "sell" his right of full control over the land in exchange for a payment of money or other benefit. For example, the landowner may do the following:

easement
The right to use the land of another for a particular purpose.

- Grant an adjoining landowner the right to use a portion of his land for a particular purpose. For example, a landowner may give a neighbour the right to take a short-cut across his land. In law, this is known as an **easement**.
- Grant a lease to a tenant, thereby giving the tenant the right to occupy the land for the specified period in exchange for rent.
- Grant a mortgage on the land as security for a loan. This makes ownership subject to repayment according to the agreed terms of the loan. The right of the lender to be repaid takes priority, and the new owner has purchased the land "subject to the mortgage."

restrictive covenant
A restriction on the use of land as specified in the deed.

deed
A document that transfers ownership of land.

- Make the land subject to **restrictive covenants**. Covenants are legally enforceable promises contained in the document transferring ownership (commonly called a **deed**). For example, deeds to lots of land in a housing development may contain covenants that prohibit or restrict certain activities (such as cutting trees or erecting storage sheds) for the purpose of preserving the character of the development and thereby enhancing its value.

These various limits on ownership raise a crucial aspect of land law for business people. Anyone contemplating the acquisition of any interest in land needs to do a thorough investigation of potential restrictions that could affect the rights to the particular piece of land. Otherwise, a buyer may end up owning land that cannot be used for its intended purpose.

Registration of Ownership

The provinces have constitutional jurisdiction over property rights.[8] A key use of this jurisdiction is a system for documenting and recording interests in land. The value of land justifies a system in which those with an ownership interest are able to record or register their interests in a public fashion. The purposes of this type of system are twofold: first, to enable owners to give notice of the land they own and the extent of their ownership; and second, to enable anyone contemplating the acquisition of an interest in land to investigate the state of ownership in order to verify its status.

Because of the provincial control, the systems of registration vary from province to province, though there are only two general types.

---

8. *Constitution Act, 1982,* s. 92(13): "property and civil rights in the province."

registry system
The system of land registration whereby the records are available to be examined.

A REGISTRY SYSTEM   The **registry system**, which originated in the eastern provinces,[9] provides the facilities for recording documents and the maintenance of the registrations. The public has access to the records and can examine or search the records to evaluate the state of ownership of a particular piece of land. This process is known as "searching the title." The main purpose of the search is to verify the seller's ownership by investigating the "chain of title" to confirm that no one has a conflicting claim to all or part of the land in question. Also required is an evaluation of the results of the search to decide whether the title is "clear" or not. If there are title defects, the parties will seek to fix those defects. For example, assume that Universal has negotiated to purchase property for its expansion, but a search reveals that there is an unregistered deed in the chain. In such circumstances, it may be possible to register the missing deed and perfect the registered record—cure the defect in the current owner's registration. If the defect cannot be cured, Universal may still decide to proceed with the deal but extract a price concession from the vendor. For example, if the search reveals a small encroachment on the property by an adjoining owner, Universal may decide to proceed with the transaction in any event but at a reduced purchase price.

The sequence of registering documents is crucial to this system. If there are conflicting claims to the same piece of land, the person who *registered* his or her interest first has priority, regardless of which *transaction* was completed first. So long as the one who registers first has no knowledge of the earlier transaction and has paid valuable consideration for the land in question, that person's interest in and claim to the land is fully protected. The party who registers second has no recourse against the land but may have actions against those who assisted in the failed transaction or who made representations concerning the status of title, for example.

paralegal
One who performs legal work under the supervision of a practising lawyer.

The administrators of a registry system take no responsibility for the validity of the documents that are filed and express no opinion on the state of the title of a particular piece of property. Lawyers retained by the buyer of property are responsible for the search and the evaluation of the results. Law clerks or **paralegals** retained by the lawyer may do the actual search.

land titles system
The system of land registration whereby the administrators guarantee the title to land.

THE LAND TITLES SYSTEM   The other system, the one in place in the western provinces,[10] is the **land titles system**. The administrators of this system assume a much more active role in that they evaluate each document presented for registration and maintain a record of the documents relating to each piece of property. They are also responsible for the accuracy of the information they provide, and they maintain an insurance fund to compensate those who suffer loss because of their errors. When someone wishes to know the state of the title to a piece of land, they need only consult the certificate of title and are not ordinarily required to do a historical search. Because the certificate itself is authoritative proof of title, there is less potential for competing claims. The greater certainty and reliability of the land titles system has caused several provinces that use the registry system, such as New Brunswick and Nova Scotia, to begin the transition toward using the land titles system.

---

9. Nova Scotia, New Brunswick, Prince Edward Island, Newfoundland, and parts of Ontario and Manitoba.
10. Saskatchewan, Alberta, British Columbia, and parts of Manitoba and Ontario.

Electronic Registration and Interests in Land

TECHNOLOGY AND THE LAW

The development of technology has huge potential for increased efficiency and accessability in the registration of interests in land. Traditionally, these systems have been paper based, involving problems and expense with indexing and storage. Several provinces operating under the registry and land titles systems are aggressively using technology to improve their systems of land registration.

Ontario has allowed electronic searching of records for several years. This eliminates the need for lawyers or other legal personnel to personally visit registry offices to check the records. Ontario will soon make electronic registration of land information mandatory. This will entail the recognition of digital signatures and will eliminate the need to register and store massive quantities of paper.

Saskatchewan is combining eight land registration districts into a single database, greatly simpli-

fying the search process. Also planned are online registration by authorized users and the availability of geodetic maps so that interested parties can see a map of a particular property along with title information.

Nova Scotia is in the process of assigning a parcel identifier number to each lot of land in the province; this should streamline the complicated searches in the registry system in place there. Also planned is the centralization of many registries and government offices with records relevant to the transfer of land in business. In British Columbia, online searching has been available since the mid-1980s.

Critical Analysis: What are the advantages of online property registration? Are there any disadvantages?

Source: Paula Kulig, "The Virtual Landscape" *The National* (May 1999) 21.

Acquisition of Ownership

There are several ways to acquire an interest in land. Universal can buy land with a building already in place, or it can buy land on which to build its own structure. Either purchase is likely to require financing, probably in the form of a loan from a financial institution secured by a mortgage on the property being purchased. If the space acquired exceeds current needs, Universal may lease the extra space to a tenant, thereby relinquishing control during the period of the lease. As an alternative to buying, Universal can lease larger premises as a tenant. By doing so, Universal gains control of the land for the term of the lease, but acquires no permanent ownership of the property.

The Purchasing Transaction

Buying land is a buyer-beware situation, expressed in law as *caveat emptor*. It is up to the buyer (also known as the purchaser) to investigate and evaluate the property both in financial and in legal terms. The seller (known as the vendor) must not mislead the buyer but generally is under no obligation to disclose information about the property, even when that information might cause the buyer to hesitate.[11]

If Universal decides on the purchase option, the first step is to identify a property that appears to be appropriate in terms of price, size, location, and suitability for Universal's manufacturing and sales operations. Universal should have its legal advisor involved from the outset to identify, among other matters, the legal significance of communication and documents used by Universal and the current owner. The technical nature of real estate transactions makes the use of professional advice a practical necessity.

Participants in the Transaction

The main participants in a real estate transaction are the buyer and the seller. In a commercial deal, such as the one Universal is contemplating, the parties to the contract of purchase and sale are likely to be corporations. Individuals from both corporations will be chosen to coordinate the deal and conclude the contract. In addition, each party may have a real estate agent, a property appraiser, a land surveyor, an engineer, and a lawyer providing expert advice and guidance. The seller, for example, will likely have engaged a real estate agent to find suitable buyers. For its part, Universal might engage an agent to identify suitable properties. The lawyers on both sides will advise on the main agreement between the buyer and the seller. Appraisers may be hired to formally value the property, based on the structure and the current market. Surveyors may be retained to determine the physical boundaries of the property. Engineers may be retained to provide an expert report on the structural integrity of the building in question. Consultants may be involved to check for any environmental hazards.

From a legal point of view, Universal's transaction is a complicated set of contracts revolving around the main contract for the transfer and sale of the property. Universal must decide which professionals it requires and be very clear on what services and advice each will provide. For example, a lawyer will normally do the investigation of title but is likely not in a position to place a value on the land.

Traditionally, lawyers have accepted responsibility for evaluating the reliability of the title of property their clients are buying. This is especially the case in registry systems, under which the lawyer searches the title and gives an opinion on its validity. Lawyers have professional liability insurance that compensates clients if lawyers are negligent in providing advice on title to property. In fact, a significant portion of claims made against lawyers arise from such situations. The cost of this insurance is reflected in the fees charged to clients in property transactions.

The concept of title insurance is well established in the United States but is a relatively new concept in Canada. The use of title insurance diverts much of the responsibility, work, and related fees from lawyers. Insurance companies offer protection to property buyers against problems with the title to the property in return for a premium that is less than the fee charged by lawyers. There is some concern for the integrity of land registration systems if property can be transferred and title documents registered without full investigation of title and the resulting repair of defects that thorough searches reveal. A title search is preventative in that it identifies problems before the transaction closes. Title insurance provides compensation if a

---

11. There are numerous exceptions to the proposition that the vendor of real estate has no duty to disclose information concerning the property. See, for example, Shannon O'Byrne, "Culpable Silence: Liability for Non-Disclosure in the Contractual Arena" (1998) 30 Can. Bus. L.J. 239.

problem is discovered later, but it may not result in the repair of the problem with the registered title.

In addition to the buyer, the seller, and professionals, others are less directly involved, as illustrated in the following examples:

- If the property is currently occupied by tenants, Universal's ownership may be subject to the rights of those tenants, depending on the jurisdiction involved and the length of the lease.
- If the property is currently mortgaged, that obligation must be discharged by the vendor or assumed by the purchaser or otherwise addressed in the financial adjustments between the parties.
- If Universal needs a loan to finance its purchase, the bank or some other lender must be brought into the equation. Universal will be required to grant the bank a mortgage on the property in question for the amount borrowed plus interest.

Stages in the Transaction

There are three stages in the transaction resulting in the transfer of the land to Universal: the agreement of purchase and sale, the investigation, and the closing.

Agreement of Purchase and Sale

agreement of purchase and sale
The contract for buying and selling land.

Of prime importance is the **agreement of purchase and sale** between Universal and the seller. Though the content of this agreement is entirely as negotiated between the parties, normal elements would include provision for Universal to conduct a full investigation of the property, the opportunity to bring matters of concern to the seller, time for Universal to arrange its financing, and a specific date for the conclusion (closing) of the transaction. This agreement can also be made conditional; for example, "subject to a satisfactory engineer's report" or "subject to financing." If, for example, Universal makes good-faith efforts to secure financing but is unable to find a willing lender, it can terminate the agreement with the vendor because the condition of being able to secure financing has not been fulfilled.[12]

Universal's agreement with the seller is the main contract and therefore must contain all requirements or terms of importance to Universal. As with any contract, once this one is signed, it is difficult to change without the agreement of both parties.[13] One legal requirement that affects this contract is that it must be in writing and signed by the parties.[14] This eliminates attempts to incorporate into the agreement items that may have been discussed but on which no formal agreement has been reached.

The contents of the agreement of purchase and sale depend on the nature of the property and the value of the transaction. The basic terms are these:

- the precise names of the parties
- a precise description of the property, including reference to the registered deed and sufficient detail so as to leave no doubt as to location, size, and boundaries
- the purchase price, deposit, and method of payment
- a statement of any conditions on which the agreement depends

---

12. For discussion of conditions precedent and conditional agreements, see Chapter 7.
13. See the law of mistake in Chapter 8.
14. See the discussion of the *Statute of Frauds* in Chapter 8.

Case

Hayward v. *Mellick* (1984), 26 B.L.R. 156 (Ont. C.A.)

The Business Context: The agreement between the buyer and the seller should include all terms and conditions that are important to them. A buyer should not rely on information outside the contract, even if the information comes from the seller or an agent. If the information is important, it should be included as a term of the contract.

Factual Background: The Mellicks owned a farm that the Haywards were interested in buying. During negotiations, the Mellicks' agent told the Haywards that the farm contained a total of 94 acres, with 65 acres under cultivation, and Mellick confirmed the statement. The offer to buy described the farm as containing 94 acres but made no mention of acres under cultivation. The agreement contained a clause indicating that there were no conditions, representations, or agreements other than those expressly contained in the offer. The deal closed, and several months later, the Haywards discovered that there were only 51.7 acres of land under cultivation.

The Legal Question: Are the Haywards entitled to 65 acres under cultivation?

Resolution: The agreement was for the purchase and sale of a 94-acre farm with two fields under cultivation. The Haywards' belief that there were 65 cultivated acres and their decision to buy were influenced by the erroneous information from Mellick and his agent; however, the agent had no authority from Mellick to provide the information. The informal way in which Mellick confirmed the agent's statement about cultivated acreage was not sufficient to make it a term of the agreement.

Mellick was negligent in making the statement without personal knowledge or measurement, but the contract contained the "entire agreement" clause, which excluded all representations (such as the one concerning acres under cultivation) from the contract. Therefore, the Haywards were limited to the terms of the agreement, which entitled them to 94 acres but made no provision for land under cultivation.

Critical Analysis: The Haywards made two errors in the agreement: they failed to include a term specifically referring to the 65 acres under cultivation, and they agreed to the clause excluding all other promises. How should the Haywards and their lawyer have acted differently? Should buyers be able to rely on statements from the seller about the property?

- a list and description of exactly what is included in the price (e.g., equipment, fixtures)
- the date for closing and a list of what each party must deliver on that date
- a statement of who is responsible for what during the period between signing and closing

Normally, Universal would submit an offer to buy, and the seller would accept it or respond to it with a counteroffer, which Universal would then accept or vary, and so on until they both agreed unconditionally on all the terms. Only then would a contract exist.[15]

The Investigation

The second stage consists of the investigation by the buyer and the seller's response to any problems the buyer may raise.

The buyer must thoroughly investigate all aspects of the property during the search period allowed in the contract. Normally, Universal's lawyer will conduct various searches on Universal's behalf. These searches are described below.

---

15. See Chapter 6.

title search
Investigation of the registered ownership of land.

TITLE TO THE PROPERTY   Since this property is located in Nova Scotia, a **title search** in the local registry of deeds[16] is needed. Normally, the search goes back 40 years to ensure clear title. Any problems that can be fixed, such as an unregistered deed, will be remedied. If there is a more serious problem (e.g., someone else owns part of the land), Universal will have the option to pull out of the deal. If the land is located in a land titles district, the search will not be necessary—Universal can obtain a certificate of title from the land titles office.

LEGAL CLAIMS AGAINST THE SELLER   Searches should be done to establish what legal claims exist against the seller of the property in question. For example, judgments registered against the seller are valid for a number of years; the exact duration varies from jurisdiction to jurisdiction. Such a judgment can form the basis of a claim against any land owned by the seller—a matter that a prospective purchaser would want to know about. Universal would not want to own a piece of land subject to such a claim because it would have less than clear title.

VERIFICATION OF BOUNDARIES   Universal will retain a surveyor to confirm that the boundaries described in the registered deed fit the physical boundaries of the land. For example, if the deed provides for 1000 metres of road frontage but the surveyor finds only 800 metres, there is a definite problem.

PHYSICAL EXAMINATION   Universal must confirm that the property is in the state it is expecting according to the agreement. If there are tenants in place, Universal must confirm the space occupied by those tenants. Universal must also confirm the building's structural integrity, as provided for in the engineer's report.

ENVIRONMENTAL AUDIT   Universal must ensure that there are no lingering or hidden environmental hazards. For example, if the property was used at some time as a gas station, Universal must ensure that there is no leaked fuel in the ground, or abandoned underground tanks that might leak.

TAXES   Universal must be sure that the municipal property taxes and any other local charges related to the property are paid up to date. If they are not, they will be deducted from the total due to the seller at closing.

LOCAL BYLAWS   Universal must verify that the property can be used for its desired purpose. If buying land on which to build or using an existing building for a new purpose, Universal must be especially careful that the zoning regulations permit that purpose.

Any problems revealed by the various searches and investigations will be dealt with according to the terms of the agreement. They will either be fixed or permit the buyer to abort the transaction.

The Closing

closing
The final stage of a real estate transaction.

The third stage, the **closing**, occurs after all price adjustments have been made. At this point final payment is made and a formal transfer of ownership occurs.

If any difficulties found during the various searches can be remedied and Universal is able to get its mortgage, the closing will proceed after the price is adjusted for such items as prepaid taxes (added to the price) or rent already received from tenants (deducted). Universal will then make the final payment, and the seller

---

16. *Registry Act,* R.S.O.1990, c. R-20; R.S.N.S. 1989, c. 392.

Responsibility for Contaminated Land

The permanence of land facilitates the tracking of ownership because it cannot be moved or hidden. One of the negative features of this permanence concerns the long-term effects of commercial activities that may be harmful to the land itself and the surrounding community. In terms of pollution to the ground from toxic substances or leakage of safe substances (such as gasoline), the legal issues concern liability for cleanup and for resulting harm to the environment and to the health of the public. Scientific advances have altered the public view of some activities. Commercial activities that were acceptable even 10 years ago may not be any longer. The difficult issue is how to allocate responsibility for the harm already caused. There is a huge risk in buying property with a long history of use for indus-

ENVIRONMENTAL PERSPECTIVE

trial purposes, i.e, how should such "tainted" property be valued? and should the buyer purchase it or not? A purchaser could face a large bill to clean up contamination caused by previous owners.

The broad social issue is how to balance the need to encourage development and commercial activity with the need to control and prohibit dangerous activities.

Critical Analysis: Who should bear the cost of environmental protection: the businesses that generate profits or the public sector? Which is more important: private property rights or the public interest? What about pollution whose source cannot be clearly traced?

will deliver the deed to the property along with keys and other means of access to the property. Universal will then immediately register its deed at the local registry office to ensure that no competing claims intervene to disrupt its ownership. At the moment of closing, Universal becomes responsible for the property. Universal must therefore arrange for insurance coverage to be transferred at that time as well.

Incomplete Transaction

The deal may fall through for a number of reasons, some of which the agreement will anticipate. For example, if the title search reveals a problem that cannot be fixed or the buyer is unable to arrange financing pursuant to a conditional agreement, the buyer normally has the right to bow out of the deal. In other situations, the buyer or the seller may find a better deal and simply refuse to complete the transaction as required by the agreement. Refusal to complete for a reason not contemplated by the agreement is a breach of contract and entitles the party not in breach to a remedy. If the buyer backs out, for example, the seller must try to mitigate by finding a replacement buyer. In such circumstances, the seller may experience costs in finding a new buyer and may, in fact, end up selling the property for less than the defaulting buyer had agreed to. In such circumstances, the seller is entitled to recover the difference between these two prices from the defaulting buyer by way of damages for breach of contract. For example, if the defaulting buyer had agreed to buy the property for $200 000 and the seller is only able to find a buyer for the property for $150 000, then the defaulting buyer is liable to pay damages to the seller in the amount of $50 000.

Figure 19.1

SUMMARY OF A REAL ESTATE TRANSACTION

SELLER

- decides to sell a piece of land
- determines the value of the land, possibly through a professional appraisal
- engages a real estate agent to find a buyer and signs a listing agreement
- engages a lawyer to advise on the legal requirements
- engages a surveyor to confirm boundaries

BUYER

- decides to buy land
- engages an agent to find suitable land
- engages an appraiser to value the seller's land
- engages a lawyer to advise on the legal requirements

SELLER AND BUYER

- negotiate, possibly with the assistance of their agents and their lawyers
- reach agreement on all terms and conclude a formal written agreement

SELLER

- addresses any problems discovered through the buyer's investigation

BUYER

- investigates all aspects of the property, including the seller's title and any outstanding claims
- confirms the boundaries of the land by retaining a land surveyor
- arranges for financing
- has an engineer assess the structural soundness of the building
- has a consultant investigate environmental soundness

SELLER AND BUYER (and/or their lawyers)

- attend the closing

SELLER

- delivers the title document (the deed)
- delivers the keys to the property

BUYER

- makes final payment
- registers the title document
- arranges for insurance
- moves in

If the seller refuses to complete, the buyer is entitled to the extra expense in acquiring a similar property. If monetary compensation is not adequate, the buyer can claim for specific performance—a special remedy for situations in which the subject of the contract is unique and the buyer cannot be compensated with anything less than the property itself.[17] In contrast, if the contract involves the purchase of goods, such as a computer, or services, such as office renovations, and the supplier fails to deliver, the customer can find another source and be fully compensated by an award for the extra cost. In such circumstances, the court will not order the party in default to specifically perform the contract but will order damages in lieu of such an order.

---

17. See Chapter 9.

Landmark Case

Semelhago v. *Paramedevan* (1996), 197 N.R. 379 (S.C.C.)

The Business Context: This a recent case in which the Supreme Court of Canada challenged the traditional wisdom that breach of contract by the seller of land automatically entitles the buyer to specific performance.

Factual Background: Paramedevan agreed to sell land to Semelhago for $205 000 and later backed out. Semelhago sued for breach of contract, initially seeking an order for specific performance, but later chose to accept damages instead. By the time the trial took place, the market value of the property had increased to $325 000. Land owned by Semelhago at the time of contract had also increased in value from $190 000 to $300 000. Since Semelhago kept his existing property, he enjoyed the benefit of the increase in value. The only issue was what compensation Semelhago should receive for Paramedevan's breach of contract.

The Legal Question: Should Semelhago be awarded the value of the property on the date of the breach of contract or the value of the property on the date of the trial? Should the increase in the value of Semelhago's property be deducted from the damage award?

Resolution: Justice Sopinka dealt with the amount of damages that would replace specific performance:

> The difference between the contract price and the value "given close to trial" as found by the trial judge is $120,000. I would not deduct from this amount the increase in value of the [buyer's] residence which he retained when the deal did not close. If the [buyer] had received a decree of specific performance, he would have had the property contracted for and retained the amount of the rise in value of his own property. Damages are to be substituted for the decree of specific performance.

The buyer ultimately recovered $120 000 less deductions for certain financing charges that he saved by remaining in his original property.

The court also discussed the right to specific performance:

> While at one time the common law regarded every piece of real estate to be unique, with the progress of modern real estate development this is no longer the case. Residential, business and industrial properties are all mass produced much in the same way as other consumer products. If a deal falls through for one property, another is frequently, though not always, readily available.

Critical Analysis: The Supreme Court of Canada said in this case that land is not automatically considered to be unique. The buyer must prove this fact in order to secure an order for specific performance. What are the features of a piece of commercial real estate that might make it unique? Is it fair to give the buyer the choice between specific performance and damages?

The Mortgage Transaction

How a Mortgage Works

If Universal requires financing to purchase the land, there are options such as borrowing or seeking further investment in the company. In this chapter, a mortgage on the land itself is discussed.[18] Universal will approach potential lenders, usually banks or other financial institutions but possibly private lenders. Assuming that Universal has a good working relationship with its own bank and is creditworthy, the bank is likely to be the lender, provided that the parties can agree on such matters as the rate of interest and a repayment schedule.

---

18. See corporate financing in Chapter 15.

mortgage
A credit arrangement
where land is security
for the loan.

A mortgage transaction has two aspects. First, a **mortgage** is a contract for the extension of credit and is a debt owed by Universal to its bank. The lender advances the principal sum to the borrower, who promises to repay the principal plus interest over the specified period. Second, the mortgage transaction also involves the bank taking a security interest in the land purchased by Universal. To attain this security protection, the bank must register the mortgage document, thereby giving notice to all creditors of Universal—as well as anyone considering purchasing the property from Universal—that the bank has first claim against the land. Registration gives the bank *secured* status, which will protect its claim against the land even if the borrower becomes bankrupt.

Any claims already registered against the land have priority over the bank and will affect the bank's decision to grant the loan. The bank's mortgage does not forbid Universal from attempting to borrow more money in future using this land as security, but those subsequent lenders will be aware that the already registered mortgage forms a prior claim. There is no legal limit to the number of mortgages against a property, but lenders' security is subject to those who have previously registered mortgages.

Under the land titles system, registration of the mortgage creates a legal charge on the land. In short, the registered mortgage amounts to a claim—or lien—on the land until repayment is complete. In provinces under the registry system, in contrast, the mortgage actually transfers ownership of the land to the lender for the duration of the lending period. The bank becomes the legal owner, but Universal remains the equitable owner. This means that Universal has the **equity of redemption**—the right to have legal ownership restored to it upon repayment.

Although the effect of the mortgage on ownership varies according to the system in place in the particular province, the practical effect on the use of the land is the same. Universal is the borrower, known as the **mortgagor**. Universal remains the occupier of the land, so there is no apparent change in control of the land. The bank as the lender is known as the **mortgagee**. As long as Universal makes the required payments on the loan, the bank is content to allow Universal to carry on normal business activities on the land.

equity of redemption
The right to regain title to mortgaged land upon repayment of the debt.

mortgagor
The borrower who grants the mortgage.

mortgagee
The lender who receives the mortgage.

Terms of the Mortgage

The focus of the mortgage is on protecting the value of the land in question. This protection is achieved by preventing the borrower from doing anything with the land that would lower its value and by giving the lender maximum flexibility in dealing with the borrower. For example, if the mortgagor does not adequately insure the property, the mortgagee (the bank) has the right to secure proper insurance and hold the borrower responsible for those additional costs.

The bank will not grant the loan unless it is confident of Universal's ability to repay. As a precaution, however, the amount of the loan is likely to be less than the current value of the land, for two reasons. First, the mortgage is a long-term arrangement, so the bank will consider the possibility of developments in Universal's business or the market that might diminish the value of the security. Second, if Universal defaults and the bank needs to use the security to recover its money, it is unlikely that the land will produce its full market value in a quick sale. A serious drop in the market could result in negative equity for the owner—that is, the amount owed on the mortgage could be more than the value of the property.

The mortgage document is normally prepared by the lender. Though each bank has its own standard form of mortgage, all of them include the following as basic terms:

- amount of the loan (known as the principal)
- interest rate
- date of renegotiation of the interest rate
- period of repayment over which the loan is amortized
- schedule of payments
- provision for payment of property taxes
- provision for full insurance coverage on the property, with the proceeds to be paid directly to the lender
- borrower's obligation to keep the property in a good state of repair and refrain from any activity that would decrease its value
- complete legal description of the land
- provision for early repayment (possible penalty)
- acceleration clause, which provides that on default of payment by the borrower, the whole amount of the loan becomes due
- remedies of the lender on default
- discharge (release) of the mortgage at the end of the term when the full loan is repaid

Of particular interest are the clauses dealing with taxes and insurance. The bank needs to be sure the taxes are paid because the appropriate municipal or provincial authorities have the right to sell the property to recover any unpaid taxes levied against the property. The land would then be owned by the purchaser at the tax sale and not available to the bank.

The bank's interest in insurance is twofold. First, the bank needs full coverage on the property so that if a fire occurs, the proceeds from the insurance will essentially replace the portion of the security destroyed by the fire. In addition, the bank needs direct access to those insurance proceeds. If paid to the lender, the money is more difficult for the bank to recover than the property would have been before the fire.

Insurance can be purchased by the borrower to pay the outstanding balance to the lender in the event of the borrower's death. This transaction is not part of the mortgage itself but is an option that a bank usually offers.

Life of a Mortgage

If the mortgage transaction proceeds as intended by both the borrower and the lender, the borrower will repay the loan as the mortgage requires and the lender's claim or charge against the land will cease. The lender will provide a document to release, or discharge, the mortgage. When this document is registered, it provides public notice that the borrower's obligations have been satisfied. However, since a mortgage is a long-term arrangement, many events can occur that result in some change to the liability, such as the following:

- Universal may choose to pay off the mortgage before it is due. The mortgagee will likely anticipate this possibility in the mortgage and require Universal to pay a "penalty" or extra charge. This is to compensate the bank for interest it loses until it finds another borrower for the money lent to Universal.
- If Universal buys more land than it needs for its operation, it may choose to sell off some of the excess. Since the mortgage forms a claim on *all* the land,

Universal needs to negotiate with the bank for a release of the piece to be sold. Only when this partial release is registered can Universal transfer clear title to that piece.

- Universal may need to renegotiate the mortgage for further financing. If the value of the land is well above the amount of the outstanding loan, the land could be used as security for an additional amount. This is a separate issue from the periodic renegotiation of the interest rate on the original loan. For example, the repayment period for the loan may be amortized—or spread out—over 25 years, with the interest rate adjusted every 5 years.

- Corporate takeover or reorganization may change the identity of the bank. The lending bank would assign all of its outstanding mortgages to the new entity. Universal must then make its payments to the new entity.

- Universal may decide to sell the land. This requires that Universal pay out the mortgage fully or negotiate with the buyer to take over or "assume" the mortgage if the terms are attractive. For example, if Universal has a lower interest rate than the current market rate, the lower rate could be used as a selling point by Universal. This "assumption" requires the agreement of the bank and likely entails a significant risk for Universal. When a mortgage is assumed, the original borrower—Universal—remains liable for payment. Hence, if the new buyer defaults under the terms of the mortgage, the bank can claim the balance owing from Universal.

- Universal's business may suffer to the point where cash flow no longer allows for payments to the bank. This is the situation that the bank most fears and that the mortgage is primarily designed to address. The bank is likely to give Universal some leeway in payment, especially if the bank is hopeful that Universal's business may recover. If this fails, the bank will proceed to exercise its legal remedies pursuant to the mortgage and applicable legislation. The rights of the lender and the procedures to be followed vary from province to province,[19] but they all involve some version of what is known as **foreclosure and sale**. Foreclosure refers to the lender's right to terminate the borrower's interest in the property by taking possession of the land. The lender can then sell the land, either by itself or through a court-supervised sale. Whichever procedure applies, the objective is to allow the lender to maximize the proceeds from the property to be applied against the outstanding loan. Most provinces[20] also permit the lender to proceed against the borrower for the shortfall—known as the **deficiency**—between the outstanding amount and the proceeds from sale of the property. At any point in the foreclosure process, the borrower is able to repay the loan and regain control of the land (assuming of course that another source of financing becomes available). If Universal cannot repay the loan, it loses the land and may be left owing a substantial debt. The bank is left with a bad debt and the knowledge that the decision to lend the money was flawed.

foreclosure and sale
The mortgagee's remedy to redeem the land to pay the mortgage debt.

deficiency
The shortfall between the outstanding mortgage balance and the proceeds from sale of the land.

---

19. Sale by the court is preferred in Alberta, Saskatchewan, and part of Manitoba and is the only remedy in Nova Scotia. Otherwise, foreclosure by the mortgagee is allowed.

20. In Alberta, Saskatchewan, and British Columbia, the mortgagee cannot sue individual borrowers and can only sue corporations that have waived their statutory protection.

Case

Bayshore Trust Company v. *Assam*, [1992] O.J. No. 715 (Gen. Div.)

The Business Context: As in most commercial transactions, the parties are expected to look out for their own interests. Lenders are concerned with the security of their loans and the borrowers' ability to repay. Borrowers must normally accept responsibility for their own financial decisions.

Factual Background: Bayshore granted a loan to Assam based on a mortgage for $210 000 with interest at 14 percent for a one-year term. The monthly payment was $2540. At the end of the term, Bayshore renewed the mortgage for another year at 14.5 percent. During that year, Assam defaulted and Bayshore sued Assam. He consented to a judgment of $241 667 and agreed to deliver possession of the property to Bayshore, but filed a counterclaim against Bayshore for inducing him into a state of financial disaster and causing him economic loss by granting a mortgage with monthly payments he could not possibly make. Assam alleged that Bayshore should never have lent him such a large sum of money to begin with. At the time of the mortgage, Assam's annual income was $28 000. He had vague plans to lease rooms in the property (which he never did).

The Legal Question: Did Bayshore as lender owe a fiduciary duty of care to Assam as borrower to look out for Assam's interests and ensure that he did not overextend himself financially?

Resolution: Bayshore was an "equity lender," granting loans up to 70 percent of the value of property. The court found that this relationship was a simple debtor–creditor arrangement, with no responsibility on the lender for the borrower's financial welfare:

> ... as a general rule, a mortgagee is not in a fiduciary relationship with the mortgagor.
>
> I do not find that Mr. Assam was vulnerable or dependent upon Bayshore Trust. He was an educated person who understood the extent of the obligation he was undertaking. He had legal counsel. The relationship between him and Bayshore was that of a lender and a borrower. There was a lot of contact between Mr. Assam and Bayshore Trust and its agents, particularly over his inability to make monthly payments, but I cannot find that Bayshore had any duty of a fiduciary nature to Mr. Assam. It is not appropriate to transform the relationship of lender and borrower into a fiduciary relationship. I cannot find that Bayshore exercised a dominating influence over Mr. Assam and there is nothing in the evidence that would bring me to the conclusion that Bayshore went beyond a normal business relationship so as to place itself in the position of a fiduciary.

Critical Analysis: Who should decide whether a lender can make payments on a loan? Should the lender be required to do anything more than protect its own interest in the mortgage?

The Real Estate Lease

The Landlord–Tenant Relationship

tenant
The occupier of land that is leased.

landlord
The owner of land that is leased.

Universal is currently in a landlord–tenant relationship because it is leasing its space. Universal is the **tenant**. The owner of the building that Universal occupies is the **landlord**. One of the options Universal is considering is whether to buy or build larger premises and lease the unneeded portion. If it proceeds on this basis, Universal will become an owner and landlord and enter into a lease with someone else.

lease
The contract that transfers control of land from the landlord to the tenant in exchange for the payment of rent.

A **lease** is a contract between a landlord and a tenant. It records the rights and obligations of both parties. Leases are of two general types—commercial and residential.

The terms of leases for commercial property are negotiated by the landlord and tenant. They are free to agree on the format and content of the lease.

Residential leases are highly regulated by provincial legislation[21] that

- prescribes the form and content of the lease
- limits the amount of security deposits that can be required of residential tenants
- defines the rights and obligations of the landlord and tenant
- requires the landlord to maintain the premises
- provides remedies for breach of the terms of the lease
- provides the procedures for resolving disputes

If Universal were the owner of an apartment complex and an office building, the leases would be under quite different regimes.

exclusive possession
The tenant's right to control land during the term of a lease.

A lease is a means of dividing ownership of property for a time. Its key feature is the idea of **exclusive possession**, which means the tenant has a high level of control and responsibility over the premises during the term of the lease. This concept of exclusive possession is doubly important because first, it is the main factor in deciding whether a lease has been created to begin with and, second, it is the major consequence of the creation of a lease. For example, a five-year lease means that the tenant has the right to occupy and control the property for the full five years and cannot be legally evicted from the land unless the lease is violated by that tenant in a major way. If Universal, as landlord, enters into a long-term lease with a tenant and later wrongfully terminates that lease, Universal is in breach of contract and will have to pay damages to the tenant. It may also be subject to an order for specific performance or an injunction preventing the eviction of the tenant.

As with any contract, the parties need to appreciate the point at which they have achieved sufficient consensus to form a legal relationship. Each party wants terms acceptable to it and wants to obligate the other party to them. At the same time, the parties want to avoid unintentional obligations. An offer to lease or an agreement to lease becomes enforceable only if it contains all the key terms and has been accepted by the other party.

In a commercial context, a number of factors will determine the lease content, including the relative bargaining positions of the parties and the nature of the market for the property in question. If suitable space is scarce, the landlord has the advantage and can largely dictate terms, especially the amount of rent. If there is a glut of property and the tenant is in no hurry to move from its current premises, the tenant may be able to negotiate significant concessions from the landlord.

Terms of the Lease

The complexity of the lease depends on the value, nature, and size of the property. A lease for an office tower is lengthy and complicated because there are many issues to address and a great deal is at stake. Conversely, a lease of a garage to store surplus equipment could be quite simple.

These are some basic terms in every commercial lease:

- identification of the parties
- description of the premises

---

21. See, for example, *Residential Tenancies Act*, R.S.N.S. 1989, c. 401; *Landlord and Tenant Act*, R.S.O. 1990, c. L-7; R.S.M. 1987, c. L-70.

Parties in a commercial lease are free to negotiate their terms.

- permitted alteration of the space
- ownership of improvements to the space
- calculation of rent (i.e., per square foot and/or based on sales)
- responsibility for repairs and maintenance to the leased space and any common areas
- security and damage deposits
- permitted uses of the space
- limits on the landlord's ability to lease space to the tenant's competitors
- time period of the lease
- provisions for renegotiation or renewal
- remedies for either party if the other fails to comply with the lease
- what happens in case of fire and other unexpected events

Rights and Obligations

The rights and obligations contained in a lease are formally known as covenants and consist largely of whatever the parties negotiate in the lease. Each lease is unique and must be reviewed closely in order to establish the rights and obligations of the parties. However, some covenants arise from the tenant's exclusive possession and corresponding responsibility:

- The tenant is responsible for repairs unless the lease imposes some obligation on the landlord.
- The tenant is entitled to exclusive and quiet possession of the premises for the full term. In return, the tenant must pay rent and observe the terms of the lease.
- The tenant cannot withhold rent, even if the landlord fails to meet a requirement in the lease. The tenant's remedy is to claim compensation from the landlord while continuing to pay rent.
- The tenant cannot terminate the lease and move out unless the landlord's breach of the lease has made the premises uninhabitable for normal purposes.
- Ordinarily, the tenant can *assign* the lease or *sublet* the property to another tenant. Assigning the lease transfers full rights and responsibilities for the remainder of the term. If the assignee fails to pay the property rent or otherwise breaches a covenant in the lease, the original tenant (the assignor) has no liability for the default. A sublease, in contrast, is simply an arrangement whereby the tenant permits someone else to occupy the leased premises for the period remaining in the term. The original tenant remains fully liable under the lease but has rights against the subtenant—should the subtenant fail to pay the subrent, for example. It is usually the case that the landlord's permission is required for both of these arrangements, and ordinarily, the landlord cannot withhold consent unreasonably.[22]

The landlord's basic obligations are to refrain from interfering with the tenant's use or enjoyment of the property and to provide any benefits or services promised in the lease. The landlord's goal is that the tenant pay rent, use the

---

22. *Supra* note 1 at 258.

distress
The right of a commercial landlord to seize the tenant's property for nonpayment of rent.

premises for acceptable purposes, and cause no damage to the property. The major risk for landlords is that the tenants may get into financial difficulties. Thus, remedies for landlords focus on collecting unpaid rent and evicting tenants for defaulting on payment or for other serious breaches. Commercial landlords also have the remedy of **distress**: if a landlord follows proper procedures, she can seize the property of the tenant located in the leased premises, sell the property, and apply the proceeds to the unpaid rent.[23]

Case

Highway Properties Ltd. v. *Kelly, Douglas & Co. Ltd.*
(1971), 17 D.L.R. (3d) 710 (S.C.C.)

The Business Context: Kelly, Douglas & Co. was a major tenant in a commercial mall. The mall was a failure and Kelly, Douglas broke their lease by failing to pay rent and abandoning the premises. The case discusses the liability of the tenant to the landlord in this situation.

Factual Background: The lease applied to space "to be used for [a] grocery store and super market" for 15 years. There was prescribed annual rent, payable monthly, with additional rent based on a formula. The tenant agreed to pay rent, taxes, and maintenance costs; to pay into a mall promotion fund; and not to do anything detrimental to insurance coverage. There were clauses dealing with renewal and repairs. The landlord promised quiet enjoyment. The lease permitted the landlord to resume possession after the rent was in arrears for 15 days by giving 15 days' notice. The tenant also agreed to carry on its business continuously for the term of the lease.

The lease was signed on August 19, 1960. By the following February, there were only five other tenants in the

mall. The Kelly, Douglas store closed on March 24, 1962. Highway Properties commenced action against Kelly, Douglas in July 1962 for failure to pay rent and for letting their premises "go dark." In September, Kelly, Douglas repudiated the lease and Highway resumed possession.

The Legal Question: Are the damages suffered by Highway Properties limited to losses as of the date of termination of the lease, or do they include prospective damages for the tenant's failure to carry on business for the full term of the lease?

Resolution: The landlord can terminate the lease based on the tenant's conduct, take possession, and claim damages for the period remaining in the lease. Therefore, the court sent the case back to the trial judge to assess the damages, based on factors such as the present value of the unpaid future rent (less the actual rental value accrued by finding a replacement tenant) and the loss that the landlord could prove resulted from the tenant's failure to stay in business in the leased property.

Critical Analysis: Does a landlord have too many options for proceeding against the tenant for unpaid rent? Should the landlord be able to end the lease and claim damages for the full term, or should the landlord be required to find a new tenant?

Termination of the Lease

The parties may be able to terminate their relationship if the terms of the lease are not followed. Normally, the lease runs its natural course and ends when the agreed period for the tenant's occupation expires.

There are two types of leases in terms of time. One identifies the exact duration of the term. If Universal's lease of its current space was for a defined term of five years, which is about to expire, the lease will automatically end on the specified date. Neither party is required to give any notice, and neither party has any obligations to

---

23. *Supra* note 1 at 264.

negotiate a renewal or extension. Therefore the landlord should realize that Universal is free to move, and Universal should realize that it has no right to stay beyond the specified date.

The other type is known as a **periodic tenancy** and automatically renews itself unless one party gives the required notice before the current term expires. For example, if Universal has a lease from year to year, that lease will automatically be renewed for another full year unless either Universal or the landlord give sufficient notice (likely about three months).

Which type of tenancy has been created depends on the actions and agreement of the parties. If they have not clearly indicated their intentions in the lease, a court will classify the lease based on their actions and other circumstances of the case. To avoid uncertainty, the parties should deal with termination in detail in the lease so that there is no doubt about the length, renewals, or the need for notice to terminate.

A lease as an interest in land is, in theory, not affected by the sale of the property by the landlord. The tenant is entitled to stay until the end of the lease with the new owner as landlord. However, long-term leases must be registered in some provinces, and in any event should be registered to give those investigating title clear notice of their existence.

Upon securing a new location, Universal's ability to terminate its current lease will depend on its terms and Universal's ability to negotiate with the landlord. If Universal chooses to lease a larger space (rather than buy), it needs to weigh the stability of a longer-term lease with the need to keep its expansion options open through a short-term arrangement. If Universal buys or builds a structure and leases part of it to a tenant, Universal should consider finding a tenant who is prepared to enter a periodic tenancy from month to month. This would permit Universal to regain full possession of the premises when the need arises. The disadvantage is that this may make the property less attractive to tenants unless their needs are short-term ones as well.

periodic tenancy
A lease that is automatically renewed unless one party gives proper notice to terminate.

Disposition of Property

The owner of the fee simple in real property has total control over the disposition of ownership in that property. The options are as follows:

- Use the land as security for a loan by granting a mortgage. The owner remains in possession of the land and retains control, subject to the obligation to repay the debt and abide by the terms of the mortgage.
- Lease all or part of the land to tenants. The owner gives up possession for a defined period of time but retains ownership. At the end of the lease, possession reverts to the owner.
- Transfer the land to family or others by gift or through a will on death. There are various legal options available to the owner in terms of dividing ownership (such as a joint tenancy).
- Sell all or part of the land. This results in a complete transfer of the fee simple in the portion of land sold. Full ownership rights are transferred to the purchaser, who becomes the registered owner.

Business Law in Practice Revisited

1. What are the key features of the various options?

A lease provides control of land for a limited period but is not ownership. It requires no purchase financing. Buying or building to meet current needs provides ownership and control, but requires financing and involves the expense and responsibility of ownership. Buying or building to provide for expansion involves the largest investment and is the most complicated. Universal will be owner of the entire property and landlord of the leased portion.

2. What factors should Universal consider in deciding how to expand?

Universal must consider the limits on ownership of land (such as zoning regulations) and the liability it entails (such as environmental damage). There is the financial risk in becoming a mortgagor (borrower) that the business will not produce sufficient income to pay the mortgagee (lender) and the mortgaged property could be lost. The temporary nature of a lease means that as tenant, Universal has no rights beyond the agreed term of its current lease. If Universal becomes a landlord of part of its new premises, it has no right to end the lease simply because it requires the leased space sooner than expected.

Of considerable importance to Universal's decision are the nonlegal factors such as its projected need for space, its financial stability, and the markets for real estate and Universal's products.

3. How can Universal use a mortgage to finance the expansion?

Universal can borrow on the security of the land under consideration for purchase. If a building is in place, the value of the land may be adequate security for a mortgage. If Universal buys vacant land on which to build, it is likely that additional assets will be required as security and shareholders may be called on to provide additional security from their personal assets.

Universal must be confident of its ability to make the mortgage payments. Default gives the lender significant rights in relation to the land.

Chapter Summary

Real property is permanent and immoveable, and the total quantity is fixed. The focus of the law is on the land itself rather than the buildings or fixtures attached to it. Ownership is called the fee simple and includes everything on, above, and below the land, subject to a wide variety of limits on use. The owner of land can transfer and divide ownership in a number of ways. Registration of any interest in land is required to preserve priority over other claimants. The most common ways to acquire ownership are to purchase the fee simple through a real estate transaction or to become a tenant through a lease. In buying land, there is considerable risk involved, which can be managed through investigation of all aspects of the land.

A mortgage is security for a loan that emphasizes the preservation of the value of the property. A mortgage gives the lender the right to have the land sold if the loan is not repaid.

The landlord transfers to the tenant the right of exclusive possession of the land for the term of the lease. In return, the landlord is entitled to rent and has the right to regain possession at the end of the lease or earlier if the tenant defaults. The lease will end when a specified term expires or when one party gives the required notice to the other.

The holder of the fee simple can dispose of her interest as she chooses: lease the land temporarily, sell it, or give it away while she is alive or in her will upon death.

Study Chapter

Key Terms and Concepts

Questions for Review

1. What are the unique features of land as a form of property?

2. What is a fee simple?

3. How does a joint tenancy operate?

4. How can ownership of land be divided by time?

5. What is the purpose of registering title to land? What are the two systems of land registration in Canada and how do they work?

6. What are the three stages in a property transaction?

7. What is clear title?

8. What happens at the closing of a property transaction?

9. What are the key features of a mortgage?

10. What are a lender's remedies if the borrower fails to make mortgage payments?

11. What are the essential terms in a lease?

12. How can the owner of land dispose of her interest?

Questions for Discussion

1. Land registration determines property rights strictly according to the order of registration. Should the system allow for late registration in exceptional circumstances, such as when a buyer either fails to consult a lawyer or the lawyer neglects to register the documents? Can you think of other exceptional circumstances?

2. Which is more cost efficient for property buyers, a title search or title insurance? To what extent is the opposition of lawyers to title insurance an attempt to protect their income?

3. Which is more important, an accurate land registry or cheaper property transactions?

4. Real property law originated as a means of protecting rights to private property. Is this purpose still valid in today's society, or are there more important public concerns?

5. Do the rules of contracts and mortgages allow the mortgagee (lender) too much protection at the expense of the mortgagor (borrower)? Should the lender bear some responsibility for a decision to lend that turns out to be a bad one?

6. Is there a need to regulate commercial tenancies to the same extent as residential tenancies?

7. Are real estate transactions unduly complicated by the involvement of so many participants? Could such transactions be simplified?

Situations for Discussion

1. Smith owns a farm on the route for a new natural gas pipeline. He has been notified that the pipeline developer has the right to come onto his property to lay the pipe and to visit in future for pipeline maintenance. Smith thinks natural gas is a dangerous substance and sees the pipeline as a hazard for his farm and family. He is strongly opposed to the pipeline being anywhere near his farm. Is the pipeline a justified imposition on landowners such as Smith along its route? Should Smith be able to refuse permission to use his land? Should he be able to claim increased compensation for the use of his land because of his opposition to natural gas?

2. Campbell's business is in financial difficulty. Technology is advancing quicker than Campbell can move. She is faced with a gradual reduction in business operations and a related need for less space. She has 20 years left in the lease of her business premises, but cannot afford to pay the monthly rent. How should Campbell approach her landlord? What are her legal options? Is the situation different if Campbell owns her business premises subject to a mortgage on which she cannot make the payments? How should she approach her banker? What are her legal options?

3. Johan is the owner and founder of his own business. Three of his children are actively involved in running the business, and one other daughter is a doctor. Johan is 52 years old and is beginning to think about retirement and the need to pass on his business to his children. How important is the ownership of the land on which the business is located for the succession of the family business? Johan can sell or give the land to some or all of his children. What factors should he consider before making his decision?

4. Bakke bought a strip mall development with a 25 percent cash payment and a 75 percent mortgage. The total price was $400 000, and her monthly mortgage payment was $3000. Traffic past the mall did not meet the expected volume. Bakke's major tenant defaulted on its lease and left. Bakke sued for unpaid rent, but the lawsuit is dragging on. She was unable to keep up her payments on the mortgage, and the bank foreclosed. The mall was eventually sold for $200 000. Because the outstanding balance on the mortgage was $280 000, the bank is now suing Bakke for the $80 000 shortfall plus its legal expenses. Bakke believes that the property was worth much more than $200 000 and wants to attack the bank's conduct of the sale and avoid the claim against her. What legal and practical difficulties does she face?

5. Harmon is interested in buying a property formerly used as a building supply outlet. When he investigates the land, he discovers that the adjacent property contains a former auto service centre with underground gasoline tanks. What is the risk to Harmon in buying the building supply land? How can he determine the extent of the risk? How should he deal with it?

6. Bresson bought a piece of land for commercial development for $3 million. He was assured that it contained an unlimited supply of water from an existing well. When construction began, it was discovered that the water was unusable due to a large cavity in the well and that half of the land was a bog covered with fill and unsuitable for building.[24] What investigation should Bresson have done before the deal closed? What can he do now?

24. Based on *Bresson* v. *Ward* (1987), 79 N.S.R. (2d) 156 (Cty. Ct.); *Edwards* v. *Boulderwood Development* (1984), 64 N.S.R. (2d) 395 (C.A.).

Twenty Chapter

Insurance

Objectives

AFTER STUDYING THIS CHAPTER, YOU SHOULD HAVE AN UNDERSTANDING OF:

► THE ROLE OF INSURANCE IN RISK MANAGEMENT
► THE VARIOUS KINDS OF INSURANCE
► THE NATURE OF AN INSURANCE CONTRACT, INCLUDING THE RIGHTS AND OBLIGATIONS OF THE INSURER AND THE INSURED

Business Law in Practice

Raj, Fionna, and Max are the sole shareholders in Wire Experts and Company Ltd. (WEC). The three are also its sole directors and devote all their time to managing and working for the company. The company is in the business of producing wires used to manufacture tires. It buys metal, formulates the alloys, extrudes the necessary wires, and then sells them to tire manufacturers both in Canada and abroad. The manufacture of the wire creates some contaminant waste products that require special storage and disposal.

A smaller part of WEC's business is consultation services. Since Fionna is an engineer, she occasionally provides advice to WEC's customers as to the kind of wire that would be suitable to their needs. For the most part, however, WEC's customers know what they want and provide their own specifications to WEC.

WEC's business office is on the first floor of its manufacturing plant. Suppliers, sales personnel, and representatives of various purchasers are frequent visitors. In addition to the plant, WEC owns several trucks, which its delivery personnel use to deliver wires to customers.

1. What risks are associated with WEC's business?
2. How can WEC use insurance to manage these risks?

Insurance Protection

Failure to secure insurance of the proper type and in sufficient quantity can bankrupt a business. For this reason, insurance is central to effective risk management, as discussed in Chapter 3. It permits a business to shift the risk of various kinds of losses because, through an **insurance policy**, the **insurer** promises to compensate the person (known as the **insured**) should the contemplated loss actually occur. The insurer provides this protection in exchange for payment, known as an insurance **premium**, from the insured.

insurance policy
A contract of insurance.

premium
The price paid for insurance coverage.

insurer
A company that sells insurance coverage.

insured
One who buys insurance coverage.

Figure 20.1

An insurance policy is a contract. By the terms of the contract, the parties agree to what kind of loss is covered, in what amount, under what circumstances, and at what cost. Insurance policies are also regulated by legislation in each of the provinces. Insurance legislation serves a number of significant purposes, including the following:

- mandating the terms that must be found in insurance contracts
- regulating the insurance industry generally by setting out licensing requirements for insurance companies, insurance brokers, and insurance adjusters
- putting in place a system for monitoring insurance companies, particularly with respect to their financial operation

The main goal of insurance legislation is to protect the public from unscrupulous, financially unstable, and otherwise problematic insurance companies. It also provides working rules that create stability within the industry at large.

The three basic kinds of insurance are as follows:

- *Life and disability insurance* provides payments on the death or disability of the insured.
- *Property insurance* (also known as fire insurance) provides payment when property of the insured is damaged or destroyed through accidents. It also can cover the costs of machine breakdown.
- *Liability insurance* (also known as casualty insurance) provides payment in circumstances where the insured is held legally responsible for causing loss or damage to another, known as the third party.[1]

---

1. The person who is injured or otherwise suffers loss is the third party in relation to the contract of insurance. In the contract of insurance, the insurer and insured are the first and second parties.

deductible
The part of a loss for which the insured is responsible.

With the exception of life insurance contracts, insurance policies can be written so that the insured pays a **deductible**. This means that the insured is responsible for the first part of the loss, and the insurer has liability for the balance. Agreeing to a deductible generally reduces the premiums that the insured must pay for the coverage. For example, WEC might agree to a $100 deductible for windshield replacement on its delivery trucks. If a WEC vehicle windshield requires replacement and the cost is $600, WEC's insurers will pay $500. The $100 deductible is WEC's responsibility, and to that extent, WEC is self-insured.

In order to secure proper coverage, a business person should assess the business operation and identify the kinds of legal risks it may encounter. For example, in its business, WEC faces a number of possible kinds of liabilities and losses, including the following:

- *Injury and property damage related to the operation of WEC's delivery trucks.* If WEC's delivery personnel drive negligently, they may be involved in traffic accidents that cause injury to other people, as well as property damage to other vehicles. Additionally, such negligence may cause injury to the WEC drivers themselves and damage to WEC vehicles.
- *Personal injury to suppliers, sales personnel, and purchasers who visit the manufacturing plant floor.* Since WEC's business office is located in its manufacturing plant, many people who are not directly involved in production may visit the plant on business. Injuries—from tripping on a carpet to being burned by the extrusion process—can be the result. As well, WEC employees who work in the manufacturing process and elsewhere face the risk of being hurt on the job.
- *Financial loss and injury to others caused by defective wire that WEC produced.* If WEC delivers defective wires that are later incorporated into tires produced by WEC customers, those tires may fail while being used or repaired, causing both physical injury and financial loss to those involved.
- *Financial loss and injury caused by Fionna's giving negligent advice to WEC customers concerning their wire needs.* If Fionna provides bad advice to WEC customers, they may end up with wire that is not appropriate for its intended use. This problem, in turn, may lead to physical injury and financial loss to WEC customers and to the ultimate consumers of the tires produced by WEC customers.
- *Injury and property damage caused by a fire or other disaster in the manufacturing plant.* If WEC experiences a fire in its plant, there can be a significant financial loss, since the building, as well as the equipment and machinery, will have to be repaired or replaced before company operations can resume.
- *Loss of profit owing to business interruption as a result of a fire or other causes of a plant shutdown.* In the event of a fire or other disaster, WEC may have to suspend business operations while it rebuilds. This loss of profit could cripple the company financially and even cause its demise.
- *Environmental damage caused by improper storage or disposal of waste products.* Environmental protection legislation in all jurisdictions prohibits businesses from discharging or spilling contaminants into the environment. Legislation may also permit the government to order the party responsible to clean up or otherwise repair the environmental damage that the contaminant caused. This cleanup can be costly for the company involved. As well, WEC can face civil actions by those who are injured or who suffer loss because WEC has improperly stored or disposed of its waste products. Since WEC produces fabricated metal products—a process that is likely to have significant environmental

implications[2]—it needs to pay particular attention to this kind of potentially catastrophic liability.

- *Death of one of the shareholders in WEC.* Should one of the WEC shareholders die, the others will likely want to buy out that person's shares. Financing the buyout will be a challenge for WEC.

Specialized Policies

While insurance is broadly divisible into three categories—life, property, and liability—insurance policies can be much more specialized. A business like WEC typically would have in place the following specialized policies.

Auto Insurance

An automobile owner is required by law to have insurance for liability arising from its ownership, use, and operation. While each jurisdiction has its own scheme in place, a common aim of these schemes is to ensure that owners are financially responsible for the liabilities that arise through use of their vehicles. Most people do not have the assets on hand to pay off a large judgment against them; insurance provides the funds to fulfill that financial responsibility, should it arise.

There are several types of auto insurance coverage. In Alberta, for example, the Standard Automobile Policy provides the insured with coverage against liability for the injury or death of someone else (third-party liability) caused by the operation of the insured vehicle. It also provides benefits to the insured for injury or death caused by an accident arising from the use or operation of the insured automobile, as well as compensation for loss or damage to the insured automobile itself. The latter is known as collision coverage.

Some people decide not to get collision coverage because the car itself is not worth very much. Purchasing third-party liability insurance, however, is not an option, but is required by law. Since a car accident causing paraplegia, for example, can result in millions of dollars of damages, owners should not be content with purchasing the minimum amount required by law. The minimum amount is simply not enough to cover a catastrophic accident. If there is a deficiency between the amount of insurance coverage and the actual damages sustained by the plaintiff, the insured will *personally* be responsible for the difference.

Each province specifies through legislation the minimum amount of coverage an owner must obtain for third-party liability. In Ontario, for example, the statutory minimum is $200 000.[3] Since this amount is insufficient to pay damages to another who has been seriously injured, the owner should purchase additional coverage.

Employees injured in car accidents on the job may have coverage through workers' compensation legislation. Under such legislation—which is in place in every Canadian province—participating employers pay premiums into a fund administered by a tribunal. Employees who are injured in the workplace or who suffer from a disease as a result, for example, of exposure to a pollutant in the work-

---

2. D. Belcher, "A Canadian Banker's Perspective on Proactive Due Diligence," at "Appendix A: Examples of Industries Likely to Have Significant Environmental Concerns," in *Managing Environmental Liability: A Practical Approach for Lenders* (Mississauga: Insight Press, 1991).

3. The *Ontario Insurance Act*, R.S.O. 1990, c. I.8, s. 251 provides: "Every contract evidenced by a motor vehicle liability policy insures, in respect of any one accident, to the limit of at least $200,000 exclusive of interest and costs, against liability resulting from bodily injury or the death of one or more persons and loss or damage to property."

place can then make a claim for benefits from this fund. When an employer participates in a workers' compensation board (WCB) plan, payment from the fund is the only compensation the employee is entitled to receive. Legislation prevents the employee from suing the employer, though there may be a right to sue others who are not participants in the workers' compensation scheme.[4]

Occupiers' Liability Insurance

WEC, as a building owner and occupier, is liable for injuries suffered to people on its premises if the injuries are due to WEC's failure to ensure that the premises are safe. Occupiers' liability insurance will compensate WEC if unsafe conditions cause injury to someone else—for example, a visitor to its plant floor. WEC should have a program in place to prevent such accidents from happening; insurance is intended to fill the gap when and if the system fails.

Comprehensive General Liability Insurance

The purpose of comprehensive general liability insurance (also known as CGL insurance) is to compensate enterprises like WEC, in a comprehensive way, for any liabilities they incur during the course of their business. For example, an important general risk faced by WEC is that its wires will fail in use and lead to some kind of loss. CGL insurance responds by compensating WEC for property damages, personal injury, loss of profit, and related losses suffered by a third party when WEC is legally responsible for such losses.[5] The CGL does *not* respond, however, to losses directly suffered by WEC itself. For this latter type of loss, WEC will need warranty insurance.

The following examples reveal the important difference between these two kinds of insurance:

EXAMPLE 1

> WEC produces wire that is seriously defective. When the customer incorporates that wire into its tire-manufacturing process, the tires fail and must be discarded. The customer loses about $50 000 in materials, time, and profit— all of which is attributable to WEC's defective product. WEC's CGL insurance policy will cover this loss.

EXAMPLE 2

> WEC produces wire that the customer notices is defective as soon as WEC attempts to deliver the shipment. Accordingly, the customer refuses to accept delivery, and WEC loses $50 000 in revenue. CGL insurance does not cover this loss because it is *not* a loss sustained by a WEC customer or other third party—it is a loss suffered directly by WEC itself. For coverage in this situation, WEC would need a warranty policy. Because its cost is so high, warranty insurance is rarely purchased. From a business perspective, WEC may be better off establishing an effective quality assurance and testing program, thereby dealing with such risks in-house, rather than looking to an insurance company for coverage.

---

4. M. Faieta, H. Kohn, et al., *Environmental Harm: Civil Actions and Compensation* (Toronto: Butterworths, 1996) at 405.

5. Note that coverage generally extends only to unintentional torts, rather than intentional acts.

Insurance Coverage for E-Business

As the volume of electronic business increases and businesses open their organizations and computer systems to those outside the company, they become more vulnerable to interference from hackers and other sources of contamination. Security concerns figure prominently in the factors that inhibit the development of e-business and increase the risks of participating in this form of business. Lloyd's of London has identified computer viruses as the single biggest risk of the 21st century.

Organizations risk the effects of viruses, such as computer downtime, damage to software, physical damage to computer installations, and lost productivity, if systems malfunction. Cyber-business insurance coverage is now available for damage to systems, security threats, and problems related to denial of service to customers if Web sites are ren-

dered unavailable. The greater the involvement of a business with the Internet, the higher the stakes if business is interrupted.

Insurance coverage and cost vary according to the type of business, the sort of computer system in place, and the level of security that exists.

Critical Analysis: Cyber-insurance has elements of property, business interruption, and third-party liability insurance. How will the insurance industry deal with major claims? If premiums increase significantly, the cost of doing business will rise accordingly. Is there a risk that major catastrophes could slow the growth of e-business? Are there other risk management strategies available to e-business?

Source: P. Pimentel, "Insurers See Interest in Cyber Policies" *The Globe and Mail* (10 May 2000) B11.

Errors and Omissions Insurance

When Fionna provides professional engineering advice to WEC customers, she is promising that it meets the standard of the reasonably competent person engaged in such activity.[6] Although this implied promise does not amount to a guarantee of perfection, she will be responsible for losses resulting from negligent advice. Through errors and omissions insurance (also known as E & O insurance), the insurer promises to pay on Fionna's behalf all the sums she is legally obligated to pay as damages resulting from the performance of her professional services. Investigation costs and Fionna's legal expenses will also be covered by her policy.[7] Like all insurance policies, Fionna's coverage will be subject to a number of conditions, such as the requirement that she give immediate notice to the insurer of a claim or *potential* claim against her. This notice allows the insurance company to carry out an investigation and otherwise gather facts associated with the alleged negligence.[8] Failure to give prompt notice or to comply with any other condition can result in the insurance company successfully denying coverage.

Corporate directors and officers also face liability for their errors and omissions related to operating their company. As discussed in Chapter 16, this risk can be insured against through directors' and officers' liability insurance—D & O insurance for short.

---

6. K.G. Neilson, "Suing the Insurer: Construction Related Insurance" in *Suing the Insurer* (Edmonton: Legal Education Society of Alberta, 1982) at 51.

7. *Ibid.* at 52.

8. *Ibid.* at 54.

Property Insurance

WEC should insure its manufacturing plant and equipment in order to fund any rebuilding or replacement that a fire or other disaster might occasion. One of the key choices WEC must make is whether to insure for the replacement value of its property or for the property's actual cash value.

If WEC chooses the second option, it will receive from the insurance company only the value of the property at the time it was destroyed, that is, not enough to purchase a replacement. If WEC chooses the first option, it will receive a higher level of compensation from the insurer—and also pay a higher premium—but the insurer also has the right to require WEC to actually rebuild or otherwise replace its property before it will pay out on the claim. WEC must also choose the coverage it wishes to purchase—for loss caused by fire, falling aircraft, earthquake, hail, water damage, malicious damage, smoke damage, and impact by vehicles, to name a few examples.[9] Not surprisingly, the more perils WEC insures against, the higher the premiums will be.

Whatever policy it ultimately chooses, WEC must be sure to fully describe its property and accurately value it in order to ensure proper and adequate coverage.

Commercial and Personal Insurance

Business owners must be careful to distinguish between personal risks and business risks, since this distinction determines the kind of policy they should purchase in the first place. Sometimes the distinction is easy to make, as many kinds of insurance are primarily business related, such as credit insurance. At other times, the distinction is more problematic, since some kinds of insurance relate to both home and business matters, such as fire, automobile, accident and sickness, third-party liability, and even life insurance.

Insurers distinguish between personal and commercial risks, as reflected in premiums and the language of policies. Failure to properly distinguish may result in the wrong type of policy and serious difficulties when making claims. The difficulties depend on the type of insurance.

Accident and sickness insurance is relatively straightforward. Although the nature of the risk is the same in both individual and commercial contexts, the packaging and nature of the contracts is different. Individuals negotiate the terms of their own policy with an insurer. Commercial insurance is provided through group contracts, which are master contracts between the insurer and an employer or organization. Individuals are entitled to coverage through their membership in the group.

The distinction in fire and liability insurance is crucial because of the policies themselves. Coverage as part of a tenant's or homeowner's package will normally exclude buildings used for commercial purposes and liability to third parties arising from professional or business activities.

Insurers selling automobile insurance policies must provide the coverage required by the applicable legislation, but they are permitted to exclude coverage for commercial activities (such as renting the vehicle or using it as a taxi) if the coverage is for private use of the vehicle.

Those buying insurance need to clarify their needs and activities with the insurer so that they acquire the appropriate type of policy with the particular coverage that their activities warrant.

Source: C. Brown & J. Menezes, *Insurance Law in Canada*, 2d ed. (Scarborough: Carswell, 1991) at 16-17.

---

9. C. Brown & J. Menezes, *Insurance Law in Canada*, 2d ed. (Scarborough: Carswell, 1991) at 182.

Business Interruption Loss Insurance

This kind of coverage—often contained in what is called an "all-risk" policy—provides the insured with financial compensation should it have to cease or reduce operations owing to a fire or another cause of damage to its plant. The insurer must compensate for loss of profits to the extent of the limits of the policy.

Case

Triple Five Corp. v. *Simcoe & Erie Group* (1994), 159 A.R. 1 (Q.B.), aff'd [1997] 5 W.W.R. 1 (C.A.), leave to appeal to the S.C.C. denied [1997] S.C.C.A. No. 263

The Business Context: The precise language of a policy is more important than what it is called or what the insured thinks is covered. This case illustrates that all-risk policies do not necessarily cover all possibilities.

Factual Background: Triple Five Corp. owned and operated West Edmonton Mall, a large shopping centre located in western Canada. One of the features of the mall was an amusement park, and more specifically, a roller coaster. A terrible accident resulted in one of the cars of the roller coaster flipping off the tracks and causing the death of two people. The claims regarding these fatalities were settled out of court. What was litigated, however, was whether Triple Five was entitled to compensation for loss of profit and other expenses that resulted from the roller coaster being out of commission for some time after the accident.

The Legal Question: Is Triple Five's insurer liable to pay Triple Five for its business interruption losses?

Resolution: The court ruled against Triple Five, and this outcome was affirmed on appeal. The fact that Triple Five lost profits because the roller coaster was out of commission for a period of time was not enough for its claim to be successful. Triple Five also had to prove that the cause of the accident itself fell within the terms of the policy. After hearing complicated expert evidence, the court ruled that the accident was caused by a design error. Since Triple Five had purchased insurance only to cover accidents external to the roller coaster itself—as opposed to something inherent or internal to the roller coaster—its loss was not insured.

Critical Analysis: Triple Five suffered a loss in gross revenues because the roller coaster was defectively designed. Would it therefore be able to sue the manufacturer of the roller coaster for breach of contract and perhaps for negligence?

Environmental Impairment Insurance

Not only may WEC face substantial fines for failing to comply with environmental protection legislation and for any clean-up costs associated with a spill or other accident, but it also can be sued by its neighbours for polluting the soil or ground water. Furthermore, if a subsequent owner of WEC's plant can trace pollutants back to WEC, WEC has civil liability for the cleanup and other associated costs, even though it no longer owns the land.

This liability explains why environmental impairment liability policies are very expensive and difficult to obtain.[10] A more viable—though not foolproof—alternative, is for WEC to ensure that it has an operational management policy in place to prevent such accidents from happening in the first place.[11]

---

10. G.J. Mannina, "Lender Liability—How to Minimize Environmental Risks" in *Managing Environmental Liability: A Practical Approach for Lenders* (Mississauga: Insight Press, 1991) at 28-29.

11. See Chapter 3.

Key Person Life Insurance

The partners in a firm or the shareholders of a small corporation likely wish their business to continue to be operated by the surviving owners if one of them dies. Their partnership agreement or shareholders' agreement will specify that the surviving owners have the right to buy the shares of the deceased owner. The effective exercise of that right requires a means of valuing the business and the shares of the deceased, as well as a means of financing the purchase of the shares by the survivors. Insurance on the lives of the owners is a means of financing the buyout. The owners need to agree on a method of evaluating the business when the insurance is purchased and at the time of death. They must then agree on how much insurance to purchase on the life of each key person. Key factors in this decision are the age of the key people, the extent of their ownership, and the payment method each prefers for their survivors.

The amount of life insurance purchased by the business for each key person will depend on the affordability of the premium, which will be higher for older owners. Because of their age or medical condition, key people may find that insurance is unobtainable. The owners must also decide whether to purchase enough coverage to provide a lump sum large enough to buy the share of the deceased outright, or whether the insurance will provide a portion of the buyout price, with the remainder paid to the heirs by the business over a period of time.

Since WEC is owned by three shareholders, with all of them working on-site and devoting considerable time to the business, it would be prudent for there to be life insurance policies on each one of them. If this proves to be uneconomic for some or all of the shareholders, an agreement between them can address how the deceased's shares will be purchased.

It may also be prudent for the main stakeholders in WEC to secure disability insurance so that if one of them is unable to work—owing to serious illness, for example—insurance will fund at least part of that person's salary or other remuneration.

The Insurance Contract

Duty to Disclose

duty of disclosure
The obligation of the insured to provide to the insurer all information that relates to the risk.

Insurance contracts are of a special nature. They are known as contracts of utmost good faith. A key consequence is that the insured has a **duty to disclose** to the insurer all information relevant to the risk; if she or he fails in that duty, the insurer may choose not to honour the policy. For example, assume that WEC wants to change insurers in an effort to save on premiums. Max, one of WEC's directors, fills in an application for fire insurance. In response to the question, "Have you ever experienced a fire?" Max writes, "Yes—in 1993." Max does not mention that WEC also had a fire in 1992, because he is convinced that WEC will end up paying an outrageously high premium. Max has failed to disclose a fact that is germane to the insurer's decision to insure, and to what the premiums should be in light of the risk. For this reason, if WEC tries to claim for fire loss should another fire occur at the plant, the insurer can refuse to honour the policy based on Max's nondisclosure.[12]

---

12. *Insurance,* 19 C.E.D. (West 3rd) para. 332.

An insurance company can deny coverage for nondisclosure even if the loss has nothing to do with the matter that was left undisclosed. For example, since WEC has failed to disclose a previous fire loss, the insurer can deny a vandalism claim that WEC might make some time in the future.

The law places a duty of disclosure on the insured for a straightforward reason: the insurer has to be in a position to fully assess the risk that the insured wants protection against. The only way the insurer can properly assess risk is if the insured is candid and forthcoming. In short, the insured is usually in the best position to provide the insurer with the information needed.

The duty to disclose is not all-encompassing, however. The law expects the insurer to be "worldly wise" and to show "personal judgment."[13] For this reason, there is no onus on the insured to inform the insurer of matters "not personal to the applicant."[14] For example, assume that in the application for fire insurance, Max notes that some welding occurs on the premises, but he does not go on to observe that welding causes sparks, which, in turn, can cause a fire. This is not a failure to disclose—after all, the insurer is expected to be worldly wise. That said, the insured is much better to err on the side of disclosure, since a miscalculation on the insured's part can lead to the policy being void.

A duty to disclose exists not just at the time of applying for the insurance—it is an ongoing duty. The insurer must be notified about any change material to the risk. For example, if WEC decides to stop producing wire and turn its attention instead to manufacturing plastic cable, the insurer should be advised of this change in writing. In the same vein, as WEC adds new property to its production plant, the insurer should be contacted so that necessary adjustments to the policy can be made.

Insurable Interest

insurable interest
A financial stake in what is being insured.

The special nature of the insurance contract also means that its validity is contingent on the insured having an **insurable interest** in the thing insured.[15] The test for whether the insured has an insurable interest is whether he or she benefits from its existence and would be prejudiced from its destruction.[16] The rationale behind this rule is that allowing people to insure property they have no real interest in may, for example, lead them to intentionally destroy the property in order to make an insurance claim. If WEC's bank holds a mortgage on the WEC production plant, it can purchase insurance on the plant because the bank has an insurable interest in property that is being used as security for a loan. The bank benefits from the continued existence of the plant and would be prejudiced from its destruction. Once the mortgage is paid off, the insurable interest of the bank no longer exists, and the bank cannot file a claim.

---

13. Brown & Menezes, *supra* note 9 at 88-89.

14. *Ibid.* at 89.

15. *Ibid.* at 65. Note that the ordinary insurable interest test is typically altered by statute for life insurance. In life insurance, the statutes generally provide that certain dependants have an insurable interest in the life insured, as does anyone else who gets the written consent of the person whose life is being insured.

16. *Lucena* v. *Craufurd* (1806), 2 B. & P. (N.R). 269 at 301 (H.L.). Discussed in Brown & Menezes, *ibid.* at 66.

Dealing with Your Insurance Company

James McGinnis, Partner at the Edmonton law firm of Parlee McLaws—

My practice is in general litigation, with a considerable number of my clients being insurance companies. Though some litigation over insurance polices can be extraordinarily complex, many problems arise because the insured has failed to keep its insurance company properly informed. In my experience, there are three simple but productive steps a business can take to avoid coverage problems.

A BUSINESS PERSPECTIVE

- *Review.* The business should review with its insurance broker the extent and nature of its insurance coverage at least once a year. This review forces the business to assess any number of matters, including what new property it has acquired and what new business activity it might engage in. It allows the broker to assess the existing policies for comprehensiveness and suggest alterations or additions to those policies. The broker then takes the matter to the insurance company so that the necessary adjustments can be made.
- *Report.* The business should report to the insurer any changes material to the risk, ideally before these changes even happen. For example, if a business person has decided to close down her operation for a month because of health problems, she must advise the insurer that the premises will be vacant for that period of time or risk being uninsured in the event of a fire. This is because most fire insurance policies will exclude coverage when the insured building has been left vacant for more than 30 consecutive days and a loss occurs. Likewise, if the business is acquiring a new piece of equipment, it should notify its insurer immediately. This is because the existing policy for property coverage may not include the equipment in question at all or not in the amount necessary to replace or repair the equipment, should that become necessary.
- *Alert.* When an incident occurs that will lead the insured to make a claim on its policy, the insured must immediately notify the insurer. However, it is advisable for the insured to alert the insurer as soon as anything happens that *may* result in the insured making a claim on the policy sometime down the road. For example, if a customer slips and falls in the business premises but seems to be OK and leaves without complaint, it would still be prudent for the insured to notify the insurer. That way, if the customer resurfaces several months later, and alleges that the fall has caused him serious back and jaw injuries, the insured is in good shape from a coverage perspective. He has already alerted the insurance company and has in no way prejudiced the insurer's right to make a proper investigation of accident itself.

It takes time for a business to keep its insurer and broker properly informed, but this time is well spent. It leads to the best outcome for everyone and means that when the insured does make a claim, the matter stands the greatest chance of being handled without controversy.

Effective insurance coverage depends on regular communication between the insured business, its broker, and its insurance company.

Indemnity

indemnity
The obligation on the
insurer to make good
the loss.

With the exception of life insurance contracts, insurance contracts are contracts of **indemnity**. This term means that the insured is not supposed to profit from the happening of the insured-against event, but at most will come out even. For example, if WEC purchases replacement-cost insurance coverage on one of its delivery vehicles and that vehicle is subsequently destroyed in an accident, WEC is entitled only to replace the vehicle with its equivalent. WEC cannot purchase a more expensive model and expect the insurer to pay the full amount.

Some policies, such as fire insurance policies, require the insured to have coverage for a specified minimum portion of the value of the property in order to fully recover from the insurer in the event of a fire. This requirement takes the form of a co-insurance clause, which is intended to discourage the insured from insuring the property for less than its value on the gamble that any loss is likely to be less than total. If such a clause is in place, the insurer will pay only the specified portion of the loss, and the insured must absorb the remainder.

Subrogation

subrogation
The right of the insurer
to recover the amount
paid on a claim from a
third party who caused
the loss.

The insurer also has what is called a right of **subrogation**. This right means that when an insurer compensates the insured, it has the right to sue a third party—the wrongdoer—who caused the loss and to recover from that party what it has already paid out to its insured. In this sense, the right of subrogation permits the insurer to "step into the shoes" of the insured and sue the wrongdoer. Because of the insurer's right of subrogation, WEC must act carefully in the face of a loss. For example, it should not admit liability for any accident that has occurred, since doing so might wrongly and unfairly jeopardize the success of any future action the insurer might commence against the wrongdoer. Instead, WEC should immediately contact its insurer, as well as legal counsel, for advice on how to proceed.

The Policy

Insurance contracts are particularly technical documents. Their content is settled to some extent by legislation, which requires standard form policies for some types of insurance. Changes in standard policy terms take the form of riders and endorsements. A rider adds to or alters the standard coverage and is part of the policy from the outset. An endorsement is an alteration to the coverage at some point during the time in which the policy is in force. Policies generally contain a number of *exclusion clauses* that exclude coverage for certain situations, occurrences, or persons for which there would otherwise be protection. For example, the standard fire policy excludes coverage when the insured building has been left unoccupied for more than 30 consecutive days. If a loss occurs after this point, the policy does not cover it.

Remedies of the Insured

Against the Broker

insurance broker
One who provides
advice and assistance to
the insured in
acquiring insurance.

It is crucial for WEC to establish a solid working relationship with an **insurance broker** in order to secure proper advice as to what kind of insurance it requires. The term *insurance broker* refers to the middle person between the insurance companies and the insured. As the party seeking insurance, WEC needs the assistance of the broker in reviewing its business operations, assessing the risks it faces, and understanding the coverages available and the policy costs. If WEC does not spend sufficient time with the broker or chooses a broker who is simply not up to the job, WEC may end up with the wrong coverage—or not enough coverage—and face a loss against which it has not been properly insured.

Should WEC face such a situation, it may have an action against its broker for negligence. If WEC is successful in its action, the broker will be required to reimburse WEC for any of its underinsured or uninsured liabilities.

The term **insurance agent** usually refers to someone who acts on behalf of an insurer to sell insurance. An agent acting in that capacity is primarily obligated to the insurer as principal, and not to the third party insured. The terms *broker* and *insurance agent* are often used interchangeably; however, the distinction between them is not always clear.

insurance agent
One who acts for an insurance company in selling insurance.

Against the Insurance Company

insurance adjuster
One who investigates and evaluates insurance claims.

When an insured makes a claim under its policy, an **insurance adjuster** will likely investigate the events and evaluate the loss. On the adjuster's advice, the insurer will offer to settle the claim. There may be disagreements between the insured and the insurer as to the nature or amount of coverage. Should they be unable to resolve these differences, the insured may have to sue the insurer for breach of contract. The claim will be that the insurer has failed to honour its obligations under the policy. This is what Triple Five (the owner of West Edmonton Mall) did when it sued its insurer for failure to pay out under its business interruption loss policy.

Business Law in Practice Revisited

1. What risks are associated with WEC's business?

A business faces many risks from many sources, including competitors, regulators, suppliers, and employees. Many of these risks are beyond the control of the business. Others, however, are controllable, or at least can be managed.

The manageable risks that WEC faces may be divided into two categories: operational and organizational. WEC's operational risks are related to its business of manufacturing and selling wires and providing consulting advice. Each aspect of its business creates the risk of loss. For example, machines may break down that prevent WEC from meeting its contractual obligations; an employee may accidentally start a fire in the plant; a potential customer may be injured while touring WEC's property; vandals could destroy WEC's inventory of raw materials; a hurricane could destroy a building; or an error could be made in the advice given to a client.

From an organizational perspective, a similar list of risks can be generated: one of WEC's key people could be injured or killed, seriously jeopardizing WEC's ability to carry out its business mission; the company could fail to properly dispose of waste products, creating personal liability for the officers for the clean-up costs; or the company could neglect to pay its taxes, with the result that the directors were personally liable for the debt.

2. How can WEC use insurance to manage these risks?

All of the risks identified above need to be addressed by management. The company should act with due diligence in this, since losses can be catastrophic for a business. Risks, however, cannot be completely eliminated, except by ceasing to do business. This is where insurance plays a crucial role. A business should ensure that proper insurance coverage is in place to protect its viability. To achieve this end, WEC will almost certainly call on an insurance broker for help in evaluating various insurance issues, including what type and amount of insurance coverage is necessary. WEC needs a comprehensive package that covers all aspects of its business.

If WEC plays by the rules governing insurance, such as abiding by its ongoing duty to disclose facts material to the risk, its insurance policies will cover many of its business risks.

Chapter Summary

Insurance is one of the simplest and most cost-effective ways of managing risk in a business environment. It permits the business to shift such risks as fire, automobile accidents, and liability for defective products onto an insurance company in exchange for the payment of premiums by the business.

A business needs to communicate effectively with its insurance broker, as well as its insurance company, in order to assess the kinds of risks its operation faces and the types of insurance coverage that can be purchased to address those risks. Though insurance policies can take a variety of forms, there are three basic kinds: life and disability insurance; property insurance; and liability insurance. More specific insurance policies are simply a variation on one of these types.

Insurance policies are technically worded and often contain exclusion clauses. These clauses identify circumstances or events for which coverage is denied. They may also identify people for whom coverage is denied.

An insurance contract is a contract of utmost good faith. This means that the insured must make full disclosure at the time of applying for insurance, as well as during the life of the policy. Failure to do so may permit the insurer to deny coverage when a loss has occurred.

The insured must have an insurable interest in the item insured to prevent moral hazards. The test for insurable interest is whether the insured benefits from the existence of the thing insured and would be prejudiced from its destruction.

Insurance contracts are not intended to improve the position of the insured should the loss occur. Rather, they are contracts of indemnity and can compensate the insured only up to the loss suffered.

When the insurer pays out under an insurance policy, it has the right of subrogation. This right permits it to sue the wrongdoer as if it were the party that had been directly injured or otherwise sustained a loss.

If the insured ends up with insurance of the wrong type or in an inadequate amount, it may have an action against its broker for breach of contract and/or negligence. If the insurance company wrongly refuses to honour the policy, the insured may have to sue the insurer in order to secure its cooperation.

Study Chapter

Questions for Review

1. What is the purpose of an insurance contract?

2. What is a premium?

3. What is a deductible? What effect does it have on insurance premiums?

4. What does an insurance broker do?

5. What are the three main types of insurance?

6. Describe comprehensive general liability insurance. How does it differ from warranty insurance?

7. What is the purpose of errors and omissions insurance?

8. When should a business consider buying key person life insurance?

9. What does it mean to say that an insured has a duty to disclose? What happens if the insured fails in this duty?

10. What is an insurable interest? Why is it important?

11. What is the right of subrogation?

12. Why are contracts of insurance known as contracts of indemnity?

Questions for Discussion

1. Why can insurance companies deny coverage on the basis of nondisclosure or misrepresentation of matters that may have occurred years before the loss? Is this rule justified?

2. How much does it take to establish an insurable interest? For example, does an adult child have an insurable interest in his parent's house? The adult child might argue that he does, since if the house burns down he will have to help his parents obtain a new residence or perhaps let them live with him. Is this a sufficient interest, or is it too tenuous? Does the adult child derive a benefit from the continued existence of his parent's house and detriment from its destruction?

3. The insurance industry has introduced a number of new insurance products aimed at reducing the risk of costly lawsuits. Lawsuit insurance, like other types of insurance, transfers some of the risks and uncertainties associated with litigation from the business to the insurance company.

   When should a business purchase this type of insurance? What factors should be considered in the purchase decision? Do you think this type of insurance is more important in some industries than in others?

4. Fraudulent insurance claims are a problem faced by the insurance industry. Common examples involve inflated property values, exaggerated personal injuries, arson and other deliberate acts of sabotage, and "insider theft." Insurance companies are entitled to question the authenticity of all claims.

   How far should the insurance company be able to go in obtaining evidence of fraud? On what basis should the insurance company be entitled to deny a claim? For example, should an unusual pattern of claims be a basis for denial?

Situations for Discussion

1. Suzanne suffered from childhood leukemia, but it has been over 20 years since she completed her treatment for this disease and was pronounced cured. When she filled in her application for life insurance, she neglected to mention her childhood illness because she thought it was too long ago to bother with anymore. On her death from a heart attack, the insurance company refused to pay her beneficiaries owing to her nondisclosure.[17] What rule of insurance law did Suzanne violate? What should she have done? Will her beneficiaries collect? Should they suffer for Suzanne's conduct?

---

17. Based on *Kanhoffen* v. *Martino* (1992), 14 C.C.L.I. (2d) 102 (B.C.S.C.), aff'd (1994), 21 C.C.L.R. (2d) 135 (C.A.).

2. Michael Bates had made a human rights complaint against Zurich Insurance because it, like every other insurance company, was charging young, single, male drivers a much higher premium rate than it was charging young, single, female drivers; young, married, male drivers; and drivers 25 years of age or over. Bates alleged that the higher rate violated the Ontario Human Rights Code because it constituted discrimination in the provision of a service based on sex, age, and marital status.

   To justify its differential premiums, Zurich had to establish that its practice was sound and accepted in the insurance industry and, furthermore, that there was no practical alternative. Zurich produced data indicating that there was a correlation between risk and the age, sex, and marital status of the insured.[18]

   Is Zurich's discrimination justified? Is it fair to treat all young, unmarried men the same? Should the insurance industry be forced instead to use neutral factors, such as driving record, in assessing risk? What would happen to the insurance premiums of those classified as lower risk if the insurance company could not automatically classify a new, young, unmarried, male driver as being in a high-risk group?

3. Dorothy is a sole proprietor who recently incorporated her business in order to take the benefits of limited liability. As part of this change, she transferred all her business assets over to her corporation, Dorothy Ltd. Unfortunately, she forgot to change her insurance policies naming the company as the new insured. The property remains insured in Dorothy's name. Soon after the transfer, there was a break-in at Dorothy Ltd.'s corporate offices, and much of the company's expensive computer equipment was stolen. Dorothy made a claim on her policy, but the insurance company took the position that she did not have an insurable interest in the corporate property.[19]

   Explain why the insurance company refused Dorothy's claim. What can she do now? What arguments can she make in support of her claim? What practical advice would Dorothy now give to other small business owners?

4. Tanic leased office space from Landrum. A term of the lease required Landrum to fully insure the property against loss caused by fire. An employee of Tanic left a coffeemaker turned on over the weekend. This caused a fire that resulted in serious damage to Tanic's furniture, computers, and business records.[20]

   Can Tanic claim under Landrum's policy? Has Tanic paid any premiums? Is Tanic an insured party? If the insurer pays the claim, does it have a right of subrogation against the employee who caused the fire? What other arrangements could Tanic and Landrum have made for insurance coverage?

---

18. Based on *Zurich Insurance Co.* v. *Ontario (Human Rights Commission)*, [1992] 2 S.C.R. 321.

19. Based on *Kosmopoulos* v. *Constitution Insurance Co. of Canada*, [1987] 1 S.C.R. 2.

20. Based on *T. Eaton Co.* v. *Smith* (1977), 92 D.L.R. (3d) 425 (S.C.C.).

Part Six

Employment and Professional Relationships

EMPLOYMENT AND PROFESSIONAL RELATIONSHIPS are essential components of business. Without the skills, knowledge, and experience of others, businesses would be unable to function and compete effectively. Most businesses require a wide range of services, including managerial, clerical, administrative, and professional services.

Businesses acquire these services by hiring employees or by contracting for the services as needed. Many professional services are acquired in the latter way.

The employment of others, whether through the employment relationship or through an independent service contract, has been affected by significant social change: the entry of women in large numbers into the workforce; recognition of the disadvantaged position of minorities; greater awareness of the needs of people with disabilities; heightened public concern for the fair treatment of workers; adaptation to technological developments; and concern for job security. Not surprisingly, there has been much legal intervention to address and account for these developments. A vast array of federal and provincial legislation, in addition to the common law, affects all aspects of employment:

► Human rights legislation prohibits discrimination in all aspects of employment.
► Employment equity laws address the hiring of historically disadvantaged groups.

► Employment insurance and pension plans provide for employees' economic security.
► Pay equity legislation addresses inequities in compensation.
► Occupational health and safety laws protect employees from unsafe working conditions.
► Protection of information laws address employee privacy.

Chapter 21 The Employment Relationship

► Chapter 21 provides an overview of the laws that affect the employment relationship, from the initial decision to hire through to the terms and conditions of employment.

Chapter 22 Terminating the Employment Relationship

► Chapter 22 addresses legal issues that arise on the termination of the employment relationship.

Chapter 23 Professional Services

► Chapter 23 canvasses the acquisition of specialized professional services.

Twenty-One

The Employment Relationship

Objectives

AFTER STUDYING THIS CHAPTER, YOU SHOULD HAVE AN
UNDERSTANDING OF:

► THE BASIC ELEMENTS OF THE EMPLOYMENT RELATIONSHIP
► THE WAYS IN WHICH THE LAW AFFECTS RECRUITMENT
  PRACTICES
► THE CONTENT OF A TYPICAL EMPLOYMENT CONTRACT
► THE LEGAL ISSUES RELATING TO THE TERMS AND CONDITIONS
  OF EMPLOYMENT

Business Law in Practice

Techroniks Inc. is a small software developer located in Fredericton, New Brunswick. The company has experienced considerable success in the rapidly expanding information technology sector. Success has provided Techroniks with the opportunity to expand its operations and to develop new markets for its products. To pursue a strategy of growth, Techroniks has decided to hire a number of software developers and several application specialists.

Charles MacNeil, the vice president of operations and the person responsible for hiring, has a number of concerns:

■ *Compatibility.* Since most of Techroniks' current employees come from similar backgrounds and have similar interests, values, and attitudes, Charles thinks that he wants to hire people who will "fit in" with the corporate culture.

- *Commitment.* Charles also wants to ensure that the people hired will be committed to Techroniks, because a great deal of time and money will be invested in their training. Techroniks does not want to hire recruits who will leave after a short period of time or who will be unable to perform their job for some reason. The information technology field is highly competitive, and Charles is concerned that people may leave with knowledge and pass it on to competitors.
- *Criminality.* Techroniks' business provides limitless opportunities for disaffected employees to engage in illegal activity. There is opportunity for employees to introduce computer bugs and viruses into software; also, Techroniks' equipment could be used to commit criminal acts, such as downloading pornography and hacking other computers. Charles would like to avoid hiring anyone with these kinds of tendencies.

1. Is Charles entitled to hire on the basis of who will "fit in" at Techroniks?
2. How can Charles' concerns about employees leaving be addressed?
3. What steps can Charles take to reduce the probability of hiring someone with criminal tendencies?

Employment Law

The employment relationship is a critical component of business activity. Engaging the services of others provides the means by which a business can carry out its mission. Employment, however, is much more than an engine of business. It is a relationship that provides a livelihood for a large proportion of society. Given the importance of this relationship to both the employer and the employee, it is not surprising that there is a vast body of law regulating employment.

Employment law in all the Canadian jurisdictions, with the exception of Quebec, is rooted in the traditions of the English common law, with an overlay of legislation. Both the federal and provincial governments have jurisdiction to pass employment legislation, and both levels have been active in this area. As a result, employment law is somewhat of a labyrinth.

The federal government has jurisdiction to make laws affecting employees of the federal government and federally regulated industries, such as the banking, airline, broadcasting, railway, and shipping industries. It is estimated that about 10 percent of all employees are subject to federal regulation. The provincial governments have jurisdiction to make laws affecting all other employees, including provincial employees. An employee is subject to either federal or provincial jurisdiction, and it is not unusual for employees working in close proximity to be subject to different employment legislation. As Techroniks is not involved in a federally regulated industry, its employees would come under provincial jurisdiction.

Both levels of government have enacted human rights legislation and an array of employee welfare legislation, such as employment standards, occupational health and safety standards, and workers' compensation. In addition to legislation of general application, governments have passed legislation that affects employees in specific jobs. Public sector employees, such as police officers, teachers, medical personnel, and civil servants, are commonly affected by specific legislation.

Employees may also be *unionized*, in which case labour legislation is applicable to the employment relationship. The federal government and all of the provinces have enacted labour or industrial relations statutes that facilitate the unionization process.

This chapter focuses on laws that affect the employment process in the private, nonunionized sector, as the majority of employees fall within this category. It examines the laws as they relate to the various phases of the employment process. At the end of the chapter, a note is provided on differences in the union environment.

The Employment Relationship

employment relationship
A contractual relationship whereby an employer provides remuneration to an employee in exchange for work or services.

independent contractor
A person who is in a working relationship that does not meet the criteria of employment.

The **employment relationship** involves a contract whereby one party, the employer, provides remuneration to another, the employee, in return for work or services.[1] Not everyone who works for another or provides services to another is an employee, however. In some situations, those who provide services are considered agents[2] or **independent contractors**. Usually, doctors and lawyers, for example, provide services in the capacity of independent contractors, rather than as employees of their patients/clients.

With the advent of "downsizing" and "right-sizing," people who traditionally worked as employees are increasingly working as independent contractors. People choose to do so for a number of reasons. A worker may prefer the status of independent contractor because of significant tax savings and flexibility and independence in arranging a work schedule. An employer may prefer to engage independent contractors because the relationship offers simplicity and fewer financial and legal obligations. In particular, many statutory obligations apply only to employees. The hiring of independent contractors is an option Techroniks may consider, particularly if it foresees that its employment needs are short term and only for specific projects. The engagement of an independent contractor would automatically end on completion of the project, with no requirement to give notice or pay in lieu of termination. However, the *nature* of the relationship is more important than what it is called.

Employee versus Independent Contractor

The distinction between an employee and an independent contractor is not always readily apparent. It is common to think of independent contractors as being short term and temporary, while employees are long term and permanent. In practice, this might be the case, but it is not a distinction based in law.

The courts have used a variety of tests to distinguish between the two relationships, including the following:

- *The degree of control exercised over the individual by the employer.* The more direction and supervision provided by the employer, the more likely it is that the relationship is employment.
- *The ownership of tools, chance of profit, and the risk of loss from performance of the requested service.*[3] Sharing profits and losses and the ownership of tools is indicative of an independent contractor.
- *The degree of integration.* The nature of the work being performed is considered in relation to the business itself. The question is whether the work being per-

---

1. The historical terms for employer and employee are master and servant.
2. The law affecting agents is discussed in Chapter 13.
3. *Montreal (City of)* v. *Montreal Locomotive Works Ltd.,* [1947] 1 D.L.R. 161 (P.C.).

formed is "integral" to the business, or is "adjunct"to the normal work of the business.[4] The more the work is integrated into the company's activities, the more likely it is that the individual is an employee.

Recently, the courts have moved away from any one test and have considered all relevant factors. In short, the nature of a relationship is a question of fact and will vary with the situation. Regardless of the test used, courts lean toward defining the relationship in question as one of employment. This bias exists as a way of ensuring that those who are entitled to benefits receive them.

Implications of an Employment Relationship

Employees have certain statutory rights and benefits, such as paid holidays and paid overtime, which are not conferred on independent contractors. Employers have certain obligations with respect to employees, namely deduction of income taxes, Canada (or Quebec) Pension Plan premiums, paid vacations, and the like, which they do not have with respect to independent contractors. A finding of employment can mean that the employer is retroactively responsible for paying these benefits.

Establishing the employment relationship is important to certain legal principles. For example, an employee can initiate an action for wrongful dismissal, but this avenue is not available to an independent contractor. An employer is responsible for the tort of an employee committed in the ordinary course of employment, whereas an employer is not usually responsible for the torts of an independent contractor committed in the course of carrying out the contract. An employer's liability is explored in the next section.

Risks in Hiring

The hiring of workers is critical to business. Hiring well can be a boon to a business, and hiring poorly can result in low productivity and possibly a costly termination. From a business perspective, hiring the candidate who is best suited for the job results in the optimal use of resources. From a legal perspective, hiring well can reduce the risks associated with the employment relationship, in particular those associated with vicarious liability and negligent hiring.

Vicarious Liability

An employer is liable for the torts of an employee committed in the ordinary or usual course of employment. For example, if an employee of Techroniks defames or injures someone in the course of employment, Techroniks is liable. Application of vicarious liability requires a determination of whether the employee was acting in the "course or scope of employment." An employee's wrongful conduct falls within the scope of employment if it is authorized by the employer or is an unauthorized mode of doing something that is, in fact, authorized by the employer.

It is difficult to distinguish between an unauthorized "mode" of performing an authorized act that attracts liability and an entirely independent "act" that does not. This problem is illustrated in the application of vicarious liability to sexual assaults committed by employees, as in the following case.

---

4. *Co-operatives Insurance Association* v. *Kearney* (1964), 48 D.L.R. (2d)1 (S.C.C.).

Case

Bazley (P.A.) v. Curry, [1999] 2 S.C.R. 534

The Business Context: In the past decade, the Canadian public has been shaken by revelations of sexual assault and abuse at some of society's most revered institutions—service clubs, charitable organizations, orphanages, residential homes, churches, and sport teams. These cases raise troubling issues concerning the responsibility, both moral and legal, of the organizations whose members or employees committed the acts.

Factual Background: A child was sexually assaulted a number of times by an employee of the residential care facility for emotionally disturbed children where the child lived. The employee was completely involved in all aspects of the child's life. He did everything a parent would do, including supervising and performing such intimate tasks as bathing and tucking in at bedtime.

The Legal Question: Was the employer vicariously liable for the employee's sexual assaults?

Resolution: First, the court stated that courts should confront the issue of whether an employer should be liable rather than hide behind semantic discussions of the meaning of "scope of employment." Second, the court stated that the fundamental question is whether the wrongful act was sufficiently related to conduct authorized by the employer to justify imposing vicarious liability. In other words, there must be a strong relationship between what the employer was asking the employee to do and the wrongful act. In the present case, there was a relationship between the power conferred on the employee (i.e., acting as a parent with close supervisory duties) and the wrong that occurred. The employer was held liable.

Critical Analysis: What is the rationale for holding the employer vicariously liable for employees' actions?

In a similar case, *Jacobi* v. *Griffiths,*[5] a brother and sister sued the Boys' and Girls' Club of Vernon, B.C., for assaults committed by the club's program director. The director used his position to befriend children and then lure them to his home, where he sexually assaulted them. The club was not held vicariously liable.

These cases are similar, yet the outcomes on the issue of vicarious liability were quite different. In *Jacobi,* the employee did not have the same supervisory duties with respect to the children as did the employee in *Curry.* The employer afforded the employee the opportunity to work with children, but the job had no element of parenting or intimacy, as was the case in *Curry.* There is a fine line between the two cases, and it is not easy to distinguish when liability will be applied to employers. This difficulty is illustrated by the fact that although the Supreme Court's decision was unanimous in *Curry,* it was split four to three in *Griffiths.*

Liability for sexual assaults is not a critical concern of Techroniks. It is not a concern for most businesses. However, cases like *Curry* illustrate the willingness of the courts to find employers responsible for the conduct of their employees, as well as the importance of hiring well.

Negligent Hiring

Another potential risk for employers in the hiring process is in the developing area of "negligent hiring."[6] If an employee injures another employee or causes harm to a

---

5. [1999] 2 S.C.R. 570.

6. This is a well-developed concept in the United States and is beginning to be referred to in Canada. See *Downey* v. *502377 Ontario Ltd.,* [1991] O.J. No. 468 (Gen. Div.) online: QL (O.J.); Stacey Ball, *Canadian Employment Law* (Aurora: Canada Law Book, 2000) at 20.66.

third party, there may be an action against the employer for being negligent in having hired that employee. This action differs from vicarious liability, which holds the employer strictly liable for the actions of the employee as long as the actions are sufficiently related to the employment. With vicarious liability, there is no requirement to prove that the employer was at fault. Negligent hiring, on the other hand, requires the plaintiff to prove that the employer was careless in, for example, hiring, training, or supervising. The court in *Jacobi* v. *Griffiths* indicated that there is much to be said for developing and refining the paths of potential direct liability against employers— a fault-based approach, as opposed to the no-fault strict liability approach of vicarious liability.

To minimize the risk in this area, an employer such as Techroniks would want to be able to show that due care was taken in all aspects of the hiring process.

The Hiring Process

The hiring process involves a number of steps. For example, in hiring employees Techroniks would normally

- develop job descriptions
- advertise the positions
- have candidates complete an application form or submit a résumé
- short-list candidates
- check backgrounds or references
- interview selected applicants

All aspects of employment are affected by human rights legislation, and in some cases by employment equity legislation. The legislation may affect the kind of advertising done, the form the application takes, the questions that are asked in the interview, and the decision of who will ultimately be hired.

Human Rights Requirements

The federal, provincial, and territorial governments have enacted human rights legislation[7] that has the objective of providing equal access to employment opportunities for all. To this end, discrimination in employment is prohibited. The Acts also provide for the establishment of **Human Rights Commissions**, which are charged with administering the legislation and investigating and hearing complaints.

Human Rights Commission
An administrative body that oversees the implementation and enforcement of human rights legislation.

Prohibited Grounds of Discrimination

Human rights legislation does not prohibit all discrimination in employment, but only discrimination on certain prohibited grounds. There are variations from jurisdiction to jurisdiction as to what are prohibited grounds, but generally these grounds are similar (see Figure 21.1).

---

7. See, for example, *Canadian Human Rights Act,* R.S.C. 1985, c. H-6.

Figure 21.1

PROHIBITED GROUNDS OF DISCRIMINATION

The following are prohibited grounds of discrimination under all Canadian legislation:

- ☒ **marital status**
- ☒ **race**
- ☒ **colour**
- ☒ **physical or mental disability**
- ☒ **religion or creed**
- ☒ **sex**
- ☒ **age**

Examples of other common grounds that are expressly included in some jurisdictions are national or ethnic origin, family status, social condition, sexual orientation, criminal record, ancestry, place of origin, language and linguistic origin, and political beliefs.

Besides the grounds specified in the legislation, other grounds may be "read in" or included. For example, alcohol dependency may be included in physical disability; pregnancy[8] and sexual orientation[9] may be included in sex. The reason for reading in other grounds relates to the broad definition given to the enumerated terms and to the impact of the *Charter of Rights and Freedoms*.[10]

The *Charter* does not apply directly to the private sector. Rather, the *Charter*'s role is to constrain government and its actions, such as government policy or legislation. When government takes the step of creating legislation that has an impact on the private sector, however, the *Charter* does become relevant. Hence, if a province passes human rights legislation prohibiting discrimination in the marketplace, the *Charter* does apply through the statute itself. In short, if the statute does not meet the mandatory standards of the *Charter*, the judiciary is entitled to strike the legislation down or "read in" provisions to make the legislation compliant with the *Charter*. This is precisely what happened in the *Vriend* case.

Case

Vriend v. *Alberta*, [1998] 1 S.C.R. 493

The Business Context: Gay men and lesbians have often been discriminated against by employers. In many instances the discrimination was covert, but in cases where it was not, it has been unclear whether such conduct violates human rights legislation, which does not expressly prohibit discrimination based on sexual orientation.

Factual background: In 1991 Delwin Vriend was dismissed from his job as a laboratory coordinator at a private Christian college in Edmonton. Though a competent employee, he was fired in 1991 when he acknowledged

---

8. See Stacey Ball, *supra* note 6 at 33-62.

9. For example, in Newfoundland, sexual orientation was "read in" in *Newfoundland (Human Rights Commission)* v. *Newfoundland (Minister of Employment and Labour Relations)* (1995), 127 D.L.R. (4th) 694 (Nfld. S.C.T.D.). The Supreme Court of Canada decided, in *Vriend* v. *Alberta*, [1998] 1 S.C.R. 493, that sexual orientation is a prohibited ground of discrimination in all jurisdictions.

10. The *Charter of Rights and Freedoms* is discussed in Chapter 2.

being homosexual[11] upon being confronted with the question by the college president. The sole reason for his termination was noncompliance with the policy of the college concerning homosexual practice.

Vriend attempted to complain to the Alberta Human Rights Commission but was told that the *Individual Rights Protection Act* (IRPA) did not prohibit discrimination on the basis of sexual orientation. In fact, the Alberta legislature had debated including such a prohibition on several occasions, but the amendments were defeated. Vriend then took the matter to court, arguing that the failure of the Alberta government to include this protection violated the equality provisions of the *Charter*.

The Legal Question: Did the Alberta law violate the *Charter*?

Resolution: The trial judge agreed with Vriend's argument, but rather than declaring the IRPA to be unconstitutional, she ordered "sexual orientation" to be read into the IRPA as a prohibited ground. The Alberta Court of Appeal did not agree, ruling that the legislature's refusal to include such protection was well within its constitutional prerogative. Vriend appealed to the Supreme Court of Canada, which upheld the trial judge's decision on the basis that gay men and lesbians, like other minority groups who had historically suffered discrimination, were entitled to legislative protection from such abuse.

Critical Analysis: Can you think of other grounds that could be read into the enumerated grounds in human rights legislation? Do you agree with the Supreme Court of Canada's overriding the wishes of the people, as evidenced by the debate and vote in the Alberta legislative assembly?

Discrimination Defined

discrimination
Treating someone differently on the basis of a prohibited ground.

adverse effects discrimination
Discrimination that occurs as a result of a rule that appears neutral but in its effects is discriminatory.

systemic discrimination
Discrimination that results from the combined effects of many rules, practices, and policies.

The Acts prohibit **discrimination** but do not define the term.[12] The usual meaning is to treat someone differently on the basis of a prohibited ground. For example, to post an advertisement that says "Wanted: Malaysian workers for Malaysian restaurant" would be an act of discrimination because it discriminates on the basis of race. Techroniks, by wanting candidates who fit in, may also be discriminating. It is entirely possible that its definition of "fit in" excludes individuals on the basis of sex, race, age, or any of the other prohibited grounds. On the other hand, it is not discrimination to require job applicants to meet certain educational or training requirements. For example, if Techroniks requires its employees to fit in by being team players or by having certain job-related experience, this is not discriminatory.

Not only is direct or explicit discrimination prohibited, but **adverse effects** and **systemic discrimination** are also prohibited. Adverse discrimination involves the application of a rule that appears to be neutral but has discriminatory effects.[13] For example, a rule that requires all workers to wear hard hats or to work every second Saturday appears to be neutral, but its effect may be to discriminate against those whose religion requires them to wear a turban or to refrain from work on Saturdays. Systemic discrimination refers to the combined effects of many rules, practices, and policies that lead to a discriminatory outcome.[14] For example, if a workforce is overwhelmingly dominated by male workers, this may mean that there is systemic discrimination.

---

11. As Professor Bruce MacDougall has observed, terminology in this area is a loaded subject. See MacDougall, "Silence in the Classroom: Limits on Homosexual Expressions and Visibility in Education and the Privileging of Homophobic Religious Theology" (1998) 61 Sask L. Rev. 41, his footnote 1. Like MacDougall, we use the term *homosexual* because it is commonly used in the case law.

12. Only the Manitoba and Quebec acts offer statutory definitions of discrimination.

13. *Ontario (Human Rights Commission)* v. *Simpson-Sears Ltd.* (1985), 23 D.L.R. (4th) 321 (S.C.C.).

14. *Action Travail des Femmes* v. *C.N.R. Co.* (1987), 40 D.L.R. (4th) 193 (S.C.C.) sub nom. *Canadian National Railway Co.* v. *Canada (Canadian Human Rights Commission)*, (1985), 20 D.L.R. (4th) 668 (F.C.A.)

Defences to Discrimination

There are situations where it is permissible to discriminate on one of the prohibited grounds. The most common defence to an allegation of discrimination is a ***bona fide occupation requirement* (BFOR)**; other defences include approved affirmative action or equity plans and group insurance and pension plans. A BFOR is a discriminatory practice that is reasonably necessary for a safe and efficient working environment. For example, a requirement that a person have a valid driver's licence discriminates against some persons with physical disabilities, but a valid driver's licence is a reasonable and necessary requirement for the job of truck driver. Similarly, the requirement of wearing a hard hat discriminates against those whose religion requires them to wear a turban, but the hard hat requirement may be reasonably necessary for a safe work environment. BFORs have been subject to much controversy, as there is little consensus on what constitute legitimate, meaningful qualifications or requirements for job applicants. For example, in one case[15] the court struck down a fire department policy requiring mandatory retirement at age 60, as this did not constitute a *bona fide* occupational requirement. The court held that it was the employer's obligation to justify the qualification as being reasonably necessary for job performance, and further, that the qualification must be imposed honestly and in good faith and not for the purposes of circumventing the Human Rights Code.

If a rule or qualification is found to be a BFOR, an employer is required to accommodate the special needs of those who are negatively affected, up to the point of undue hardship for the employer. The employer may have to modify rules, practices, and requirements in the workplace. For example, an employer may have to reschedule work, redefine job descriptions, or alter the physical workplace to accommodate the special needs of those who are being discriminated against. As with BFORs, the **duty to accommodate** has been subject to much controversy, as it is unclear how far an employer must go to accommodate special needs. Some of the factors are the cost of modification of equipment, the size of the organization, and the disruption to the business, its workers, and its customers.[16]

Case

British Columbia (Public Service Employee Relations Commission) v. *BCGSEU*, [1999] 3 S.C.R. 3

The Business Context: Employers often implement physical performance standards or requirements for particular jobs. Standards are easy to apply and appear to be an objective or neutral basis for evaluating employees.

Factual Background: The province of British Columbia established a number of fitness standards for forest firefighters. Among the standards, which included sit-up, pull-up, and push-up components, was an aerobic standard. The aerobic standard required a firefighter to run 2.5 kilometres in 11 minutes. Tawney Meiorin, a three-year veteran of the service, was terminated from her job because she could not meet the standard. She needed an extra 49.4 seconds. Meiorin complained to the B.C. Human Rights Commission.

The Legal Question: Did the aerobic standard discriminate on the basis of sex?

Resolution: The court held that the standard on its face was discriminatory, owing to physiological differences between males and females. Most women have a lower aerobic capacity than most men and cannot increase their aerobic capacity enough with training to meet the aerobic standard.

---

15. *Ontario (Human Rights Commission)* v. *Etobicoke (Borough)* (1982), 132 D.L.R. (3d) 14 (S.C.C.).
16. See *Central Alberta Dairy Pool* v. *Alberta (Human Rights Commission)*, [1990] 2 S.C.R. 489.

To justify the standard as a BFOR, the employer would have to show that the standard was rationally connected to the job; that it adopted the standard in an honest and good-faith belief that it was necessary to fulfill a legitimate, work-related purpose; and that the standard was reasonably necessary to the accomplishment of that purpose. Applying the approach, the court concluded that passing the aerobic standard was not reasonably necessary to the safe and efficient operation of the work of a forest firefighter. The government had not established that it would experience undue hardship if a different standard were used. In other words, the employer failed to establish that the aerobic standard was reasonably necessary to identify those who are unable to perform the tasks of a forest firefighter safely and efficiently.

Critical Analysis: What must a business do in order to establish performance standards for certain jobs?

Penalties

Failure to avoid or eliminate discriminatory practices can result in a complaint to the Human Rights Commission. This, in turn, can result in a Board of Inquiry investigating the complaint. If the board finds the complaint to be valid, it can order that the employer stop its practices, hire a particular individual, pay monetary compensation, write a letter of apology, reinstate an employee, or institute an affirmative action plan. Regardless of the outcome, a complaint may result in unwelcome publicity, expenditures of time and money to answer the complaint, and an unsettled work environment. To reduce the risk of a human rights complaint, an employer needs to review all aspects of the employment process. The following box provides some examples of ways to reduce the risks.

Avoiding Discrimination in Hiring Practices

A human rights complaint can be a costly and embarrassing situation for a company. Each step of the hiring process should be reviewed to ensure that the company is not discriminating.

BUSINESS APPLICATION OF THE LAW

JOB DESCRIPTION
Do develop a list of job-related duties and responsibilities.
Don't describe job openings in terms of prohibited grounds (e.g., busboy, hostess, policeman, waitress).

ADVERTISEMENTS
Do advertise for qualifications related to ability to do the job.
Don't advertise for qualifications unrelated to ability to do the job (e.g., single, Canadian-born, young).

APPLICATION FORMS
Do solicit information that is related to the applicant's ability to do the job.

Don't ask for information that suggests prohibited grounds are being considered—for example, age, sex, photograph, or title (Miss, Ms, Mr., Mrs.).

INTERVIEW
Do ask questions related to the applicant's suitability for the job
Don't ask questions related to prohibited grounds (e.g., Are you planning to start a family? Do you have any physical disabilities? Have you ever been treated for a mental illness? How old are you? What church do you attend?)

An employer should provide human rights training for supervisors and other employees and also develop policies prohibiting discrimination. Employees need to be made aware of the policies.

Source: The New Brunswick Human Rights Commission, *Fact Sheets* (Fredericton: The New Brunswick Human Rights Commission, 1998).

Employment Equity

Employment equity may also affect hiring decisions. Employment equity attempts to achieve equality in the workplace by giving underrepresented groups special consideration in hiring. Human rights legislation prohibits discrimination; **employment equity legislation** requires employers to take positive steps to make the workplace more equitable.

The federal *Employment Equity Act*[17] targets the underrepresentation of women, Aboriginal peoples, people with disabilities, and visible minorities in the workforce. The Act applies to businesses that have one hundred or more employees and that are under the regulation of the federal government. It requires employers to

employment equity legislation
Laws designed to improve the status of certain designated groups.

Diversity is good for business.

- consult with employee representatives regarding the implementation of employment equity
- identify and eliminate barriers to the employment of the designated groups
- institute policies and practices and make reasonable efforts at accommodation to ensure that the designated groups have a degree of representation in the portion of the workforce from which the employer can reasonably be expected to draw employees
- prepare a plan that sets out the goals to be achieved and a timetable for implementation

There has been much debate about whether such programs are a form of reverse discrimination; however, the equality provision of the *Charter* specifically permits them.

None of the provincial jurisdictions has legislation in this area.[18] However, many employers have their own voluntary employment equity programs. As well, the federal government has a nonlegislated federal contractors program. This program seeks to ensure that all contractors that have one hundred or more employees and are bidding on federal contracts worth more than $200 000 achieve and maintain a fair and representative workforce. Techroniks is not affected by the federal legislation, and given its small size is unlikely to be affected by the federal contractors program. Any program Techroniks instituted would be voluntary.

Privacy Concerns

reference
A person who will testify to the ability and qualities of an applicant.

The process of hiring involves gathering a wealth of information about prospective candidates. For example, at some point in the hiring process Techroniks will probably check a prospective employee's **references** or verify the accuracy of the information provided. This verification is particularly important because technological advances have made it very easy to forge documents, records, transcripts, and letters. References are also checked because it is thought that past performance is an indi-

---

17. *Employment Equity Act*, S.C. 1995, c. 44.

18. The only provincial government to pass legislation in this area was Ontario. However its legislation, passed in 1993 by a NDP government, was repealed in 1996 after the Progressive Conservative Party

cator of future success. There is no *legal obligation* to check references or verify information provided by a job applicant; however, the risks of vicarious liability and negligent hiring provide incentive for doing so. Checking references and backgrounds cannot entirely eliminate Techronkics' concerns about hiring someone with criminal tendencies, but it does eliminate the most obvious threats.

Could checking into someone's background be considered an invasion of privacy?[19] The law in this area is uncertain. Privacy is not an explicit right protected under the *Charter,* nor is it a right set out in the human rights legislation. The extent to which there is a common law right to privacy or an actionable tort of "invasion of privacy" is also unclear. The federal government, however, has recently enacted the *Personal Information Protection and Electronic Document Act,*[20] which supports and promotes electronic commerce by protecting personal information. This Act establishes a right of privacy for personal information that is collected, used, and disclosed in the private sector.[21] It applies to all personal information, including information about an employee. A key provision of the legislation is the requirement that organizations obtain an individual's consent before collecting, using, or disclosing the individual's personal information.

An employer should get permission from an applicant to do a background search, particularly in situations where the search goes beyond the references named on the application form or listed on the résumé. It is also useful for the employer to keep a record of the inquiries made, as well as the result of the inquiries, so that it can demonstrate that "reasonable care" was taken in hiring.

Formation of the Employment Contract

During the negotiations leading to an offer of employment, a lot of information is exchanged. In many cases disputes have arisen upon termination, based on representations in the negotiations leading up to the offer. There may have been prehiring promises, or representations made concerning the nature of the employment that did not materialize. On termination, the employee may be able to allege breach of oral promises, as *Queen* v. *Cognos* illustrates.

Case

Queen v. *Cognos Inc.* (1993), 99 D.L.R. (4th) 626 (S.C.C.)

The Business Context: A company seeking to attract the most qualified candidate may sometimes oversell itself or the job. Promises and representations are often freely made.

Factual Background: Douglas Queen was hired by Cognos to help develop an accounting software package. Queen was told by an employee of Cognos that the project would run for a number of years and would be well funded. Based on these representations and a signed employment contract, Queen quit a secure job in Calgary and moved to Ottawa. About two weeks later, the company shifted funding into a different product. Queen was kept on for 18 months, during which time he had a number of fill-in jobs. After being dismissed, he brought

---

19. In Ontario, the *Consumer Reporting Act,* R.S.O. 1990, c. 33, s. 11 prohibits employers from seeking a reference unless the applicant has given permission in writing for it to do so.

20. *Personal Information and Electronic Documents Act,* S.C. 2000, c. 4. The Act received Royal Assent on 13 April 2000 and is expected to come into force in early 2001.

21. The Act applies to the federal private sector but has provisions for application to the provincial private sectors. If provinces do not enact their own legislation, then after three years the federal legislation becomes applicable to the provincial private sector. Quebec is the only province with privacy legislation that applies to the private sector.

an action against Cognos for negligent misrepresentation. He claimed that he would not have accepted the position had it not been for the representations about the scope and viability of the job.

The Legal Question: Does an interviewer owe a duty of care to a prospective employee?

Resolution: The trial judge ruled in Queen's favour. The Court of Appeal also recognized that a duty of care would be owed but found, in effect, that the written employment contract overrode the prior representations. The Supreme Court of Canada restored the trial court's decision. It held that an interviewer has a duty to take reasonable care to avoid making misleading statements. Here,

the interviewer failed by misrepresenting the security of the job. Although the contract Queen signed had a disclaimer that allowed the company to reassign or dismiss him, the disclaimer did not save the company from liability for making false promises about the job. Cognos was required to pay damages for Queen's loss of income, loss on the sale of his house in Calgary and the purchase of his house in Ottawa, emotional stress, and expenses incurred in finding a new job.

Critical Analysis: Is it realistic to expect employers to control what is said by their employees when engaged in recruiting candidates? Does the applicant have an obligation to check out the company?

Employees may make statements that are inaccurate by embellishing their qualifications. This is an added reason for carefully checking backgrounds and stating in employment contracts that misrepresentations by the employee can lead to termination.

Offer of Employment

After Techronniks has recruited job applicants, interviewed them, and checked their references, the next step is usually an offer of employment. The offer normally comes from the employer to the employee, but there is no legal requirement that it must.

Like offers in other types of contracts, the offer must be reasonably certain to constitute an "offer" in law. Thus, the statement, "We would like you to work for us" is not considered an offer, as it does not define the job, remuneration, or any of the other terms of employment. The offer, however, need not be in a particular form or in writing. As long as the statements are reasonably complete and certain, casual comments may be considered offers. Once made, the offer is capable of acceptance until it is terminated. Therefore, an offer of employment made to two candidates could result in two acceptances and two employment contracts for the one job. Offers should have time limits so that there are no problems with ascertaining when the offer expires.

Prior to making an offer, the employer should determine whether the candidate has any obligations to her most recent employer. These obligations may impede her ability to perform the job and could result in legal action against the new employer, such as in the following ways:

- *Inducing breach of contract.* If the newly hired employee breaks an existing employment contract in order to accept an offer, the former employer may sue new employer for the tort of "inducing a breach of contract."[22]
- *Restrictive covenants.* It is also not uncommon for employment contracts to contain restrictive covenants limiting the former employee's ability to compete against the former employer. The contract may seek to restrict the solicitation of customers and employees or the use of confidential information, for example.

---

22. The tort of inducing breach of contract is discussed in Chapter 12.

These restrictions are particularly common in industries in which businesses are highly dependent on customer contacts or skilled employees and there is a lot of confidential information and trade secrets.[23]

- *Fiduciary obligations.* A potential employee may also be considered to be in a "fiduciary" relationship with his or her former employer. Whether or not an employee is a fiduciary will be determined by the position held by the employee, the employee's duties and responsibilities, the nature of the business, and the organizational structure. Generally, only senior employees are considered to be in this relationship, but there does appear to be support for broadening the scope of the definition to include any "key" employee.[24] A finding of a fiduciary relationship may mean that such employees are prohibited from soliciting customers from their former employer and from taking advantage of business opportunities discovered through the former employer.

The Employment Contract

fixed or definite term contract
A contract for a specified period of time which automatically ends on the expiry date.

indefinite term contract
A contract for no fixed period which can end on giving reasonable notice.

The employment relationship is contractual. The contract may be for a specified period of time, in which case the contract is known as a **fixed or definite term contract**. The contract, however, need not specify any period of time. Contracts such as these are known as **indefinite term contracts**. The distinction is particularly important with respect to termination. Historically, most employment contracts were indefinite, but term contracts are becoming more common. The contract may be oral or in writing,[25] but most commonly it is written.

Express and Implied Terms

Whether it is oral or in writing, the contract may include express terms and implied terms.[26] Express terms are those that have been actually agreed upon by the parties. They are included in the contract or incorporated by reference. Benefits packages, job descriptions, and company rules and policies are often in separate documents and included by reference. Implied terms are those that have not been specifically agreed upon by the parties but are what the courts believe the parties *would* have agreed to, had they sat down and negotiated the point. Employment is an area where traditionally there have been a great many implied terms. For example, if the parties do not specify the duration of the contract, it is implied that the contract is for an indefinite period of time. Therefore, the contract does not come to an end until one of the parties gives notice of termination. This term leads to another implied term that the notice of termination must be *reasonable.*[27]

Content of the Contract

Most employers and employees now see the need to introduce certainty into the employment relationship by putting their relationship into writing.

Besides the advantage of certainty, a written employment contract offers other advantages, including a forum for negotiating terms and conditions that are tailored

---

23. Restrictive covenants in contracts are discussed in Chapter 9.
24. See *Canadian Aero Service Ltd.* v. *O'Malley,* [1974] S.C.R. 592.
25. Writing requirements are discussed in Chapter 8.
26. Implied terms in contracts are discussed in Chapter 7.
27. Notice and termination are discussed in Chapter 22.

to the situation—notice periods, restrictive covenants, and limitation of precontractual promises, to name a few (see Figure 21.2). Written terms will override terms that are implied at law.

ESSENTIAL CONTENT OF AN EMPLOYMENT CONTRACT

An employment contract should contain the following information:

- ✔ names of the parties
- ✔ date on which the contract begins
- ✔ position and description of the work to be performed
- ✔ compensation (i.e., salary, wages, benefits)
- ✔ vacation and vacation pay
- ✔ duration of the contract, if any
- ✔ termination provisions
- ✔ recital of management rights (i.e., employer has a right to make changes to job duties and responsibilities)
- ✔ confidentiality clause, if appropriate
- ✔ restrictive covenants, if any
- ✔ "entire agreement" clause (i.e., the written contract contains the whole agreement)

Written employment contracts provide a mechanism for Techroniks to address its concerns about employees leaving. Although Techroniks cannot prevent its employees from leaving, it can negotiate for terms in the contract that prohibit the employees from working for competitors for a period of time or from revealing confidential information. More important is providing favourable working conditions so that employees are disinclined to leave.

Terms and Conditions

The ability of an employer and an employee to negotiate their contract has been abrogated to some extent by legislation designed to protect the employee. The terms of the employment contract are affected by legislation, and so are the conditions of employment. The terms of the employment contract and the conditions of employment are affected by legislation relating to employee welfare, workplace discrimination, and workplace privacy. This is by no means an exhaustive list of all the issues related to the terms and conditions of employment.

Employee Welfare Issues

Employment Standards

employment standards legislation
Laws that specify minimum standards in the workplace.

All the provinces and territories, as well as the federal government,[28] have **employment standards legislation** that sets out minimum standards in the workplace. This legislation has often been referred to as the collective agreement for nonunionized employees. It sets a floor of rights for employees. An employer may provide greater benefits than those provided for in the legislation but not lesser. In short, any contractual provisions that provide lesser benefits than those set out in the legislation are not enforceable.

There are variations in the details of the legislation from province to province. Most, however, cover the same general categories of benefits:

- hours of work and overtime
- minimum wages
- equal pay for equal work
- statutory holidays
- maternity and parental leave
- bereavement and sick leave
- vacations and vacation pay
- termination and severance pay

Certain employees, such as doctors, farmers, and domestic workers, may be exempt from certain provisions, such as hours of work, minimum wages, and overtime pay. The legislation also provides a mechanism for enforcing employment standards. In Ontario, for example, employment standards officers, employed by the Employment Standards Branch, investigate complaints, carry on general investigations, and, when necessary, issue orders requiring compliance with provisions of the *Employment Standards Act*.

Employment Standards Abroad

ETHICAL CONSIDERATIONS

Many Canadian companies manufacture goods abroad, often because of the reduced costs of manufacturing attributable to lower wage rates in developing countries. Most legal agreements for manufacturing in a foreign country include a "Compliance with Local Laws" provision. This stipulation requires the Canadian company to comply with all regulations in the foreign country that apply to the production, sale, and delivery of goods and to the supply of labour services. This mere compliance with local laws, however, may be problematic. For example, in many developing countries the minimum working age permits children to work, and the working day is 12 hours long. Also, in many countries the minimum wage is extremely low and often at or below poverty levels. In short, sweatshop conditions can exist in a lawful environment.

Critical Analysis: What are the risks for Canadian companies in manufacturing abroad using "sweatshop" labour? Why may "mere" compliance with local laws be problematic?

Source: James M. Klotz, "The Sweatshop Predicament for Canadians" *The Globe and Mail* (25 June 1998) A25.

---

28. Federal employment standards are contained in the *Canada Labour Code*, R.S.C. 1985, c. L-2.

Safety and Compensation

Workers' compensation legislation is designed to address accidents and injuries in the workplace. It provides for a type of no-fault insurance scheme. Employers are required to pay into a fund, and workers who have job-related injuries, accidents, or illnesses are compensated out of the fund, regardless of fault. Compensation covers lost wages, medical aid, and rehabilitation. The scheme prevents a civil suit by the employee against the employer relating to a workplace injury or accident. Not all employees, accidents, or illnesses are covered by the legislation, however. Illness must be job related, which is not always easy to determine, particularly as the causes of many illnesses are unclear and the illnesses themselves can take decades to develop.

Most jurisdictions have enacted comprehensive occupational health and safety legislation that generally applies to all sectors of the economy. In addition to general provisions applicable to most workplaces, there are industry-specific provisions and hazard-oriented provisions. The purpose of the legislation is to protect workers in the workplace by giving them a right to participate in safety issues, a right to know about hazards in the workplace, and a right to refuse to work in unsafe conditions.

Employee Economic Safety

Two legislative schemes in the area of employee economic safety are employment insurance and the Canada and Quebec pension plans.

The *Employment Insurance Act*[29] is federal legislation that applies to both the federally and provincially regulated sectors. The basic concept of employment insurance is that the employer and employee contribute to a fund that provides insurance against loss of income. The plan provides benefits for unemployment, maternity leave, and sickness, as well as some retirement benefits. A limited number of employees are not covered by the scheme. The most common exclusions are casual workers, some part-time workers, and those employed in agriculture.

The *Canada* (and *Quebec) Pension Plan*[30] is an insurance plan designed to provide pensions on retirement and financial assistance in the case of disability or death. Both the employer and the employee contribute to the plan.

Workplace Discrimination

Discrimination on certain grounds is prohibited in all aspects of employment, including promotions and terminations. One area that has received a great deal of attention is workplace harassment, particularly sexual harassment.

Sexual Harassment

sexual harassment
Unwelcome conduct of a sexual nature.

In some jurisdictions, the human rights legislation specifically prohibits **sexual harassment** of employees in the workplace. In other jurisdictions where it is not specifically prohibited, it is included within the prohibition against sex discrimination.

Sexual harassment is defined as unwelcome conduct of a sexual nature that detrimentally affects the work environment or leads to adverse job-related consequences for the victims of harassment. Such behaviour may include touching, telling inappropriate jokes, making sexual requests or suggestions, staring, making comments about a person's appearance, and displaying suggestive pictures, drawings, or slogans.

---

29. S.C. 1996, c. 23. The Act was formerly known as the *Unemployment Insurance Act* but was renamed in 1996 as part of a general reform package. It covers provincial sectors as a result of a specific amendment to the Constitution.

30. R.S.C. 1985, c. P-21.

A workplace harassment policy addresses inappropriate behaviour.

Sexual Harassment in the Workplace

INTERNATIONAL PERSPECTIVE

In 1996, the U.S. Equal Employment Opportunity Commission sued Mitsubishi Motors, the giant Japanese conglomerate, over sexual harassment complaints. The commission alleged that women at an Illinois factory were groped, insulted, and subjected to "raunchy" pranks and that managers did nothing to stop it.

Mitsubishi initially fought the accusations, even organizing an employee protest outside the commission's Chicago office. But it soon reversed its stand after getting bad publicity over the hardline approach.

The company agreed to pay a record US $34 million to settle—the biggest sexual harassment settlement ever obtained by the U.S. government. The settlement was shared by 350 women who had worked on the auto plant's assembly line since 1987. The payout for each woman ranged from a few thousand dollars to $300 000.

Critical Analysis: Should there be different standards of conduct in an industrial setting, as opposed to other types of work environments?

Source: "Shop-Floor Harassment Costs $34M US" *The Edmonton Journal* (12 June 1998) E1.

The prohibition against sexual harassment extends not only to employers but also to their employees. In some jurisdictions the legislation provides that an employer will be vicariously liable for the acts of its employees. Even in the absence of such a provision, the Supreme Court of Canada has imposed liability against the employer.[31]

It is incumbent on employers to develop and implement a workplace harassment policy. Such action may affect the remedy awarded to a victim. The wronged employee may end up receiving less compensation if it is found that the employer took some action to prevent the wrongful conduct from occurring in the first place.

Figure 21.3

ESSENTIAL CONTENT OF A HARASSMENT POLICY

A workplace harassment policy should contain the following:

- ☑ **an explanation of the underlying philosophy of the policy**
- ☑ **a definition of the prohibited conduct**
- ☑ **a warning of penalties that will be invoked for violating the policy**
- ☑ **a procedural guideline for filing a complaint**
- ☑ **an outline of what might occur once a complaint has been filed**

Pay Equity

Discrimination in pay scales between males and females has led to legislation designed to ensure that female and male employees receive the same compensation for performing the same or substantially similar work.[32] Some jurisdictions provide equal pay for equal work. Other jurisdictions have gone one step further and have provided for equal pay for work of equal value. In addition to these provisions, some jurisdictions have enacted specific **pay equity** statutes.[33]

Pay equity provisions are designed to redress systemic discrimination in compensation for work performed. They require an employer to evaluate the work performed by employees in order to divide the workforce into job classes. The classes can then be considered to determine whether they are male or female dominated. Employers must then value each of the job classes in terms of duties, responsibilities, and required qualifications; compare like classes; and then endeavour to compensate each female job class with a wage rate comparable to the male job class performing work of equal value. This procedure, however, has been extremely difficult to administer and apply.

pay equity
Provisions designed to ensure that female and male employees receive the same compensation for performing similar or substantially similar work.

31. *Robichaud* v. *The Queen* (1987), 40 D.L.R. (4th) 577 (S.C.C.).

32. These provisions may be in human rights or employment standards legislation.

33. The provinces of Manitoba, New Brunswick, Nova Scotia, Prince Edward Island, and Ontario have specific pay equity legislation. Ontario is the only province in which the legislation applies to the private sector. The other provinces limit the legislation's application to the public sector. See *Pay Equity Act,* R.S.O. 1990, c. P-7.

Pay Equity at Bell Canada

Many employees' experiences with pay equity have been less than happy. Consider the experience of employees at Bell Canada.

In the 1980s a number of wage discrimination complaints were filed with the Canadian Human Rights Commission by unions representing employees at Bell Canada. The commission investigated and dismissed the complaints. However, in 1991 an internal study conducted by Bell and the unions showed a wage gap of between $1.99 and $5.35. In September 1993, Bell made a "pay equity" adjustment of approximately 1 percent for each affected employee. It also announced a similar adjustment for 1994.

The unions rejected these adjustments, claiming that they failed to close the gap. In 1994 the unions and a group of employees filed a complaint with the Canadian Human Rights Commission alleging that Bell had followed a discriminatory practice contrary to the *Canadian Human Rights Act*. They alleged that Bell had established or maintained "differences in wages" between men and women in the same establishment performing work of equal value.

The commission investigated the complaint and determined that it merited a hearing before the Canadian Human Rights Tribunal. The tribunal is set up to hear both sides of the issue and make a decision. Bell objected and requested a review of the commission's decision to refer the matter to a tri-

A BUSINESS PERSPECTIVE

bunal. This preliminary matter of whether the complaint merited a hearing before a tribunal went all the way to the Appeal Division of the Federal Court. The court determined that it did merit a hearing. Shortly thereafter, the union representing the employees and Bell reached a settlement of about $59 million, which would have provided about $3000 for each of the 20 000 current and former workers affected. The employees rejected the settlement, and the dispute is back in litigation.

The experience of the Bell employees is not unique. A similar pay equity dispute between the federal government and 230 000 clerks, librarians, secretaries, and other federal employees went on for over 15 years until a settlement was reached. The federal government finally agreed to pay over $3.6 billion in settlement. Other pay equity disputes that are ongoing involve Air Canada, Canada Post, and the government of the Northwest Territories.

Critical Analysis: Is the integrity of the pay equity regime called into question when the government of Canada has difficulty implementing its own legislation? What do you think might be the problems with implementing pay equity?

Source: *Bell Canada* v. *C.E.P.* (1998), 167 D.L.R. (4th) 432 (F.C.A.).

Drug Testing

Mandatory drug testing in the workplace is a contentious issue. Policies have often been introduced into the Canadian workplace because a U.S. parent company of the Canadian subsidiary has required it. The policies are controversial because they appear to offend human rights legislation by discriminating on the basis of a disability (drug or alcohol dependency). To meet a challenge on this ground, a company needs to show that the policy is a *bona fide* occupational requirement. The policy must have been developed honestly and in good faith and be "reasonably necessary" to ensure the safe, economical, and efficient performance of the job. As well, the means adopted in the policy to address substance abuse must be the least intrusive methods possible. *Canadian Civil Liberties Assn.* v. *Toronto-Dominion Bank* illustrates the court's approach to drug-testing policies.

Case

Canadian Civil Liberties Assn. v. *Toronto Dominion Bank* (1998), 163 D.L.R. (4th) 193 (F.C.A.)

The Business Context: The publicity associated with drug and alcohol abuse has often spurred employers to take actions to prevent and eliminate substance abuse in the workplace.

Factual Background: In the mid-1980s the Toronto-Dominion Bank (TD), in response to a general concern about substance abuse in the workplace, established a drug-testing policy. Under this policy, all applicants to the TD bank are notified on the application form that, as a condition of employment, they will be tested for drugs. Once an offer of employment has been accepted, the new employee is advised to appear at a clinic within 48 hours to provide a urine sample. Samples are screened for marijuana, hashish, codeine, morphine, and heroin. If the result is negative, the employee is notified and that is the end of the matter; if the result is positive, there is an elaborate follow-up with assessment and treatment. An employee is terminated if she or he tests positive on three occasions or refuses to comply with any step in the procedure.

The Canadian Civil Liberties Association filed a complaint with the Canadian Human Rights Commission, alleging that the bank's policy offended the *Canadian Human Rights Act*.

The Legal Question: Is the policy discriminatory in that it "deprives or tends to deprive persons of employment by forcing all new and returning employees to undergo a mandatory drug test because of a disability (perceived drug dependency)"?

Resolution: The Federal Court (Appeal) held that the policy runs afoul of the *Canadian Human Rights Act*. The Act forbids an employer from establishing a policy that discriminates on the basis of a disability, which includes "previous or existing dependency on alcohol or a drug." The discrimination can be justified only if it is "rationally connected" to job performance. In other words, there must be evidence that drug use is affecting job performance at the bank. The bank did not present evidence of a drug problem at the bank or scientific evidence of drug use affecting job performance. The court ordered the case sent back to a human rights tribunal, where an appropriate remedy would be fashioned.

Critical Analysis: What sort of drug testing might not offend human rights legislation? What might be an appropriate remedy in this case?

Workplace Privacy

Privacy, particularly since technological developments have made it easier to "watch" or monitor employees, has become a real concern in the workplace. Issues centre on watching and searching employees, collecting and disseminating information about employees, and, more recently, monitoring employees' electronic communications.

Surveillance and Searches

There is very little law concerning the surveillance and searching of employees in a nonunionized setting. However, because these issues are often covered by a collective agreement, there are arbitration decisions providing some guidance for employers. The surveillance of employees with video cameras or closed-circuit television may not be an invasion of privacy, as the workplace is the employer's property. The employee has no expectation of privacy there except in some areas, such as washrooms and locker rooms. Nonetheless, it is unlikely that cameras would be condoned anywhere unless they were reasonably necessary to protect the employer's interests.[34]

---

34. Employment standards legislation prohibits the use of lie-detector tests in the workplace.

Intrusive searches of employees or their belongings would be carefully scrutinized by the courts. An employer would need to have some particularly compelling reasons, such as bomb threats being issued or thefts occurring, to undertake such practices. Additionally, the employer would need to demonstrate that all other alternatives for dealing with the threats had been exhausted. Employees should be informed in advance of any policy in this regard, and any searches would need to be conducted in a systematic and nonarbitrary manner; otherwise, the employer may be vulnerable to charges of discrimination.

Collection and Dissemination of Information

Employers have the ability to collect and store, in hard copy or electronically, a great deal of employee data—performance reviews, work activity reports, medical records, credit ratings, and letters of recommendation. The issue is whether the employee has any right to control the release and dissemination of this information.

A wide array of legislation in the public sector, at both the federal and provincial levels, gives individuals the right to control personal information. For example, the federal *Privacy Act*[35] regulates the collection and use of personal information held by the federal government. The Act gives individuals the right to see information and to request corrections if it is inaccurate. Similar provincial legislation applies to information held by provincial governments. The *Personal Information and Electronic Documents Act*[36] will extend these rights to the private sector. The Act limits the collection of personal information to that which is reasonably necessary for the purposes identified by the organization collecting the information. It also puts limits on the use, disclosure, and retention of the collected information. Businesses will be required to respect a code of fair information practices, which will require that the employee consent to the collection, use, and disclosure of personal information.

Monitoring of Communications

The *Criminal Code*[37] provides that it is an offence to intercept—that is, tap—a telephone or voice-mail communication by various means. The section, however, does not apply to oral communications that are not private or to interception that is consented to by one of the parties. A communication is private only if all parties have an expectation that it will not be intercepted. Thus, the issue is whether a reasonable expectation of privacy is attached to communications made on systems that the employer pays for during working hours. The argument could be made that there is no such expectation, and the argument would be further strengthened by notice of and consent to monitoring.

This issue is also applicable to the monitoring of employee e-mail, which can be easily monitored through technology.

Technology has many business applications.

35. R.S.C. 1985. c. P-21.
36. *Supra,* note 20.
37. *Criminal Code of Canada,* R.S.C 1985, c. C-46, s. 184.

"Can Your Boss Spy on Your E-Mail?"

How carefully are employees' privacy rights protected?

Privacy issues in the workplace used to be straightforward, as they dealt with little more than the employer's right to open employees' mail, check their references, or search their bags, purses, and lockers. Technology has changed that.

An employer's surveillance of the workplace, access to medical information, and, more recently, access to employees' computer files, interception of electronic mail messages, and monitoring of Internet surfing are new examples of the erosion of employees' privacy rights.

E-mail messages in particular pose an interesting question. Are employers permitted to intercept them?

If e-mail communications are found by a court to be "private communications," it is arguable that anyone intercepting them could be held criminally liable. The law regarding whether e-mail messages are private communications that could create criminal liability remains unclear.

An employee who uses a password will have a greater expectation that communication will be private. The argument is then stronger that an employer's interception might be criminal.

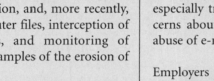

An organization that uses a two-tier storage system for e-mail—one tier for the employee's personal information and the other for business information—may be able to access the tier storing business information without offending the law. These messages are interoffice communications intended to be used for business purposes. Although, again, the law is unclear, it is generally assumed that an employer has the right to intercept them. This is especially true if the employer has legitimate concerns about illegal activity, improper conduct, or abuse of e-mail.

Employers should have written corporate policies establishing that management reserves the right to intercept e-mail communication at any time or in clearly defined circumstances. That policy should be given to employees in advance. Employers that do so will have the right to monitor e-mail in the manner they have defined.

The law will evolve case by case as it attempts to balance the employee's right to privacy with the employer's right to monitor and control the workplace.

Source: Howard Levitt, "Can Your Boss Spy on Your E-Mail? *The Toronto Star* (27 April 1998) D3.

The Union Relationship

Discussion in this chapter, thus far, has focused on the hiring and employment of nonunionized employees. It has also focused on private as opposed to public sector employees, as there is often specific legislation that affects their employment.

In a unionized environment, many of the same employment issues that arise in a nonunionized environment are also relevant—recruiting, terms and conditions of employment, and so on. However, negotiating and entering an employment contract is a much different process.

Both the federal and provincial governments have enacted labour or industrial relations legislation that guarantees the right of employees to join trade unions. The

certification
The process by which a union is recognized as a bargaining agent for a group of employees.

Labour Relations Board
A body that administers labour relations legislation.

collective bargaining
A mechanism by which parties enter a collective agreement or contract.

collective agreement
The employment agreement reached between the union and employer setting out the bargaining unit employees' terms and conditions of employment.

Acts apply to most employees, but certain employees—namely, managers and those in specific occupations, such as domestic workers and farmhands—are excluded. The legislative enactments provide for a **certification** process, by which the union is recognized as the bargaining agent for a group of employees. An employer, however, can voluntarily recognize the union as the bargaining agent for the employees without the necessity of the certification process. The certification process is basically a method by which the **Labour Relations Board** approves the union as the employees' representative, upon the union being able to show that a majority of the employees in the bargaining unit want the union to represent them.

The legislation provides a mechanism known as **collective bargaining**, by which the parties enter a collective agreement or contract. The contract applies to all employees in the bargaining unit, regardless of whether they voted for the union representation. The union and the employer have a duty to bargain in good faith—that is, they must make a substantive effort to negotiate the agreement. The collective agreement, like an individual employment contract, sets out the terms and conditions of employment. The two types of contracts cover many of the same issues, such as wages, benefits, and the like, but a **collective agreement** is usually far more comprehensive. As well, a union bargaining on behalf of many employees generally has far more bargaining power than a single individual negotiating with an employer (although some highly skilled or specialized employees do have a lot of individual bargaining power). During the term of the collective agreement, there can be no legal strikes by the employees or lock-outs by the employer.

In return, the legislation provides a process involving *grievance and arbitration* procedures for resolving disputes. These procedures are discussed in Chapter 22.

Business Law in Practice Revisited

1. Is Charles entitled to hire on the basis of who will "fit in" at Techroniks?

Hiring is the prerogative of the owner or manager of a company; however, discrimination is prohibited. By hiring employees on the basis of who will fit in, as determined by in-house values and attitudes, it is possible that Techroniks is either intentionally or unintentionally discriminating. The company may be eliminating candidates on the basis of their race, religion, age, and sex, for example. Techroniks should develop job-related qualifications and use these in the recruiting and hiring process.

2. How can Charles' concerns about employees leaving be addressed?

There are no guarantees with hiring employees that they will be committed and stay with the organization. Techroniks, however, may want to consider term contracts, as giving them to employees may result in a commitment for at least a specific period of time. The risk of hiring an employee who ultimately turns out to be unstable can be reduced somewhat by collecting as much information as possible about the candidate through the application process, interviews, and references. However, Techroniks is cautioned about running afoul of the human rights legislation. For example, an employer cannot discriminate on the basis of sex, and as pregnancy is considered to be part of this ground, an employer is not entitled to ask a female candidate if she is pregnant or intends to have children.

Protection of the company's intellectual assets is a legitimate concern, and the company should consider including a confidentiality clause and a restrictive covenant in the employment contract. A confidentiality clause restricts the disclosure of trade secrets. It also draws to the employee's attention the importance of confidentiality. A noncompetition clause prevents an employee from commencing employment with a competitor. Clauses need to be carefully drafted to balance an employee's ability to earn a livelihood using the skills and experience they have gained with the employer's interests in protecting intellectual assets.

3. What steps can Charles take to reduce the probability of hiring someone with criminal tendencies?

Techroniks can reduce the chances of this occurring by carefully following all the steps in the hiring process. In particular, Techroniks should carefully verify employee information and check references.

Chapter Summary

The employment relationship is one of the most fundamental relationships in business. The cornerstone of this relationship is a contract, either individual or collective, whereby one party provides services to another in return for remuneration. However, not everyone who provides services to another through the vehicle of a contract is an "employee." The distinction is crucial because common law, as well as statutory rights and obligations, in most cases applies only to employees and not to independent contractors.

The hiring process has a number of phases—advertising, application submission, interviewing, and reference checking. Legal issues such as discrimination, employment equity, and privacy apply to each of these steps and provide the opportunity for potential liability for the unwary employer. Most of the costly mistakes made by employers who end up the subject of a human rights investigation or the recipient of a wrongful dismissal suit can be avoided. Organizations need to be proactive by designing and implementing policies, practices, and procedures to address the legal issues at all stages of the employment relationship.

A well-drafted employment contract sets out the terms and conditions of employment. It describes the employment relationship and at a minimum sets out the job to be performed and the remuneration to be provided. The employment contract can be advantageous for both the employer and employee, as it contributes to certainty and clarity in the relationship.

The ability to freely negotiate an employment contract has been somewhat curtailed by a host of legislation designed to protect employees. This protection is provided not only with respect to the terms of employment, such as wages, vacation, and hours of work, but also with respect to the conditions of employment. There is a vast array of legislation affecting employee welfare, discrimination in the workplace, and privacy.

When a union is in place, negotiating and entering into an employment contract takes place through a process known as collective bargaining. The collective agreement that emerges from negotiations applies to all employees, regardless of whether they voted for union representation.

Study Chapter

Key Terms and Concepts

adverse effects discrimination (p. 469)

bona fide **occupational requirement (BFOR)** (p. 470)

certification (p. 485)

collective agreement (p. 485)

collective bargaining (p. 485)

discrimination (p. 469)

duty to accommodate (p. 470)

employment equity legislation (p. 472)

employment relationship (p. 464)

employment standards legislation (p. 477)

fixed or definite term contract (p. 475)

Human Rights Commission (p. 467)

indefinite term contract (p. 475)

independent contractor (p. 464)

Labour Relations Board (p. 485)

pay equity (p. 480)

reference (p. 472)

sexual harassment (p. 478)

systemic discrimination (p. 469)

Questions for Review

1. Which level of government has jurisdiction to make laws in the area of employment?

2. What are the tests for determining the difference between an employee and an independent contractor?

3. Define vicarious liability and negligent hiring. How do they differ?

4. The *Human Rights Acts* attempt to prohibit discrimination in employment. What is meant by "discrimination"?

5. What is a *bona fide* occupational requirement? Give an example.

6. What is the "duty to accommodate"?

7. What is meant by "employment equity"?

8. Are employers under a legal obligation to check the references of prospective employees? What are the legal risks associated with checking references? With not checking references?

9. Do employment contracts need to be in writing to be enforceable? What are the advantages of a written employment contract? Can you think of any disadvantages?

10. What is the purpose of employment standards legislation? Give an example of an employment standard.

11. Explain how the freedom to contract in employment has been affected by legislation, and give examples.

12. What is the purpose of workers' compensation legislation?

13. Would displaying a picture of a nude person be an example of sexual harassment in the workplace? Explain.

14. What is the purpose of pay equity?

15. Do employees have a right to privacy? Explain.

Questions for Discussion

1. It has long been recognized that addiction to alcohol is a disability under human rights legislation. Should addiction to nicotine also be recognized as a disability? How would such a finding affect an employer's ability to regulate the workplace?

2. An advertisement that reads "Wanted: Vietnamese waiters for a Vietnamese restaurant" is discriminatory. On what basis does the advertisement discriminate? Could or should ethnicity qualify as a *bona fide* occupational requirement? Would it make any difference where the restaurant was located?

3. The concept of vicarious liability developed in the business world, where the company is out to make a profit and its activities are for the most part directed to generating profit. Is it appropriate to apply a test developed in this context to a charitable organization? What are the pros and cons for holding organizations liable for the conduct of their employees?

4. Technological developments have allowed business to obtain, share, and disseminate information with an ease and speed unimaginable less than a decade ago. The tools, however, are susceptible to abuse by employees who use them for personal, improper, or illegal purposes. For example, in 1999 Xerox fired a number of employees for accessing Web sites deemed inappropriate in the workplace. Employers can easily monitor and track employees' use of the technology. What are the legal and personnel issues that should be considered before embarking on such a course of action?

5. Mandatory drug testing in the workplace is a contentious issue. Under what circumstances should companies attempt to introduce drug testing? What specifications should the drug-testing policy contain?

Situations for Discussion

1. In 1991, Cindy Choung became British Columbia's first accredited Chinese-language court interpreter. Interpreters are called by court services (a branch of the government) when needed and are selected from a list in rotation. They are paid an hourly rate, plus expenses. All travel arrangements are made by and paid for by court services. There is no guarantee of a minimum amount of work, and there is no prohibition against working for other agencies. Court services make no deductions for income tax, employment insurance, or pension plans. A code of professional conduct implemented by court services governs how interpreters are to translate and to dress in court. It also sets out rules of confidentiality and prohibits interpreters from assigning their work to another interpreter.

   In 1994 the court services' executive director received complaints about Cindy's work and decided to remove her name from the list of interpreters. Cindy is considering bringing an action for wrongful dismissal. Is she entitled to bring such an action? What does she need to prove? Explain.[38]

2. Jan Delaney was hired by Tulay Cosmetics and Skin-Care Products Ltd. as a sales consultant and technical trainer. This position involved selling and providing information seminars to other salespersons on Tulay's skin-care products. When hired, Jan signed an employment contract that contained a two-year nonsolicitation covenant.

   The relationship between Jan and Tulay eventually deteriorated, and Jan subsequently secured a similar position with a competitor. Tulay brought an action for an injunction to restrain Jan from working for the competitor. What factors would the court consider in deciding whether to grant an injunction? What additional information would be helpful? [39]

3. Pierre Légère was a marketing representative for Compu-plus, a consulting firm that provided computer services to various government departments in New Brunswick. As a marketing representative, he developed contacts within government and among independent contractors who were retained to provide the computer services on a contract basis. Pierre, without giving any notice, left Compu-plus and joined a competitor that had actively pursued him and had offered substantially more money. Compu-plus is concerned about the impact that Pierre's defection will have on its business. What should Compu-plus do? What potential actions does it have? What factors should Compu-plus consider before it proceeds?[40]

4. **a.** Bill Reyno owns and operates a bottle-recycling plant. He has recently experienced a rash of thefts and break-ins and wants to hire a night watchman or security guard. Bill wants someone large and feisty in case there are any problems. What steps should Bill take in hiring someone to fill the position?

   b. Jon Blondin applied for the position. When he showed up for the interview, he seemed to be a little "unstable." In fact, Bill thought he might have been drinking, but he wasn't sure. Other than this concern, Jon seemed to be perfect for the job. Bill would like Jon to take a drug and alcohol test. Is it permissible for Bill to make this request?

---

38. Based on *Truong* v. *British Columbia*, (1999) 178 D.L.R. (4th) 644 (B.C.C.A.).
39. Based on *Phytoderm* v. *Urwin*, [1999] O.J. No. 383 (Ont. Gen. Div.).
40. Based on *MacDonald* v. *Klein*, [1998] O.J. No. 4922 (Ont. Gen. Div.).

5. Jodene recently got a job with a company that sells herbal medicines and related products. There are two aspects to her job: part of the time she is located in a small booth in a mall, and part of the time she demonstrates and sells products at home parties. In both situations she is paid by commission. One day, on her way from the mall to a home party, she accidently runs over a very valuable dog. Assuming that Jodene is negligent, who is liable to pay for the dog? Assuming the company was liable, how can it avoid liability in future?

6. Jennifer Moxley is a recent university graduate employed in the human resources department of a medium-sized firm in the textile industry. This is Jennifer's first full-time position. The company has a very small HR department. In fact, there is only Jennifer and her manager, who has other responsibilities in the company. Jennifer's manager is away at a convention and the following situation has arisen:

   The company is in the process of hiring a new employee for the design department. One of the vice presidents has given her the résumé of a person who went to school with his daughter, with the following comment: "Don't bother wasting time checking this kid's background—I can vouch for him." On examining the résumé, Jennifer finds that the person has no previous employment either full or part time, that he graduated with distinction from a computer design course at a well-known institution, that he has listed the vice president as his only reference, and that he has done volunteer work at the Pilgrim House Retreat.

   Advise Jennifer.

Chapter Twenty-Two

Terminating the Employment Relationship

Objectives

AFTER STUDYING THIS CHAPTER, YOU SHOULD HAVE AN
UNDERSTANDING OF:

► HOW THE EMPLOYMENT RELATIONSHIP ENDS
► THE DIFFERENCES AMONG DISMISSALS FOR JUST CAUSE, DIS-
  MISSALS WITH NOTICE, CONSTRUCTIVE DISMISSALS, AND
  WRONGFUL DISMISSALS
► THE ISSUES ARISING FROM A WRONGFUL DISMISSAL SUIT
► THE COMPONENTS OF A TERMINATION SETTLEMENT

Business Law in Practice

MegaBites, a manufacturer of wooden toys, has suffered serious economic setbacks owing in large measure to loss in market share to popular electronic games for children. Charlotte Delmar, the president, has come to the conclusion that several employees will have to go. Charlotte sees this as an opportunity to deal with a couple of marginal employees. In particular, she is thinking of Freda Jones, a 53-year-old clerical worker who has been with the company for 23 years, but who is chronically late for work and has shown an aversion to technology. The other employee is 40-year-old Ray Martinelli, the regional sales manager, who has been with the company

491

for 4 years. Charlotte had high hopes for Ray when she lured him away from Pouchez Electronics, one of MegaBites' major competitors, but his personality and demeanour are at odds with how things are done at MegaBites. Charlotte can't quite put her finger on what is wrong, but she has heard rumours about an office affair. She thinks, however, that he should be given another chance—perhaps if he is given the opportunity to be product manager of one of the company's poorer performers, he will rise to the challenge.

1. Is Charlotte justified in terminating Freda Jones?
2. Is Charlotte justified in transferring Ray Martinelli?
3. What course of action would you advise Charlotte to pursue?

Ending the Relationship

In many instances, the employment relationship ends in an amicable fashion. An employee resigns to pursue other interests, retires, or simply leaves at the end of a fixed-term employment contract.

The employment relationship can also come to an end through less pleasant means, as when the employer

- summarily dismisses, or fires, an employee
- gives the employee notice of termination
- acts in such a manner that the employment relationship becomes untenable

It is an implied term of an employment contract that an employer may terminate the employment relationship without any notice if there is "just cause." This implied term is subject to collective agreements and individual employment contracts, which may specify the terms for ending the employment relationship. The term is also subject to legislation that may give to certain employees, such as teachers, police officers, and firefighters, special rights in the case of dismissal.

It is also an implied term that an employer may terminate the employment contract by giving the employee reasonable notice of the termination. In this case the employer is not required to have a reason or cause for the termination. The implied term is also subject to collective agreements and individual employment contracts that provide for notice periods and rights on dismissal. As well, provincial and federal employment standards legislation provides for notice periods and procedures on dismissal. The periods of notice provided by the legislation are only minimum periods, and often employees are entitled to more notice.

This area of the law has become increasingly important for employers owing to the courts' recognition of the importance of work in people's lives. It has been the subject of much litigation over the last couple of decades and thus has seen profound changes.

just cause
Employee conduct that amounts to a fundamental breach of the employment contract.

Dismissals for Just Cause

When there is **just cause**, an employer may dismiss an employee without notice. Just cause for dismissal means, in effect, that the employee has breached a fundamental term of the employment contract.

Just cause exists when the employee is guilty of one or more of the following:

- serious misconduct
- habitual neglect of duty
- incompetence
- conduct incompatible with duties or prejudicial to the employer's business
- willful disobedience in a matter of substance[1]

The grounds for dismissal with cause are easy to articulate but difficult to apply in practice because the severity of conduct is a question of fact to be determined by a court. It is impossible to specify all of the conduct that may constitute just cause; however, it is possible to make some general comments about the various categories.

Serious Misconduct

A minor infraction by an employee is insufficient to justify dismissal, although the cumulative effect of many minor instances may be sufficient. The cumulative effect must be such that there is a serious impact on the employment relationship. For example, the telling of one off-colour joke would be insufficient grounds for dismissal. However, if the telling of the joke is combined with a number of other incidents, such as showing a picture of semi-nude women, winking at a co-worker, and telling another off-colour joke, then the cumulative effect of the incidents may be considered **serious misconduct** and may be sufficient to terminate.

serious misconduct
Intentional, harmful conduct of the employee that permits the employer to dismiss without notice.

If the employer wants to terminate on the basis of an accumulation of a number of minor incidents, then the employer usually has a duty to warn the employee and give an opportunity to improve performance. This duty is particularly important in situations where the employer has a **progressive discipline policy** in place. This is a system whereby the employer applies discipline for relatively minor infractions on a progressive basis. Each step in the progression carries a more serious penalty, until the last step—dismissal—is reached. The warning may be oral[2] or in writing and should be clear and understood by the employee. The employee should be advised not just about the unacceptable conduct, but also about the consequences of failure to improve.

progressive discipline policy
A system that follows a sequence of employee discipline from less to more severe punishment.

A single act of misconduct can justify dismissal if it is sufficiently serious. A single act of dishonesty has been held to be sufficient grounds for dismissal, as when an employee steals a large sum of money from the employer. Other conduct, although less serious than stealing, may also constitute serious misconduct. Examples include lying to an employer, forging signatures and documents, and cheating. What constitutes serious misconduct may also be affected by workforce policies. For example, Ray's rumoured office affair may constitute grounds for dismissal if the affair can be proven and if MegaBites has a policy in place forbidding fraternization among co-workers. Without the existence of such a policy, it is unlikely that an affair that occurs outside the office is grounds for dismissal, unless there is evidence that the workplace has been negatively affected.

condonation
Employer behaviour that indicates to the employee that misconduct is being overlooked.

An important principle with respect to any of the grounds for dismissal is **condonation**. Condonation occurs when an employer indicates through words or actions that behaviour constituting grounds for dismissal is being overlooked. For example, an employer who is aware of the harassing activities of an employee and who ignores or tolerates the activities cannot then fire an employee for harassment. Condonation occurs only if the employer is fully aware of the wrongful behaviour.

---

1. *R. v. Arthur, Ex parte Port Arthur Shipbuilding Co.* (1967), 62 D.L.R. (2d) 342 (Ont. C.A.).
2. Warnings, especially oral warnings, need to be documented so that an employer can establish that the duty to warn was fulfilled.

Personal Use of the Employer's Property

The introduction of technologies such as fax machines, e-mail, and the Internet into the workplace has greatly increased the possibility of employees using company property for personal use. It is a new spin on the old nuisance of employees making personal phone calls at work—but with greatly magnified consequences. Use of the technologies by employees ranges from occasional online shopping ventures to hours spent surfing on the Net and the use of a company computer to run a personal business.

Critical Analysis: Should excessive Internet use be grounds for dismissal? Under what circumstances? Other than to prevent lost productivity, why would an employer may want to control an employee's Internet use?

Habitual Neglect of Duty

habitual neglect of duty
Customary failure to perform employment duties.

An employee may be terminated with cause for chronic absenteeism and lateness that are considered **habitual neglect of duty**. The absenteeism must be without the employer's permission or authorization and be more than an occasional absence. Important to this ground is whether warnings were issued, whether there was any excuse for the absence, and whether the absence occurred at a critical time for the employer.

It is more difficult to establish lateness than absenteeism as grounds for dismissal. The courts will consider whether the employee had a valid excuse, whether there were warnings concerning lateness, and whether the time was ever made up, as well as related factors.

Freda, for example, has exhibited chronic lateness, but at this point it is unlikely that Charlotte can use this as just cause to terminate. Warnings may not have been issued, and it appears that the behaviour has been condoned.

Incompetence

incompetence
Lack of ability, knowledge, or qualification to perform employment obligations.

To dismiss on the ground of incompetence, the employer must be more than merely dissatisfied with an employee's work. There must be actual **incompetence**. The substandard level of performance must be evident after the employee has been given a warning and an opportunity to improve. An employer must establish fair and reasonable performance standards against which to measure performance. An employee can raise a number of issues to explain poor performance—inadequate training, insufficient volume of business, inexperience, and condonation of performance problems. Freda has exhibited an aversion to technology, but that does not necessarily equal incompetence. Charlotte would need to determine what impact technology has on Freda's job, whether Freda received adequate training, and whether she was given any warning about her performance. Similarly, Ray's less than stellar performance as a product manager may not be incompetence, particularly if the company has not instituted performance standards against which to assess his work.

A single act of incompetence is rarely grounds for dismissal, unless it shows a complete lack of skills that an employee claimed to have possessed.

Conduct Incompatible

conduct incompatible
Personal behaviour that is irreconcilable with employment duties.

An employer may be justified in terminating with cause for **conduct incompatible** with the employee's duties or prejudicial to the employer's business—for example, accepting lavish and inappropriate gifts from the employer's clients. The conduct complained of is not limited to conduct on the job—it can also apply to conduct outside of working hours. For example, a school board was justified in dismissing a school superintendent who was convicted of a petty fraud outside the performance of his duties.[3]

Closely related to incompatible conduct is the ground for dismissal related to an employee's conflict of interest. For example, if an employee were to run a business that was in direct competition with the employer's business, that could be a breach of the employee's duty of loyalty and good faith to the employer.[4]

Willful Disobedience

willful disobedience
Deliberate failure to carry out lawful and reasonable orders.

An employer is entitled to expect an employee to carry out lawful and reasonable orders. Failure to do otherwise is considered **willful disobedience**. A single act of disobedience would not ordinarily constitute grounds for dismissal, unless that act was very serious, such as not attending an important meeting or refusing to follow important safety rules. To rely on this ground, the employer would have to establish that the instructions or directions given to the employee were unambiguous and that the employee had no reasonable excuse for disobeying. Less serious instances of disobedience may justify dismissal when combined with other types of misconduct, such as insolence and insubordination.

An employer is entitled to expect an employee to carry out orders without extended debate and with respect. Whether an employer is justified in terminating an employee who fails to meet this standard depends on a number of factors, such as whether the employee was provoked, whether the employee was upset, and whether it was a moment of temporary anger.

Other Causes

In addition to the above grounds, there can be other legitimate bases for termination without notice. However, each situation needs to be analyzed on its facts and examined in relation to whether

- the conduct was a single act
- the conduct was condoned in some manner
- the employee had a disability
- the employee had been warned about conduct and the consequences of failure to improve

---

3. *Cherniwchan* v. *Two Hills No. 21* (1982), 21 Alta. L.R. (2d) 353 (Q.B.).
4. Stacey Ball, *Canadian Employment Law* (Aurora: Canada Law Book, 2000) at 11-24.

Case

Ditchburn v. *Landis & Gyr Powers Ltd.* (1997), 34 O.R. (3d) 578 (Ont. C.A.)

The Business Context: A business has a vested interest in maintaining positive customer relations. Assaulting a customer would normally be grounds for immediate dismissal.

Factual Background: Kenneth Ditchburn, age 59, was a senior sales executive earning $80 000 annually and with over 30 years' service when he was dismissed by Landis. A few days prior to his dismissal, Ditchburn had lunch with a representative of an important client. Following a number of drinks at a local strip club, the pair, who had been long-term friends, had a physical altercation over an insulting remark the representative made about Ditchburn's wife. Ditchburn told his employer about the incident and was fired a few days later. He was offered two months' salary. He refused and sued for wrongful dismissal.

The Legal Question: Did the employer have just cause to dismiss Ditchburn?

Resolution: Both the trial and appeal court held that there was not just cause to dismiss Ditchburn. The court determined that the incident differed significantly from a calculated act of dishonesty, such as theft, which could constitute just cause for dismissal after a single incident. The court was influenced by Ditchburn's lengthy, pristine service record—he had no previous history of bad judgment. What constitutes just cause for terminating an employee with 6 months' service is not the same as just cause for terminating a long-term employee. As the relationship progresses, the expectations change, and the responsibilities of the employer to the employee increase.

Critical Analysis: Good customer relations is important to business. What kind of proven customer complaints might justify the immediate dismissal of an employee?

Non-Cause and Near Cause

There are many potential reasons or situations that may constitute just cause for dismissal. However, it is important to note that what might seem to be a good reason for terminating an employee is not necessarily just cause. For example, MegaBites has suffered economic setbacks, but although this is a good reason to scale back its workforce, it is not "just cause" for termination. Similarly, Freda is a marginal employee who is averse to technology, and Ray's personality and demeanour are at odds with how things have been traditionally done at MegaBites, but although these may be good reasons to terminate their employment, again, they are not "just cause."

In the absence of just cause, the employer who wishes to terminate employees is required to give notice or pay in lieu of notice. The period of notice will either be the term agreed upon in the employment contract or **reasonable notice**. What constitutes "reasonable" notice is to be determined in relation to such factors as age, length of service, availability of employment, and the status of the employee.

reasonable notice
A period of time for an employee to find similar employment.

In some situations, an employer may have an employee who is neither particularly good nor bad. Is an employer entitled to give the "so-so" employee a lesser period of notice? In a recent decision,[5] a long-service stationary engineer who would have been entitled to about 24 months' notice on termination had the notice period reduced to 6 months by the employer because of some inappropriate conduct—favouring one contractor over another and making work difficult for the competing contractor. The Supreme Court flatly refused to accept any argument by the employer that the reduction was justified because of near cause and sent the matter back to the trial judge for an assessment of reasonable notice. Thus, either an employer has just cause to dismiss an employee and the employee is not entitled to

---

5. *Dowling v. Halifax (City)*, [1998] 1 S.C.R. 22.

any notice, or the employer does not have just cause to dismiss and the employee is entitled to the full period of reasonable notice. There is no halfway position.

Risks in Just Cause Dismissals

The employer should be cautioned by the results of one study of court decisions across Canada, which reported that employers won only 37 percent of wrongful dismissal cases in which they argued just cause.[6] Since an employee is not entitled to any compensation when dismissed for cause, the employee is more likely to bring a suit against the employer. An employer should carefully consider all of the potential costs of dismissing for cause and consider a termination settlement.

An employer who determines that dismissal for cause is justified can reduce the risks considerably by ensuring that sound policies and procedures for dismissal with just cause are established and practised.

Dismissal with Notice

An employee who has been hired for an indefinite period of time may be dismissed at any time and without cause as long as the employer gives notice of the termination (or pay in lieu of notice).[7] While indefinite-term employment contracts are the norm in most industries, many individuals do work for fixed periods of time. For those employees, their contracts end without any notice when the term expires. Termination of a fixed term contract prior to its expiry is a breach of contract.

The period of notice required to terminate an indefinite-term employment contract would be either the period agreed upon in the employment contract, or the period specified in employment standards legislation, or reasonable notice. In many cases the parties do not agree in the employment contract on a period of notice, and even in cases when they do, the courts do not always uphold the provisions. This is particularly the case when the agreed-upon notice is considerably less than what would be implied by the courts as reasonable notice. The courts may justify ignoring the contractual provisions on the basis that the circumstances of the employment contract had changed or that the contract was unfair and unconscionable. It is therefore often the case that employees are entitled to reasonable notice, despite the contractual terms. The period of notice provided in employment standards legislation is a minimum period, and most employees would be entitled to considerably more notice. As Charlotte is unlikely to establish just cause for terminating Freda or Ray (if Charlotte decides to terminate rather than transfer him), the better course of action is to give reasonable notice.

Reasonable Notice Periods

In theory, notice is a period of time to enable the soon-to-be terminated employee to find alternative employment. In determining how much notice, the primary factors to be considered are those set out in *Bardal* v. *Globe & Mail Ltd.*.[8]

---

6. Margot Gibb-Clark, "Employers Win Less than Half of Wrongful Dismissals for Just Cause" *The Lawyers Weekly* (31 May 1996) 13.

7. Note that employers cannot give effective notice or payment in lieu of notice to someone who is unable to work, since an employee who is disabled or on pregnancy or parental leave cannot take advantage of the notice period to look for other work.

8. (1960), 24 D.L.R. (2d) 140 (Ont. H.C.). These factors were endorsed by the Supreme Court of Canada in *Machtinger* v. *HOJ Industries Ltd.*, [1992] 1 S.C.R. 986.

- character of employment
- length of service
- age
- availability of similar employment

Character of Employment

This factor refers to whether the employee was at a high-status position in the organization. Generally, a senior, high-level, or management employee would be entitled to more notice than a junior, nonmanagement employee. For example, Ray occupies a higher position at MegaBites than Freda, so on this basis Ray is entitled to more notice than Freda. The rationale behind this factor is the assumption that it takes a higher-level employee a longer period of time to find alternative employment than it does a lower-level employee. In recent years, however, this distinction has been called into question, as illustrated in the following case.

Although Cronk ultimately lost her case on appeal and was not awarded a lengthy period of notice, the case is important as it signals a willingness on the part of the judiciary to re-examine the notice factors. Since *Cronk,* a number of courts have awarded long periods of notice to low-level, nonmanagement employees.[9]

Case

Cronk v. *Canadian General Insurance* (1995), 25 O.R. (3d) 505 (C.A.)

The Business Context: The employee's place in the employer's hierarchy has always been an important factor in calculating reasonable notice of termination.

Factual Background: Edna Cronk, 55 years of age, had 35 years' service with Canadian General Insurance (CGI) when her employment was terminated as a result of an internal reorganization. She had begun her employment as a clerk-stenographer and had attained the position of assistant underwriter at the time of her termination. Her duties, however, were essentially clerical. Her annual salary was $32 000. CGI offered her 9 months' notice. She refused and requested 20 months.

The Legal Question: How much notice was Cronk entitled to?

Resolution: The trial judge noted that although the length of notice requested by Cronk had traditionally been reserved for more senior employees, he could find no principled reason why this should be so. He stated that managerial and professional employees are better, not worse, positioned than clerical workers to find employment after dismissal. In support of this assertion, he cited two social science studies that he discovered through his own research. He granted judgment for Cronk based on a period of notice of 20 months.

On appeal the court reduced the period of notice to 12 months. The appellate judge stated that the trial judge had erred in departing from the established principle that clerical workers are generally entitled to lesser notice than senior management employees. The trial judge was not entitled to consider his own sociological research without providing the defendant the opportunity to challenge it.

Critical Analysis: Do you think "character of employment" should remain a relevant factor in determining notice? Do you agree with the trial or the appeal result?

---

9. See, for example, *Byers* v. *Prince George (City) Downtown Parking Commission,* [1999] 2 W.W.R. 335 (B.C.C.A.), where a parking attendant was awarded 8 months' notice; *Jones* v. *Consumers Packaging Inc.* (1995), 14 C.C.E.L. (2d) 273 (Ont. Gen. Div.), where a customer service representative won 20 months' notice; and *Laister* v. *Zenon Environmental Inc.,* [1999] O.J. No. 922 (Ont. Gen. Div.) online: QL (O.J.), where a 58-year-old clerical worker with seven and a half years of experience received 8 months' notice.

Length of Service

A longer-term employee is entitled to more notice than a shorter-term employee. On this basis Freda, with 23 years' service, is entitled to more notice than Ray, with a mere 4 years' service. The rationale behind this factor is that a long-serving employee does not have the same degree or breadth of experience as an employee who has had several shorter-term jobs. In essence, a long-serving employee has a smaller range of comparable re-employment prospects.

Reasonable notice is *not* calculated by a rule of thumb of one month of notice for every year of service.[10] Short-term employees, in particular, have often received notice periods well above the one-month per year of service benchmark.

Age

Older employees, particularly those over 50 years of age, are entitled to more notice than younger employees because they have more difficulty finding employment. Many employers are unwilling to hire older persons. Freda, at 53 years of age, is entitled to more notice than 40-year-old Ray.

The rationale for the age distinction is questionable in view of the high rates of unemployment experienced by youth in Canada. It is arguable that younger employees have as much difficulty as older employees in obtaining employment.

Availability of Similar Employment

The more employment opportunities available, the shorter the period of notice to which the employee will be entitled. The availability of employment opportunities may be gauged by expert opinion of job openings, advertisements, and other indicators of market conditions. From a practical perspective, the availability of job opportunities will be affected by an employee's experience, training, and qualifications.

Developments in Notice

Although the factors in *Bardal* v. *Globe & Mail* remain of prime importance in determining reasonable notice, they are not an exhaustive list. Other factors that tend to lengthen notice are

- a high degree of specialization
- inducement to join an organization
- company policy
- custom and industry practice
- personal characteristics
- economic climate[11]

Risks in Dismissal with Notice

The calculation of reasonable notice is a task fraught with uncertainty. Although the factors used in the calculation are well known, the weight to be given to each is uncertain. Most courts list the factors and then state a period of notice without indicating whether one factor should be given more weight than another.[12] Notice

---

10. *Supra* note 4 at 9-13.
11. See generally Ellen Mole, *The Wrongful Dismissal Handbook,* 2d ed. (Toronto: Butterworths, 1997) at 170-196.
12. An exception to this approach is *McKay* v. *Eaton Yale Ltd.* (1996), 31 O.R. (3d) 216 (Gen. Div.).

Competing for Employees

In some industries, competition is fierce for employees with certain skills, qualifications, and experience. Employers go to great lengths to entice a prospective employee to join their organization. Employers often succeed in hiring employees away from competitors by promising security, bonuses, stock options, and a host of other benefits. There is no guarantee, however, that the employment relationship will be a mutually profitable one, and sometimes it may be necessary to terminate the employment of the very person the employer went to great lengths to hire.

Critical Analysis: What role, if any, should the "enticement" of the employee have in the dismissal process? Should it lengthen the notice period? By how much? Should inducement as a factor in notice be discounted after a period of years?

periods have increased, so that in a number of cases the notice period has exceeded two years.[13] This development suggests that there is not a general cap on notice, although at one time in some jurisdictions, it was thought to be 24 months for high-level employees and 12 months for low-level employees.

How much notice would Freda and Ray be entitled to? Freda is a 53-year-old low-level employee with 23 years' experience and unknown employment opportunities. She would be entitled to approximately 12 months' notice. Ray is a 40-year-old middle manager with 4 years' experience and unknown employment opportunities. His case is complicated by MegaBites having lured him away from employment with a competitor. What was said to him about the security of his position with MegaBites would be an important factor in valuing inducement. He would probably be entitled to notice in the range of 8 to 10 months.

Constructive Dismissal

constructive dismissal
Employer conduct that amounts to a fundamental breach of the employment contract.

An employer has no entitlement to change a fundamental or key term of the employment contract without the employee's consent. The employee may accept the change and create a new employment contract or refuse to accept the change, quit, and sue for what is called **constructive dismissal**. The dismissal is not express—the employer has not said to the employee, "You're fired"—but changing a key aspect of the employment contract may be equivalent to dismissal.

Fundamental Changes

fundamental term
A term that underlies the entire contract.

For constructive dismissal to arise, the employer must make a significant change to a **fundamental term** of the contract. A minor change will not trigger a constructive dismissal. As well, the employment contract may reserve for the employer the right to make certain unilateral changes without triggering a constructive dismissal. For example, geographical transfers are often provided for in the contract.

---

13. See, for example, *Dey* v. *Valley Forest Products Ltd.* (1995), 162 N.B.R. (2d) 207 (C.A.), where the NB Court of Appeal awarded 28 months; *Donovan* v. *N.B. Publishing* (1996), 184 N.B.R. (2d) 40 (N.B.C.A.), where the NB Court of Appeal awarded 28 months; and *Clendenning* v. *Lowndes Lambert (B.C.) Ltd.* (1998), 41 C.C.E.L. (2d) 58 (B.C.S.C.), where the B.C. Supreme Court awarded 42 months.

Generally, the changes that are considered to be fundamental are adverse changes to salary/benefits, job function, responsibility, and the power/reporting structures, although other changes may be considered fundamental depending on the circumstances. It is negative changes that trigger constructive dismissal, as employees normally readily accept positive changes. Charlotte's contemplated transfer of Ray to product manager of one of MegaBites' poorer-performing toys may trigger a constructive dismissal. Even though Ray may have the same job title and may be earning the same money, being in charge of one of the "poorer performers" may be in effect a demotion.

Case

Farber v. *Royal Trust Co.,* [1997] 1 S.C.R. 846

The Business Context: In the 1980s, it was common to see whole industries restructure and downsize. Many employees lost their jobs; others saw their jobs changed.

Factual Background: In June 1984, as part of a major restructuring of its real estate arm in Quebec, Royal Trust decided to eliminate all but one of its regional manager positions.[14] At the time, David Farber, age 44, was the highly regarded regional manager for western Quebec. He had been with the company for 18 years and had received many promotions. As regional manager, he supervised 400 real estate agents and administered 21 offices, whose real estate sales exceeded $16 million in 1983. He had a base salary of $48 800, but with commissions and benefits, his earnings were $150 000 in 1983.

Royal Trust offered him the manager's job at one of the company's least profitable branches in Quebec—a position he had been promoted from eight years previously. The branch employed 20 real estate agents and had sales of $616 000 in 1983. As well, the company proposed to eliminate his base salary and to pay him by commission only. Farber estimated that his income would be reduced by half. He tried to negotiate with the company, but to no avail. He was told to appear at the new branch on a certain date; if he did not, he would be deemed to have resigned. Farber did not show up for work and sued.

The Legal Question: Had Farber been constructively dismissed from his job?

Resolution: Farber lost both at trial and on appeal largely owing to the admission of evidence showing that sales at the new branch were very good in 1984 and that Farber would have earned about the same as he had earned in 1983. The trial judge, in particular, thought that Royal Trust's offer was reasonable and adequate, both in terms of money and prestige, and that Farber should have accepted it.

The Supreme Court of Canada overturned the decision and awarded Farber damages equivalent to one year's pay. The court held that where an employer decides unilaterally to make substantial changes to the essential terms of an employee's contract and the employee does not agree to the changes and leaves his or her job, the employee has not resigned, but has been dismissed. This is a constructive dismissal. The test for determining whether a substantial change is made is an objective one; the basic question is whether at the time of the change the reasonable person would believe that essential terms of the employment contract were being changed. Subsequent evidence of what actually happened is not relevant—the critical time for assessment is the time the changes were made. The change to Farber's employment was substantial, since it amounted to a demotion with less income.

The court also noted that an employer can make changes to an employee's position, but the extent of the changes depends on what the parties agreed to at the time of entering into the contract. Constructive dismissal does not have to involve bad faith on the part of the employer. There need be no intent on the employer's part to force the employer out. In other words, sound business reasons for making changes are not a defence in a constructive dismissal suit.

Critical Analysis: Do you think the doctrine of constructive dismissal unduly affects a company's ability to manage its affairs?

14. Although this case arose in Quebec and was decided pursuant to the civil law, the court noted that the doctrine of constructive dismissal, a creature of the common law, is now also part of the civil law. The case therefore has application to Canadian jurisdictions outside Quebec.

Minimizing the Risks of Triggering Constructive Dismissal

BUSINESS APPLICATION OF THE LAW

1. Is the change being contemplated a change to a fundamental term of the employment contract?
2. Is the change itself fundamental? Is the change a demotion in the overall context of the position?
3. Is the employee likely to accept the change? Is the change being negotiated with the employee?
4. Why is the change being made? Is there a *bona fide* reason for the change? Or is there some other reason?
5. Are there contractual provisions that permit the contemplated changes? Are there implied terms that would make the change permissible?

"Bad" Behaviour

Although most constructive dismissal cases involve demotions and pay cuts, the doctrine is not limited to these kinds of factors. Unacceptable or unethical practices by an employer may amount to constructive dismissal. For example, the B.C. Supreme Court awarded constructive dismissal damages to an employee who quit when he discovered that his boss was sending out fraudulent bills.[15] Humiliating or abusive behaviour, such as shouting and swearing, and threats of dismissal can also constitute constructive dismissal.[16]

Risks in Constructive Dismissal

Constructive dismissal may cost the organization a lot of time, effort, and money. Companies should have policies and guidelines for appropriate and acceptable treatment of employees. They should also have procedures and systems in place for dealing with incidents or complaints of "bad" behaviour. As well, prior to unilaterally introducing change, an employer should consider whether the change may trigger constructive dismissal.

Wrongful Dismissal Suit

A wrongful dismissal suit may arise in several situations. It may arise when an employee has been dismissed for cause and the employee claims there was no just cause, or it may arise when an employee is given notice of dismissal and the employee claims the notice was inadequate. It can also arise from a constructive dismissal. An employee is not obligated to go to a court but may proceed by making a claim to an employment standards tribunal. This action would limit an employee's

---

15. *Nethery* v. *Lindsey Morden Claim Services Ltd.* (1999), 127 B.C.A.C. 237 (B.C.C.A.).
16. See *Lloyd* v. *Imperial Parking Ltd.* (1996), 25 C.C.E.L. (2d) 97 (Alta. Q.B.).

Ending employment can be a traumatic experience.

compensation to an amount equivalent to the statutory period of notice. It is the route most often used by low-level employees, as they are often entitled to no more than the statutory notice and it is considerably less expensive.

Specific performance or reinstatement is rarely an option in the nonunionized sector.[17] The common law does not provide for this remedy, on the rationale that after a termination the employment relationship is usually irreparably damaged.

Manner of Dismissal

An employer who conducts a dismissal "in bad faith" may be vulnerable to additional damages beyond those required for reasonable notice. This circumstance is becoming known as the *Wallace* factor.

Case

Wallace v. *United Grain Growers*, [1997] 3 S.C.R. 701

The Business Context: Termination of employment can be a traumatic event for the employee. When such an event is handled in bad faith, it can be especially devastating.

Factual Background: Jack Wallace, age 59, had been a marketing manager for United for 14 years when he was terminated without explanation. Prior to his employment with United, he had worked for a competitor for 25 years. When he was originally approached by United, he was disinclined to leave his stable job. However, he was assured that if he performed satisfactorily he could work until retirement. In fact, he was their top sales representative in each year prior to his abrupt termination. He sued for wrongful dismissal, whereupon the company alleged that they had cause to fire him. The company claimed that he was insubordinate and failed to carry out his duties. This allegation was abandoned at trial. The termination of employment and the allegations of cause created emotional difficulties for Wallace. He was forced to seek psychiatric help, was unable to find another job, and eventually declared bankruptcy.

The Legal Question: How much notice was Wallace entitled to?

Resolution: The Supreme Court awarded Wallace 24 months' notice—14 months for reasonable notice based

on age, length of service, and limited prospects for re-employment, and another 10 months for United's bad-faith conduct in the manner of dismissal.

The court stated that the end of the employment relationship is a very traumatic time for an employee—a time when the employee is most vulnerable and in need of protection. To ensure that the employee receives protection, employers ought to be held to an obligation of good faith and fair dealing in the manner of the dismissal. Mr Justice Iacobucci wrote,

> The obligation of good faith and fair dealing is incapable of precise definition. However, at a minimum, I believe that in the course of dismissal employers ought to be candid, reasonable, honest and forthright with their employees and should refrain from engaging in conduct which is unfair or in bad faith by being for example, untruthful, misleading or unduly insensitive.

The court found several examples of bad faith on the part of United—the abrupt manner of dismissal after complimenting him on his work only days before; unfounded allegations of cause, which were maintained until the day of the trial; and the conscious decision of United to play "hardball" with Wallace.

Critical Analysis: The Supreme Court decision requires an employer to pay extra damages when unfounded allegations are made in the termination process or the employer otherwise treats the dismissed employee in a reprehensible fashion. Should employees be required to pay extra damages when they make unfounded, dam-

---

17. Human rights legislation, however, provides for reinstatement.

The *Wallace* decision has introduced a new factor or standard into the workplace: "bad faith" conduct. In addition to the instance of alleging cause when there is none, the Supreme Court gave several examples of bad faith:

- refusing to provide a deserved letter of reference
- terminating while on disability leave
- failing to communicate a termination decision in a timely manner
- communicating false allegations to potential employers

Since *Wallace* there have been numerous cases that have suggested other factors—failing to conduct a proper investigation prior to dismissal, neglecting to give an employee an opportunity to explain his or her version of events, conducting the termination insensitively, withholding statutory severance unless the employee signs a release, being insensitive in timing the termination, escorting an employee out the door, and making it difficult for an employee to find new employment.[18] It has been estimated that courts that have applied the findings in *Wallace* have increased severance awards by an average of one-third.

Wrongful Dismissal Damages

Once a court determines how many months' notice a successful claimant is entitled to, the general approach is to multiply this number by the salary and the benefits that the employee was entitled to for each month. In addition, the claimant may be entitled to other special damages for out-of-pocket losses associated with the termination. From the total, a deduction is made for any money earned (income from a new job) or received (employment insurance) during the notice period. As well, a deduction can be made for a failure to mitigate damages by promptly seeking replacement employment. Figure 22.1 illustrates a typical damage award in a successful wrongful dismissal case.

Figure 22.1

A TYPICAL DAMAGE AWARD FOR WRONGFUL DISMISSAL

	Salary ($34 500 x 15 months' notice)	$43 125.00
	Fringe benefits @ 22	9487.50
Less:	Pay in lieu of notice paid (3 weeks)	2602.00
	Income from new job during notice period	11 645.00
	Unemployment insurance	3351.00
Total damages		**$35 014.50**

Source: *Burton* v. *MacMillan Bloedel Limited*, [1976] 4 W.W.R. 267 (B.C.S.C.).

A claimant may also be entitled to other types of damages, such as aggravated and punitive damages. These will be awarded only where the damages arise from a separate, actionable wrong, such as deceit, breach of fiduciary duty, abuse of power, or defamation. Therefore, these damages will be awarded only in very exceptional circumstances.

---

18. Bill Rogers, "The 'Wallace Factor': Where's the Top?" *The Lawyers Weekly* (2 April 1999) 7.

Duty to Mitigate

Employees who have been terminated or constructively dismissed have a duty to mitigate their damages. This is not a duty that is unique to employment law. As was pointed out in Chapter 9, this duty arises on the breach of most contracts.

The duty requires that an employee take reasonable steps to find comparable employment. What is required of an employee depends on the nature of the job, on the job market, and on the way that a job would normally be obtained in that market (e.g., by searching newspaper advertisements, registering at a human resource centre, or engaging the services of an employment agency).

The duty requires the employee to look for comparable or similar employment. It does not require an employee to take or look for a lower-level job. Nor does it require an employee to take a lower position with the same employer, since working at the same place after a dismissal may be untenable.[19]

Whether the duty to mitigate requires an employee to move to look for employment depends on a host of factors, including age of employee, family situation, attachment to the community, prospects of employment in the present area, and the housing market. A failure to mitigate will result in a deduction from the damage award.

Dealing with Wrongful Dismissal Suits

BUSINESS APPLICATION OF THE LAW

1. Review the claim carefully. Is it a claim you want to defend? Make sure you have not overlooked anything that could negatively affect your position.
2. Choose the right lawyer. Find a lawyer who specializes in employment law and who has the same philosophy as your organization on how such matters should be handled.
3. Ask for a legal opinion early on. It is better to be informed of a weak position at the beginning than to find out at trial.
4. Provide all relevant information and documentation to your lawyer, as your case will only be as good as the facts.
5. Never allege cause when none exists—just cause is difficult to defend, it usually means a lengthy trial, and if it is unsuccessfully argued it could cost you a lot of money.
6. Investigate even after termination. Evidence of improper conduct by the employee may come to light later, and this evidence may be used to strengthen your case.
7. Avoid defamatory statements, as they may lead to an action for defamation.
8. Consider providing a reference letter even if you have alleged cause. An accurate, factual reference will not automatically undermine your allegation of cause, but failure to provide a letter may increase the damages if the employee succeeds in a wrongful dismissal suit.
9. Always consider whether an offer to settle should be made, as a settlement may avoid further time and costs.
10. Consider mediation. Generally, neither party fares as well as it would like to, but the downside is never as bad either.

Source: Malcolm MacKillop, "Ten Ways to Deal with a Wrongful Dismissal Suit" *The Globe and Mail* (8 April 1997) B13.

---

19. See *Farquhar* v. *Butler Bros. Supplies Ltd.* (1988), 23 B.C.L.R. (2d) 89 (C.A.).

Developments in Wrongful Dismissal Suits

As the courts have narrowed the grounds upon which a dismissed employee may claim aggravated and punitive damages, some employees have turned to other avenues to procure relief. In some situations the dismissed employee can sue for defamation. The advantage of this route is that damages for defamation are usually significantly higher than those for breach of the employment contract, as the amount of damages is not limited by the notice period. As well, the courts are more willing to award punitive damages pursuant to a defamation claim, although this may become less relevant in light of the precedent set by *Wallace*, which allowed the court to award damages for "bad faith."

Regardless of the action taken by a dismissed employee, litigation is an expensive process. It is a particularly expensive proposition in cases where an employee may not be entitled to a large sum of money in compensation if successful, even though there is legitimate cause of action. However, the availability of the class-action suit and alternative dispute mechanisms is changing these dynamics somewhat and making it feasible for a group of ill-treated employees to pursue small claims.

Class-Action Suits and ADR

BUSINESS APPLICATION OF THE LAW

Silicorp Limited is a large convenience store chain based in Ontario and operating under the names Mac's Milk and Mike's Mart. In 1996 it acquired the 530 stores of the Becker Milk Co., a rival. Consequently, Silicorp closed 30 stores and dismissed 90 redundant employees.

A former Becker's manager, Sherrie Gagne, initiated a class-action suit claiming that Silicorp had delayed payments of termination pay provided for under the *Employment Standards Act* (ESA), and had not provided reasonable notice as required under the common law. On behalf of all former employees dismissed in Ontario, she sought compensatory damages of $11 million, punitive damages of $1 million, and injunctive relief compelling payment of benefits required by the ESA.

Silicorp quickly opted to settle the suit, and the parties entered into a settlement agreement, which was approved by a Justice of the Ontario Court (General Division). Certification of the action as a class-action suit was granted by consent. It was the first mass class-action lawsuit for wrongful dismissal anywhere in Canada, and both parties claimed victory.

The settlement provided for the determination of individual claims for compensatory damages through a comprehensive ADR procedure. Silicorp agreed to pay ESA entitlements and party costs. The claim for punitive damages was dismissed. Within five months, most of the claims had been settled—half by mediation and half by arbitration. This was breathtaking speed, compared with litigation. Most employees received considerably more than the employment standards minimums. In total, the 60-plus members of the class-action suit recovered over $2 million in damages.

Critical Analysis: Why do you think both parties claimed victory?

Source: Jeff Burtt, "Class Action, ADR Give Downsized Workers Speedy Remedy" *The Lawyers Weekly* (8 October 1998) at 8.

Termination Settlements

The costs associated with a wrongful dismissal suit can be high. Therefore, it may be incumbent on an employer to make a termination settlement.

Career counselling is often part of a termination settlement.

Negotiation of the Settlement

The settlement offered to the employee should be fair. This is not the time to take a "cookie-cutter" or standardized approach to severance packages. It is important to consider all the factors noted in the calculation of appropriate notice. Cash is not the only item a terminated employee can be offered; pension benefits, medical or dental coverage, disability insurance, tax-sheltered income, and financial or career counselling are all considerations. As well, an employer should consider providing a factual letter of reference to assist the employee. An employee should be given a period of time (one to two weeks) to consider the termination settlement and should be encouraged to seek independent advice on the fairness of the offer.

The termination settlement may help the departed employee feel better about the termination. A fair offer and settlement may also help keep remaining employees motivated. A fair settlement may ultimately avoid a lawsuit and be less costly in the long run. It also helps maintain a positive corporate image.

The Release

release
A written or oral statement discharging another from an existing duty.

When an employee accepts a termination package, it is customary to have the employee sign a **release**. The release normally indicates that the employee has been dismissed and been paid a sum of money in return for giving up any right of action against the employer. The release form may include a stipulation that the employee will not pursue an action for wrongful dismissal, as well as a statement that the employee has not been discriminated against and therefore will not pursue a claim under human rights legislation. It may also contain provisions to keep the settlement confidential and restrictions preventing the employee from competing against the former employer.

A release will normally be binding on the employee, provided that the settlement was fair and reasonable, the release was clear and unambiguous, and the employee had ample time to consider the package and obtain independent advice. On the other hand, a release will likely be unenforceable if the termination package was "unconscionable" and the employee did not obtain independent advice.

The provisions of a collective agreement will vary depending on the nature of the industry involved and the issues the parties bring to the negotiating table. The agreement will provide for a process for settling disputes arising from the agreement. This procedure is the only route an employee has to challenge an employer's dismissal decision. The final step in the procedure is arbitration, which is binding on the parties. Unlike the situation in the nonunionized sector, courts do not make the final decision.

In addition, most agreements will have specific provisions relating to termination.

Grievance and Arbitration

grievance process
A procedure for resolving disputes contained in union contracts.

Regardless of the individual content of collective agreements, disputes about their interpretation, administration, or application are required to be submitted to a **grievance process**. The grievance procedure will vary widely from organization to organization. Some procedures involve only a couple of steps; others have several. All usually have time limits attached to the steps, and most begin with an informal consultation. The final step in almost all jurisdictions is third-party binding arbitration.[20] This step arises when the dispute cannot be resolved by less formal means and all the other steps in the grievance process have failed.

The arbitration itself usually involves either a single arbitrator or a three-person panel, which conducts a hearing of the grievance and renders a decision. The arbitrator may dismiss the grievance; order compensation for breach of the collective agreement; order reinstatement of the employee without loss of seniority and with back wages and benefits; or, in most jurisdictions, fashion a remedy somewhere in between dismissal and full reinstatement. The arbitration award can be filed with the court and enforced in the same manner as a judicial decision.

Seniority

Most collective agreements contain an extensive clause dealing with seniority (the length of time the employee has been with the company). These clauses usually provide that an employer cannot promote, demote, transfer, lay off (usually defined as temporary suspension of the employment relationship), or recall without giving some consideration to the seniority of the employee. These clauses do not, however, affect the employer's ability to terminate the employment relationship (usually referred to as "discharge" in labour law).

Discipline and Discharge

The general rule in the union context is that an employer may not discipline or discharge an employee without justification or just cause.

The discipline and discharge of employees is the largest category of grievances carried to arbitration. In assessing whether the penalty imposed by the employer was appropriate in the circumstances, the arbitrator will look for evidence of progressive discipline. In other words, discipline should progress from warnings to suspensions

---

20. Saskatchewan is the exception.

and only finally to discharge. In upholding a particular penalty imposed by an employer, the arbitrator will consider many factors, including the following:

- the record and service of the employee
- provocation
- any special economic hardship imposed on the employee by the penalty
- the seriousness of the offence
- premeditation
- uniform enforcement of policies and rules
- circumstances negating intent
- condonation

The arbitrator has the authority to mitigate or soften the severity of the penalty imposed by the employer. In other words, the arbitrator may substitute her or his judgment for that of management (unless the collective agreement mandates a specific penalty for the infraction).

Business Law in Action Revisited

1. Is Charlotte justified in terminating Freda Jones?

An economic downturn that results in a genuine lack of work is a good reason for terminating an employee, but it is not legal or just cause, which deprives an employee of severance pay. Charlotte also raises the issue of Freda's chronic lateness and aversion to technology. It is possible that chronic lateness may amount to "habitual neglect of duty" and an aversion to technology may amount to "incompetence." However, in order to use either as grounds to dismiss without notice, the employer must consider the following questions: Was Freda given a warning about her behaviour? Did she understand that failure to improve could lead to termination? Did she make up for the time she missed as a result of lateness? Was her behaviour condoned by the employer? Was she provided with training in the use of technology? Were there performance standards set for the use of technology? Were they communicated to her?

2. Is Charlotte justified in transferring Ray Martinelli?

Charlotte does not have grounds for dismissing Ray without notice. Personality differences are not just cause, and vague rumours about an office affair do not amount to "conduct incompatible with the employee's duties or prejudicial to the employer's business." Even if the alleged rumours prove to be true, the conduct may still not amount to just cause. A transfer to a product manager position may trigger a constructive dismissal, as it appears to be an obvious demotion. Charlotte may want to consider whether Ray is likely to accept the transfer and whether there are sufficient benefits to the transfer that in the overall context, the employee will not view the transfer negatively. An employer is entitled to make some changes without triggering a dismissal; Charlotte should check Ray's employment contract to see what is permissible.

3. What course of action would you advise Charlotte to pursue?

As it is highly unlikely that Charlotte has grounds to dismiss either employee, she needs to consider what a reasonable settlement would be. Freda is an older, long-serving, low-level employee, so she is probably entitled to notice somewhere in the 12-month range. This amount of notice could be affected in either direction by the availability of alternative employment. Charlotte should seek legal advice on this issue, as this area of the law is somewhat unpredictable and subject to rapid change.

Charlotte should know that the proposed transfer of Ray may result in a constructive dismissal. She should reconsider this move, and if she decides to terminate, consider giving him reasonable notice. He is a younger, shorter-term, high-level employee who was induced to join the organization. Reasonable notice would probably be somewhere in the 8- to 10-month range, depending, again, on alternative employment opportunities.

Charlotte should carefully choose the manner of dismissal. The predicted range of notice for both employees could be severely affected by any bad-faith conduct on her part, such as alleging cause when there is none, escorting the employee out the door, refusing to provide a fair reference, or otherwise acting in bad faith.

Chapter Summary

Employment ends when an employee resigns or retires, or when the employer dismisses, gives notice, or otherwise terminates the relationship. An employer may, subject to contractual provisions, summarily terminate an employee if just cause exists. What constitutes just cause is a question of fact, but it must involve a situation where the employee has breached a fundamental term of the employment contract. In the absence of just cause, an employer must give notice (or pay in lieu) of termination. Notice is either what is specified in the employment contract or reasonable notice. The latter is determined by reference to the employee's age, position within the organization, and length of service, and by the availability of alternative employment. When the employer breaches a fundamental term of the employment contract (i.e., demotes or cuts pay), the employee may treat the breach as a constructive dismissal. The termination of employment by the employer is often a traumatic event in the life of the employee. Courts have increasingly put an onus on the employer to act fairly and decently toward the terminated employee. In the event of a successful wrongful dismissal suit, an employer may be required to compensate for unfair and harsh conduct in the termination process. Wrongful dismissal suits can be costly, time-consuming, and embarrassing. An employer may want to reduce the risks by considering a termination settlement that provides a measure of compensation to an employee. It may be much cheaper in the long run.

Study Chapter

Questions for Review

1. In what circumstances may an employee be terminated?

2. What is meant by "just cause"?

3. When does incompetence amount to just cause for dismissal?

4. How much notice of termination must an employee be given?

5. How is reasonable notice calculated?

6. What is constructive dismissal? Give an example.

7. Why is the manner of termination important?

8. What is the duty to mitigate? When does it arise?

9. What should a termination settlement contain?

10. How does the process for termination differ between the union and nonunion sectors?

Questions for Discussion

1. Some lower courts have suggested that there are or should be caps on notice periods—12 months for low-level employees and 24 months for high-level employees. What are the advantages and disadvantages of caps?

2. Cleo was fired shortly after a leak from her company resulted in sensitive information being aired on a radio news show. A search of company phone records revealed that Cleo had made a call to the radio station.[21] Do you think she has an action for wrongful dismissal?

3. Are superior employees entitled to more notice than mediocre ones? Should they be? Should there be less notice for mediocre employees (as in near cause)? What would be the problems with such a system?

4. The rationale for not awarding specific performance or reinstatement in wrongful dismissal cases is that the employment relationship may be irreparably damaged. How would you argue against this rationale?

5. It has been reported that employers win less than half of all wrongful dismissal cases. What factors do you think contribute to this success rate?

Situations for Discussion

1. The Consumers Association of Canada had been without an executive director for a number of months when it hired David Simpson in 1989. Over the next couple of years, Simpson received positive evaluations on his performance, particularly in respect to securing maximum potential funding from the federal government. In 1992 the board of directors received several complaints about Simpson's inappropriate conduct—he had invited his staff to his cottage, stripped down, and gone skinny-dipping; he invited staff members to a strip club; he had an affair with a subordinate; and on another occasion, he jumped naked into a hot tub, joining others who were partially dressed.[22] Is the board of directors justified in dismissing Simpson? Explain.

2. Ramone Johnson, age 34, was fired from her job as assistant spa manager at the luxurious Ocean Pointe Resort Hotel in Victoria after five years' employment. She had returned from maternity leave just one month prior to her termination. At that time she found that her duties had been taken over by other employees. The hotel manager offered Ramone five weeks' statutory severance pay on the condition that she sign a release protecting the hotel from any further action. She signed the release but now feels "exploited."[23] What should she do?

3. William A. Campbell worked for Hong Kong-based Wellfund Audio-Visual Ltd. at a salary of $8000 a month. He had been with the company for only eight months when he was terminated. The company claimed that he was dismissed for financial irregularities, but the real reason was that he had refused to cooperate when asked to create reasons for terminating the company's controller. When Campbell refused to cooperate, Wellfund executives began harassing and threatening him. He took a six-week leave for stress and on his return was fired.

21. "Cleo Makes an Unfortunate Call" *The Globe and Mail* (11 August 1998) B15.
22. Based on *Simpson* v. *Consumers' Assn. of Canada* (1999), 41 C.C.E.L. (2d) 179 (Ont. Gen. Div.).
23. Based on *Stolle* v. *Daishinpan (Canada) Inc.* (1998), 37 C.C.E.L. (2d) 18 (B.C.S.C.).

At the time of his termination, Campbell's health had deteriorated from stress caused by the harassment. As well, a genetic predisposition to migraine headaches had been exacerbated. Following his termination, he suffered nightmares, panic attacks, paranoia, depression, and other anxiety-related disorders. He was unable to work for two years after his termination, and at one point he had to go on social assistance to support himself and his family. Campbell successfully sued Wellfund for wrongful dismissal.[24] What factors would the courts consider in an award of damages?

4. Randal Martin joined International Maple Leaf Springs Water Corp. of Vancouver, B.C., in July 1994. He was hired to assist with the construction of a bottling plant at a spring near Chilliwack, B.C., and to develop markets in North America and Asia. He had been running a similar operation in Saskatchewan but left on the assurance that the B.C. company was viable and would be able to finance the new plant and fund the marketing initiatives. By March 1995, Martin had settled contracts with six companies and was close to three more, including a major deal with an American brewery that wanted to use its own brand name on Maple Leaf's products.

   In April 1995 the company fired Martin, accusing him of dishonesty and of coming to work drunk. Martin had registered trade names personally, as Maple Leaf did not have the funds to do this itself. The president of Maple Leaf knew about Martin's action and knew that the trade names would be transferred to the company as soon as Martin was repaid. There was no evidence of Martin's coming to work drunk. Martin successfully sued for wrongful dismissal.[25] What would be reasonable notice in this situation? What factors would the courts consider in awarding a period of notice?

5. Clyde Peters has worked as a senior systems analyst for 17 years at NJ Industries. He has a good work record and a positive image throughout the company. Recently, he has come under the supervision of the new controller, John Baxter, who has quickly found himself dissatisfied with Peters' performance. Baxter believes that Peters has failed to properly implement the company's new computerized financial system. As well, he feels that Peters has failed to design a strategic plan for his department.

   These two matters have caused considerable problems between the two. Baxter is considering recommending Peters' termination.[26] How should the problem be resolved? Do grounds for termination exist?

24. Based on *Campbell* v. *Wellfund Audio-Visual Ltd.* (1995), 14 C.C.E.L. (2d) 240 (B.C.S.C.).

25. Based on *Martin* v. *International Maple Leaf Springs Water Corp.* (1998), 38 C.C.E.L. (2d) 128 (B.C.S.C.).

26. Based on *Fussell* v. *Nova Scotia Power* (1996), 150 N.S.R. (2d) 271 (S.C.).

Twenty-Three

Professional Services

Objectives

AFTER STUDYING THIS CHAPTER, YOU SHOULD HAVE AN UNDER-
STANDING OF:

▶ THE LEGAL RESPONSIBILITIES PROFESSIONALS OWE THEIR
CLIENTS

▶ THE GOVERNANCE STRUCTURES OF THE PROFESSIONS

▶ THE RELATIONSHIP BETWEEN THE LEGAL AND ETHICAL
OBLIGATIONS OF THE PROFESSIONS

Business Law in Practice

Jean Dubé is president of Dry Cleaners Inc. (DC), an old family business operating
a chain of dry-cleaning stores across the Prairies. The business is under considerable
financial stress owing to both the diminishing market for its service and environmental concerns with some former sites it wishes to sell. Dubé, however, is the classic
optimist and firmly believes the business will weather all storms.

DC recently engaged the services of a consulting environmental engineer, who
advised that there was extensive soil contamination in the balance of its properties
as a result of unsound chemical disposal practices, which has lowered the net worth
of several properties substantially. An environmental cleanup would require a major
cash infusion. Dubé and Sandra Roberts, the CFO and a professional accountant,
were advised by their bank that it would not lend further before seeing audited

financial statements. They contacted their firm of accountants, Lam Wolf LLP, for the audit. This firm has been used primarily for tax preparation services, since DC has not until now required audited financial statements. Roberts advised the auditors of the reason for the audit and said that she and Dubé would be showing the audited statements to two or three different banks from which DC might borrow in order to finance the cleanup. The audit was conducted, Lam Wolf gave an unqualified audit opinion, and Provincial Bank, after carefully reviewing the audited financial statements, lent $500 000 to DC.

Six months following the loan, DC is struggling to make repayments. On closer investigation, it turns out that the audited financial statements were in error as, with hindsight, DC was not a viable entity at the time of the audit. In such situations, professional standards require that the auditor provide a notification to readers that the firm is not a going concern.

Compounding the cash crisis is another issue. A purchaser of a former DC site has served DC with a statement of claim alleging misrepresentation about the environmental condition of the property. Dubé is surprised that Ralph Cricket, a firm of lawyers DC recently retained, has asked for a $20 000 retainer before filing a defence and has already billed a sizable amount for basic advice in the matter.

Provincial Bank is exploring its own rights. Meanwhile, it is insisting that DC have a further audit conducted by a different accounting firm. Dubé is beginning to panic and has proposed to Roberts that DC adopt some aggressive accounting practices to improve the apparent state of DC's financial affairs. Roberts is deeply troubled. She believes these practices are pushing the limit of what is acceptable under generally accepted accounting principles, and, in particular, she considers that Dubé's suggestion involves premature recognition of revenue and deferral of expenses. Furthermore, she feels that these proposals may result in the new auditor's failing to uncover the true state of DC's affairs.

Finally, last year Dubé asked Lam Wolf for advice on his personal financial affairs and, in particular, requested advice on a sound, high-yield investment with tax advantages. Wolf recommended that Dubé invest in a promising local business venture conducted by another of its clients. Dubé, relying on this recommendation, invested a significant portion of his personal assets. He now discovers that the venture is in serious trouble and that Wolf's brother-in-law has a controlling interest in it—a fact Wolf had not previously disclosed.

1. What legal responsibilities does Lam Wolf LLP have toward DC and other users of the audited financial statements?
2. What is the legal significance of the letters "LLP" after the firm name Lam Wolf?
3. How should DC deal with the statement of claim and its lawyer's fees?
4. How should Roberts address the concerns she has with Dubé's proposals?
5. Are Dubé's concerns about his personal investment addressed by Wolf's professional responsibilities?

Businesses and Professionals

professional
A person with specific expertise and skills in an accepted area of knowledge.

Businesses depend on **professional** services, which can be either supplied in-house or contracted out to private firms. DC is typical of many businesses. Its CFO is a professional accountant. It hires external legal services because there is insufficient work to warrant having an in-house department. Other professional services, such as those of the engineer or architect, are hired in on an ad hoc or project basis.

Whether the professional is an employee or an independent supplier of a service, that person owes a series of responsibilities to the business. In many respects, these responsibilities are those already addressed in this text. Thus, professionals as employees are governed by the basic principles of employment law, and relationships with external professional service providers are defined by contract law. However, in other respects, professionals and professional services are unique. The professional–client relationship is a special relationship of trust and loyalty that goes beyond the protection normally provided by contract. In return, professionals are usually held to higher standards than other service providers. These standards come in part from the rules of the profession itself. They also flow from legal principles that, where applied, result in the client—the employer of those services—typically being afforded protection beyond that normally provided by contract.

Responsibilities of Professionals

Professionals owe a range of responsibilities to their clients, many of which are identical to those of all service providers. The environmental engineer, Lam Wolf LLP, and Ralph Cricket all owe contractual responsibilities to DC. Likewise, professionals owe tort duties, most obviously those arising from negligence. Finally, beyond contract and tort duties, professionals commonly owe fiduciary responsibilities to their clients.

Responsibilities in Contract

Professional responsibilities in any given engagement are defined, in part, by contract. The nature of the service to be provided, the timeliness of the delivery of the service, and the way in which that service will be billed are established by the terms of the contract entered into. The legal rules governing the contract are those already described in Part 2 of this text.[1]

In practice, contractual terms are often determined by the professional, and only a well-prepared user might think to negotiate additional or alternative provisions. In the Business Law in Practice scenario, Dubé has not paid much attention to the terms of any contract DC has with its new law firm, Ralph Cricket. It is clear that he is unaware of how the contract provides for the way work will be billed and how and when **retainers** will be required. Dubé is certainly surprised by the firm's request. It is unlikely that DC would pay so little attention to the terms of any other contracts for goods and services that it entered into.

Both professional and client must comply with the terms of the contract negotiated. The most contentious issues in practice tend to be those relating to quality of service and to the fee. If a client wishes to avoid enforcing the contract through the court of law, most, if not all, professional associations have mechanisms for advising on and even investigating fee and quality-of-service disputes. Lawyer–client bills are subject to special provisions.[2] Clients may submit lawyers' bills to taxing officers for review. This officer of the court reviews the bill and considers related issues, including the entirety of the work performed and any agreements that were entered into between lawyer and client. Then the officer determines whether the sum

retainer
An advance payment requested to fund services to be provided and thereby minimize the professional's exposure to risk.

---

1. With the exception of bills for legal services; see *infra* notes 2 and 3.
2. For example, *Legal Profession Act*, R.S.B.C. 1996, c. 255, ss. 78-83.

Prior to engaging a professional's services, a client needs to address the key terms of the contract. Of particular importance are the following:

- How will fees be charged—on an hourly or a per-job basis? Although the per-job approach provides certainty, it is not a panacea. To be effective, the client must be satisfied that the charges are appropriate for the nature of the service. Hourly rates can, with proper monitoring, provide greater control over costs.

- What expertise is required for the work? Will the project be "overengineered" for what is required? Does the professional fully understand the client's business needs? Are the client's expectations appropriate and reasonable?
- When is the project to be completed? How will the changes to the schedule be addressed?
- How frequently will the professional contact the client?

charged was generally fair and reasonable. If the bill is reduced through this process by more than a minor amount, the cost of the exercise is usually borne by the lawyer.[3]

If a contract price is not stated, the principle of *quantum meruit* applies—the professional provides an appropriate level of service, and the client pays a reasonable amount for that service. For small tasks performed by a familiar service provider, this situation is entirely satisfactory because fee disputes are unlikely and there is little at risk. However, for larger engagements or contracts with a new service provider, such a situation would leave too many issues unresolved.

What can Dubé do if he feels that the bill for the advice is too high? He can request an itemized statement of all work performed (including by whom), and in most cases this resolves the issue. He can seek advice from the Law Society or another lawyer. He can also get the statement taxed. Although this move may end the relationship, if Dubé is concerned that Ralph Cricket does not meet DC's needs, this consequence may be appropriate. The request for a retainer, however, is standard when a law firm takes on a new client (or the existing client has a troubled payment record), since the law firm is not expected to absorb the risk of nonpayment.

Fiduciary Responsibilities

fiduciary

A person who has an obligation to act primarily in the interest of the person to whom a responsibility is owed because of the relationship between the two parties.

The term *fiduciary* was introduced in chapters 13 and 16. Directors owe fiduciary responsibilities to the corporation, partners owe fiduciary responsibilities to one another, and agents owe fiduciary responsibilities to their principals. The essence of the professional–client relationship is also often fiduciary. In simple terms, it goes beyond a contractual or tort obligation and flows from a concept of trust. Professionals hold considerable privilege in society because of their unique expertise, training, and commitment to codes of professional conduct.[4] The relationships they

---

3. *Ibid.* For example, under the British Columbia legislation, where the bill has been reduced by one-sixth or more, the lawyer pays the cost of the review (s. 78(11)). Note, in general, contracts for legal services must be fair and reasonable. This principle stems from general as well as equitable principles that guide a registrar under legislation providing for the taxing of legal bills. See *Abel* v. *Burke,* [2000] B.C.C.A. 284.

4. T.J. Johnson, *Professions and Power* (London: Macmillan, 1972).

enter into with their clients (or patients) are often ones of inequality or vulnerability[5] because of the disparity in knowledge base, the dependency on specific skills, and the necessity for the client (or patient) at times to disclose often highly personal information. Where such conditions exist, professionals act in a fiduciary capacity and will be deemed by law to owe duties of loyalty, trust, and confidence that go beyond those contractual or tort responsibilities which they also owe and which are expected of the nonprofessional service provider.[6]

A fiduciary must act primarily in the interest of the person to whom a responsibility is owed. This is a broad and overriding concept captured by the notions of loyalty and trust. It is also expressed in terms of specific obligations. For example, the fiduciary must

- not be in any conflict of interest
- refrain from using the position for personal profit beyond charging a reasonable fee for services provided
- follow all instructions given
- disclose all information
- act honestly, in good faith, and with due care
- maintain confidentiality of client information

The fiduciary must comply with the *spirit* of the obligation and not merely the letter. The following case illustrates the fiduciary obligation.

Case

Hodgkinson v. *Simms,* [1993] 3 S.C.R. 377

The Business Context: Professionals sometimes blur their professional and business activities. This tendency raises questions of where the boundaries of the fiduciary obligations begin and end.

Factual Background: In 1980 Hodgkinson hired Simms, a chartered accountant, for independent advice about tax shelters. Simms recommended investment in multi-unit residential buildings (MURBs). The relationship between the parties, and in particular Hodgkinson's confidence in Simms, was such that Hodgkinson did not ask many questions regarding the investments. He trusted Simms to do the necessary analysis and believed that if Simms recommended a project, it was a good investment. Hodgkinson made substantial investments in four MURBs recommended by Simms. In 1981 the real estate market in British Columbia collapsed, and Hodgkinson lost most of his investment. His claim against Simms was based on breach of fiduciary duty. Specifically, by not

advising Hodgkinson that he had a personal stake in the MURBs (the developers were also Simms' clients and, in addition to fees, Simms received a bonus for MURBs sold), Simms failed to provide the independent advice for which he was hired and thus breached his fiduciary duties to Hodgkinson.

The Legal Question: Did Simms owe a fiduciary responsibility to Hodgkinson, and if so, did his actions amount to a violation of that fiduciary responsibility?

Resolution: Justice La Forest examined the nature of the relationship between Simms and Hodgkinson closely and found that a fiduciary duty was owed; specifically, he found "the elements of trust and confidence and reliance on skill and knowledge and advice ... present." In the course of the examination he discussed the relationship between fiduciary responsibilities and the rules of the respective professions. He stated that the rules of the accounting profession of which Simms was a member required that "all real and apparent conflicts of interest be fully disclosed to clients, particularly in the area of tax-related investment advice. The basis of this requirement is the maintenance of the independence and honesty which is the linchpin of the profession's credibility with the public."

---

5. *Frame* v. *Smith,* [1987] 2 S.C.R. 99.
6. *Hodgkinson* v. *Simms,* [1993] 3 S.C.R. 377.

Justice La Forest stated further that the fiduciary duties imposed by courts should not be any lower than those of a self-regulating profession.

The court held that Simms had been in a clear conflict of interest. It accepted Hodgkinson's evidence that he never would have purchased the MURBs had he been aware of Simms' interest in selling them. The breach of fiduciary obligation was deemed to be so serious that the court was prepared to place all risk of market failure on Simms.

Critical Analysis: Arguably, Hodgkinson got exactly what he had contracted for from the seller of the MURB, and one could take the position that the loss he suffered was the result of the failure of the real estate market in British Columbia. Is it fair that, because he used Simms as an intermediary advisor in order to select these particular purchases, Hodgkinson should be sheltered from his investment losses?

In the Business Law in Practice scenario, Dubé has apparently suffered serious personal financial loss from the failure of the investment he made based on Wolf's advice. The relevant question is whether Wolf owed Dubé any fiduciary obligation. This question will, in turn, depend on whether the relationship itself was one of a fiduciary. Did it have "the elements of trust and confidence and reliance on skill and knowledge and advice" found to exist in *Hodgkinson* v. *Simms*? Of critical importance will be the details of the discussion between the two at the time the advice was requested and then given. If Dubé exhibited the equivalent dependency of Hodgkinson, likely a fiduciary duty is owed. The professional rules governing Wolf would have required disclosure of the interest of the brother-in-law in the project. Applying these circumstances as the minimum fiduciary standard would suggest that a violation of the fiduciary duty has occurred. In any event, failure to disclose a personal interest or a non-arm's length relationship in such an investment, is typically considered a violation of a fiduciary obligation.

The fiduciary obligation to give independent advice or advice free from self-interest has a distinct meaning in the case of the audit. The auditor, besides acting without self-interest, must also act independently of any interest of the company, since he or she is fulfilling a public function—namely, providing assurance to shareholders (and, indirectly, to the financial markets, in the case of publicly listed companies) that the financial statements have been prepared according to certain established guidelines.

confidentiality

The obligation of a professional not to disclose any information provided by the client without the client's consent.

Professionals must maintain client **confidentiality** because of both fiduciary principles and professional rules of conduct.[7] For example, a rule of conduct for professional engineers is the following:

> 4.10 Engineers shall not disclose information concerning the business affairs or technical processes of clients or employers without their consent.[8]

Had the consulting engineer, for example, divulged the results of the testing of DC properties to any third party without DC's permission, it would have seriously violated both professional and fiduciary obligations to maintain client confidentiality. Related to confidentiality is the concept of professional–client **privilege**. When Dubé seeks legal advice on behalf of DC, his lawyer must not divulge the contents of that advice to others. The basis for this principle is the overriding need of clients in specific circumstances to be able to put their entire trust in their professional advisor.

privilege

The client's right not to have information divulged to third parties.

---

7. In very limited circumstances, confidentiality must be violated, such as when a patient tells her doctor that she plans to harm seriously herself or others.

8. Association of Professional Engineers of New Brunswick, "Foreword" in *Code of Ethics*, Part B, s. 2 (1999), online: Association of Professional Engineers and Geoscientists of New Brunswick <http:www.apegnb.com/documents/bylaw99.pdf>.

A construction disaster leads to questions about the soundness of the engineering design.

From a business perspective, the only advice to which privilege attaches is legal advice. Privilege may extend to the advice given by other professionals only where, for example, an accountant or engineer prepares documentation at a lawyer's request and solely as part of the lawyer's advice to the client.[9]

Responsibilities in Tort

General Responsibility

Professionals have duties in tort equivalent to those of other service providers. While they can be responsible for a range of torts, negligence is most common. The professional must perform the services in accordance with the standards of the reasonably competent member of that profession.

Professional groups often talk of a "liability crisis" when describing the burden of tort liability. Any such crisis is usually a product of two factors: the extent of liability and the affordability of liability insurance. Professionals have experienced the same consequences of consumerism as has business in general. In some respects, however, the impact has been more marked for professionals, since traditionally clients rarely questioned the quality of professional services received and, for some professions, third-party liability was once virtually nonexistent. Furthermore, at times, different professions have found affordable insurance coverage difficult to attain, making continued practice problematic. While insurance is not a complete protection—it cannot, for example, adequately compensate for damage to reputation—it is a prerequisite to viable professional practice and is often mandated by law.

Professional liability for negligence was introduced in Chapter 11. It is useful now to distinguish four categories of negligent activity:

1. Professionals perform physical tasks or procedures carelessly and *physically harm* clients/patients. If a doctor improperly performs surgery or a pharmacist provides the wrong medication, the patient/client has traditionally been able to sue for negligence.
2. Professionals give careless advice—utter words or make negligent statements (misrepresentations)—that have negative *physical* consequences. An architect may design a building that collapses, or a doctor may prescribe medication that has avoidable adverse consequences. Negligent misrepresentations resulting in physical harm fall within the normal scope of negligence.
3. Professionals give careless advice—make negligent misrepresentations—with negative *economic* consequences for *the client*. For example, DC intends to make a claim under a provincial business assistance program; however, its lawyer fails to read the terms of the program correctly, and the application is submitted after the relevant deadline and is rejected. Provided it is the client who is harmed, a claim in negligence may well be established against the lawyer.

9. *Cineplex Odeon Corp.* v. *M.N.R.* (1994), 114 D.L.R. (4th) 141 (Ont. Gen. Div.).

4. Professionals give careless advice—make misrepresentations—with negative *economic* consequences for *third parties*. For example, DC's consulting engineer may incorrectly report that a particular property is free from soil contamination. A purchaser, having relied on the report prepared for DC, subsequently discovers the error and is now advised that the property is worth substantially less than it paid.

This last category of negligent misrepresentation, or negligent misstatement, is most problematic. On the one hand, why should this be any different from any other form of negligence liability? What is the difference between a negligently prepared appraisal or audit and a negligently manufactured widget? On the other hand, there are practical problems that flow from imposing liability, as noted in Chapter 11. Words are easily uttered and, once out, are hard to retract. Is there a risk of imposing liability "in an indeterminate amount for an indeterminate time to an indeterminate class"[10]?

The remainder of this section will focus on this fourth category of professional responsibility.

Responsibility to Third Parties

Traditionally, courts have denied the claims of third parties who relied on negligent misstatements. Underlying these decisions has been the public-policy concern of maintaining the economic viability of those professions in the business of giving advice. While a property appraiser can manage the risk exposure to the client, extending such risk to all subsequent purchasers of property may be economically oppressive. If all existing and potential investors could sue for negligence as a result of depending on a negligently prepared audit opinion for a public company, the delivery of audit services might no longer be economically feasible. Nonetheless, denying claims does not necessarily leave the user without remedy. The purchaser of contaminated land can sue the vendor. Audit failures typically are uncovered because of some significant failure in the company itself. Shareholders can pursue their rights in company law and also sue the directors. The professions have been attractive targets for plaintiffs principally because they have the "deep pockets" otherwise lacking in these contexts. They may be the only persons left with the economic resources necessary to meet claims.

The potential for third-party claims for economic loss resulting from negligent misrepresentations was first recognized in Britain in 1964.[11] In 1976 the Supreme Court of Canada addressed the issue of auditor's liability.

Case

Haig v. *Bamford* (1976), 72 D.L.R. (3d) 68 (S.C.C.)

The Business Context: An audit is most commonly conducted because legislation requires it. However, businesses not requiring an audit by statute may still seek one in order to provide information to third parties (such as lenders) who are prevented by the constraints of the corporate structure from having access to financial records.

Factual Background: A mill-work business required additional funding. The Saskatchewan Economic Development Corporation (Sedco) agreed to provide a portion of the funding on the following conditions: that

---

10. This remains the best-known statement of this problem and comes from a U.S. case: *Ultramares Corp.* v. *Touche* (1931), 255 N.Y. 170 (C.A.) at 444.

11. *Hedley Byrne & Co.* v. *Heller & Partners*, [1964] A.C. 465 (H.L.). In fact, an exclusion clause protected the Heller Bank.

the business attain satisfactory audited financial statements and that it acquire additional equity capital from a further investor or investors. The business approached R.L. Bamford & Co., an accounting firm, and asked it to prepare the audited statements. It was made known to the firm that these statements would be shown to potential investors. Haig invested on the basis of favourable audited statements. In fact, the business's bookkeeper had made an error in crediting a sum to revenue that should have been shown as a liability, and the accountants failed to spot the error. The business failed, and Haig lost his investment.

The Legal Question: Should Haig, a third party, be allowed to recover for his loss because he lent money based on a negligently prepared audit?

Resolution: The Supreme Court found that the accountants had not performed a competent audit. In determining whether a duty of care was owed to the third party, it applied a test appropriate for the particular circumstances: A duty of care is owed where the defendant had "actual knowledge of the limited class that will use and rely on the statement."

In this case, the careful wording of the test was important. The accountants knew the statements would be shown to a small group of investors but did not know their names. Knowledge of the *actual* identity of the users was not necessary.

Critical Analysis: What should the liability of the negligent auditor be, if the actual existence of potential end users was not known, but they were merely "foreseeable"?

From the auditor's perspective of risk management, imposing liability in a *Haig* v. *Bamford* context, while novel, did not extend liability beyond that of most other providers of goods and services. The existence of the limited group of third parties who might use the audit opinion was known at the time of the engagement. Furthermore, from a business perspective, what other reliable information would third parties have in order to make their critical decisions?

The difficult question that was left unstated by *Haig* v. *Bamford* was whether liability should extend beyond this relatively narrow scope. Of critical importance was the question of whether liability would also exist in situations where third parties were neither known nor limited in number. Specifically, would a court apply the general "foreseeability" test from *Donoghue* v. *Stevenson*[12] in cases of negligent misrepresentation resulting in economic loss? In the context of auditing, would investors in a public company be entitled to make claims if the audit opinion they relied on for their investment decision was negligently prepared?

For many years, these issues were widely debated in Canada and elsewhere.[13] In 1997, a case that dealt directly with these points, *Hercules Managements Ltd.* v. *Ernst & Young*, came before the Supreme Court of Canada.

Case

Hercules Managements Ltd. v. *Ernst & Young*, [1997] 2 S.C.R. 165

The Business Context: Investors in public companies often make decisions based on the audited financial statements appearing in the annual report. What happens if there is a material error in these statements?

Factual Background: Shareholder investors in a company brought action against the auditing firm Ernst & Young. They argued that the audit was negligently prepared and that they would not have invested or maintained their investments in the company, had they known the company's correct financial position.

The Legal Question: Were the shareholders foreseeable users of the audit? Should the auditors be liable to them?

---

12. [1932] A.C. 562 (H.L.).

13. In a further case, the Supreme Court of Canada referred to the requirement of a "special relationship" between plaintiff and defendant: *Queen* v. *Cognos Inc.* (1993), 99 D.L.R. (4th) 626 (S.C.C.).

Resolution: The Supreme Court held that, in determining the duty of care for negligent misrepresentations, the test should be as for negligence in general. A two-step approach is applied.[14]

Step One: Is there a relationship of proximity between the parties? Put another way, are the parties neighbours? Put another way still, is it reasonably foreseeable that carelessness by one party would adversely affect the other? If the answer is yes, then a duty of care is owed, subject to Step Two.

Step Two: Are there any considerations that should limit the duty owed or eliminate it entirely?

The court found that in the case of an audit, it is almost always reasonably foreseeable that a large number of persons will use and rely on the statements. Applying the first stage of the test, a duty of care exists. However, in applying the second step and evaluating possible policy considerations, the court examined the purposes of the audited financial statements as set out in the relevant legislation:

> ... the directors of a corporation are required to place the auditors' report before the shareholders at the annual meeting in order to permit the share-holders, as a body, to make decisions as to the manner in which they want the corporation to be managed, to assess the performance of the directors and officers, and to decide whether or not they wish to retain the existing management or to have them replaced. On this basis, it may be said that the respondent auditors' purpose in preparing the reports at issue in this case was, precisely, to assist the collectivity of shareholders of the audited companies in their task of overseeing management.

The court held that the duty of care to foreseeable investors was negated by the statutorily defined purpose of the audit and stated that to decide the case otherwise "would be to expose auditors to the possibility of indeterminate liability, since such a finding would imply that auditors owe a duty of care to any known class of potential plaintiffs regardless of the purpose to which they put the auditors' reports." The only remedy investor plaintiffs have is the indirect right to bring a derivative action on behalf of the company (see Chapter 16).

Critical Analysis: While recognizing the need for some limiting principle to be applied, is it appropriate to define the purpose of the audit in such a restrictive manner? Why are the financial markets so dependent on the audit, if this is the case?

This issue of third-party liability for negligently uttered words remains contentious, particularly in the context of the audit. The *Hercules* decision, while popular with the public accounting profession, was controversial among the business community. For example, one commentator observed that the "Hercules decision reinforces the need for a statutory regime of civil liability for all corporate disclosure."[15] To date, however, there have been no judicial or statutory changes, and the *Hercules* decision prevails.

Returning to the Business Law in Practice scenario, DC and Provincial Bank may now consider suing Lam Wolf LLP for negligence:

- Lam Wolf LLP owes DC (its client) a duty of care using the two-step test.
- Lam Wolf LLP may owe Provincial Bank, a third-party claimant, a duty only under limited circumstances. The key remains whether any policy considerations exist that would limit the duty of care as defined by foreseeability. Such considerations would prevent liability extending to third-party investors relying on a negligently prepared audit where that audit was mandated by law. In contrast, when DC approaches Lam Wolf LLP for an audit to show to "two or three" banks from which it is seeking a loan, Lam Wolf LLP accepts the engagement knowing who will see the results. If the audit is negligently prepared, Lam Wolf LLP likely owes a duty of care to one of those "two or three" banks that made

---

14. *Anns* v. *Merton London Borough Council*, [1977] 2 All E.R. 492 (H.L.).

15. P. Anisman, "Investors Need More Protection Against Negligent Auditing" *The Financial Post* (10 June 1997).

loans based on the audit. A court is unlikely to consider that there are policy reasons for the duty of care not to apply. The liability is not unlimited—it is exactly as described at the time Wolf and Lam elected to assume the audit. This is not a statutorily mandated audit. The purpose has been clearly stated: to provide an independent audit opinion for two or three banks where no other reliable financial information exists for dependent third parties.

- DC and Provincial Bank must prove that Lam Wolf LLP breached the standard of care. Professional testimony as to generally accepted auditing standards (GAAS) will guide a court in determining the answer to this question. Even had the work been conducted *pro bono* (without fee), the same responsibilities exist.
- DC and Provincial Bank must be able to establish the requisite causation and lack of remoteness of damage. Did the claimants, for example, actually use the audited financial statements? If so, did they rely on them to make their decision, and did that reliance cause the loss?
- The principles of contributory negligence also apply. If users ignored cautions or other significant advice, they may be partially responsible for their loss.

Governance Structures of Professions

Legislation

Professions are "self-regulating"—that is, there are provincial statutes that establish the rights of the professions to self-governance. The Acts create the governing body for the profession and specify when individuals may represent themselves as being qualified to practise in that province. The legislation gives autonomy and sometimes a monopoly over specific activities to professional bodies sanctioned by the legislation. For example, the *Legal Profession Act*[16] governs the practice of law in British Columbia:

- It provides a very detailed definition of the "practice of law."
- It recognizes the legal status of the Law Society of British Columbia.
- It defines members of the Law Society as those barristers and solicitors who hold a practising certificate for the current year.
- It states that only members of the Law Society in good standing are allowed to engage in the practise of law.
- It recognizes that the society is governed by elected members of the profession (benchers).
- It states that the benchers govern and administer the affairs of the society, including determining whether or not a person is a member in good standing of the society and establishing and maintaining a system of legal education and training.

Each profession is governed by similar legislation in each province. The provincial professional associations are often linked to federal associations.

The organization of the accounting profession in Canada is more complex than others, since there are three professional accounting bodies: the Certified General Accountants Association of Canada (CGA-Canada), the Canadian Institute of Chartered Accountants (CICA), and Certified Management Accountants of Canada (CMA-Canada). The key distinction between the associations relates to the right to

---

16. S.B.C. 1998, c. 9.

perform the audit as defined by provincial legislation. Each province approaches the issue slightly differently, with some provinces allowing only CAs to perform audits (for example, Prince Edward Island) and some having no restrictions (licensing requirements) on who can perform audits (for example, New Brunswick). The right to audit continues to be strongly contested, particularly between the CA and CGA professional bodies. Any change to the CA monopoly or near monopoly in those provinces where it exists will, however, have to come through the political process, as the status quo has been held to be constitutional.[17]

In the DC organization, Sandra Roberts is described simply as a "professional accountant." In practice, she could be a member of any one of the three professional accounting bodies.

Right to Practice

From a business perspective, the licensing of professionals may seem an issue of little relevance. However, any business operating across several provinces, like DC, may need to seek advice in different jurisdictions. How does Dubé, for example, select a lawyer out of province and ensure adequate delivery of service?

Business has recently been assisted by the removal of many of the interprovincial barriers to professional practice that once existed. Professionals must belong to provincial societies or associations in order to practise within the particular province. They attain the right to practise in different provinces by demonstrating familiarity with local legislation and rules.[18] For all professions there are firms that operate nationally, with practitioners in different provinces. If DC is sued out of province, for example, Dubé can do one of two things. He can employ the services of a regional or national law firm, or he can ask his existing firm, Ralph Cricket, to hire a local firm in the other jurisdiction on DC's behalf.

Increasingly, professional firms are finding means of organizing themselves to better meet the needs of clients. Some firms operate internationally. While accounting firms (now often known as "professional service firms") were the leaders in international practice, other professions are increasingly moving in the same direction. Other firms are combining the services of different types of professionals within one practice, in what is known as a multi-disciplinary practice (MDP) (see the following box).

MDPs are only one example of significant change in the delivery of professional services. In the United States, for example, major corporations[19] are creating nationwide, one-stop financial and professional service firms. There are collectives of law firms that are expanding rapidly in the United States and in Canada. Some are linked to the concept of pre-paying for services (a form of insurance). From the client's perspective, many of these changes offer increased convenience and better service. However, these benefits can come at a price. Consider the implications for DC of attaining legal and audit services from an MDP. If the audit was improperly conducted, causing harm to DC, how confident will Dubé feel that he will attain competent, independent legal advice? DC may now feel the need to change not only its auditor, but perhaps its lawyer as well.

---

17. *Walker* v. *Prince Edward Island* (1993), 111 Nfld. & P.E.I.R. 150 (P.E.I. S.C.A.D.), aff'd [1995] 2 S.C.R. 407.
18. For engineers in Nova Scotia, for example, the licensing is automatic upon proof of membership in good standing of an equivalent, recognized association and payment of appropriate fees; see *Engineering Profession Act*, R.S.N.S. 1989, c. 148, s. 8.
19. For example, American Express and H&R Block.

The Multidisciplinary Practice

A relatively new form of practice is the multidisciplinary practice, which is based on the notion of "one-stop shopping" for professional services. For many years the large accounting practices have been hiring a variety of professionals, but traditionally the lawyer or engineer in the accounting firm would be engaged in work complementing different arms of the practice. The MDP provides, within the one professional firm, different forms of professional practice. Thus, a client can go to A and B Partners to acquire a full range of legal, accounting, and engineering services, for example. The initial focus of the MDP has been on accounting and law, and the first examples have been the major accounting firms offering legal services.

Some professions oppose MDPs. There are important concerns related to conflicts of interest. Will the long-established and well-crafted standards of each profession be maintained in a merged practice? On a professional governance level, will the law profession maintain its traditional independence

BUSINESS APPLICATION OF THE LAW

and autonomy, particularly if law firms become part of the far larger multinational accounting firms?

There are different legal and practice restrictions in each country in which MDPs are being either introduced or contemplated, although in many respects these restrictions are more relevant to the professions than to the users of the services. It is too soon to know how the legal requirements for these practices will eventually unfold. However, if the individual professional groups believe that there is an economic future for this form of professional practice, it will undoubtedly exist in some form.[20]

Critical Analysis: Businesses are already faced with a growing concentration in the market of professional advisors as major firms get larger through mergers. How great a threat might MDPs become to the ability, particularly of large businesses, to obtain independent advice?

Disciplining Professionals

Each profession in Canada has established rules of professional conduct or codes of ethics that prescribe acceptable behaviour. Each has established mechanisms for enforcing these rules and disciplining any member who violates them. The rules governing professional behaviour must be consistent with both statute and common law. In the event of conflict, statute or common law prevails.

Professional rules and codes are critical for the protection of the client. Most professional associations or societies now have materials (usually on Web sites) outlining the processes for users to follow if they have a complaint. In the disciplinary process itself, clients (complainants) are, however, only facilitators (witnesses) and observers. For damages or other compensation, the client must sue the professional involved. Depending on the nature of the claim, the professional may have insurance to draw upon. In addition, the legal profession has an indemnification or assurance fund to compensate clients whose money has been stolen by members of the profession, usually from trust funds.

To be effective, the investigatory and disciplinary process must protect both complainants' and professionals' rights. Any investigation is a serious matter for the professional, who must respond and who will usually need legal representation. If

20. K. Roach. "Multi-disciplinary Organizations" (The 1999 Isaac Pitblado Lectures, Law Society of Manitoba. 19-20 November 1999); K. Roach & E.M. Iacobucci, "Multidisciplinary Practices and Partnerships: Prospects, Problems and Policy Options" (2000) 79 The Can. Bar Rev. 1.

the process proceeds and the professional is found to have violated the rules, the consequences can extend to withdrawal of the right to practise. If the process is in any way flawed, the professional may complain to a civil court to have the decision overturned.

Figure 23.1 shows the process in Alberta when a complaint is brought against a member of the Law Society.[21]

Figure 23.1

THE COMPLAINT PROCESS OF THE LAW SOCIETY OF ALBERTA

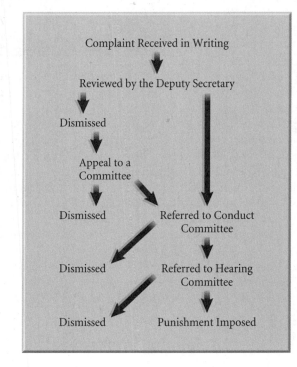

Complaint Received in Writing

Reviewed by the Deputy Secretary

Dismissed

Appeal to a Committee

Dismissed

Referred to Conduct Committee

Dismissed

Referred to Hearing Committee

Dismissed

Punishment Imposed

Employing Professionals

Most mid- or large-sized businesses have professionals on staff. For example, DC employs a professional accountant. The legal or ethical obligations these professionals owe the business vary according to the capacity in which they are hired. For example, some professionals may move into purely managerial functions, and the individual will declare him- or herself to be "nonpractising" with the relevant professional body. That person's obligations are now equivalent to those of any other manager.

Other employees choose to retain their professional status and are hired in this capacity. Corporate counsel are practising members of the provincial bar and are hired for their professional expertise. The comptroller or chief financial officer may hold one or more of the three professional accounting designations and be a member in good standing of the relevant provincial body.

In principle, the legal obligations of employed professionals are the same as those working in private practices outside the firm. They may be in a fiduciary relationship with their employer, where there exist elements of trust, confidence, and

---

21. "Reviewing the Conduct of Lawyers" (1999), online: Law Society of Alberta <http://www.lawsocietyalberta.com/public_legal/review_conduct.asp>.

reliance on the professionals' skill, knowledge, and advice. They can be liable for negligence, although realistically, it is the employer who is sued in most cases through vicarious liability.

Of more significance to the employer are ethical obligations. When managers are questioned, they often report that they value the services of, say, employed lawyers, because of the independence and ethical training they bring to the task. Professionals retaining their active membership in the profession continue to be bound by the rules of professional conduct and codes of ethics of their professional bodies. It is these obligations that bring objectivity and independence to the function and that distinguish a professional employee from a manager. Both owe ethical obligations to themselves and the business, but the professional has additional external professional obligations.

Ethical conflicts or dilemmas tend to arise when the business is under stress. Sandra Roberts' position is not unusual. Dubé is pressuring her to adopt aggressive accounting practices that she believes are counter to her professional obligations. The motive appears honourable—to "save the company." However, the accounting profession had good reasons for establishing the rules Sandra believes she must follow. If she violates these rules, she is breaching her own professional responsibilities and risking sanction (up to and including removal from the profession). Moreover, she undoubtedly will be placing DC at further risk, since outsiders reviewing the conduct will hold DC responsible for any harm that results.

Potential Conflicts between Ethical Obligations

Few of the professional codes of ethics or rules of conduct include rules specifically for those members employed outside of private practice. One exception is the *Management Accountants Handbook*, likely because the majority of management accountants work in employed capacities. It specifically addresses the very real dilemma or conflicts between ethical obligations and identifies five separate categories of obligations a member will owe:

1. the ethics required by the law
2. the implied, but unwritten, rules of behaviour, or societal norms, expected of all members of society
3. The Society of Management Accountant's *Code of Ethics* (for Certified Management Accountants)
4. the code of ethics of the member's employer
5. the member's personal code of ethics[22]

The code provides several pages of guidance as to how to handle any conflicts that might arise between these five categories of obligations. It concludes with the following specific directive:

> Where there is a clear conflict between stated organization ethics and The Society of Management Accountants' *Code of Ethics*, the member's choice is clear; resign from the Society, or resign from the organization.

If the accountant cannot resolve conflicts between professional and business obligations, the professional obligations must prevail if the accountant is to retain her or his professional status.

Critical Analysis: What practical steps might an accountant follow in order to resolve a conflict between professional and business obligations?

---

22. Society of Management Accountants of Ontario, *Management Accountants Handbook* (Toronto: The Society, 1992) 5400 at 5-12.

Changing Professional Service Providers

Clients change professional service providers from time to time, as DC clearly has. Perhaps a lawyer does not have the requisite expertise, or a conflict of interest arises. The professional may be retiring and another is taking over the practice. The client may want a change. In all situations, the transition is a formal process. The new professional must be satisfied that she or he understands the reasons for the change. The former service provider will not hand over documentation until paid for work completed. If there is a fee dispute, this will have to be resolved first.

With the audit, transition rules are subject to additional regulation. Both the rules of professional conduct and the *Canada Business Corporations Act*[23] require the future auditor to communicate with the predecessor in evaluating whether to accept the engagement. Before making inquiries, the auditor must obtain permission from the client. If that permission is not granted, the auditor is unlikely to take on the engagement. In the communication, the potential successor may be told that there are problems with client integrity, or that there have been disputes about accounting principles, procedures, or fees.[24] In the case of DC, any information Lam Wolf LLP provides a new auditor will presumably extend only to the nature of the disputes DC should have already described.

Any change in professional service providers may prove costly to the client. The professional who takes over the work usually assumes responsibility for that which is already done. Tasks may be duplicated if the new professional requires additional assurance before assuming responsibility for work performed by others.

Finally, if the impetus for change comes from the professional and not the client, clients should negotiate an arrangement whereby the professional assumes the financial burden of the change.

Professionals' Risk Management Practices

How professionals manage risk exposure has a direct impact on the businesses that hire them. Three options are exclusion clauses, incorporation or limited liability partnerships, and insurance.

Exclusion Clauses

Whether a professional specifically excludes responsibility is a function mostly of the contract negotiated, but sometimes it also relates to custom. For example, with accounting services, liability for negligence cannot be excluded in the case of the audit, but typically it is excluded for all other engagements. Clients should check contracts carefully to ensure that their interests are protected.

Incorporation and Limited Liability Partnerships

Historically, businesses have managed risk through limited liability corporations, while professional service providers have been required to assume liability personally. Now there are three models governing professional liability.

---

23. R.S. 1985, c. C-44, s. 168(7).
24. A.J. Arens, J.K. Loebbecke, W. M. Lemon, & I. B.Splettstoesser, *Auditing,* 8th Can. ed. (Scarborough: Prentice Hall, 1999).

1. Some professions may incorporate using limited liability corporations. Generally, professions may incorporate only if they are specifically permitted to do so by the legislation governing the particular profession in that province.[25] A standard approach is found in the Nova Scotia Act regulating engineers:

> A partnership, association of persons or body corporate, may undertake and carry out the application of engineering in its own name provided that one of its principal and customary functions is the application of engineering and such application of engineering is done under the supervision of a member or a full-time permanent employee thereof.[26]

Note that even where incorporation exists, it typically does not protect the professional from the liability of greatest concern—namely, personal liability for negligence. In Nova Scotia, for example, the rules of professional conduct explicitly state that while the corporation can be liable in contract, the individual engineer remains personally liable in negligence (and must carry appropriate insurance coverage).[27] Furthermore, that same individual may be subject to disciplinary action under the rules of professional conduct.

Again, where accountants have been able to incorporate, the Act establishing the right to practise specifies that the personal liability of the accountant will not be affected by the limited liability of the corporation of which the accountant is a shareholder and/or director/officer.[28]

From the client's perspective, the individual professional generally remains personally liable for negligent work, and the assets of the professional organization (the corporation) can be accessed.

2. Partnerships may register as limited liability partnerships (LLPs) (see Chapter 14). These are relatively new structures. The impetus for allowing this business form came from the large professional partnerships that considered it unfair that a partner in Vancouver should be responsible for the negligence of, say, a partner in Ontario. LLPs have been introduced by amendments to the provincial Partnership Acts. Whether or not individual professions allow members to form LLPs is determined by the provincial legislation governing that profession.[29]

Typically, LLPs protect individual partners from personal responsibility arising from negligence claims that are brought against the partnership in general or other partners in the firm. Individual partners remain liable for their own negligence and also for the negligence of those whom they supervise. Likewise, the firm itself retains liability, and firm assets (and insurance) can be used to compensate for losses. As each province debates the introduction of LLPs, the extent of the protection is one critical issue to be resolved.

3. Traditionally law and accountancy were denied the right to incorporate. The alternative form was either the sole proprietorship or the partnership.

The differences between the two forms of partnership (or sole proprietorship) are of greatest significance in the case of catastrophic claims. In practice, partnership agreements allow for losses to be paid out of general partnership funds

---

25. For example, *Business Corporations Act*, R.S.N.B. 1982, c. B-9.1, s. 13(3)(d); *Business Corporations Act*, R.S.O. 1990, c. B.16, s. 3(1).
26. *Engineering Profession Act*, R.S.N.S. 1989, c. 148, s. 11(2).
27. Association of Professional Engineers of Nova Scotia, *Manual of Professional Practice*, Part C, "Guidelines to Professional Practice," s. 6 "Liability Issues."
28. For example, *Public Accountants Act*, 1989, R.S.N.S., c. 369, s. 22A(2).
29. For example, *Partnerships Act*, R.S.O. 1990, c. P.5, s. 10(2). In Alberta, see *Partnership Act*, R.S.A. c. P-2, s. 11.1(1). Also, the *Law Society Act*, R.S.O. 1990, c. L.8, s. 61.1 as am. by S.O. 1998, c. 21, s. 28.

(or insurance). If any one partner is sued individually, the uninsured portion of the loss will be paid first out of those funds or from other individual partners.

From the perspective of the client/user who is suing, the only concern is whether there will be compensation. The focus then becomes the availability of insurance.

Insurance

Errors and omission insurance was described in Chapter 20. It is a condition of practice in most professions that members carry this professional liability insurance. In the legal profession, in which lawyers traditionally hold large trust accounts, separate coverage is provided through a mandatory professional insurance program.

At times, real crises have evolved in terms of the affordability and even availability of insurance. For the client/user, guarantees of insurance coverage are essential. Insurance coverage, however, has an important consequence for claimants. Professional insurers, such as the Canadian Medical Protection Association, are highly specialized and expert at defending claims. If the loss could be significant, the user should not contemplate litigation without hiring a lawyer who has the equivalent expertise. Where contingency fees are unavailable, the cost associated with hiring such lawyers can effectively prevent many legitimate claimants from bringing suit.

Business Law in Practice Revisited

1. **What legal responsibilities does Lam Wolf LLP have toward DC and other users of the audited financial statements?**

Lam Wolf has breached its contract with DC to provide an audit in accordance with GAAS, assuming that Lam Wolf has indeed made the error stated. At issue is the measure of damages. Damages would include the cost of the further audit. DC could also sue for breach of the fiduciary duty of care or competence, and the measure of damages would be equivalent to that for a claim based on breach of contract.

DC may sue Lam Wolf for negligence. Since DC hired Lam Wolf, the duty of care will be found to exist; the foreseeability duty will not be limited by policy reasons. The standard of care that must be applied is that of the professional auditor, and GAAS will be used in order to evaluate the performance. Assuming there is evidence of breach, causality and lack of remoteness of damage must be established. Since the DC claim will include the cost of the audit and any additional cost of a replacement audit, these are likely proven.

Provincial Bank can sue only for negligence, and its principal obstacle will be establishing that a duty of care was owed it. The difficulty will not be in terms of establishing that the bank was a foreseeable user of the audited financial statements. Rather, Provincial must establish that no policy considerations exist that might limit this duty. This issue will depend on the stated purpose of the audit. In this stituation, the audit was not mandated by companies legislation, and therefore it is not relevant to interpret the provisions of that legislation as in the *Hercules* case. Determining the stated purpose will call for an interpretation of what Dubé told Lam Wolf at the time the engagement contract was formed. If Lam Wolf was told that the audit was required solely in order that DC could show two or three banks its audited financial statements, and so those same banks could assess whether they should extend credit to DC, that limited group of third-party users would likely be owed a duty of care. If

Dubé failed to be this explicit, then a court, applying a policy analysis, would be unlikely to find that a duty of care was owed.

Provincial will need to prove the balance of the negligence elements. The standard of care issues are equivalent to those in DC's claims. More critical will be the need to prove that Provincial did indeed use the audited financial statements for the described purposes and that this reliance caused its loss. Since Provincial had no other source of information about the financial state of DC, these last issues in this particular case should be reasonably easy to prove. If the claim is successful, damages will include the amount lost on the loan.

2. What is the legal significance of the letters "LLP" after the firm name Lam Wolf?

LLP is short for Limited Liability Partnership and denotes that the firm operates in provinces where legislation permits this legal form. The significance is that partners are responsible only for their own negligence and for that of anyone whom they supervise. The LLP contrasts with a regular partnership, in which all partners are jointly and personally liable for the negligence of any one partner.

3. How should DC deal with the statement of claim and its lawyer's fees?

Dubé is concerned about two issues—the existing bill and the retainer. Whether the bill must be paid as presented will depend, in part, on what the agreement between DC and Ralph Cricket LLP provided, although the sum must also be fair and reasonable.[30] If, as the facts seem to suggest, there was no formal agreement entered into for this particular service, then, applying the *quantum meruit* principle, DC must pay whatever is a reasonable amount for the service. Dubé is entitled to a complete statement of the services provided and of how costs were assessed. He should express his concerns, and this alone may be enough to persuade Ralph Cricket to reduce the amount claimed. Alternatively, a complete explanation might satisfy Dubé. If Dubé remains genuinely concerned about the size of the bill, he can seek advice from another lawyer or from the relevant law society. He may also go to a taxing officer. If Ralph Cricket is adamant that the sum must be paid in full, litigation may be the final outcome.

Requesting a retainer for litigation services is an entirely appropriate business practice on the part of the lawyer, who has no prior experience of DC's ability or willingness to pay for what might be lengthy litigation. Whether or not the sum of $20 000 is reasonable depends on the complexity and value of the case. Dubé should be discussing the cost and risk of litigation, in any event, before deciding whether to settle or defend the claim.

4. How should Roberts address the concerns she has with Dubé's proposals?

Roberts is facing the classic conflict between ethical obligations owed to the employer and to the profession, as well as possible conflicts with her own personal values. In terms of ethical obligations owed to the employer and those owed to the profession, the latter must prevail, even if that calls for her to quit her position with DC. In practice, her first step must be to explain to Dubé the reasons for the audit itself and the rules the company must follow in presenting its financial information. There may be legitimate alternatives she can present to Dubé that at least partially meet his objectives. However, under no circumstances can Roberts engage in any practices that violate the rules of professional conduct. To do so would not only be

---

30. *Supra* note 1.

ethically wrong, but would also expose Roberts to the risk of professional discipline and herself, the company, and Dubé to legal risk.

5. Are Dubé's concerns about his personal investment addressed by Wolf's professional responsibilities?

Whether Wolf is liable to Dubé in contract will be determined by the promises made at the time, the advice given, and whether an implied term existed that Wolf would fully disclose conflicts of interest. Given the nature of the professional service contract between Wolf and Dubé, the implied term likely existed. If Dubé can establish that he would not have invested had he known about the non-arm's length relationship between Wolf and the business venture, he can claim damages at least for breach of the implied term.

Whether or not there was tort liability for negligence will depend, in part, on the competency of Wolf's assessment of the potential investment. If it was competently (not negligently) performed, there has been no negligence from this perspective, and Wolf has no liability. The business has since failed, but a competent assessment would not have disclosed underlying difficulties. Furthermore, since there is no evidence that Wolf's failure to disclose the relationship was a result of oversight—it appears to be an intentional, not negligent, action—Dubé is again unlikely to succeed on this possible ground of negligence.

The obvious further area of responsibility owed is that of the fiduciary. How did Dubé express his dependency upon Wolf's advice, and what was Lam's undertaking? If the relationship can be described as fiduciary, which it probably is under the circumstances, a violation has occurred. Wolf had a personal interest, through his brother-in-law, in the enterprise that he failed to disclose. This detail goes to the heart of the requirement of independence expected of a fiduciary and of a professional accountant. If Wolf is found liable to Dubé, he will be obliged to account for those losses Dubé suffered as a result of making this investment, provided Dubé can establish that he would not have made the investment had he known the true state of affairs.

Chapter Summary

Professionals owe a range of duties to their clients. Most obviously, they are governed by contract and tort law. They must deliver services as contracted for and in accordance with the requisite professional expertise. If they are negligent in performing their responsibilities, they will likely be responsible for damages. In addition, professionals may be in a fiduciary relationship with their clients where there exist "the elements of trust and confidence and reliance on skill and knowledge and advice."[31] Because of inherent vulnerability or dependency, the client is owed this duty of loyalty and trust.

The professions are governed by legislation that establishes them as self-regulating entities. The professions create codes of conduct or rules of practice, and these determine the standards by which the professional must operate, and provide a measure of the expected standard of care in contracts, torts, and the exercising of fiduciary obligations.

Most professions have created dispute resolution services or complaint procedures that are of assistance to clients (patients). They also maintain a disciplining

---

31. *Supra* note 6.

process that provides assurance to users that professionals violating professional rules will be disciplined, up to and including removal from the rolls of practitioners.

Professional service providers manage risk for the same reasons as businesses in general, but without necessarily the same freedom of choice. From the client's perspective, insurance is critical, and many professions make such coverage obligatory. Different types of business vehicles are increasingly an option for professionals, although other trends have greater immediate impact for clients. In particular, new forms of practice, such as national and international firms and multidisciplinary practices, offer real benefits for users.

The challenge facing clients and professionals today is to ensure that the individual professionals continue to comply with the ethical obligations of their profession, despite increasing pressures, both from their own members and from clients, to become more "business minded."

Study Chapter

Questions for Review

1. What is the meaning of "fiduciary"?

2. What is a retainer?

3. What is the basis for determining the cost of a professional service if there is no formal contractual term addressing the issue?

4. What was the basic attribute of negligence actions against accountants that traditionally protected them from third-party claims?

5. How did the Supreme Court of Canada define the duty of care for negligently uttered statements in the *Hercules* decision?

6. What is the meaning of a "self-regulating" profession?

7. In the basic contract between the accounting firm and the client, for which services can liability be excluded and for which ones can it not?

8. During a disciplinary process, why is it of such importance to protect the rights of the professional against whom a complaint has been made?

9. What are LLPs?

10. What law establishes who can be a member of a particular profession?

11. If there is a conflict between a professional's ethical obligations to the profession and those to the organization that cannot be resolved, which prevails?

12. What is the responsibility of an auditor who is asked to take over the audit from another auditor?

Questions for Discussion

1. The following is an example of the standard unqualified auditor's report:

   To the Shareholders of ABC Ltd.

   We have audited the balance sheet of ABC Ltd. as at X date, and the statements of income, retained earnings, and cash flows for the year then ended. These financial statements are the responsibility of the company's management. Our responsibility is to express an opinion on these financial statements based on our audit.

   We conducted our audit in accordance with generally accepted auditing standards. Those standards require that we plan and perform an audit to obtain reasonable assurance whether the financial statements are free of material misstatement. An audit includes examining, on a test basis, evidence supporting the amounts and disclosures in the financial statements. An audit also includes assessing the accounting principles used and significant estimates made by management, as well as evaluating the overall financial statement presentation.

   In our opinion, these financial statements present fairly, in all material respects, the financial position of the company as at X date, and the results of its operations and cash flows for the year then ended are in accordance with generally accepted accounting principles.

   EFG,

   Chartered Accountants[32]

   There are many standard practices auditors follow. For example, auditors are not responsible for detecting management fraud (unless they ignore "red flags" warning them of improper activities). They may test on a sampling basis. Do you think that the report they issue could be written in such a way as to make it clearer to users the extent of their responsibilities?

2. Assume you are the manager in an organization responsible for finalizing contracts with professional service providers. What are the pros and cons of having the professional charge on an hourly basis versus a per job basis? What protections might you build into the contract?

3. The *Hercules* decision was heavily criticized by some members of the business press, but was also received with great relief by public accountants. Critically analyze this decision in terms of the interpretation the Supreme Court of Canada gave to the purpose of the audit.

4. What are the pros and cons of protecting professionals through allowing their professional organizations to incorporate?

Situations for Discussion

1. Lan Nguyen had, over the years of running her small business, acquired sizable savings. She was concerned about how to get the best return on this money and discussed this with her lawyer, John Smith. Smith advised her that this was an excellent time to get into real estate. He had many clients who required financing. Nguyen could provide either first or second mortgages, depending on her desired level of risk and return. Smith said he had some clients involved in a large townhouse development. Nguyen trusted Smith implicitly, as he had been

---

32. Adapted from a standard audit report presented in Arens, Loebbecke, Lemon & Splettstoesser, *supra* note 24 at 36.

her lawyer since she had first started her business. Thus, she provided the bulk of her savings—$200 000—as a second mortgage, which would earn interest at 19 percent per annum over five years.

Within eight months the real estate market collapsed. The mortgagees defaulted on payment, and once the first mortgage holders had foreclosed, there was virtually nothing left for Nguyen. When Nguyen complained to Smith, he said there was little that could be done. Investments of any sort carry inherent risk. His personal investment company, for example, had been one of the partners in the townhouse development, and he too had lost his entire investment.

Nguyen is shattered by Smith's lack of concern and seeks advice about what she can do to recoup her losses. Discuss Nguyen's options.

2. Good Property engaged the services of a professional real estate appraisal firm, McGee and McGee, prior to purchasing a large tract of property on the outskirts of town. There were a number of complex easements affecting the land and proposals for new roads. When Dan, the CFO of Good Property, first discussed the appraisal with Andy McGee, he said the appraisal had to be completed by January 10. Andy said this was impossible owing to other commitments and proposed the 26th. It was agreed that Andy McGee would be the appraiser. Dan said he would get back to Andy about the date.

    The project was far more complex than either Good Property or the appraisers expected. The local Water Conservation Authority was about to issue a report that seriously affected the land, and evaluating the proposals the Authority was considering delayed the survey further. The appraisal was not handed to Good Property until January 29. By this time, another purchaser had come in and acquired the property. When Dan was handed the sizable invoice for the work, he was furious. He claimed that McGee had violated the contract by finishing the work late, and he had therefore lost out on being able to buy the land. Furthermore, the invoice was far more than he expected to pay.

    How are these matters likely to be resolved? What will be the primary arguments both Good Property and McGee will raise?

3. Assume the same facts as in situation 2 above, except that the appraisal is completed on time and without dispute. Good Properties acquires the properties. Some months later, the Water Conservation Authority publishes its report, which seriously affects the value of the land. On closer inspection, it turns out that McGee made a basic mistake in interpreting the impact of the proposals it had received from the authority. What rights does Good Property have against McGee?

4. Phelps Development (PD) is proposing a new property development that will require major debt financing. It has contacted its bank and several venture capital firms, and has been advised that it must first present audited financial statements. Phelps, the CEO of PD, approaches its accounting firm and tells the partner, Kaur, of PD's plans and why it needs an audit. Kaur accepts the engagement.

    The audit is complete and Phelps shows it to several interested parties, including Money Lenders (ML). ML has heard about PD's proposals and is anxious to join this venture, since it already has several other successful interests in the vicinity. ML provides $500 000 debt financing. Eight months later, PD faces a serious cash crisis and is unable to meet its debts as they fall due. ML loses most of its investment. On closer examination, it turns out that the audited financial statements included a serious material misstatement: $250 000 in liabilities were overstated.

ML is now attempting to recover its losses. Since PD is unable to pay, it seeks compensation from the accounting firm and Kaur as the individual partner responsible for the audit. Present arguments for both parties.

5. Big Clean-Ups is a public company that has developed products used to address environmental clean-ups. Its market performance has attracted considerable investor attention. One particular investor, Max Find Inc., acquired a significant holding in Big Clean-Ups over a five-year period. It tracked all performance announcements closely and increased its holdings with each favourable announcement.

   In the past year there were rumours of some underlying problems with Big Clean-Ups' technology. The CEO and principal shareholder of Max Find Inc., Max Find, therefore paid particularly close attention to the most recent annual report. Somewhat unexpectedly, the report indicated further strong performance and Max Find, on the basis of the report, increased the holdings of Max Find Inc. in Big Clean-Ups and made a significant personal investment.

   Some months later, the third-quarter results for Big Clean-Ups are published. They show unexpected losses and the share price precipitously declines. The company requests that trading be halted. The auditor withdraws the audited statements and later issues new statements, which now show a large loss.

   Trading resumes, but share prices are substantially lower. Max Find Inc. now claims that its losses are due to the allegedly misleading audit report. If it had known the true state of affairs it would have reduced, not increased, its holdings in the company. Max Find, the individual, also claims for losses on the basis that he would not have invested had the audited statements available when he made his investment showed the true state of affairs. The auditor claims that the audit was prepared according to GAAS and that it was not responsible for this turn of events.

   Outline the primary arguments for Max Find Inc., Max Find, and the auditors, assuming these disputes lead to litigation.

6. Lemon is a CA working as comptroller for Jones Manufacturing. He is deeply concerned about the cash flow position of the company. There have been large orders, but Jones (the CEO) has insisted on an aggressive pricing policy, and, quite simply, prices charged do not cover costs. The company is rapidly approaching a cash flow crisis.

   Lemon approaches Jones with his concerns, but Jones will not listen. Jones is a high-profile member of the local community; the success of the company means that it can hire a large number of people in this economically depressed area; and it is inconceivable to Jones that booming sales could translate into losses. Lemon tries another approach. He explains that the auditors will be coming in soon and, if he doesn't expose the current position, they will uncover it anyway. Jones tells him that she understands, but that she wants Lemon to do whatever it takes to get through this audit. Afterwards, prices can be raised, since by then the company will be in a very strong position in the marketplace and this temporary hurdle will have been overcome.

   Lemon is trying to devise a strategy to follow. His professional responsibilities seem clear. At the same time, the survival of this company is critical to the lives of many people. It would be devastating to see the company close if he is unable to find a way of presenting the information to satisfy the auditors.

   Discuss the pressures Lemon faces. What should he do now?

Part Seven

The Market

"Marketing is the process of creating, distributing, promoting, and pricing goods, services and ideas to facilitate satisfying exchange relationships in a dynamic environment.... [A]n exchange is the provision or transfer of goods, services, or ideas in return for something of value."[1]

While modern marketing theory never loses sight of the sale as the ultimate goal, that sale is always recognized as an inevitable consequence of establishing a relationship that meets the needs of both the seller and the purchaser. Marketing texts say that "marketing activities should attempt to create and maintain satisfying exchange relationships,"[2] and "the marketing concept [is based on the notion that] the social and economic justification for an organization's existence is the satisfaction of customer wants and needs while meeting organizational objectives."[3] Why this concern for the customer? A satisfied customer is a return customer. Where sales to individual purchasers are a one-time event, future business depends as much on word of mouth as on the effectiveness of advertising.

What is the role of law in the marketing process? The lawyer is often caricatured as putting a "red light" before every creative effort. The law that affects marketing is, however, only an expression of the public will. It has evolved to ensure that the customers' needs are indeed met and that the transaction is conducted according to terms that would generally be considered fair to both parties. If marketing is genuinely about effecting "satisfying exchange relationships," marketing law is the regulatory tool that assures producers that all market participants operate according to the same principles. The law is there to protect the end-user. It is also there to protect the honest seller from unscrupulous operators who are competing unfairly.

In the chapters that follow, legal provisions will be presented in terms of the traditional marketing components or variables that compose the marketing mix: product, promotion, price, and place of distribution. This is a presentation of convenience: the four factors should not be considered as discrete entities.

The materials in both marketing chapters must be considered as an integrated whole. For example, whether a product is considered appropriate for a particular use will depend not only on its design, but also on the words expressed on its labels and promotion, the price for which it is sold, and the way it is shipped to distributers and users. Often, it will be the mix or interrelationship as much as the individual factors that will determine not only the success of the marketing venture, but also whether the producer complies with the provisions of the law.

Chapter 24   Marketing Practices: Product and Promotion

► Chapter 24 presents legal obligations relating to product and promotion.

Chapter 25   Marketing Practices: Price and Distribution

► Chapter 25 discusses legal obligations that affect price and distribution.

---

1. W.M. Pride, O.C. Ferrell, H.F. MacKenzie & K. Snow, *Marketing: Concepts and Strategies,* Can. ed. (Scarborough: ITP Nelson, 1998) at 4.
2. *Ibid.* at 6.
3. C.W. Lamb, J.E. Hair, C. McDaniel & A.J. Faria, *Marketing,* 3d Can. ed. (Scarborough: ITP Nelson, 1997) at 9.

Twenty-Four

Marketing Practices: Product and Promotion

Objectives

AFTER STUDYING THIS CHAPTER, YOU SHOULD HAVE AN
UNDERSTANDING OF:

► THE SCOPE OF MARKETING LAW

► THE LEGAL OBLIGATIONS ASSOCIATED WITH THE PRODUCT
COMPONENT OF MARKETING

► THE LEGAL OBLIGATIONS ASSOCIATED WITH THE PROMOTION
COMPONENT OF MARKETING

Business Law in Practice

Kids Climb Naturally Inc (KCN), a corporation based in Prince George, is in the
process of developing a new product—children's playground equipment made from
wood. Despite the current market trend of using metal for playground equipment in
general, the CEO of KCN, Lisa Patel, believes there is still room for a wood product
for home purchases, since long-term durability is not such a major concern and
KCN's products may prove to be appreciated by those wanting a natural-looking
alternative in their backyards.

KCN intends to promote, distribute, and sell its products nationally. The equipment will be sold partially assembled and will be boxed with graphics of the product on the outside. Final assembly instructions and all required parts will be included in the packaging. Initially, products will be designed for relatively young children (under the age of 8), although the present strategy is to have equipment "grow" with the children, with add-ons becoming available over time. Sales will be through national hardware and toy retail chains. The marketing theme will stress the environmental friendliness of the product, the creativity of the design, and its inherent safety. The premium pricing will reflect the strategy of selling to parents who are reasonably affluent and eager to ensure that their children have access to products that maximize play value. Promotion will be primarily through in-store displays and print media, with a special focus on advertising in parenting magazines.

Lisa is aware that her company is moving into a new market and that there are likely many regulations and general legal concerns she will need to address. Since playground equipment is used by small children, safety is a major consideration. Lisa understands that risk management is critical in this business.

1. How does the law affect KCN's marketing strategy?
2. What impact does the law have on KCN's product?
3. What impact does the law have on the promotion of KCN's product?
4. How can KCN effectively manage its exposure to legal risk?

What Is Marketing Law?

Marketing practices, like other business decisions, are directed and influenced by laws and regulation. The most fundamental laws affecting the marketing process are the common law principles explained in Parts 2 and 3. Marketing is also regulated by all three levels of government: federal, provincial, and municipal. The main objectives of these laws are:

- to protect consumers from physical harm
- to foster fair competition
- to protect consumers from unfair selling practices

These objectives give rise to laws regulating a multitude of issues, including safety standards products must meet, quality of disclosure on packaging, minimum standards for honest promotion, implied conditions and warranties for the sale of goods, anti-competitive practices, and safe transportation and delivery of goods.

If a business engages in international distribution of its product, then the marketing practices of that business are exposed to the laws and regulations of other countries as well.

Marketing law is presented here in terms of the traditional four "Ps" of the marketing mix: product, promotion, price, and place or distribution. This chapter considers the product and promotion components of the marketing mix, and Chapter 25 addresses price and distribution.

marketing law
All areas of law that influence and direct the creation, distribution, promotion, and pricing of goods, services, or ideas.

The Product

Basic Principles

Traditionally, the term *product* implied a tangible good, and this was the focus of early regulation. Today, the term and the regulations that apply to it are far broader in scope. A product is anything a business sells. It may be goods, services, and ideas, or any combination of these.

Businesses must comply with general, common law standards for product safety and legislation regulating product design and labelling. In addition, businesses will normally follow voluntary industry codes.

KCN is developing a product that involves inherent and practically unavoidable risks that are obvious and legally acceptable. Children may fall off even the best-designed climbing frames and break limbs. However, provided the climbing frame is properly built and not dangerously high, KCN is unlikely to have any legal responsibility for such unfortunate incidents. On the other hand, were KCN irresponsible enough to leave large raised bolts exposed that could catch the hood strings of a jacket—an avoidable design feature—it would face a successful lawsuit should a child become injured in this way. In addition to being legally accountable for injuries suffered by children as a result of poor product design, KCN's entire marketing effort and business reputation would be compromised by such a preventable accident.

In essence, doing the right thing in terms of safe product design coincides with what the law demands from business enterprises. KCN is required by the law of negligence to avoid causing harm that is reasonably foreseeable. KCN is required by contract law to supply a safe product. Finally, KCN is required to meet regulatory standards designed to protect the public, over and above what the common law requires. These regulatory standards, in relation to product design, manufacture, and labelling, are discussed below.

Product Design and Manufacture

Governments, through legislation, impose minimum standards for many goods and services where they consider it to be in the public interest to reduce the risk of harm. They create licensing systems for those offering certain kinds of services, such as realtors, doctors, lawyers, and engineers. Governments also establish standards for product design and patent protection. For example, KCN cannot produce or sell particular playground equipment if that industrial design has been registered by another person or company, unless KCN obtains their explicit permission (licence).

Canadian Standards Association
The nonprofit, nongovernmental organization that sets standards for products in Canada in association with the International Organization for Standardization (ISO).

In addition, such organizations as the **Canadian Standards Association** develop voluntary guidelines for use by both producers and users of goods. Guidelines are developed with the assistance of a broad range of experts, including representatives from industry.[1] These guidelines may be adopted by regulators as mandatory standards, and they will typically represent the measure of the standard of care for tort liability.

All businesses should be familiar with voluntary guidelines that apply to their goods or services. They must become familiar with the standards in their field of operation that are mandatory:

---

1. The *Standards Council of Canada Act*, R.S.C. 1985, c. S-16, s. 3 creates a Standards Council, which, in turn, accredits bodies, including the Canadian Standards Association, that create different standards. The Canadian Standards Association also provides testing and certification of products under its brand name CSA International. The international standards-setting body is the International Organization for Standardization (ISO).

- Some industries must comply with specific legislation. For example, the *Motor Vehicle Safety Act:*

    ... regulate[s] the manufacture and importation of motor vehicles and motor vehicle equipment to reduce the risk of death, injury and damage to property and the environment.[2]

    All aspects of the production of vehicles for the Canadian market, including rules relating to emissions, are governed by this Act and its regulations.

- Importers, advertisers, and vendors of certain products are subject to specific legislative requirements. For example, the regulations to the *Hazardous Products Act (HPA)*[3] require that

    A person may advertise, sell or import a product only if it meets the requirements of the National Standard of Canada CAN/CSA-Z262.1-M90, Ice Hockey Helmets, published by the Canadian Standards Association, as amended from time to time.[4]

- In certain cases, the sale or distribution of products or substances is simply prohibited. For example, if KCN sold painted playground equipment, its actions would be illegal if the paint contained lead.[5] If goods are inherently dangerous and have no overriding value, they are banned by the *HPA.*

    Producers of goods and services may consider both regulations and voluntary guidelines to be impediments to their right to develop an effective marketing mix. It is more accurate and certainly more useful, however, to view them as the collective opinion of specialists in risk assessment. For example, the voluntary standards on Children's Playspaces and Equipment[6] developed by the Canadian Standards Association represent the consensus of qualified experts, industry participants included, as to what is reasonable to maintain child safety. Viewed in this light, they are a valuable resource for producers like KCN. Ignoring the standards would seriously compromise KCN's marketplace reputation and significantly increase its exposure to legal liability.

The result of good product design is children playing safely.

Product Attributes/Characteristics

Most producers of goods and services like to think that they supply the best product they can, given its price and intended purpose. Consumers do not always agree, although they sometimes have unreasonable expectations. The common law of contract maintains a limited role in issues of product quality. **Caveat emptor**, or let the buyer beware, defines its standard. Only where goods almost completely fail or a con-

caveat emptor
Let the buyer beware, or let the buyer take care.

---

2. S.C. 1993, c. 16.
3. R.S.C. 1985, c. H-3.
4. *Hazardous Products (Ice Hockey Helmets) Regulations,* S.O.R./89-257, s. 3.
5. *Ibid.,* Sch. 1, part 1, s. 9(a).
6. Canadian Standards Association International, *A Guideline on Children's Playspaces and Equipment* Doc. No. CSA Z614-98 (Toronto: CSA International, 1998).

Sale of Goods Act

All Canadian provinces and territories, with the exception of Quebec,[7] have their own *Sale of Goods* legislation.[8] While some have amended the legislation (see below), all the Acts have a great deal in common. The *Sale of Goods Acts* originated with 19th-century British legislation that incorporated many existing common law rules. Most common law jurisdictions adopted this British model.

Today, the legislation supplements existing common law contract rules (explored in Part 2). As the name suggests, the legislation applies only to the sale of goods, and not, for example, to transactions such as bartering. Goods are defined as "all chattels personal other than things in action or money"[9]—

LANDMARK IN THE LAW

that is, generally, all tangible items and not, for example, interests in real property or intellectual property or services. A contract of sale of goods is defined to include both sales and agreements to sell. The critical element of the contract of sale is that it transfers property ownership or title rights in the goods.

Different provisions of the *Sale of Goods Acts* have been introduced throughout this text. In Part 7, two issues of particular significance to the marketing effort will be explored. First, the *Sale of Goods Acts* imply certain conditions and warranties into contracts of sale. Second, they define when title or ownership rights shift between the seller and the buyer (see Chapter 25), which in turn defines when risk shifts.

---

tract term is breached does the common law provide a remedy. For this reason, concern for the state of products (goods) was one of the early areas of statutory intervention, starting in the 19th century with the *Sale of Goods Act.*

Caveat emptor remains a guiding principle in contracts, particularly where buyers have the opportunity to inspect goods. The focus of the *Sale of Goods Acts* has always been on sales where there is either no such opportunity or buyers make it known that they are dependent on the advice of the seller. In addition, the Acts have addressed the need for buyers to acquire clear title to goods.

The Acts provide these assurances through **conditions** and **warranties**, which are implied into all sales of goods—both to business and to consumers—unless the parties agree to the contrary, including specifically contracting out of their application. Generally, conditions are terms that are important or essential to the purpose of the contract.[10] Since warranties can also be important, they are best understood as all terms that are not conditions.[11]

The following conditions and warranties are implied into all sales transactions:

- the condition that the seller has the right to sell the goods (i.e., holds title to the goods) and is therefore able to pass title to the purchaser
- the condition that the goods are equivalent to their description

condition
An essential or important term under Sale of Goods legislation.

warranty
A term that is not classified as a condition under Sale of Goods legislation.

---

7. Although Quebec has no *Sale of Goods Act,* articles 1726-1731 of the *Civil Code of Quebec* contain warranties implied in sales transactions.

8. *Sale of Goods Act,* R.S.A. 1980, c. S-2; *Sale of Goods Act,* R.S.B.C. 1979, c. 370; *Sale of Goods Act,* R.S.M. 1987, c. S10; *Sale of Goods Act,* R.S.N.B., 1973. c. S-1; *Sale of Goods Act,* R.S.N. 1990, c. S-6; *Sale of Goods Act,* R.S.N.W.T. 1938, c. S -6; *Sale of Goods Act,* R.S.N.S. 1989, c. 408; *Sale of Goods Act,* R.S.O. 1990, c. S-1; *Sale of Goods Act,* R.S.P.E.I. 1988, c. S-1; *Sale of Goods Act,* R.S.S. 1978, c. S-1; *Sale of Goods Act,* R.S.Y. 1986, c. 154.

9. *Sale of Goods Act,* R.S.A. 1980, s. 1.

10. Per Jenkins J., *Michael's Pizzeria Ltd.* v. *LP Computer Solutions Ind.* (1996), 139 Nfld. & P.E.I.R. 295 (P.E.I. S.C.T.D.).

11. Note also the discussion of innominate terms in Chapter 9—namely, terms not easily classified as either conditions or warranties; G.H.L. Fridman, *Sale of Goods in Canada,* 4th ed. (Scarborough: Carswell, 1995) at 159-160.

- the condition that the goods will be reasonably fit for the intended purpose where the buyer, expressly or by implication, makes it known what the intended purpose of the goods will be, in such a way as to show that he or she is relying on the skill and judgment of the seller
- the condition that the goods are of merchantable quality (meaning of reasonable quality, considering the price paid) if bought by description or if the defects were not observable by inspection; the reasonable purchaser would not have bought the goods at that price and in that state if the deficiencies had been known
- the condition that the goods sold are equivalent to the sample shown the prospective buyer
- the warranty that the buyer will receive quiet possession to the goods—that is, a third party will not claim rights against them
- the warranty that the goods are free of encumbrances such as liens

Consider the application of these provisions to a KCN sale:

EXAMPLE 1

KCN sells play equipment prepackaged through the Internet. There is a three-dimensional photographic representation of the equipment that potential consumers can manipulate. Furthermore, KCN has introduced an online "let us help you find equipment that meets your needs" service. Prospective purchasers describe their needs, and a salesperson for KCN identifies the equipment that best meets those needs.

The customer e-mail service has received two complaints. Customer Kathy, who ordered a climbing frame exactly as presented in the graphic on the Web page, received one that had some significant differences. Customer Kurt, relying on the online advisor, was expecting a play set suitable for eight- to ten-year-olds. Instead, he received a set that could be used only by children under five.

In both cases, KCN will have violated a condition implied by the *Sale of Goods Act*. In Kathy's case, the goods do not meet the description. In Kurt's case, they are not suitable for the purpose described and he relied on the advice of a KCN employee.

EXAMPLE 2

Customer Kadish bought a top-of-the-line KCN play set described as "the very best money can buy." Within two years it began to deteriorate significantly, to the point that there are now genuine safety concerns.

There is likely a violation of the condition that the goods will be of merchantable quality, since it is reasonable to expect that high-priced goods of this type should last for more than two years under normal conditions of use.

The distinction between conditions and warranties is important because of the difference in remedies provided.

A breach of an implied condition may give the innocent party the right not only to sue for damages, but also to reject the goods and treat the contract as ended. This is known as the right of repudiation, and it means that if he so chooses, the nondefaulting party can consider himself to be freed from the balance of the contract and to have no further obligations under it. For example, customer Kurt, who received play equipment that was not suitable for the purpose sold, is not obligated to accept further shipments from KCN. Kurt can bring his contract with KCN to an end, return the equipment, and find another supplier.

In contrast, when an implied warranty is breached, the sale-of-goods legislation permits the buyer to maintain an action for damages or ask the court to reduce the purchase price.[12] The buyer cannot return the goods and is still obligated to continue with the contract in question and perform any outstanding terms. In short, the buyer must continue to perform after breach of warranty or be in breach herself.

In practice, the distinctions between the remedies for breach of implied conditions and warranties can lead to results that are inconsistent with the severity of the harm. For example, a minor breach that is classified as a condition will allow recission or repudiation, whereas a serious breach that is classified as a warranty may still result in the buyer having to continue with the contract.[13]

While the provisions of conditions and warranties may seem useful, particularly to consumers, they have some serious limitations in addition to those already described. They can be explicitly excluded, they apply only to sales of goods (not to leases or purchases of services, for example), there must be privity of contract between the complainant and the "defaulting party," and there is no addressing of any oral assurances given prior to contract that seriously affected a consumer's purchasing decision.

All provinces today have some form of legislation intended to overcome at least some of these deficiencies for consumer sales, although there is little uniformity between provinces:

- Most provinces no longer allow the exclusion of implied conditions and warranties in consumer contracts.[14]
- In Saskatchewan[15] (and in more limited respects, New Brunswick and Quebec[16]), for example, privity is no longer an obstacle to suing any party along the supply chain.
- In New Brunswick, for example, conditions and warranties apply to a wider range of transactions, including leases and the provision of services.[17]
- The sometimes artificial distinction between remedies for warranties and those for conditions has been removed in some provinces, typically by having remedies depend on the seriousness of the breach. For example, in New Brunswick, if the problem is relatively minor and repairable, the onus is generally on the consumer to attempt to have the problem corrected by allowing the party at fault a reasonable time to correct the defect. If that does not occur, then there is an entitlement to compensation. If the problem is more major or serious, the consumer is entitled to revoke the contract and to receive compensation where relevant. In either case, the onus is on the consumer to act quickly. The Act also permits recovery of any reasonably foreseeable damages.[18]

Are these imposed provisions unfair to the producer? The legislation strives to balance consumer expectations and practical business concerns.

---

12. For example, see s. 51 of the Ontario *Sale of Goods Act*, R.S.O. 1990, c. S.1.

13. D.M.W. Young & B.R.F. Fraser, *Canadian Advertising and Marketing Law,* vol. 1 (Toronto: Carswell, 1990) at 4-30.

14. *Ibid.* at 4-30.2.

15. For example, Saskatchewan, *Consumer Protection Act*, R.S.S. 1996, c. C-30.1, s. 45(3).

16. New Brunswick, *Consumer Product Warranty and Liability Act,* S.N.B. 1978, c. C-18; Quebec, *Consumer Protection Act*, R.S.Q. c. P-40.1; Young & Fraser, *supra* note 13 at 4-40.3 - 4-41.

17. *Supra* note 13 at 4-31.

18. *Consumer Product Warranty and Liability Act* (New Brunswick), *supra* note 16, ss. 14-22.

Case

Grabka v. *Regina Motor Products (1970) Ltd.,* [1997] S.J. No. 770 (Prov. Ct.), online: QL (SJ)

The Business Context: Those engaged in selling goods secondhand have unique problems in terms of disclosing quality and durability of goods. Where do the seller's responsibilities for disclosure end and the purchaser's responsibilities for discovery begin?

Factual Background: Grabka bought an 11-year-old car "wholesale" and "as is." He had ample opportunity to inspect it. Within a short time, there were problems with the car that required costly repairs.

The Legal Issue: In the context of the Saskatchewan *Consumer Protection Act,* and in the context of second-hand cars sold "as is," how far do the seller's obligations related to "acceptable quality" and "durability" extend?

Resolution: The court held that the obligations of the seller should be determined by the factual context. Here, it was relevant that the purchaser knew the vehicle was 11 years old with over 170 000 kilometres on the odometer (the expert testimony was that automatic transmissions in cars of this type and year commonly wear out around that time or even earlier); that the vehicle had the appearance of not being well maintained; that it was only recently received by the seller as a trade-in; and that it was being "wholesaled" to the buyer, suggesting that this was a discount price. Furthermore, it was important to the court that the purchaser had ample opportunity to examine the vehicle prior to purchase and have it professionally examined. For these reasons, it was found not only that the vehicle was of acceptable quality as defined by the legislation, but also that the period of durability for which the purchaser was entitled to expect a warranty to cover his vehicle was something less than the relevant period in this case (3800 kilometres).

> Buyers acquiring high kilometrage older model vehicles for modest prices are engaged in a somewhat risky activity. It is to be expected that such vehicles will at any time require major and costly repairs. Such buyers must expect that the risk for such repairs will remain with retail sellers under those circumstances for a short period of time only.

Critical Analysis: Did the court strike a fair balance between the rights of the dealer and the purchaser in this case?

Contracts for the International Sale of Goods

In 1980 the United Nations Commission on International Trade Law (UNCITRAL) produced a treaty, the Convention on the International Sale of Goods (CISG). The treaty went into force in 1988 and has been ratified by more than 30 countries, including Canada and the United States. The goal of the convention is to create a uniform body of international commercial law.

INTERNATIONAL PERSPECTIVE

The CISG applies to business-to-business contracts for the sale of goods. The convention automatically applies to the contract if the parties are from ratifying countries, unless they contracted out of its provisions. It does not apply to contracts for services and technology, leases and licences, or goods bought for personal, family, or household use.

The convention provides a uniform set of rules for forming contracts and establishes the obligations of the buyer and seller. It addresses such issues as the requirement of writing; acceptance; implied terms; performance of the contract, including the buyer's and seller's obligations; and breach of contract.

Critical Analysis: The CISG is a compromise agreed to by many nations and encompassing aspects of many different legal systems. Questions regarding, for example, what constitutes an offer and whether the contract must be in writing may have different answers under the convention than under domestic law. How useful is this convention to Canadian business?

Source: *Convention on the International Sale of Goods,* online: United Nations Commission on International Trade Law (UNCITRAL) <UNDoc.A/Conf.97/18> (10 April 1980).

Product Packaging and Labelling

Marketing is often as much about designing the product packaging as creating the product itself. Packaging and labelling are the primary means the manufacturer has of "talking to" consumers. While package design will be carefully considered in terms of attracting customers, it must also comply with laws concerning safety and honesty.

Part 3 of this text considered the impact of tort law on product packaging. When designing packaging and drafting the label contents, the law of negligence is of primary concern.

Labelling and packaging legislation complements common law, as its primary focus is the imposition of standards in order to prevent harm. It is also supplemented by trademark law (see Chapter 18). Most packaging and labelling legislation is fed-

Product Packaging and Labelling and the Law of Negligence

Acme Face Creams produces high-priced night creams. The creams consist primarily of natural substances, but one ingredient can result in an allergic reaction in a small minority of users. The product must be packaged in glass, as its properties can become unstable when in contact with plastic. Designers have created a smoky (opaque) navy blue pot with a plastic rim inside the lid.

What harm can come from both the product and the packaging? There are two obvious areas of concern: the possible allergic reactions and the fragility of the pot. How does tort law apply to each? Acme must warn potential users of the allergenic properties. Typically, it does so via clearly written statements both on the packaging in which the pot comes and on the pot itself, so that the consumer/purchaser can read the warning before buying the product and after external packaging has been thrown away. If glass is the only viable packaging material, Acme must ensure that each bottle is packed and shipped so that it reaches the consumer undamaged.

If a consumer uses the product and is harmed because of an allergic reaction or glass shards from a broken bottle, the relevant question will be whether, given the potential for harm associated with this product, Acme has done everything reasonably possible to ensure that risks were minimized.

Critical Analysis: Does the law of negligence provide adequate protection to consumers in this situation?

eral and therefore applies throughout the country.[19] Some legislation is industry specific—for example, the *Food and Drugs Act*[20] (food, drugs, cosmetics, and other therapeutic devices), the *Textile Labelling Act,*[21] and the *Tobacco Act.*[22] Other legislation regulates across most consumer products.

Labelling of Prepackaged Goods

The *Consumer Packaging and Labelling Act (CPLA)*[23] sets out minimum packaging and labelling requirements for almost all prepackaged goods sold in Canada, other than drugs, cosmetics, and medical devices.[24] The Act encourages fair competition between manufacturers and other sellers by ensuring that consumers can compare the price and quantity of products. It is enforced by the federal department, Industry Canada.

The *CPLA* requires manufacturers to

- provide the consumer with certain basic essential information; specifically, the generic description, net quantity, and identity of manufacturer or importer; and
- eliminate any misleading information about the nature or quantity of the product that might flow either from statements made on the container or from the shape or size of the container.[25]

What is the impact of these provisions on KCN? Marketing is about providing customers with the product information required to make purchasing decisions. KCN proposes to sell its playground equipment partially assembled, in boxes. If KCN prints only its name and a graphic on the packaging, purchasers will not know how big the equipment is, whether all the parts are included and holes predrilled, whether the wood requires a sealant, and who should be contacted if there are any questions or parts are missing. Failure to provide this information can anger consumers and may also violate the *CPLA*.

Much of the information required by law must be disclosed in both French and English. The regulations can also be very specific. For example, wrapping paper and tinfoil (bi-dimensional products) must be described in appropriate units—square metres, or dimensions of roll, ply, and the number of perforated individual units for paper towels. All information must be prominently and clearly presented.

This degree of detail is not an illustration of bureaucratic excess. Its purpose is to foster competition through comparative information. The Act does not require the manufacturer to provide any information it does not readily have. It addresses, however, obvious limitations as to what the consumer can see when buying a product. Without a statement of total square metres of wrapping paper, for example, the prospective purchaser would have to guess, and a manufacturer could become expert in making the product look bigger than it is.

---

19. The principal exception to this is the Quebec language legislation, most importantly that found in section 51 of the *Charter of the French Language*, R.S.Q. c. C-11. Otherwise, provincial legislation tends to apply to specialized industries such as alcohol, milk, and margarine.

20. R.S.C. 1985, c. F-27.

21. R.S.C. 1985, c. T-10. The voluntary Canadian Care Labelling Program was devised under the direction of National Standards of Canada; see *Guide to the Canadian Care Labelling Program,* Fair Business Practices Branch, Competition Bureau, 9 March 2000.

22. S.C. 1997, c. 13.

23. R.S.C. 1985, c. C-38.

24. Drugs, cosmetics, and medical devices are governed by the *Food and Drugs Act, supra* note 20. There is a small group of other products not covered, either because they are exclusively for commercial or industrial use or export or because they are are covered by some other legislation, such as the *Textile Labelling Act, supra* note 21, or an assortment of agriculture-related legislation, such as the *Feeds Act,* R.S.C. 1985, c. F-9.

25. Young & Fraser, *supra* note 13, at 6-4–6-5.

Product Warnings

Some products are inherently hazardous, and there is a clear need both to warn of hazards and to provide critical information about what to do if the product causes harm to the user.

The *HPA* provides at least 23 identified categories of "restricted" products—products that must be labelled in a specific manner or meet certain standards in order to be sold legally in Canada.[26] About half of these are chemicals (for example, household cleaners) or petroleum distillates, and the rest include a wide range of goods, such as pressurized metal cans, flammable carpets, baby cribs and car seats, tents, cigarette lighters, and children's sleepwear.

Warnings must be clearly present and usually in an established form, including first aid and related information. Also, the packaging itself must be "child resistant," where relevant, and meet specific standards in this regard.

Product warnings usually must be written in an established form and must include first aid information.

Language Requirements

KCN is proposing a national marketing strategy using major retail outlets, and it will likely have all labelling in bilingual format to avoid the expense of separate labelling for different markets. This strategy will also comply with the legal requirements for bilingual labelling scattered throughout a number of Acts. For example, under the *Food and Drugs Act* and the *HPA*, all prescribed wording must be in both French and English.

Disclosure of Weight of Contents

The *Weights and Measures Act*[27] regulates both the measurement and the presentation of the measurement of the product. Likewise, the "tools" of measurement are controlled for accuracy.

Promotion

A leading marketing text defines promotion as "communication by marketers that informs, persuades, and reminds potential buyers of a product in order to influence their opinion or elicit a response."[28] This influencing of the consumer is achieved through an optimal mix of the key elements of promotion—namely, advertising, public relations, personal selling, and sales promotion.[29]

---

26. These restricted products are set out in the *Hazardous Products Act, supra* note 3, Sch. 1, part 2.

27. R.S.C. 1985, c. W-6.

28. C.W. Lamb, J.E. Hair, C. McDaniel & A.J. Faria, *Marketing,* 3d Can. ed. (Scarborough: ITP Nelson, 1997) at 403.

29. *Ibid.*

Industry Standards and Legislation

For both business and consumers, promotion is the most visible component of the marketing mix. As with design and production, promotion is governed by both voluntary industry standards and legislation. The most important voluntary standards are those of Advertising Standards Canada (ASC), an organization established by the advertising community to promote public confidence in its products and services, and those of the Canadian Broadcast Standards Council (CBSC), a council supported by the Canadian Association of Broadcasters (CAB) with the approval of the Canadian Radio-television and Telecommunications Commission (CRTC).

The ASC addresses advertising in general and has a detailed code of industry guidelines. It provides the mechanism for public complaints concerning violations of that code, as well as business-to-business complaints:

> The Canadian Code of Advertising Standards is widely supported by all participating organizations, and is designed to help set and maintain standards of honesty, truth, accuracy, fairness and propriety in advertising.
>
> No advertising shall be prepared or knowingly exhibited by the participating organizations which contravenes this Code of Standards.
>
> The provisions of the Code should be adhered to both in letter and in spirit. Advertisers and their representatives must substantiate their advertised claims promptly when requested to do so by one or more of the Councils.[30]

Complaints are investigated, and if found to be of substance, result in a finding that the advertiser should change or remove the offending promotion. Since this is a voluntary process, enforcement relies on moral suasion. However, findings will be publicized, and members of the advertising community can ill afford to ignore a ruling made against them by their peers.

The CBSC has an equivalent code of ethics and complaints process, related specifically to promotion in broadcast media. In addition, it has developed more specialized codes, such as those related to sex stereotyping and violence.

The promotion of goods is also regulated by legislation. KCN will again discover that an effective legal compliance plan and good marketing practices coincide.

Misleading Advertising

false or misleading advertising
Promotional statements that either are false or have the ability to mislead a consumer as to their truth.

The most important provision relating to **false or misleading advertising** is the federal *Competition Act*.[31] The Act defines false or misleading advertising as arising where

> A person .... who, for the purpose of promoting, directly or indirectly, the supply or use of a product or for the purpose of promoting, directly or indirectly, any business interest, by any means whatever,
>
> (a) makes a representation to the public that is false or misleading in a material respect.[32]

---

30. *Canadian Code of Advertising Standards*, Advertising Standards Canada (May 1999 Revision).
31. R.S.C. 1985, c. C-34. Other legislation tends to focus on specific issues. For example, the *Consumer Packaging and Labelling Act, supra* note 23, prohibits misleading advertising, specifically in the context of prepackaged goods; it would be misleading to describe the product box as "full" or "large" if this is not the case.
32. *Ibid.*, s. 74.01(1).

prohibited offences
Offences under the *Competition Act* that are criminal in nature.

reviewable matters
Offences under the *Competition Act* that are assessed according to a civil burden of proof and resolved by voluntary agreement or by order of the Competition Tribunal.

This provision is stated in broad terms so as to capture not only those who deliberately make false statements, but also those who push the limits of truth—intentionally or otherwise—in the impressions given.

Falsity is judged by an objective test. Whether or not a statement is misleading is measured by what might be the impression formed by the average member of the group of persons to whom the statement is directed. Furthermore, what is important is the impression created by the advertisement in its entirety, including illustrations and disclaimers.

The misrepresentation must be "material"—that is, it must apply to statements that entice prospective purchasers to the place of business[33] or that influence the customer's decision to purchase the particular item.

The *Competition Act*

LANDMARK IN THE LAW

The federal *Competition Act* has its origins in anti-trust legislation passed first in Canada in 1889.[34] While it retains a critical role in proscribing behaviour that manipulates a competitive market (see Chapter 25), today it also plays a very important part in regulating activities that improperly benefit one producer over another through misleading or unfair practices affecting consumers.

The Commissioner of Competition, appointed by the Governor-in-Council, is responsible for enforcing and administering the Act. The commissioner is an independent official and is solely responsible for the conduct of examinations and inquiries under the Act. For administrative purposes, the commissioner is the head of the Competition Bureau, which is part of Industry Canada. Under the Act, the Minister of Industry receives reports of discontinued inquiries and can, under section 10 of the Act, direct the commissioner to make an inquiry. However, the conduct of inquiries is at the discretion of the commissioner.

The commissioner is also responsible for administering and enforcing the *Consumer Packaging and Labelling Act*, the *Textile Labelling Act*, and the *Precious Metals Marking Act*.[35]

Provisions in the *Competition Act* are either criminal or civil in nature. Mergers are also subject to civil law review, and certain large transactions are notifiable (see Chapter 25). Criminal matters are called **prohibited offences** and are considered by legislators to be of a more serious nature than civil **reviewable matters**. Alleged offences are investigated by the bureau, and evidence obtained in criminal matters can, at any stage of an inquiry, be referred by the commissioner to the Attorney General of Canada, who will, in turn, decide whether to proceed to prosecution, as is the normal practice with criminal matters.

In the case of civil reviewable matters, the commissioner has authority to apply for a remedial order to a judge of the Competition Tribunal, the tribunal established to hear such matters.[36] The burden of proof for reviewable matters is less than that for criminal cases, and the outcome, if successful, is typically an order to desist from the offending behaviour. Violation of that order itself carries penalties.

For some offences, under the Act there is a choice as to whether to proceed criminally or civilly (see below).

Source: *Competition Act*, R.S.C. 1985, c. C-34.

---

33. *R* v. *Whitehall Development Corp.* (1977), 43 C.P.R. (2d) 64 (Ont. Co. Ct.).
34. *Act for the Prevention and Suppression of Combinations formed in restraint of Trade*, S.C. 1889, c. 41.
35. R.S.C. 1985, c. P-19.
36. *Competition Tribunal Act*, R.S. 1985, c.19 (2nd Supp.), C-36.4.

Investigation of Complaints

If a business is suspected of false or misleading advertising of goods or services, officers of the Competition Bureau will conduct an investigation, which may have one of two consequences. If the misrepresentation is sufficiently serious, criminal charges under the *Competition Act* may be laid,[37] in which case the prosecutor will need to prove that the misrepresentation was "[made] knowingly and recklessly."[38] More frequently, a complaint of false or misleading advertising will be pursued through the civil track process (see below). This process can be swift, particularly where there is a risk of immediate harm, and can result in an order to halt the deceptive practice and/or an administrative penalty.

Section 36 of the *Competition Act* allows for civil actions to be brought by individuals. In practice, the costs of litigation discourage most consumers, who instead might complain either to the Competition Bureau or to ASC or CBCS, the industry associations.[39] Such complaints do not provide direct monetary benefit to consumers but may result in the advertising being pulled and/or the advertiser being prosecuted or disciplined by a third party.

Section 36 may now be used by commercial complainants who are seriously concerned about the actions of competitors, particularly in the context of comparative advertising. Since stopping the advertising campaign is of primary importance, the complainant may seek an injunction, as well as pursue claims for damages if the loss is quantifiable. The *Mead Johnson Canada*[40] case, discussed in Chapter 12, was the first case in which an injunction under section 36 was allowed.

Civil or Fast Track Processes

The **civil track,** or fast track, process was introduced in 1999 for a number of deceptive marketing practices proscribed under the *Competition Act*, as a result of concerns about the time and difficulty of proving criminal cases. The primary purpose of the civil track process is to stop the misleading activity. The Competition Bureau will typically seek an order prohibiting the use of the deceptive practice. Persons found responsible for deceptive practices may also be ordered to publish an information notice and may be ordered to pay an administrative penalty. Any violation of an order may itself be a criminal offence. While the penalties are not as severe as in the criminal provision, the cases are far easier to prove and proof of intent is not necessary.

Defences

The best defence to allegations of misleading advertising is that the elements of the offence have not been proven.

Civil track claims have an additional defence, namely that of **due diligence**:[41]

... consideration of what a reasonable man would have done in the circumstances. The defence will be available if the accused reasonably believed in a mistaken set of facts which, if true, would render the act or omission innocent, or if he took all reasonable steps to avoid the particular event.[42]

civil track
The process by which the Competition Bureau may order a promoter to desist from engaging in false or misleading advertising.

due diligence
A defence based on having a reasonable belief in the truth of the statement made or adopting reasonable steps to avoid the utterance of false or misleading statements.

---

37. *Competition Act, supra* note 31, s. 52. These offences are often known as "regulatory or public welfare" (see Chapter 16).
38. *Ibid.*, s. 52(1).
39. See ASC's homepage, online: <http//www.canad/com/asc/mainmenu.html>.
40. (1996), 31 O.R. (3d) 237, 70 C.P.R. (3d) 189 (Gen. Div.).
41. This defence is available for all reviewable conduct applications.
42. *R v. Sault Ste. Marie (City)*, [1978] 2 S.C.R. 1299 at 181-182.

Civil or Criminal Offence?

BUSINESS APPLICATION OF THE LAW

When the civil track was introduced, the Competition Bureau issued guidelines explaining what would be considered in determining whether a complaint was serious enough to give rise to a criminal prosecution:

... consideration [should be given to]:

(a) whether there was substantial harm to consumers or competitors which could not be adequately dealt with by available civil remedies;

(b) whether the deceptive practices targeted or took unfair advantage of vulnerable groups (e.g., children and seniors);

(c) whether the persons involved failed to make timely and effective attempts to remedy the adverse effects of the conduct, or whether the conduct continued after corporate officials became aware of it;

(d) whether the conduct involved a failure to comply with a previous undertaking, a promised voluntary corrective action, or a prohibition order; and

(e) whether the persons had engaged in similar conduct in the past.

Mitigating factors will include:

(a) whether the consequence of a prosecution or conviction would be disproportionately harsh or oppressive; and

(b) whether the company or entity has in place an effective compliance program.[43]

Critical Analysis: Has the availability of the civil process removed the need for difficult criminal prosecutions?

Since this is a defence, the onus is on the accused, not the Crown, to prove due diligence. Consider the following examples.[44]

Example 1

KCN imports some products from overseas. It is advised by the exporter that the goods meet Canadian Standards Association standards, and thus, KCN makes this statement in all publicity. In fact, the goods meet some lesser standards, and there has been no attempt by the exporter or KCN to establish that Canadian standards have been met.

KCN will fail to prove due diligence. As a seller in Canada, KCN should have exercised reasonable care; failing to make any checks is inadequate.

---

43. Information Bulletin *Misleading Representations and Deceptive Marketing Practices: Choice of Criminal or Civil Track under the Competition Act*, Competition Bureau, 22 September 1999.

44. These examples are based on cases brought under the old, pre–civil track procedure, when all complaints were criminal. Now that intent is required for the criminal offence, due diligence is no longer available.

EXAMPLE 2

> KCN received the goods and had them analyzed by an industrial engineer, who provided a detailed technical report that affirmed compliance with Canadian Standards Association standards. In fact, the engineer had made an error, and the goods did not comply.

> KCN has likely exercised due diligence. Provided it can show that the controls it put in place over experts hired or its own employees were reasonable under the circumstances, and that there were no other extenuating factors that would suggest KCN's actions were less than reasonable, it will be successful in its defence.[45]

EXAMPLE 3

> KCN publishes and distributes the KCN Children's Play Catalogue, a biannual publication. The catalogue lists 2500 items, and it is found to have a high incidence of errors in their descriptions. KCN's defence is that it spot checks every twentieth product listed for accuracy.

> The sampling is unlikely to be considered adequate for this type of catalogue. "Reasonableness" may not involve the checking of each individual description, but it certainly involves more than one in twenty.[46]

The Competition Bureau will be influenced by whether or not the advertiser has sought to correct errors. Speedy retraction may also be evidence of due diligence. The advertiser should retract an error quickly and in a manner consistent with the original advertisement. A pattern of similar errors consistently corrected, however, may suggest both a cynical marketing strategy and a clear lack of due diligence.

Others involved in the misleading advertising—such as an advertising agency, newspapers that run the ad, and retailers displaying in-store promotion signs—also face potential liability. If an advertising agency actually prepares the copy, it is responsible for verifying any promises made. If it simply accepts the advertisement for dissemination, it is still responsible for following up any suspect claims and must establish that it acted "in good faith."[47] The media are better protected. If the advertisement is accepted "as is," the good faith defence applies. That is, there is no liability if it can be shown that the media outlet had no knowledge of any inaccuracy and, in the circumstances, should not have had knowledge.[48]

The retailer using materials provided by the producer (or another party in the distribution chain) does not face *Competition Act* liability unless it has transformed the representation made by the manufacturer into its own advertisement and promoted the product itself.[49]

Performance Claims

Statements about the performance of a product or service may fall within the general provisions described above under misleading advertising.

---

45. *R.* v. *Consumers Distributing Co.* (1980), 54 C.P.R. (2d) 50, 57 C.C.C. (2d) 317 (Ont. C.A.).

46. *R.* v. *Tege Investments Ltd.* (1981), 51 C.P.R. (2d) 216 (Alta. Prov. Ct.).

47. Director of Investigation and Research, Competition Bureau, Industry Canada, *Misleading Advertising Guidelines,* special ed. (Hull, Que.: Competition Bureau, September 1991) at para. 8.A.

48. *Competition Act, supra* note 31, s. 60.

49. *Misleading Advertising Guidelines, supra* note 47, at para. 5.A.

The *Competition Act* also has a specific provision directed to performance claims. It is reviewable conduct to make a representation about a quality of a product that is not based on an "adequate and proper test."[50] Statements such as "the KCN climber develops your child's gross motor skills better than any other play equipment on the market" and "KCN's environmentally friendly harvesting of woods enhances regeneration of local forests" must be neither false nor misleading. KCN must also establish that before making these claims there was appropriate testing of their accuracy, and that the testing met the state of the art in scientific tests or consumer analysis.[51] The marketing department must have a close working relationship with those who have the expertise to provide the appropriate level of assurance for any statements made.

The following are examples of statements that have led to investigation:[52]

Fleecy in the rinse softens right through the wash for three times more softness than any dryer product ... Fleecy beats the best. It's the softest touch of all.[53]

In only 90 minutes you will lose excess fat. Without exhausting exercises, costly medicines or strict dieting.[54]

Cleans better than any leading cleanser.[55]

[In relation to fabric softener] No static cling.[56]

Case

R. v. Fuel Base Industries Inc. (1992), 44 C.P.R. (3d) 184 (Alta. Prov. Ct.)

The Business Context: Performance-enhancing products are common, but the manufacturer cannot make claims about their effectiveness unless prior proof of their truth exists.

Factual Background: Fuel Base Industries imported and marketed the Vitalizer, a fuel-saving device claiming to increase fuel consumption efficiency in automobiles by 10 to 20 percent.

The Legal Question: Who has the onus of proving the truth of performance claims such as that made about the Vitalizer?

Resolution: The onus of proving the truth of performance claims lies with the party making the claim. Since the accused in this case was unable to prove the truth of its assertions, it was found guilty and fined $50 000. Although the business was essentially bankrupt at the time of sentencing, the court applied the following considerations in determining an appropriate fine:

[G]eneral deterrence is of paramount concern in cases involving gas-saving additives. It is very convenient for corporations to advance such claims to the consumer without ensuring the accuracy of those claims through proper testing. Corporations cannot hide behind their own failure to properly test products in order to reduce their liability under the law.

Critical Analysis: Why does the onus lie with the accused in this context, when the Crown is responsible for proving the case?

50. *Competition Act. supra* note 31, s. 74.01(1)(b).

51. Advertising Standards Canada, *Guidelines for the Use of Research and Survey Data in Comparative Food Commercials* (Toronto: Advertising Standards Council of Canada, 1983).

52. These examples are found in Young & Fraser, *supra* note 13 at 1-46 - 1-47 and elsewhere in materials on misleading advertising. They are all from the old criminal provisions of the *Competition Act, supra* note 31.

53. *R. v. Bristol-Meyers Canada Ltd.* (1979), 48 C.C.C. (2d) 384 (Ont. Co. Ct.).

54. *R. v. Gregory, Chcquette & Hebert* (1973), 12 C.C.C. (2d) 137 (Que. Co. Ct.).

55. *R. v. Colgate-Palmolive Ltd.* (1977), 20 O.R. (2d) 691, 37 C.P.R. (2d) 276 (Co. Ct.).

56. *R. v. Bristol-Meyers Can. Ltd.*, [1980] O.J. No. 2760 (Co. Ct.), online: QL (O.J.).

Claims to Environmental Benefits

Claims to environmental benefits have become a popular method of promoting products. KCN's marketing strategy in this regard is typical. All environmental claims are subject to the general requirements already described in this section. Any claims that a product is biodegradable or recyclable, for example, must be supported by prior "adequate and proper testing."

Industry Canada brought together a team of industry associations and experts to develop guidelines for environmental claims within the context of the *CPLA* and the *Competition Act*.[57] The Guiding Principles are as follows:

It is recognized that all participants in the marketplace have an important role to play in reducing the environmental impacts resulting from the production, use and disposal of products. Environmental claims and/or representations should provide accurate and relevant information to allow meaningful comparisons to be made, thereby enabling consumer purchasing power to influence the marketplace through informed product selection.

ENVIRONMENTAL PERSPECTIVE

1) Those making environmental claims are responsible for ensuring that any claims and/or representations are accurate, and in compliance with the relevant legislation.

2) Consumers are responsible, to the extent possible, for appropriately using the information made available to them in labelling and advertising, thereby enhancing their role in the marketplace.

3) Environmental claims and/or representations that are ambiguous, vague, incomplete, misleading, or irrelevant, and that cannot be substantiated through credible information and/or test methods should not be used.

4) Claims and/or representations should indicate whether they are related to the product or the packaging materials.

Critical Analysis: In light of the popularity of "green" advertising, are these guidelines adequate to protect both consumers and the environment?

Tests and Testimonials

Advertisers often promote products and services either by presenting supportive test results or by using the assurances of convincing spokespersons, real or hypothetical. Tests must be carried out prior to the promotion.[58] If conducted by a third party, there must be permission to draw from the tests or they must already be in the public domain.

KCN may claim to have tested its products on a sample of nursery schools in the Prince George area. Provided it quotes accurately from these tests and they are fairly presented, this is in compliance with the Act. Alternatively, suppose *Consumer Reports* or *Today's Parent* has published surveys of different play equipment, and

---

57. Director of Investigation and Research, Bureau of Competition Policy, Consumer and Corporate Affairs Canada, *Principles and Guidelines for Environmental Labelling and Advertising* (Hull, Que.: Competition Bureau, 2 July 1993).

58. *Competition Act, supra* note 31, s. 74.02. This is reviewable conduct.

KCN wishes to quote from these surveys in promotional material. If copyright approval is required and received, and the quotes are accurately represented, this form of promotion is acceptable.

KCN may also wish to use testimonials,[59] for example, from a child care professional, an expert in child development, or a parent. These testimonials will be acceptable provided they are accurately stated and reasonably current, *and* provided the persons providing the testimonials have actually used or evaluated the KCN product. Using a well-known personality to provide the desired testimonial will attract close scrutiny. If, however, KCN is using an actor to represent, say, a hypothetical parent, the statements will be measured by the provisions for false and misleading advertising in general.

Warranty and Service Promises

Generally, any promises must meet the same standards for truthfulness as set out in the false and misleading provisions. These provisions are reinforced by provincial statutes that bind the advertiser to the promises made in the promotion, whether or not that was the meaning set out in the "fine print" in the final agreement.[60]

Promotion through Selling Practices

Promotion is more than advertising. Where practices are considered unfair to consumers, specific provisions have evolved to regulate or prohibit them. The following are some examples.

Bait and Switch

bait and switch
Advertising a product at a very low price to attract customers, then encouraging them to accept another product that is usually more expensive.

A particularly unscrupulous[61] promotional practice is **bait and switch**. The product is advertised at a very low price (the bait) but is in insufficient supply to meet expected demand. When consumers take the bait, they are informed that this product is "not in stock," "of poor quality," or "inferior to Product B." They are then persuaded to purchase the higher-priced Product B (the switch). It is, of course, Product B that the promoter intended to sell all along, usually because it has better profit margins.

Businesses may protect themselves from accusations under these provisions by establishing that they did indeed have a reasonable supply to meet expected demand and that they, for example, provided a "rain check" when supplies ran out. Note that rain checks alone will not protect a seller, since when used cynically, they become merely a means of encouraging return visits.

Unfair Practices

Provinces have legislated to address selling practices that can generally be described as unfair, usually because they prey on ill-informed consumers.[62]

The term "unfair" typically arises in the context of unequal bargaining power.

---

59. Guidelines are provided in *Misleading Advertising Guidelines, supra* note 47, at 5-6.

60. For example, *Consumer Protection Act,* (Sask), *supra* note 15.

61. It is reviewable conduct under *Competition Act, supra* note 31, s. 74.04.

62. For example, British Columbia, *Trade Practices Act,* R.S.B.C. 1979, c. 406; Newfoundland, *Trade Practices Act,* R.S.N. 1990, c. T-7; Ontario, *Business Practices Act,* R.S.O. 1990, c. B-18; Prince Edward Island, *Business Practices Act,* R.S.P.E.I. 1988, c. B-7; Quebec, *Consumer Protection Act,* c. P-40.1.

unfair practices
Illegal business practices that exploit the unequal bargaining position of consumers.

Unfair practices arise when the business intentionally (actual or implied)[63]

- targets customers with "physical infirmity, ignorance, illiteracy, inability to understand the language or the agreement, or other similar factors"[64] and who are therefore unable to understand the serious nature of the agreement
- sells at a price that "grossly exceeds the price at which similar goods or services are readily available to like consumers"[65]
- engages in a calculated and cynical marketing scheme that is "subjecting the consumer to undue pressure to enter into the transaction"[66]
- persuades a customer to buy where there "is no reasonable probability of payment of the obligation in full by the consumer"[67]
- imposes terms and conditions "of the proposed transaction [which] are so adverse to the consumer as to be inequitable"[68]

Should a vendor's actions be unfair, the consumer is typically entitled to recision or to a return of money paid. The relevant government agency may also choose to prosecute the seller when a complaint is made.

Contests

Contests are a common form of promotion. They are also highly regulated. Organizations embarking upon any form of promotion incorporating a game of chance should receive sound legal advice, since noncompliant contests may be indictable offences under the *Criminal Code*[69] or may be reviewable under the *Competition Act*.[70]

Provinces also have statutes that establish licensing systems for contests. Provided a contest or game of chance is licensed provincially, it is typically not in violation of the *Criminal Code* provisions.

The *Criminal Code* prohibits competitions that require participants to buy goods or services in order to participate. For this reason, promoters will allow contestants to draw "reasonable facsimiles," for example, of the product packaging or UPC code, or they will distribute free entry forms. The *Criminal Code* provisions also require participants to engage in a skill test before becoming eligible to receive a prize. What amounts to a skill-testing question is itself unclear. However, solving mathematical questions of sufficient skill level appears to satisfy the requirement, provided the exercise is not a sham.[71]

The *Competition Act* provisions focus on disclosure. For example, the number and approximate value of prizes, the geographic area in which the competition is being conducted, and the odds of winning all must be disclosed.[72] Furthermore, prizes must be distributed promptly, and winners must be selected either randomly or on the basis of skill.

A quick glance at the provisions of a contest on any consumer product will indicate the extent to which the law intervenes in what might appear to be a very simple marketing scheme.[73]

---

63. Note that these are only examples of the many circumstances covered in the various legislation.
64. *Business Practices Act, supra* note 62, s. 2(2)(i).
65. *Ibid.,* s. 2(2)(ii).
66. *Ibid.,* s. 2(2)(viii).
67. *Ibid.,* s. 2(2)(iv).
68. *Ibid.,* s. 2(2)(vi).
69. *Criminal Code*, R.S.C. 1985, C. c-46, s. 206(1).
70. *Competition Act, supra* note 31, s. 74.06.
71. Young & Fraser, *supra* note 13 at 3-15–3-17.
72. *Ibid.,* s. 74.06.
73. See the Director of Investigation and Research, Bureau of Competition Policy, *Section 74.06 of the Competition Act: Promotional Contests* (Hull, Que.: Competition Bureau, 28 July 1999).

Risk Management

Sound risk management practices call for consideration of many of the issues already discussed in Chapter 3 and the contracts and torts sections (Parts 2 and 3) of this text. The products and services must perform as intended, the design of any products must be fundamentally sound and address all reasonably foreseeable risks, and promises must not exceed what it is possible to deliver. Whether a producer or service provider meets these objectives will in large part be a function of its willingness to accept that planning for risk is essential. A business that is preoccupied with refining the design, production, and marketability of its product, and with ensuring adequate financing, sometimes finds it difficult to find the time to step back and ask the difficult questions that will prevent fundamental flaws or ill-conceived practices from evolving.

What then are the basic practices that a business such as KCN should adopt in order to minimize its risk exposure?

- KCN must establish a climate in which maximizing safety of the product is considered paramount. For any business producing goods or services for children, this is essential. Even one preventable injury can destroy the viability of the product line. Product designers must be familiar with all relevant design regulations. They must also monitor changes in standards. Perhaps KCN is unaware of the safety considerations associated with a market shift to metal products. Product designers must assume a critical mindset that always asks, "What are the reasonably foreseeable risks that all reasonably foreseeable users of this product might face, and can they be avoided?" They should observe children at play. Senior management should support this approach to design, even when faced with competing pressures.

- The organization should acquire, through its trade association and specialized professional advisors (for KCN, lawyers and industrial engineers) the knowledge of what standards must be met for both the production and the labelling of the goods. What is the age span of the intended users? If goods or services are unsuitable for the very young, this information must be effectively communicated on product labelling, and all promotions must be consistent with this message. Are the design features optimal for the particular age group? If the goods come partially assembled, as is the case with KCN, what information has to be provided so that prospective purchasers understand the final form of the product? How should labelling be expressed, and do both official languages need to be used?

- KCN should follow the basic guidelines for promotion—that is, ensure that statements and promises are both honest and clear. In the middle of a marketing campaign, it is easy to allow wording to go beyond the bounds of what it is possible to deliver. Those responsible for advertising must be well versed in the properties of the product or service. They should understand what it can and cannot deliver. This requirement extends beyond the obvious category of persons writing advertising copy. Those directly responsible for creating in-store promotions and for explaining products or services to customers must be well educated in the qualities of a product, even when they are not the producer's employees.

- KCN should establish an informed and properly responsive customer relations process. This is the primary line of communication between the producer and the customer. It can ward off serious problems. It can also reassure customers and reduce the potential for subsequent complaints and claims. It can also be an early warning system of the need to reconsider design or production techniques.
- Since no organization can prevent all untoward events, KCN must have adequate insurance coverage to address expected risk. It must have access to professional advisors who understand the business, including specialized insurance brokers and lawyers, where appropriate.

The irony of risk management is that it represents no more than corporate common sense. Businesses fail to implement sound plans not because of the complexity of the exercise, but rather because of the time it takes. While no pressing need exists, planning all too often is postponed or forgotten.

Business Law in Practice Revisited

1. How does the law affect KCN's marketing strategy?

KCN's marketing strategy covers the four aspects of the marketing mix: the product, its promotion, its retail price, and the way it reaches the consumer (distribution or place). This entire mix is designed to present the product in the best light and to maximize the potential for sales. Even though the industry in which KCN operates cannot be described as highly regulated, both common law and statute law affect every aspect of the marketing mix.

KCN is selling to children, so safety is paramount. In practice, it must comply with the Canadian Standards Association safety standards, and these will provide further guidance for the minimum standard of care both in tort and in contract. The goods are sold boxed and therefore must comply with the *Consumer Packaging and Labelling Act (CPLA)*. KCN is promoting mainly through the print media and in-store displays. It must be familiar with the provisions related to false and misleading advertising and to tests and testimonials (if relevant) in the *Competition Act*. Since KCN is intending to make environmental claims, it must ensure that it complies with Industry Canada Guiding Principles. Finally, KCN should be aware of how the implied conditions and warranties of the *Sale of Goods Acts* affect its contract obligations. Most importantly, the goods must match the description KCN provides on the box and be of merchantable quality.

2. What impact does the law have on KCN's product?

The producer must meet the terms of its contract; otherwise, the purchasers may claim that a breach has occurred. As well, statute law—for example, the *Sale of Goods Act*—imposes some conditions and warranties concerning the quality of the product. The federal *CPLA* will govern how KCN packages the goods by providing minimum disclosure requirements. While the law does not require all information to be in both official languages, practical marketing considerations will ensure that it is, since this is a national marketing campaign. For the same reason, KCN will need to comply with the maximum requirements of provincial legislation that supplements the *Sale of Goods Act*. Under tort law, and the law of negligence or product liability in particular, privity is not relevant. KCN must avoid any reasonably foreseeable harm to reasonably foreseeable users of its products. It should limit any potential liability through "warnings." For example, if climbing equipment is not appropriate for children under five, labelling should clearly state so. KCN must also consider the full range of voluntary guidelines that affect the products, since these, in practice, will define the standard of care in negligence.

3. What impact does the law have on the promotion of KCN's product?

Promotion of the product introduces additional requirements, most found in the federal *Competition Act*, although compliance with provincial legislation will also be required where applicable. Representations must be neither false nor misleading, and will be evaluated in their entirety. Graphics that are inconsistent with wording may result in an overall misleading impression. In general, KCN's best defence under the *Competition Act* is honesty. Where civil provisions are at issue, the due diligence defence will apply, and KCN must establish both that it had a reasonable belief in the accuracy of any representations and that it took reasonable steps to avoid any inaccuracies. KCN must be particularly careful if it makes claims about the performance capabilities of its products—for example, a claim that they develop gross motor skills better than other products. All such claims must be backed by prior and fully supportive testing. If KCN uses testimonials, these must be given by real people who are familiar with the products, or be obviously stated by actors. If it cites tests, these must be current, used with permission if appropriate, and accurately stated. Finally, any environmental claims must comply with the Guiding Principles developed by the Competition Bureau.

4. How can KCN effectively manage its exposure to legal risk?

KCN is making and selling goods that have significant legal risk exposure, as they are designed for children. Any untoward event has the potential of destroying market confidence in the products. KCN must ensure that it maintains a "safety first" strategy, with all employees buying into this fundamental notion. Likewise, all promotion must be truthful, as well as effective. Maximizing safety and honesty will minimize risk. Using all the resources provided by the relevant federal and provincial governments, Advertising Standards Canada, and the Canadian Standards Association will also assist. Finally, KCN should ensure that it has full insurance coverage.

Chapter Summary

Two parts of the marketing mix that are affected by the law are product and promotion. Compliance with the relevant laws coincides, for the most part, with good marketing practice. Providing reliable and safe products and ensuring that consumers are accurately and fully informed goes a long way toward meeting the important feature of good marketing policy—namely, meeting customer expectations.

Inevitably, however, some market participants disregard these basic principles and will attempt to profit at the customers' expense. If there were no regulations in place, such practices would clearly place "good" producers at a distinct disadvantage. The legislation introduced in this chapter should therefore be recognized for its important goal of ensuring fair competition.

Regulation relating to the product component addresses both the product (or service) itself and its packaging and labelling. The producer must be familiar with voluntary and statutory guidelines for product design and standards. It must be aware of the implied conditions and warranties of the *Sale of Goods Acts*. Product labelling regulation is particularly important where the customer cannot see the goods and there are explicit requirements for disclosure. In promoting goods, the most important regulation is the false and misleading advertising provision of the *Competition Act*. More specific legislative provisions also apply—for example, to tests and testimonials, performance, and environmental claims. Finally, close attention will be paid to any practices that induce purchases through unfair or improper means. Here, both provincial and federal legislation applies.

Study Chapter

Key Terms and Concepts

bait and switch (p. 560)
condition (p. 546)
Canadian Standards Association (p. 544)
caveat emptor (p. 545)
civil track (p. 555)
due diligence (p. 555)
false or misleading advertising (p. 553)
marketing law (p. 543)
prohibited offences (p. 554)
reviewable matters (p. 554)
unfair practices (p. 561)
warranty (p. 546)

Questions for Review

1. What is the relationship between voluntary standards such as those created by the Canadian Standards Association and common law obligations in tort and contract?

2. What are the two different ways the *Hazardous Products Act* regulates inherently dangerous products?

3. What is the primary difference between an implied condition and a warranty in the *Sale of Goods Act*?

4. Give one example of a condition implied by the *Sale of Goods Act* into a contract of sale.

5. Give one example of a change to the *Sale of Goods Act* provisions applying to consumer contracts of sale.

6. What is the broad problem that the *Consumer Packaging and Labelling Act* addresses?

7. There are two separate provisions relating to misleading advertising in the *Competition Act*. What are the critical differences between the two?

8. How could an advertising company defend itself from an accusation of misleading advertising related to a campaign it worked on?

9. What is the due diligence defence, and in what circumstances does it apply?

10. What are the rights of an individual to enforce the misleading advertising provisions of the *Competition Act*?

11. If KCN is investigated for an improper performance claim about its products, what might be its most important defence?

12. What is the general practice related to contests that the Criminal Code seeks to outlaw?

Questions for Discussion

1. If consumer protection legislation equates to good marketing practices, why have legislators gone to such inordinate lengths to pass legislation? Wouldn't basic market forces sort these issues out without state intervention?

2. The common law exposes KCN to extensive potential tort liability. What would be the foundations of a sound risk minimization program for KCN in this regard?

3. The standards relating to children's playground equipment have become somewhat controversial. They are seen as being too cautious and as imposing undue burdens on service providers who might have to replace all equipment. Why might this controversy have arisen? What is the balancing act these provisions attempt to achieve?

4. Compare the details of the regulations in the *Consumer Packaging and Labelling Act* relating to disclosure for prepackaged goods with some of the conditions or warranties that have been provided for many years by the *Sale of Goods Act*. Why is it necessary to provide this extent of detail in the newer legislation?

5. Why does the *Competition Act* not encourage claims by individuals? Is this good policy?

6. Compare and contrast the criminal and civil procedures relating to consumer offences in the *Competition Act*. Which problems were civil track provisions implemented to overcome?

Situations for Discussion

1. The Best Foods Supermarket chain is seeking to gain a marketing edge over its principal competitors. It feels that a "green" approach will encourage consumers to believe that it is socially responsible to shop in its stores. It proposes to concentrate on the packaging of its "own-label" products. Specifically, it wants to reduce its dependency on double packaging materials (typically paper and cardboard) and plastic boxes for produce and delicatessen goods. The marketing team has devised packaging for dry goods products, whereby heavy cellophane

will replace paper and cardboard. For delicatessen and produce, a fibre product (made out of recycled materials) will replace the standard plastic containers.

The marketing team is now finalizing the theme shown below for the advertising campaign.

For those who care
about the future.

The wording "Best Foods goods are always packaged to please Mother Nature because we care about the future for your children and ours" will appear on all ads.

What message is Best Foods selling? Consider all the provisions of the *Competition Act*, including the Guiding Principles related to environmental advertising. Might Best Foods be in violation of some of these provisions? If so, how? What evidence will Best Foods have to produce in order to defend any action taken against it? Who might bring a claim against Best Foods?

2. Hammer and Nails Hardware, a nationwide chain, has devised a new product line. It has discerned a growing niche in the market among new home owners, whom it describes as typically very young and not having much in the way of know-how or basic tools and equipment, and older "empty nesters," who are moving into apartments or condominiums from a home. It has devised a "We meet all your basic ... needs" campaign that prepackages home repair and paint and wallpapering products. It intends to introduce a series of 10 different lines over a six-month period. They will all be boxed in an attractive, consistent style of cardboard packaging that includes "how-to" books. The goods inside will be the basic ones needed (for example, there will be only two styles of screwdriver). The price will reflect the basic quality. Purchasers are either first-time buyers, who will typically replace items over time, or buyers who will use the items infrequently.

Focus on the provisions of the *Consumer Packaging and Labelling Act* and the *Competition Act*. How will these two pieces of legislation affect the Hammer and Nails campaign? What must it do in order to comply with these provisions?

3. Outdoor World sells new and used snowmobiles. It makes most of its money from new products and attempts to move secondhand ones quickly, particularly since the season is relatively short and it doesn't want to be caught with extensive storage costs throughout the summer. Each January it has a major "blowout" sale, which is heavily promoted and provides genuine savings.

   Morley is in the market for a used snowmobile. Since he does not go snowmobiling often, he is anxious to get a good price. He tells the salesperson he wants a basic machine, "no hassles," and as good a deal as he can get. The salesperson shows him three; he starts each one and says that they are roughly equivalent. Morley takes a quick look and picks one basically on colour, since he knows little about any other differentiating qualities. The starting price was $3500, but because Outdoors is anxious to clear the line and Morley is extremely price-sensitive, he is able to bargain down the price to $2000.

   Two days later there is a good snowfall and Morley takes the machine out for a run. On the way home, but still five kilometres out, the snowmobile splutters to a stop. Morley is a competent mechanic, but he can't make it work. In the end, a friend rescues him, and Morley gets the machine towed straight back to Outdoor World.

   What are Morley's rights under the common law? Do the *Sale of Goods Act* warranties and conditions help? Do Morley's rights vary according to the province the sale occurred in?

4. Huge Electronics sells a full range of home entertainment systems. Recently, it has extended its product line into computers. It sells "packages" that are put together by major manufacturers and designed to meet basic consumer needs. The systems are such that the basic, stripped-down package, while doing most things required of it for the average user, provides the seller with little markup. It is with the middle- and high-priced lines that Huge makes its money. The market is highly competitive, and Huge is always looking for an edge over its competitors. Two-thirds of computer packages are sold in the summer months as "back-to-school" specials.

   Huge salespeople work on commission. The incentive scheme is consistent with profit margins, so there is a far greater commission "reward" for selling higher-priced computer packages. Furthermore, Huge does not carry extensive stock in the low price range, as it simply does not feel it is worth its while to do so. Nonetheless, these products are an important part of its advertising campaign, as the low prices get the customers in the door. Huge ensures that its low-price-range computers are priced sufficiently lower than those of its competitors in order to be attractive. Once consumers are in the store, they are encouraged to buy a system that "better meets their needs," and typically this pitch works.

   The Competition Bureau has received complaints about Huge's marketing practices and is now investigating. What might the problem be with this marketing strategy? What kind of conduct might this be considered to be? Can Huge use any defences? If so, how and what kind? What will be the likely outcome? What might Huge do differently to avoid this problem?

5. Softest Diapers is one of two leading producers of diapers for infants. It has spent several years researching and testing a new brand of super-absorbent diaper. It is now devising an advertising campaign that will make direct comparison with its competitor's products. The marketing team has spent months comparing the two lines of products and genuinely believes that the new Softest diapers absorb significantly more moisture than do the equivalently priced products of the competitor. They have asked the scientists to confirm their

results, and after several months of testing, the scientists report that there is, on average, a 10 percent increase in absorbency. The campaign materials are as follows:

This is the first breakthrough in diaper science for several years, and the campaign is an immediate success. The competitor, recognizing the threat, immediately seeks an injunction to stop this campaign under the provisions of section 36 of the *Competition Act*. What provisions of the Act and what arguments will the competitor rely upon? What will Softest use in its defence? What is the likely outcome?

THIS FAMILY HAS DISCOVERED

new *Softest* **Diapers**

....10 percent* more absorbent than those of the leading competitor.

* on average under simulated use conditions

6. Better Booksellers, a major international bookseller, has a new promotional scheme. It knows that if it can get purchasers in the door to buy one book, they frequently will buy several others. The new promotion centres around a competition. Specifically, if a customer buys a first book, he or she has a one-in-two chance of winning one other (lower price) book free. There is a massive advertising campaign promoting this contest in the six weeks leading up to Christmas. It immediately works just as the managers expected: there is an increase in customers over normal patterns, and, on average, each customer buys an additional three books. Better Booksellers finds it hard to keep track of the "one-in-two" aspect of the contest, but it is confident that there is a good proportion of customers receiving free books when they present their winning tickets.

What legislation affects this scheme? Are there aspects of the scheme that might get Better Booksellers into trouble? What should Better Booksellers do in order to avoid these problems? Why is there legislative concern about this kind of contest?

Twenty-Five

Marketing Practices: Price and Distribution

Objectives

AFTER STUDYING THIS CHAPTER, YOU SHOULD HAVE AN
UNDERSTANDING OF:

► THE LEGAL OBLIGATIONS ASSOCIATED WITH THE PRICE
COMPONENT OF THE MARKETING MIX
► THE LEGAL OBLIGATIONS ASSOCIATED WITH THE
DISTRIBUTION (PLACE) COMPONENT OF THE MARKETING MIX
► THE ROLE OF CORPORATE COMPLIANCE PROGRAMS

Business Law in Practice

Lighting Beautiful Inc. (Lighting) is a Mississauga-based company that imports and
distributes lights and other decorative goods for homes and gardens throughout
Canada. It has been in business for a number of years and dominates its market. It
sells through retailers, primarily those with high-volume business. It has two principal selling periods: the spring/summer season, when people are buying products
for their decks and gardens, and the period leading up to Christmas, when
Christmas lights are a major consumer item. All goods are manufactured offshore

but are made to meet Canadian standards. Lighting has never had a problem with either product quality or labelling. However, in the last few years some major changes in the retail market in Canada have exerted pressure on Lighting's pricing and distribution policies.

Steve, the head of sales, has reported that some retailers are engaging in ruthless competitive practices, and he is worried that Lighting is being challenged to cross the line of legality in what it does. In particular, there is a new, aggressive market participant asking for terms and conditions that would give it a distinct advantage over long-established competitors. The most recent demand has been for a higher discount and longer payment terms. Furthermore, Steve is concerned about the way this new market participant promotes Lighting products, and he is considering imposing restrictions on retailers, although he is not sure how legal such action would be. He is anxious to stop the product line being used as a loss leader and proposes to place a "recommended retail price" sticker on the packaging.

In-store promotions are the primary method of communicating price to the customer.

Lighting has recently hired a new distribution manager, Gerry, who needs guidance. Gerry is not sure whether Lighting's insurance coverage for lost or damaged goods is adequate, considering its recently revised shipping practices. She also has concerns that staff are inadequately trained in basic shipping practices and terminology. She has talked to Steve, and they have agreed to put together new guidelines for sales and shipping staff.

1. How does the law affect Lighting's pricing strategy?
2. How does the law affect Lighting's distribution strategy?
3. What topics should be included in the new guidelines for sales and shipping staff?

Price

Generally, price is freely negotiated when forming a contract.[1] Parties settle on a sum that is as much or as little as they can agree on. For the most part, the legal regulation of price is directed toward pricing practices that will create an unfair or uneven playing field between market participants, thus destroying competition, or treat consumer purchasers unfairly. Regulations aim to protect the right to set prices freely.

In reviewing the relevant issues surrounding pricing, it is useful to separate pricing between producer and seller from pricing between seller (including, at times, producer) and consumer. Furthermore, it will continue to be important, when discussing provisions found in the *Competition Act*,[2] to remember the distinction

---

1. Note that prices in a few industries in Canada continue to be regulated by government or government agencies or are subject to regulatory bodies that set prices between producers/growers and users—for example, utilities and agricultural marketing boards.

between prohibited offences and reviewable matters explained in Chapter 24. In broad terms, prohibited offences, which are criminal in nature, are more serious, are referred to the Attorney General for prosecution, and are more difficult to prove because of the higher burden of proof necessitated by the more serious consequences of a guilty verdict. Reviewable matters, if not resolved by voluntary agreement, may result in a remedial order from a judge of the Competition Tribunal.

Pricing Practices between Producer and Commercial Purchaser

The federal *Competition Act* prohibits unfair pricing practices, including those involving the producer and its (commercial) purchaser. An important policy objective of the legislation is to create a level playing field with respect to **channel power**—that is, the respective powers members of the marketing or distribution channel may exert over one another. The Act seeks to ensure that commercial customers are not subject to unfair differential treatment that could seriously reduce competition in the marketplace.

channel power
The ability of one member of the marketing or distribution channel to influence another.

The *Competition Act* defines many pricing practices as criminal in nature. While it is possible that a business can "inadvertently" commit illegal acts, it is far more likely that these offences are the actions of aberrant participants acting knowingly or with willful ignorance. Offences committed under the following provisions have to be put in perspective. Most individuals and most businesses do not commit serious criminal acts. Nonetheless, it is important to understand the scope of the law and the protection it provides businesses.

Pricing Conspiracies

One of the most obvious ways for business to manipulate a market is through conspiring with direct competitors to control prices. For example, assume there are only three suppliers of light bulbs from which Lighting can purchase. Lighting observes that all three suppliers quote equivalent prices for equivalent orders. There are certainly innocent explanations for this practice. Each supplier likely faces similar costs, and all three may have similar profit expectations. It could also be the case, however, that this is part of a conspiracy to control the cost of bulbs to major producers such as Lighting. If this can be proven, the bulb suppliers will be guilty of a criminal offence under section 45 of the *Competition Act*.

Section 45 is a broad provision that addresses more than simply pricing conspiracies. It proscribes the practices that were the original focus of anti-trust legislation in Canada and elsewhere:

> 45. (1) Every one who conspires, combines, agrees or arranges with another person
>
> > (a) to limit unduly the facilities for transporting, producing, manufacturing, supplying, storing or dealing in any product,
> > (b) to prevent, limit or lessen, unduly, the manufacture or production of a product or to enhance unreasonably the price thereof,
> > (c) to prevent or lessen, unduly, competition in the production, manufacture, purchase, barter, sale, storage, rental, transportation or supply of a product, or in the price of insurance on persons or property, or

2. R.S.C. 1985, c. C-34, s. 45.

(d) to otherwise restrain or injure competition unduly, is guilty of an indictable offence and liable to imprisonment for a term not exceeding five years or to a fine not exceeding ten million dollars or to both.

For a criminal offence to be proven, it must be established not only that there was an agreement or a conspiracy to set prices (in this case), but also that this agreement unduly lessened competition.

R. v. Nova Scotia Pharmaceutical Society et al.

The Nova Scotia Pharmaceutical Society argued that the term "unduly" in section 45 of the *Competition Act* violated the provisions of the *Canadian Charter of Rights and Freedoms* because of its vagueness. In reaching its decision that the provision did not violate the *Charter*, the Supreme Court of Canada considered the history of this provision and what is required in order to find a conspiracy under it. Specifically, it identified the *Competition Act* as a "central and established feature of Canadian economic policy" and the prohibition against conspiracies in restraint of trade as "the epitome of competition law" in Canada and elsewhere.

The court examined the two elements for proof of "unduly" lessening competition:

1. *The structure of the market.* What is the degree of market power of the parties to the conspiracy agreement? Here, the court identified a nonexhaustive list of factors as relevant:

   1. the number of competitors and the concentration of competition, 2. barriers to entry 3. geographical distribution of buyers and sellers, 4. differences in the degree of integration among competitors, 5. product differentiation, 6. countervailing power, and 7. cross-elasticity of demand.

   It must be proven that, by means of such factors, the parties can behave independently of the market and free competition will no longer exist.

2. *The behaviour of the parties.* Specifically, there must be some behaviour—for example, an agreement to fix prices or market share—that, in combination with the market power, would be likely to injure competition. The term "unduly" is used to connote the requisite seriousness.

How is the conspiracy or agreement proven? First, it must be established that there was an intention to enter into the agreement and knowledge of its terms. From this, it would ordinarily be reasonable to infer that the accused intended to carry out the agreement, unless there is evidence to the contrary. Second, it must be established that the effect of the agreement will be to prevent competition or to lessen it unduly. It is sufficient then to establish that a reasonable business person would or should have known that this was the likely effect of the agreement.

Critical Analysis: In the trial following this case,[3] the court found that the pharmacies had entered into an agreement that unduly lessened competition but that there was insufficient evidence that the accused would or should have been aware that the agreement had that effect. What are the practical obstacles to proving this offence?

Source: *R. v. Nova Scotia Pharmaceutical Society et al.,* [1992] 2 S.C.R. 606.

---

3. *R. v. Nova Scotia Pharmaceutical Society et al.,* [1992] 2 S.C.R. 606.

Convictions under section 45 are common, mostly as a consequence of guilty pleas. Fines can be heavy, as in the following example: [4]

- Following the exposure of the international conspiracy by Archer Daniels Midland and others to fix prices and allocate markets for lysine (1998) and citric acid (1998–99), fines (following guilty pleas) of $17 570 000 and $9 575 000, respectively, were levied by the Federal Court of Canada.
- In 1999 seven companies and two individuals pleaded guilty to involvement in an international cartel to fix prices and allocate markets for bulk vitamins and were fined $91 125 000 in Canada.

If the conspiracy is considered sufficiently serious, violators can be incarcerated. In two cases since 1996, jail sentences of up to one year have been imposed.[5]

If the conspiracy or agreement is entered into outside of Canada but implemented within Canada on the directive of those outside, a criminal offence will be committed, even if those implementing the agreement have no knowledge of it.[6]

Price Discrimination

price discrimination
The offence of failing to provide similar pricing terms and conditions to competing wholesalers or retailers for equivalent volume sales at an equivalent time.

Price discrimination[7] is the practice of failing to provide similar pricing terms and conditions to competitors for equivalent volume sales at an equivalent time. This situation may arise either because a producer, unsolicited, offers discriminatory prices, or, more commonly, because the producer responds to a customer's pressure tactics. The producer may see this as the only way of maintaining its position in the market.

For example, ABC Discounter has a strategy of attaining rapid market penetration in Canada by taking market share away from XYZ Discounter, an established player in the market. It has identified certain products that it will discount and is applying pressure to manufacturers to sell to it at significantly lower prices and allow longer payment terms than it would to XYZ. Lighting Beautiful Inc., believing it has little choice, is prepared to accommodate ABC.

Price discrimination between genuine competitors is a criminal offence under section 50 of the *Competition Act*, since it can destroy or restrict competition. In practice, convictions have been rare under this provision because of the difficulty of overcoming the criminal burden of proof. Nonetheless, the bureau reports "many" requests for advice and interpretation and considers this to be evidence of the business community's desire to comply with the law.[8]

What is the difference between legitimate discounts that may vary among customers and illegal discrimination? Differential discounts are legal provided it can be shown that customers who were prepared to purchase under equivalent conditions were offered the same terms. Any differences must be a direct reflection of cost differentials, say, in terms of volume or delivery.

---

4. Harry Chandler, Deputy Commissioner of Competition, Criminal Matters, & Robert Jackson, *Beyond Merriment and Diversion: The Treatment of Conspiracies under Canada's Competition Act* (Toronto: Competition Bureau, 25 May 2000).

5. *Ibid. (Sherbrooke Driving Schools* case 1996 and 1997; *Chlorine Chloride* case 1999).

6. *Competition Act, supra* note 2, s. 46. Note that other examples of conspiracies can be found in s. 47 (bid rigging), s. 48 (conspiracies relating to professional sports), and s. 49 (conspiracies among federal financial institutions).

7. *Ibid.,* s. 50(1)(a). See also Director of Investigation and Research, Bureau of Competition Policy, Consumer and Corporate Affairs Canada, *Price Discrimination Enforcement Guidelines* (Hull, Que.: 17 August 1992).

8. There have been only three convictions in the entire history of the provision. All were noncontested, and fines ranged from $15 000 to $50 000. *Ibid.*, Part 1.4.

It should be noted that in cases of price discrimination, the buyer is considered as culpable as the seller. If Lighting bends to ABC's demands, both risk prosecution if XYZ becomes aware of Lighting's actions and reports them to the Competition Bureau.

Predatory Pricing

predatory pricing
The offence of setting unreasonably low prices to eliminate competition.

Predatory pricing[9] occurs when the seller sets prices unreasonably low with the intent of driving out a competitor. This offence can be committed at different levels of the distribution chain.

Predatory pricing is a criminal offence under the *Competition Act*. To attain a conviction, it must be shown that prices are unreasonably low and that they effectively reduced competition. Because of this burden of proof, relatively few charges have ever been brought. As an alternative to criminal prosecution, the Competition Bureau now also refers complaints under the reviewable anti-competitive behaviour provision of section 79 to the Competition Tribunal. The tribunal applies the civil burden of proof and has the authority to make orders preventing or stopping the particular behaviour. Should such orders be ignored, penalties could be imposed. Today, the threat of the civil, reviewable provisions may well lead to a voluntary agreement between the offending party and the bureau.

The Competition Bureau uses a two-step approach to evaluate predatory pricing practices:

1. Does the alleged predator have the ability unilaterally to affect industry pricing?
2. Will that dominant position or power be used to recoup the losses incurred during the period of predatory pricing, once the competitor is gone?

What amounts to "unreasonably low prices" and predatory effect is seldom clear-cut. Most intervention by the Competition Bureau follows complaints made by competitors[10] or concerned suppliers, such as Lighting. ABC Discounting may be committing the offence of predatory pricing if it can be shown that ABC's dominant position will affect pricing and that, if the practice reduces competition, ABC will likely recoup losses by subsequently raising prices.

Price Maintenance

price maintenance
The offence of attempting to drive the final retail price of goods upward and imposing recriminations upon noncompliant retailers.

The producer can commit the criminal offence known as **price maintenance** by attempting to drive upwards the final retail price at which its goods are sold to the public. The producer might commit this offence by exerting pressure on the retailer/customer, placing notice on the goods themselves, or combining both practices.

For example, because of its increasing concern that widely advertised sales of its products will damage product image, Lighting instructs sales staff to advise retailers to cease dropping prices, and to monitor their compliance. Lighting also begins to print on the packaging the "recommended retail price." Any retailer selling below this price will be refused supplies.

Two aspects of this strategy are illegal:[11] the attempt to influence the final retail price *upwards* and the recriminations against noncompliant retailers. Both attempt to prevent competition and to discipline the marketplace. Lighting can use the words

---

9. *Competition Act, supra* note 2, s. 50(1)(c). See also Director of Investigation and Research, Bureau of Competition Policy, Consumer and Corporate Affairs Canada, *Predatory Pricing Enforcement Guidelines* (Hull, Que.: 17 August 1992).

10. Competitors can also bring civil actions under the *Competition Act, supra* note 2, s. 36.

11. *Ibid.,* s. 61.

"recommended retail price," provided this statement determines only maximum and not minimum prices.

Lighting does have a defence here. It can refuse to sell to retailers who are selling at unreasonably low prices, provided it can show that the retailers were using its products in any of the following ways:

- as loss leaders (typically, below actual purchase price)
- for bait-and-switch selling
- in misleading advertising
- in sales, where they fail to provide a reasonable level of service

Bid Rigging

bid rigging
Conspiring to fix the bidding process to suit the collective needs of the producers suppliers.

Bid rigging is a specialized form of conspiracy by producers/suppliers to manipulate a market through price.[12] **Bid rigging** occurs when suppliers conspire to "fix" the bidding process in a manner that suits their collective needs or wishes. It is a serious criminal offence, since it attacks the heart of the competitive process. Penalties include fines and/or up to five years' imprisonment. The most usual forms of bid-rigging are as follows:

- *Cover bidding* gives the impression of competitive bidding; in reality, suppliers have agreed to submit token bids that are usually too high.
- *Bid suppression* is an agreement among suppliers to either abstain from bidding or withdraw bids.
- *Bid rotation* is a process whereby the preselected supplier submits the lowest bid on a systematic or rotating basis.
- *Market division* is an agreement among suppliers not to compete in designated geographic regions or for specific customers.[13]

Certificate of Independent Bid Determination

Anyone calling for bids, tenders, or quotations can require the Certificate of Independent Bid Determination. This certificate, developed by the Competition Bureau, can deter bid rigging by requiring bidders to disclose all material facts about any communications and arrangements they have entered into with competitors regarding the tender call. Specifically, the bidder must certify that it has

- arrived at the bid "independently from and without consultation, communications agreement or arrangement with, any competitor" about any relevant factor

BUSINESS APPLICATION OF THE LAW

- not engaged in any "consultations, communications, agreements or arrangements with one or more competitors regarding this call for bids," other than those disclosed in the certificate
- not knowingly disclosed "directly or indirectly, to any competitor, prior to the date and time of the official bid opening, or of the awarding of the contract," the terms of the bid (other than if described in the certificate)

Critical Analysis: In practice, how effective will this requirement be in preventing bid rigging?

12. *Ibid*, s. 47.

13. Director of Investigation and Research, Bureau of Competition Policy, Consumer and Corporate Affairs Canada, *Bid-Rigging*, pamphlet (Hull, Que.: Competition Bureau, 2 June 1999).

Bid-rigging prosecutions are not uncommon. For example, suppliers of bulk compressed gases to hospitals and medical centres across Canada pleaded guilty to controlling the selling price of gases for many years through bid rigging.[14] The Competition Bureau reports fines for bid-rigging offences totalling approximately $9 million since 1980.[15]

Protection for Whistle Blowers

Successful criminal prosecutions under trade practices legislation typically depend on the willingness of members of offending businesses to come forward with evidence of criminal activity and testify in court. The standard term for such people is "whistle blowers," since they are reporting information about improper practices that is secret and would otherwise remain unknown.

Whistle blowing is often presented in the press or entertainment business as a noble or heroic activity. After Roger Boisjoly exposed the defective O-rings connecting segments of Morton Thiokol's solid rocket booster, a defect that resulted in the crash of the *Challenger* in 1986—he became an important public speaker in this field. Similarly, the employee of Pacific Gas & Electric Co. who "blew the whistle" on the employer, leading to successful litigation against the company by Erin Brokovitch and others, was presented as a hero in a movie of the events.

Whistle blowing, however, carries with it inevitable risks. Employers may go to extraordinary efforts to suppress information and effect retribution. Increasingly, there is recognition that since the public very often depends on the efforts of whistle blowers, such persons should receive protection. At the same time, there are the inevitable cases of whistle blowers being either disaffected employees seeking vengeance or misguided employees lacking the perspective to understand the true nature of the employer's activity. In other words, not all information brought forward by a whistle blower is neces-

ETHICAL CONSIDERATIONS

sarily evidence of wrongful acts, and its disclosure can be very harmful to the employer.

Regulators, such as officers of the Competition Bureau, who rely on whistle blowers must screen information carefully. When there is substance to the accusations, traditionally, regulators have entered into informal arrangements or plea bargains whereby, for example, if the whistle blower was a participant in a conspiracy or other criminal offence, lesser charges will be brought against the informer or a lesser penalty will be sought. For individuals who are not the subject of prosecution themselves, this arrangement is obviously ineffective. Moreover, it is no protection against, for example, dismissal from employment.

Section 66 of the *Competition Act* now provides basic protection for these individuals. The Act protects the confidentiality for whistle blowers (employees and independent contractors) who supply information. Should they be required to testify, this confidentiality cannot be maintained; however, simply providing the evidence at the investigative stage often leads to a guilty plea. The Act also provides protection from reprisals, such as dismissal or other adverse employment-related action, against any employee who supplies evidence acting in good faith. It is an offence for an employer to violate this provision.

Critical Analysis: How adequate is this protection? Why are the words "in good faith" used here?

---

14. *North York Branson Hospital* v. *Praxair Canada Inc.* (1998), 84 C.P.R. (3d) 12 (Ont. Ct. (Gen. Div.)).
15. Chandler & Jackson, *supra* note 4.

Pricing Practices between Seller and Consumer

The main protection for consumers is through the civil and criminal misleading advertising offences (see Chapter 24). This section addresses more specific provisions.

Sale or Bargain Prices

If goods are promoted as bargains, how do consumers tell what their real price is? Generally, it is a reviewable offence for the seller to state that a price is less than the ordinary price ("on sale," "reduced," "clearance") when it is not.[16] An advertiser may legitimately claim a price to be the **ordinary price** if:

> [it] reflects the price at which suppliers generally in the relevant market area have either:
> - sold a substantial volume of the product within a reasonable period of time before or after making the representation *(volume test)* or
> - offered the product for sale in good faith for a substantial period of time recently before or immediately after making the representation *(time test)*.[17]

ordinary price
The price at which goods are normally sold in a given market at specified volumes and in a given period.

Both the volume test and time test are applied according to specific guidelines established by the Competition Bureau.[18] Any review by the Competition Bureau requires the supply of extensive sales data for the entire relevant market. Placing a restriction to the promise in small print on the advertisement is no protection if the overall impression remains misleading.

When does stating that prices are "subject to error" protect the advertiser? Generally, such a clause provides protection only in the context of catalogue sales, since catalogues are not printed regularly and some protection is reasonable for the seller. However, because this is a reviewable offence, the due diligence defence applies, and the promoter should always correct errors quickly and in a manner consistent with the original promotion.

Double Ticketing

Sellers can commit pricing offences in their direct contact with the customer. For example, if there are two or more prices on goods, the product must be sold at the lower of those prices. To do otherwise amounts to the (criminal) offence of **double ticketing**.[19] Obligations extend to in-store promotions and displays, as well as prices listed in store computers. If goods are obviously misplaced and the seller can prove it has taken reasonable steps to prevent such an occurrence, likely the goods do not have to be sold at the reduced price. If consumers intentionally move the goods (or change pricing labels), they themselves are likely committing fraud.

double ticketing
The offence of failing to sell at the lower of the two prices appearing on a product.

The Competition Bureau is particularly concerned about differentials between prices posted on store shelves and those stored in automatic price-scanning systems, since it is easy for customers to fail to notice an increased price at the checkout.

---

16. *Competition Act, supra* note 2, s. 74.01(2), 74.01(3), and 74.1(1); Director of Investigation and Research, Bureau of Competition Policy, Consumer and Corporate Affairs Canada, *Ordinary Price Claims,* information bulletin (Hull, Que.: Competition Bureau, 22 September 1999).

17. *Competition Act, ibid.,* s. 74.01(2), 74.01(3), and 74.1(1).

18. *Ordinary Price Claims, supra* note 16.

19. *Competition Act, supra* note 2, s. 54(1).

Distribution (Place)

Distribution is defined in a leading marketing text as "focus[ing] on the decisions and actions involved in making products available to consumers when and where they want to purchase them. Choosing which channels of distribution to use is a major decision in the development of marketing strategies."[20]

Distribution includes the process of ensuring that goods get into the customers' hands—that is, shipping and transportation. Distribution decisions also determine whether goods will be sold by retailers, wholesalers, door-to-door salespeople, or e-commerce vendors. How corporations are structured, including merger decisions resulting in horizontal or vertical integration, is part of the broad notion of distribution.

Organizational Structure

Typically, businesses are free to structure themselves in a manner that best meets their needs. However, if competition is adversely affected, particularly through mergers, acquisitions, or takeovers, regulators may step in.

Mergers, Acquisitions, and Takeovers

In Canada it has always been recognized that there is a fine line between allowing business to expand through merger, acquisition, or takeover in order to operate profitably in what is a relatively small market, and avoiding the negative consequences of what might through these processes become harmful, monopolistic behaviour.

The *Competition Act* sets out the conditions under which the bureau can seek an order ending a proposed or actual merger. A merger is the union of two or more companies to form one larger company. The critical question in each case is "whether the tribunal finds that a merger or proposed merger prevents or lessens, or is likely to prevent or lessen, competition substantially."[21] What is considered "substantial" is described by the bureau in its guidelines as follows:

> In general, a prevention or lessening of competition will be considered to be "substantial" where the price of the relevant product is likely to be materially greater, in a substantial part of the relevant market, than it would be in the absence of the merger, and where this price differential would not likely be eliminated within two years by new or increased competition from foreign or domestic sources. What constitutes a "materially greater" price varies from industry to industry, and may be a differential that is less than the "significant" price increase that is postulated for the purpose of market definition.[22]

The *Competition Act* recognizes the complexity of examining mergers and has a notification requirement for large proposed mergers. Here, the businesses proposing the merger must notify the director of their intentions prior to the merger; within a specified time, they will be provided with a determination as to whether the director considers that the merger will substantially prevent or lessen competition.

---

20. W.M. Pride, O.C. Ferrell, H.F. MacKenzie & K. Snow, *Marketing: Concepts and Strategies,* Can. ed. (Scarborough: ITP Nelson, 1998) at 299.

21. *Competition Act, supra* note 2, s. 92(1).

22. *Merger Enforcement Guidelines* (Hull, Que.: Competition Bureau, 24 January 1997).

Multilevel and Pyramid Selling[23]

multilevel marketing
A scheme for distributing products or services that involves participants supplying them to other participants to earn a profit.

Multilevel marketing plans arise through what are known as distributorships. Income is earned through commissions to distributors, and fees are paid upwards to those creating the schemes.

Multilevel marketing or selling can be either entirely legitimate or illegal. The legitimacy of the activity will be determined by such factors as whether there is a genuine selling opportunity for those buying distributorships in the plan; whether the goal of each distributorship is truly the selling of actual goods or services or, rather, primarily channelling monies back up the chain; and whether there is a realistic opportunity for distributorships to expand. If a genuine business activity cannot be seen to exist, the multilevel selling scheme is likely illegal. Such schemes are inherently unstable, and inevitably those joining at the late stages receive little or no value as the scheme collapses for lack of new participants.

Legal multilevel selling schemes are the subject of regulation, in particular, relating to disclosure. There must be "fair, reasonable and timely disclosure" of earnings or expected earnings.[24]

pyramid selling
An illegal form of multilevel selling under the *Competition Act*.

Pyramid selling is illegal. It is a criminal act under the provisions of the *Competition Act* if

- participants pay money for the right to receive compensation for recruiting new participants;
- a participant is required to buy a specific quantity of products, other than at cost price for the purpose of advertising before the participant is allowed to join the plan or advance within the plan;
- participants are knowingly sold commercially unreasonable quantities of the product or products (this practice is called inventory loading); or
- participants are not allowed to return products on reasonable commercial terms.[25]

Case

R. v. Partridge (1996), 32 W.C.B. (2d) 259 (Sask. C.A.)

The Business Context: A business person accused of conducting a pyramid marketing scheme must establish that what is involved is a genuine commercial exchange. Where multiple sales levels exist and goods are sold vastly in excess of their true value, proof of legitimacy is difficult to establish.

Factual Background: The scheme under investigation involved the purchase and sale of travel vouchers. The travel vouchers had little or no real value for sale purposes. A person purchased a packet of travel vouchers for $500 but knew that the broker selling it had paid only $62.50. It was found that the person purchased the packet not to acquire and use the vouchers, but only to become a seller of packets and benefit from the markup when selling to new participants. There was no evidence that any participant had ever used the travel vouchers or knew anyone else who had.

The Legal Question: Was this a legitimate selling venture or a pyramid scheme prohibited by law?

Resolution: The court found the scheme to be illegal:

The ostensible purpose of the scheme, multi-level marketing of travel vouchers, was a mere sham or window dressing designed to conceal the true purpose of the scheme, namely eventual receipt by a participant of a sum of money larger than that he paid in by reason of payments into the scheme by new recruits.

Critical Analysis: How should legitimate businesses operate in order to avoid being accused of conducting a pyramid scheme?

---

23. *Competition Act, supra* note 2, ss. 55, 55.1. Also *Franchises Act*, S.A. 1995, c. F-17.1 (Alta); *Pyramid Franchises Act*, R.S.S. 1978, c. P-50 (Sask.); *Consumer Protection Act*, c. P-40.1 (Que); *Criminal Code*, R.S.C. 1985, C. c-46, s. 206(1)(e).
24. *Competition Act, supra* note 2, s. 55(2).
25. Director of Investigation and Research, Bureau of Competition Policy, Consumer and Corporate Affairs Canada *Pyramid Selling and Multi-level Marketing Schemes,* pamphlet (Hull, Que.: Competition Bureau) 2 June, 1999).

For businesses, it is essential that any multilevel marketing scheme comply with the provisions of the *Competition Act*. The very term *pyramid selling* carries serious negative connotations. Even an accusation that this is the basis of the distribution scheme will be extremely damaging.

Discriminatory Distribution Practices

Producers may discriminate unfairly between customers through distribution policies as well as pricing practices. The consequence in either case is the same: the practice reduces or eliminates competition.

Many practices that discriminate in this way are reviewable matters.[26] The Competition Bureau will investigate the activity and, if it believes an offence is being committed, seek a remedial order. These offences are best illustrated through practical examples.

EXAMPLE 1

Lighting supplies one dominant brand of outdoor lights. All major discount retailers are using these as a means of attracting customers. XYZ finds that Lighting will not supply it with the lights, even though XYZ is willing and able to meet the same conditions of sale as ABC.

refusal to deal
Conduct that is reviewable under the *Competition Act* because the seller refuses to sell to a purchaser even under comparable conditions to the purchaser's competitor.

This practice likely falls within the definition of **refusal to deal**[27] and will be reviewable provided that it is "substantially" affecting XYZ, that XYZ is willing to meet the usual trade terms offered to ABC, and that Lighting has an adequate supply of the lights that it refuses to provide.

EXAMPLE 2

Lighting is owned by Electric Supplies Inc. Lighting tells ABC that it will supply lights to it only if ABC buys from no other lighting supplier and also buys all other electrical supplies from Electric Supplies.

exclusive dealing
Conduct that is reviewable under the *Competition Act* because the seller agrees to sell to the purchaser only if the purchaser buys from it exclusively.

If this practice lessens competition substantially, it falls within the definition of **exclusive dealing**[28] and is therefore reviewable.

EXAMPLE 3

Lighting advises XYZ that it will supply the "hottest" lighting product of the holiday season only if XYZ also buys a number of less popular products both from it and from Electric Supply, and refrains from buying from any competitor.

tied selling
Conduct that is reviewable under the *Competition Act* because the seller will sell to the purchaser only if the purchaser buys other, less desirable goods as well.

This practice may be **tied selling**[29] and is reviewable provided, again, that the action lessens competition substantially.

---

26. *Competition Act, supra* note 2, s. 75-107.
27. *Ibid,,* s. 75(1).
28. *Ibid.,* s. 77(1)(2).
29. *Ibid.*

EXAMPLE 4

Lighting considers adopting the following practices:

- dropping prices significantly to prevent Bright Lights from expanding in the market; Bright Lights does not have the same benefits of vertical integration as does Lighting
- buying D & E Hardware Chain, Bright Lights' major customer, in order to squeeze Bright Lights out of the market

These practices may be reviewable as **anti-competitive behaviour**.[30]

Direct Marketing

Direct marketing is "the use of the telephone and nonpersonal media to communicate product and organizational information to customers, who then can purchase products by mail, e-mail, or telephone. Direct marketing can occur through catalogue marketing, direct-response marketing, telemarketing, home shopping, and on-line marketing."[31]

Regulators traditionally focused on door-to-door sellers, but over time, legislators began to look for ways to protect consumers from intrusion by other means. The 1999 amendments to the *Competition Act* addressed telemarketing specifically for the first time. Online shopping remains regulated by more general provisions in the *Competition Act*, such as those related to promotion and pricing.

Door-to-Door Selling

Regulation in the area of **door-to-door selling** focuses on protecting consumers from untoward pressure and on allowing them the chance for second thought and the opportunity to cancel the sale.

Door-to-door selling is regulated provincially under consumer protection legislation.[32] Typically, legislation requires

- those selling door-to-door to be licensed
- contracts in excess of a certain dollar figure to be in writing and to disclose specific matters
- consumers who sign a contract to be allowed a "cooling off" period[33] during which they may cancel the contract

Direct-Response Marketing

Direct-response marketing is any form of marketing where the retailer "advertises a product and makes it available though mail or telephone orders."[34] This approach is regulated by consumer protection legislation (described under Promotion in Chapter 24). Marketing through mail-order catalogues is a common form of direct-response marketing.

---

anti-competitive behaviour
Conduct that restricts competition and is reviewable under the *Competition Act*.

direct marketing
Using the telephone and nonpersonal media to communicate product information to customers.

door-to-door selling
The act of selling in person directly to a customer's residence.

direct-response marketing
Advertising a product to be made available through mail or telephone orders.

---

30. *Ibid.*, s. 78.
31. Pride, Ferrell, MacKenzie & Snow, *supra* note 20 at 355.
32. For example, *Fair Trading Act*, S.A. 1998, c. F-1.05; *Direct Sellers' Licensing Act*, R.S.N.S. 1989, c. 129.
33. In Alberta and Nova Scotia, 10 days; see *Fair Trading Act*, ibid., s. 27 and *Direct Sellers' Licensing Act*, ibid., s. 20(1)(g).
34. Pride, Ferrell, MacKenzie & Snow, *supra* note 20 at 355.

Telemarketing

telemarketing
The use of telephone to communicate product and organizational information to customers.

Marketers typically define **telemarketing**[35] as including both *inbound* sales calls, such as those included in direct-response marketing above, and *outbound* calls, where the focus is on unsolicited calls to consumers in their homes.

Regulation is similar to that affecting door-to-door sellers. It protects the consumer from high-pressure tactics. Basic information about the vendor and the product must be disclosed, and deceptive practices are defined as offences. The regulations apply to any "interactive telephone communication" but do not extend to fax, Internet communications, or automated, prerecorded messages.

Home-Shopping Networks

Shop-at-home television networks are governed by consumer protection legislation and are regulated by the *Broadcasting Act*[36] and the Canadian Radio-television and Telecommunications Commission, an independent government agency that regulates radio, television, specialty services, cable television, and pay television.

Online Retailing

Internet selling is the fastest-growing area of retailing. To date, however, regulation is limited primarily to general consumer protection provisions in the *Competition Act* and elsewhere that affect all sales of goods and services. Marketers and their industry organizations are instituting means—often through contract law—of gaining the trust of prospective purchasers. For example, sellers may guarantee that consumers can return goods at no cost if the goods do not meet expectations. Consumers, however, have few protections against fraudulent sellers beyond phoning the police.

Regulation of Online Retailing

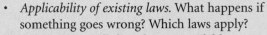

Consumers are often reluctant to buy through e-commerce because of the following concerns:

- *Identity of the business.* Web sites come and go, and the location of the vendor is often unknown. Consumers tend to favour well-known brands and companies at the expense of smaller, less familiar businesses.
- *Privacy and personal information.* Private information supplied by consumers may become a resource that other marketers use and abuse.
- *Security.* How effective are the current encryption devices in protecting financial information?

- *Applicability of existing laws.* What happens if something goes wrong? Which laws apply? Will there be any available redress?

The Government of Canada proposes to address these issues through the following means:
- *Establishing principles for protecting e-commerce customers.* These will be established by both industry groups and governments. For example, a group of interested parties (industry groups, consumers, and government) is currently working to create a framework of principles upon which e-commerce will be based. The OECD is working on a comparable set of principles relating to

---

35. *Competition Act, supra* note 2 s. 52.1.
36. S.C. 1991, c. 11.

online advertising. Different industry groups have already established guidelines and codes. The Canadian Marketing Association has amended its codes of ethics and standards of practice to address issues of consumer consent. The Canadian Association of Internet Providers (CAIP) has a new voluntary code of conduct. There already are third-party seal programs, such as the CA WebTrust program created in 1997 by the Canadian Institute of Chartered Accountants and the American Institute of Public Accountants. This program provides an electronic "seal of assurance" signifying that a commercial Web site complies with specific practices and standards.

- *Applying provisions of the* Competition Act. The *Competition Act* provisions concerning anti-competitive practices already apply to Web sites, cybermalls, electronic bulletin boards where advertisements may be posted, banner ads in browser programs and search engines, and the use of e-mail.

    Section 52.(1.2) of the *Competition Act*, which refers to permitting a representation to be made, likely applies to third parties such as Web page designers, proprietors of cybermalls, proprietors of electronic bulletin boards, and Internet service providers. In criminal prosecutions, it would need to be proven that these third parties acted "knowingly or willfully." Otherwise, the bureau would rely on civil orders or on the other forms of compliance already available.

- *Enacting privacy legislation.* The federal government has recently passed the *Personal Information Protection and Electronic Documents Act,*[37] which requires all organizations to obtain consent for the collection, use, or disclosure of personal information.
- *Encouraging international cooperation.* There is a strong need for international cooperation, particularly between enforcement agencies.

The Competition Bureau sees the *Competition Act* as a "key component of the legal and regulatory framework for electronic commerce. The study and analysis of enforcement issues will be an ongoing process, and the bureau will continue to adapt its compliance and enforcement techniques to ensure low-cost, effective enforcement in the global economy and the electronic marketplace."[38]

Source: N. Ladouceur, Assistant Deputy Commissioner of Competition, Amendments Unit, Competition Bureau, "Calibrating the Electronic Scales: Tipping the Balance in Favour of a Vigorous and Competitive Electronic Market for Consumers" (Address to the Canadian/United States Law Institute, The Impact of Technological Change in the Canada/United States Context, 16-18 April 1999).

Management of Distribution Channels

Distribution includes ensuring that goods reach end users in a timely and sound fashion, whether through post, courier, or the Internet.

This part considers two related issues—namely, the transfer of title to goods and the regulation of the transportation process.

Transfer of Title

The question of when title or ownership to goods changes is fundamental to the marketing process and has an impact on a number of basic business concerns, especially the transfer of risk. Consider these examples:

---

37. S.C. 2000, c. 5.

- If a truckload of goods is destroyed by fire in mid-delivery, who owns them and who bears the risk if they are destroyed?
- If goods are to be paid for within 30 days of sale, when does the 30 days begin and end? Upon delivery or at some earlier point?
- When an auditor is valuing finished goods and inventory, has title to the goods passed to the customers? Who owns a completed custom-built machine that has yet to be delivered?

At the heart of this issue is the notion that possession and ownership of goods are two distinct conditions. Possessing goods without owning them (i.e., without having title) confers certain obligations and rights, which were discussed in Chapter 17. Ownership confers additional rights.

The best way for parties to ensure clarity is to write the contract in a way that specifies completion and transfer. If the contract is silent, there are statutory provisions that resolve the issue. In addition, there are trade terms that are often used as "shorthand" for different forms of transfer.

specific goods
Goods that are identified and agreed on at the time a contract of sale is made.

unascertained goods
Goods not yet set aside and identifiable as the subject of the contract at the time the contract is formed.

STATUTORY RULES   The provincial *Sale of Goods Acts* set out a series of rules that determine when title changes in the absence of terms in a contract. The following examples explain these rules (each illustrates one of the five rules established in the Acts).[38] In broad terms, the Acts address two contrasting sets of circumstances. In most contracts for sale, goods are already in existence and can be clearly identified when the contract is formed (examples 1 through 4 below). These are known as **specific goods**. However, sometimes goods either are yet to be set aside and identified as being the subject of the contract or have not yet been produced. In this scenario, described in Example 5, goods are said to be **unascertained**.

EXAMPLE 1

Lighting Beautiful has the best-selling Christmas lights of the season, and supplies are short. In order to guarantee supplies, ABC Discounter goes to Lighting's warehouse, orders, and pays on the spot for all the remaining lights. The lights are immediately set aside in the loading dock for pickup the next day. There is a major fire at the warehouse that night, and all the supplies are destroyed. Whose lights were they: Lighting's or ABC's? In other words, had ABC acquired title to these lights?

The destroyed goods belonged to ABC. Title shifted *when the contract was made,* since the goods were ready for delivery at that time.

EXAMPLE 2

XYZ Discounter places an order for standard Christmas lights at the spring trade show in Toronto. The sale specifies that Lighting will pack the lights in boxes carrying the XYZ name and logo.

In this case, XYZ does not become owner of (acquire title to) these goods until Lighting has notified it that the goods have been packed in the appropriate boxes. If the warehouse burns either before XYZ is told the goods are ready or before the goods are packed in the XYZ boxes, Lighting remains owner of the lights and incurs the loss. *Title does not change until* the goods have been put in a *deliverable state* and XYZ has been notified.

---

38. *Sale of Goods Act*, R.S.O. 1990, c. S-1, s. 19.

EXAMPLE 3

Lighting buys Christmas lights offshore. Since quality is important, the contract specifies that each string must be tested to ensure that it works before shipping. The contract is signed; the lights have already been manufactured but have not been tested. This particular item becomes the hot item for this year's Christmas season, and at this point the manufacturer sells and delivers the same lights elsewhere. It advises Lighting that it is unlikely it will be able to meet the order before a certain date.

Who owned the goods the manufacturer sold? Until the goods have been tested, title has not passed. There is an act or event that must take place as a condition of the agreement for sale, and *until that act or event has taken place, Lighting does not acquire title.*

EXAMPLE 4

Lighting has a standing contract with ABC Discounter that it will ship out seasonal lights at set times and in set amounts to the ABC warehouse, and that ABC can return these goods should it determine they are not required. Lighting ships out 50 cases of lights to the ABC Discounter's warehouse as per this agreement. After three weeks, there is severe water damage in the ABC warehouse and the lights in storage are destroyed. ABC now argues that the lights were owned by Lighting, as it intended to return them.

Where goods are for "sale or return," title changes when there is some indication from ABC that it has accepted the order. If there is no specified time in which this should occur, it should be within *a reasonable time*. What is a reasonable time will depend on the circumstances and prior practices between Lighting and ABC. If ABC had always returned goods within two to three days of delivery in the past and this was typical of the trade, acceptance has likely occurred, and ABC will have title. If, on the other hand, ABC informed Lighting of acceptance anytime between two and six weeks after delivery, title may still lie with Lighting.

EXAMPLE 5

XYZ places an order with Lighting for 50 cases of standard outdoor lights. The operator of the forklift truck in the Lighting warehouse accidentally drops some lights that could have been sent to XYZ. Who has title to these lights?

Since the order is generic or unascertained (there is no way of knowing which lights in the warehouse will be used to fill XYZ's order), *title changes when the goods are unconditionally appropriated to the contract.* Here, title has not shifted, as lights for XYZ are still mixed in with general inventory. If, however, the forklift had dropped XYZ's order as it was loading it onto the truck or the truck was involved in an accident en route to XYZ and the order destroyed, XYZ would have title and incur the risk.

The rules determining when title to goods shifts affect the damages the seller is entitled to in the event of breach by the buyer. Specifically, if title has not shifted

damages for nonacceptance
Damages to which a seller is entitled if a buyer refuses to accept goods prior to the title shifting.

action for the price
The obligation of buyers of goods, once title to goods has passed, to pay the seller the full price of the goods.

bill of lading
A shipping document that serves as a contract between the seller and the carrier.

stoppage in transitu
The right of a seller to demand that goods be returned by a shipper at the seller's expense even after title has transferred, provided the purchaser is insolvent.

according to these rules, the seller still owns the goods. The seller is therefore entitled to the normal measure of **damages for nonacceptance**, always recognizing that the seller has an obligation to mitigate the loss.[39] If title has shifted, the buyer owns the goods and must pay the full amount of its obligation under the contract.[40] This principle is known as **action for the price**.

Although the *Sale of Goods Act* rules are important, in practice, it is always preferable to draft contracts that set out clearly when the parties want title to shift.

Delivery of Goods

It is beyond the scope of this text to address specialized laws affecting the transportation of goods. More general principles applying to carriers were described under the bailment section in Chapter 17.

Business has developed standardized terms that describe documentation in particular types of contracts. For illustration of these points, assume that Lighting contracts to sell $10 000 worth of Halloween Lights to Lumière, a Montreal-based retailer.

BILL OF LADING   The **bill of lading**, generically known as a "shipping document," is the contract between the seller (Lighting) and the carrier (Custom Trucking). It specifies to whom the goods must be delivered and provides evidence that the goods have been transferred from the seller to the carrier. If title to the goods shifts to the purchaser before delivery—for example, when they leave the seller—the bill of lading can be used by the purchaser as security against a loan.

STOPPAGE IN TRANSITU   The time it takes for goods to reach their destination can be significant, particularly in foreign trade. What happens when, one day after shipping, Lighting learns that Lumière is insolvent? At this time, Lighting has the right to exercise **stoppage in transitu**. It can direct the carrier to return the goods, even

Shipping goods gives rise to new legal responsibilities.

though title may have moved to Lumière. Provided Custom receives this direction before it has delivered the goods to Lumière, it *must* return them (at Lighting's expense) to Lighting. If Custom ignores this direction, it may be liable for the tort of conversion. Once the goods have been delivered to Lumière, however, Lighting's rights are governed by the *Bankruptcy and Insolvency Act* (see Chapter 28, and in particular the section of the Act dealing with the right of suppliers to recover goods received by the bankrupt in the 30 days preceding a bankruptcy or receivership order).[41]

---

39. *Sale of Goods Act*, R.S.A., 1980, c. S-2., s. 50.
40. *Ibid*, s. 49.
41. *Bankruptcy and Insolvency Act*, R.S.C. 1985, c. B-3 81.1

c.i.f.
A contractual term making the seller responsible for arranging the insurance (in the buyer's name) and shipping.

f.o.b.
A contractual term whereby the buyer specifies the type of transportation and the seller arranges that transportation and delivery of goods to the shipper at the buyer's expense.

c.o.d.
A contractual term requiring the purchaser to pay the shipper cash on delivery of goods.

COST, INSURANCE, AND FREIGHT   The initials **c.i.f.** stand for "cost, insurance, freight." In a c.i.f. contract, the seller is responsible for arranging the insurance (in the buyer's name) and shipping. The purchase price includes the cost of the goods, insurance, and shipping.[42] The seller must deliver the goods to the carrier and send copies of all documentation and a full statement of costs to the buyer. If the contract between Lighting and Lumière is "c.i.f. Montreal," Lighting must arrange shipping and insurance and will not have fulfilled its contractual obligations to deliver to Lumière until it has transferred the goods to the shipper and provided Lumière with all necessary documentation.

FREE ON BOARD   The initials **f.o.b.** stand for "free on board." In an f.o.b. contract, the buyer specifies the type of transportation to be used, and the seller arranges this and delivers the goods to that shipper. The seller's responsibilities are over when the goods are delivered to the shipper. The seller incurs the cost of delivering the goods to the shipper, and generally the buyer pays for shipping and insurance.[43] So if the contract is "f.o.b. Mississauga," Lumière will advise how the goods are to be transported, and Lighting will arrange for that transportation and ensure that the goods are delivered to the relevant carrier.

CASH ON DELIVERY   A **c.o.d.** or "cash on delivery" contract was once common with consumer orders, particularly before credit cards. The purchaser is obliged to pay for the goods upon delivery.

Commercial Terms

INTERNATIONAL PERSPECTIVE

In international trade it is important that shipping terms be standardized to ensure that there is a common understanding between jurisdictions.

The International Chamber of Commerce has published a set of definitions for trade terms, known as INCOTERMS. These definitions do not have the force of law but are often adopted by contracting parties. They may differ from the terms outlined above or from those, for example, used in the Uniform Commercial Code of the United States.

Business people need to be familiar with the appropriate terms applying to their specific transaction.

Source: International Chamber of Commerce, *INCCTERMS 2000* (Incoterms 2000, Publication 560).

---

42. G.H.L. Fridman, *Sale of Goods in Canada*, 4th ed. (Scarborough: Carswell, 1995) at 483.
43. *Ibid.* at 487.

Reputable businesses, for the most part, comply with legal requirements. As with every other aspect of business, however, prevention and minimization of risk must be conscious processes; thus, adequate and appropriate insurance coverage must be in place. The need for preventive action was outlined in full in Chapter 3, and the factors that hinder its implementation were acknowledged in Chapter 24. A potential public relations nightmare is the public disclosure of violations of regulations in the marketing effort. Although the public often appears to have a remarkably short memory, a poor reputation in the marketplace can have a lasting effect. If there are choices, why would customers choose to buy a product when they are not convinced that the price is fair or the selling practices are ethical?

The position of the regulators is typically one that encourages prevention. The goal of the Competition Bureau is compliance before harm; thus, it has devised guidelines for a sound corporate compliance program, as outlined in the following box.

Corporate Compliance Program

In 1997 the Competition Bureau released an information bulletin designed to assist businesses in creating a corporate program of compliance with the provisions of the *Competition Act*. The bureau outlined the components of a credible and effective corporate compliance program and highlighted its benefits—most notably, that the bureau will consider the existence of an effective compliance program in determining how to proceed in any investigation.

The bureau suggested that the essential elements of such a program are as follows:
- *The involvement and support of senior management.* Senior management should create a corporate culture or climate within the company to encourage compliance with the Act. Senior management must send the message that violations of the Act are unacceptable business practices.
- *The development of relevant policies and procedures.* The company should create materials outlining the content of the corporate compliance program in order to ensure that employees are aware of the program. Such

BUSINESS APPLICATION OF THE LAW

policies and procedures should be updated to account for changes in the law and company practices.
- *The ongoing education of management and employees.* The company should include a training program that targets personnel at all levels who are in a position to engage in or be exposed to anti-competitive behaviour.
- *Monitoring, auditing, and reporting mechanisms.* The company should include a review and assessment component to ensure that the program is being adhered to and to identify where adjustments may be necessary.
- *Disciplinary procedures.* The company should have a discipline code addressing violations, not only to deter anti-competitive conduct, but also to reflect the company's policy against such conduct.

Critical Analysis: How effective will such programs be in minimizing risk?

Source: *Corporate Compliance Programs, Industry Canada* (Hull, Que.: Competition Bureau, 3 July 1997).

Business Law in Practice Revisited

1. How does the law affect Lighting's pricing strategy?

Generally, the law requires Lighting to treat its customers in similar fashion when they are purchasing under similar conditions. Lighting has good reason to be concerned about the practices that retailers are pressuring it to partake in, since these practices may violate the provisions of the *Competition Act* and Lighting will be the obvious subject of any investigation. If the retailer insists that Lighting sell to the competitor under less favourable purchasing terms, Lighting may be subject to investigation for the criminal offence of price discrimination. The fact that Lighting is being pressured to partake in such illegal schemes will provide no defence. Lighting has limited rights to control the final price at which its goods are sold. Directives can only be toward providing a maximum selling price, not a minimum. The exception is where Lighting seeks to prevent a retailer, for example, from using its products as loss leaders or engaging in improper activity such as bait-and-switch selling.

2. How does the law affect Lighting's distribution strategy?

Lighting is not selling directly to the consumer, so many of the concerns about channel selection, for example, do not apply to its strategy. However, Lighting is selling to an increasingly competitive retail market and is likely finding its margins under attack. Under these conditions, Lighting finds itself considering imposing terms on customers that violate regulations. It cannot, for example, insist that customers purchase less popular goods along with popular items, and it must not differentiate between comparable customers who are willing and able to purchase under similar conditions. If a dominant retailer insists that Lighting stop selling to a major competitor, Lighting may be the subject of investigation for refusing to deal, which is a reviewable offence (an offence evaluated by the civil burden of proof). Lighting is entitled to refuse to deal with retailers who might harm the reputation of the company or its products through their selling practices. If the retailer fails to support the product or promote it fairly, Lighting can discontinue supplying.

3. What topics should be included in the new guidelines for sales and shipping staff?

The guidelines should set out all pricing and distribution practices that Lighting might be tempted or pressured to participate in and all those that are prohibited. Both the nature of the practices and the penalties imposed for engaging in them should be described. A clear protocol must be established for decision making and for addressing questionable practices. Steve and Gerry can turn to the compliance program materials provided by the Competition Bureau for guidance in this.

It is important also to provide information about all aspects of shipping the goods. Lighting will have standard practices that transfer title or risk. Employees should know the significance of these practices to the risk of the business. Also, basic shipping terminology should be defined so that employees understand the implications of contractual terms. Finally, all relevant aspects of insurance coverage and claims management must be explained.

Chapter Summary

Price and distribution are two of the four components of the marketing mix. Price includes more than the provisions designed to protect consumers. There is a strong public interest in ensuring that businesses compete fairly. If unfair practices are permitted, honest businesses will find themselves at a competitive disadvantage or will be squeezed out of the marketplace. While it is perhaps a common perception that anything goes in competition between businesses, the regulations outlined in this chapter related to business-to-business dealings show that this assumption is incorrect. Laws have evolved to address some of the issues that are of particular concern to Canadians, given the enormous size of this country and its relatively small population. Businesses may have to become dominant in the marketplace to achieve economies of scale. Nonetheless, such market dominance cannot be allowed to lead to unfair or discriminatory practices.

The term *distribution* covers a range of activities and practices. Distribution practices that discriminate between customers and thereby substantially reduce competition may be categorized as reviewable by the *Competition Act*. Direct-marketing practices are regulated both provincially and federally. The process for establishing when title to goods shifts is set out in the *Sale of Goods Acts* unless otherwise provided by contract. Finally, understanding distribution calls for knowledge of the meaning of a series of standard terms used in shipping of goods, such as bill of lading, c.i.f., and f.o.b.

A corporate compliance program is a critical defence in any investigation by the Competition Bureau. More importantly, it positions the business so that compliance with all legislation is a fundamental principle by which it operates.

Study Chapter

Key Terms and Concepts

action for the price (p. 588)

anti-competitive behaviour (p. 583)

bid rigging (p. 577)

bill of lading (p. 588)

channel power (p. 573)

c.i.f. (p. 589)

c.o.d. (p. 589)

damages for nonacceptance (p. 588)

direct marketing (p. 583)

direct-response marketing (p. 583)

door-to-door selling (p. 583)

double ticketing (p. 579)

exclusive dealing (page 582)

f.o.b. (p. 589)

multilevel marketing (p. 581)

ordinary price (p. 579)

predatory pricing (p. 576)

price discrimination (p. 575)

price maintenance (p. 576)

pyramid selling (p. 581)

refusal to deal (p. 582)

specific goods (p. 586)

stoppage in transitu (p. 588)

telemarketing (p. 584)

tied selling (p. 582)

unascertained goods (p. 586)

Questions for Review

1. What are two important facts that must be proven in order to establish illegal price discrimination?

2. What is a pricing conspiracy, and how is it proven?

3. What is predatory pricing?

4. Under what conditions is it acceptable to state "recommended retail price" on a product?

5. What are two situations where it is legitimate for a seller to refuse to supply to a retailer?

6. What is bid rigging?

7. What is the meaning of "ordinary price" in evaluating the promotion of goods?

8. What is double ticketing?

9. What is the difference between legal multilevel selling and pyramid selling?

10. How are door-to-door sellers regulated?

11. What are two primary concerns of consumers buying online?

12. Give one example of the shifting of title under the *Sale of Goods Act*.

13. What is stoppage in transitu?

14. What is a c.i.f. contract?

Questions for Discussion

1. Internet shopping opens up a broad range of risks to consumers. What recommendations would you have for federal and provincial governments moving to regulate in this area to enhance consumer confidence?

2. Insisting on a Certificate of Independent Bid Determination sounds like prudent practice. However, since bid rigging is criminal activity, how much protection do you think it offers? Is it still a good idea to insist on it?

3. The rules related to when title shifts under the *Sale of Goods Act* appear complex, but they are still important. Take two of the rules, and prepare examples of where and how, in practice, these might apply.

4. Assume you are a relatively new marketing manager in a fast-moving consumer products business. You are concerned because the firm encourages managers to operate quickly, independently, and aggressively. You are aware of the need for a corporate compliance program under the *Competition Act*. How could you persuade management to implement and apply such a program, given the existing corporate culture?

Situations for Discussion

1. Home Goods Inc. is a major discount retailer operating throughout Canada. The Home Co-op is also a nationwide chain, but it is a co-operative buying group of smaller retailers who band together in order to achieve buying power. Both retailers buy large volumes of plastic food containers from the major manufacturer (PFC Inc.) in the market. The product line is an important customer draw and is often used in special promotions.

    Home Goods is eager to increase its market share, particularly with the introduction of a multinational, U.S.-based discounter into the Canadian market. It decides that one of its first defensive tactics must be to remove the direct competition from the Co-op in smaller centres. Home Goods approaches PFC and requests changed conditions of purchase. Specifically, it asks for a significant drop in price in return for a reduced payment period. This change will place it at a distinct advantage over the Co-op, as the Co-op cannot pay quickly because of its membership structure. Home Goods intends to approach all other major suppliers if this proposal works.

    PFC management is quite concerned, as the Co-op is a long-standing customer and is easy to work with. PFC fears that this proposal will be only one of many by Home Goods, particularly if the U.S. company moves into the market and becomes a major competitor. Would supplying on Home Goods' terms be legal?

2. There are three major suppliers of highly specialized industrial chemicals in Canada. They have all operated for many years and respect each other and the quality of their products. They recognize that the market, while profitable, is finite, and that for each to survive, none can assume a greater market portion than presently held. For many years, it has been accepted that when calls for supplies are made by various industries, Company A will respond for western Canada, Company B for Ontario, and Company C for Quebec and the Maritimes.

    Recently, purchasers from these suppliers have been questioning why, of all supplies purchased, these chemicals are subject to the least price fluctuation. Word is getting back to the three suppliers that questions are being asked. Do they have any reason to be concerned? Is this the only way all three can survive?

3. John Smith is an employee of Company A in situation 2 above. He is not a happy man, having been overlooked for promotions for many years. Today, he has a serious drinking problem and is unlikely to hold on to his job for very much longer. If he were more pleasant he would undoubtedly attract more sympathy, since he hasn't had an easy life. However, he is thoroughly miserable to everyone he works with and his "moods" are often highly disruptive.

    Smith recognizes the threat to his employment and decides to take action of his own against the company. He knows that no one will ever know about the arrangements between the three chemical suppliers unless an insider tells. He starts researching in his local library to find out where this information can be conveyed and what protection he will receive if he conveys it.

    What is Smith likely to find out? Is his planned behaviour worthy of protection?

4. Brown Publishers sells textbooks to university bookshops on a sale-or-return basis. The three weeks at the beginning of the fall term is the peak period for most sales. Typically, the bookshops return unsold books within the first five weeks of the term, as they take up valuable retail space.

   The bookshop at Suddaby University routinely places large orders with Brown. This year, however, its management practices may politely be described as "confused." The long-time manager is on leave for illness, and the acting manager has little experience and is out of his depth. Orders have been placed, but tracking of sales has been poor. After six weeks, staff are only beginning to count stock—a necessary step prior to sending books back. That same weekend, a pipe bursts in the store and all stock is effectively destroyed. The acting manager calls the sales rep at Brown and relates this turn of events. Within two days, he receives by certified mail an invoice for the cost of the entire original order.

   Is the Suddaby bookshop obliged to pay? Where does the risk of this loss lie?

5. Textiles Inc. is a major chain of fabric sellers. In this market, there are a few high-end sellers of designer fabrics, some small independents, and three chains, with Textiles being the largest and most profitable. Textiles thrives on its ability to attract customers, often through discount pricing.

   Every few weeks Textiles has a major promotion, with certain materials being sold at a reduced cost. The business sells both "commodity" fabrics and fashion fabrics. Textiles tends to discount the commodity fabrics to get purchasers in the door, who are then inevitably drawn to the attractively arranged, high-markup fashion fabrics with sample clothing and patterns prominently displayed. After a while, even though advertisements state that fabric prices are reduced by 30 percent and even 50 percent, regular customers have become so used to these reductions that they seldom expect to pay the full price.

   These practices are attracting the attention of competitors, who have notified the Competition Bureau. Is the bureau likely to be interested, and why?

Part Eight

Financing the Business

THE DECISIONS RELATED TO FINANCING A BUSINESS range from paying a supplier to financing an expansion of operations and dealing with financial difficulties. Virtually all financial aspects of starting, operating, and terminating a business have legal implications. As with other sectors of a business, an understanding of the legal aspects of finance can be used to structure activities in a way that minimizes unfavourable legal consequences.

Part 8 presents the various aspects of financing a business not simply in a legal fashion, but rather as a business person might encounter them.

Chapter 26 Business and Banking

► Chapter 26 deals with the relationship between banks and business customers. It indicates what the business person can expect from a bank. Negotiable instruments are documents such as cheques and promissory notes that are used in financial transactions. The chapter outlines the rights, obligations, benefits, and risks related to their use. The chapter concludes with a look at the legal challenges created by the various developments in electronic banking.

Chapter 27 The Legal Aspects of Credit

► Chapter 27 provides an overview of credit transactions, including their regulation and the negotiation of credit arrangements. It deals with security for debt, the priorities among creditors, and the remedies to which creditors are entitled. The chapter concludes with an examination of the implications of giving personal guarantees for the debts of others.

Chapter 28 Bankruptcy and Insolvency

► Chapter 28 deals with the challenge of business failure by examining the complex rules that apply and the ways that the business person can cope with those rules. It includes a detailed review of the *Bankruptcy and Insolvency Act.*

Twenty-Six

Business and Banking

Objectives

AFTER STUDYING THIS CHAPTER, YOU SHOULD HAVE AN
UNDERSTANDING OF:

► THE RELATIONSHIP BETWEEN A BUSINESS AND ITS BANK
► THE LEGAL FRAMEWORK OF NEGOTIABLE INSTRUMENTS
► THE RIGHTS AND OBLIGATIONS OF THOSE CONNECTED WITH
  NEGOTIABLE INSTRUMENTS
► THE LEGAL CHALLENGES INVOLVED IN ELECTRONIC BANKING

Business Law in Practice

Michelle Chu lives in Surrey, British Columbia. She has been employed by the municipal government as an information officer for 15 years. Michelle has some spare time and has saved some money. She also has a passion for the movies and is frustrated by the limited selection of video rentals in her area. She has decided to open a small video rental shop to cater to specialty tastes not served by the existing outlets. Michelle has no experience in running a business. One of the many challenges she faces is establishing banking arrangements. She knows she needs a bank account for making deposits and writing cheques, but she is unsure of what other banking services she may need. Michelle has heard of banks collecting excessive service charges. She has some interest in computers and knows that banks are heavily

involved in technology. She has heard of packages of electronic banking services developed especially to assist small businesses like hers. Michelle also needs to decide how to accept payments from customers—whether to accept cheques, credit cards, or debit cards.

1. What does Michelle need to know about the legal aspects of the relationship between her business and a bank?
2. What are the risks and benefits of using cheques to pay bills and allowing customers to pay her by cheque?
3. What are the added risks and benefits to doing her banking electronically?

Starting a video shop requires many financial decisions with legal consequences.

The Banking Relationship

In its simplest form, the relationship between a business and its bank consists of one bank account into which the business deposits its cash receipts from customers and from which it makes payments to suppliers, government, and owners. As a result of regulatory changes and decisions by banks to broaden their range of services, the relationship now can be much more comprehensive. Banks have become financial marketplaces, offering services in cash management, investment advice and brokerage, and business financing. Therefore, it is a challenge for someone in Michelle's position to decide what banking services she needs, which services she can afford, and who will do the best job of providing them. It is not as simple as choosing a bank and opening an account.

Regulation of Banks

Traditionally, the Canadian financial services industry had four distinct sectors: banks, trust companies, stockbrokers, and insurance companies. To ensure stability within each sector and to avoid conflicts of interest resulting from institutions providing services from several sectors, each was separately regulated, and institutions in one sector were prohibited from conducting business beyond that sector.

The internationalization of the financial services industry in the 1980s placed pressure on governments to deregulate and relax the strict separation of the four sectors. In 1987 the legislation was reviewed and revised in Canada. Banks were allowed to go beyond traditional banking and engage in all of the other sectors, except insurance, in their branches or through subsidiary firms. The legislation is now revisited every five years; the next review will be in 2002.

Banks are under federal jurisdiction and are regulated through the federal *Bank Act*.[1] The main purposes of the *Bank Act* are to ensure the stability and liquidity of banks and to identify and regulate the types of business they are permitted to conduct. The relationship between a bank and its individual customers is not a primary

---

1. S.C. 1991, c. 46, as am. by S.C. 1998, c. 30.

concern of the Act. The terms and conditions of that relationship are, instead, found primarily in the agreements made between the bank and its customers, which are influenced by banking practice and common law rules. Contract law is the prime source of guidance in interpreting and enforcing the rights and obligations of the parties in this relationship.

Banks are increasingly offering international banking services, such as letters of credit, cross-border transfers, and accounts in different currencies. These services are governed largely by voluntary rules created by international bodies, such as the Bank for International Settlements and the International Chamber of Commerce. Parties involved in international transactions frequently incorporate these rules into their agreements.

The Bank–Customer Agreement

banking agreement
A document that contains the rights and obligations of a bank and a customer.

The purpose of the **banking agreement** is twofold:

- to specify who has the authority to issue instructions to the bank on behalf of the customer
- to allocate the risk of loss resulting from problems with verifying the customer's authority and carrying out the customer's instructions

The customer designates those with authority to issue instructions to the bank, such as cheque-signing authority. At this point in Michelle's business, she will be the only person with that authority.

The second focus of the banking agreement—namely, the allocation of loss—is of greater significance. Michelle must be cautious in her dealings because the bank–customer agreement is invariably drafted by the bank to limit its duties and liabilities. For example, a clause commonly found in banking documents gives the customer 30 days to detect and report any unauthorized payments that the bank makes from the customer's account. Beyond that period, the customer absorbs the loss. Typically, the bank also has flexibility in dealing with all of the customer's accounts. For example, the bank can transfer funds from an account with a positive balance to one that is overdrawn.

The key document involved in opening a bank account is the *operation of account agreement*, which includes provisions dealing with issues such as

- the bank's ability to apply charges to the customer's accounts (commonly known as service charges);
- arrangements concerning the issue of cheques and instructions for payment by the customer
- confirmations and stop payments
- release of information by the bank about the customer

Duties of the Bank and the Customer

The common law and banking practice imply additional duties on both parties to the banking contract. For example, the bank must

- honour cheques and repay deposits
- collect cheques for the customer
- provide account information to the customer on a regular basis
- maintain secrecy of the customer's affairs[2]

---

2. Alison R. Manzer & Jordan S. Bernamoff, *The Corporate Counsel Guide to Banking and Credit Relationships* (Aurora, Ont.: Canada Law Book, 1999) at 14.

Customer Information and Money Laundering

The bank's duty to maintain secrecy of customer information is subject to the law concerning money laundering—that is, the false reporting of income obtained through criminal activity as income gained through legitimate business enterprises. The law imposes obligations on banks

- to verify the identity of customers (including proper incorporation of corporate customers and identification of directors and officers)
- to verify that customers are engaged in valid business activities
- to determine the source of transfers exceeding $10 000[3]

New legislation was introduced in Parliament in 1999[4] to combat **money laundering**. The legislation

BUSINESS APPLICATION OF THE LAW

creates a mandatory reporting system in which banks, trust companies, insurance companies, and professionals must report to a new independent body—the Financial Transactions and Reports Analysis Centre—suspicious financial transactions (such as transactions that result in a conspicuous increase in an account balance) and large cross-border currency transfers.

Critical Analysis: To what extent should the confidentiality of individual customer accounts be compromised to combat money laundering by a small minority of bank customers? Should banks be designated informants? Is the basis of the bank–customer relationship being undermined?

---

money laundering
The false reporting of income from criminal activity as income from legitimate business.

Customers also have implied duties to the bank. They must

- take reasonable steps to provide documentation as to who is authorized to give instructions to the bank, in order to prevent fraud and forgery
- keep authorizations current
- notify the bank of any suspected problems
- provide safeguards for electronic communications (including telephone, fax, and computer)[5]

As long as Michelle is the only one with signing authority at the bank, authorization should not be a problem. When she reaches the point at which she needs to share that responsibility, she must make the terms of the arrangement clear to the person receiving the authority and to the bank. Michelle must also familiarize herself with the practices of her bank related to authorization by phone, fax, or computer if she chooses to use them.

---

3. *Proceeds of Crime (Money Laundering) Act,* S.C. 1991, c. 26.
4. Bill C-22, *Proceeds of Crime (Money Laundering) Bill,* 15 December 1999 (assented to 29 June 2000, S.C. 2000, c. 17).
5. *Supra* note 2 at 15.

The Bank–Customer Relationship

Standard banking documents are designed to protect the bank, not the customer. Large customers may have some bargaining power, but small businesses such as Michelle's have very little. Understanding the terms and conditions in the agreement will enable Michelle to identify risks arising from her business. She can then establish practices to avoid activities resulting in loss for which the banking agreement would make her responsible.

The legal nature of the relationship is clear. In terms of the customer's money on deposit with the bank, the relationship is purely that of the bank as debtor and the customer as creditor. Normally, the bank is not obligated to give advice or to look out for the best interest of the customer, unless, for example, the bank provides services such as financial advice, which are outside the normal scope of traditional banking services. In that situation a fiduciary relationship does exist, and the bank has several additional onerous duties:

- to provide advice with care and skill
- to disclose any actual or potential conflicts of interest
- to consider the interests of the customer ahead of those of the bank[6]

If Michelle has sought and received advice from her banker as to the amount and structure of the financing she needs to start her business, she can expect to receive competent advice from the bank and to be encouraged to seek independent advice before agreeing to a financing arrangement operating heavily in the bank's favour.

The practical advice for customers is to appreciate the basic nature of the relationship and to understand that banks generally have no obligation to look beyond their own self-interest. Customers are on their own. On the political front, banks are under considerable pressure to deal fairly with customers and to refrain from strict enforcement of agreements that are onerous for their customers. In 1998, for example, customer service was a key factor in the ruling by the Competition Bureau against proposed mergers by the major banks. The bureau paid considerable attention to the decreased competition and possible branch closures resulting from the mergers.[7]

Negotiable Instruments

cheque
An order to a bank to pay money to a specified person.

promissory note
A written promise to pay a specified amount.

bill of exchange
An order to a person to pay an amount to another person.

When Michelle pays an account with one of her suppliers, she has several options. She can use cash, with the inconvenience and risk of having adequate cash on hand to pay bills, or she can pay by **cheque** (a written order to her bank) or by electronic funds transfer (a paperless transaction). The rules for cheques are well defined and are part of the law of negotiable instruments. Electronic transfers are more recent and create some special legal challenges, which are considered later in the chapter.

A cheque is the most common example of a negotiable instrument, but the rules also apply to other documents, such as **promissory notes** and **bills of exchange**. A promissory note is a written promise by one person to pay a specified amount on a certain date or on demand to another person. A bill of exchange is an order to someone else to pay funds to another person. A cheque is a special type of bill of exchange, which is payable on demand and where the party instructed to pay is a

---

6. *Supra* note 2 at 36.

7. See various documents, including bank merger guidelines and letters from the bureau to the banks, at the Competition Bureau Web site <http://competition.ic.gc.ca>.

bank. These instruments are federally regulated by the *Bills of Exchange Act*.[8] The rules in this legislation focus on the attributes and transferability of pieces of paper called *negotiable instruments*. The development of electronic transfers without paper undermines the utility of the existing rules for resolving disputes. Electronic transactions by nature are paperless and consist of a series of transfers, rather than the circulation of a single paper instrument from one party to another.

There are several technical requirements for an instrument (a document) to become negotiable, but the essence is that it must be a self-contained obligation. It must specify an amount of money to be paid, and the obligation must be unconditional. This latter feature enables the instrument to be negotiated or transferred without the need to investigate its validity through reference to the circumstances of its creation or other documents. For example, if a promise is made to pay "the balance due" on a construction contract, the promise cannot be a negotiable instrument because the balance can be determined only by consulting the original contract and investigating the work done and payments already made. A **negotiable instrument** must be for a specific sum without conditions. When Michelle issues a cheque to a supplier of goods or services, she gives a written order to her bank to pay a specified sum to the supplier.

As indicated in Figure 26.1, Michelle is the *creator* of the instrument. The supplier is the *payee* (the business entitled to payment). Michelle is formally known as the *drawer* because she is ordering her bank to pay the supplier. The bank, as the recipient of Michelle's instructions, is known as the *drawee*.

negotiable instrument
A document that meets the requirements for circulation without reference to other sources.

Figure 26.1

AN ANNOTATED CHEQUE

Michelle's instructions to her bank in the form of a cheque and the bank's actions to carry out her instructions by paying money from her account to the designated supplier are at the centre of the bank–customer relationship. The written agreement will address these transactions in some detail, but a number of duties are imposed on the two parties through the common law. For example, the customer must keep adequate funds in her or his accounts to pay any cheques that are issued, and must provide clear and unambiguous instructions to the bank concerning payment. The bank must take reasonable care in honouring instructions to pay out the money, provided there are sufficient funds in the customer's account.[9]

8. R.S.C. 1985, c. B-4.
9. *Supra* note 2 at 30.

Michelle's supplier will likely take the cheque to its bank for deposit. Through the centralized clearing process, the cheque will find its way from the supplier's bank to Michelle's bank, and the specified sum will be taken from Michelle's account.

Figure 26.2

STEPS IN THE CHEQUE CIRCULATION PROCESS

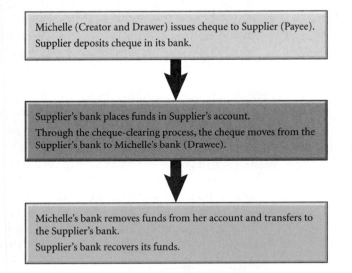

As long as Michelle has funds in her account and there is no defect in the cheque, it will proceed smoothly through the steps. If she accepts cheques as payment from her customers, the customer is the drawer and Michelle is the payee, in relation to the steps in Figure 26.2. The following sections describe the potential problems and risks for the participants if difficulties arise in the circulation or cashing of the cheque.

Implications of Creating a Cheque

When Michelle chooses to pay a supplier by cheque, she is discharging a debt that she owes as debtor to the supplier as creditor. That debt has arisen through the contract between Michelle and the supplier for the provision of goods or services. Assuming that Michelle buys or rents her videos from a number of distributors, she will have regular payment obligations arising from her contractual arrangements with those distributors. If she encounters problems with the videos, she will have a valid complaint against the supplier (subject to their contract). She can pursue that complaint as she would any breach of contract.

However, her claim on the contract is a totally different matter from her obligation to pay the cheque. By issuing the cheque, she has made an unconditional promise to pay the specified sum not just to the supplier, but to anyone who presents the cheque to her bank for payment. The person presenting the cheque for payment is known as a **holder** and is not affected by any terms of Michelle's contract with the supplier. Michelle must allow her bank to pay out the cheque, and she must then seek compensation separately from the supplier. The special status of the cheque and the holder are confirmed by legislation,[10] which deliberately places the holder in a strong

holder
A person who presents a negotiable instrument for payment.

---

10. *Bills of Exchange Act,* s. 55.

position in terms of collecting on the cheque. If the holder has acted in good faith (meaning he or she has no reason to doubt the validity of the cheque), there are limited arguments that Michelle can use to justify refusing payment (for example, a forged signature or an alteration of the cheque).

A cheque involves a radically different situation from an ordinary assignment of contractual rights, where there can be any number of defences against paying. For example, if Michelle owes money to a distributor, that distributor can assign the right to collect to someone else (known as an assignee). In the absence of a negotiable instrument, the assignee's right to collect from Michelle is subject to any problems with the contract between Michelle and the distributor. Thus, if Michelle has a valid reason for refusing to pay the distributor's claim, she can use the same reason to avoid paying the assignee. In law, this idea is captured in the expression "an assignee can have no better rights than the assignor."[11]

Consumer Loans and Negotiable Instruments

A consumer sale is one in which the buyer is the final user of the goods for a noncommercial purpose. Prior to 1970, the separation of obligations arising from the negotiable instrument and the contract of sale was abused in some consumer transactions. If a consumer bought something on credit and signed a promissory note in favour of the seller, that seller could sell the note to another party (such as a finance company). The legal result of the transfer of the note was that the financier became a holder of the note with special status. The buyer's obligation to pay the financier was then nearly absolute and independent of problems with the quality and performance of the purchased goods. Such problems could be pursued against the seller based on the contract of sale, but they did not affect the consumer's continuing obligation to make payments to the holder of the note. These rules enabled collusion

ETHICAL CONSIDERATIONS

between unscrupulous sellers and financiers to sell substandard goods to consumers and require them to make all payments, even when the goods were defective or worthless.

In 1970, the *Bills of Exchange Act*[12] was amended to classify these promissory notes arising from consumer credit sales as **consumer notes**. They must be stamped as "consumer purchases." The holder of a consumer note is not accorded the special status of a normal holder of a negotiable instrument and is subject to claims arising from the original contract of sale. The consumer's obligation to pay the note is subject to remedies against the seller if the goods are defective.

Critical Analysis: Was the law changed to impose ethical standards on businesses that were acting within pre-1970 law? Is this a valid use of legislative power?

consumer note
A promissory note arising in a consumer credit sale.

---

11. See Chapter 9 for a more complete discussion of assignments.
12. *Supra* note 10, s. 191.

negotiation
The process of
transferring negotiable
instruments from one
person to another.

A cheque normally follows a relatively short route, as shown in Figure 26.2, but it may also be transferred many times. Eventually, it is presented by a holder to the maker's bank for payment. The transfer process is known as **negotiation**—hence the name of the instrument. However, negotiation in this context has a distinct meaning from its more common use as a process for resolving disputes. All that is needed for the negotiation of an instrument is for the current holder to **endorse**, or sign, the instrument over to a new holder, who then becomes entitled to either present the instrument for payment or transfer it to yet another holder.

endorsement
The process of signing
a negotiable
instrument to enable
negotiation.

Figure 26.3

COMPARISON OF PAYMENT AND COLLECTION ARRANGEMENTS

Type of arrangement	Parties involved	Enforcement rights
Contract	Buyer (debtor) Seller (creditor)	Seller can collect subject to performance of its obligations.
Assignment of contractual right	Debtor Creditor (assignor) Assignee	Assignee's right to collect is subject to the debtor's obligation to pay the assignor.
Negotiable instrument (i.e., a cheque)	Drawer (debtor) Payee (creditor) Holder	Holder's right to collect is not tied to the original contract.
Consumer note	Consumer Seller Financier	Financier does not have the status of a holder—consumer's obligation depends on the original contract.

The essential point for the creator of a cheque is that the cheque is a self-contained obligation, the validity of which does not depend on any circumstances outside the cheque. The creator has issued instructions to the bank to pay the designated payee or the holder. As long as the cheque contains the necessary endorsements (signatures) to confirm the holder's right to possession of the cheque, the bank will pay it. Despite the holder's strong position, there are certain risks for holders of negotiable instruments.

Implications of Accepting a Cheque

The major risk involved in accepting a cheque relates to the financial health of the maker, rather than any legal rules. The holder's strong and secure legal position is of no value if the drawer's account does not contain enough money to cover the cheque when it is presented for payment. The likelihood of that happening is the key consideration in Michelle's decision whether to accept any payments by cheque from customers. Deciding to accept cheques is equivalent to extending credit, since there are several days between handing over goods and receiving payment from a cheque.

In major transactions, the method of payment that overcomes the above risk is the certified cheque. **Certification** is a process in which the drawer (or sometimes the payee) takes the cheque to the drawer's bank and has the bank certify it for payment. The bank immediately removes the money from the customer's account and holds it in reserve until the cheque is presented for payment. This process removes

certification
The process whereby a
bank guarantees
payment of a cheque.

stop payment
The process whereby the person who writes a cheque orders the bank not to pay the holder who presents it for payment.

the risk of there being insufficient funds in the drawer's account when the cheque is cashed.

Certification usually prevents the drawer from putting a **stop payment** on the cheque. A stop payment means that the drawer (as the bank's customer) countermands (or cancels) its instructions to pay the cheque and orders the bank to refuse payment when the cheque is presented. These instructions can be issued at any time before a cheque has been charged against the drawer's account. However, the bank will likely require the customer's agreement that the bank will not be responsible if the cheque is cashed accidentally, despite the stop payment order. Once a cheque is presented for payment, it is too late to stop the bank from cashing it.

Despite the secure position of holders of negotiable instruments, those who are called upon to accept the transfer of a cheque may be reluctant to do so without verification of the various endorsements on the cheque and some means of recovering funds advanced on a cheque that turns out to be invalid. Thus, banks are reluctant to cash cheques for anyone who is not a customer of that bank and who does not hold a significant balance on account. If the cheque comes back to the bank owing to a lack of funds in the drawer's account, the amount can be deducted from the customer's account (likely in accordance with the bank–customer agreement). The bank, therefore, will not suffer the ultimate loss on the cheque. This is a significant risk for Michelle if she accepts cheques from customers in her store. If the bank cashes a cheque for someone who is not a customer, it will be much more difficult to recover the funds if the cheque turns out to be worthless.

A bank or anyone else who gives money in return for a cheque runs the risk that the drawer is not able or obligated to honour it. In these rare situations, anyone who has endorsed the cheque is potentially liable for the amount.

A bank's responsibility to carry out the instructions of its customers includes verifying a customer's signature on a cheque. The bank and its customers both have obligations when forgery is involved. The bank has a duty to detect unauthorized instructions (such as a forged signature), and customers must take reasonable steps to prevent forgeries and immediately report any potential problems to the bank. If a bank is left with liability for a forged cheque, it can look to prior endorsers of the cheque to recover its money. Therefore, anyone accepting a cheque should verify the authenticity of the endorsements on it.

Case

Canadian Pacific Hotels Ltd. v. *Bank of Montreal*
(1987), 40 D.L.R. (4th) 385 (S.C.C.)

The Business Context: There are situations where the bank fails to detect forged signatures and the customer does not immediately notice that the forged cheques have been cashed from its account. In these cases, the courts will look to the bank–customer agreement. If there is none, the common law rules apply.

Factual Background: Sands was the accountant for a business unit of Canadian Pacific (CP). He forged the signatures on a number of cheques payable from the CP account to companies he controlled. CP eventually discovered the forgeries and sued to recover its money from the bank. There was no verification agreement between CP and the bank, which would have made CP responsible for unauthorized cheques if not detected and reported by CP within a specified period. The lower courts dismissed the action on the basis that CP, through its lack of care, was responsible for its own loss.

The Legal Question: Was the customer, CP, responsible for detecting the forgeries?

Resolution: The Supreme Court of Canada found in favour of CP. Justice LeDain ruled that

> a customer of a bank does not, in the absence of a verification agreement, owe a duty to the bank to examine his bank statements and vouchers with reasonable care and to report any discrepancies within a reasonable time, nor does a customer, "sophisticated" or otherwise, owe a duty to its bank to maintain an adequate system of internal accounting controls for the prevention and minimization of loss through forgery.

Justice LaForest suggested a broader basis for the decision:

> the necessity for clear rules of general application. In the case of forged cheques the rule was clear.

The banker was supposed to know his customer's signature and the liability was his if he honoured a cheque on which his customer's signature had been forged.

Critical Analysis:
Most banking contracts now have a verification clause that shifts responsibility for undetected forgeries from the bank to the customer. There is also an emerging implied duty on the part of the customer to undertake reasonable procedures to prevent fraud and forgery.[13] What would those procedures be? Should the customer bear this responsibility? Who is in the best position to detect forgeries?

---

endorsement in blank
Signing a cheque without any special instructions.

restrictive endorsement
Signing a cheque for deposit only to a particular bank account.

special endorsement
Signing a cheque and making it payable to a specific person.

Those in possession of cheques should take steps to safeguard them and transfer them by endorsing in a way that minimizes the risk that others may illegally obtain and cash them. Simply signing a cheque on the back is known as an **endorsement in blank**. This means that the signatures are complete and that anyone who acquires the cheque can cash it (subject to a bank's willingness to do so). Holders should therefore take care with the form of endorsements. Businesses commonly endorse cheques "for deposit only." These are known as **restrictive endorsements**; they stop the circulation of cheques and remove the risk of anyone else acquiring and cashing them. If Michelle accepts cheques from customers, she should routinely endorse them in this manner as soon as possible. If a cheque received by a payee is to be transferred to someone other than a bank, it is wise to endorse it directly to that person (for example, "Pay to Desmond Chu/signed Michelle Chu"). This is known as a **special endorsement**; it ensures that only the designated person is able to deal with the cheque further.

Those accepting cheques should realize that there are financial and legal reasons why collection may be a problem. Apart from a certified cheque, there is no guaranteed payment. Michelle must understand that if a customer's cheque is returned to her by her bank because of insufficient funds in the customer's account, she will recover the funds only if she can collect from the customer. If the customer cannot be located or is unable to pay the amount, Michelle will ultimately bear the loss. However, if she can locate the customer, the cheque is valuable evidence of the customer's contractual obligation.

A negotiable instrument has a life of its own, quite separate from the contract that produced it. Liability for payment is independent of the original debtor–creditor relationship. The purpose of the rules is to produce convenience and dependability with the negotiable instruments in the commercial environment. The tradeoff is that a relatively small but still significant number of the instruments must be honoured by makers in situations where there is a good reason for liability to be borne by another party.

---

13. *Supra* note 2 at 15.

Electronic Banking

electronic banking
Financial transactions
through the use of
computers, telephones,
or other electronic
means.

Electronic banking includes a growing range and variety of transactions that previously required formal documentation. Some examples are automatic payments from chequing accounts, direct deposit of cheques, automatic teller machines (ATMs), payment by telephone, and point-of-sale transfers with debit cards. Credit card transactions are now processed electronically as well. They involve two contracts—one between the card issuer and the user, and the second between the credit card company and the merchant.

The basis of the well-established and comprehensive set of rules governing negotiable instruments is the instrument itself—the piece of paper. The information it contains and where it goes are the key features of any dispute. How does the law of negotiable instruments (constructed on the basis of hard copy documents) apply to paperless transactions? Electronic transfers present several challenges. First, since there is no key piece of paper that circulates through the system, there is no paper trail in the event of a dispute. Second, electronic transfers are instantaneous, so there is no opportunity to change the instructions for payment (for example, by issuing a stop payment). There is no need for the certification process because the transfer is unlikely to be effective unless the account from which the transfer is made has sufficient funds. Electronic deposits may result in problems if no one verifies the validity of the instruments being deposited. For example, if there is a serious defect in a deposited cheque, the amount will initially be added to the customer's balance, but it

ATMs are only one vehicle for electronic banking.

will be deducted later when the defect is discovered. By this time, the customer may have already withdrawn the money.

There is a tradeoff between increased efficiency and the absence of rules. Electronic transfers are cheap and efficient. The absence of paper is a distinct advantage. There is no need to track or store the documents. Instructions can be issued by the customer to the bank instantly, and the funds are transferred to the recipient immediately. However, safeguarding the authority for such transfers becomes a major challenge for customers. Rather than verifying signatures on cheques, banks are looking for the necessary authorization codes in electronic messages. If the codes are there, the bank will have no reason to question the authority. The methods and potential for forgery and fraud are changed and expanded.

Another potential problem for customers is the occasional transmission failure. As business comes to rely increasingly on instant payments, possibly at the last minute, the potential loss from a failed or delayed transfer is significant.

Most of the problems surrounding electronic banking are the result of the irrelevance of existing legislation to a paperless environment. The process and timing of electronic transactions do not fit with existing rules related to risk allocation for authentication, verification, and finalization of payments.[14]

The gap in the rules governing electronic banking is being filled in two ways. Banking contracts now include provisions for the risks of electronic transactions that specify the customer's duties to report problems to the bank and the bank's responsibility for electronic failures. There is also greater reliance on international rules, such as the UNCITRAL Model Law for International Credit Transfers,[15] since electronic transfers are completed as easily across the world as within the local community. If the sending and receiving banks are in different countries, these international rules deal with the obligations of the parties, timing for payment, consequences for technical problems, and liability and damages.

The Cashless Society and Virtual Banks

TECHNOLOGY AND THE LAW

A wide variety of technological developments are changing the ways that business deals with banks, customers, and other businesses. Banks are encouraging customers to conduct their banking business through various electronic means, rather than through traditional in-person transactions in bank branches. These new methods can be more convenient for customers and significantly less expensive for the banks. An electronic transaction costs the bank a fraction of the cost of the same transaction in person. Some new banks have no physical branches at all and conduct all their business as virtual banks in cyberspace.

Customers are offered a range of electronic options by the traditional banks. Automatic teller machines are available for deposits, withdrawals, transfers between accounts, and bill payments. Telephone banking and online banking can be used for everything other than cash transactions, including applications for mortgages and loans.

Apart from banking innovations, there are other models for cashless transactions. Debit cards allow buyers to purchase goods and services and to transfer payment directly from a bank account to the seller. Money cards carry a computer chip that enables virtual money to be loaded on the card and transferred directly from the card to the seller. Electronic money or digital cash takes no physical form, but instead is loaded onto computer hard drives or electronic wallets, enabling payment to be made as easily as sending e-mail.

There are many potential problems with the various forms of electronic banking and cashless transactions. Existing laws apply to documented or paper transactions. Electronic storage means that data are subject to system crashes or hackers. Counterfeiting, fraud, and money laundering may become easier. The developers of electronic options are faced with significant challenges to build the confidence of business and consumers through secure and confidential systems.

Critical Analysis: What are the potential legal problems arising from the use of these substitutes for cash and negotiable instruments? Is the absence of regulation a major problem? Can the law keep up with technology?

---

14. *Supra* note 2 at 41.
15. "UNCITRAL Model Law on International Credit Transfers" (1993), 32 I.L.M. 587.

There is little evidence yet of real legal problems arising from electronic transfers. Business customers of banks are interested in security, convenience, and low costs in terms of banking services. As long as banks can assure customers that their needs are being met without significant risks, electronic banking will prosper. In legal terms, electronic banking is an expansion of the tradeoff that makes negotiable instruments work. The convenience and volume of electronic transactions outweighs the occasional injustice resulting from a defective transaction. Tracing the cause of an electronic loss may be difficult. Someone must bear that loss, but in terms of the public good, the reliability and convenience of the transfer system may be more important than identifying the one responsible.

Michelle needs to ask the relevant questions of her bank related to the risks and to what happens if, for example, an electronic transfer simply does not happen or the bank transfers funds without proper authorization. She needs to make sure that the bank has anticipated potential problems and has a reasonable way of dealing with them. In risk management terms, she needs to evaluate the risk against the potential benefits of electronic banking.

Methods of Payment

The factors in Michelle's decision as to the methods of payment she will accept from her customers relate to marketing and finance, as well as to legal risks. She must be responsive to the needs and demands of her customers and sensitive to the cost of various payment options.

Before deciding to accept debit cards or credit cards, Michelle needs to understand the implications of the agreements she will be required to sign with those service providers. If Michelle accepts the cards, she will pay a portion of the proceeds of those sales to the card providers. In return, she will get immediate payment for debit card sales and a guarantee of payment on credit card sales, as long as she complies with the requirements in her agreements, such as verification of signatures.

The possibility of extending credit to customers is the subject of Chapter 27.

Figure 26.4

COMPARATIVE RISKS OF METHODS OF ACCEPTING PAYMENT

Form of payment	Nature of payment	Risk for person accepting payment
Cash	Immediate	The money may be counterfeit or the proceeds of a crime.
Cheque	Deposited	There may be insufficient funds in the account on which the cheque was drawn; the cheque may be forged.
Credit card	Guaranteed	Risk is borne largely by the card provider.
Debit card	Immediate transfer	Risk is borne largely by the payments system.
Credit	Payment at a later date	The debtor may be unable or unwilling to pay.

Business Law in Practice Revisited

1. What does Michelle need to know about the legal aspects of the relationship between her business and a bank?

Michelle needs to appreciate that her basic relationship with the bank is one in which the bank must safeguard her money and follow her payment instructions but is otherwise not responsible for her interests. She needs to appreciate the importance of her contract with the bank and become familiar with her basic rights and obligations.

2. What are the risks and benefits of using cheques to pay bills and allowing customers to pay her by cheque?

The risk of paying by cheque is that Michelle cannot avoid her obligation to honour the cheque if she has a problem with the goods or services she used it to pay for. The risk of allowing customers to pay by cheque is that they may have insufficient funds in their accounts, they may be engaged in fraud or forgery, they might issue a stop payment, or there may be a technical defect in the cheque.

The legal benefits of paying by cheque are the relative security compared with cash, the paper trail provided by the cheque, and the ability to issue a stop payment before the cheque is cashed. Accepting payments by cheque is more risky than taking only cash, but it is safer than credit. As the holder of a cheque, Michelle has an instrument in her possession that provides proof of her right to collect.

3. What are the added risks and benefits to doing her banking electronically?

If Michelle engages in electronic banking, it will likely be cheaper and faster, but she risks having transmission problems, she cannot easily cancel e-transactions because they are instantaneous, and she is left with no paper trail to follow the transaction, should that become desirable. Michelle needs to thoroughly discuss these risks with her bank so that she feels comfortable with her banking arrangements. She should not simply sign whatever documents the bank requests and hope for the best. If Michelle decides to accept payments by credit card or debit card, she will need to negotiate with the providers of those services and be prepared to pay their fees. Such arrangements are not part of her package of banking services.

Chapter Summary

Customers should be wary of their relationship with their banks, not because banks attempt to take advantage of them, but because the relationship is a contractual one. The rights and obligations are found in the contract, and because the banks write the contracts, the language tends to favour the banks' interests more than those of the customers. The chief effect of a banking contract is to transfer risk from the bank to the customer. If the customer appreciates this reality, the level of disappointment, frustration, and financial loss is likely to be less than if her or his expectations of the bank are unrealistic.

The established system for negotiable instruments focuses on the commercial convenience of instruments circulating freely, with little need for the various holders to be concerned about their validity. It is a paper-based system that places prime importance on the piece of paper and the secure status of those in possession of it.

The primary right is the ability of a holder to collect from the creator of the instrument—the person whose promise to pay originated the transaction. The main obligation is that of the creator or drawer of the instrument to pay regardless of events that preceded or followed the creation of the instrument.

The instantaneous nature of electronic transactions greatly improves efficiency, but it also makes the transfers irrevocable. The absence of paper and the inapplicability of the rules that govern paper transactions are the major challenges.

Study Chapter

Questions for Review

1. What is the basic nature of the bank–customer relationship?

2. How are banks regulated?

3. What are the key issues addressed in a banking contract?

4. What are the key duties of the customer and the bank?

5. How are negotiable instruments regulated?

6. Why are electronic transfers not subject to the same regulations as paper transactions?

7. Who are the drawer, the drawee, and the payee of a cheque?

8. Who is responsible for a forged cheque if the forger has disappeared?

9. What are the key risks in creating and accepting cheques?

10. What is the status of a holder of a cheque who presents it for payment?

Questions for Discussion

1. Should banks be responsible to a greater extent than they currently are for managing the financial affairs of their customers?

2. Should banking contracts be regulated to ensure greater protection for customers?

3. What are the key aspects of electronic banking that need to be regulated? What are the problems with creating and enforcing those regulations?

4. Is it a good idea to allow banks to give advice and sell investments?

5. Considering the number of negotiable instruments and electronic transfers, there are relatively few legal disputes arising from them. Does that mean the system is working well? What else might it mean?

6. Does the convenience of using payment methods other than cash outweigh the risks? How can a business manage the risk involved in cashless methods of payment?

Situations for Discussion

1. Paul, a bookkeeper employed by Harvey's Car Lot, forged Harvey's signature on a number of cheques over the course of a year. The cheques were made payable to fictitious payees. Paul deposited the cheques in his account at Y Bank. He forged the endorsement on some and was able to deposit the rest with no endorsement. The Y Bank accepted them all, as did Z Bank when they came to be deducted from the account that Harvey maintains there. Paul was able to conceal his fraudulent transactions in the course of his work. The fraud was not discovered for more than a year, when Harvey hired a new audit firm that detected the fraud in a random check. Meanwhile, Paul has left Harvey's and left town.[16] Who should bear the loss from Paul's fraud—Y Bank, Z Bank, or Harvey? What practices should Harvey put in place to prevent future fraud?

2. Michelle needs to borrow $50 000 to start her video rental business. She applies for a loan from W Bank. Pamela is the loans officer at the bank and assures Michelle that there should be no problem with her loan. The approval process takes longer than normal, and Michelle goes ahead and signs a lease for space for her shop and a three-year video rental contract with a distributor. Eventually, W Bank rejects Michelle's application. Based on recent experience, the bank has decided that video rental shops are too risky and hardly ever last beyond six months. Michelle is unable to arrange alternative financing in time and suffers a

---

16. Based on *Boma Manufacturing Ltd.* v. *CIBC* (1996), 203 N.R. 321 (S.C.C.).

large loss in her shop.[17] Does Pamela or the W Bank have any responsibility for Michelle's plight? What should Michelle and the bank have done differently?

3. Ratty Publications wrote a cheque payable to LePage on its account at CIBC in payment for the first month's rent on an office lease. Ratty changed its mind about the lease and instructed CIBC to stop payment on the cheque. The following day, LePage got the cheque certified at another branch of CIBC and deposited the cheque in its account at TD Bank. When TD presented the cheque to CIBC for payment, CIBC refused to honour it.[18] What happens to the cheque? Which prevails—the stop payment or the certification? Does the validity of the cheque depend on the lease agreement between Ratty and LePage? Which of the four parties should bear the loss?

4. Harvey's Car Lot bought a used car from Luke. When Luke delivered the car, Harvey gave him a cheque for $5000. When Harvey put the car in the garage, he discovered that the bottom was severely rusted and the engine was shot. The next day Harvey was contacted by the Magna Bank and informed that Luke still owed the bank $1000 on the car.[19] What can Harvey do about the cheque? What additional information do you need? How should Harvey change his purchasing practices?

5. Ravanello is a computer hacker. He is motivated primarily by the challenge of breaking systems, but he figures he might as well make some money at the same time. After many months of dedicated effort, he penetrated the electronic customer files of EZ Bank. Not wanting to appear greedy or be caught, Ravenello devised a system to skim $10 from random accounts every month. He began to accumulate money in his account faster than he could spend it. It was nine months before a customer of EZ convinced the bank that his account was short by three $10 withdrawals and the bank was able to trace the reason. What does this scenario reveal about the perils of electronic banking? Do you think this scenario could really happen? Would banking practices, contracts, or the law prevent it from happening?

6. Rubin and Russell were partners in RRP Associates. They did their personal and business banking with Colossal Bank, where they arranged their accounts so that transfers from one to the other could be made by either partner online, by phone, or in person. Although the business prospered, Rubin and Russell had difficulty working together. Following a serious disagreement, Russell went online and transferred $50 000 from the RRP account to his personal account. When Rubin discovered this transaction, he complained to the bank and was told that the transfer was done in accordance with the agreement between RRP and the bank. How can partners best balance the risks arising from banking arrangements with the need for convenient banking? What action can Rubin take now?

17. Based on *Royal Bank of Canada* v. *Woloszyn* (1998), 170 N.S.R. (2d) 122 (S.C.).
18. Based on *A.E. Lepage Real Estate Services Ltd.* v. *Rattray Publications* (1994), 21 O.R. (3d) 164 (C.A.).
19. Based on *William Ciurluini* v. *Royal Bank of Canada* (1972), 26 D.L.R. (3d) 552 (Ont. H.C.).

Chapter Twenty-Seven

The Legal Aspects of Credit

Objectives

AFTER STUDYING THIS CHAPTER, YOU SHOULD HAVE AN UNDERSTANDING OF:

► THE LEGAL SIGNIFICANCE OF CREDIT TRANSACTIONS IN BUSINESS

► THE DIFFERENCE BETWEEN SECURED AND UNSECURED CREDITORS

► THE WAYS THAT LENDERS AND BORROWERS ARE PROTECTED

► THE IMPLICATIONS OF GUARANTEEING A DEBT

Business Law in Practice

RST Ltd. is an independent printing company in a medium-sized town in Saskatchewan. It was established 15 years ago by Ron, Sandra, and Tara, who each own one-third of the shares in the company. Last year, RST revenues were $4 million, mainly from local contracts for such items as customized office stationery, business cards, advertising posters, calendars, and entertainment programs. Because the business is prospering, the owners are planning to expand their printing and sales space. They know that significant financing is required for the expanded facilities and the

Expanding a business
requires financing.

increased business. RST is currently financed 60 percent by the owners' shares and 40 percent by debt. The owners are prepared to put more equity into the business by purchasing additional shares, but they need $300 000 more to properly finance the project. They have decided to have RST Ltd. borrow that amount, rather than bring new shareholders into the company.

1. What are potential lenders likely to require from RST?
2. What are the risks for the business in borrowing $300 000?
3. What restrictions is a lender likely to put on the operation of the business?
4. Is there potential personal liability for Ron, Sandra, and Tara?
5. What will happen if the loan is not repaid?

Overview of Credit

A business engages in an array of transactions on a daily basis that involve credit. Some credit arrangements are formal and deliberate, with carefully negotiated terms, while others are an incidental feature of routine transactions. A business like RST is involved in numerous credit transactions—some as a borrower (debtor), and others as a lender (creditor). When RST orders paper from suppliers, the shipment is delivered with an invoice, likely requiring payment within 30 days. When RST fills orders for its customers, they are expected to pay on a similar basis.

unsecured credit
Debts that are not backed by specific assets of the debtor.

These examples illustrate what is known as **unsecured credit**. RST's suppliers have a contractual right to payment from RST for goods delivered, and RST has a similar right to collect from its customers. In the majority of these transactions, payment is made within the designated period and collection remedies are not needed, as a result of careful selection through such means as credit checks of those to whom credit will be granted. RST will have no trouble receiving orders on credit from suppliers it has dealt with before. RST will not hesitate to fill customer orders in advance of actual payment if those customers have paid as expected in the past. The "unsecured" element of these transactions becomes obvious if a debtor fails to pay what is due. The creditor then has a contractual right to collect and may sue the debtor for payment, but the creditor has no special security for payment. A judgment obtained against the debtor is satisfied from its general financial resources. If the debtor is financially healthy, the creditor is likely to receive payment. When the debtor is in financial difficulty and is unable to respond to claims from many creditors, the lack of security becomes a problem.

Credit arrangements outside normal business activities tend to be more formal and to provide more security to the lender. Borrowing a large amount of money to purchase a major asset or to finance an expansion, as RST is planning to do, is an example of a credit transaction in which the rights and obligations of the parties are carefully negotiated. When RST approaches a bank or another potential lender to request a loan of $300 000, the lender will require extensive documentation, such as a business plan and cash-flow projections. The lender will then consider two major criteria in evaluating the loan application. First, the lender will focus on RST's finan-

collateral
Security for a borrower's promise to repay a loan.

default
Failure to make required payments on a loan.

cial health—in particular, the likelihood that the expansion plans will succeed and that RST will be able to repay the loan in a period of time that the lender considers reasonable. This evaluation of risk will determine whether the lender grants the loan, and if so, on what terms (i.e., the interest rate will reflect the risk). Second, the lender will investigate the security RST can provide for repayment. Even healthy borrowers can get into financial difficulty and become unable to make loan payments as planned. A lender wants security, or **collateral**, to back up the borrower's promise to pay. The lender therefore carefully examines the borrower's assets (such as land, buildings, inventory, accounts receivable, and intellectual property) in terms of their current value and any other claims from existing creditors. For example, RST may own the land and building on which its business is located, but if the property is already mortgaged to another lender, its utility as security for a new loan is limited.

If the creditor approves the application for a loan, the resulting arrangement is a credit agreement (a contract). The lender agrees to lend the money based on the terms of the agreement, which essentially require the borrower to repay the loan on a specified schedule and provide security in the event of **default**. The security may be specific assets or a blanket coverage of all assets, and it may include assets that the borrower acquires in the future. The lender may officially register its claim against the borrower's assets and acquire priority over other creditors with subsequent claims. If the debtor defaults, the creditor can take action to have the assets seized and sold to satisfy the unpaid debt. As extra security, the lender may also seek assurance from persons other than the lender. In the RST situation, the lender may call upon the three shareholders to give their personal guarantees for repayment of the loan by RST.

The result of this system of credit granting is that the lender can extract whatever promises of security it deems necessary to protect its loan. Borrowers can shop around for better terms or less restrictive lending conditions, but ultimately they must meet a lender's requirements in order to get the loan.

Credit Risk in International Trade

Canadian companies import products from countries around the world to sell in Canada. For example, an international trade relationship might originate with a visit by representatives of the Canadian government and importers to a country that is identified as a potential source of trade, say, China. Let's say that Star Clothing, based in Toronto, participates in such a trip and identifies two manufacturers in China who could supply high-quality clothing at a lower cost than suppliers in Canada can. Representatives of

INTERNATIONAL PERSPECTIVE

Star communicate with their counterparts in the two Chinese companies and choose one of them (Beijing Clothing) as the best prospect. Star and Beijing eventually negotiate a contract worth $25 000 for clothing to be delivered in time for the spring fashion season in Canada. The contract includes quantity, price, and delivery date, and it specifies who is responsible for insurance and freight.

Since these companies are dealing with each other for the first time, they are sensitive to the risks involved. Beijing wants payment as soon as possible, ideally before shipment, to finance the production of the clothing. There is a large risk if Beijing ships the clothing to Canada with no means of ensuring payment. Beijing appreciates the difficulties involved in suing a Canadian company to recover payment, so it is unwilling to transfer title to the clothing before being paid and wishes to receive payment through its own bank in China.

On the other side of the transaction, Star is reluctant to pay for the clothing until it has received the agreed quality and quantity of clothing at the agreed time and place. Star is unwilling to pay before the clothing is manufactured and shipped and insists on at least receiving the title documents before making payment. Star knows that suing a Chinese company for breach of contract is difficult.

The services of international bankers and letters of credit are a common means of distributing these risks and dealing with the challenges of distance, unfamiliarity of the parties, and different legal rules and enforcement mechanisms. A **letter of credit** is a written promise made by the importer's bank (on the importer's instructions) and given to the exporter's bank to make payment to the exporter when specified conditions are met. These conditions relate to the exporter's delivery of documents, such as an invoice, shipping receipt, proof of insurance, and customs declaration. Although these documents are often presented and payment is made to the seller well before the importer receives the goods, the importer has considerable assurance that the goods will arrive.

Critical Analysis: Is the letter of credit a device that could be used in domestic transactions? What level of security does it provide? How does it relate to reputation and reliability in commercial dealings?

Source: Mary Jo Nicholson, *Legal Aspects of International Business* (Scarborough: Prentice Hall, 1997), at 190.

letter of credit
A written promise by a buyer's bank to a seller's bank to pay the seller when specified conditions are met.

consumer debt
A loan to an individual for a noncommercial purpose.

Regulation of Credit

Government intervention in the system of credit is mainly through provincial consumer protection legislation, which applies to transactions that lead to **consumer debt**, where the borrower is a *consumer* rather than a business. Its main purpose is to protect the consumer from the potentially unfair bargaining advantage that lenders enjoy. Enforcement is generally left to the consumer, so if the consumer is unaware of legislative protection or is unsure of how to enforce her or his rights, the protection is of little practical utility. This is a problem that governments seek to address by providing consumer information and counselling (for example, in Nova Scotia through the Department of Service Nova Scotia and Municipal Relations).

Within each province, the forms of protection are often scattered throughout a number of statutes but are united by the theme of seeking to regulate the provision of credit in the areas of licensing, permitted activities, and terms of credit.

A review of the various consumer credit regulations illustrates

- that there are specific rules a business must follow when it extends credit to consumers; otherwise, it risks any number of penalties, including the credit being declared unenforceable, licence suspension or revocation, and fines
- that these same rules function as a guide that businesses can use to protect themselves and to ensure good customer relations

The particular areas of consumer credit that are subject to regulation are as follows:

Reporting

credit bureau
An agency that compiles credit information on borrowers.

Credit bureaus provide a service to lenders by compiling credit information on consumers and reporting on their credit history. Lenders use this information to evaluate requests for loans. Because consumers may be unaware that this is happening, there are licensing systems to ensure the respectability of credit bureaus, and regulations to ensure the accuracy of the information that is compiled. Consumers have access to their files and the opportunity to correct any errors.[1] For example, if Sandra applied for a loan and was refused, the lender must supply her with the particulars of the reporting agency that provided the information on her credit history. She can then contact the reporting agency, examine the information in its files, and address any inaccuracies. The agency must amend its files accordingly.

Negotiation of Terms

Lenders are specifically prohibited from making misleading statements in the application and negotiation process. These regulations bolster contract law protection against misrepresentation.

Terms of Credit

In order to protect the consumer from those who would provide credit at exorbitant rates, the *Criminal Code*[2] prohibits lending at a rate of interest above 60 percent on an annual basis. Provincial legislation is more general. The courts are able to reopen transactions where "the cost of the loan is excessive and the transaction is harsh and unconscionable."[3] Most provinces now have legislation regulating business practices (including credit transactions) that prohibits, for example, transactions where there is "no reasonable probability of making payment in full" or where there is no substantial benefit to the consumer.[4]

Disclosure of Cost of the Credit

The unsophisticated consumer may not realize just how expensive credit can be. Legislation seeks to address this reality by requiring disclosure of the true cost of lending in terms of the following:

- the amount borrowed, the amount of interest, any other charges such as registration fees or insurance, and the total balance payable
- the annual rate of interest (as a percentage) and the period over which the rate applies

The goal is to prevent hidden charges by the lender and to better enable the borrower to appreciate the implications of the transaction.[5]

Remedies

The remedies that a borrower can seek where a lender has failed to observe the regulations are varied. They include filing a complaint against the lender with a regula-

---

1. See, for example, *Consumer Reporting Act*, R.S.O. 1990, c. C-33, s. 280.
2. R.S.C. 1985, c. C-46, s. 347.
3. *Unconscionable Transactions Relief Act*, R.S.N.S. 1989, c. 481, s. 3.
4. *Business Practices Act*, R.S.O. 1990, c. B-18, s. 2. See Chapter 24.
5. *Consumer Protection Act*, R.S.B.C. 1996, c. 69, s. 41.

tory body (which can lead to fines, licence suspension or revocation, and orders prohibiting further violations), or applying to the courts to have the terms of the loan adjusted, or in some situations claiming damages.

Collection

Collection agencies provide a service to lenders who have serious difficulty recovering loans. These agencies are subject to a licensing scheme and cannot harass, threaten, or exert undue pressure on defaulting borrowers. They are also prohibited from contacting anyone other than the borrower (such as a family member or business associates). Only those with contractual responsibility for the debt can be subject to any efforts to collect, even when the debtor is bankrupt or deceased.[6] Agencies that go beyond allowed means of collection risk having their licence to operate revoked.

Negotiation of the Credit Agreement

The aspects of credit that are regulated in relation to consumer loans are left to the parties themselves in the commercial context. RST must look after its own interests. The process of applying for a loan and formulating the terms of credit is much the same as for the negotiation of any other contract. Key factors are the needs and bargaining power of the lender and the borrower. RST's need for $300 000 is major in terms of its expansion plans, but it is an insignificant transaction to a large commercial lender. The lender has the advantage in bargaining power. When RST applies for the loan, the lender will demand whatever information it deems necessary in order to assess the risk and determine how much, if anything, it is prepared to lend to RST and on what basis. If the lender decides to grant the loan, it will offer terms to RST in the form of a **letter of commitment**,which sets out in detail the basic terms dealing with

letter of commitment
A document that is provided by a bank to a borrower and sets out the terms of a loan.

- amount of the loan
- interest
- repayment terms
- renewal
- security
- requirements for maintenance of the borrower's financial position
- events that constitute default
- lender's remedies

This letter may be the actual agreement (if the borrower agrees), or it may lead to other formal documentation. RST can try to negotiate adjustments in those terms, but ultimately, if RST wants the loan, it must meet the lender's terms or seek another lender (whose terms are likely to be similar).

Security

The two major elements of the credit agreement are the borrower's promise to repay the loan and the lender's collateral or security if the borrower fails to repay. Security for the loan can be any interest in property that is of value to the lender, namely

---

6. *Collection Agencies Act*, R.S.O. 1990, c. C-14.

- *Real property.* This is accomplished through a mortgage, as discussed in Chapter 19.
- *All forms of personal property.* For example, if RST borrows in order to buy a new piece of printing equipment, the security for the loan may be the equipment itself.

general security agreement
A loan contract that includes all of the assets of a business as collateral.

In RST's current application for expansion funds, the lender will likely require broader security in the form of a **general security agreement**, sometimes known as a floating charge. In this agreement, the lender will probably want to include all specific assets currently held by RST, as well as all other assets of the business either currently owned or acquired during the term of the loan. RST is free to carry on business and use its assets as long as it makes the required payments on the loan. If RST defaults on the loan, the floating charge crystallizes and attaches to the assets covered by the agreement and held by RST at the time of default.

From this perspective, assets used as security can be classified in terms of whether they are meant to be retained in the business by the debtor. For example, if RST buys a printing machine for use in the business over the course of its useful life, it is available as security for a substantial length of time. Other assets, such as inventory and accounts receivable, are meant to circulate through the business on a regular basis. The security is the value of those assets at any given time. The loan agreement will require the borrower to maintain certain levels of those assets. However, it is understood and expected that the business will regularly be selling inventory and buying more, and that it will be collecting accounts from customers while delivering more orders on credit. In addition, the agreement will require the borrower to submit financial reports to the lender at specified intervals and maintain a specified debt–equity ratio.

Security may also consist of assets to be produced in the future. For example, a manufacturer may need financing in order to convert raw materials into finished goods. The federal *Bank Act*[7] enables the finished goods to be the security for the loan. As the goods are manufactured, the bank gains priority over the inventory against other creditors.

RST should appreciate the implications of the credit agreement—in particular, the degree of control over its assets that the lender will acquire should RST default. RST's ability to repay depends on the success of the expanded business, so it is not surprising that the lender wants considerable control over the business and its assets.

Lenders demand as much security as possible, to the extent that its value may even appear to exceed the extent of the lender's risk. One reason for this demand for excessive security is the uncertain value of the assets. If RST borrows money to buy one piece of equipment and defaults on the loan, the lender's security is a used piece of equipment. The lender knows that the proceeds from a forced sale of the asset are likely to be much less than its value to RST in its ongoing business. Similarly, if RST gives a general security agreement, the value of all of RST's assets in the event of the business failing is much less than it appears at the time a financially healthy RST receives the loan.

---

7. *Bank Act,* S.C. 1991, c. 46, s. 427.

Credit and Environmental Risk

ENVIRONMENTAL PERSPECTIVE

Financial institutions engaged in commercial lending with real property as security generally require environmental assurance as part of the credit documentation. This assurance consists of representations and warranties by the borrower regarding the environmental status of the property, supplemented by surveys and questionnaires in the standard form of the particular lender. In addition, lenders may require more detailed environmental reviews and investigations from the borrower.

These reviews may be in two stages. The first stage identifies clearly visible contamination resulting from current or past use of the property. It consists of

- review of the borrower's records concerning such things as site history and documented contamination
- site visits
- inventory of hazardous materials
- interviews with site personnel and others involved with the borrower's use of the property

The results of the first stage of investigation may cause the lender to require a secondary report, either to eliminate questions raised by the environmental consultant or to address possible contamination. The second stage involves more intensive investigation, such as taking core samples, sampling underground water, and reviewing surrounding properties. This stage may help eliminate concerns raised by the consultants in the first stage, particularly with regard to adjoining properties, but it may also identify contamination leading to potential environmental liability.

Critical Analysis: Why would a lender require such extensive environmental information as part of the credit application process? Is this a significant requirement for the borrower?

Source: Alison R. Manzer & Jordan S. Bernamoff, *The Corporate Counsel Guide to Banking and Credit Relationships* (Aurora: Canada Law Book, 1999) at 70.

Creditors are aware of the impact environmental hazards can have on the value of their security.

Priority among Creditors

For a security to be of value as collateral, the lender must be confident of its claim to the assets in the event of default. When considering the loan application, the lender needs a means of verifying ownership of the assets being offered as possible collateral and of determining whether the assets already form security for a loan. Assets that are free and clear—or otherwise unencumbered—are most attractive as security. Assets already used as security for debt may be considered if they are worth more than the debt. Once the loan is granted, the lender needs a means of informing existing and future creditors and potential purchasers of the assets that it has a claim against the property. If the borrower seeks additional financing, potential creditors need an accurate picture of the borrower's assets as security.

All provinces have two systems in place to provide creditors with priority over others regarding their security for loans. The system in place for real property was discussed in Chapter 19. The system for the other form of property—personal property—takes the form of personal property security legislation. All provinces (except Newfoundland) have one statute[8] that applies to all forms of personal property security arrangements. These comprehensive provincial statutes have several common features:

registration
The process of recording a security interest in a public registry system.

financing statement
The document registered as evidence of security against personal property.

- There is one set of **registration** rules in each province for all arrangements using personal property as security.
- The creditor registers a **financing statement,** which identifies the debtor and the property that is security for the loan. Specific items are identified by serial number where possible.
- Financing statements are maintained in a central computerized registry, which is public.
- Anyone interested in the degree of encumbrance of the assets of a business or an individual need conduct only one search within the province in order to discover all registered claims against the assets of that business or person.
- Anyone who discovers a relevant registered financing statement can obtain from the creditor the full details as contained in the written security agreement.
- In the event of conflicting claims for the same assets, priority goes to the creditor who registered the financing statement first.
- The priority of registration is subject to the limitation that specific security agreements (i.e., RST's purchase of the piece of equipment) have priority over clauses in general security agreements that apply to **after-acquired property** (property acquired after the agreement was signed).

after-acquired property
Assets purchased after a secured loan is granted.

These centralized and uniform systems are a vast improvement over the earlier patchwork of different statutes and rules. However, they do not remove inconsistencies among provinces or address the practical problem that personal property is portable and may easily be moved beyond the ambit of a single province's registration system.

Provincial Variations

The Canadian Constitution gives the provinces jurisdiction over property and civil rights. Thus, each province has its own system and rules for the registration of property as security for credit. The rationale is to allow provincial governments to take local and regional conditions into account when developing legislation. The result for corporations doing business in several provinces is major inconvenience and expense stemming from the need to comply with many different sets of rules. The

BUSINESS APPLICATION OF THE LAW

United States has the Uniform Commercial Code, which has been adopted in all states to provide uniform registration rules for secured transactions.

Critical Analysis: Do the benefits to the provinces of autonomy outweigh the burden on business? Is there a political or legal mechanism in Canada to harmonize rules that are already very similar from province to province?

---

8. See, for example, *Personal Property Security Act*, R.S.O. 1990, c. P-10 and S.N.S. 1995-96, c. 13.

Other weaknesses in the current system include the cost of registration and the fact that in the interest of simplicity and consistency of registration, a common financing statement is used. It is necessary to contact the creditor to obtain the details of the credit agreement. Although the initial search is straightforward, obtaining the full details from the creditor is more cumbersome.

The system does provide creditors with a considerable level of protection, however. They have a means of informing the borrower's other creditors what their security is. Borrowers' credit agreements are public knowledge. Any subsequent credit arrangements are subject to those registered commitments. The same assets can provide security for more than one credit arrangement, but the claims of competing lenders are subject to priority according to the order of registration of their agreements.

Remedies

Status of the Creditor

secured creditor
A lender who has the right to seize and sell specific assets of a borrower to pay off a loan.

The major distinction in status is between secured and unsecured creditors. Unsecured or general creditors have the right to sue the debtor for unpaid debts and at the end of that process achieve a judgment against any assets of the debtor that are not already claimed by other creditors. Creditors who have a registered claim against all or a portion of the debtors' assets are known as **secured creditors**. They have the remedies enjoyed by unsecured creditors, but in addition they have first claim against the assets covered by their security agreement with the debtor. These secured assets are unavailable for the claims of unsecured creditors, even if the debtor becomes bankrupt. From the distribution of assets in a bankruptcy, secured creditors recover a higher portion of what they are owed than unsecured creditors do (see Chapter 28).

Lenders' Remedies

If the borrower defaults on the loan, secured lenders have a variety of remedies from two sources: the credit agreement and the legislation under which the agreement is registered.

acceleration clause
A term of a loan agreement that makes the entire loan due if one payment is missed.

Credit agreements normally permit the lender to call the entire loan based on default of one payment, through what is known as an **acceleration clause**. The default accelerates the time when the entire debt is due to the date of the default, thereby giving the debtor an incentive to make timely payments. The lender can enter the borrower's premises (possibly with authorization from the courts) and seize the secured assets. The lender can then proceed to collect on the collateral (such as accounts receivable) or sell or otherwise dispose of it (in the case of inventory or equipment, for example) in order to generate funds to cover the unpaid balance.

deficiency
The shortfall if a secured asset is sold for less than the amount of the outstanding loan.

At this point, the lender's evaluation of the security at the time the loan was granted is tested. If the lender valued the security conservatively and granted credit for less than the full value, the recovery on default should be complete. But if the lender took a less cautious approach (by overvaluing the security or lending its full value), the proceeds of sale may be inadequate. The lender then has an action (as a general creditor) against the borrower for the shortfall or **deficiency** in what is owed and shares the remaining unsecured assets with all general creditors. If the sale of the security generates funds in excess of those needed to repay the loan, that excess must be paid to the borrower for the benefit of other creditors.

Legislation generally confirms and supplements the contractual remedies, enabling the creditor to begin legal action for arrears, retain or take possession of collateral, and appoint a receiver or manager if there is a general security agreement in place.[9]

Limits on Lenders' Remedies

Creditors are generally prohibited from seizing assets that provide security for their purchase if the debtor has already made payments equal to two-thirds of the loan.[10] In some provinces the lender is limited to the proceeds from the seized assets and is therefore unable to sue the debtor for any deficiency between the outstanding balance and the proceeds from the seized assets. In all provinces, the creditor must deal with assets in a commercially reasonable manner.[11] This means taking reasonable steps to realize as much from the seized assets as possible. Creditors are not expected to retain assets until the ideal buyer can be found because the courts recognize that creditors are in the lending business—they are not dealers in a wide variety of vehicles, equipment, and other assets. Creditors must avoid conflicts of interest through buying assets themselves or selling to related businesses at a price less than fair market value.

The major restraint on creditors' remedies is the requirement to give the debtor reasonable notice before calling a loan, appointing a receiver, and seizing assets. This notice is especially important in situations where a general security agreement gives the creditor first claim over the bulk of the debtors' assets and allows the creditor to appoint a receiver in the event of default. Receivers essentially control the business and can exclude the debtor from making decisions. The debtor is anxious to salvage the business, perhaps by refinancing and generating revenue to pay creditors and carry on business. The creditor has already made the decision to call the loan and, as always, has the primary objective of redeeming sufficient assets to clear the loan. The survival of the business is secondary to the creditor.

Case

Murano v. *Bank of Montreal* (1995), 20 B.L.R. (2d) 61 (Ont. Gen. Div.), varied (1998), 41 B.L.R. (2d) 10 (Ont. C.A.)

The Business Context: A creditor with a general security agreement has considerable power that threatens the survival of the business. As a result, the courts have developed the requirement of notice to provide an opportunity for the debtor to raise funds from other sources to pay the loan. Creditors are reluctant to give such notice, as they are fearful that valuable assets may disappear during the notice period.

Factual Background: Murano owned and operated a chain of video rental stores called the Hilton division. He also owned five "Top 30" video stores and had plans to open 70 more. He had also agreed to buy 52 stores in the Bandito Video chain. When one of the Hilton stores changed locations, the bank immediately demanded payment of its loans on the basis of terms in the credit agreement and appointed a receiver for the Hilton division two hours later. Murano was not told of the bank's reasons for its actions. The bank told other lenders, business associates of Murano, and suppliers that it acted because of Murano's dishonest activities related to his desperate financial situation. Murano claimed that the bank's actions destroyed the Hilton division and prevented the Top 30 and Bandito

---

9. See, for example, the Ontario *Personal Property Security Act,* R.S.O. 1990, c. P-10.
10. This limitation applies, for example, in New Brunswick, Nova Scotia, and Ontario.
11. For example, *Personal Property Security Act,* S.N.S. 1996-96, c. 13 s. 66(2).

projects from proceeding. In addition, Murano could not maintain payments on several real estate loans or refinance his business operations. The bank's actions caused the real estate lenders to seize those assets and sell them at distressed prices. The bank defended its conduct on the basis that Murano's businesses were a highly leveraged "house of cards" waiting to fall.

The Legal Question: Was the bank justified in acting as quickly as it did? If not, what losses did the bank cause to Murano?

Resolution: A creditor must give a debtor reasonable notice that repayment of a loan is required, even where the loan is payable on demand. The length of notice depends on the circumstances in each case, including the amount of the loan, the risk to the creditor, the length of the relationship between debtor and creditor, the character and reputation of the debtor, and the potential for the debtor to quickly raise the funds to pay the loan.

The bank did not give Murano reasonable notice of its intentions. There were no special circumstances beyond the normal fears of all lenders that the borrower may default. There was no indication that

Murano planned to disappear with his assets. The bank used the move of the one Hilton store as a pretext for acting quickly. The bank's disclosure of information about Murano to others was unnecessary to protect the bank or the public and was therefore a breach of the bank's duty of confidentiality in relation to its customer's affairs.

The court awarded Murano a total of $3.37 million in damages, composed of $1.55 million for the loss on the Hilton division, $1 million for each of the Top 30 and Bandito transactions, and $220 000 for real estate losses. With the exception of the real estate losses, the Court of Appeal confirmed the award.

Critical Analysis: A key factor in the case was the bank's mismanagement of Murano's account, largely a result of turnover of account managers and lack of information in his file. Can a customer assume that a bank is monitoring the file? Does the result of this case ask too much of banks, which need to protect their security? Did the court go too far in holding the bank responsible for losses on business deals other than those directly connected to the loan?

Borrowers' Remedies

The borrower has the basic right to limit the lender to the remedies permitted by legislation and defined by the agreement. Therefore, the borrower can best protect its interest by trying to negotiate flexible terms when the business is relatively prosperous. If the borrower later has financial difficulties, the lender will quickly focus on damage control and be less inclined to be flexible.

On an ongoing basis, the borrower is entitled to an accounting of the state of the loan, mainly in terms of the outstanding balance. If default occurs, the borrower has several rights in relation to the lender's seizure and sale of assets. The borrower is entitled to prescribed or reasonable notice of seizure and sale in order to be able to monitor the process and know when an infusion of funds could halt the collection process and enable the borrower to carry on. The borrower can challenge a sale that is improperly conducted or that produces unreasonably low proceeds, known as an **improvident sale**, and recover surplus proceeds from a sale of assets, or any property seized but not sold to satisfy the debt.[12]

These rights and remedies available to the borrower relate to credit agreements with particular creditors. If the borrower is in serious financial difficulty, there are

improvident sale
A sale of the borrower's assets by the lender for less than fair market value.

---

12. Alison R. Manzer & Jordan S. Bernamoff, *The Corporate Counsel Guide to Banking and Credit Relationships* (Aurora: Canada Law Book, 1999) at 65.

ADR in the Banking Industry

The Canadian Bankers Association has an ADR model for credit disputes between its member banks and their small-business customers. The model recognizes that there are complaints from customers dealing with banks' decisions to decrease or remove credit or call their security. Each bank has a resolution procedure for addressing these complaints. If that procedure fails to resolve the complaint to the customer's satisfaction, each member bank must have a code of conduct that makes an ADR process available to the customer.

The model contains several key elements that each bank must include in its process:

- The individual conducting the process must be independent and impartial.
- Information shared during the process must remain confidential.
- There must be guidelines indicating which customers can use the process and under what circumstances.
- Customers must follow the bank's procedure in accessing the process.
- The cost must be made known before the process begins.
- The process must begin within 15 days of receipt of the customer's request.

The process itself must be voluntary for the customer. The facilitator will help the bank and the customer to try to reach a resolution but has no authority to overturn the bank's decision. During the process, the bank will not take legal action to enforce its remedies and the customer will not dispose of assets. The process does not affect the legal rights of the parties, unless they reach a resolution, in which case they are bound by their agreement.

Each bank must report annually the number of customers requesting ADR and the outcome of each case to the Superintendent of Financial Institutions. Each bank must annually review its process for effectiveness and compliance with the model.

Critical Analysis: What disputes between bankers and customers do you think this process could resolve? What are some of the uncertainties in how the process would work? Does one side have the upper hand? What are the benefits for banks and customers?

Source: Canadian Bankers Association Web site, online <http://www.cba.ca/cba/eng/Publications/ADR/adr.htm> (date accessed: 4 September 2000).

---

broader remedies available whose purpose is to facilitate the refinancing of businesses that are in trouble but that have potential for recovery (see Chapter 28). For example, the borrower can file notice of intention to make a proposal to creditors under the *Bankruptcy and Insolvency Act.*[13]

Personal Guarantees

If RST's bank grants the loan for expansion, it is highly likely that one of the requirements will be personal guarantees from Ron, Sandra, and Tara. These guarantees provide more collateral for the loan to RST because the personal assets of the three shareholders will be available to the bank if RST defaults. The bank's rights against RST

---

13. R.S.C. 1985, c. B-3, s. 50.4(1).

are found in the credit agreement and the legislation and may be limited to certain assets owned by RST. Potential claims against Ron, Sandra, and Tara personally are defined by the contracts of guarantee they sign with the bank and are likely unlimited in terms of which assets of the three the bank can pursue as an unsecured creditor.

Figure 27.1

RELATIONSHIPS IN PERSONAL GUARANTEES

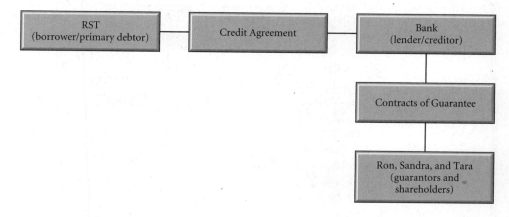

guarantor
A person who signs a guarantee.

A guarantee is a contract between the bank as creditor and the shareholders as **guarantors**. Therefore, the terms and conditions are those contained in the guarantee agreement. Any arrangements between the guarantors and the debtor (RST) do not affect the rights of the bank. The essence of the guarantee is a promise by those who sign it that if the debtor fails to repay its loan, the guarantors will. Their promises are conditional or secondary to the primary obligation of the borrower. Ron, Sandra, and Tara may also be called upon to cosign RST's loans, but only then will they become primarily liable for repayment along with RST.

The implications for shareholders (or others) who sign personal guarantees are significant. They lose their limited liability protection to the extent of their promises to the bank by putting their personal assets at risk. As officers of RST, the three shareholders sign many documents on behalf of RST, but the guarantees create personal obligations.

Another major danger of guarantees is their continuing nature. They often include the total debt owed to the bank at any given time. When the initial loan is granted, the guarantors are confident in RST's future and comfortable with the amount of the loan. As time passes, the amount of credit may increase, and RST's financial health may deteriorate. Meanwhile, the bank holds the guarantees. If financial disaster strikes and the bank proceeds on the guarantees, Ron, Sandra, and Tara will view their commitment and risk much differently than they did when they signed several years earlier. In a typical disaster situation, where the sums owed by the corporate debtor are substantial, the guarantors may be unable to respond to the bank's demands on the guarantees and may be forced into personal bankruptcy.

The Guarantee Agreement

A guarantee is one of the few contracts that must be in written form and signed by the guarantor in order to be enforceable.[14] A written record is important because the

---

14. Manitoba is the exception. The writing requirement is in place in all other provinces, generally in the *Statute of Frauds*.

guarantee has major implications for the individuals who sign, and it may be in force for a long period.

A guarantee is not normally a freely negotiated arrangement. It is part of a larger credit arrangement where the lender requires that guarantees be provided on the lender's standard form. These contracts are designed to maximize the lender's ability to obligate the guarantors—by severely limiting ways for the guarantors to avoid liability—and to give the lender maximum flexibility in dealing with the debtor. The guarantors may be compelled to sign in order for the loan to be granted, but they need to make this commitment in a deliberate rather than casual manner. In the RST situation, guarantees from the shareholders will be a condition for the loan to RST, so the three need to consider this as an important factor in their decision to seek debt rather than equity financing.

The following are some typical terms in a contract of guarantee:

- All guarantors are liable for the full amount; thus, if Ron, Sandra, and Tara sign a guarantee for the $300 000 loan, they are each 100 percent liable for that full amount. The bank can recover the total amount of the loan from any one of them because the guarantors are jointly liable. It is up to the individuals to seek recovery from one another.
- The guarantee normally applies to all credit extended to the debtor while the guarantee is in force. If the shareholders wish to limit their liability to $300 000, they must negotiate this term with the bank and ensure that the contract they sign states that limit in clear terms.
- Guarantees are normally in force for an unlimited period. Those who sign must realize the risk this term entails and try to negotiate either a time limit or a clause that allows them to terminate their obligations by giving notice to the bank.
- Guarantees normally exclude any terms, conditions, statements, or representations that are not in the agreement. Guarantors should not sign based on any assurances or assumptions that are not expressly stated.
- A standard guarantee ordinarily provides that the creditor is authorized to deal with the debtor and the terms of credit without affecting the guarantors' liability (for example, by increasing the amount of the loan). This is a direct reversal of the common law rule that ends the guarantee if the terms of the debt are changed without the guarantors' consent.

Avoiding Guarantor Obligations

When the arrangement is first made, guarantors can see the benefits of guaranteeing a loan. Without the guarantee, the bank is unlikely to advance the money. But by the time the bank takes action to enforce the guarantee, the debtor's situation is hopeless, and there is no benefit for the guarantors in making payments because the business is failing. However, when and if the guarantors do make payments on behalf of the primary debtor, they have a right of **subrogation** against the debtor. This means that if RST defaults on its loan and the shareholders are required to pay through their guarantees, they have the right to recover their money from RST. However, if RST were able to repay the guarantors, it is unlikely the default would have occurred in the first place.

subrogation
The right of a guarantor to recover from the debtor any payments made to the creditor.

Guarantors have some common law defences. For example, the guarantors' obligation is limited to the terms of the debt they guaranteed. If the terms of that loan are changed in any way that increases the risk to the guarantors, the agreement is terminated unless the guarantors have agreed to the changes. Changes having this effect include increasing the amount of the loan or the rate of interest, extending the time for payment, or altering the collateral the debtor has provided for the loan. These and other defences are often eliminated by the words of modern guarantees that specifically prevent the guarantor from using the common law defences to payment.

Landmark Case

Hawrish v. *Bank of Montreal* (1969), 2 D.L.R. (3d) 600 (S.C.C.)

The Business Context: This case illustrates the importance of the written guarantee agreement.

Factual Background: Crescent Dairies Ltd. was a company formed to buy a cheese factory. When Crescent exhausted its line of credit with the bank, Hawrish was asked to sign a guarantee. He signed the bank's usual form, which stated that it was a continuing guarantee and covered existing and future debt of Crescent up to $6000. There was also a clause in which the guarantor acknowledged that no representations had been made to him on behalf of the bank and that the guarantee had nothing to do with any other guarantee. Hawrish claimed that he was assured by the assistant manager of the bank branch that the guarantee was to cover only debt outstanding at the time of signing and that

he would be released from his obligation when the bank received a joint guarantee from the company directors. He claimed that he did not read the guarantee before he signed.

The Legal Question: Was the liability of Hawrish subject to the assurances he received from the bank before he signed the guarantee?

Resolution: The court found in favour of the bank. Even if the statements were made by the bank, they directly contradicted the terms of the written guarantee, which clearly stated that the guarantee was a continuing obligation. Even though Crescent's directors gave the joint guarantee to the bank, Hawrish was not released.

Critical Analysis: Should a bank be able to make statements such as those made to Hawrish and then later rely on the contradictory terms of the written agreement? Why is this unfair to guarantors? What is the danger if guarantors are released because of such statements?

A defence available to some guarantors is their lack of understanding of the terms of the contract and their risk. If the signors are individuals who are not directly involved in the debtor's business or in the particular credit transaction, they should obtain independent advice before signing. Spouses or other relatives of Ron, Sandra, and Tara with little or no involvement in RST may sign under pressure from family and personal relationships. Without independent advice, they may make commitments that they fail to understand and may as a result be relieved of their obligations. Ron, Sandra, and Tara are directly involved in the RST business, so this defence is not available to them. They are presumed to know the implications of RST's loan request and how their guarantees affect that arrangement. Bank personnel may also make assumptions about the willingness and level of knowledge of the prospective guarantors. Subject to the various exceptional possibilities for avoiding contractual obligations (see Chapter 8), guarantors have little chance to escape liability if the debtor defaults.

Case

Manulife Bank of Canada v. Conlin (1996), 203 N.R. 81 (S.C.C.)

The Business Context: Although the terms of guarantees tend to favour the creditor over the guarantor and the chances of a guarantor avoiding liability are slim, the courts are prepared to closely scrutinize the terms and to hold the guarantor responsible only to the extent that the terms clearly indicate.

Factual Background: In 1987 Dina Conlin signed a three-year mortgage on an apartment building in favour of Manulife in the amount of $275 000 at 11.5 percent interest. Her husband, John Conlin, signed the mortgage as guarantor. The guarantee clause of the mortgage stated that the guarantor was obligated despite "the giving of time for payment ... or the varying of the terms of payment ... or the rate of interest." It also stated that the guarantor's liability was continuous and that he was liable until payment in full by the borrower. Another clause of the mortgage provided for renewal by agreement in writing. The Conlins separated in 1989, and the next year the mortgage was renewed at 13 percent interest. Only Dina signed the renewal agreement. John was not notified, even though the agreement provided space for a guarantor's signature. In 1992 Dina defaulted, and Manulife foreclosed and sued John on his 1987 guarantee.

The Legal Question: Was John Conlin released from his guarantee by the renewal of the mortgage?

Resolution: The trial judge found that the original terms held John liable for the renewal, even though he was not notified. The appeal court disagreed, and the Supreme Court confirmed John's release by a 4–3 majority based on the following points:

- Any material alteration of the contract of debt will change the terms upon which the guarantor was to be liable and will result in a change in the guarantor's risk.
- A guarantor will be released from liability when the creditor and the debtor agree to a material alteration of the terms of the contract of debt without the consent of the guarantor.
- The guarantor and the creditor can agree to opt out of this rule.
- Where the creditor argues that the guarantee agreement provides a blanket authorization to make material alterations to the contract of debt, the wording must be very clear that such a right was intended.
- If there is doubt or ambiguity about the meaning of the clauses in the agreement, they must be resolved in favour of the guarantor.
- When the guarantee clause is interpreted, it must be considered in the context of the entire transaction, including the terms and arrangements for the renewal agreement.

Critical Analysis: Are guarantors in a vulnerable position and in need of protection? Why was the decision in the Supreme Court so close? How is a bank and the banking industry likely to react to a decision like this? What risk management action is appropriate?

The only government regulation of guarantees in Canada is a statute in Alberta.[15] It provides that for any guarantee to be valid in that province, it must be certified by a notary public that the guarantors were aware of the contents of the guarantee and understood them. The statute places no limits on the content of the guarantee, so creditors can make the terms as restrictive as they like without affecting the validity of the guarantee.

---

15. *Guarantees Acknowledgment Act*, R.S.A. 1980, c. G-12.

Business Law in Practice Revisited

1. What are potential lenders likely to require from RST?

RST will be asked to provide detailed financial statements and a business plan for the expansion. Lenders will also require RST to pledge assets of sufficient worth to cover the loan.

2. What are the risks for the business in borrowing $300 000?

The major risk is the possibility that the business will be less profitable than planned and that cash-flow problems will result in default on the loan payments. Default will lead to loss of assets to the lender and possibly the end of the business.

3. What restrictions is a lender likely to put on the operation of the business?

RST will be required to maintain minimum levels of accounts receivable and inventory, to stay within a specified debt–equity ratio, and to report to the bank at specified intervals. RST will also need the lender's permission to deal with secured assets.

4. Is there potential personal liability for Ron, Sandra, and Tara?

The three shareholders will be required to personally guarantee the loan to RST. If RST defaults, their personal assets are available to the lender. They lose their limited liability protection to the extent of this loan.

5. What will happen if the loan is not repaid?

If RST fails to repay, the secured assets can be seized and sold by the lender, and probably the lender will have the power to appoint a receiver to assume control of the business. Only if RST can refinance will it be able to recover and carry on.

Chapter Summary

Credit transactions are an important and normal part of every business. A business can be a debtor or a creditor, depending on the transaction. Some arrangements are continuous and revolving, such as with a customer and supplier. Others are major individual transactions and involve a formal credit agreement specifying the rights and obligations of the borrower and the lender.

Unsecured creditors have equal claim against the assets of the borrowing business. They can sue and obtain a judgment and apply that against the debtor's unsecured assets. If a business is involved in significant debt financing, most of its assets will be covered by credit agreements, which secured creditors will register to obtain priority over unsecured creditors. If the business defaults, secured creditors have first claim over the assets covered by their registered agreements.

Lenders are protected by the contracts that borrowers sign and by the legislation that provides for security through registration. Unsecured creditors have the right to litigate their claims.

Borrowers are also protected through their agreements with creditors and legislation. Lenders can exercise only the rights provided by contract and legislation and must act reasonably in doing so.

Guarantors place their personal assets at risk when they sign a guarantee. They should be aware of the onerous terms in most guarantees and ensure that they limit their exposure to the extent possible in the standard form agreements.

StudyChapter

Key Terms and Concepts

acceleration clause (p. 628)
after-acquired property (p. 627)
collateral (p. 621)
consumer debt (p. 622)
credit bureau (p. 623)
default (p. 621)
deficiency (p. 628)
financing statement (p. 627)
general security agreement (p. 625)
guarantor (p. 632)
improvident sale (p. 630)
letter of commitment (p. 624)
letter of credit (p. 622)
registration (p. 627)
secured creditor (p. 628)
subrogation (p. 633)
unsecured credit (p. 620)

Questions for Review

1. What are some examples of credit transactions?

2. What is the position of an unsecured creditor?

3. What are the two key aspects of a secured credit transaction?

4. What are the disclosure requirements for a consumer loan?

5. What is a general security agreement?

6. What is the role of a financing statement in personal property security registration?

7. What are the practical differences between real and personal property in terms of registering security interests?

8. To what extent do we have uniform personal property registration rules in Canada?

9. What is the role of a receiver appointed by a creditor?

10. Who are the parties in a contract of guarantee?

11. Who writes the language in most guarantees?

Questions for Discussion

1. When a business fails, most of the assets are claimed by secured creditors. Other creditors receive very little, and the shareholders are left with nothing. Are secured creditors given too much protection by the current law?

2. There is a complex web of rules governing consumer credit. Should commercial credit be regulated the way consumer credit is now? Would we benefit from uniform rules across the country?

3. The registration systems used by secured creditors give priority to the creditors who register first, regardless of when the credit agreement was finalized. Are there situations where the rule of strict priority in registration should be waived?

4. How should a secured creditor decide how much notice to give a debtor before appointing a receiver?

5. Creditors who demand guarantees dictate the terms of the agreements. Should the content of guarantees be regulated to give guarantors some protection against standard form agreements?

6. In light of this chapter, what advice would you give to Ron, Sandra, and Tara about financing their expansion?

Situations for Discussion

1. Careful Bank made a loan to Sampson and took his truck as security in a credit agreement. The bank filed a financing statement in Ontario. Sampson took the truck to Manitoba and used it as a trade-in on a new one. The truck dealer knew Sampson was not from Manitoba but never asked where exactly he was from. The bank discovered Sampson's move and registered a financing statement in Manitoba. When Sampson defaulted on his loan, the bank seized the truck from the dealer's lot.[16] Who is entitled to the truck—the dealer or the bank? What should each have done differently? How likely is it that the bank could trace the truck in circumstances such as these?

2. Two corporations gave promissory notes to a bank and gave a security interest in their assets to secure the amounts due in the notes, which were also guaranteed by the major shareholders of the two corporations. When the corporations

---

16. Based on *Westman Equipment Corp.* v. *Royal Bank of Canada* (1982), 19 B.L.R. 56 (Man. Cty. Ct.).

failed to pay the notes when they became due, the bank seized and sold the assets, without informing the corporations or the shareholders of the time, place, or nature of the sale. The sale proceeds were not enough to pay the balance on the notes, so the bank is now suing the corporations and the guarantors for the shortfall.[17] On what basis can the defendants challenge the bank's actions and defend the claims against them? How important are the terms of the security agreement and the guarantees?

3. The Weiss Brothers operated a successful business in Montreal for 30 years. They bought a bankrupt hardware business in Ottawa, even though they had no experience in Ottawa or in selling hardware. Their bank, Toronto Dominion, got nervous about their financial stability and suggested they seek financing elsewhere. They contacted a former employee of TD who was then with Aetna Financial Services and negotiated a new credit arrangement with Aetna, consisting of a line of credit up to $1 million with conditions attached related to accounts receivable and inventory. Security for the loan was a demand debenture (general security agreement), pledge of accounts receivable, mortgage on land, and guarantees by the Weiss brothers. Six months later, the brothers defaulted on their loan. Aetna demanded payment in full and appointed a receiver, who seized all the assets three hours later.[18] What can the Weiss Brothers do now to save the business and their personal assets? What could they have done to prevent this disaster? How should they have analyzed the risk before buying the hardware business?

4. Protech borrowed $100 000 from Savin based on a general security agreement that covered all of Protech's assets. The agreement permitted Protech to deal with its assets in the ordinary course of business, but it prohibited Protech from pledging any current or future assets as security to another creditor. Protech later borrowed $50 000 from Catliff and gave a real property mortgage as security. Protech defaulted on both loans. The land is worth $55 000. The other assets are valued at $25 000.[19] What information is needed to define the rights of the two creditors? Who has priority over the land?

5. Dave and Betty Wilder arranged a loan for their company, Wilder Enterprises Ltd., and personally guaranteed the loan. Janson was the manager of their bank branch and told them that he thought he could get authorization from his regional office for a fixed term at a fixed rate of interest. However, the loan documents showed a loan repayable on demand with a floating interest rate. When the company got into financial difficulty, the Wilders negotiated an arrangement whereby the bank increased its credit to the company, agreed to honour the company's cheques, and agreed to refrain from demanding payment for a specified time. In return, the Wilders gave more security. Without warning, the bank stopped honouring cheques and appointed a receiver. Wilder Enterprises went bankrupt, and the bank called the guarantees, all of which permitted the bank to "deal with the customer as the bank may see fit."[20] Will the Wilders be obligated on their guarantees? How sympathetic are the courts likely to be? Is there any way for those in the position of the Wilders to avoid high personal risk for the escalating debts of a failing business?

---

17. Based on *Royal Bank of Canada* v. *Segreto Construction Ltd.* (1988), 38 B.L.R. 134 (Ont. C.A.).
18. Based on *Kavcar Investments* v. *Aetna Financial Services* (1989), 62 D.L.R. (4th) 277 (Ont. C.A.).
19. Based on *Savin Canada Inc.* v. *Protech Office Electronics Ltd.* (1981), 14 B.L.R. 108 (B.C.S.C.); rev'd (1984) 27 B.L.R. 93 (B.C.C.A.).
20. Based on *Bank of Montreal* v. *Wilder* (1986), 32 D.L.R. (4th) 9 (S.C.C.).

6. Kyle owned and operated a retail sporting goods shop. A new ski resort was built in the area, and to take advantage of increased activity, Kyle decided to expand his shop. He borrowed money from his bank, which took a security interest in his present inventory and any after-acquired inventory as collateral for the loan. A year later an avalanche destroyed the ski lodge. Kyle's business suffered, and he was left with double the inventory he had when he obtained the loan. When he defaulted on his payments, the bank seized all of his inventory. Kyle claims the bank is entitled only to the value of the inventory at the time of the loan. Who is entitled to the inventory? Could Kyle have negotiated better terms in the beginning?

7. Excel is a new business engaged in manufacturing and selling ski equipment to large retail stores, as well as to smaller sports shops. Excel has been unable to get customers to pay before or at the time of delivery, so most sales are now made on credit. Customers have 30 days to pay for the equipment they buy from Excel. If payment is not made within 30 days, Excel wants to be able to repossess the equipment. What questions should Excel ask prospective customers before granting them credit? What criteria should Excel use in evaluating customers' applications for credit? What steps can Excel take to enable it to repossess equipment for nonpayment? What about the payments due for equipment already sold to the retailers' customers?

8. Kings Tire Shop agreed to buy a vacant building-supply outlet to expand its tire business. To finance the purchase, Kings negotiated a loan from its bank, with the land and building as security. As part of the loan documentation, the bank required a report stating that the property was not environmentally contaminated in any way. Kings engaged a local environmental consulting firm to investigate and prepare the report for the bank. The firm gave the property a clean bill of health, and the loan was granted. Two years later, it was discovered that the adjacent property, which was formerly a gas station, had seriously contaminated the soil and pollution was leaching into the soil of Kings' property. The cleanup cost is significant, and Kings cannot afford it. As a result, Kings' property is seriously devalued and the bank is concerned about its security, especially since Kings' business is not doing well. Who is responsible for this environmental damage? How does it affect the credit agreement between Kings and the Bank? How could the problem have been avoided?

Twenty-Eight

Bankruptcy and Insolvency

Objectives

AFTER STUDYING THIS CHAPTER, YOU SHOULD HAVE AN
UNDERSTANDING OF:

► THE LEGAL ASPECTS OF BUSINESS FAILURE

► THE RIGHTS AND OBLIGATIONS OF DEBTORS AND
CREDITORS

► THE VARIOUS STAGES IN THE BANKRUPTCY PROCESS

Business Law in Practice

Ikeda Plumbing Inc. has been operating successfully in Timmins, Ontario, for the
past 35 years. Bill Ikeda is the present owner and CEO of the company. Eighteen
months ago a major international hardware supply chain opened on the outskirts of
town. Ikeda has experienced at least a 30 percent drop off in the routine, do-it-your-
self plumbing sales and, of even greater concern, a 25 percent drop in sales to local
tradespersons. There is no evidence that this decline is abating.

When the chain first announced its intention to locate in Timmins, Bill reacted
with a costly promotional campaign. To cover this unexpected expense, Bill borrowed $20 000 from his sister, Annie. More recently, he felt obliged to bring in new
inventory in response to the competition and this time borrowed $10 000 from a
close friend, Tom, since the bank would not extend the company's line of credit.

Bill now believes that the business is no longer viable, and he intends to close permanently in the winter (in nine months' time) when business is slowest. He wants to sell off adjacent land owned by the company now so that he can immediately repay Tom and Annie. The company owns the property (subject to a mortgage) on which the business is located but leases several vehicles and pieces of machinery. He thinks he can continue to draw his regular salary from the business and make regular payments to the bank and lessors. He can also continue to hire his wife on a part-time basis as bookkeeper.

1. What choices does a business like this have when faced with a serious financial crisis?
2. Is Bill entitled to make the arrangements with individuals that he proposes?
3. What steps are involved in addressing a business failure?

Business Failure

Business failure is often overlooked in the study of business, which emphasizes success and entrepreneurship in new ventures. Even when the economy booms, the majority of new businesses fail, and others face fundamental threats to their viability. Whether these threats bring the business to an end or result in major reorganizations, they affect many people in addition to the business owners. If a local builder

Eaton's Bankruptcy

In 1999 the Canadian retailing icon Eaton's (now owned by Sears) was failing. The decline was very public and was followed closely in both the business and popular press. In the months preceding the filing of a proposal under the *Bankruptcy and Insolvency Act*, the company walked a fine line. If it was to have any chance of succeeding—for example, by selling parts of its operations as a going concern—it had to appear healthy and have well-stocked stores. At the same time, given its precarious financial position, any supplier shipping stock was taking a gamble on getting paid.

Tommy Hilfiger Canada Inc. stopped shipping to Eaton's in July 1999 but started shipping again in early August after Eaton's announced it had secured $35 million in additional financing. In fact, the financing deal was part of a package that included entering into a deal that would allow a liquidator to

liquidate the inventory of about 30 stores, in the hope that the balance of Eaton's stores could be sold.

This second part of the plan failed, and Eaton's filed a notice of proposal later in the same month. Hilfiger argued that it never would have shipped goods if it had known the significant role of the liquidator. It was now owed about $2.5 million.[1]

Critical Analysis: Were Eaton's actions fair to suppliers such as Hilfiger? Was it ethical to make an announcement that effectively told only part of the story? If it had told all, might any chance of recovery have been lost? To whom did Eaton's owe responsibilities, and what choices did it have? Who determines when the "point of no return" has been reached? In the meantime, are suppliers and other unsecured creditors merely pawns in the process?

---

1. G. Livingston, "Judge Lets Eaton's Liquidation Sales Go On—For Now" *Canadian Press Newstex* (20 August 1999); G. Livingston, "Eaton's Liquidator Appointed, Stock Plummets" *Canadian Press Newstex* (27 August 1999).

fails, there will be subcontractors and suppliers who are seriously harmed. House purchasers may be left with no remedies for defects if the contractor is now out of business. How the law addresses the respective interests of creditors and what it allows in terms of reorganization are critical for a wide section of the local community—business and otherwise.

In order to ensure that both the business in difficulty and its creditors are treated fairly, a body of law, generically called *insolvency law,* has evolved. In addition to negotiated agreements between debtor and creditor and informal arrangements, there are four possible outcomes for financially troubled businesses:

- The debtor and creditors may agree to a proposal.
- The debtor can make an assignment in bankruptcy.
- Secured creditors can appoint receivers.
- Creditors can petition the debtor into bankruptcy.

Each of these possible outcomes is discussed in this chapter.

Negotiated Settlements

Bill Ikeda is anxious to move straight to a bankruptcy process. In fact, many in his position first attempt to solve their financial distress by way of a negotiated settlement. This settlement can be more or less formal, depending on the circumstances. Often, if the facts are either very simple or seen to be hopeless, creditors will meet with the debtor and, typically using the services of a professional facilitator (an accountant, a lawyer, or a debt counsellor), will reach an agreement that is fair to all interested parties and brings the claims to an end.

The key to negotiated settlements is ensuring that all creditors genuinely agree to the arrangement. One of the real dangers is that some creditors will attempt to push through an agreement that is unfair or that simply ignores others. The value of using a facilitator with appropriate expertise is that he or she is trained to identify these risks. Furthermore, the parties collectively may not recognize alternatives that would result in greater returns overall, and, again, a skilled facilitator will direct attention to these choices. When parties can reach agreement, it is typically concluded with a contract that binds all. Provided there is compliance by the debtor, debt obligations will come to an end.

In truly hopeless cases, there may be no negotiations at all. Creditors may recognize that it is not worth their time to pursue their claims. It is then up to the debtor to seek remedies through insolvency law, to bring closure to her or his obligations. In the case of a corporation, the entity will be left to "die" through deregistration.

When agreement cannot be reached as to what is a fair settlement, debtor or creditors may turn to legislative provisions to address their concerns. Discussion of these more formal requirements forms the balance of this chapter.

Administration of Bankruptcy

If a negotiated settlement with creditors fails or is simply not feasible, formal proceedings under the *Bankruptcy and Insolvency Act*[2] may be unavoidable.

---

2. *Bankruptcy and Insolvency Act,* R.S.C. 1985, c. B-3.

Origins and Purposes of Bankruptcy Legislation

The most famous observer of the miseries of insolvency was Charles Dickens. In the early 19th century, debtors prisons still existed in most countries. The dubious logic of imprisoning a person for failing to pay creditors was not lost on Dickens, whose own father was imprisoned in the Marshalsea Prison when Charles was 12.

Dickens' writings made a powerful impact on the reading public throughout the English-speaking world. The desperate plight of the debtor was, however, only one concern. Clearly not all creditors

were, even in Dickens' novels, sleazy and undeserving. For every miserable debtor there are undoubtedly several equally miserable and worthy creditors who may themselves be pushed into insolvency by this failure to pay. Moreover, some debtors themselves may have less than honourable intentions, and even the most honest may be inclined to favour one creditor over another when money gets tight.

Largely as a result of Dickens' writings, bankruptcy legislation was introduced in England and elsewhere. Today, the purpose of the legislation in Canada remains threefold:

- to provide a means for the honest but unfortunate debtors to get beyond their insolvent position and be free from debts[3]

- to establish priorities between creditors

- to impose punishment in the case of debtors who commit bankruptcy offences

Increasingly, there is a fourth purpose:

- to ensure, if possible, that potentially viable businesses are reorganized so they can continue operating for the benefit of creditors

Marshalsea Prison, the debtors prison where Dickens' father was incarcerated.

superintendent of bankruptcy
The most senior ministerial appointment with general supervisory authority for all functions prescribed under the *Bankruptcy and Insolvency Act*.

The *Bankruptcy and Insolvency Act* is federal legislation that falls within the mandate of Industry Canada. The administrative process resembles a pyramid, with the **superintendent of bankruptcy** having overriding supervisory authority. The country is divided into manageable-sized units or **bankruptcy districts**, with at least one **official receiver** in each district. This administrative official is legally responsible for all aspects of the bankrupt's estate upon the making of the bankruptcy order. The

---

3. *Re: Newsome,* [1927] 3 D.L.R. 828 (Ont. S.C.).

bankruptcy district
An administrative unit for a specific geographic area under the *Bankruptcy and Insolvency Act*.

official receiver
The administrative official legally responsible for all aspects of the bankrupt's estate.

trustee in bankruptcy
The officer assigned legal responsibility by the official receiver for administering the bankrupt's estate.

inspector
A person appointed by a creditor to act on his or her behalf and supervise the actions of the trustee.

estate
The collective term for the assets and liabilities of the insolvent or bankrupt.

official receiver transfers responsibility for the administration of the estate to the **trustee**. This position requires extraordinary trust and competency. Most often, the early training of the trustee is as a public accountant.

The trustee must be licensed by the superintendent in bankruptcy in order to practise. The professional body to which most trustees belong is the Chartered Insolvency Practitioners Association (CIPA). In order to become a certified insolvency practitioner (a member of CIPA) you must hold a CA, CGA, or CMA designation or be employed by a corporate trustee (generally a part or an affiliate of a public accounting practice). Candidates for CIP take a three-year course culminating in rigorous written and oral qualifying exams. Trustees must comply with the Code of Conduct as set out in the General Rules of the *Bankruptcy and Insolvency Act*.[4]

Finally, creditors appoint **inspectors** to act on their behalf and supervise the actions of the trustee.[5] In practice, an inspector is usually an employee or officer of one of the major creditors—for example, the comptroller or production manager—with knowledge of the debtor and the debt. While inspectors have fiduciary obligations to all creditors, they tend to focus on the interests of the creditor with which they are associated.

Proceedings Initiated by the Debtor

Pre-bankruptcy Processes

The initial task for the debtor is to find a trustee. Perhaps a colleague or a lawyer can make a recommendation. Trustees are also listed in the phone book and the local newspaper. There is, however, no obligation on the part of a trustee to take on a case. The trustee's decision will be based on two factors: is there any conflict of interest (perhaps a creditor is an existing client), and are there sufficient assets in the estate to ensure payment for the services offered? If debtors cannot find a trustee willing to accept the appointment—a relatively common occurrence—their only recourse may be some form of debt counselling service.

At the first meeting of the trustee and debtor, the trustee outlines the nature of the services offered. The trustee also begins assessing the **estate** and prepares a preliminary statement of assets and obligations. Often, this assessment calls for an untangling of business from personal affairs. In Ikeda's case, the pending bankruptcy is that of Ikeda the corporation, since it owns the business and assets, although it is possible that Bill the individual (and even other family members) may ultimately also become bankrupt.

Bill has met with the trustee, who has now prepared the statement shown in Figure 28.1.

---

4. *Bankruptcy and Insolvency General Rules,* C.R.C., c. 368, s. 34-53.
5. *Supra* note 2, s. 116. The trustee must post a bond representing the estimated value of the assets in the estate. The security is almost always in the form of a bond with a guarantee company (s. 16).

Figure 28.1

PRELIMINARY STATEMENT OF ASSETS AND OBLIGATIONS

Assets* at estimated cash value

Cash	$ 1 000
Accounts receivable	1 000
Inventory of plumbing supplies	7 000
Land and Building	105 000
Equipment	10 000
	$ 124 000

Obligations

Unremitted payroll deductions (due to Revenue Canada)	$24 000
Accounts payable to suppliers	67 000
Mortgage on land and building	97 000
Line of credit at bank	85 000
Salaries due to employees	7 000
	$280 000

* Leased property is not an asset of the estate but will revert to the lessors upon default.

insolvent
A person or company that owes more than $1000 and is unable to meet or has ceased paying financial obligations as they fall due, or has insufficient assets to meet obligations.

From this initial assessment, it is obvious that Ikeda Plumbing Inc. is **insolvent**—that is, it is not bankrupt, but it

- owes more than $1000, and
- is unable to meet financial obligations as they fall due, *or*
- has ceased paying obligations as they fall due, *or*
- has insufficient assets to meet obligations.[6]

If the trustee agrees with Ikeda's assessment of the prospects for the business, the next step is bankruptcy. If Ikeda wanted to keep the business going, and if the financial situation were not so bleak, the alternative at this stage would be to make a **proposal**.

proposal
A contractual agreement between the debtor and creditors for the payment of debts that allows the business to continue.

Proposals are contractual arrangements for the payment of debts between the debtor and creditors that allow the business to continue; in contrast, a negotiated settlement brings the business to an end. Under a successful proposal, if the business is reorganized and allowed some breathing room, not only will the debtor benefit, but creditors, under the right conditions, will receive more than if the business were to end. An alternative to a proposal is an **arrangement** under the *Companies' Creditors Arrangement Act*,[7] which typically is used for corporations that have extensive debts and the affairs of which tend to have considerable impact on the broader business community.

arrangement
A proposal governed by the Companies' Creditors Arrangement Act.

It is a prerequisite for filing a proposal that the debtor be insolvent. While the goal is to allow the business to continue, this can occur only if it makes sense to do so *and* the majority of creditors agree to such an arrangement.

The proposal is designed to achieve a combination of three alternative purposes:

composition
A proposal that reduces the amount of monies to be paid to creditors while the debtor retains assets.

- a reduction in the amount of monies to be paid to creditors while the debtor retains assets (a **composition**)
- an extension of time for payment of claims ("extension of time")

---

6. *Supra* note 2, s. 2(1).
7. R.S.C. 1985, c. C-36.

scheme of arrangement
A proposal in which the trustee controls assets for the benefit of creditors for the duration of the proposal.

- an arrangement whereby the trustee has control of assets for the benefit of the creditors for the period of the proposal (a **scheme of arrangement**)[8]

Because of the risk of proposals being used as delaying tactics, they operate under rigid time lines. The proposals themselves are simply contracts between debtor and creditors, and as such, there is an almost infinite variety of forms they might take, provided certain basic obligations are met—for example, employees are paid as they would be under bankruptcy, and preferred creditors retain their priority over ordinary unsecured creditors. All classes of creditors must separately approve the final proposal. If any does not, there is a deemed assignment in bankruptcy by the debtor.[9] When the proposal is approved by creditors, it must then be approved by the court. The business continues to function in accordance with the terms of the proposal and under the supervision of the trustee. All creditors, including those who voted against the terms of the proposal, are bound. New debts are not covered by the proposal and typically must be paid in full. Any default on the proposal terms can lead to bankruptcy.

Bankruptcy

assignment in bankruptcy
The debtor's voluntary assignment to the trustee in bankruptcy of legal title to all the debtor's property for the general benefit of creditors.

bankruptcy order
A document that assigns legal responsibility of assets and liabilities from the debtor to the official receiver through the appointed trustee.

bankrupt
The legal status defined by the *Bankruptcy and Insolvency Act* that prevents a person from having control of his or her assets and debts.

Since Ikeda Plumbing Inc. is insolvent, it can now make an **assignment in bankruptcy**. Here, the debtor voluntarily assigns "all his property for the general benefit of his creditors"[10] to the trustee in bankruptcy.

Following formal processes, a **bankruptcy order** is made that assigns all legal responsibility for assets and liabilities from the debtor to the official receiver through the services of the appointed trustee. The debtor now is **bankrupt**, which has a distinct legal meaning from *insolvent*.

Upon the making of a bankruptcy order, the trustee gives public notice of the change of status as a first step in order to identify and protect assets and to identify all liabilities.

Protecting Assets

Even in voluntary assignments, such as Ikeda's, the trustee must take extraordinary care to protect assets. Typically, the trustee will

- change the locks on the business premises and secure storage facilities
- post notice on the doors of the business
- conduct a detailed examination of assets
- prepare the appropriate statements
- ensure that assets are adequately protected, including arranging insurance
- establish the appropriate books and accounts for handling the estate finances
- sell any perishable goods immediately

Only in very exceptional circumstances would the trustee continue running the business.

Protection of assets calls for a review not only of what assets exist at the time of bankruptcy, but also of what has happened to assets before. Typically, if debtors made payments to creditors in the ordinary course of business, there will now be no question of recovering them. However, if payments were made to favour one creditor over another, the primary purpose of the Act—namely, ensuring that creditors

---

8. *Supra* note 2, s. 2(1).
9. *Ibid.,* s. 57(a).
10. *Ibid., s.* 49(1).

are treated equitably and according to the priorities of the Act—will have been defeated. Payments ahead of bankruptcy fall within three categories: fraudulent preferences, reviewable transactions, and settlements and fraudulent conveyances.

Assume that the Ikeda company sold the adjacent land in December as proposed and immediately repaid Annie and Tom.

FRAUDULENT PREFERENCES Any payment made within three months of bankruptcy that favours one creditor over another is deemed by the *Bankruptcy and Insolvency Act* to be a **fraudulent preference**[11] and, as such, is void. The key to this provision is that the bankrupt has been preferring, or favouring, one or more creditors to the detriment of the others. Not all creditors have been treated fairly, and therefore the trustee can insist (through court order if necessary) that the transaction be reversed and the assets returned to the estate. However, some specific requirements must be met:

fraudulent preference
A payment made by an insolvent debtor within three months of bankruptcy with the intent of favouring one creditor over another.

- The payment must have been made at a time when the debtor was insolvent, hence the significance of understanding the meaning of insolvency.
- The payment to the creditor must have been made in the three-month period preceding the bankruptcy order.
- The payment must have been made with the *intention* of giving this particular creditor priority over at least one other creditor.

In evaluating whether the requisite intention existed, it is irrelevant that Bill Ikeda acted with good intentions in paying Tom. If, however, the payment was made in the ordinary course of business, or if the debtor genuinely believed that making this payment would allow the business to continue, it may not be recoverable.

In the Ikeda example, the payment to Tom was within three months of bankruptcy and likely when the corporation was insolvent. Ikeda intended to give Tom priority over other creditors. The payment was a fraudulent preference, and Tom will need to repay the money and join other unsecured creditors. Provided the salaries paid to Bill Ikeda and his wife were genuine payments for services given, they will not be categorized as fraudulent preferences and will not be recoverable. The payments to trade creditors in the relevant period were likely made in the normal course of business, and, as such would not be recoverable.

reviewable transaction
A payment made to a person related to the bankrupt within one year of the bankruptcy order with the intention of giving the related person priority over at least one other creditor.

REVIEWABLE TRANSACTIONS Debtors in financial trouble are often tempted to repay close relatives before other creditors, which clearly defeats the purpose of bankruptcy. A **reviewable transaction** is a payment made to a person *related*[12] to the bankrupt within one year of the bankruptcy order and with the intention of giving this particular creditor priority over at least one other creditor.

If the bankrupt is a corporation, a **related person** is any person who is a blood relative (or relative by marriage or adoption) of a person with a controlling interest in the corporation.[13] In the Ikeda case, Annie's blood relationship with Bill Ikeda makes her a related person. Since payment to Annie was within the year preceding bankruptcy and was intended to give her priority over other creditors, provided the business was insolvent at the time, the payment will be recoverable and Annie, like Tom, will become an unsecured creditor.

related person
Any person who is a blood relative (or related by marriage or adoption) of the bankrupt or of the person with controlling interest in the bankrupt corporation.

---

11. *Ibid.,* s. 95.
12. *Ibid.,* s. 4(2)(b)(iii).
13. *Ibid.,* s. 96.

SETTLEMENTS AND FRAUDULENT CONVEYANCES   Here the transaction is one between the then debtor and a *noncreditor*. Perhaps Bill Ikeda, recognizing the predicament of the business, transferred valuable assets to his children or spouse for $1 six months before the bankruptcy. Such an action obviously violates the intent of the *Bankruptcy and Insolvency Act*. It is categorized as a **settlement** under the Act,[14] and the transfer is void if it was

- within one year of the bankruptcy order[15]
- within five years of the bankruptcy order and it can be shown that the debtor at that time was unable to pay his debts without the relevant property[16]

The most important exception to this provision is if the transfer was made in good faith and for valuable consideration. The transfer of assets by Ikeda to his family for $1 was undoubtedly a settlement and therefore void.

Provincial *Fraudulent Conveyances Acts* complement the federal legislation and affect conveyances of real or personal property made with the intent to defeat, hinder, delay, or defraud creditors.[17] If the transfer was for consideration, it is necessary to prove fraud on the part of both parties in order to avoid it. If the transfer was *not* for good consideration, it is only necessary to show fraud on the part of the debtor making the transfer. The sale by the Ikeda company of its adjacent piece of land will be examined as being a possible settlement. However, since the vendor and purchaser can, in all likelihood, show good faith and prove that the sale was for valuable consideration—albeit not top price—the transaction will not be void as a **fraudulent conveyance**.

Identifying Debts

Creditors find out about the bankruptcy through formal notice. Details are provided at the first meeting of creditors, held usually at the office of the official receiver for business bankruptcies or at the office of the trustee for personal bankruptcies.

Each creditor must file a **proof of claim**[18] as formal notice of the amount owed. Filing this document entitles them to participate in the creditors' meetings through voting and, ultimately, to receive a proportion of whatever money is available for distribution. The trustee examines each proof of claim or security and either asks for more evidence to support it, or allows or disallows it in full or in part. The trustee will reject a security or priority of payment if she or he believes there is inadequate evidence either of the debt itself or of its status as secured or preferred.

The trustee must establish priorities for payment according to the three broad categories of creditors: secured, preferred, and ordinary or unsecured. The implications of creditors being secured and unsecured were described in Chapter 27.

Revenue Canada is in a unique position in the case of unremitted payroll deductions. These debts are considered not to be part of the estate and as such will be payable ahead of all creditors, including those who are secured.[19]

---

settlement
A sale that can be declared void because it was not made in good faith or for valuable consideration.

fraudulent conveyance
A transfer of real or personal property made to defeat, hinder, delay, or defraud.

proof of claim
A formal notice provided by the creditor of the amount owed and the nature of the debt.

---

14. *Ibid.,* s. 91.
15. *Ibid.,* s. 91(1).
16. *Ibid.,* s. 91(2).
17. *Fraudulent Conveyances Act,* R.S.O. 1990, c. F-29, s. 2.
18. *Supra* note 2, s. 124.
19. The provision for source deductions is somewhat complex. The *Bankruptcy and Insolvency Act, supra* note 2, recognizes "trusts" as exempt property (s. 67). Source deductions fall within this definition by s. 227 of the *Income Tax Act,* R.S.C. 1985, c. 1 and the equivalent provincial legislation. As exempt property, they are considered not part of the property of the estate and are monies payable immediately to Revenue Canada.

Preferred creditors exhibit characteristics both of the secured and unsecured creditors. They are paid after secured creditors and before unsecured creditors and in order of priority, as set out in section 136 of the *Bankruptcy and Insolvency Act.*

The list of preferred creditors reflects the value that society has placed on the debts incurred. Funeral expenses and trustee fees are examples of preferred debts. Preferred creditors will be paid a reasonable amount for the services they have provided if the money is available.

In the Ikeda estate, the lender holding the mortgage over the land is a secured creditor. The bank that provided the line of credit likely holds personal guarantees from Bill Ikeda and/or his spouse, and it is these guarantees that may push Ikeda, the individual, into personal bankruptcy. There are at least two preferred creditors: the trustee and the unpaid employees. Employees are entitled to a maximum of $2000 for wages for the six-month period preceding bankruptcy, and the bankruptcy order terminates the contract of employment with no allowance for severance payments. Any severance payment owed prior to bankruptcy is unsecured debt. There are several unsecured creditors who will be paid ratably. So, for example, in the final distribution of Ikeda assets, the bank lent $85 000 on the line of credit (see Figure 28.2). The amount available on distribution for unsecured creditors is 0·11846 on the dollar (total remaining assets over total unsecured debts). Thus, the bank will receive $85 000 x 0·11846 = $10 069.10. The guarantor, if one exists, must pay the balance of that debt.

Suppliers are given special protection under the Act. They are allowed to recover any goods shipped in the past 30 days, provided the debtor is now bankrupt and the goods are in the same condition as when shipped.[20]

Figure 28.2

FINAL DISTRIBUTION OF ASSETS BY CLASS OF CREDITOR

Revised Statement of Assets

Assets at estimated cash value

Cash	$31 000*
Accounts receivable	1 000
Inventory of plumbing supplies	3 500**
Land and building	105 000
Equipment	10 000
Cash available for distribution	$150 500

Revised Statement of Liabilities

Liabilities at estimated cash value

Revenue Canada payroll deductions	24 000
Mortgage on land and building	97 000
Trustee's fees and expenses	4 000
Preferred part of salaries due***	4 000
Accounts payable to suppliers	63 500
Salaries due to employees	3 000
Amounts owed Tom	10 000
Amounts owed Annie	20 000
Line of credit at bank****	85 000
	$310 500

---

20. *Supra* note 2, s. 81.1.

Schedule 1: Distribution of Cash to Secured Creditors

Opening balance available	$150 500
Pay Revenue Canada payroll deductions	24 000
	126 500
Secured Creditors	
Pay mortgage on land and building	97 000
	$ 29 500
Preferred Creditors:	
Trustee's fees and expenses	$ 4 000
Pay preferred part of salaries due	4 000
Balance available for unsecured creditors	$ 21 500

Schedule 2: Distribution of cash to unsecured creditors

Balance available for Unsecured Creditors	$ 21 500
Balance due to Unsecured Creditors:	
Accounts payable to suppliers	63 500
Salaries due to employees	3 000
Amounts owed Tom	10 000
Amounts owed Annie	20 000
Line of credit at bank	85 000
	$181 500

Proportion of amount to be paid per dollar of unsecured debt: $\frac{21\ 500}{181\ 500} = .11846$

Payments to Unsecured Creditors*****

Accounts payable to suppliers	$ 7 522.10
Salaries due to employees	355.30
Payment to Tom	1184.40
Payment to Annie	2369.10
Line of credit at bank	10 069.10
Total payments to Unsecured Creditors	$ 21 500.00

Balance 0

Bill Ikeda personally owes the bank the unpaid balance of the line of credit if he has guaranteed the debt: ($85 000 − 10 069.10 = $74 930.90).

* Includes original balance ($1000) plus monies recovered from Tom and Annie ($10 000 + $20 000).
** Half of original ($3500) was taken back by suppliers (reducing accounts payable from $7000 to $3500).
*** Two employees were owed a total of $7000 ($3000 and $4000). Each employee has a pre-ferred claim of $2000, while the remainder of $3000 is unsecured.
**** If Bill Ikeda has provided a personal guarantee for the line of credit, he will be personally liable for any outstanding balance, after distribution.
***** Amounts rounded.

Discharge of Bankruptcy

discharge of bankruptcy
The formal process releasing the bankrupt of most liabilities.

The **discharge of bankruptcy** formally releases the honest but unfortunate bankrupt from most liabilities. While the discharge is not a right, it comes automatically for first-time (only) individual bankrupts nine months following the bankruptcy order, provided it has not been opposed by the superintendent, trustee, or creditors. A discharge is not available to a corporation, unless debts have been paid in full.[21]

The discharge will be opposed, for example, if a bankruptcy offence has been committed (see below), or where there is evidence of real extravagance prior to the bankruptcy, or where the unsecured creditors will receive less than 50 cents on each dollar owed. In the Ikeda case, there will be no discharge of the corporation, since its debts cannot be paid in full.

Action by Creditors

Creditors may take one of two formal actions: a secured creditor can take private action using a specific asset, or any or all creditors may petition the debtor into bankruptcy[22] pursuant to a court order.

Actions Taken by Secured Creditors against Specific Assets

This is the most common action taken by secured creditors, since what happens to the balance of the estate is of no concern to them, unless the value of their security does not cover money owed. Here, the secured creditor is enforcing the terms of the debt contract.

receiver
A person appointed by the secured creditor to retrieve the asset and realize the debt.

Creditors often appoint a **receiver** for the purpose of retrieving the asset and realizing the debt. The receiver owes a fiduciary obligation not only to the secured creditor, but also to all others with an interest in the insolvent's estate. So, for example, if the receiver for the mortgagee of the Ikeda land and buildings sells the property, there should be some excess available for other creditors, provided reasonable efforts have been made to get the best price.

Potential Liability from Repossession

Negative environmental factors affect a number of the parties involved in a bankruptcy or an insolvency. They obviously lower the value of the property itself. If the loan was made without a competent environmental assessment, at the time the receiver sells the property its value may be substantially less than what is required to cover the debt.

The concern for trustees or receivers repossessing property is the risk of potential personal liability for environmental harm. The trustee and the receiver are now protected by the *Bankruptcy and Insolvency Act* against personal liability for claims arising from the state of the property, unless the harm is the result of their "gross negligence or wilful misconduct."[23] The trustee is obliged to notify the appropriate authority in accordance with specific environmental legislation or regulations.[24] The bankrupt's estate, however, remains liable for any harm.

Critical Analysis: Has the legislature struck the right balance between concern for the environment and the viability of the bankruptcy or receivership process? Would the environment have been any better protected if this change had not been made?

---

21. *Ibid.,* s. 169(4).
22. *Ibid.,* s. 43 allows for petitions by all categories of creditors.
23. *Ibid.,* s. 14.06(2).
24. *Ibid.,* s. 14.06(3).

652 • PART 8 FINANCING THE BUSINESS

Creditors Petitioning the Debtor into Bankruptcy

When creditors petition the debtor into bankruptcy, the steps are identical to those outlined under the bankruptcy process commenced by the debtor, with the exception of the initiating processes.

Creditors initiate action by filing a **petition**, which is a statement of what is owed and to whom. In order for the creditors' actions to proceed, the debtor must owe at least $1000 and have committed an **act of bankruptcy**.[25]

petition
The statement filed by the creditor claiming that the debtor owes at least $1000 and has committed at least one act of bankruptcy.

act of bankruptcy
One of ten acts that the debtor must commit before a creditor can petition the debtor into bankruptcy.

Figure 28.3

ACTS OF BANKRUPTCY

An act of bankruptcy occurs when the debtor commits one of the following acts:

- ✓ makes an assignment to the trustee
- ✓ makes a fraudulent transfer of property of any kind
- ✓ makes a fraudulent preference
- ✓ tries physically to avoid creditors, for example, by leaving Canada or moving to another location and failing to notify creditors
- ✓ permits the sheriff to take (execute an order against) property when there is insufficient value in the property to pay the debt
- ✓ advises creditors that he or she is insolvent or cannot pay any debts
- ✓ attempts to deceive creditors by disposing of property in any way
- ✓ advises creditors that she or he has suspended payment on debts
- ✓ defaults on an approved proposal
- ✓ stops meeting liabilities as they fall due

Creditors of the Ikeda estate will have no difficulty meeting these formal requirements. Several acts of bankruptcy have occurred, and the company owes more than $1000.

The petition is filed in the bankruptcy court, and if approved, the court issues a **receiving order**. This is the equivalent of the assignment in bankruptcy. The debtor becomes bankrupt, and responsibility for the estate is taken out of the hands of the debtor and given to a trustee.

The interval between when the petition is filed and the order is made may well be one of considerable risk to assets. When the petition is filed, the creditor(s) can also apply for the appointment of a licensed trustee as **interim receiver**.[26] An interim receiver is considered an officer of the court and has the same fiduciary responsibilities as the official receiver or trustee. In practice, however, the role is best described as that of watchdog or caretaker.

receiving order
The court order following a creditor's petition that formally declares the debtor to be bankrupt and transfers legal control of the estate to the trustee.

interim receiver
The official appointed to take care of the estate in the period between the filing of the petition and the making of the receiving order.

---

25. *Ibid.*, s. 43(1).
26. *Ibid.*, s. 46.

International Insolvencies

In 1997 the *Bankruptcy and Insolvency Act* was amended to introduce Part XIII, dealing with international insolvencies. Generally, these provisions address two questions: What happens when a Canadian bankrupt has assets in a foreign jurisdiction? And what happens when a foreign creditor wishes to realize assets that are located in Canada pursuant to a foreign order? There are a number of important public interests at stake here. Given the importance of international trade to the Canadian economy, it is critical that participants both in Canada and abroad feel confident that the bankruptcy laws of all countries will be respected and, in the event of a bankruptcy order being made, that assets will be accessible wherever they are located. Furthermore, it would be highly offensive if a Canadian bankrupt could shield assets from Canadian creditors by ensuring that they are located outside the jurisdiction. Finally, it is also important that only foreign orders that generally equate to similar provisions in Canadian law be capable of execution in Canada.

Sections 267–275 of the *Bankruptcy and Insolvency Act* provide for these concerns. Generally, a foreign creditor can gain access to a debtor's assets located in Canada pursuant to a foreign order. Furthermore, Canadian creditors can gain access to assets located outside the jurisdiction. Note, however, that such actions are also subject to international treaties. Should a Canadian bankrupt have assets in a foreign country where reciprocity does not exist, and should that same bankrupt choose to relocate to that country, Canadian creditors will likely have no chance of recovery.

Critical Analysis: In practice, how effective are these provisions, particularly against a determined debtor?

Bankruptcy Offences

bankruptcy offences
Criminal acts defined by the *Bankruptcy and Insolvency Act* and committed by any participant in the bankruptcy and insolvency process.

For the *Bankruptcy and Insolvency Act* to be respected, it must also provide penalties for those who violate its provisions. These violations are known as **bankruptcy offences**.[27] They are criminal acts and can be committed by any of the key participants, including debtors, creditors, and trustees.

To ensure that the bankrupt knows what he or she can and cannot do, the trustee is obliged to give specific notice of what amounts to an offence. In general, offences occur if bankrupts are not truthful in any declaration made or if they attempt to dispose of property or otherwise defeat the purposes of the Act. Some offences may have occurred in the 12 months prior to bankruptcy. For example, if Ikeda acted fraudulently when disposing of the land before bankruptcy, a bankruptcy offence has been committed.

Creditors commit bankruptcy offences if they, for example, make false claims. Inspectors commit offences if they accept payments over and above their entitlement provided for in the Act. Finally, trustees may commit offences by violating specific duties established in the legislation or in any way acting in what could generally be described as a conflict of interest.

---

27. *Ibid.*, s. 198-208.

Personal Bankruptcy

Personal bankruptcies affect businesses mainly in the sense that they will be unable to collect money owed to them by bankrupt individuals. Otherwise, a personal bankruptcy may arise in situations where the "owner" of the business—whether a sole proprietor, a partner, or a director/officer of a corporation—has been obliged to provide a personal guarantee or co-sign for debts of that business. Bill Ikeda may have personally guaranteed the line of credit for the business, and may have mortgaged the family home in order to obtain inventory.

The *Bankruptcy and Insolvency Act* provides a streamlined process for small consumer estates. For example, any estate with debts (other than those secured by the family residence) under $75 000 may fall within the provisions for Consumer Proposals.[28] Likewise, in certain provinces[29] there is provision for "orderly payment of debts." In all other situations, the general bankruptcy provisions of the Act apply

Bill Goss, Insolvency Partner

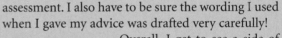

I have been an insolvency practitioner almost my entire career as a public accountant; I became a licensed trustee first in 1973. Insolvency practice is not for everyone. It requires a person who copes well with risk and uncertainty and who enjoys being in the midst of controversy. By definition, there is a scarcity of assets, and competing interests have to be resolved.

The variety of work is enormous. I can't think of any type of business I haven't been in over my career either to assess or run. As I speak I am running three different businesses, one with four separate unions and between 600 and 700 employees.

The risk I assume under conditions of uncertainty is huge. In these kinds of situations I am recommending to the bank that the business should be run and incur further losses because selling it as a whole will realize more than the break-up value. When the losses start mounting up and I can't find a buyer, I have to be really confident in my initial assessment. I also have to be sure the wording I used when I gave my advice was drafted very carefully!

Overall, I get to see a side of businesses that few others see. After all these years I believe I can look at any business and see decisions and events that will precipitate problems in the future.

Would I recommend insolvency practice to a young accountant? Yes, always provided they have the type of personality that deals well with unpredictability, uncertainty, and risk.

Bill Goss is an insolvency partner with Ernst & Young Inc.

---

28. *Ibid.*, s. 66.11-66.4.

29. Manitoba and Alberta, *Ibid.*, s. 217; British Columbia, Saskatchewan, Northwest Territories, Nova Scotia, and Prince Edward Island, *Bankruptcy and Insolvency General Rules*, C.R.C. 1978, c. 368, ss. 34-53.

up to and including discharge. Note that in all of these processes, debtors are entitled to retain sufficient assets to support themselves and their families. There are a number of statutes containing exemptions with respect to the seizing of assets to satisfy court orders. For example, all provinces have the equivalent of the *Ontario Execution Act*,[30] which provides exemptions for items such as tools of the trade up to $2000, necessary wearing apparel up to $1000, and household furniture and utensils up to $2000.[31]

Not all liabilities are expunged by the discharge. Fines, penalties, alimony or support payments, and student loans are among the liabilities that survive the discharge. These exemptions serve the public interest. Allowing a debtor to avoid liability for debts arising, for example, out of fraudulent acts by declaring bankruptcy and subsequently receiving a discharge would defeat the purpose of the original penalty.[32]

Business Law in Practice Revisited

1. What choices does a business like this have when faced with a serious financial crisis?

Ikeda Plumbing has three "choices," although the term choice is in quotation marks because others may impose decisions upon the company. The company can seek a voluntary negotiated settlement with creditors, bringing the business to an end. It can seek bankruptcy protection as Bill is proposing, and again, this will bring the business to an end. Finally, it can make a proposal to creditors that would allow the business to continue under conditions that meet both creditor and debtor needs and wishes. There is a fourth alternative: creditors may themselves petition the company into bankruptcy.

2. Is Bill entitled to make the arrangements with individuals that he proposes?

The answer depends on whether Ikeda Plumbing is insolvent. If it is not, and provided proposed payments will not make it insolvent, Bill can pay any creditor he chooses. However, since it is probable that Ikeda Plumbing is insolvent, payments to any creditors in order to give them priority over others are likely fraudulent preferences and, as such, are reviewable and recoverable.

3. What steps are involved in addressing a business failure?

If the financial situation is truly hopeless, the likely outcome is either a negotiated settlement or no action at all (particularly in the case of a corporation). It takes time and money for all parties to participate in the formal bankruptcy process. Secured creditors will recoup their losses from a particular secured asset, using the services of a receiver. If the debtor and/or creditors see value in taking additional steps, they will first seek the services of a trustee, who is trained to take the parties through the required stages of the bankruptcy process. Trustees have a fiduciary obligation to act in the best interests of all. If the parties so wish, and if there is good reason to believe there is value in the business continuing, a proposal will be the likely outcome. If this is not the case, a formal bankruptcy order will result, debts and assets will be identified and realized, and a final distribution will be made before the bankrupt is discharged.

---

30. R.S.O. 1990, c. E-24.
31. *Ibid.,* s. 2.
32. *Supra* note 2, s. 178.

Chapter Summary

The provisions of the *Bankruptcy and Insolvency Act* and related legislation are complex and arise generally under circumstances of great confusion. The role of highly skilled experts with strong ethical obligations is critical to the fair distribution of assets. Even with the best of motives, debtors like Bill Ikeda may treat the rights of creditors in an arbitrary and unfair manner. The provisions of the Act provide for certainty and equity.

The key feature of the law providing for business failure is that the owners of the business have two alternatives: they can have the business continue in a reorganized fashion, or they can bring it to an end. In either case, the law provides the process for ensuring that the rights and obligations of both creditors and debtor are met. Furthermore, while understanding the basic steps in the process is important, in practice specialized professionals will provide the appropriate guidance.

When there are secured assets, the most common consequence of a failure to pay a debt as it falls due is the secured creditor enforcing the debt agreement directly.

If a debtor's position is indeed hopeless, there is little point in spending good money attempting to recover what is not there. In practice, creditors usually resort to the proceedings provided for under *the Bankruptcy and Insolvency Act* only when they are seeking to reverse priorities or defeat other claims. Otherwise, the most they might do is participate if someone else bears the cost of initiating the process. Likewise, for businesses organized in the corporate form, under which there is no personal liability for the "owners" (other than the loss of investment in the corporation), owners typically simply abandon the corporation. Secured creditors will take that to which they are entitled. For other creditors, there is generally little, if anything, left over, and eventually the company will be struck from the relevant registry.

Study Chapter

Key Terms and Concepts

act of bankruptcy (p. 653)

arrangement (p. 646)

assignment in bankruptcy (p. 647)

bankrupt (p. 647)

bankruptcy district (p. 645)

bankruptcy offences (p. 654)

bankruptcy order (p. 647)

composition (p. 646)

discharge of bankruptcy (p. 651)

estate (p. 645)

fraudulent conveyance (p. 649)

fraudulent preference (p. 648)

insolvent (p. 646)

inspector (p. 645)

interim receiver (p. 653)

official receiver (p. 645)

petition (p. 653)

preferred creditors (p. 650)

proof of claim (p. 649)

proposal (p. 646)

receiver (p. 652)

receiving order (p. 653)

related person (p. 648)

reviewable transaction (p. 648)

scheme of arrangement (p. 647)

settlement (p. 649)

superintendent of bankruptcy (p. 644)

trustee in bankruptcy (p. 645)

Questions for Review

1. Why is it so important to know the precise meaning of insolvency?

2. What is the meaning of insolvency, and how does it contrast with bankruptcy?

3. Sometimes companies are brought to an end voluntarily by their owners. Under what legislation would this occur, and what is the critical distinction between this and the bankruptcy process?

4. What is the difference between an assignment in bankruptcy and petitioning into bankruptcy?

5. What are two different acts of bankruptcy?

6. What is a fraudulent preference? Is intention a prerequisite?

7. What are two key purposes of the initial meeting of creditors?

8. What are preferred creditors, and how do they differ from either secured or ordinary unsecured creditors?

9. Under what conditions will a bankrupt likely not be discharged automatically from bankruptcy?

10. What is the purpose of a proposal, and when might it not be approved by a court?

11. What happens if ordinary unsecured creditors do not vote to approve a proposal?

12. What is one bankruptcy offence that may be committed by a debtor?

Questions for Discussion

1. In the Ikeda example, the payments to Tom and Annie were likely recoverable as reviewable transactions or as preference payments. Is this fair? Why is proof of actual fraud not the appropriate measure?

2. One of the shortcomings of the bankruptcy process is that it still offers few choices when a debtor cannot pay a trustee, there are insufficient assets for the trustee to be assured that fees will be paid, and the creditors have no interest in pursuing the matter as the economic incentive is not there. Potentially, the debtor is left with continuing obligations and without the possibility of getting "out from under" that is available to other debtors. Might there be better or more fair alternatives?

3. What factors might have discouraged Bill Ikeda from pursuing a negotiated settlement? What would have been the difference in outcomes between such a settlement and his preferred bankruptcy option?

4. Proposals are an important part of the bankruptcy and insolvency legislation. At the same time, they can, despite the controls that exist, have the effect of delaying alternative actions by creditors to protect their interests. Do the benefits from proposals outweigh the obvious potential harm?

5. The category of preferred creditors is not found in many bankruptcy jurisdictions. Clearly, there are social costs both to having them and to not having them. What are these costs, and do they outweigh the benefits?

6. What is the right balance between the need to protect the environment and the need to ensure that trustees and receivers are themselves protected?

Situations for Discussion

1. It is a requirement of an assignment in bankruptcy that there first be an act of bankruptcy. Review the Ikeda case and identify all possible events that fall within the definition of an act of bankruptcy.

2. Ontario Realty is a major property developer based in Toronto. It is primarily in the business of building offices and other commercial sites. In the past year, the Ontario economy has suffered a serious downturn and commercial properties have been particularly hard-hit. Ontario Realty now finds itself holding onto several major city sites for which there is little chance of development, at least until the economy recovers. Debts now amount to some $150 million, and assets at today's values are worth $80 million. Interest rates are slowly but steadily rising. Two banks hold security for 90 percent of the debt. The balance of the debt is unsecured.

   John, the CEO of the company, has weathered these kinds of crises before. He is convinced (with some good reason) that a recovery should begin within a year. His discussions with the two major creditors suggest that only one would be prepared to negotiate a more favourable payment scheme. John seeks advice from an insolvency practitioner about the pros and cons of making a proposal.

   What advice will John likely receive? What are the roles of the respective creditors, and how will they likely seek to protect their interests?

3. Designer Shirts is a supplier to a major national retail outlet. There have been rumours circulating for months that the retailer is in trouble, but the company has been in trouble before and has always managed to recover. The perception is that there are too many interests at stake for the company to fail. Furthermore, this is a notoriously troubled industry, and if all suppliers believed all things that were said about all companies, they would be out of business for fear of making a sale.

   The retailer has recently made an announcement about an infusion of cash from a major investor. On the basis of this news, Designer agrees to make deliveries, although it insists on a shorter payment period than normal. Designer makes the first delivery of summer stock at the end of March. It receives its payment within the specified twenty days. It then makes a second delivery, but this time payment is not forthcoming at twenty days. Based on further promises that the payment will be made "within two days," Designer makes a third shipment. Within ten days there is an announcement that the retailer has filed for bankruptcy protection. Designer has never received payment for either the second or third shipment and is owed $1.5 million.

   What are Designer's rights and prospects? What will happen next?

4. Mary is the owner-operator of an incorporated consulting practice, which owns the building in which it is located. Mary lives above the offices and rents the apartment from the company. There are five employees working in the business,

two of whom are her cousins, who have been close to her over the years. The business has a standing line of credit with a local bank. It rents office equipment and vehicles for Mary and the office manager (one of her cousins).

Mary has developed the business successfully, but in recent years poor health has limited the number of hours she can devote to the business. She is reluctant to lay off any of the employees, as she knows they depend on their income. She has switched those actively engaged in projects to primarily a "commission" basis of payment, and this allows her to keep paying the office staff. She has negotiated an extension of the payment schedule with the bank and is meeting payments. She is extremely anxious about the building, as this remains her only security in her retirement. Her lawyer has for many years been encouraging her to buy the building from the company, and finally she does this. Six months later she suffers a severe stroke and is unable to work. There is no income for wages, but her two cousins keep the office open for two months out of loyalty. The business is then forced into bankruptcy.

Make a list of assets and liabilities and outline how the assets will be distributed to the creditors.

5. Kim owns a family business that is experiencing serious difficulties because of changing economic circumstances. It operates as a sole proprietorship and has borrowed from a number of sources (some commercial, but increasingly from friends and family) over the last three years to keep the business afloat. There are three employees, without whose services Kim could no longer run the business. He is beginning to feel overwhelmed and needs some basic advice as to what he can and cannot do. For example, should he create a corporation and sell the business assets to that corporation? It seems to him an obvious choice to make. Should he consolidate his loans and pay off as many as he can now by extending his borrowing with the bank? Who should get paid first? He remembers a business acquaintance finding herself in a terrible mess when her business finally failed. The worst part was that many payments she had made to relatives had to be retrieved. Clearly, she had done something wrong, but what was it? Consider yourself Kim's advisor. Outline some basic guidelines he should follow.

6. The Great Big Bank has recently conducted a review of its small-loan failure rates and is concerned about what it has found. There is strong evidence that failures are increasing disproportionately to loans made, and that amounts recovered are decreasing. Spot interviews of local loans managers suggest a good deal of confusion about how to assess risk, when the bank should call a loan, and what mechanism best meets the bank's needs after the loan has been called. On the strength of this information, the bank is redesigning its basic training manual. The primary focus now is on the section entitled "The loan has gone bad. Now what do you do?" Develop guidelines that would offer practical advice and basic information for loans officers to act upon. Address all options, from informal arrangements through to bankruptcy. Ensure that the guidelines identify the circumstances under which each might be appropriate.

Appendix A

Canadian Charter of Rights and Freedoms

Constitution Act, 1982, Part I

Whereas Canada is founded upon principles that recognize the supremacy of God and the rule of law:

Guarantee of Rights and Freedoms

Rights and Freedoms in Canada

Gov't ⇒ individual rights
Gov't can limit rights if reasonable

1. The *Canadian Charter of Rights and Freedoms* guarantees the rights and freedoms set out in it subject only to such reasonable limits prescribed by law as can be demonstrably justified in a free and democratic society.

Fundamental Freedoms

Fundamental Freedoms

2. Everyone has the following fundamental freedoms:

(a) freedom of conscience and religion;

(b) freedom of thought, belief, opinion and expression, including freedom of the press and other media of communication;

(c) freedom of peaceful assembly; and

(d) freedom of association.

Democratic Rights

Democratic Rights of Citizens

3. Every citizen of Canada has the right to vote in an election of members of the House of Commons or of a legislative assembly and to be qualified for membership therein.

Maximum Duration of Legislative Bodies

4. (1) No House of Commons and no legislative assembly shall continue for longer than five years from the date fixed for the return of the writs at a general election of its members.

Continuation in Special Circumstances

(2) In time of real or apprehended war, invasion or insurrection, a House of Commons may be continued by Parliament and a legislative assembly may be continued by the legislature beyond five years if such continuation is not opposed by the votes of more than one-third of the members of the House of Commons or the legislative assembly, as the case may be.

Annual Sitting of Legislative Bodies

5. There shall be a sitting of Parliament and of each legislature at least once every twelve months.

Mobility Rights

Mobility of Citizens

6. (1) Every citizen of Canada has the right to enter, remain in and leave Canada.

Rights to Move and Gain Livelihood

(2) Every citizen of Canada and every person who has the status of a permanent resident of Canada has the right

(a) to move and take up residence in any province; and

(b) to pursue the gaining of a livelihood in any province.

Limitation

(3) The rights specified in subsection (2) are subject to

(a) any laws or practices of general application in force in a province other than those that discriminate among persons primarily on the basis of

662

province of present or previous residence; and

(b) any laws providing for reasonable residency requirements as a qualification for the receipt of publicly provided social services.

Affirmative Action Programs

(4) Subsections (2) and (3) do not preclude any law, program or activity that has as its object the amelioration in a province of conditions of individuals in that province who are socially or economically disadvantaged if the rate of employment in that province is below the rate of employment in Canada.

Legal Rights

Life, Liberty and Security of Person

7. Everyone has the right to life, liberty and security of the person and the right not to be deprived thereof except in accordance with the principles of fundamental justice.

Search or Seizure

8. Everyone has the right to be secure against unreasonable search or seizure.

Detention or Imprisonment

9. Everyone has the right not to be arbitrarily detained or imprisoned.

Arrest or Detention

10. Everyone has the right on arrest or detention

(a) to be informed promptly of the reasons therefor;

(b) to retain and instruct counsel without delay and to be informed of that right; and

(c) to have the validity of the detention determined by way of *habeas corpus* and to be released if the detention is not lawful.

Proceedings in Criminal and Penal Matters

11. Any person charged with an offence has the right

(a) to be informed without unreasonable delay of the specific offence;

(b) to be tried within a reasonable time;

(c) not to be compelled to be a witness in proceedings against that person in respect of the offence;

(d) to be presumed innocent until proven guilty according to law in a fair and public hearing by an independent and impartial tribunal;

(e) not to be denied reasonable bail without just cause;

(f) except in the case of an offence under military law tried before a military tribunal, to the benefit of trial by jury where the maximum punishment for the offence is imprisonment for five years or a more severe punishment;

(g) not to be found guilty on account of any act or omission unless, at the time of the act or omission, it constituted an offence under Canadian or international law or was criminal according to the general principles of law recognized by the community of nations;

(h) if finally acquitted of the offence, not to be tried for it again and, if finally found guilty and punished for the offence, not to be tried or punished for it again; and

(i) if found guilty of the offence and if the punishment for the offence has been varied between the time of commission and the time of sentencing, to the benefit of the lesser punishment.

12. Everyone has the right not to be subjected to any cruel and unusual treatment or punishment.

Treatment or Punishment

13. A witness who testifies in any proceedings has the right not to have any incriminating evidence so given used to incriminate that witness in any other proceedings, except in a prosecution for perjury or for the giving of contradictory evidence.

Self-Crimination

14. A party or witness in any proceedings who does not understand

Interpreter

or speak the language in which the proceedings are conducted or who is deaf has the right to the assistance of an interpreter.

Equality Rights

Equality before and under Law and Equal Protection and Benefit of Law

15. (1) Every individual is equal before and under the law and has the right to the equal protection and equal benefit of the law without discrimination and, in particular, without discrimination based on race, national or ethnic origin, colour, religion, sex, age or mental or physical disability.

Affirmative Action Programs

(2) Subsection (1) does not preclude any law, program or activity that has as its object the amelioration of conditions of disadvantaged individuals or groups including those that are disadvantaged because of race, national or ethnic origin, colour, religion, sex, age or mental or physical disability.

Official Languages of Canada

Official Languages of Canada

16. (1) English and French are the official languages of Canada and have equality of status and equal rights and privileges as to their use in all institutions of the Parliament and government of Canada.

Official Languages of New Brunswick

(2) English and French are the official languages of New Brunswick and have equality of status and equal rights and privileges as to their use in all institutions of the legislature and government of New Brunswick.

Advancement of Status and Use

(3) Nothing in this Charter limits the authority of Parliament or a legislature to advance the equality of status or use of English and French.

Proceedings of Parliament

17. (1) Everyone has the right to use English or French in any debates and other proceedings of Parliament.

(2) Everyone has the right to use English or French in any debates and other proceedings of the legislature of New Brunswick.

Proceedings of New Brunswick Legislature

18. (1) The statutes, records and journals of Parliament shall be printed and published in English and French and both language versions are equally authoritative.

Parliamentary Statutes and Records

(2) The statutes, records and journals of the legislature of New Brunswick shall be printed and published in English and French and both language versions are equally authoritative.

New Brunswick Statutes and Records

19. (1) Either English or French may be used by any person in, or in any pleading in or process issuing from, any court established by Parliament.

Proceedings in Courts Established by Parliament

(2) Either English or French may be used by any person in, or in any pleading in or process issuing from, any court of New Brunswick.

Proceedings in New Brunswick Courts

20. (1) Any member of the public in Canada has the right to communicate with, and to receive available services from, any head or central office of an institution of the Parliament or government of Canada in English or French, and has the same right with respect to any other office of any such institution where

Communications by Public with Federal Institutions

(a) there is a significant demand for communications with and services from that office in such language; or

(b) due to the nature of the office, it is reasonable that communications with and services from that office be available in both English and French.

(2) Any member of the public in New Brunswick has the right to communicate with, and to receive available services from, any office of an institution of the legislature or

Communications by Public with New Brunswick Institutions

government of New Brunswick in English or French.

Continuation of Existing Constitutional Provisions

21. Nothing in sections 16 to 20 abrogates or derogates from any right, privilege or obligation with respect to the English or French languages, or either of them, that exists or is continued by virtue of any other provision of the Constitution of Canada.

Rights and Privileges Preserved

22. Nothing in sections 16 to 20 abrogates or derogates from any legal or customary right or privilege acquired or enjoyed either before or after the coming into force of this Charter with respect to any language that is not English or French.

Minority Language Educational Rights

Language of Instruction

23. (1) Citizens of Canada

(a) whose first language learned and still understood is that of the English or French linguistic minority population of the province in which they reside, or

(b) who have received their primary school instruction in Canada in English or French and reside in a province where the language in which they received that instruction is the language of the English or French linguistic minority population of the province, have the right to have their children receive primary and secondary school instruction in that language in that province.

Continuity of Language Instruction

(2) Citizens of Canada of whom any child has received or is receiving primary or secondary school instruction in English or French in Canada, have the right to have all their children receive primary and secondary school instruction in the same language.

(3) The right of citizens of Canada under subsections (1) and (2) to have their children receive primary and secondary school instruction in the language of the English or French linguistic minority population of a province

(a) applies wherever in the province the number of children of citizens who have such a right is sufficient to warrant the provision to them out of public funds of minority language instruction; and

(b) includes, where the number of those children so warrants, the right to have them receive that instruction in minority language educational facilities provided out of public funds.

Application Where Numbers Warrant

Enforcement

24. (1) Anyone whose rights or freedoms, as guaranteed by this Charter, have been infringed or denied may apply to a court of competent jurisdiction to obtain such remedy as the court considers appropriate and just in the circumstances.

Enforcement of Guaranteed Rights and Freedoms

(2) Where, in proceedings under subsection (1), a court concludes that evidence was obtained in a manner that infringed or denied any rights or freedoms guaranteed by this Charter, the evidence shall be excluded if it is established that, having regard to all the circumstances, the admission of it in the proceedings would bring the administration of justice into disrepute.

Exclusion of Evidence Bringing Administration of Justice into Disrepute

General

25. The guarantee in this Charter of certain rights and freedoms shall not be construed so as to abrogate or derogate from any aboriginal treaty or other rights of freedoms that pertain to the aboriginal peoples of Canada including

Aboriginal Rights and Freedoms not Affected by Charter

(a) any rights or freedoms that have been recognized by the Royal Proclamation of October 7, 1763; and

(b) any rights or freedoms that now exist by way of land claims agreements or may be so acquired.

Other Rights and Freedoms not Affected by Charter

26. The guarantee in this Charter of certain rights and freedoms shall not be construed as denying the existence of any other rights or freedoms that exist in Canada.

Multicultural Heritage

27. This Charter shall be interpreted in a manner consistent with the preservation and enhancement of the multicultural heritage of Canadians.

Rights Guaranteed Equally to Both Sexes

28. Notwithstanding anything in this Charter, the rights and freedoms referred to in it are guaranteed equally to male and female persons.

Rights Respecting Certain Schools Preserved

29. Nothing in this Charter abrogates or derogates from any rights or privileges guaranteed by or under the Constitution of Canada in respect of denominational, separate or dissentient schools.

Application to Territories and Territorial Authorities

30. A reference in this Charter to a province or to the legislative assembly or legislature of a province shall be deemed to include a reference to the Yukon Territory and the Northwest Territories, or to the appropriate legislative authority thereof, as the case may be.

Legislative Powers not Extended

31. Nothing in this Charter extends the legislative powers of any body or authority.

Application of Charter

Application of Charter

32. (1) This Charter applies

(a) to the Parliament and government of Canada in respect of all matters within the authority of Parliament including all matters relating to the Yukon Territory and Northwest Territories; and

(b) to the legislature and government of each province in respect of all matters within the authority of the legislature of each province.

(2) Notwithstanding subsection (1), section 15 shall not have effect until three years after this section comes into force.

Exception

33. (1) Parliament or the legislature of a province may expressly declare in an Act of Parliament or of the legislature, as the case may be, that the Act or a provision thereof shall operate notwithstanding a provision included in section 2 or sections 7 to 15 of this Charter.

Exception Where Express Declaration

(referred to & applied to parliament or legislature i.e. munt)

(2) An Act or a provision of an Act in respect of which a declaration made under this section is in effect shall have such operation as it would have but for the provision of this Charter referred to in the declaration.

Operation of Exception

(doesn't have to be too reasonable)

(3) A declaration made under subsection (1) shall cease to have effect five years after it comes into force or on such earlier date as may be specified in the declaration.

Five Year Limitation

(4) Parliament or a legislature of a province may re-enact a declaration made under subsection (1).

Re-enactment

(5) Subsection (3) applies in respect of a re-enactment made under subsection (4).

Five Year Limitation

Citation

34. This Part may be cited as the *Canadian Charter of Rights and Freedoms.*

Citation

Appendix B

Business Law on the Internet

A growing amount of information related to business law is becoming available online. This appendix provides addresses for many Web sites relevant to business and the law, as well as a brief summary of the content of each site. For ease of access, direct links to these sites are available on the *Canadian Business and the Law* home page at www.businesslaw.nelson.com. This regularly updated home page also provides addresses and descriptions of new or more specialized Internet sites.

Because Web sites may be inaccessible for a variety of reasons—such as the server being temporarily disabled, the site being upgraded, or the site changing addresses—this guide offers alternative routes for obtaining the same information wherever possible.

Canadian Government and Business Information

Federal, Provincial, and Territorial Governments

These sites have links to a wide range of government information, including government departments, services, publications, and programs.

Canada	www.gc.ca
Alberta	www.gov.ab.ca
British Columbia	www.gov.bc.ca
Manitoba	www.gov.mb.ca
New Brunswick	www.gov.nb.ca
Newfoundland	www.gov.nf.ca/
Nova Scotia	www.gov.ns.ca
Ontario	www.gov.on.ca
Quebec	www.gouv.qc.ca
Saskatchewan	www.gov.sk.ca
Northwest Territories	www.gov.nt.ca/
Yukon Territory	www.gov.yk.ca/
Nunavut Territory	www.gov.nu.ca/

Selected Government Organizations and Agencies

Business Centre for the Aboriginal Community (Industry Canada)
www.abc.gc.ca

Provides information on opportunities for Aboriginals, as well as a history of Aboriginal businesses, services, and business support.

Canada Business Service Centres (Government of Canada)
www.cbsc.org/

Offers information on starting a business in any part of Canada, descriptions of government programs and services, and links to provincial and territorial Business Services Centres.

Canadian Governments On-Line (CGOL)
www.intergov.gc.ca/

Includes federal, provincial, territorial, and municipal government information, government news, and an online services catelogue.

Canadian Human Rights Commission (Government of Canada)
www.chrc.ccdp.ca
or through the Government of Canada home page
www.gc.ca

Details the work of the commission, with links to provincial human rights commissions; describes the steps in filing a human rights complaint; and provides examples of tribunal decisions.

Canadian Intellectual Property Office (Industry Canada)
http://cipo.gc.ca/

Provides searchable patent and trademark databases and describes intellectual property legislation and regulations.

Competition Bureau (Industry Canada)
http://strategis.ic.gc.ca/SSG/ct01250e.html

Outlines the role and function of the Competition Bureau, lists the legislation and regulations administered by the bureau, and provides business and consumer information.

Environment Canada (Government of Canada)
www.ec.gc.ca

Describes the new *Canada Environmental Protection Act;* also provides news releases and listings of publications.

Human Resources Canada (Government of Canada)
www.hrdc-drhc.gc.ca

Provides information on employment equity and employment insurance; links to regional offices and employment centres; and a link to the Canadian Employment Insurance Commission.

Industry Canada
>http://strategis.ic.gc.ca/

Tells you what you need to know to start up a business, including information on business support; financing licences, legislation, and regulations, with links to a broad range of government agencies and legal information sites; and employment and learning resources. Also provides company directories; trade and investment business information by sector; economic analyses; and statistics.

Superintendent of Bankruptcy (Industry Canada)
>http://strategis.ic.gc.ca/sc_marks/bankrupt/engdoc/superint.html
>or through Industry Canada's homepage
>http://strategis.ic.gc.ca/

Outlines bankruptcy and insolvency legislation, consumer and debtor information, and bankruptcy statistics.

Task Force on Electronic Commerce (Industry Canada)
>http://e-com.ic.gc.ca

Describes global initiatives in electronic commerce; provides tips on e-commerce safety; and offers useful e-commerce links, including legal resources related to electronic signatures and the United Nations Model law on Electronic Commerce.

Note: Many of the Web sites of government organizations and agencies can be accessed through the main home page of the federal government at www.gc.ca and through the home page for Industry Canada at www.ic.gc.ca/.

Selected Industry Associations and Professional Organizations

Advertising Standards Canada
>www.canad.com/asc/mainmenu.html

Describes advertising codes and guidelines and provides consumer information.

Canadian Association of Certified General Accountants
>www.cga-canada.org

Provides information on the CGA profession, articles, and links to CGA affiliates.

Canadian Bankers Association
>www.cba.ca

Offers information about the association; outlines media, industry, and small business issues; and lists publications and statistics.

Canadian Bar Association
>www.cba.org/Gate.asp

Describes the CBA and opportunities for continuing legal education for lawyers. Also provides links to all the provincial law societies.

Canadian Broadcast Standards Council
>www.ccnr.ca/english/home.htm

Provides information on broadcast standards and related legal links.

Canadian Civil Liberties Association
www.ccla.org/
Outlines the history of the association and offers information on the protection of Canadians' rights and freedoms.

Canadian Council for International Business
www.ccib.org
Describes publications of the International Chamber of Commerce and rules concerning the interpretation of international trade terms. Also offers links to other sites.

Canadian Franchise Association
www.cfa.ca
Offers information on franchising in Canada, the association's code of ethics, and government relations.

Canadian Institute of Chartered Accountants
www.cica.ca
Provides information on the CA profession and accounting standards and services.

Canadian Labour Congress
www.clc-ctc.ca
Describes publications and offers links to related organizations.

Canadian Real Estate Association
http://realtors.mls.ca/crea/
Provides real estate information in Canada, legal information, and links to provincial associations.

Cancopy
www.cancopy.com
Describes copyright regulations and various publications.

CMA Canada
www.cma-canada.org
Provides information on the CMA profession and links to provincial bodies and related materials.

Insurance Canada
www.insurance-canada/ca/
Provides consumer insurance information for both individuals and business, a directory of insurance providers and related services, information on industry news and events, and links to related sites.

Insurance Council of Canada
www.ibc.ca/English/intro.htm
Provides information on all types of insurance for the home and business, as well as loss prevention. Describes articles dealing with issues pertinent to the auto industry, consumer awareness issues, and industry news. Supplies links to the Insurance Bureau of Canada, including its legal division.

Canadian Legislation

Access to Justice Network
http://legis.acjnet.org
Provides access to statutes and regulations for most Canadian jurisdictions and links to international law resources.

Government of Canada
www.canada.justice.gc.ca
Describes federal statutes and regulations. Includes press releases, information on judicial appointments, and descriptions of government initiatives.

Government of Canada
www.parl.gc.ca
Provides an overview of the Parliament of Canada and explains the workings of the parliamentary system.

Government of Alberta
www.gov.ab.ca/qp/
Outlines statutes and regulations, rules of court, bills, orders in council, and recent judgments.

Government of British Columbia
www.legis.gov.bc.ca
Provides the full text of bills and their status, the 1996 Revised Statutes of British Columbia and regulations, and orders-in-council.

Government of Manitoba
www.gov.mb.ca/chc/statpub/free/index.html
Gives access to statutes, the full text of bills, and court rules.

Government of Manitoba
www.gov.mb.ca/leg-asmb/index.html
Lists bills and their status; outlines debates and proceedings.

Government of New Brunswick
www.gov.nb.ca/justice/index.htm
Provides a complete list of all New Brunswick Acts and regulations and identifies the officials who administer the Acts.

Government of New Brunswick
www.gov.nb.ca/legis/status/status.htm
Lists New Brunswick bills, along with an account of their status.

Government of Newfoundland
www.gov.nf.ca/hoa/sr/
Provides statutes and regulations. The site is searchable by keyword.

Government of Northwest Territories
    http://legis.acjnet.org/TNO/Loi/a_en.html
Outlines statutes.

Government of Northwest Territories
    http://legis.acjnet.org/TNO/reg/index_en.html
Provides regulations.

Government of Nova Scotia
    www.gov.ns.ca/legi/index.htm
Lists Nova Scotia bills and gives an account of their status.

Government of Nova Scotia
    www.gov.ns.ca/just/regulations/regs/conregs.htm
Provides the text of Nova Scotia regulations.

Government of Nunavut
    http://pooka.nunanet.com/~ncjlib/legislation.html
Lists statutes and regulations.

Government of Ontario
    http://209.195.107.57/en/index.html or www.gov.on.ca/MBS/
    english/publications/statregs/contents.html
Provides access to Ontario's statutes and regulations. Searchable by keyword or by the table of contents.

Government of Ontario
    www.ontla.on.ca/
Provides the full text of bills and the status of bills.

Government of Prince Edward Island
    www.gov.pe.ca/law/index.php3
Describes statutes; searchable by keyword.

Government of Prince Edward Island
    www.gov.pe.ca/leg/bills/index.php3
Outlines the progress of bills.

Government of Quebec
    www.lexum.umontreal.ca/ccq/en/index.html
Provides the text of the Civil Code of Quebec in English.

Government of Quebec
    http://doc.gouv.qc.ca/servlets/Dbml/index2.html
Provides the text of the Civil Code of Quebec in French.

Government of Quebec
    www.gazette.gouv.qc.ca
Provides the most recent three weeks of Quebec's official gazette (in French).

Government of Saskatchewan
> **www.legassembly.sk.ca/legassembly/docs/docs.htm**

Offers a complete list of bills and their status.

Government of Yukon
> **http://legis.acjnet.org/Yukon/index_en.html**

Summarizes statutes and regulations.

Links to legislation across the country via the University of Calgary
> **www.ucalgary.ca/library/law/**

Canadian Courts and Their Judgments

Supreme Court of Canada
> **www.scc-csc.gc.ca/**

Describes the Supreme Court, including its role in the legal system, and provides links to judgments.

Supreme Court of Canada
> **www.lexum.umontreal.ca/csc-scs/en**

Gives access to decisions of the Supreme Court of Canada via the University of Montreal.

Supreme Court of Canada via QuickLaw
> **www.quicklaw.com (select "Recent Decisions," then "Supreme Court of Canada Service")**

Gives access to recent Supreme Court of Canada decisions, via QuickLaw, within an hour of release by the court.

Federal Court of Canada
> **www.fja.gc.ca/**

Describes the federal courts, including the appointment process, and supplies links to judgments.

Alberta Courts
> **www.albertacourts.ab.ca/**

Describes the Alberta courts and provides links to judgments of the Court of Appeal and provincial courts. Queen's Bench judgments are not yet available (as of November 2000).

British Columbia Courts
> **www.courts.gov.bc.ca/**

Provides information on British Columbia's courts and links to judgments of the Court of Appeal and Supreme Court. Also supplies a link to Chief Justice McEachern's home page and access to a three-volume guide to the judiciary, the *Criminal Code,* and the *Canadian Charter of Rights and Freedoms.*

Manitoba Courts
> **www.jus.gov.mb.ca/registry/**

Records all documents filed and hearings scheduled in the Manitoba Court of Appeal and the Manitoba Court of Queen's Bench.

Northwest Territories Courts
> **www.andomot.com/nwt/**

Supplies a link to judgments via the Northwest Territories court library.

Nova Scotia
> **www.nsbs.ns.ca (select "Library Services" icon and then "Law News Online")**

Provides digests of decisions from July 1997 (primarily Supreme and Appeal) and full text of decisions from January 1999.

Ontario Courts
> **www.ontariocourts.on.ca/english.htm**

Describes the Ontario courts and links to judgments from the Court of Appeal. Judgments from the Ontario Court and Superior Court not yet available (as of November 2000).

Prince Edward Courts
> **www.gov.pe.ca/courts/**

Describes the P.E.I. courts and provides links to judgments of the P.E.I. Supreme Court.

Links to Homepages for Canadian Courts via the University of Calgary
> **www.ucalgary.ca/library/law/decision.htm**

Canadian Judicial Council
> **www.cjc-ccm.gc.ca**

Explains the purposes of the council, including its role in improving the quality of judicial service and in handling complaints against federally appointed judges.

LAW/NET from QuickLaw
> **www.quicklaw.com (select "Recent Decisions" and then "LAW/NET Legal Update Service")**

Provides digests of recent newsworthy cases from courts across the country.

Note: For information on case reporter abbreviations, consult the Legal Citations List via Nahum Gelber Law Library (McGill University)
> **www.law.library.mcgill.ca/abbreviations/**

Selected International Law Sites

Access to Justice Network
http://legis.acjnet.org
Gives access to constitutional statutes and other important documents for foreign countries. Also provides information on international courts and international law generally.

Canadian Governments On-Line (CGOL)
www.intergov.gc.ca
Provides access to government information for foreign countries

Organization for Economic Cooperation and Development
www.oecd.org
Provides information by country on competition and regulatory reform; offers an international regulation database; and describes international developments and articles on electronic commerce.

United Kingdom Courts via the University of Calgary
www.ucalgary.ca/library/law/decision.htm
Gives links to the British and Irish Legal Information Institute and outlines the decisions of various courts.

United Nations
www.un.or.at/uncitral
Offers information on international trade law and model laws.

United States Courts via the University of Calgary
www.ucalgary.ca/library/law/decision.htm
Gives links to the United States Supreme Court and judgments and to many state courts.

U.S. Department of Justice
www.usdoj.gov/
Provides information on the U.S. legal system and links to other government departments.

U.S. Patent and Trademark Office
www.uspto.gov/
Offers databases for searching U.S. patents and trademarks.

World Intellectual Property Office (the WIPO)
www.wipo.org
Provides information on the WIPO and links to related organizations such as e-commerce sites.

World Trade Organization (the WTO)
www.wto.org
Describes the WTO, analyzes trade topics, and provides dispute reports.

Conducting Legal Research

The Law Library at the University of Calgary
www.ucalgary.ca/library/law

Provides links to legislation and judicial sites, international law sites, legal databases, and government agencies.

Hieros-Gamos
www.hg.org

Offers a comprehensive international law and government portal; law-related discussion groups; links to legal associations; and business and consumer centre sites.

Lloyd Duhaime's Legal Information Centre
www.wwlia.org/ or www.duhaime.org/

Provides legal information on a variety of topics, such as contracts, bankruptcy, torts, and real estate.

Roger Batchelor, Queen's University Contract Law Page
http://qsilver.queensu.ca/~law20/

Provides a contract law study guide for first-year law students at Queen's University.

Surfing Lawyer
www.netlegal.com

Offers Canadian legislation and government information; updates on decisions, statutes, and rules; a link to the Canadian judges home page; a selection of publications; and news groups.

Canadian Legal Information
www.CanadaLegal.com

Contains articles by lawyers indexed by area of law, by category of information, and by jurisdiction. The site is searchable by keyword.

Michigan State University's International Business Resources
http://ciber.bus.msu.edu/busres.htm

Describes trade law and government resources.

Hugh Kindred et al.'s home page for *International Law: Chiefly as Interpreted and Applied in Canada*
http://is.dal.ca/~wwwlaw/kindred.intlaw/index.html

A Web site supporting the textbook, it offers links to treaties and cases, as well as to international law sites and databases of international law materials.

Legal Information Ontario
www.LegalLine.ca

A nonprofit organization providing free legal information. Also offers frequently asked questions and answers pertaining to various areas of the law and information on finding a lawyer.

Legal Terminology

Duhaime's Law Dictionary
    www.duhaime.org/ or http://www.duhaime.org/diction.htm
Offers a comprehensive legal dictionary written in plain language.

Ray August (University of Washington)
    http://august1.com/pubs/dict
Provides a dictionary of international legal terms.

'Lectric Law Library
    www.lectlaw.com/da.htm
Supplies definitions and explanations of legal terms.

Glossary

acceleration clause   A term of a loan agreement that makes the entire loan due if one payment is missed.

acceptance   An unqualified willingness to enter into a contract on the terms in the offer.

act of bankruptcy   One of ten acts that the debtor must commit before a creditor can petition the debtor into bankruptcy.

action for the price   The obligation of buyers of goods, once title to goods has passed, to pay the seller the full price of the goods.

actual authority   The power of an agent that derives from either express or implied agreement.

administrative law   Rules created and applied by those having governmental powers.

adverse effects discrimination   Discrimination that occurs as a result of a rule that appears neutral but in its effects is discriminatory.

after-acquired property   Assets purchased after a secured loan is granted.

agency   A relationship that exists when one party represents another party in the formation of legal relations.

agency by estoppel   An agency relationship created when the principal acts such that third parties reasonably conclude that an agency relationship exists.

agency by ratification   An agency relationship created when one party adopts a contract entered into on his or her behalf by another who at the time acted without authority.

agent   A person who is authorized to act on behalf of another.

age of majority   The age at which a person becomes an adult for legal purposes.

aggravated damages   Compensation for intangible injuries such as distress and humiliation caused by the defendant's reprehensible conduct.

agreement of purchase and sale   The contract for buying and selling land.

alternative dispute resolution (ADR)   A range of options for resolving disputes as an alternative to litigation.

anticipatory breach   A breach that occurs before the date for performance.

anti-competitive behaviour   Conduct that restricts competition and is reviewable under the *Competition Act*.

apparent authority   The power that an agent appears to have because of conduct or statements of the principal.

appeal   The process of arguing to a higher court that a court decision is wrong.

arbitration   A process through which a neutral party makes a decision (usually binding) that resolves a dispute.

arbitrator   A person who listens to both sides of a dispute and makes a ruling that is binding on the parties.

arrangement   A proposal governed by the Companies' Creditors Arrangement Act.

articles of association   Rules specifying day-to-day operating procedures of a company in memorandum of association jurisdictions.

articles of incorporation   The incorporating document and constitution of a corporation in Newfoundland, New Brunswick, Ontario, Manitoba, Saskatchewan, Alberta, and the federal jurisdiction.

assault   The threat of imminent physical harm.

assignment   The transfer of a contractual right by an assignor to an assignee.

assignment in bankruptcy   The debtor's voluntary assignment to the trustee in bankruptcy of legal title to all the debtor's property for the general benefit of creditors.

bailee   The person who gains possession in a bailment.

bailment   Temporary transfer of possession of personal property.

bailment for value   Bailment involving payment for use or a service.

bailor   The owner of property in a bailment.

bait and switch   Advertising a product at a very low price to attract customers, then encouraging them to accept another product that is usually more expensive.

balance of probabilities   Proof that there is a better than 50 percent chance that the circumstances are as the plaintiff contends.

banking agreement   A document that contains the rights and obligations of a bank and a customer.

bankrupt   The legal status defined by the *Bankruptcy and Insolvency Act* that prevents a person from having control of his or her assets and debts.

bankruptcy district   An administrative unit for a specific geographic area under the *Bankruptcy and Insolvency Act.*

bankruptcy offences   Criminal acts defined by the *Bankruptcy and Insolvency Act* and committed by any participant in the bankruptcy and insolvency process.

bankruptcy order   A document that assigns legal responsibility of assets and liabilities from the debtor to the official receiver through the appointed trustee.

battery   Nonconsensual physical contact that violates an individual's bodily security.

bid rigging   Conspiring to fix the bidding process to suit the collective needs of the producers/suppliers.

bill of exchange   An order to a person to pay an amount to another person.

bill of lading   A shipping document that serves as a contract between the seller and the carrier.

binding   Final and enforceable in the courts.

bona fide occupational requirement (BFOR)   A defence that excuses discrimination on a prohibited ground when it is done in good faith and for a legitimate business reason.

bond   A document evidencing a debt owed by the corporation, often used to refer to a secured debt.

breach of contract   Failure to comply with a contractual promise.

burden of proof   The obligation of the plaintiff to prove its case.

business law   A set of established rules governing commercial relationships, including the enforcement of rights.

bylaw   A law made by the municipal level of government.

bylaws   Rules specifying day-to-day operating procedures of a company in letters patent and articles of incorporation jurisdictions.

Cabinet   A body composed of all ministers heading government departments, as well as the prime minister or premier.

Canadian Charter of Rights and Freedoms   A guarantee of specific rights and freedoms enshrined in the Constitution and enforceable by the judiciary.

Canadian Standards Association The nonprofit, nongovernmental organization that sets standards for products in Canada in association with the International Organization for Standardization (ISO).

carrier A bailee who transports personal property.

causation The relationship that must exist between the defendant's action and the plaintiff's loss.

caveat emptor Let the buyer beware, or let the buyer take care.

certification The process by which a union is recognized as a bargaining agent for a group of employees; also, the process whereby a bank guarantees payment of a cheque.

channel power The ability of one member of the marketing or distribution channel to influence another.

chattel lease A contract where a lessee pays for the use of a lessor's personal property.

cheque An order to a bank to pay money to a specified person.

c.i.f. Cost, insurance, and freight. A contractual term making the seller responsible for arranging the insurance (in the buyer's name) and shipping.

civil track The process by which the Competition Bureau may order a promoter to desist from engaging in false or misleading advertising.

claims What a patented invention can do.

closely held corporation A corporation that does not sell its shares to the public.

closing The final stage of a real estate transaction.

c.o.d. Cash on delivery. A contractual term requiring the purchaser to pay the shipper cash on delivery of goods.

collateral Security for a borrower's promise to repay a loan.

collective agreement The employment agreement reached between the union and employer setting out the bargaining unit employees' terms and conditions of employment.

collective bargaining A mechanism by which parties enter a collective agreement or contract.

common law Rules that are formulated in judgments.

common share A share that generally has a right to vote, to share in dividends, and to share in proceeds on dissolution.

compensation in tort Financial compensation awarded for the harm suffered by the plaintiff.

composition A proposal that reduces the amount of monies to be paid to creditors while the debtor retains assets.

condition An important term, which, if breached, gives the innocent party the right to terminate the contract and claim damages; also, a term as defined under *Sale of Goods* legislation.

condition precedent A condition that, until it occurs, suspends the parties' obligation to *perform* their contractual obligations.

condition subsequent A condition that, when it occurs, brings an existing contract to an end.

condonation Employer behaviour that indicates to the employee that misconduct is being overlooked.

conduct incompatible Personal behaviour that is irreconcilable with employment duties.

confidential business information Information that provides a business advantage as a result of the fact that it is kept secret.

confidentiality The obligation of a professional not to disclose any information provided by the client without the client's consent.

consideration The price paid for a promise.

constitutional law The body of law governing the individual–state relationship, including the permissible scope of legislative power.

constructive dismissal Employer conduct that amounts to a fundamental breach of the employment contract.

consumer debt A loan to an individual for a noncommercial purpose.

consumer note A promissory note arising in a consumer credit sale.

contract An agreement between two parties that is enforceable in a court of law.

contract law Rules that make agreements binding and therefore facilitate planning and the enforcement of expectations.

contractual entrant Any person who has paid (contracted) for the right to enter the premises.

contributory negligence A defence claiming that the plaintiff is at least partially responsible for the harm that has occurred.

convention Important rules that are not enforceable by a court of law but that practically determine or constrain how a given legal power is exercised.

conversion right The right to convert one type of security into another type.

copyright The right to prevent others from copying or modifying certain works.

corporate law department A group of lawyers hired as in-house counsel to do the legal work of a business.

corporate opportunity A business opportunity in which the corporation has an interest.

costs Legal expenses that a judge orders the loser to pay the winner.

counterclaim A claim by the defendant against the plaintiff.

counteroffer The rejection of one offer and proposal of a new one.

credit bureau An agency that compiles credit information on borrowers.

cumulative dividend right The right of the holder of a preferred share to be paid arrears.

damages Monetary compensation awarded in a lawsuit.

damages for nonacceptance Damages to which a seller is entitled if a buyer refuses to accept goods prior to the title shifting.

debenture A document evidencing a debt owed by the corporation, often used to refer to an unsecured debt.

deceit Fraudulent misrepresentation that induces another to enter a contract.

decision The judgment of the court that specifies which party is successful and why.

deductible The part of a loss for which the insured is responsible.

deed A document that transfers ownership of land.

defamation The public utterance of a false statement of fact or opinion that harms another's reputation.

default Failure to make required payments on a loan.

defendant The party being sued.

deficiency The shortfall between the outstanding mortgage balance and the proceeds from sale of the land; also, the shortfall if a secured asset is sold for less than the amount of the outstanding loan.

derivative action A suit by a shareholder on behalf of the corporation to enforce a corporate cause of action.

direct marketing   Using the telephone and nonpersonal media to communicate product information to customers.

director   A person elected by shareholders to manage a corporation.

direct-response marketing   Advertising a product to be made available through mail or telephone orders.

discharge of bankruptcy   The formal process releasing the bankrupt of most liabilities.

discovery   The process of disclosing evidence to support both claims in a lawsuit.

discrimination   Treating someone differently on the basis of a prohibited ground.

distinguishing guise   A shaping of wares or their container, or a mode of wrapping or packaging wares.

distress   The right of a commercial landlord to seize the tenant's property for nonpayment of rent.

dividend   A division of profits payable to shareholders.

doctrine of constructive notice   Deemed notice of publicly filed documents.

domestic law   The internal law of a given country, which includes both statute and case law.

door-to-door selling   The act of selling in person directly to a customer's residence.

double ticketing   The offence of failing to sell at the lower of the two prices appearing on a product.

due diligence   A defence based on having a reasonable belief in the truth of the statement made or adopting reasonable steps to avoid the utterance of false or misleading statements.

duress   The threat of physical or economic harm that results in a contract.

duty of care   The responsibility owed to avoid careless acts that cause harm to others.

duty of disclosure   The obligation of the insured to provide to the insurer all information that relates to the risk.

duty to accommodate   The duty of an employer to modify work rules, practices, and requirements to meet the needs of individuals who would otherwise be subjected to unlawful discrimination.

duty to mitigate   The obligation to take reasonable steps to minimize the losses resulting from a breach of contract or other wrong.

easement   The right to use the land of another for a particular purpose.

electronic banking   Financial transactions through the use of computers, telephones, or other electronic means.

employment equity legislation   Laws designed to improve the status of certain designated groups.

employment relationship   A contractual relationship whereby an employer provides remuneration to an employee in exchange for work or services.

employment standards legislation   Laws that specify minimum standards in the workplace.

endorsement   The process of signing a negotiable instrument to enable negotiation.

endorsement in blank   Signing a cheque without any special instructions.

entire contract clause   A term in a contract in which the parties agree that their contract is complete as written.

equality of bargaining power   The legal assumption that parties to a contract are able to look out for their own interests.

equity   Rules that focus on what would be fair given the specific circumstances of the case, as opposed to what the strict rules of common law might dictate.

equity of redemption   The right to regain title to mortgaged land upon repayment of the debt.

estate   The collective term for the assets and liabilities of the insolvent or bankrupt.

evidence   Proof presented in court to support a claim.

exclusive dealing   Conduct that is reviewable under the *Competition Act* because the seller agrees to sell to the purchaser only if the purchaser buys from it exclusively.

exclusive possession   The tenant's right to control land during the term of a lease.

exemption clause   A term of a contract that identifies events causing loss for which there is no liability.

express term   A provision of a contract that states a promise explicitly.

fair dealing   A defence to copyright infringement.

false imprisonment   Unlawful detention or physical restraint or the perception thereof.

false or misleading advertising   Promotional statements that either are false or have the ability to mislead a consumer as to their truth.

Federal Court of Canada   The court that deals with litigation involving the federal government.

fee simple   The highest level of land ownership.

fiduciary   A person who has an obligation to act primarily in the interest of the person to whom a responsibility is owed because of the relationship between the two parties.

fiduciary duty   A duty imposed on a person who has a special relationship of trust with another.

financing lease   A lease that enables the lessee to finance the acquisition of personal property.

financing statement   The document registered as evidence of security against personal property.

fixed or definite term contract   A contract for a specified period of time which automatically ends on the expiry date.

fixtures   Anything permanently attached to land.

f.o.b.   Free on board. A contractual term whereby the buyer specifies the type of transportation and the seller arranges that transportation and delivery of goods to the shipper at the buyer's expense.

foreclosure and sale   The mortgagee's remedy to sell the land to pay the mortgage debt.

formal executive   The branch of government responsible for the ceremonial features of government.

franchise   An agreement whereby an owner of a trademark or trade name permits another to sell a product or service under that trademark or name.

fraudulent conveyance   A transfer of real or personal property made to defeat, hinder, delay, or defraud.

fraudulent preference   A payment made by an insolvent debtor within three months of bankruptcy with the intent of favouring one creditor over another.

frustration   Termination of a contract by an unexpected event or change that makes performance functionally impossible or illegal.

functional areas   Traditional departments for organizing a business.

fundamental breach   A breach of contract that affects the foundation of the contract.

fundamental term   A term that underlies the entire contract.

general security agreement   A loan contract that includes all of the assets of a business as collateral.

government policy   The central ideas or principles that guide government in its work, including the kinds of laws it passes.

gratuitous bailment Bailment that involves no payment.

gratuitous promise A promise for which no consideration is given.

grievance process A procedure for resolving disputes contained in union contracts.

guarantee A promise to pay the debt of someone else, should that person default on the obligation.

guarantor A person who signs a guarantee.

habitual neglect of duty Customary failure to perform employment duties.

hacker A person who attempts to gain unauthorized access to computers.

holder A person who presents a negotiable instrument for payment.

Human Rights Commission An administrative body that oversees the implementation and enforcement of human rights legislation.

identification theory A theory specifying that a corporation is liable when the person committing the wrong is the corporation's directing mind.

illegal contract A contract that cannot be enforced because it is contrary to legislation or public policy.

implied term A provision that is not expressly included in a contract but that is necessary to give effect to the parties' intention.

improvident sale A sale of the borrower's assets by the lender for less than fair market value.

incompetence Lack of ability, knowledge, or qualification to perform employment obligations.

incomplete agreement An agreement that is not contractual because its content is not sufficiently comprehensive.

incorporator The person who sets the incorporation process in motion.

indefinite term contract A contract for no fixed period which can end on giving reasonable notice.

indemnification The corporate practice of paying litigation expenses of officers and directors for lawsuits related to corporate affairs.

indemnity The obligation on the insurer to make good the loss.

independent contractor A person who is in a working relationship that does not meet the criteria of employment.

industrial design Ornamentation or shape of functional objects.

injurious or malicious falsehood The utterance of a false statement about another's goods or services that is harmful to the reputation of those goods or services.

innominate term A term that cannot easily be classified as either a condition or a warranty.

insider A person who has a special relationship with a corporation.

insider trading Transactions in shares based on confidential information of a material nature.

insolvent Unable to pay debts or having liabilities in excess of assets; under the *Bankruptcy Act,* a person or company that owes more than $1000 and is unable to meet or has ceased paying financial obligations as they fall due, or has insufficient assets to meet obligations.

inspector A person appointed by a creditor to act on his or her behalf and supervise the actions of the trustee.

insurable interest A financial stake in what is being insured.

insurance adjuster One who investigates and evaluates insurance claims.

insurance agent One who acts for an insurance company in selling insurance.

insurance broker One who provides advice and assistance to the insured in acquiring insurance.

insurance policy A contract of insurance.

insured One who buys insurance coverage.

insurer A company that sells insurance coverage.

intangible property Personal property, the value of which comes from legal rights.

intellectual property The results of the creative process.

intentional tort A harmful act that is committed on purpose.

interference with contractual relations Incitement to break the contractual obligations of another.

interim receiver The official appointed to take care of the estate in the period between the filing of the petition and the making of the receiving order.

interlocutory injunction An order to refrain from doing something for a limited period of time.

international law Law that governs relations between states and other entities with international legal status.

invitation to treat An expression of willingness to do business.

invitee Any person who comes onto the property to provide the occupier with a benefit.

joint and several liability Responsibility together and individually.

joint liability Full responsibility for all debts.

joint tenancy Co-ownership whereby the survivor inherits the undivided interest of the deceased.

joint venture A grouping of two or more businesses to undertake a particular project.

judges Those appointed by federal and provincial governments to adjudicate on a variety of disputes, as well as to preside over criminal proceedings.

judgment debtor The party ordered by the court to pay a specified amount to the winner of a lawsuit.

judiciary A collective reference to judges.

jurisdiction The power that a given level of government has to enact laws.

just cause Employee conduct that amounts to a fundamental breach of the employment contract.

Labour Relations Board A body that administers labour relations legislation.

landlord The owner of land that is leased.

land titles system The system of land registration whereby the administrators guarantee the title to land.

lapse The expiration of an offer after a specified or reasonable period.

law The set of rules and principles guiding conduct in society.

law firm A partnership formed by lawyers.

law of agency The law governing the relationship where one party acts on behalf of another.

lawyer A person who is legally qualified to practise law.

lease The contract that transfers control of land from the landlord to the tenant in exchange for the payment of rent.

legal capacity The ability to make binding contracts.

legal risk A business risk with legal implications.

legal risk management plan A comprehensive action plan for dealing with the legal risks involved in operating a business.

legislative branch The branch of government that creates statute law.

letter of commitment A document that is provided by a bank to a borrower and sets out the terms of a loan.

letter of credit A written promise by a buyer's bank to a seller's bank to pay the seller when specified conditions are met.

letters patent The incorporating document and constitution of a corporation in Quebec and Prince Edward Island.

liability Legal responsibility for the event or loss that has occurred.

liberalism A political philosophy that elevates individual freedom and autonomy as its key organizing value.

licence Consent given by the owner of rights to someone to do something that only the owner can do.

licensee Any person whose presence is not a benefit to the occupier but to which the occupier has no objection; also, the holder of a licence.

lien The right to retain possession of personal property until payment for service is received.

limitation of liability clause A term in a contract that sets a monetary limit on the financial responsibility for failure to perform as agreed; also, a term of a contract that limits liability for breach to something less than would otherwise be recoverable.

limitation period The time period specified by legislation for commencing legal action.

limited liability Responsibility for obligations restricted to the amount of investment.

limited liability partnership (LLP) A partnership in which the partners have unlimited liability for their own malpractice but limited liability for other partners' malpractice.

limited partnership A partnership in which the liability of some partners is limited to their capital contribution.

liquidated damages clause A term of a contract that specifies how much one party must pay the other in the event of breach.

litigation The process involved when one person sues another.

marketing law All areas of law that influence and direct the creation, distribution, promotion, and pricing of goods, services, or ideas.

mediation A process through which the parties to a dispute endeavour to reach a resolution with the assistance of a neutral person.

mediator A person who helps the parties to a dispute reach a compromise.

memorandum of association The incorporating document and constitution of a corporation in Nova Scotia and British Columbia.

misrepresentation A false statement of fact that causes someone to enter a contract.

mistake An error made by one or both parties that seriously undermines a contract.

money laundering The false reporting of income from criminal activity as income from legitimate business.

moral rights The author's rights to have work properly attributed and not prejudicially modified or associated with products.

mortgage A credit arrangement where land is security for the loan.

mortgagee The lender who receives the mortgage.

mortgagor The borrower who grants the mortgage.

multilevel marketing A scheme for distributing products or services that involves participants supplying them to other participants to earn a profit.

negligence A careless act or omission that causes harm to another.

negligent misstatement or misrepresentation Negligence that arises out of uttering a misleading statement with less than the appropriate standard of care.

negotiable instrument A document that meets the requirements for circulation without reference to other sources.

negotiation A process of deliberation and discussion used to reach a mutually acceptable resolution to a dispute; also, the process of transferring negotiable instruments from one person to another.

neighbour Anyone who might reasonably be affected by another's conduct.

nonpecuniary damages Compensation for pain and suffering, loss of enjoyment of life, and loss of life expectancy.

novation The substitution of parties in a contract or the replacement of one contract with another.

NUANS report A document that shows the result of a search for business names.

nuisance Any activity on an occupier's property that unreasonably and substantially interferes with the neighbour's rights to enjoyment of his or her property.

objective standard test The test applied in dealing with a contractual dispute based on how a "reasonable person" would view the conduct of the parties.

occupier Any person with a legal right to occupy premises.

offer A promise to perform specified acts on certain terms.

offeree The person to whom an offer is made.

offeror The person who makes an offer.

official receiver The administrative official legally responsible for all aspects of the bankrupt's estate.

operating lease A lease where the property is returned to the lessor when the term is up.

oppression remedy A statutory remedy available to shareholders and other stakeholders to protect their corporate interests.

option agreement An agreement where, in exchange for payment, an offeror is obligated to keep an offer open for a specified time.

ordinary price The price at which goods are normally sold in a given market at specified volumes and in a given period.

outsider The party with whom the agent does business on behalf of the principal.

paralegal One who performs legal work under the supervision of a practising lawyer.

paramountcy A doctrine that provides that federal laws prevail when there are conflicting or inconsistent federal and provincial laws.

parol evidence rule A rule that limits the evidence a party can introduce concerning the contents of the contract.

partnership A business carried on by two or more persons that is not a corporation.

passing off Presenting another's goods or services as one's own.

patent A monopoly to make, use, or sell an invention.

patent agent A professional trained in patent law and practice who can assist in the preparation of a patent application.

pay equity Provisions designed to ensure that female and male employees receive the same compensation for performing similar or substantially similar work.

pecuniary damages Compensation for out-of-pocket expenses, loss of future income, and cost of future care.

periodic tenancy A lease that is automatically renewed unless one party gives proper notice to terminate.

personal property All property other than land.

petition The statement filed by the creditor claiming that the debtor owes at least $1000 and has committed at least one act of bankruptcy.

piercing the corporate veil Holding the owners of a corporation personally liable for the corporation's acts.

plaintiff The party that initiates a lawsuit against another party.

pleadings The formal documents concerning the basis for a lawsuit.

political executive The branch of government responsible for day-to-day operations, including formulating and executing government policy, as well as administering all departments of government.

precedent An earlier case used to resolve a current case because of its similarity.

predatory pricing The offence of setting unreasonably low prices to eliminate competition.

preemptive right A shareholder's right to maintain a proportionate share of ownership by purchasing a proportionate share of any new stock issue.

pre-existing legal duty A legal obligation that a person already owes.

preferred creditors Those creditors identified in section 136 of the *Bankruptcy and Insolvency Act* who are paid after secured creditors and before unsecured creditors.

preferred share A share or stock that has a preference in the distribution of dividends and the proceeds on dissolution.

premium The price paid for insurance coverage.

price discrimination The offence of failing to provide similar pricing terms and conditions to competing wholesalers or retailers for equivalent volume sales at an equivalent time.

price maintenance The offence of attempting to drive the final retail price of goods upward and imposing recriminations upon noncompliant retailers.

principal A person who has permitted another to act on her or his behalf.

private law Areas of law that concern dealings between persons.

privilege The client's right not to have information divulged to third parties.

privity of contract A doctrine providing that only parties to a contract have rights and obligations under the contract.

procedural law The law governing the procedure to enforce rights, duties, and liabilities.

product liability The manufacturer's liability for negligently made goods that cause harm to the consumer.

professional A person with specific expertise and skills in an accepted area of knowledge.

progressive discipline policy A system that follows a sequence of employee discipline from less to more severe punishment.

prohibited offences Offences under the *Competition Act* that are criminal in nature.

promissory estoppel A principle whereby someone who relies on a gratuitous promise may be able to enforce it.

promissory note A written promise to pay a specified amount.

proof of claim A formal notice provided by the creditor of the amount owed and the nature of the debt.

proposal A contractual agreement between the debtor and creditors for the payment of debts that allows the business to continue.

prospectus The document a corporation must publish when offering securities to the public.

proxy A person who acts for another in a meeting or a public body.

public law Areas of the law that relate to or regulate the relationship between persons and government at all levels.

public policy The community's common sense and common conscience.

punitive damages Compensation awarded to the plaintiff to punish the defendant for particularly offensive behaviour.

pure economic loss Financial loss that results from a negligent act where there has been no accompanying property or personal injury damage.

pyramid selling An illegal form of multilevel selling under the *Competition Act*.

Quebec Civil Code The rules of private law that govern Quebec.

real property Land or real estate.

reasonable care The care a reasonable person would exhibit in a similar situation.

reasonable notice A period of time for an employee to find similar employment.

reasonable person The standard used to judge whether a person's conduct in a particular situation is negligent.

receiver A person appointed by the secured creditor to retrieve the asset and realize the debt.

receiving order The court order following a creditor's petition that formally declares the debtor to be bankrupt and transfers legal control of the estate to the trustee.

reference A person who will testify to the ability and qualities of an applicant.

refusal to deal Conduct that is reviewable under the *Competition Act* because the seller refuses to sell to a purchaser even under comparable conditions to the purchaser's competitor.

registration The process of recording a security interest in a public registry system.

registry system The system of land registration whereby the records are available to be examined.

regulations Rules created by the political executive that have the force of law.

regulatory offence An offence contrary to the public interest.

rejection The refusal to accept an offer.

related person Any person who is a blood relative (or related by marriage or adoption) of the bankrupt or of the person with controlling interest in the bankrupt corporation.

release A written or oral statement discharging another from an existing duty.

remoteness of damage The absence of a sufficiently close relationship between the defendant's action and the plaintiff's loss.

rescission The remedy that results in the parties being returned to their precontractual positions.

responsible government Government that abides by conventions prescribing how governmental power is to be exercised.

restrictive covenant A restriction on the use of land as specified in the deed.

restrictive endorsement Signing a cheque for deposit only to a particular bank account.

retainer An advance payment requested to fund services to be provided and thereby minimize the professional's exposure to risk.

reviewable matters Offences under the *Competition Act* that are assessed according to a civil burden of proof and are resolved either by voluntary agreement or by order of the Competition Tribunal.

reviewable transaction A payment made to a person related to the bankrupt within one year of the bankruptcy order with the intention of giving the related person priority over at least one other creditor.

revocation The withdrawal of an offer.

risk avoidance The decision to cease a business activity because the legal risk is too great.

risk reduction Implementation of practices in a business to lower the probability of loss and its severity.

risk retention The decision to absorb the loss if a legal risk materializes.

risk transference The decision to shift the risk to someone else through a contract.

royal charter An official document that established a corporation as a separate legal entity.

royal prerogative Historical rights and privileges of the Crown, including the right to conduct foreign affairs and to declare war.

rules of construction Guiding principles for interpreting the terms of a contract.

scheme of arrangement A proposal in which the trustee controls assets for the benefit of creditors for the duration of the proposal.

secured creditor A lender who has the right to seize and sell specific assets of a borrower to pay off a loan.

securities Shares and bonds issued by a corporation.

securities legislation Laws designed to regulate transactions involving shares and bonds of a corporation.

self-dealing contract A contract in which a fiduciary has a conflict of interest.

serious misconduct Intentional, harmful conduct of the employee that permits the employer to dismiss without notice.

settlement A sale that can be declared void because it was not made in good faith or for valuable consideration.

settlement out of court A negotiated resolution of a lawsuit after litigation begins, but before going to trial.

sexual harassment Unwelcome conduct of a sexual nature.

shareholder A person who has an ownership interest in a corporation.

shareholder agreement An agreement that defines the relationship among people who have an ownership interest in a corporation.

share structure The shares that a corporation is permitted to issue by its constitution.

shelf company A company that does not engage in active business.

small claims court A court that deals with claims up to a specified amount.

sole proprietorship A business organization that has only one owner.

special endorsement Signing a cheque and making it payable to a specific person.

specialized standard of care The standard of care exhibited by average persons with the requisite specialized training.

specifications The description of an invention contained in a patent.

specific goods Goods that are identified and agreed on at the time a contract of sale is made.

stakeholder One who has an interest in a corporation.

standard form contract A form of agreement that imposes the same set of terms on every customer.

standard of care The standard by which reasonableness is determined.

statute law Formal, written laws created or enacted by the legislative branch of government.

stop payment The process whereby the person who writes a cheque orders the bank not to pay the holder who presents it for payment.

stoppage in transitu The right of a seller to demand that goods be returned by a shipper at the seller's expense even after title has transferred, provided the purchaser is insolvent.

strict liability The principle that liability will be imposed irrespective of proof of negligence.

subrogation The right of the insurer to recover the amount paid on a claim from a third party who caused the loss; also, the right of a guarantor to recover from the debtor any payments made to the creditor.

substantive law Law that defines rights, duties, and liabilities.

suing The process of instituting formal legal proceedings against someone to enforce a right.

superintendent of bankruptcy The most senior ministerial appointment with general supervisory authority for all functions prescribed under the *Bankruptcy and Insolvency Act*.

superior court A court with unlimited financial jurisdiction.

Supreme Court of Canada The final court for appeals in the country.

systemic discrimination Discrimination that results from the combined effects of many rules, practices, and policies.

tangible property Personal property, the value of which comes from its physical form.

telemarketing The use of telephone to communicate product and organizational information to customers.

tenancy in common Co-ownership whereby each owner of an undivided interest can dispose of that interest.

tenant The occupier of land that is leased.

terms of the contract Binding commitments that form part of a contract.

thin skull rule The principle that a defendant is liable for the full extent of a plaintiff's loss even where a prior vulnerability makes the harm more serious than it otherwise might be.

tied selling Conduct that is reviewable under the *Competition Act* because the seller will sell to the purchaser only if the purchaser buys other, less desirable goods as well.

tippee A person who acquires confidential information from an insider.

title search Investigation of the registered ownership of land.

tort A harm caused by one person to another, other than through breach of contract, and for which the law provides a remedy.

trademark A mark used to distinguish the source of goods or services.

trade name The name under which a sole proprietorship, a partnership, or a corporation does business.

treaty An agreement between two or more states that is governed by international law.

trespass The act of coming onto another's property without the occupier's express or implied consent.

trespasser Any person who is not invited onto property and whose presence is either unknown to the occupier or is objected to by the occupier.

trial A formal hearing before a judge that results in a binding decision.

trustee in bankruptcy The officer assigned legal responsibility by the official receiver for administering the bankrupt's estate.

unanimous shareholder agreement (USA) An agreement among all shareholders that restricts the powers of the directors to manage the corporation.

unascertained goods Goods not yet set aside and identifiable as the subject of the contract at the time the contract is formed.

unconscionable contract An unwise contract formed when one party takes advantage of the weakness of another.

undisclosed principal A principal whose identity is unknown to a third party, who has no knowledge that the agent is acting in an agency capacity.

undue influence Unfair manipulation that compromises someone's free will.

unfair practices Illegal business practices that exploit the unequal bargaining position of consumers.

unlimited liability Unrestricted responsibility for obligations.

unsecured credit Debts that are not backed by specific assets of the debtor.

vicarious liability The liability of the employer for the tortious acts of an employee committed in the normal course of employment.

vicarious performance Performance of contractual obligations through others.

voidable contract A contract that in certain circumstances an aggrieved party can choose to keep in force or bring to an end.

void contract A contract involving a defect so substantial that it is of no force or effect.

voluntary assumption of risk The defence that no liability exists as the plaintiff agreed to accept the risk inherent in the activity.

warehouseman A bailee who stores personal property.

warranty A minor term, which, if breached, gives the innocent party the right to claim damages only; also, a term that is not classified as a condition under *Sale of Goods* legislation.

widely held corporation A corporation whose shares are normally traded on a stock exchange.

willful disobedience Deliberate failure to carry out lawful and reasonable orders.

winding up The process of dissolving a corporation.

workers' compensation legislation Provincial legislation that provides no-fault compensation for injured employees in lieu of their right to sue in tort.

Index

Economic breach, 101

887574 Ont. v. *Pizza Pizza*, 305

Electronic banking, 611–613

Electronic commerce. *See* E-commerce

Electronic Commerce Act, 138, 170

Electronic money, 612

Electronic wallet, 612

Elsley v. *J.G. Collins Insurance Agencies Limited*, 168

Employee vs. independent contractor, 464, 465

Employment contract, 475, 476

Employment equity, 472

Employment equity legislation, 472

Employment insurance, 478

Employment relationship, 462–513

   collection/dissemination of information, 483

   CPP/QPP, 478

   defined, 464

   discrimination. *See* Discrimination

   drug testing, 481

   employee vs. independent contractor, 464, 465

   employment contract, 475, 476

   employment equity, 472

   employment insurance, 478

   employment standards, 477

   fiduciary obligations, 475

   formation of employment contract, 473–475

   hiring process, 467

   human rights, 467–472

   monitoring of communications, 483, 484

   negligent hiring, 466, 467

   offer of employment, 474

   pay equity, 480, 481

   privacy, 472, 473, 482–484

   professionals, 528

   safety, 478

   sexual harassment, 478–480

   surveillance/searches, 482, 483

   termination, 491–513. *See also* Terminating the employment relationship

   unions, 484, 485, 508, 509

   vicarious liability, 465, 466

   workers' compensation, 478

Employment standards, 477

Employment standards legislation, 477

Endorsement, 454, 608

Endorsement in blank, 610

Enduring power of attorney, 273

Enforcement of judgment, 83

Entire contract clause, 134

Environmental claims, 559

Environmental hazards, 227

Environmental impairment insurance, 450

Equality of bargaining power, 96

Equality rights, 27

Equitable remedies, 192–194

Equity, 32

Equity of redemption, 430

Ernst & Young v. *Stuart*, 252

Errors and omissions insurance, 448, 532

Estate, 645

Exclusive dealing, 582

Exclusive possession, 434

Executive branch of government, 25

Exemplary damages, 212

Exemption clause, 142

Express terms, 131

External stakeholders, 318

f.o.b., 589

Fair dealing, 402

False advertising, 553–557

False imprisonment, 248

Family agreements, 122, 123

Farber v. *Royal Trust Co.*, 501

Fast track, 555

Federal Court of Canada, 78

Federal jurisdiction, 21, 22

Fee simple, 418

Fiduciary, 518

Fiduciary duty, 277, 342–345

Financing lease, 377

Financing statement, 627

Fine's Flowers Ltd. v. *General Accident Assurance Co.*, 277

Fire insurance, 444

First reading, 23

Fixed term contract, 475

Fixtures, 418

Floating charge, 625

Force majeure clause, 184

Foreclosure and sale, 432

Foreign agent, 269

Foreign presence in another country, 308

Formal executive, 25

Forms of business organizations. *See* Business forms/arrangements

Four Ps of marketing mix, 543

Franchise, 304–306

Fraudulent conveyance, 649

Fraudulent misrepresentation, 165

Fraudulent preference, 648

Frustration, 183, 184

Functional areas, 45

Fundamental breach, 187

Fundamental freedoms, 27

Fundamental term, 500

Gateway v. *Arton Holdings Ltd.*, 132

General acts of incorporation, 320

General damages, 211, 212

General Motors, 50

General Motors of Canada, 20

General security agreement, 625

Gilbert Steel Ltd. v. *University Construction Ltd.*, 119

Goss, Bill, 655

Government policy, 20

Grabka v. *Regina Motor Products (1970) Ltd.*, 549

Gratuitous bailment, 370

Gratuitous promise, 118

Green advertising, 559

Grievance process, 508

Guarantee, 169

causation, 226, 227
contributory, 229
defences, 229, 230
duty of care, 223–225
negligent misstatement, 232
product liability, 230–232
product packaging, 550
professionals, 521–525
remoteness of damage, 227, 228
standard of care, 225, 226
steps in bringing action, 223
thin skull rule, 228
voluntary assumption of risk, 229, 230
Negligent hiring, 466, 467
Negligent misstatement/misrepresentation, 232, 521, 522
Negotiation, 69–71, 85, 608
Neighbour, 223
New York Convention on the Recognition and Enforcement of Foreign Arbitral Awards, 76
Newell v. *Canadian Pacific Airlines Ltd.*, 191
No-fault liability, 232
Noncompetition clauses, 168, 474, 475
Nonpecuniary damages, 190, 191, 211
Nonvoting shareholders, 351
Notice of the claim, 79
Notwithstanding clause, 30
Novation, 181
NUANS report, 324
Nuisance, 245–247
Numbered company, 325

Objective standard test, 95
Occupational health and safety legislation, 478
Occupier, 243
Occupier's liability, 243–245, 255
Occupiers' liability insurance, 447
Offer, 107–111
Offeree, 108
Offeror, 108
Officers. *See* Directors/officers
Official receiver, 644, 645
Online retailing, 584, 585

Operating lease, 377
Operation of account agreement, 602
Oppression remedy, 353
Option agreement, 110
Ordinance, 37
Ordinary price, 579
Ostensible authority, 273
Outsider, 270
Outsider-principal relationship, 270

Packaging, 550–552
Panorama Developments (Guildford) Ltd. v. *Fidelis Furnishing Fabrics Ltd.*, 274
Paralegal, 421
Paramountcy, 22
Paris Convention for the Protection of Industrial Property, 410
Parliament, 22
Parol evidence rule, 136, 137
Partial payment of debt, 121
Partnership, 291–300
creation, 294
decision making, 293
financial liability, 292
legislation, 294, 296
limited, 299
LLP, 300
overview (chart), 303
profit sharing, 292, 293
pros/cons, 298
relations of partners to one another, 294, 295
relations of partners to outsiders, 296, 297
sources of capital, 293
taxation, 293
termination, 298
transferability, 293
Partnership Act, 294, 296
Partnership agreement, 295
Passing off, 250
Patent agent, 393
Patent Co-operation Treaty, 410
Patents, 389–394
abuse, 408
application for, 393
defined, 390, 391

infringement, 408
international treaties, 410
overview (chart), 406
protection of, 393, 394
requirements for patentability, 392, 393
Paws Pet Food & Accessories Ltd. v. *Paws & Shop Inc.*, 324
Pay equity, 480, 481
Pecuniary damages, 191, 192, 212
Performance claims, 557, 558
Periodic tenancy, 437
Personal bankruptcy, 655, 656
Personal guarantees, 631–635
Personal Information and Electronic Documents Act, 473, 483
Personal property, 366–385
bailment, 369–381. *See also* Bailment
defined, 367
ownership/possession, 367–369
Personal use of employer's property, 494
Petition, 653
Physique Health Club Ltd. v. *Carlsen*, 406
Piercing the corporate veil, 349
Place. *See* Distribution (place)
Plaintiff, 78
Pleadings, 79
Political executive, 25
Power of attorney, 273
Pre-existing legal duty, 118
Pre-incorporation contracts, 339
Precedent, 31, 32
Predatory pricing, 576
Preemptive rights, 351
Preferred creditors, 650
Preferred shares, 350, 351
Premium, 444
Price discrimination, 575
Price maintenance, 576, 577
Pricing conspiracies, 573–575
Pricing practices, 572–579
bid rigging, 577, 578
conspiracies, 573–575
double ticketing, 579
predatory pricing, 576

price discrimination, 575
price maintenance, 576, 577
sale/bargain prices, 579
Principal, 267
Privacy Act, 483
Private law, 34
Private prosecutions, 209n
Privilege, 520, 521
Privity of contract, 185
Procedural law, 34
Procuring breach of contract, 251
Product
  attributes/characteristics, 545–549
  basic principles, 544
  conditions/warranties, 546–548
  design/manufacture, 544, 545
  packaging/labelling, 550–552
Product dealership, 307
Product defamation, 253, 254
Product licensing, 308
Product packaging, 550–552
Product warnings, 552
Professional, 516
Professional associations, 525, 526
Professional-client privilege, 520, 521
Professional law societies, 56
Professional service firms, 526
Professional services, 515–539
  changing service providers, 530
  client confidentiality, 520
  disciplinary process, 527, 528
  employing professionals, 528
  ethics, 528, 529
  exclusion clauses, 530
  fiduciary responsibilities, 518–521
  form of organization, 530–532
  governance structure, 525–530
  insurance, 532
  limited liability, 531

MDPs, 526, 527
negligence, 521–525
privilege, 520, 521
responsibilities in contract, 517, 518
right to practice, 526
risk management, 530–532
self-regulation, 525, 526
Progressive discipline policy, 493
Prohibited offences, 554
Promissory estoppel, 120, 121
Promissory note, 604
Promotion, 552–561
  bait and switch, 560
  contests, 561
  defined, 552
  industry standards, 553
  misleading advertising, 553–557
  performance claims, 557, 558
  tests/testimonials, 559, 560
  unfair practices, 560, 561
  warranty/service promises, 560
Proof of claim, 649
Property
  insurance, and, 443–459
  intellectual, 387–415
  personal, 366–385
  real, 417–442
Property insurance, 444, 449
Proposal, 646
Prosecution, 208
Prospectus, 330
Provincial jurisdiction, 22
Provincial legislative bodies, 23
Proving the case on the balance of probabilities, 81
Proxy, 350
Public law, 34
Public policy, 168
Punch v. *Savoy's Jewellers Ltd.*, 375
Punitive damages, 212, 213
Pure economic loss, 228
Pyramid selling, 581, 582

Quebec Civil Code, 35
Quebec Pension Plan (QPP), 473
Queen v. *Cognos*, 473

R. v. *Bata Industries Ltd.*, 347
R. v. *Fuel Base Industries Inc.*, 558
R. v. *Nova Scotia Pharmaceutical Society*, 574
R. v. *Partridge*, 581
Re City Equitable Fire Insurance Co., 342
Real estate agents, 268
Real estate lease, 433–437
Real estate transaction, 422–428
  agreement of purchase and sale, 424, 425
  closing, 426, 427
  investigation of title, 421, 425, 426
  overview (chart), 428
  refusal to complete, 427, 428
  title insurance, 423
Real property, 417–442
  defined, 418
  disposition of property, 437
  electronic registration, 422
  land titles system, 421
  leases (landlord and tenant), 433–437
  limits on ownership, 419, 420
  mortgage, 429–432
  ownership, 418–420
  purchase of, 422–428. *See also* Real estate transaction
  registration of ownership, 420–422
  registry system, 421
Reasonable apprehension of bias, 37
Reasonable care, 222
Reasonable notice, 496–499
Reasonable person, 225
Receiver, 652
Receiving order, 653
Recommended retail price, 576, 577
Record, 255
Reference, 472
Reference checking, 472, 473
Refusal to deal, 582
Registration, 627
Registry system, 421

Regulations, 25
Regulatory offences, 341
Rejection, 110
Related person, 648
Release, 507
Remoteness of damage, 189, 190, 228
Repairs, 379
Rescission, 160, 193
Responsible government, 26
Restrictive covenants, 420, 474
Restrictive endorsement, 610
Retainer, 517
Reviewable matters, 554
Reviewable transaction, 648
Revocation, 109
Rhône (The) v. *Peter A.B. Widener*, 340
Rider, 454
Right of repudiation, 547
Risk avoidance, 48, 49
Risk management. *See* Legal risk management plan
Risk reduction, 49
Risk retention, 49, 50
Risk transference, 50, 51
RJR-MacDonald Inc. v. *Canada*, 31
Rockland Industries Inc. v. *Amerada Minerals Corporation of Canada*, 275
Royal charter, 319
Royal prerogative, 31
Rules of construction, 134

Sale/bargain prices, 579
Sale-of-goods legislation, 133, 134, 546, 548, 549
Sales agency, 307
Salomon v. *Salomon Ltd.*, 317
Scheme of arrangement, 647
Seal, 120
Searching the title, 421, 426
Second reading, 23
Secured creditors, 628
Securities, 329
Securities legislation, 328–331
Seeking legal advice, 56, 57
Self-dealing contract, 343
Semelhago v. *Paramedevan*, 429

Senate, 23
Seniority, 508
Serious misconduct, 493
Service, 79
Service dealership, 307
Settlement, 649
Settlement out of court, 79
Severance package, 507
Sexual harassment, 478–480
Share structure, 325
Shareholder agreement, 354–356
Shareholders
    financial rights, 351
    liability, 349
    remedies, 352–354
    right to information, 351
    rights, 350–352
    shareholder agreements (USA), 354–356
    voting, 350, 351
Shares, 328
Shelf company, 325
Shipping document, 588
Shipping terms, 589
Shop-at-home television networks, 584
Shoplifting, 248, 249
Signature, 170
Silicorp Limited, 506
Slander, 252
Small claims court, 78
Snow v. *The Eaton Centre Ltd.*, 402
Solar U.S.A. Inc. v. *Saskatchewan Minerals*, 135
Sole proprietorship, 288–291, 303
Solicitor and client costs, 82
Solicitors, 56
Sources of law, 31
Special acts of incorporation, 320
Special damages, 212
Special endorsement, 610
Specialized standard of care, 226
Specific goods, 586
Specific performance, 192, 193
Specifications, 393
Stakeholders, 317, 318

Standard form contract, 46, 98, 143, 144
Standard of care, 225
State Street Bank & Trust v. *Signature Financial Group*, 391
Statute law, 21
Statute of Frauds, 169–171
Stewart v. *Pettie*, 233
Stop payment, 609
Stoppage in transitu, 588
Storage, 378, 379
Strategic alliance, 307
Strict liability, 231, 232
Structured settlement, 210
Subrogation, 454, 633
Substantive law, 33
Suing, 11
Superintendent of bankruptcy, 644
Superior court, 78
Supreme Court of Canada, 78
Systemic discrimination, 469

Takeovers, 580
Tangible property, 367
Tardiness, 494
Taylor v. *Caldwell*, 183
Telemarketing, 584
Tenancy in common, 419
Tenant, 433
Terminating the employment relationship, 491–513
    constructive dismissal, 500–502
    dismissal with notice, 497–500
    duty to mitigate, 505
    fundamental changes, 500, 501
    grievance/arbitration, 508, 509
    just cause, 492–497
    near cause, 496
    reasonable notice, 497–499
    severance package, 507
    wrongful dismissal, 502–506
Terms of the contract, 93, 131
Test for remoteness, 189
Tests/testimonials, 559, 560

Photo Credits

Part 1
Page 2: Top: The Canadian Press; Middle, left: CORBIS; Middle, right: PhotoDisc; Bottom: The Canadian Press

Chapter 1
Page 4: PhotoDisc
Page 7: Courtesy of Dick Hemingway
Page 8: Courtesy of Kathryn Dykstra
Page 12: The Canadian Press
Page 13: Courtesy of Le Journal de Montreal

Chapter 2
Page 19: The Canadian Press

Chapter 3
Page 43: Kit Kittle, CORBIS
Page 47: The Canadian Press
Page 59: Courtesy of Richard Bailey

Chapter 4
Page 65: CORBIS

Part 2
Page 90: Top, left: PhotoDisc; Top, right: CORBIS; Bottom: Corel

Chapter 5
Page 92: CORBIS
Page 93: PhotoDisc
Page 97: CORBIS
Page 98: Superstock

Chapter 6
Page 105: PhotoDisc
Page 108: Courtesy of Dick Hemingway
Page 111: CORBIS

Chapter 7
Page 129: PhotoDisc
Page 133: DILBERT reprinted by permission of Universal Feature Syndicate, Inc.
Page 139: Courtesy of Dick Hemingway

Chapter 8
Page 155: CORBIS
Page 162: Comstock

Chapter 9
Page 177: PhotoDisc
Page 179: CORBIS

Part 3
Page 202: Top, left: PhotoDisc; Top, right: CORBIS; Bottom, left: Corel; Bottom, right: The Canadian Press

Chapter 10
Page 204: The Canadian Press
Page 206: CORBIS
Page 215: Courtesy of Glen McCurdie

Chapter 11
Page 221: PhotoDisc
Page 223: Photographed with permission by Bio-Lab Canada, Inc.

Chapter 12
Page 241: Corel
Page 245: Courtesy of Dick Hemingway
Page 248: Courtesy of Mas Kikuta
Page 256: Courtesy of Mr. McCurdy

Part 4
Page 264: All: CORBIS

Chapter 13
Page 266: CORBIS
Page 268: Courtesy of Dick Hemingway
Page 272: Corel
Page 278: The Canadian Press

Chapter 14
Page 287: Corel
Page 288: Courtesy of Dick Hemingway
Page 291: Courtesy of Dick Hemingway

To the owner of this book

We hope that you have enjoyed *Canadian Business and the Law,* (ISBN 0-17-607372-8), by DuPlessis, Enman, Gunz, and O'Byrne, and we would like to know as much about your experiences with this text as you would care to offer. Only through your comments and those of others can we learn how to make this a better text for future readers.

School _____ Your instructor's name _____

Course _____ Was the text required? _____ Recommended? _____

1. What did you like the most about *Canadian Business and the Law*?

_____

_____

_____

2. How useful was this text for your course?

_____

_____

_____

3. Do you have any recommendations for ways to improve the next edition of this text?

_____

_____

_____

4. In the space below or in a separate letter, please write any other comments you have about the book. (For example, please feel free to comment on reading level, writing style, terminology, design features, and learning aids.)

_____

_____

_____

_____

Optional

Your name _____ Date _____

May Nelson Thomson Learning quote you, either in promotion for *Canadian Business and the Law,* or in future publishing ventures?

Yes _____ No _____

Thanks!

You can also send your comments to us via e-mail at
college@nelson.com

PLEASE TAPE SHUT. DO NOT STAPLE.

TAPE SHUT

TAPE SHUT

- - - FOLD HERE - - -

NELSON

THOMSON LEARNING ™

MAIL ≫ POSTE
Canada Post Corporation
Société canadienne des postes
Postage paid   Port payé
if mailed in Canada si posté au Canada
Business Reply   Réponse d'affaires
0066102399   01

0066102399-M1K5G4-BR01

NELSON THOMSON LEARNING
HIGHER EDUCATION
PO BOX 60225 STN BRM B
TORONTO ON M7Y 2H1

TAPE SHUT

TAPE SHUT